The Evolution of Policing

Worldwide Innovations and Insights

International Police Executive Symposium Co-Publications

Dilip K. Das, *Founding President-IPES*

PUBLISHED

Examining Political Violence: Studies of Terrorism, Counterterrorism, and Internal Wars
By David Lowe, Austin Turk, and Dilip K. Das ISBN: 978-1-4665-8820-2

The Evolution of Policing: Worldwide Innovations and Insights
By Melchor C. de Guzman, Aiedeo Mintie Das, and Dilip K. Das, ISBN: 978-1-4665-6715-3

Policing Global Movement: Tourism, Migration, Human Trafficking, and Terrorism
By S. Caroline Taylor, Daniel Joseph Torpy, and Dilip K. Das, ISBN: 978-1-4665-0726-5

Global Community Policing: Problems and Challenges
By Arvind Verma, Dilip K. Das, Manoj Abraham, ISBN 978-1-4398-8416-4

Global Environment of Policing
By Darren Palmer, Michael M. Berlin, and Dilip K. Das, ISBN: 978-1-4200-6590-9

Strategic Responses to Crime: Thinking Locally, Acting Globally
By Melchor de Guzman, Aiedeo Mintie Das, and Dilip K. Das, ISBN: 978-1-4200-7669-1

Police without Borders: The Fading Distinction between Local and Global
By Cliff Roberson, Dilip K. Das, and Jennie K. Singer, ISBN: 978-1-4398-0501-5

Effective Crime Reduction Strategies: International Perspectives
By James F. Albrecht and Dilip K. Das, ISBN: 978-1-4200-7838-1

Urbanization, Policing, and Security: Global Perspectives
By Gary Cordner, Ann Marie Cordner, and Dilip K. Das, ISBN: 978-1-4200-8557-0

Criminal Abuse of Women and Children: An International Perspective
By Obi N.I. Ebbe and Dilip K. Das, ISBN: 978-1-4200-8803-8

Contemporary Issues in Law Enforcement and Policing
By Andrew Millie and Dilip K. Das, ISBN: 978-1-4200-7215-0

Global Trafficking in Women and Children
By Obi N.I. Ebbe and Dilip K. Das, ISBN: 978-1-4200-5943-4

FORTHCOMING

Police Reform: The Effects of International Economic Development, Armed Violence, and Public Safety
By Garth den Heyer and Dilip K. Das, ISBN: 978-1-4822-0456-8

Policing Major Events: Perspectives from around the World
by Martha Dow, Darryl Plecas, and Dilip K. Das, ISBN: 978-1-4665-8805-9

The Evolution of Policing

Worldwide Innovations and Insights

Edited by
Melchor C. de Guzman
Aiedeo Mintie Das
Dilip K. Das

International Police Executive Symposium Co-Publication

CRC Press is an imprint of the
Taylor & Francis Group, an **informa** business

CRC Press
Taylor & Francis Group
6000 Broken Sound Parkway NW, Suite 300
Boca Raton, FL 33487-2742

First issued in paperback 2019

© 2014 by Taylor & Francis Group, LLC
CRC Press is an imprint of Taylor & Francis Group, an Informa business

No claim to original U.S. Government works

ISBN-13: 978-1-4665-6715-3 (hbk)
ISBN-13: 978-0-367-86769-0 (pbk)

Library of Congress Cataloging-in-Publication Data

The evolution of policing : worldwide innovations and insights / edited by Melchor C. de
    Guzman, Aiedeo Mintie Das, and Dilip K. Das.
        pages cm
    Includes bibliographical references and index.
    ISBN 978-1-4665-6715-3 (hardcover : alk. paper)
    1. Police. I. De Guzman, Melchor. II. Das, Aiedeo Mintie. III. Das, Dilip K.

HV7921.E96 2014
363.2'3--dc23   2013030838

Visit the Taylor & Francis Web site at
http://www.taylorandfrancis.com

and the CRC Press Web site at
http://www.crcpress.com

Table of Contents

Section I

THE EVOLVING NATURE OF POLICE ROLES IN DEMOCRATIC AND DEMOCRATIZING SOCIETIES

Section III
THE EVOLVING NATURE OF POLICE TRAINING AND PERSONNEL MANAGEMENT

Section IV

THE EVOLVING NATURE OF POLICE OPERATIONAL MANAGEMENT

Section V

EMERGING ISSUES

Prologue

Every year the International Police Executive Symposium (IPES) holds an international conference for police scholars and practitioners to have the opportunity to engage and exchange information about the latest trends in police practice and research. Some of the presentations at the conferences have been accepted for publication in the affiliated journal of the organization, *Police Practice & Research: An International Journal*, based on their intellectual stimulations. Other manuscripts from the conference are collated to form chapters for a book that represents the most current themes on policing across the globe.

This book presents a survey of the evolving roles and practices in policing across the world that emanated from the conferences and some submissions to the above-mentioned journal. The objective of this book is to combine the latest trends in policing and to provide readers with some tools and knowledge that could (1) assist them in seeking directions in their current scholarly endeavors and (2) implement new programs or fine tune their current practices. The strategy of the book in presenting these evolutions in policing roles and practices is fourfold. First, we exerted enormous efforts to gather original manuscripts from experts in policing around the world to provide a snapshot of these evolving police roles and practices. Second, we tried to combine the best sources of manuscripts from two fields: the police practitioners' field and the police scholars' field. We think there is a multitude of benefits to be derived when practice is guided by research and when research is grounded in practice. Third, we touched on different evolutionary aspects of policing, from training to operations as well as philosophical and organizational changes in organizations. Fourth, the manuscripts were selected and edited for a wide readership by using language that has universal appeal rather than catering to the technical jargon of both practitioners and scholars. We made an extra effort in selecting manuscripts that were not muddled by technicalities so that the readers do not miss the usefulness of the manuscripts. We hoped that these strategic directions would help the book serve as a valuable reference for a vast number of readers and appeal to different audiences interested in policing research and practice. Thus, it could become a reference for beginning readers as well as readers who are well exposed to policing literature.

This book comprises five sections that cover the following topics. Section I covers the trends in the evolving police roles among democratic and democratizing states. It provides convergence among different states in the pursuit of more democratic policing models. Section II informs the readers about the evolution that takes place with the most dominant philosophy in policing: community-oriented policing. It presents the models that other countries have undertaken in implementation of community-oriented policing. It aims to deliver a message that though policing agencies are unidimensional in the philosophy they adopt, they are quite varied in the implementation of the same philosophy. Section III guides the readers to several innovations happening in training and personnel management. Those pursuing the ideals of scientific management would certainly be provided with several perspectives on these issues of administration. Police training and management keep evolving due to the vigorous efforts of the police to attain or maintain the status of a professional organization. Section IV covers the volatile world of police operations. Persistent issues such as ethics, technology, investigations, and handling public relations are tackled. Section V covers the challenges that may bring about future changes to police practice. The issues of terrorism, decentralization, and policing of indigenous and special population groups are presented to the reader as food for thought rather than definitive factors that may change the idea of policing.

There are 25 chapters in this book and they are evenly distributed in five sections. In Section I, five chapters discuss the evolving police roles and practices among democratic and democratizing countries. In Chapter 1, Kusha presents historical accounts of the challenges of establishing a professional police force in Iran. Interestingly, Lesotho and South Africa are also experiencing challenges that democratic policing demands. Specifically, in Chapters 2 and 5, Monyane and Roelofse, respectively, deal with establishing mechanisms of accountability to control the police as well as the challenge of promoting human rights. In Chapter 4, Lauritz and Karp identified the image of police as a problem for police and suggested that the police are searching for a new identity. In this search for identity, in Chapter 3, Borglund and Nuldén suggest that the police use a soap opera approach.

Section II has five chapters. In this, the reader is treated to a global perspective on the implementation of community policing, starting with Chapter 6 by Rolle on the Bahamas and ending with Chapter 10 by Fernandes on the implementation of community policing in Portugal. Chapters 7 to 9 narrate the innovations in implementation of community policing in other jurisdictions. Chapter 7 by Wallace describes a different model of community participation in policing in Trinidad and Tobago. These variations in community participation in policing are likewise discussed through examples from the Czech Republic in Chapter 9 by Hrinko and Binkova. In Chapter 8, Adewale's essay on community policing engages the readers with his thoughts on whether community policing is a panacea or a Pandora's box to the crime problem in South Africa.

Section III consists of five chapters. Chapter 11 by Ask deals with training in writing memoranda. Writing reports and memoranda is key to effective policing, and her analysis is instructive on these issues. Likewise, Chapter 15 by Byrman on writing techniques in police interviews supplements Chapter 11 by Ask. Chapters 12 to 14 deal with management of police personnel particularly coping with workplace challenges. In Chapter 12, Pattanaik and Worley tackle the perennial issue of coping mechanisms among women police officers. Another important police personnel issue is stress, and in Chapter 13, Bertillson et al. show how to conduct simulated activities for stress training. Finally, in Chapter 14, Gyamfi traces the development and establishment of a police personnel unit in Ghana.

Section IV presents a potpourri of police operational issues and innovations. Chapters 16 to 20 tackle the issues of ethics, public relations, technology, and database management. In Chapter 16, Lambri, Cook, and Jackson narrate the evolution of a policing database in the United Kingdom. In Chapter 17, Butler, Thompson, and Bel present the utility of head-mounted cameras as a tool for policing. Similarly, in Chapter 18, Cook presents a strategy to classify crime as "wicked." In Chapter 19, Jenks, Johnson, and Matthews present their research on ethics in policing. This chapter contributes to the growing use of corruption vignettes as an approach to teaching ethics in policing. Lastly, in Chapter 20, Marsh analyzes the presentation of police officers in the media, which could become a major public relations challenge for the police.

Section V comprises five chapters. Chapters 21 and 22 deal with policing innovations related to terrorism. In Chapter 21, Roberts approaches the issue through his analysis of innovations in investigations, whereas in Chapter 22, Awan presents the effect of the law, that is, control orders in the United Kingdom. Chapters 23 and 24 discuss special populations. In Chapter 24, Lowe touches on England's policing strategies involving mentally ill clients. In Chapter 23, Luna-Firebaugh presents issues involving the policing of tribal populations. As an added chapter in the section, Chapter 25 by Park and Johnstone presents the prospects for a more decentralized police administration in South Korea.

As we strive to present more evidence of these evolutions, we know that we cannot fully capture the whole story of the evolutions in policing that are happening across the world. Part of the reason for this limitation is space. There is a vast number of materials that would require a project the size of an encyclopedia to include full coverage on police innovations. Thus, we could only contribute part of the accounts of these policing innovations. Though only presenting a partial picture of police innovations, we strive to provide the readers with meaningful insights through these compiled manuscripts. This is just the beginning.

We thank all the contributors of this volume who are the stars of this project. We would also like to thank our families because they served as inspiration to us most of the time while assembling these chapters. In addition, CRC Press/Taylor & Francis deserve our gratitude for publishing this book. Their unfailing trust and support in the pursuit of this project enabled us to bring it to conclusion.

Melchor C. de Guzman
State University of New York

Aiedeo Mintie Das
International Police Executive Symposium

Dilip K. Das
International Police Executive Symposium

IPES Preface

The International Police Executive Symposium (IPES) was convened in 1994 to address one major challenge, that is, the two fields of research and practice remain disconnected even though cooperation between them is growing. A major reason for this is that the two groups speak in different languages. The research is published in hard-to-access journals and presented in a manner that is difficult for some to comprehend. On the other hand, police practitioners tend not to mix with researchers and remain secretive about their work. Consequently, there is little dialogue between the two and almost no attempt to learn from one another. The global dialogue among police researchers and practitioners is limited. It is true that the literature on police is growing exponentially. But its impact on day-to-day policing, however, is negligible.

The aims and objectives of the IPES are to provide a forum for fostering closer relationships among police researchers and practitioners on a global scale; facilitating cross-cultural, international, and interdisciplinary exchanges for the enrichment of the law enforcement profession; encouraging discussion; and publishing research on challenging and contemporary problems facing the profession of policing. One of the most important activities of the IPES is the organization of an annual meeting under the auspices of a police agency or an educational institution. Now in its 17th year, the annual meeting, a 5-day initiative on specific issues relevant to the policing profession, brings together ministers of interior and justice, police commissioners and chiefs, members of academia representing world-renowned institutions, and many more criminal justice elite from over 60 countries. It facilitates the interaction and exchange of ideas and opinions on all aspects of policing. The agenda is structured to encourage dialogue in both formal and informal settings.

Another important aspect of the meeting is the publication of the best presented papers edited by well-known criminal justice scholars and police professionals who attend the meetings. The best papers are selected, thoroughly revised, fully updated, meticulously edited, and published as books based on the theme of each meeting. This repository of knowledge under the copublication imprint of IPES and CRC Press/Taylor & Francis Group chronicles the important contributions of the IPES over the past two decades. As a result, in 2011 the United Nations awarded IPES a *Special Consultative Status* for the Economic and Social Council (ECSOC), honoring its importance in the global security community.

In addition to this book series, the IPES also has a research journal, *Police Practice & Research: An International Journal* (PPR). The PPR contains research articles on police issues from practitioners and researchers. It is an international journal in the true sense of the term and is distributed worldwide. For more information on the PPR, visit http://www.tandf.co.uk/journals/GPPR.

This book emerges from collections of papers from the IPES conferences and *Police Practice & Research: An International Journal*. It combines the latest trends in policing and provides the readers with some tools and knowledge that could advance the craft of policing. This book on evolutions in policing roles and practices aims to achieve four goals. First, we gathered original manuscripts from experts in policing around the world to provide a snapshot of these evolving police roles and practices. Second, we combined the best sources of manuscripts from two fields—the police practitioners' field and the police scholars' field. We think that there is a multitude of benefits to be derived when practice is guided by research and when research is grounded in practice. Third, we touched on different evolutionary aspects of policing, from training to operations as well as philosophical and organizational changes.

The IPES advocates, promotes, and propagates that policing is one of the most basic and essential avenues for improving the quality of life in all nations: rich and poor, modern and traditional, large and small, as well as peaceful and strife-ridden. IPES actively works to drive home to all its office bearers, supporters, and admirers that, in order to reach its full potential as an instrument of service to humanity, policing must be fully and enthusiastically open to collaboration between research and practice, global exchange of information between police practitioners and academics, universal disseminations and sharing of best practices, generating thinking police leaders and followers, as well as reflecting and writing on the issues challenging to the profession.

Through its annual meetings, hosts, institutional supporters, and publications, IPES reaffirms that policing is a moral profession with unflinching adherence to the rule of law and human rights as the embodiment of humane values.

Dilip K. Das, PhD
Founding President,
International Police Executive Symposium,
www.ipes.info

Book Series Editor,
Advances in Police Theory and Practice,
CRC Press/Taylor & Francis Group.

Book Series Editor,
Interviews with Global Leaders in Criminal Justice,
CRC Press/Taylor & Francis Group.

Book Series Editor,
PPR Special Issues as Books,
Routledge/Taylor & Francis Group.

Founding Editor-in-Chief,
Police Practice & Research: An International Journal *(PPR),*
http://www.tandf.co.uk/journals/GPPR

Editors

Melchor C. de Guzman, PhD, is an associate professor of criminal justice at the College of Brockport at the State University of New York. He earned his doctorate degree in criminal justice from the University of Cincinnati. De Guzman's research includes the examination of citizen participation in the control of the police. He also investigates organizational and environmental factors that influence police behavior. His most recent research includes the utilization of websites by police departments in the delivery of police services and the role of the police in homeland security. Prior to joining the academy, de Guzman was serving the government of the Philippines. He was a senate committee secretary for National Defense and Security in the Philippine Senate. Later, he was appointed by the president of the Republic of the Philippines as Director II of the Philippine Veterans Affairs Office. He recently edited *Strategic Responses to Crime: Thinking Globally, Acting Locally* with Mintie Das and Dilip K. Das. De Guzman is also the production editor of *Police Practice & Research: An International Journal* and the book editor of *International Police Executive Symposium*. He can be contacted by e-mail at mdeguzma@brockport.edu or bookeditoripes@yahoo.com and by phone at +1 585-395-5785.

Aiedeo Mintie Das has served as editor and associate editor for six academic titles published by Taylor & Francis, Lexington Books, Rovio, and Prentice Hall. She serves as publicity and public relations editor of *Police Practice & Research: An International Journal* (PPR). As director of public relations of the International Police Executive Symposium (IPES; www.ipes.info), she organizes international criminal justice symposia, coordinating with ministries of interior/justice to bring together well-known academics and top police leaders in global venues. So far she has organized symposia in Bulgaria, Dubai, Hungary, India, Macedonia, Malta, and the United States. Mintie Das has 15 years of experience in corporate public relations and marketing, serving as the director of two public relations departments. She continues to work as a digital media/content marketing specialist. Currently, she is pursuing graduate studies in Helsinki, Finland.

Dilip K. Das, PhD, has years of experience in police practice, research, writing, and education. After obtaining a master's degree in English literature, he joined the Indian Police Service, an elite national service with a distinguished tradition. After 14 years of service as a police executive, including a term as a chief of police, he moved to the United States, where he earned a master's degree and a PhD in criminal justice.

Das is a professor of criminal justice, a former police chief, and a human rights consultant for the United Nations. He is the founding president of the International Police Executive Symposium (IPES), where he manages the affairs of the organization in cooperation with an appointed group of police practitioners, academia members, and individuals from around the world. Das is also the founding editor-in-chief of *Police Practice & Research: An International Journal*. He is the author, editor, or coeditor of more than 40 books and numerous articles. Das has received several faculty excellence awards and was a distinguished faculty lecturer.

Contributors

Sofia A. Ask is a senior lecturer in Swedish at Linnaeus University, Sweden. Her field of interest is writing in academic and workplace settings. Currently, she is involved in a project that studies writing in the exercise of authority as it is performed in education and occupational life in three professions: police, teachers, and social workers.

Imran Awan is a senior lecturer in criminology at Birmingham City University. He has published extensively on counterterrorism, human rights, and policing, and he recently coedited *Policing Cyber Hate, Cyber Threats and Cyber Terrorism*. Currently, he is involved in a project that examines the impact of counterterrorism legislation upon Muslim families in Cardiff. He is an ambassador for the Make Justice Work Campaign and a fellow of the Higher Education Academy. He is also the director and founder of the Ethnic Minority Research Network in Criminology.

Éric Bel started his career at Teesside University, Tees Valley, UK, as a language teacher before becoming the head of Languages. Since then, he has specialized in postcompulsory education, more specifically in learning and teaching in higher education. Bel's main responsibilities are on the Postgraduate Certificate in Learning and Teaching in Higher Education. He also contributes to the master's program in education and supervises PhD students.

Johan Bertilsson is a sergeant and firearms and tactics instructor and has been working since 2005 as chief self-defense instructor at Skåne County Police Department, Swedish National Police Force. Since 2009, he has been a PhD student at the Department of Clinical Sciences, Lund University. His research interests include perceptive, cognitive, and motor skill performance depending on the effects of internal and external pressures such as pretraining and psychological and physical stress.

Petra Binkova is a senior officer at the Ministry of the Interior of the Czech Republic (Crime Prevention Department). She focuses on the prevention of violence on children, searching for missing children, and international collaboration on human rights issues and/or crime prevention. She is a national coordinator of the European Crime Prevention Award and a member of the Committee for the Rights of the Child of the Czech Republic. Moreover, she is a lecturer and member of the external comprehensive exam committee at the School of Humanities, Charles University, Prague.

Erik Borglund has a doctorate in computer and systems science and is a researcher at the Archival and Information Management School of Mid Sweden University. His main research interests are digital recordkeeping, document management, information systems in crisis management, information systems design, and computer-supported cooperative work. He has been a sworn police officer for 20 years.

Mark Butler is a former UK Police Assistant Senior Scenes of Crime Officer and crime scene investigator instructor at the National Training School. His main area of work is teaching undergraduate crime scene science students. He has advised the UK police forces on training and developing expertise in crime scene investigation. He is also a member of the Institution of Fire Engineers. Butler is a senior lecturer in crime scene science, School of Science and Engineering, Teesside University, Tees Valley, UK.

Gunilla K. Byrman is a professor in Swedish at Linnaeus University in Växjö, Sweden. She earned her PhD in Scandinavian languages at Lund University in 1989. Her primary research interests are text, gender, and discourse analysis in professional contexts and the media. Since 2008, she has been doing research in forensic linguistics. Currently, she is involved in a project that studies writing in education and occupational life with a special focus on the police.

Neil Cook is a police inspector serving for Greater Manchester Police. Cook is a member of the national High Potential Development Scheme and is studying postgraduate diploma in police leadership and management at Warwick Business School, University of Warwick, Coventry, UK. His research topic for his dissertation was on the links between fitness and on-duty performance among police officers, where supporting evidence was found that increasing an officer's aerobic fitness levels increased his self-rated performance levels.

Louise Cooke is the director of postgraduate programmes in the Centre for Information Management at Loughborough University, UK. Her research interests focus on information and knowledge management; information law, policy, and ethics; and the dynamics of online communication and interaction in online forums. Her research has been widely published and cited in international journals. She was the recipient of the Loughborough

University 2012 Enterprise Award (Knowledge Transfer) for her research undertaken with Leicestershire Police. She has won a number of awards for teaching excellence.

Luís Fiães Fernandes holds a master's degree in strategy, a postgraduate degree in political and international sciences, and a police sciences degree from the Advanced Institute of Police Sciences and Internal Security. He is a lieutenant colonel of the Public Security Police, and he has served as an advisor to several ministers of internal affairs of the Portuguese government. He teaches at the Advanced Institute of Police Sciences and Internal Security. He has written more than a dozen scientific articles and book chapters about police, policing, and terrorism.

Per-Anders Fransson earned a PhD in medical science from Lund University, Sweden, in 2005 and was an associate professor in 2009. He holds a senior researcher position at the Department of Clinical Sciences at Lund University. His research interests include the human central nervous system, the sensory and motor systems, and the functional decline or adaptation of these systems as an effect of physical and psychological stress, drugs, and new training paradigms.

Peter J. Fredriksson is a police sergeant who worked as both a firefighter and a paramedic before becoming a police officer. He is a self-defense instructor and a developer of strategies concerning tactics, firearms, self-defense, and training at the Skåne County Police Department. His research interests include performance under pressure and adaptation needed for different, common, or dangerous situations.

Gerald Dapaah Gyamfi is a PhD student at the University of Phoenix. He has a master's degree in human resource development from the University of Manchester, UK. He is a fellow of the Institute of Chartered Secretaries and Administrators, UK. In addition, he is a senior lecturer and the dean of Management Faculty and teaches risk management and operations management at the University of Professional Studies in Ghana. He has authored articles and books on policing in Ghana.

Martin Hrinko has worked for 19 years in various positions in the Police of the Czech Republic. He is the author or coauthor of several key texts and publications focusing on community policing (CP) and CP-related issues in the Czech Republic. He participated in several research projects centered on security issues, most often in collaboration with researchers from the

Technical University of Ostrava, where he works as an external lecturer and researcher. He is an author of the Meeting with Citizens project and coauthor and tutor of the CP implementation strategy in Latvia.

Thomas W. Jackson is a chair of Information and Knowledge Management and is the director of the Centre for Information Management. His research areas are electronic communications and information retrieval and applied and theory-based knowledge management, including natural language processing email knowledge extraction (EKE) system that has the world's best F-ranking measure. He is on a number of editorial boards of international journals and is a reviewer for many more journals. He has published more than 130 papers in peer-reviewed journals and conferences.

David Jenks is a professor and founding chair of the Department of Criminology at the University of West Georgia. His research interests include police structure and organization, comparative/international policing, research methodology, and terrorism. He is currently working on a book, *Crime and Globalization*. He previously worked for or with the International Scientific and Professional Advisory Council of the United Nations, the Geneva Centre for the Democratic Control of Armed Forces, the Los Angeles Police Department, and the US Department of State. More recently, he completed a fellowship in Israel awarded by the Foundation for the Defense of Democracies.

Lee Michael Johnson is an associate professor of criminology at the University of West Georgia. He earned a PhD in sociology at Iowa State University in 2001. Professor Johnson's current research interests are juvenile delinquency, victimology, and criminal justice policy and practice. He has published articles on the subjects of juvenile delinquency, victimization, corrections, and policing. He is also the editor of *Experiencing Corrections: From Practitioner to Professor.*

Peter Johnstone is a professor of criminal justice at the University of North Texas. He holds a BA (Hons), an LLM in international criminal law, and a PhD in comparative law. He has written a number of books and articles on policing, financial crime, and the history of crime. Before leaving the United Kingdom in 2001, Johnstone was reader-in-law at Northampton University and research fellow at the Institute of Advanced Legal Studies, University of London. He has been an advisor to Her Majesty's government and the recipient of grants from UK and European funding councils.

Staffan Karp is an associate professor of pedagogy at the Department of Education at Umeå University in Sweden. His research interests are values and norms in the police culture with a focus on development and change. He has an extensive experience in teaching students training to become police officers, and he is also the chairman of Police Education at Umeå University, Umeå, Sweden.

Hamid R. Kusha is an associate professor of criminal justice in the School of Justice and Social Sciences at Anna Maria College, Paxton, Massachusetts. Besides publishing refereed and invited articles, he has authored three scholarly books with two more in progress. He has taught and written on comparative crime, law and justice, policing, and international terrorism.

Tessa Lambri is a doctoral candidate at the Centre for Information Management at Loughborough University. Lambri studied criminology at Middlesex University. She is a police officer working as an intelligence analyst for a regional counterterrorism unit. She also worked as part of a peer review team on the internalization and evaluation of the UK National Intelligence Model. Lambri is currently working with the Home Office and British police forces and has developed a police system acceptance tool kit to assist the police organization in the implementation and adoption of new technology.

Lars Erik Lauritz is the director of Police Education at Umeå University and has 15 years of experience as a police officer. His main interests in police research are identity construction, personality, and learning preferences among police students and police officers. He has been engaged in several longitudinal studies involving police in Sweden and South Africa, particularly tracking police students and focusing on their learning preferences and changes during their police education. Currently, he leads a project studying the processes in which lonesome-coming refugee juveniles receive negative decisions in the asylum process.

David Lowe is principal lecturer at Liverpool John Moores University, UK. He teaches criminal law, public law, and policing and terrorism studies. Until 2007, he was a police officer in a large metropolitan force in England where most of his services were in Special Branch's counterterrorism unit. Besides policing in general, terrorism is his main interest. Along with providing expert commentary for the UK and European media, he has publications in policing and counterterrorism. Likewise, he has been frequently called upon by the UK media for expert commentaries on these areas.

Eileen M. Luna-Firebaugh is an associate professor of American Indian law and policy at the University of Arizona. She is Choctaw and Cherokee. She is an attorney and also holds an MPA from the Kennedy School at Harvard University with an emphasis on criminal justice policy and law. For 10 years, she has been a justice of the Colorado River Indian Tribes Appellate Court, and in 2013 she was chosen to serve as a visiting judge in the New Zealand Rangatahi Court. She authored a number of articles, chapters, and monographs in policing, tribal justice, and juvenile diversion programs for American Indian youth.

Mans Magnusson earned an MD in 1981 and a PhD in 1986 from Lund University, Sweden. He became an associate professor of otorhinolaryngology in 1988 and received full professorship in 1999. He presently holds a position as senior consultant and head of the Division of Otolaryngology and is head of the Section of Senses, Neuroscience and Psychiatry of the Department of Clinical Sciences, Lund University. His research interests involve inner ear and vestibular disorders and postural control and orientation.

Ian Marsh is a principal lecturer in criminology and criminal justice at Liverpool Hope University, UK, where he is the director of the master's program in criminal justice. He has authored, coauthored, and edited a number of books, including *Crime and Criminal Justice* (Routledge 2011), *Crime, Justice and the Media* (Routledge 2009), and *Sociology: Making Sense of Society*, 4th ed. (Pearson 2009).

Todd L. Matthews earned his doctorate at Mississippi State University and is currently an associate professor and coordinator of the organizational leadership program at the University of Maryland–Eastern Shore. Dr. Matthews' research focuses on the issues of social trust, civic participation, religion, inequality, and environment. He has published widely in the social sciences, including highly rated journals such as *Social Forces, Journal for the Scientific Study of Religion,* and *Journal of Homosexuality,* among many others. He has also published chapters in several books.

Chelete Monyane is a senior researcher at the Centre for Sociological Research, University of Johannesburg, South Africa. He has published widely on interdisciplinary issues ranging from political economy of criminal justice and criminal law, socioeconomic rights, consolidation of democratic institutions, and electoral reforms. His publications include "Operation Rachel: A case study in cross-border police cooperation," "What is democratic consolidation," "Theory and practice of criminal justice in Southern Africa," and "Adjudicating non-justiciable rights: Socio-economic rights and South African Constitutional Court" (2011). His research interests include constitutionalism, socioeconomic rights, and democratic governance.

Urban Nuldén is an associate professor of information systems and the head of the Department of Applied IT at the University of Gothenburg and Chalmers University of Technology. He has a research interest in IT in the police domain and has for many years been a head of a research group that studies IT in various crisis management contexts.

Adewale A. Olutola holds LLB (Hons) and LLM degrees in law from Nigeria and a doctoral degree in policing from the Tshwane University of Technology, South Africa. Olutola is a member of the Criminological and Victimological Society of Southern Africa, the Policing Association of Southern Africa, and the Nigerian Bar Association. His research focuses on legal issues, crime prevention, and comparative criminal justice systems.

Jinwoo Park is a police lieutenant for the national police force of South Korea. In 2006, he was given a scholarship to pursue a master's degree in criminal justice at the University of North Texas. During this time, he also visited a number of agencies in the Dallas area and spent some time with the Dallas Police Department. He is particularly interested in comparative policing methods and has returned to active duty in South Korea with the intention of pursuing a PhD in the near future. He currently serves in Seoul, the nation's capital.

Mitesh Patel earned a PhD in medical science from Lund University, Sweden, in 2009. He is a research associate in the Department of Neuro-Otology, Charing Cross Hospital, Imperial College London, London, UK, and lecturer in balance and spatial orientation in the Department of Medicine at Imperial College London. His research interests include the control and disorders of the vestibular system, posture, and gait. He has authored a number of studies and speaks regularly at international and national conferences in the field of vestibular science.

Jisu Ketan Pattanaik earned a PhD in sociology from the National Institute of Criminology and Forensic Science, New Delhi, India. He is currently an assistant professor at the National University of Study and Research in Law, Ranchi. His research interest includes women police, women prisoners, girls' education, human development, gender, and governance. He has worked with several agencies of the United Nations and the Administrative Staff College of India (ASCI) in Odisha. He has published 16 articles in national and international journals and also a book on women police in India.

Lars-Folke Piledahl is the district police commissioner of Malmo, Sweden. He became the chief of staff of the Skåne County Police Department in 2005, and since 2011 he has been the chief of the South Skåne Police District. He is interested in education and strives to expand science- and experience-based knowledge aimed at enhancing the safety of police officers by improving their skills through better training methods and equipment.

Karl Roberts is the director of research at the Centre for Policing, Intelligence and Counter Terrorism at Macquarie University, Sydney, NSW, Australia, and an associate professor of criminal justice at the University of Massachusetts, Amherst, Massachusetts. He is a forensic psychologist and specializes in the study of investigative interviewing and threat assessment, focusing particularly on violent extremism and stalking behaviors. He works closely with the police and other agencies in interview and investigation training and provides operational advice.

Cornelis Roelofse is an associate professor of criminology and criminal justice at the University of Limpopo, Mankweng, South Africa. Formerly, he was an elected member of the Provincial Parliament of Limpopo. Roelofse chaired the 2010 IPES conference in Malta and organized the All Africa Conference on Organised Crime and Other Criminal Justice Issues in 2012. He founded the All Africa Criminal Justice Society (ACJUS) and launched its journal, *Just Africa*. He is deputy president of ACJUS, a member of the board of the Criminological and Victimological Society of Southern Africa, and a member of the executive committee of the Policing Association of Southern Africa (POLSA).

Paul A. Rolle has been a police officer since 1983. In May 2011 he was appointed director and officer in charge of the Central Detective Unit of the Royal Bahamas Police Force, Nassau. He graduated from the College of the Bahamas in 1998 with a degree in public administration, and he was the recipient of the President's Award. He completed studies for the advanced certificate in public administration at the University of the West Indies. In 2004, he was awarded the prestigious Chevening Scholarship by the British Foreign and Commonwealth Office to pursue graduate studies in the United Kingdom, where he graduated in 2006, with a master's degree in criminology from the University of Leicester.

Tim Thompson is a reader at Teesside University, Tees Valley, UK. He has a background in biological anthropology. He is a fellow of the Forensic Science Society and is on the council for the British Association for Biological Anthropology and Osteoarchaeology. He has an active research interest in the application of forensic and crime scene science within society.

Wendell C. Wallace is a doctoral candidate of the Criminology and Criminal Justice program at the University of the West Indies at St. Augustine. He earned a bachelor's degree in history and human resource management and a master's degree in criminology and criminal justice (with distinction) from the University of London, UK (External Program), and he is currently preparing for his call to the Bar in England and Wales. His research interests include juvenile delinquency, gangs, policing, law reform, and the tourism–crime relationship.

Vidisha Barua Worley is an assistant professor of criminal justice at the University of North Texas at Dallas. She is a founding member of the Institute for Legal Studies in Criminal Justice, Sam Houston State University, Huntsville, Texas. Her research areas include police and prison officers' liabilities for the use of tasers and stun guns, police stress, ethical issues in criminal justice, sexual assault in prisons, crime and media, and terrorism. Her published books include *Press & Media: Law Manual* (2002) and *Terrorism in India* (2006).

Acknowledgments

The editors of this book thank the tremendous contributions of the following individuals: Carolyn Spence (senior editor), Ed Curtis (project editor), and Marsha Pronin (project coordinator) from the CRC Press/Taylor & Francis Group, who together steered this project from inception to completion; Amrin Sahay (project manager) and her supervisor, Muhilan Selvaraj (production manager), from Datamatics Global Services Limited for patiently copyediting this book and providing professional assistance, tremendously enhancing its overall appearance and readability; and Amanda Chestnut, our graduate assistant from the College at Brockport in the State University of New York, who helped us manage the administrative aspects in compiling the manuscripts.

We also acknowledge our institutions that have extended tremendous support for this project. The International Police Executive Symposium has truly created a forum for international police scholars and practitioners to contribute to the advancement of policing knowledge. The able stewardship of its founding president, Dilip K. Das, made the completion of this book less demanding. Finally, we acknowledge the logistical support that the College at Brockport in the State University of New York has extended to its editors. The college has provided office space and personnel that facilitated the job for finishing this book.

We extend our sincerest gratitude to all of you.

Introduction
Environmental Factors for Policing Evolutions

MELCHOR C. DE GUZMAN,
AIEDEO MINTIE DAS, AND DILIP K. DAS

Lundman (1980) suggests that the evolution of policing follows the ever-changing landscapes of social, technological, political, and crime environments where the police operate. In particular, he attributed the evolution of policing to the developments in society that he called "patterns of solidarity," that is, the development of communities from mechanistic to organic societies. Alongside this societal evolution, he suggests that two other developments accompany such changes. He identifies the rates and images of criminality and the emergence of a dominant elite in society as additional influences on the evolution of policing. He claims that, as societies evolve, crime rates and disorder problems become more pronounced. Likewise, he adds that the evolution of society has produced social classes that trigger competitions for dominance and formulation of safety forces to secure that dominance (Bayley and Shearing 2001; de Guzman and Kumar 2011).

Lundman's theory was supported by historical facts as outlined in a book by Travis and Langworthy (2008), who traced the histories of different societies, such as those of Rome, Italy, and Japan, and found evidence of the proposed influences of the patterns of solidarity on the types of policing. However, the emergence of public-paid policing is not the only evolutionary effect of these factors. Other environmental factors have added several dimensions to the present police character and behavior. In a test of Lundman's theory, de Guzman and Kumar (2011) proposed that the rates and images of criminality influence the quantity of police, while the emergence and struggles for dominance by different classes predict the quality of policing in society. Indeed, in their retest of Lundman's theory, using India as a setting, de Guzman and Kumar (2011) found that as crime and disorders become more pronounced, the number of police officers and police units increase. Likewise, they found that the police behaved according to the preferences of the social elite. Thus, their study provided explanations for the quantity and quality of policing apart from the forms (i.e., formal and informal) of policing. These findings highlighted the ever-changing nature of policing. However, research has not provided insights into the ever-changing roles, practices, and management of the police, especially across countries.

Several other factors shape policing evolutions: social environments, technology, political environments, and criminality in society. The later sections present discussions on how these four societal developments relate to policing evolutions. One caveat, the literature in this analysis essay is mostly from Western annals. This introductory piece presents the foreground for which the rich experiences of other countries could provide context to readers in the presentation of evolving police roles, practices, and administration across the world.

Social Environments and Policing Evolution

Social environments refer mostly to the human ecological changes that are happening within the working environments of policing. For example, Caldero and Crank (2004) suggest that US policing has dealt with a multiplicity of races, cultures, and beliefs that shaped its evolution. Furthermore, they claim that these human ecological changes are accompanied by nonadherence to the assimilation philosophy that has been long held in US society. Instead, Caldero and Crank (2004) stated that the United States has adopted the distinctiveness theory. Distinctiveness theory suggests that not only are the people encouraged to perpetuate their culture but the state encourages the practice and retention of these cultural practices (Caldero and Crank 2004). In other words, inhabitants, especially immigrants, are no longer required to embrace US culture but are allowed to retain their original cultures. Thus, the police have to adapt to these new social realities in order to perform their work and survive as organizations. They have to educate themselves on the cultures of their constituents, which includes learning the language, behaviors, and attitudes that will allow them to effectively interact with their constituents. Thus, a huge challenge for the police emerges, that is, how they would be able to cope with these emerging social conditions. Thus, it is not merely just patterns of solidarity that shapes policing but also emerging new cultures and philosophies.

The US experience is not unique. Countries around the world have experiences about globalization and the social changes that emerge from these globalization phenomena (Sheptyki 1999). These global changes have redefined policing and have led to the marketization of security, including the provision of policing services. Other social phenomena are the changing dominant elites in different societies. These changes would certainly shift the nature and character of the police. Take, for instance, the changes happening in Afghanistan, Burma, Iraq, the states of the former Soviet Union, the Middle Eastern states, and the African states. The changing social landscapes of the countries have included a redefinition of women's rights, enhancements of human rights for marginalized and indigenous communities, tolerance for different beliefs and persuasions, and the policing of special populations such as the mentally ill or the homeless. The chapters in this book present some of these developments alongside the developments of "new" policing in these democratic and democratizing countries.

Technology and Policing Evolution

Technology could be defined as the level of knowledge that society has acquired (see Travis and Langworthy (2008) for the conceptualizations of technology). This technology takes two dimensions: soft and hard. Soft policing technology refers to innovations in the training and management of police organizations. Soft technology is produced by formal education, training, and experiences. The evolution of soft technology is also accompanied by the evolution of hard technology (Wilson and Kelling 1982). Hard technology refers to the equipment that police use in the performance of their functions. Several scholars have analyzed the effects of technology on the police. For example, Wilson and Kelling's (1982) analysis of the impact of technology in policing considered technology to have played a major role in police evolution in the United States from the political era to the professional era and finally to the community era. They believed that policing technology has improved how policing was done but was responsible for the turbulent relations of the police with the public. In contrast, Walker (2001) presents arguments to show that technology has really made the police closer to the public and has improved their performance of these roles: quick response, directed patrol, differential response, and other innovative ideas. Finally, the use of computers has taken hold on policing technology. Police are now using modern communications systems on the Internet such as Facebook, Twitter, YouTube, and other social media (de Guzman and Jones 2012; International Association of Chiefs of Police 2010).

Hard technology is not the only significant factor for change. Soft technology, too, is being developed and has an impact on policing and police officers. Police officers are now being trained in cultural and gender sensitivity and how to deal with special populations and terrorists. Thus, police officers are developing means and ways of learning different languages and different communication levels. New techniques in investigative interrogation and interviewing are being developed (see Gordom and Fleisher (2011) for these developments in investigations). Higher-educated police applicants are getting to be the norm when selecting police officers (Cole and Smith 2011). Departments are no longer placing premiums on experiences that emphasize an authoritarian character and strong presence as qualifications for becoming a police officer. Instead, unbiased or nondiscriminatory attitudes, interpersonal skills, communication skills, and people skills in general are slowly being used as criteria for hiring (Swanson, Territo, and Taylor 2012).

Technology will continue to play a huge part in the evolution of policing. Lundman (1980) has predicted it as having an impact on the rates and images of criminality as well as the emergence of the dominant elite. In fact, the new elite are those that have command over technology and are slowly creeping into the policing domain. Scientists now have major roles in policing with the use of forensic technology such as DNA, fingerprint analysis, and psychological profiling (Orthmann and Hess 2013). Alongside these uses of hard science, police departments have slowly adopted business and management theories to screen, train, and supervise officers (Swanson et al. 2012). People who are technologically savvy are also becoming ubiquitous in policing. Crime analysts, intelligence analysts, and information systems experts are now slowly becoming integral parts of the police department personnel. This development is because of adoption of computer technology such as Compstat, fusion centers, intelligence centers, and crime mapping technologies (Henry 2003; Ratcliffe 2008). Therefore, officers should learn either new technologies or collaborate with technical people to carry out their mandates.

Political Environments and Policing Evolution

Power arrangements in a state create ideological upheavals that tend to put the police at the center of these changes. The police are the political instruments of the state in its maintenance of the *status quo* (Lenin 2010). Travis and Langworthy (2008) based their whole book on policing on the thesis that the police are involved in balance-of-power struggles. Alongside these political changes are the ethical and management reforms in policing, whether on being more rights conscious or catering to the needs of the marginalized groups in the society. Sometimes these political reforms create ripples that shake regional arrangements such as the formation of police regional cooperation or even multinational or global police cooperation (Das and Kratcoski 2001). In most circumstances, we could only document reforms in emerging democratic states as they tend to democratize their police. However, even more established democratic states continue to reform their police, such as the ever-continuing adoption of and innovations on the implementation of community policing. Police departments tweak community-oriented policing in their particular jurisdiction to accommodate cravings for citizen participation and inputs in policing (Albrecht 2012; Mesko and Maver 2012).

The other effects of changing political landscapes and ideologies result in the redefinition of the meaning of safety and who should be responsible for it. This notion was first propounded by Bayley and Shearing (2001) who suggested that policing would undergo a revolution due to the nonmonopoly by the state of the ability to define the meaning of public safety and the growing permissiveness by states in allowing nongovernmental entities to provide this safety. In these emerging arrangements, the police no longer have the monopoly of delivering police service. Thus, it can start seeing itself being more managed using civilian bureaucratic principles rather than along military doctrines (Coleman 2012).

In countries that have experienced successful political revolutions, these changes in power are accompanied by the reorganization of their respective police as well as the reorientation of the police missions. Countries such as India, during its transition to self-rule (de Guzman and Kumar 2011), South Africa, with its eventful change to a nonapartheid state (Singh 2004), the Philippines, after its people power revolution (Campos 1991), and many other countries have experienced major reforms in their police forces. However, major social upheavals are not necessary for these policing changes to occur. The United States has had several reforms implemented throughout the course of its history (Kelling and Moore 1988). Law enforcement in the United States has moved from the political era to the reform era and, more recently, to the community era. Writers document the political and ideological shifts as responsible for these eras. For example, scholars attribute the transition of US policing from political to reform due to the emergence of universalistic principles (Travis and Langworthy 2008). Likewise, the transition of US police from the reform era to the community era was due to the civil rights revolutions that occurred in the 1960s (Walker 2001). These political and ideological changes reflect the changing nature of the character as well as the practices of policing.

Crimes and Their Effects on Police Evolution

Perhaps, of all the factors in the evolution of policing, the notion about crime is the most influential force for police innovations. Historical accounts of the emergence of the police and police reforms are mostly argued through the evolution of crime. For example, the London bobbies were organized in response to the growing menace of crime (Cole and Smith 2011). Colonial powers also used the police in response to the emergence of disorders in society (Bayley 1983; de Guzman and Kumar 2011; Travis and Langworthy 2008). In fact, more recent history in the United States attests to this tremendous influence of crime on the evolution of the police. In 1994, the rate of crime was the impetus for enactment of the Comprehensive Crime Control Act, and its major component was the recruitment and training of police officers for community policing (Evans and Owens 2007). Following the 2001 attacks on the United States by terrorists, the Patriot Act was enacted and eventually the Homeland Security Department was created. This increased level of disorder has produced an evident shift in policing strategies and priorities (Beresford 2004; Kim and de Guzman 2012). The major components of these legislations were the training and development of law enforcement for counterterrorism (Greene and Herzog 2009). Numerous other crime phenomena have shaped the evolution of how policing is done. Experiences with street crimes have resulted in different patrol experiments and strategies (Groff, Johnson, Ratcliffe, and Wood 2013). Domestic violence became a major catalyst for mandatory arrest policies (Sherman and Cohn 1989). The war on drugs has increased police aggressiveness in interdiction strategies and surveillance work (Lyman 2011). The list could go on as to how crime influences police practices and creates waves for police innovation.

Currently, the emergence of transnational and global crimes has precipitated the debate for new security arrangements (Sheptyki 1999). Crimes such as money laundering, drug trafficking, human trafficking, smuggling, and hooliganism have led to regional as well as international cooperation (Gerspacher 2008). For instance, Interpol's role has taken central stage again with the emergence of these transnational crimes (Gagliardi 2012).

The police have been considered to be agents of social change. The evidence seems to indicate that this perception about the police might be a misconception. The police have been reacting to their environment (Maguire 2001). Simon (1964) suggested that the organizational goals should be construed as constraint sets that have to be minimally satisfied in order to be effective and survive. Following that argument, Travis and Langworthy (2008) argued that police are indeed just reacting to a whole host of constraints. Furthermore, they explained that police in a democratic society are typically going to be reactive rather than proactive (Travis and Langworthy 2008). Apparently, the paradigm has shifted—the police are changed by their environments more than they change their environment. No longer should the police be perceived as catalysts for change but should simply react to the world around them and be shaped by the forces surrounding them (Zhao, Lovrich, and Thurman 1999).

References

Albrecht, J. F. (2012). Analyzing the implementation and evolution of community policing in the United States and Scandinavia. In de Guzman, M. C., Das, D. K., and Das, M. A. (eds), *Strategic Responses to Crime: Thinking Locally, Acting Globally*, pp. 3–26. Boca Raton, FL: CRC Press.

Bayley, D. H. (1983). The police and political order in India. *Asian Survey*, 23(4): 484–496.

Bayley, D. H. and Shearing, C. D. (2001). *The New Structure of Policing: Description, Conceptualization, and Research Agenda*. Washington, DC: National Institute of Justice, Office of Justice Programs.

Beresford, A. D. (2004). Homeland security as an American ideology: Implications for US policy and action. *Journal of Homeland Security and Emergency Management*, 1(3): 1–22.

Caldero, M. A. and Crank, J. P. (2004). *Police Ethics: The Corruption of Noble Cause* (2nd edition). Cincinnati, OH: LexisNexis.

Campos, C. C. (1991). Law enforcement policy and strategy in the Republic of the Philippines. *Police Studies*, 14(2): 76–104.

Cole, G. F. and Smith, C. E. (2011). *Criminal Justice in America* (6th edition). Belmont, CA: Cengage Learning.

Coleman, T. G. (2012). 2010! But is anyone counting? In de Guzman, M. C., Das, D. K., and Das, M. A. (eds.), *Strategic Responses to Crime: Thinking Locally, Acting Globally*, pp. 43–67. Boca Raton, FL: CRC Press.

Das, D. K. and Kratcoski, P. C. (2001). International police cooperation: A world perspective. In Koenig, D. J. and Das, D. K. (eds.), *International Police Cooperation: A World Perspective*, pp. 2–27. Lanham, MD: Lexington Books.

de Guzman, M. C. and Jones, M. A. (2012). E-policing: Environmental and organizational correlates of website features and characteristics among large police departments in the United States of America. *International Journal of Electronic Government Research*, 8(1): 64–82.

de Guzman, M. C. and Kumar, K. S. (2011). Extending Lundman's theory on policing: The evidence from the literature focusing on India. *Policing: An International Journal of Police Strategies & Management*, 34(3): 403–418.

Evans, W. N. and Owens, E. G. (2007). COPS and crime. *Journal of Public Economics*, 91(1–2): 181–201.

Gagliardi, P. (2012). Transnational organized crime and gun violence: A case for firearm forensic intelligence sharing. *International Review of Law, Computers & Technology*, 25(1): 83–95.

Gerspacher, N. (2008). The history of international police: A 150-year evolution in trends and approaches. *Global Crime*, 9(1–2): 169–184.

Gordom, N. J. and Fleisher, W. L. (2011). *Effective Interviewing and Interrogation Techniques* (3rd edition). Burlington, MA: Elsevier.

Greene, J. R. and Herzog, S. (2009). The implications of terrorism on the formal and social organization of the police. In Weisburd, D., Feucht, T. E., Hakimi, I., Mock, L. F., and Perry, S. (eds.), *To Protect and to Serve: Policing in Age of Terrorism*, pp. 143–176. New York: Springer.

Groff, E. R., Johnson, L., Ratcliffe, J. H. and Wood, J. (2013). Exploring the relationship between foot and car patrol in violent crime areas. *Policing: An International Journal of Police Strategies & Management*, 36(1): 119–139.

Henry, V. E. (2003). *The Compstat Paradigm: Management Accountability in Policing, Business and the Public Sector*. Flushing, NY: Looseleaf Law Publications.

International Association of Chiefs of Police (IACP). (2010). *IACP Center for Social Media 2010 Survey Results*. Retrieved November 11, 2010, from http://www. iacpsocial media.org/Resources/Publications/SurveyResults.aspx

Kelling, G. L. and Moore, M. H. (1988). *The Evolving Strategy of Policing*. Washington, DC: US Department of Justice.

Kim, M. and de Guzman, M. C. (2012). Police paradigm shift after the 9/11 terrorist attacks: the empirical evidence from the United States municipal police departments. *Criminal Justice Studies: A Critical Journal of Crime, Law and Society*, 25(4): 323–342.

Lenin, V. I. (2010). *State and Revolution*. Whitefish, MT: Kessinger Publishing.

Lundman, R. J. (1980). *Police and Policing: An Introduction*. New York: Holt, Rinehart and Winston.

Lyman, M. D. (2011). *Drugs in Society: Causes, Concepts and Control* (6th edition). Burlington, MA: Elsevier.

Maguire, E. (2001). *Organizational Structure in American Police Agencies: Context, Complexity, and Control.* Albany, NY: SUNY Press.

Mesko, G. and Maver, D. (2012). Think globally, solve locally: Security threats—From public opinion to a proper response. In de Guzman, M. C., Das, D. K., and Das, M. A. (eds.), *Strategic Responses to Crime: Thinking Locally, Acting Globally*, pp. 27–42. Boca Raton, FL: CRC Press.

Orthmann, C. H. and Hess, K. M. (2013). *Criminal Investigation* (10th edition). Clifton Park, NY: Delmar Cengage Learning.

Ratcliffe, J. H. (2008). *Intelligence-Led Policing.* Portland, OR: Willan Publishing.

Sheptycki, J. (1999). Policing, postmodernism and transnationalization. In Smandych, R. (ed.), *Governable Places: Readings on Governmentality and Crime Control*, pp. 215–238. Brookfield, VT: Ashgate.

Sherman, L. W. and Cohn, E. G. (1989). The impact of research on legal policy: The Minneapolis domestic violence experiment. *Law & Society Review*, 23(1): 117–144.

Simon, H. (1964). On the concept of organizational goal. *Administrative Science Quarterly*, 9: 1–22.

Singh, D. (2004). Violators and victims: A historical review of policing in South Africa after a decade of democracy. *Acta Criminologica*, 17(3): 86–98.

Swanson, C. R., Territo, L. and Taylor, R. W. (2012). *Police Administration: Structures, Processes, and Behaviors* (8th edition). Upper Saddle River, NJ: Pearson.

Travis III, L. F. and Langworthy, R. H. (2008). *Policing in America: A Balance of Forces* (4th edition). Cincinnati, OH: Prentice Hall.

Walker, S. (2001). Broken windows and fractured history: The use and misuse of history in recent police patrol analysis. In Dunham, R. and Alpert, G. (eds.), *Critical Issues in Policing* (4th edition), pp. 480–492. Prospect Heights, IL: Waveland Press.

Wilson, J. Q. and Kelling, G. L. (1982). Broken windows: The police and neighborhood safety. *Atlantic Monthly*, 249(3): 29–38.

Zhao, J., Lovrich, N. and Thurman, Q. (1999). The status of community policing in American cities: Facilitators and impediments revisited. *Policing: An International Journal of Police Strategies & Management*, 22(1): 74–92.

The Evolving Nature of Police Roles in Democratic and Democratizing Societies

I

A Clash of Modern Professionalism and Oriental Despotism
The Case of Iran, 1878–1979

1

HAMID R. KUSHA

Contents

Introduction

Iran is a major Middle Eastern country with 25 centuries of continuous existence. Historians have divided Iran's long history into pre- and post-Islamic periods. During the pre-Islamic period (708 BC–AD 642), five imperial dynasties ruled the country with varying degrees of sophistication in law enforcement structure and philosophy: the Medes (708–550 BC), the Achaemenids (550–330 BC), the Seleucids (312–247 BC), the Arsacids (also known as the Parthians) (247 BC–AD 224), and the Sasanids (AD 224–642). In the post-Islamic period that commenced with Iran's invasion by Muslim Arabs in AD 642, nearly 30 major and minor dynasties ruled the country, the last one being the Pahlavi dynasty (r. 1925–1979) that was overthrown in 1979, replaced by the Islamic Republic that the Ayatollah Ruhollah Khomeini built (r. 1979–1989). Although the genesis of Iran's socioeconomic and legal modernization took shape in the late nineteenth and early twentieth centuries as the country was being ruled by a number of relatively enlightened Qajar monarchs [e.g., Nasser al-Din Shah (1848–1896), Mozaffar al-Din Shah (1896–1907), and Ahmad Shah (1809–1924)], it was under the rule of the two Pahlavi monarchs, Reza Shah (r. 1925–1941) and Mohammad Reza Shah (r. 1941–1979), whose comprehensive plans for modern policing were undertaken throughout the country (Alibabaie 1385/1999; Bakhash 1978, 1981, 1992; Keddie 1999; Kusha 2000, 2006; Yarshater 1992). However, the Pahlavi monarchs, like their Qajar predecessors, were unable to inculcate the core principle of Western professionalism in Iranian policing because the centuries-old philosophy of law and order in Iran was antithetical to the new policing philosophy enunciated by the European reformers, for example, Sir Robert Peel. In addition, monarchs in Iran ruled on the basis of the centuries-old despotic principles that were conceived of the police as organized force at the service of the reigning monarchs rather than at the service of their subjects (Amaanat 1997; Arjomand 1984; Keddie 1999). Therefore, with the overthrow of the despotic Pahlavi monarchy in 1979, it was hoped that republicanism would bring a more democratic policing philosophy to Iran, a philosophy that would be harmonious with the initial democratization ideals of the 1979 revolution.

However, the ideal has not eventuated during the past three decades because the Islamic Republic, as defined by its theocratic constitution (that replaced Iran's 1906 modern constitution), is not an ordinary republican form of governance as understood in modern political vernacular. Islamic Republic is lofty "divine governance" whose stated objective is the creation of a "model society," based on Islamic criteria that, among others, cover policing. The reconstruction of this utopian society and policing philosophy is not just hyperbola, but a strategic aim of the Islamic state expressed in postrevolutionary police literature and police training manuals. Therefore, from 1979 till present, an Islamic policing philosophy whose mottos are *Jaameh-e Mas'ul* (Responsible Society) and *Polis-e Paasokhgoo* (Accountable Police) has emerged. At first glance, these mottos sound novel, considering the fact that prior to the rise of the Islamic Republic, the thrust of Iranian policing discourse was that although police functioned as an organized deterrent force against criminogenic social elements, in order to protect society against crime and perversion, police—like other organs of the state—served the wishes and commands of the monarch in accordance with the Persian theory of kingship, the hegemonic political theory upon which the Persian monarchs had ruled from the time of the Achaemenids. The theory maintained that monarchs ruled on the basis of divine authority; thus, it was incumbent upon the state and its organs (e.g., police) to submit to the reigning monarch's wishes and commands. It was through this total submission that both the realm (*molk*) and the nation (*mellat*) would be secured, the taxes would be collected on time, and the malcontents would be vanquished. Reflecting this rationale, under the Pahlavi monarchy the mottos of the state and its organs, including police, were *Cheh Farman-e Yazdan* (Whether the Command of God) and *Cheh Farman-e Shah* (Whether the Command of the King). These mottos, in essence, put the reigning monarch(s) authority at par with that of the Almighty. As will be discussed shortly, the Iranian National Police functioned in the capacity of both the ideological and the Praetorian Guard of the monarchy. Modern police in Iran (be it under the Qajar or Pahlavi) were utilized for both ordinary law enforcement operations and suppressing political dissent (Alibabaie 1385/1999; Kusha 2006).

With the overthrow of the monarchy in 1979, there was much public anticipation and hope for a new policing philosophy that would be harmonious with the democratic ideals of the Islamic revolution. In fact, the dignitaries of the Islamic Republic are on record that during the past three decades (1979–2009), policing philosophy has dramatically changed in Iran due to the success of the Islamizing mandates of the revolution. Accordingly, Islamization of society and economy as well as legal relations has transformed police from their Praetorian Guard functionality to the one that responds to the service and security needs of the Iranian society.

Modern Policing in Advanced Democracies

What we consider as "modern policing" adhered to in advanced democracies of the world, most of which are located in the Western part of the Northern hemisphere, has its historical roots in societies that have gone through full capitalization in economy and society since the time of the Industrial Revolution (from 1840s till present). Due to these developments, modernity in policing implies that police are more than law enforcers per se; police are professional public servants whose main responsibility is to help the state serve and protect the public. Serving and protecting the public under modern policing is a balancing act between law and order on the one end and respect for the privacy and civil rights of the tax-paying citizens on the other end of the scale. Therefore, although police are authorized to investigate, gather intelligence, conduct surveillance, search, seize as well as use the construct of the so-called "force continuum" for garnering compliance (Thomas 2011). However, police powers are of a discretionary nature given under the collar of the state to help expediting the state's constitutionally mandated objectives. Modern police are held liable for their law enforcement activities; therefore, police ranks and files must exercise caution in utilizing each and every element of police authority as each is capable of functioning as a double-edged sword: the proper use of police authority can enhance the public trust in the police, as against the improper use of it that can be undermined, especially if it is of a chronic nature. This may sound common to seneschal and those who live in advanced democracies of the world accustomed to the operational dynamics of organized and discriminate professional policing modalities (Del Pozo 2004). In less advanced societies of the world, most of which are located in Asia, Africa, and Latin and Central Americas, the dynamics of police–community relationship is markedly different, to which reference will be made shortly. Iran is a classic example of a less democratized authoritarian society whose modern in-form yet despotic policing in-content is the main subject of this chapter. For the sake of clarity, the comparative thrust of this chapter is not that Western professionalism in policing is "good," or "spotless," whereas others are "bad," or criminogenic; but the thrust of this chapter is that the whole structure of policing in advanced democracies is subjected to a much more rigorous and orderly organizational as well as legal (constitutional) checks and balances in comparison with those of the less democratized ones. It is upon the structural viability of such checks and balances that police–citizen relations are regulated. Therefore, policing advanced democratic societies is not arbitrary, but is based on the recognition of, and respect for, the inviolability of the citizen rights by the police as articulated by the law. It is through adherence to these features of modern policing that a relatively healthy police–community relationship is being structured in the bulk of the advanced democracies whose organizational and cultural heritage is being passed on from one generation of police ranks and files to the next (Braga et al. 2006; Goldstein 1987; O'Hara 2005; Reichel 2008; Reiss 1992; Schafer 2007; Skolnick 1994; Stojkovic et al. 2010; Thomas 2011; Uchida 2010). On the contrary, police–community relationships in Iran have historically been engendered through arbitrary means and structures (Kusha 2006). This is despite the fact that police in Iran, like many others in developing Asian, African, Latin American, and the Middle Eastern societies, are modernized in form, but seldom in content. The end result has been one of the anomic incompatibilities between form and content: police seem modern in form (uniformed, relatively well equipped, and trained in use of the force continuum), but policing strategies and operations are geared for moral control of the public at large as exemplified by the Monkerat Preventive Patrol strategies or suppression of social and political dissent regardless of their root causes and merits. By and large, Iranian police ranks and files do not tolerate any form of challenge to their personal authorities in their day-to-day operations. In addition, compared to advanced democracies, Iranian police utilize their policing authority with impunity in depriving citizens of their constitutional rights. This is despite the fact that the Constitution of the Islamic Republic of Iran has recognized a wide range of civil and political rights, provided that the exercise of such rights does not violate a set of Islamic criteria. However, as pointed out above, in the Amnesty International Iran Report (2009), these criteria are vague or, as will be discussed shortly, contradict the letter and the spirit of the very Islamic sources from which they have been extracted and legalized in order to be enforced by the police.

An example is the Procedural Law for Enforcing Public Chastity and [female] Coverage (*Maten-e Kamel-e Qaanun-e Gostaresh-e Raah-kaarhaay-e Ejraiy-e Efaaf wa Hejaab*). This law has a preamble and 20 articles. The preamble states that "Hijaab is the most valued and becoming social and cultural icon of the Iranian-Islamic civilization whose history dates back Islam's entrance [in Iran]. However, it is under the Islamic culture that it reaches its most sacrosanct nature" (MHCIP Portal 2010). To achieve this objective, 23 state and national organizations are being authorized with detailed procedural laws as how to enforce the law for female coverage rules and regulations on the rationale that it is through the "adequacy of female coverage" that Islam's social mores and values can be protected in postrevolutionary Iran against the corrupting onslaught of the Western culture. Considering the historical significance of safeguarding Islam's high ideals that were being dismantled under Western-imposed modernization schemes under the Pahlavids, this law has empowered the Islamic state to police the propriety and unification of appearance of young and adult women throughout the country. In this attempt, what is completely ignored by those who have drafted the law and its enforcement mechanism is the fact that attempts to change human behavior by the penal force of the state have proven criminogenic throughout the world. Examples include the American Prohibition Era (1923–1933) that led to the rise and institutionalization of the organized crime; the Bolshevik attempt to uproot once and for religious faith in the USSR (1917–1992) that led to religious and political persecutions during the Stalinist Era (1929–1953) in the Gulags; the Cultural Revolution (1965–1975) under Maoist China; and so on. During the past three decades, attempts to force women into Islamic garb in Iran have also failed to the effect that the state now has to employ the whole state apparatus into cajoling millions of young and adult women into uniformity in appearance. The end result has been one of turning the Islamic police into instruments of gender-based violence whose presence in the daily lives of women in Iran has proven quite criminogenic rather than improving police–community relationship in postrevolutionary Iran. In addition, Iranian culture has historically been protective of any form of entanglement with females, especially in public. The involvement of police in forced Islamization of female Hijaab, as reported by the media, is a rebel-rousing endeavor. The Monkerat Preventive Patrol involves both moral lecturing and arresting women for violating the rules of appearance in public, engaging with the opposite sex, and commuting in public transportation system. Such engagements are reported of being dangerous for both male and female police officers because they engender public hostility and even violence against the arresting officer(s). Therefore, it could be argued that although police in Iran seem modern in form (uniformed, relatively well equipped, and trained in use of the force continuum), policing strategies and operations are geared for control of the social and political dissent regardless of their root causes and merits (Kusha 2000).

On the contrary, advanced democracies have gradually recognized the importance of enforcing variegated checks and balances in relation to the use of police authority under the collar of the state, a modern legal construct that by holding police liable for their actions allows redressing of wrongs committed by the police against citizens; by extension, it also holds the state responsible for the unauthorized, illegal, or criminal acts of the police. A classic example is the "New Police" that Sir Robert Peel created in 1828 in the persona of the London Metropolitan Police; most scholars agree that the modern policing principles set forth by Peel were the precursors of what we consider as the modality of the Western professionalism in policing. Peel modernized police not only in form, but also in content. He achieved this feat by making the new police a highly trained organized force under the strict government control which in essence made the successive British governments (thus the state) legally responsible for their proper utilization of the police. The new police were no longer supposed to act as booted thugs and hooligans, but as organized force that represented law and order on the one hand. On the other hand, the new police agents, known as the Bobbies (alluding to their Peelian heritage), were an entrenched part of the community whose presence was welcomed as a protector rather than an oppressor of the community. The Peelian modality of congruency between form and content in policing has historically become the hall mark of modern professionalism in policing (Reichel 2008; Uchida 2010).

From a Peelian modality perspective, the propriety in police conduct unless subjected to institutionalized norms, and procedures enforced at the departmental and state levels, is left to arbitrary criteria. Constitutional as well as organizational rules and procedures may abound on paper, but unregulated police conduct is a reflection of the fact that police are not adequately controlled by the government, or that the propriety of police conduct is ignored by the state for ulterior motives. In either case, the congruency between form and content in policing suffers. Following the Peelian modality, the rules of propriety in policing have gradually been institutionalized within the policing academies and training manuals from 1828 till present. In addition, police–community relationship has engendered a police–citizen dynamics whereby citizens do not necessarily conceive of the police as instruments of indiscriminate and unjust coercion per se, but as arbiters in their capacity as the server and protector of the public. Therefore, once in police custody, everyone is expected to be presumed innocent regardless of extraneous parameters [e.g., socioeconomic status (SES) as well as race, gender, religion, or ethnicity]. It is not up to the police to determine the guilt or innocence of the suspect in custody, but to ascertain that the legally proscribed custodial safeguards are adhered to by the arresting officer(s). Modern police are deemed obligated to protect both the victim and the alleged victimizers as the police, under the collar of the state, enforce laws (Dunham and Alpert 2010).

This balancing function of modern policing is maintained by the inculcation of the codes of professionalism in police subculture that include (1) the code of honor and integrity, (2) the code of bravery, (3) the code of dedication to the cause of justice, (4) the code of serving and protecting the community, and (5) the code of equity, social justice, and impartiality in enforcement (Uchida 2010). This, of course, is an *ideal* picture in relation to Western professional policing; it does not mean that police in advanced democracies do not violate citizens' rights; they do, but not with impunity. For example, the Anglo-American police literature is replete with both academic and investigative commissions' findings in relation to the abuse of police authority. Examples include the Wickersham (1931), the Seabury (1932), the Knapp (1973), the Christopher (1991), the Mellon (1994), and the Commission of Police Integrity in Chicago (1997). However, it is also an established fact that the level and intensity of such abuses differ in terms of their degree of seriousness (Dunham and Alpert 2010; Goldstein 1975). The same literature has also shown that the police in advanced democracies have been subjected to a wide range of reforms and innovations in both enforcement and police use of modern technology (Maureen 1992) or community relationships (Stojkovic et al. 2010).

Incongruence between Form and Content

The Peelian modality in policing is created on the basis of gradual adaptation of police conduct to the ideals of modern social and legal norms, which proffers that "all are equal" before the proverbial eye of the law. Police conduct in authoritarian societies—of which Iran is a classic example—is more convoluted. Although equity is given lip service to Iranian policing modality, in reality "all" are not equal before the proverbial eye of the law (Uchida 2010). One reason has got to do with the fact that Iran, like many authoritarian societies around the world, has gone through different stages of capitalization of the society and economy in the past century. However, despite the fact that the country does have a comprehensive constitution that subjects policing to checks and balances—be in mundane daily traffic enforcement or in the more sensitive issues of custodial arrest, search, and seizure, including the use of force continuum, this subjugation has remained on paper. As a result of the incongruence between modernity in form and modernity in content, police in Iran, like other authoritarian police in Asian, African, and Latin and Central American societies, have been involved in continuous and egregious violation of citizens' rights, a fact that is consistently being borne out by comparative research in policing (Barak 2000; Ebbe 2000; Kusha 2006) as well as internationally recognized human rights groups and watches. Thus, one could argue that it is not enough to have on-paper checks and balances in policing. Neither is it enough to opt for modern police uniforms, training manuals, and operations strategies, hoping that through academic training congruency between form and content in police professionalism is garnered. Police academies are important for the foundation of professionalism modalities; however, it is wishful thinking to believe that theoretical academic modeling, by and of itself, is capable of garnering congruency between form and content: what is sorely needed is the recognition by the police (rank and file) as well as the community at large that police are public servants rather than instruments of oppression and legalized terror at the service of regime politics. The problem with nondemocratic attempts to professionalize police in many authoritarian societies around the world, including Iran, has stemmed from the fact that the structure of the state and its political theory has remained nondemocratic/ authoritarian and/or totalitarian. It is for this reason that "on-paper" professionalism modalities in Asia, Africa, and Latin and Central Americas share commonalities in their policing culture, typologies, and instrumental functionalities at the service of regime politics (Kusha 2000; Tolefson 1999).

In sum, it is plausible to propose that the transition of the modern policing from its traditional law enforcer functionality to one of "serve and protect" professionalism is due to the larger democratization processes that have taken place in modern market economies during the past century. Extending this rationale to the case of police modernization in Iran, this chapter raises an important yet unexplored problem in Iranian policing: the issue of historical incongruence between Western professionalism and oriental despotism in policing. This dichotomy in Iranian policing has its socioeconomic as well as philosophical bases that this chapter articulates. The theoretical thrust of the chapter is that police in Iran are modern in form yet despotic in content. This is an anomic result that the chapter proposes is due to the cultural and organizational impacts of Iran's long-established theory of the state, the Persian theory of kingship (*Resaaleh-e Shahriyari*), on all aspects of law and justice including policing. The historical clash between Western professionalism and oriental despotism in policing explored in this chapter is not an exclusive to Iranian policing, but has its parallelism in other major

Middle Eastern societies that have gone through similar modernization and developmental schemes in the late first and early twentieth centuries. Examples include Egypt (Tolefson 1999).

Oriental Despotism in Policing

Oriental despotism can be conceived as a paradigmatic approach to the rise and entrenchment of the culture of autocracy in "hydraulic societies" theorized by Karl Witffogel (1982), which were originally formed in the arid zones of Asia, Africa, Latin and Central Americas, and the Middle East; it was in this extensive zone that ancient civilizations gradually were formed, for example, in China, Japan, Korea, India, Iran, Mesopotamia, and Egypt; there were others in Central and Latin Americas, for example, the Aztecs–Mayan civilizations (Kusha 2000). The defining material characteristic of the hydraulic societies was the chronic inadequacy of water resources that necessitated the heavy and systemic involvement of the organizing power of the state in the construction, maintenance, and safeguarding of complex and costly irrigation networks, dams, aqueducts as well as defense-related posts, roads, and communication facilities (Witfogel 1981). In addition, ancient hydraulic societies were vulnerable to the so-called barbarian invasion that, if not prevented, could and did wreak havoc and irreparable existential damage to the permanency of settled life—as the invaders would destroy the irrigation networks to subdue local resistance. It has been for this functional role of the state—as a builder and protector of the very material base of the hydraulic societies—that despotism in both political philosophy and interpersonal relationship evolved through ions; Iran has been an important constituent from antiquity until recent times (Kusha 2000, 2006).

Cultural Autocracy in Policing

The thrust of the Witffogel typology is that despotism in the hydraulic societies was a natural outcome of the material conditions surrounding societies in the arid zones of the Old World. Therefore, be it the Egyptian Pharos, the Persian Shahanshahs, the Japanese Shoguns, the Korean Wangs, the Indian Rajahs, or the Muslim Caliphs and Sultans, all ruled for centuries as despots with impunity legitimated by norms and values that collectively have comprised the foundational base of the culture of autocracy (Kusha 2000). The recrudescence of despotism in the state and its organs (e.g., policing) is a direct outcome of the culture of autocracy that has both individual and institutional bases to its formation, appropriation, and reappropriation, be it within the family, the education, or the religious or political institutions. In other words, autocratic policing philosophy and typology of the hydraulic societies is not solely due to the nature of the police work that calls for autocratic means and strategies, but also due to a larger culture whose norms and values amenable to autocracy are produced and reproduced from generation to generation despite the fact that the hydraulic societies are no longer at the mercy of the harsh climatic conditions as in the past, thanks to the emancipating power of modern technology.

It is noteworthy that deference to power holders as promoted by the culture of autocracy does not mean, nor is it this chapter's contention, that it is the root cause of malevolence in policing in Iran, or in other societies mentioned above. In fact, respect for police authority is quite functional in garnering compliance much easier, be it hydraulic or nonhydraulic societies, provided that the police are not conceived as the chronically oppressive long arm of the state bent on suppressing any form of dissent, regardless of its merits, under the guise of law and order. However, as will be discussed shortly, the history of police modernization in Iran attests to the fact that from the late nineteenth century to the present, police have functioned as one among a number of other instruments of oppression (e.g., the army, the Gendarmerie, the Army Intelligence Bureau, the justice system) of the state, be it under the monarchy (the Qajar or the Pahlavi) or under the Islamic Republic that replaced monarchy in 1979. For example, under the Pahlavi monarchy, the functioning rationale of the state and its organs, including police, was to serve the wishes of the person of the monarch because the state propagated the idea that he was the erstwhile shadow of the Almighty in accordance with the Persian theory of kingship. Thus, under the monarchy, the motto of the state and its organs (e.g., the police) was "God, King, and Motherland" (*Khodaa, Shah, Mihan*) and in that order (Kusha 2000). Under the Islamic Republic, the functioning rationale of the Islamic state police is to serve the core ideals of the Islamic Revolution under the spiritual and moral guidance of the supreme religious leader in accordance with the Article V of the Constitution of the Islamic Republic of Iran. Therefore, regardless of a formal change from monarchy to republicanism, the whole apparatus of the state, including the police, has remained the same from the standpoint of their serving one central figure—the person of the monarch in the past and the supreme religious leader now. However, compared to the Pahlavi monarchy whose development and modernization strategy was one of the dependent capitalization of the Iranian society and economy, the Islamic Republic's motto is one of Islamizing Iranian society and economy, making the Islamic Republic way more ruthless in its utilization of the police and its "revolutionary" paramilitary and militia at the service of the supreme religious leader (aka the Waliy-e Faqih). This structure has led to the intensification of the role of the police as an ideological instrument of Islamizing "everything" in Iran as mandated by Article IV of the Constitution of the Islamic Republic of Iran. This state of affairs will not change for the better unless comprehensive democratization processes were to be undertaken by the state, a prospect that is in stark contrast to the Islamizing mandate of the police in the present Iran (Kusha 2000, 2006).

A Clash of Two Policing Philosophies in Iran

Police modernization in Iran can be resembled to a clash between two policing philosophies that are antithetical to one another despite the fact that four police modernization periods have been identified in Iran as follows: the Nasseri period (1878–1896), the Constitutional period (1906–1924), the First Pahlavi period (1925–1941), and the Second Pahlavi period (1941–1979) (Alibabaie 1385/1999; Kusha 2006, 2011). Prior to the rise of the Islamic Republic, Iran was a constitutional monarchy. Iran's law enforcement philosophy had had a symbiotic relationship with Iran's centuries-old theory of governance, the Persian theory of kingship which in turn had formed in the past. Due to this historical longevity, modern Iran's traditional state thus the structured polity (e.g., the relationship between the state and its subjects) were both antithetical to modern state and polity. Iran's traditional theory of governance is known by its Persian epithet, the *Resaaleh-e Shariyari* (Kusha 2000). The theory proposed that kingship (*Shariyari*) was a divinely ordained right to governance bestowed upon individuals who were endowed with the *Farr-e Izadi* (a divine guiding light), which accompanied them as long as they reigned on the principles of just rule. The theory, since the time of the Achaemenids (550–330 BC), had obligated the Persian kings with a set of reciprocal governing rights and responsibilities that, if performed diligently, would make the kings' reign legitimate and beneficial to their subjects. In return for the subjects' unequivocal loyalty to the reigning king(s), the king(s) pledged to establish peace and tranquility in the realm, to safeguard the frontiers against external threats, and to apply swift justice against malcontents (criminals or those who attempted to disrupt the sociopolitical status quo that ideally functioned for the highest amount of the common good). Thus, historically speaking, law and order in Iran meant the enforcement and/or preservation of the reigning monarch's wishes and commands. In addition, law enforcement had had a long history of gestation extending as far back as the time of the Median Empire (Kusha 2000, 2006). This longevity gave to Iranian policing a culture that resonated deeply with Iran's deeply authoritarian culture in social and legal relationships to which reference will be made shortly.

Historical Roots of Oriental Despotism in Iran

The Persian emperors and local kings employed various "means of legitimate coercion" to borrow the term from the German sociologist Max Weber, to impose order on the realm, and to bring criminal culprits to justice. These ranged from law enforcement activities of the standing armies who pursued criminal gangs that raided villages and towns and then fled, to policing activities of the military garrisons stationed in strategic locations of a sophisticated and well-maintained highway network that linked the main cities of the Achaemenid Empire that covered nearly 2.5 million square miles at the zenith of its power under the emperor Darius I, the Great (521–486 BC). There were also local militia groups who helped the army and local garrisons in performing their order-imposing duties throughout the realm. One of these was the *Arkpat* that acted in the capacity of the so-called the Ears and the Eyes of the Monarch. Etymologically, *Arkpat* means the commander of military garrison whose main duty was to police cities and highways that fell under his jurisdiction in accordance with a meticulous division of the empire into different administrative units (Kusha 2000). Being different than regular military commander, the *Arkpat* had the authority to imprison thieves and highway robbers before their cases were heard by trial judges known as *Dat*. Capital cases were brought before the local kings or the person of emperor himself, the *Shahanshah* (King of Kings). It goes without saying that he could pardon, commute, or dismiss the case without any repercussions. In doing so, the emperor could and did utilize his agents, the so-called the *ears and eyes of the Monarch*. They were the highly trusted confidants of the emperor appointed by him whose main responsibility was to travel throughout the empire, conduct surveillance on local authorities, and report to the emperor of the manner in which the *Arkpat* performed their order-imposing and law enforcement duties. The actual identity of the "ears" and "eyes" that was kept secret was only known by few individuals very close to the emperor (Kusha 2000).

Later, when Iran was invaded by Alexander, the Great, around 330 BC, the organizational structure of the *Polis* was adapted from the Greek system of local administration. The Hellenized version of *Polis* was now responsible for the management of the city including policing and other security-related matters. An official named *Epistat*, appointed by the monarch, oversaw the manner in which the *Polis* performed its duties. It is very likely that the term police in Western languages has its source in the Greek notion of *Polis*. The *Shahrik* and the *Dayhik* were two additional administrative and governing bodies whose development goes to the time of the Sassanid Empire (Kusha 2000). The *Shahrik* was responsible for law enforcement and security matters pertaining to cities, whereas the *Dayhik* performed these duties in villages. It is logical to assume that these order-imposing institutions borrowed legal and administrative concepts and technical know-how from their predecessors, for instance, from the Hellenistic institution of *Polis* mentioned above. The established wisdom is that the efficacy of these institutions rests on the strength and efficacy of the central government, the economic prosperity of the realm, and a general state of justice that linked the average free tax-paying citizens with the local and imperial governing structures in pre-Islamic Iran (Kusha 2000).

In the post-Islamic period, law enforcement was organized on the basis of an admixture of Islamic and Middle Eastern (e.g., Sassanid–Byzantine, Turkic–Mongol) policing philosophies, structures, and operation principles. The most prominent among these were the *Shorteh* (local police), the *Shabgard* (night watches and vigils), the *Saahib al-barid* (postal authority who also conducted surveillance), the *Gazmeh* (a Turk–Mongol institution of mobile quasilegal vigilantes at the service of local authorities), the *Saaheb-e diwaan* (a Turk–Mongol invention that oversaw financial as well as legal security of the realm), the *Yarghu* (a Turk–Mongol invention created to hear allegations of wrong doings of those in the position of authority), the *Diwaan beygi* (acted as the order-imposing council of the chieftains responsible for hearing public grievances), and the *Darugheh* (a Turkish invention that represented the main law enforcement authority in the capital city). Historical records of the time indicate that the efficacy of these order-imposing institutions also depended on factors such as the strength of the central government, the personal character of the monarch, and the overall economic prosperity and the security of the frontiers. Iran's traditional culture (Kusha 2000) has been authoritarian as legitimated through its long gestation and internalization of the tripartite ethos of (1) respect for authority, (2) aversion to law-infracting behavior, and (3) concern for the honor of the family. Putatively, these ideals have made order imposing a relatively easy task for the official organs of state.

Iran's First Modern Police Charter, 1878–1906

By the time of the ascendency of the Nasser al-Din Shah to the Qajar thrown in 1848, Iran's traditional policing philosophy and variegated structures had proven beneficial to a long list of dynasties that had ruled the country; the theory had helped the governing elite under successive dynasties to preserve the prevailing status quo by enforcing the reigning king's wishes and commands, including those of the Qajar kings in stark contrast to the mandates of modern policing philosophy that had been devised and made operational by Sir Robert Peel in the creation of the London Metropolitan Police in 1828. It is noteworthy that the Qajar monarch was cognizant of the fact that nineteenth-century Europe was way ahead of the rest of the world, including Qajar Iran (Kusha 2006, 2011). Nasser al-Din Shah was a relatively enlightened monarch credited with a number of reform measures in state bureaucracy, transportation, customs, and policing. He traveled three times to Europe (1873, 1878, and 1889). He also appointed able administrators such as Mirza Taqi Khan Amir Kabir (1848–1851), Mirza Agha Khan Nuri (1851–1858), and Mirza Hossein Khan Moshir ad-Dowlah (1873–1875) to the post of the Prime Minister in order to expedite his reform measures. The Qajar shah was also reported of having had consulted with the European monarch and emperors during his state visits enquiring about various European modernization schemes and experts that the Iranian government could hire for that purpose (Amaanat 1997; Yarshater 1992). One such expert in modern policing was an Italian police professional, Count de Montfort, who had served the Austrian police in Wien with dignity and exemplary professionalism. He was reported of having been offered and accepted a contract of employment during Nasser al-Din Shah's visit to Austria in 1878. The purpose of the contract was to relocate to Iran in order to reform Iran's traditional Nazmiyeh Police (Kusha 2011).

Upon arrival in Tehran, the capital of Iran, in 1878, the Count and his advisors studied the actual structure and layout of the city and gave a report to the shah, proposing how a modern police organization could reduce Tehran's crime problem. The Count also studied Iran's traditional law enforcement structure and philosophy as he wrote a comprehensive modern police charter titled the *Nezam Naameh* that was put into commission after being reviewed and signed by the shah. Based on the principles of modern bureaucracy, and modeled after the Prussian–Austrian system of policing, the Count's Nezam Naameh reorganized the Nazmiyeh Police into professional units (Alibabaie 1385/1999; Kusha 2011). The new police was also put under the jurisdictional authority of the Governor of Tehran, rather than that of the Minister of War as in the past. This change was important as it allowed the Governor of Tehran, rather than the Minister of War, to have jurisdiction over the police, making it more responsive to the law enforcement requisites of Tehran, Iran's largest and most important city (Alibabaie 1385/1999). The significance of the Count's Nezam Naameh stemmed from the fact that it constituted Iran's first modern police charter to hold police rank and file accountable to the procedural requisites of a coherently written Western-style police professional principles (Kusha 2011). It later became the organizational charter of the Ministry of the Nazmiyeh (*Wezarat-e Nazmiyeh*), elevating the Nazmiyeh Police to a national stature whose modern policing mandates were to be enforced throughout the country. This feature of the Count's Nezam Naameh argues that Alibabaie's (1385/1999) concept of policing was not welcomed by a cadre of Qajar governing elite in Tehran as well as in the provinces because the new police charter was deemed antithetical to Iran's centuries-old policing philosophy that had articulated a "King's Peace" type of law enforcement structure throughout the realm for centuries. The primary objective of the new Nazmiyeh Police was systemic uprooting of urban crime in Tehran as the city was facing growth-related social ailments. The main crime problems were opium-related offenses, gambling, prostitution, as well as residential burglary, next to predatory street crimes committed by a horde of local thugs and criminal gangs who shared their loots with the law enforcement agents as a form of graft and payback. By diligently enforcing the policing principles of the Nezam Naameh, the Count tried to put a decisive end to this long-established corruptive and criminogenic practice in policing. This was another reason for the dislike of the Nezam Naameh by those officials who not only tolerated but in fact benefitted, handsomely, from such graft and corruption in the Nazmiyeh (Kusha 2011).

Modern Training and Uniformed Police

Attempts were also made to uniform police agents and modernize police training and recruitment standards (Alibabaie 1385/1999; Bagley 1992; Floor 1973; Kusha 2006; Shuster 1912). For example, the Nezam Naameh established new policing principles that obligated the Nazmiyeh rank and file to report their law enforcement activities in their precincts. The Nazmiyeh agents had to report on time for their shifts and meticulously carry out their night watch and patrol duties. Police interrogators were no longer allowed to maltreat those in police custody. Stolen goods recovered by the police were to be warehoused and logged in police inventory sheets subjected to periodical inspections for adjudicative and/or claimant purposes. The Nazmiyeh detectives were also trained in modern policing principles in relation to criminal investigation and interrogation procedures that were drastically different than the traditional investigation norms utilized in the past. Unlike traditional methods that allowed both physical and mental torture of the suspect for getting forced confession to guilt, the new police had to get confession through modern methods such as forensic dactylographic identification of Tehran's known thieves, residential burglars, and thugs who formed drug, gambling, and prostitution rings in Tehran and other large cities throughout the country (Kusha 2011).

Traditional Persian State and Policing

Count de Montfort's Nezam Naameh aimed to replicate a set of modern policing principles in Iran that were alien to Iran's traditional state and polity. These principles, if institutionalized, could work against the "Just Order" (*Nezam-e 'Aadel*) that the Persian monarchs had built in the past passing its heritage to the next dynasty all the way to the Qajars (Ballantine 1879; Bayat 1992; Nezam-Mafi 1989; Yarshater 1992). Therefore, the Nazmiyeh was more than law enforcement philosophy per se, but one that had historically acted as the guardian of an established balance of power between the Persian kings and their subjects. Any tempering with the traditional policing philosophy could gradually undermine the balance to the detriment of the monarchy. Police could be modernized in form, but not in their philosophical content. Put it differently, the Qajar governing elite did not object to a well-trained, uniformed, and efficient police force at the service of the status quo, provided that policing philosophy was not corrupted by "alien" ideas. In the late nineteenth- and early twentieth-century Qajar Iran, the source of these "alien" ideas was Europe (aka *Farang* in colloquial Persian) (Abrahamian 1982; Floor 1973; Kusha 2000; Nezam-Mafi 1989).

The Persian theory of kingship in its late nineteenth- and early twentieth-century format had gone through changes; nonetheless, it manifestly represented the socioeconomic and political interests of the Qajar feudal lords and their cohorts. Qajar Iran's land division rationale, tillage, and tax farming measures were based on the *Iqta'a* principles that provided the Asiatic equivalent of the European feudalism (Alibabaie 1385/1999; Kusha 2000). Although there were structural as well as ideological differences between the two, both operated on a hierarchical division of power and its utilization based on the amount of land that one controlled. At the apex of the Qajar Iqta'a system, the king who theoretically owned the *molk-e Iranzamin* (the whole country of Iran) was thus authorized to appoint whomever he wished to various offices of the government, from the Grand Vizier (*Sadr-e A'azaam*) to the Chief of the Standing Army (*Sardar-e Sepah*) or the Governor General (*Waali* and in Pahlavi times, *Ostandaar*) (Kusha 2006).

Under the tutelage of the king, there was a complex bureaucratic governing structure known as the *Nezam-e Diwaani*; it comprised highly educated professional scribes, accountants, and tax and revenue assessors who served the Qajar Crown and its interests throughout the country. By the time of the Nasser al-Din Shah, the system had long since established a corroding and criminogenic practice of cash bidding for appointment to high governmental posts especially to the post of the provincial governor (Browne 1893; Shuster 1912). The more prosperous a province, the more financially lucrative the post of the governor of such provinces, thus the costlier the bidding processes; the amount of cash garnered by the bidding procedure was a lucrative source of income for the Qajar monarchs (Keddie 1971, 1999; Kusha 2000).

Although in theory the provincial governors were appointees of the Qajar Crown, serving at the pleasure of the reigning monarch, the practice of cash bidding had long since created de facto, if not de jure, sense of entitlement to the provinces. Barring exceptions, the Qajar governors considered the provinces as their personal fiefdoms (*molk-e talq*); in essence, the governors ruled with the same feudal servitude principles that the Qajar monarchs enjoyed. Because the Qajar governors ruled with impunity only answerable to the king in enforcing his wishes and commands, they jealously guarded their discretionary power and enforcement means (Kusha 2011). The Count's Nezam Naameh aimed to reform police on the basis of modern bureaucratic principles with checks and balances that were alien to the Persian theory of kingship and thus to its law enforcement mandates. Although traditional as well as new policing mandates served and protected the political status quo, there were strategic differences between the two at a time that the Qajar political establishment was going through a deepening legitimacy crisis that led to Iran's first revolution that is known as the Constitutional Revolution (1906–1911). As will be discussed shortly, police played an important political role in subduing the revolutionary forces, thus opening the road to the criminalization of dissent throughout the past century. For this reason, modern policing profession in Iran has not evolved as a neutral server and protector of the public as in the Western advanced free-market economies (Kusha 2006).

Traditional Serve and Protect Mandates

Iran's traditional law enforcement philosophy and structure was not arbitrary per se; laws were enforced to serve and protect "The Order" (*Nezam*) that the Qajar kings had established by "meticulously" observing the principles of the "Just Rule" (*Edalat*) of the Persian theory of kingship. For the Qajar governing elite and their political cohorts, the Qajar Order had "embraced" within its just and protective arms the People of Iran who had unequivocally submitted to the legitimate authority of the reigning monarch(s), the sin qua non prerequisite of living under law. Thus, the established feudal–agrarian order was "legitimate" and "beneficial" to both the prince and the pauper. In addition, state functionaries (from the provincial governors all the way down to police chiefs and local law enforcement officials, *Kalantar*) were not authorized to utilize police against people without cause; Iranians, regardless of their social status, were considered as the *Ru'aya* of the king, a term that does not have an exact English equivalence, but has historically signified the town and rural populace with a set of rights and responsibilities within the Iqta'a system. The governors were obligated to protect the king's Ru'aya against crime, social perversion as well as any abuse in the utilization of the arable land, seed, water, labor, and foliage in their jurisdictions; violation of these traditional agrarian rights and responsibilities could entice grievances that the governors had to handle by a combination of political tact and threat of force (Alibabaie 1385/1999; Floor 1992; Kusha 2006).

The principles of the "Just Rule" under the Persian theory of kingship also obligated the governors to periodically hold public audience (*baar-e 'aam*) to listen to the Ru'aya and their concerns over the conduct of the government agents, for example, tax collectors, or law enforcement. In addition, the theory obligated the governors to investigate and apply swift justice to state functionaries who were found guilty of abusing their office. The contemporary Qajar literature gives a distinct impression as if by the late nineteenth century the Qajar governors resorted to whatever means that they found expedient in "suppressing" as against "resolving" the root causes of social and political grievances for the benefit of the presumed "Just Order," regardless of the nature of the grievances (Abrahamian 1982; Bakhash 1978, 1992; Floor 1992; Keddie 1999). The pre-reform Nazmiyeh Police played an important suppressive role in these deeply socioeconomically engendered crises that were gradually becoming anti-establishment in nature (Abrahamian 1982; Amaanat 1997; Arjomand 1984; Floor 1992; Keddie 1966, 1971, 1981; Nashat 1982).

The new police was also suspect in the eyes of the Qajar governing elite for two reasons. First, they soon realized that the reformed Nazmiyeh Police was to be marching to the beats of new law enforcement drums alien to the modus operandi of the traditional Nazmiyeh Police. Second, these changes were taken place under a non-Muslim police commissioner who could gradually intervene in Muslim affairs to undermine the growing power of the Shiite clerics in running these affairs. To alleviate some of these fears, the Count pledged that the new police would not interfere in civil issues that were traditionally handled by the Shiite divines (*Ayaat-e A'azaam*), for example, marriage, divorce, and funeral and religious processions. The Count also pledged that police agents would not enter the mosques or the Shiite seminaries and mausoleums in pursuit of those who sought asylum; in such situations, the cases would be handled by the religious authority in charge of the mausoleum, known as the *khoddaam*. Despite these assurances, the contemporary Qajar literature gives the impression that from the standpoint of what we may characterize as "traditionalist" state functionaries, the Count's Nezam Naameh was subversive of the "Just Order" that was built by Muslim men of right genealogy, faculties, knowledge, and expertise appointed to the governing posts throughout the country. The Qajar literature makes reference to incompetent and corrupt law enforcement functionaries here and there, but is adamant that the pillars of the dynasty were firmly built on the traditional Perso-Islamic principles of justice and good governance (Kusha 2011; Nezam-Mafi 1989; Wright 1977).

An Agrarian Social and Economic System in Crisis

By the time of the ascendance of Nasser al-Din Shah to the Qajar throne in 1848, it was becoming more difficult to convince the public and a large segment of the progressive, as against the traditionalist, Qajar Intelligentsia that the prevailing status quo was on the right track especially in relation to the state functionaries' chronic abuse of their vested authority. This abuse was most prevalent in the tax levy and collection methods. Depending on the personality of the appointed governor, and the initial costs incurred for the procurement of the post of the governor, the tax levy and collection methods could turn into a daunting law and order issue, which was even the cause célèbre of bloody revolts especially in agriculturally poor provinces (Browne 1893; Floor 1973; Kusha 2000; Nezam-Mafi 1989; Shuster 1912). In such exigencies, the governors were allowed to use force to quell tax revolts and punish the social malcontents who resorted to rioting rather than appealing to the governor's sense of justice. Thus, ideally speaking, organized force (e.g., the police) at the disposal of the state played an important role in keeping the status quo intact at the time that the Qajar political system was going through a deepening legitimacy crisis, either in Tehran or in the provincial capitals (Alibabaie 1385/1999; Kusha 2000). This state of affairs could not tolerate a drastic change in traditional law enforcement philosophy as mandated by the Nezam Naameh once it became the foundational charter of Ministry of Nazmiyeh. It was one thing for the new police to carry out the Count's Western-style policing mandates in Tehran, but once elevated to a ministerial level, the modern policing mandates took a national urgency to their implementation that could drastically deprive the Qajar governing elite of one of their instruments of impunity to rule (Kusha 2011).

Studies on the late nineteenth- and early twentieth-century Iran are indicative of the fact that by the time of the Nasser al-Din Shah, there had emerged an entrenched political machine (akin to its American counterpart of it, ca. 1840s–1920s) that ran the affairs of the Qajar Crown in Tehran and, by extension, in the provinces (Gilbar 1986; Wright 1977; Yarshater 1992). The main function of this political machine was preserving the political status quo by balancing the interests of various social classes and strata; in reality, it served the interests of the traditionalist governing elite, the provincial feudal lords, and the Shiite clergy; this trio, barring exceptions, were the trilateral bases of the Qajar political machine thus beneficiaries of a retrogressively defunct Asiatic agrarian social and political system that was doomed to extinction in lieu of the emerging forces and relations of production of modern entrepreneurial capitalism in Europe and North America (Abrahamian 1982; Bagley 1992; Bakhash 1992). By the time of the Nasser al-Din Shah, modern entrepreneurial capitalism had already reached the status of a world dynamic force transcending national boundaries and cultures. The late nineteenth- and early twentieth-century Qajar Iran was one among a multitude of defunct Middle Eastern structures being subjected to the modernizing impacts of the entrepreneurial capitalism (Afary 1994; Keddie 1999; Yarshater 1992).

Success in Modern Police Professionalism

It is plausible to suggest that success in modern police professionalism depends on the degree of democratization of the state and the manner in which the state has regulated its governance mandates with those who live under its jurisdiction (Thomas 2011). The European history of police modernization is indicative of the fact that since French Revolution (1787), monarchies were gradually forced to respond to the emerging social, political, and legal realities of entrepreneurial capitalism by allowing the construct of impunity to rule be subjected to the construct of the rule of law (Lane 1992). The kings and queens gradually realized that they were no longer semidivine entities representing the will of Almighty on the earth, but were regal symbols of national unity; thus, they could not rule with impunity as in the past. The emerging political philosophy in Western Europe (and later in North America) conceptualized the organized power of the state as one that was constitutional in nature. Because modern state operated on the basis of constitutionally mandated law and regulations, so did modern police. Modern professionalism in police gradually emerged as a distinct value separating police from their "peace and order" imposing functionality to one of serving the public (Lane 1992; Uchida 2010).

Modernization in the late nineteenth- and early twentieth-century Europe and North America was both in form and in content symbiotic with the democratization of the state and polity in the emerging market economies (Uchida 2010). Modern police gradually started serving and protecting an enterprising (entrepreneurial) capitalist system and those who promoted capitalist relations of production. Modern police were no longer Praetorian Guards at the service of the European monarchs and cohorts as in the past, but at the service of the new emerging "Order," the Entrepreneurial Capitalism. As this Order has been of a dynamic and expansionist nature from its inception to the present, the two constructs of "modernization" and "development" have historically been symbiotic with capitalism and capitalization processes (Wallersteine 1974; Wittfogel 1981). This does not mean that everything is good and dandy under capitalism in so far as this chapter is concerned. However, capitalism is the prevailing dynamic force whose socioeconomic impacts are socially and culturally transcendental. Modernization of police in market economies has deeply been impacted by the capitalization processes, including the Middle Eastern societies of which Iran is an important constituent (Tolefson 1999).

The Geopolitics of Police Modernization in Iran

One impediment to police modernization in content, as against in form, was a set of intertwined external geopolitical forces that played a significant role in the overall modernization and development of the Qajar Iran in the late nineteenth and early twentieth centuries; although these forces were external, their operational dynamics and impacts on police modernization had a lot to do with Iran's geopolitical significance in a region that has provided the bulk of the world's carbon-based energy supplies in the past century (Bakhash 1981; Keddie 1999; Kusha 2000). For example, in 1908 Knox Darcy, a British subject, discovered natural oil reservoirs in Masjed Soleyman in Khuzestan Province of Iran that borders the Persian Gulf. This discovery in conjunction with the British geopolitical rivalry with Czarist Russia, Iran's giant neighbor to the North, prompted the British Admiralty to declare a strategic shift from coal to oil-powered engines, upgrading the thrust power of the British fleets in the Persian Gulf. Concomitantly, the British undertook the creation of the Southern Persian Rifles that on the surface acted in the capacity of law enforcement, but in reality it was a highly trained force counterbalancing the Kazak Brigade that served Czarist Russia's imperialist designs and interests in northern Iran (Alibabaie 1385/1999). In fact, in 1907, the two major powers had clandestinely divided the country into two zones of interests with their respective law enforcement organizations on the pretext that the Iranian government(s) was incapable of securing the national routes throughout the country. Although the outbreak of the Great War in 1914 stopped the actual partition of Iran between the two, the rivalry between Britain and Russia made police modernization deeply political in nature. For example, Nasser al-Din Shah is reported of having had consulted with the Russian Czar for reforming the Nazmiyeh Police (Alibabaie 1385/1999; Floor 1973). Alarmed over the adage to the influence of the Russians, the British intervened and asked the Austrian emperor to suggest the service of the Count de Montfort for that purpose (Lenczowski 1992; Yarshater 1992). Modernization of the Nazmiyeh Police and later Iran's National Police was therefore not primed for purely administrative–organizational issues. Modernity in policing was related to the strategic role the police were to perform against internal factors that opposed the transformation of Iran from a defunct Asiatic social formation to a modernizing capitalist albeit peripheral one with an externally imposed division of labor to serve the interests of the larger capitalist world economy. In a nutshell, police were among the slew of traditional forces and structures that had to be modernized as Iran had to become a functioning stable state within the emerging world capitalist forces and relations of production (Kusha 2006).

The Double-Edged Role of the Shiite Clergy

There were also internal impediments to police modernization, for example, Iran's influential Shiite clergy; historically speaking, the Shiite clergy has proven time and again was capable of expediting or negating social reform by giving its seal of approval for, or against, such endeavors. This ability of the clerics is due to the fact that the clergy rank and file, besides their Islamic learning (e.g., the Koran and the Hadith), are also trained in the arts religious oratory in delivering sermons in mosques and Friday public prayers. This religious function of the clergy is unique as it has traditionally enabled influential clerics to reach mass audiences throughout the country giving Shiite Islam's perspective on important social issues, for example, whether modernization is compatible with Shiite Islam (Afary 1994; Arjomand 1984; Bayat 1992). The provincial governors and the clergy perceived the police as an organized force whose main function was to safeguard the prevailing status quo from the standpoint of both Shiite Islam and Iran's traditional law enforcement philosophy. Neither group had any problem with the police force that was efficacious in keeping the peace of the established order, but was adamantly against a force that wanted to hold every one accountable to propriety in conduct as defined by law, be it modern or the Shari'a (Floor 1973; Kusha 2000).

However, based on the historical evidence, one could argue that by the time of the appointment of the Count de Montfort to the post of the Chief of the Nazmiyeh Police, the Qajar political machine was at a crossroad. On the one hand, it had already built for itself the reputation of all things that made the state and its functionaries, including law enforcement, oppressive and criminogenic especially toward the weaklings of society. On the other hand, there were modernizing monarchs, the likes of the Nasser al-Din Shah as well as Qajar Intelligentsia, who were desirous of a European-style modernization and development (Amaanat 1997; Bakhash 1992; Gilbar 1987; Keddie 1999; Kusha 2000; Yarshater 1992). The question remained as to whether modernization was antithetical to Islam at that juncture (Arjomand 1984). The question was partially settled in 1906 when Iran's first constitutional charter, *Farman-e Mashrutiyat*, was drafted during the reign of another modernizing Qajar, Mozaffar al-Din Shah (r. 1898–1907) (Abrahamian 1982; Wickens 1992).

Modern Citizenship versus the Ru'aya

Unlike citizenship status conferred on free and tax-paying men and women in emerging modern nation states of the nineteenth century, the concept of modern citizen was not accepted in Qajar Iran (thus in the King's Peace policing philosophy) until the Constitutional Revolution (1906–1911). Prior to this date, Iranians, regardless of their social status, were the Ru'aya of the Qajar shahs, as mentioned earlier. They had a set of traditional rights and responsibilities in accordance with the Persian theory of kingship, but such rights were not secured as a matter of a constitutionally mandated law (as was the case in Western Europe or North America), but as a matter of tradition (*urf wa 'adaat*) (Floor 1973). In the same manner that just kings had recognized these rights and responsibilities, the unjust ones including police circumvented them with impunity. The classic problem was one formulated by Ann K.S. Lambton in her famous *quis custodiet ipsos custodies* (who shall guard the guardians) question.

In modern constitutional systems, it is the province of law to guard the guardians; the police are duty bound to apply law to the prince or the pauper alike, but not a police system that is operating on the basis of the King's Peace philosophy. The Ru'aya of the Qajar kings was not equal to the king because it was the king who was the law giver and it was the commands of the king that protected the public. Naturally, the law giver was not at par with his subjects, nor those who enforced the king's law (e.g., state functionaries, including the police). Therefore, from the standpoint of the traditional law enforcement philosophy, police in Qajar Iran did not represent law, nor did they enforce anything other than the commands of the sovereign that had been codified into the King's Peace mandates (Kusha 2011). This philosophy was different than policing philosophy that was emerging in modern market economies, a philosophy that considered police as law enforcers rather than peace enforcers. There were strategic differences between the two: the peace maintained in agrarian society was qualitatively different than its counterpart in the thriving entrepreneurial capitalist societies of the late nineteenth and early twentieth centuries (Tolefson 1999).

The Construct of Social and Political Peace in Modern Capitalism

Modern capitalism has historically built its construct of peace on the basis of a thriving economic system that provides jobs and services in what Immanuel Wallersteine (1974) has characterized as the world capitalist system. Accordingly, the hierarchically dominant capitalist economies in the center exploit the semi- and peripheral satellite economies as they create the world capitalist system with its global capitalist division of labor. Social systems enter into this scheme and are assigned a certain role as the provider of raw material and cheap labor for the dominant economies. Thus, the construct of peace in the world capitalist system is of a market economy nature amenable to capitalism and its ideals. The Count's police charter aimed to gradually extricate the Nazmiyeh Police from its traditional King's Peace thus Praetorian Guard functionality to one of Western-professionalized urban policing with regulated conduct and law enforcement responsibilities (Alibabaie 1385/1999; Kusha 2006, 2011). However, as previously mentioned, the Count's police reforms were antithetical to the manner in which traditionalist provincial governors ran the affairs of the Ru'aya in their jurisdictions. The Shiite clergy was also resentful of the fact that a non-Muslim was given authority to regulate policing in a major Islamic country such as Iran. After 14 years of trial and error, the Count de Montfort was forced to resign his post in 1890.

With the departure of the Count, the Nazmiyeh Police reverted back to its old malaise under 13 Director General(s) who followed each other's short and ineffective tenures until the beginning of Iran's Constitutional Revolution (1906–1911) (Kusha 2011).

Police Modernization, the Constitutional Era, 1906–1911

From the mid-nineteenth century onward, and influenced by the European Enlightenment, there had emerged the genesis of a Qajar Enlightenment movement spearheaded by the writings and political activism of a cadre of Western-educated elite and intelligentsia who deeply despised the abject backwardness of the country as they compared and contrasted it with the European supremacy and cultural efflorescence in all fields. By and large, they blamed Iran's abject backwardness (including policing) on the prevalence of despotism that permeated all layers of social, political, and legal relationships and institutions in Qajar Iran (Floor 1992; Keddie 1999). For example, Iran's traditional law enforcement methods were critiqued for having had remained almost impervious to the wonders of modern science and technology that had prompted Europe's supremacy in all fields, including in the science of policing and security. The same criticism was applied to education, religion, and family and its dynamics. This segment of the intelligentsia was by and large supportive of any Nezam Naameh type of organized force, be it the state or its agents, provided that the rule of law was applied to all, be it the prince or the pauper (Kusha 2011).

Nasser al-Din Shah was assassinated in 1896 by a political dissident, as the shah was entering the M'asumah mausoleum in the Rey township situated to the west of Tehran. The assassin, Mirza Reza Kermani (a disciple of a revolutionary Iranian intellectual, Jamal ad-Din Asadabadi who preached Islamic modernization), was later arrested and subjected to traditional interrogation methods. He confessed his guilt and was subsequently hanged in public. The assassinated shah was given the epithet of the martyred shah (*Shah-e Shahid*) and was buried in the same mausoleum conferring a highly honorable status on one of the most celebrated Qajar kings whose true legacy in Iran's modernization and development has yet to be determined without prejudice. His successor, Mozaffar al-Din Shah (r. 1896–1907), enunciated the *Farman-e Mashrutiyat* (The Decree of Constitutionalism) in 1906 which subjected the despotic power of the Qajar Crown to the restriction of Iran's first modern constitution, *Qaanun-e Mashruteh*. It authorized the creation of Iran's modern parliament, the *Majles-e Showray-e Melli* based on electoral processes. The new shah's reign ended with his sudden death in 1907. His successor, Mohammad Ali Shah (r. 1907–1909), was a ruthless tyrant who deeply despised the emerging constitutional form of governance and its parliament; there were powerful Shiite clerics, for example, the Grand Ayatollah Fazlollah Nuri who rejected constitutional governance antithetical to Islam characterizing it as a diabolical Western plot against Shiite Islam and its "Just Sultan," Mohammad Ali Shah. Instead of attempts to create a constitutional monarchy, Nuri proposed a Shari'a-based monarchy. This proposal led to the rise of two opposing camps. One camp belonged to the supporters of the *Mashruteh* (the constitution) and the other to the supporters of the *Mashr'ueh* (the Shari'a-based governance) (Gilbar 1986; Keddie 1981, 1999; Lenczowski 1992; Yarshater 1992). Each camp had their prominent Shiite clerics as well as secular intellectual supporters and foot soldiers. The Nazmiyeh Police as an organized force played an important political role in this period (Kusha 2011).

Police Modernization, the Pahlavi Era, 1925–1975

With the conclusion of the Great War (1914–1919), Iran, like other Middle Eastern countries, went through structural changes, be it in socioeconomic or legal bases of relationship (Keddie 1971). The founder of the new dynasty, Reza Khan Sawadkoohi (aka Reza Khan Mirpanj), was a soldier by training with a charismatic personality well suited to the post-World War I (WWI) social psychology that sought political stability next to social and economic reconstruction. Although the Great War was quite bloody and disruptive, it aimed at the redistribution of the world markets (including the Greater Middle

East) among the great powers in Europe. However, the Bolshevik Revolution of 1917 in Czarist Russia made Communism a formidable international foe for the post-WWI and emerging world capitalist order (Lenczowski 1992). Reza Khan was the ideal strong man that the British policy makers in the 10 Downing Street in London had their eye on for post-Qajar Iran. It was reasoned that Iran needed a strong man at the top because if left to its own devices, the country could easily be engulfed by a Bolshevik-inspired revolution. Internally, Reza Khan had already been portrayed by the Anglophile Iranian press and political circles as a progressive, yet iron-willed modernizer who could steer Iran's reconstruction efforts. In reality, Reza Khan had successfully expropriated the remnants of the Qajar political machine and with the acquiescence of the British managed to engineer the abdication of the last Qajar monarch, Ahmad Shah in 1921. He was first elected to the most powerful post of the Minister of War that facilitated his ascendency as he commanded the only viable force in Iran, the Kazak Brigade composed of 1,200 highly trained professional soldiers (Alibabaie 1385/1999; Kusha 2000).

In 1921, the Kazak Brigade under the command of Reza Khan marched to Tehran and established himself as the strong man of Iran, an event that led to the foundation of the Pahlavi dynasty in 1925 (Keddie 1999; Kusha 2000). Next, building on the police modernization efforts of the Constitutional Revolution as well as those of the Count's Nezam Naameh, Reza Shah established the National Police and Municipality (*Polis wa Shahrebani Koll-e Keshwar*). Headquartered in Tehran, the National Police was charged with urban policing and a municipality-based law enforcement mandate under the Ministry of Interior. Its main function was to serve and protect the citizens against crime, to regulate traffic, to investigate crime scenes, and to enforce laws in the urban areas (Alibabaie 1385/1999; Kusha 2000, 2006). Despite its modern serve and protect mandate, the National Police gradually resorted to the centuries-old King's Peace philosophy in law enforcement, but this time as an instrument of the king's modernization efforts. For example, Reza Shah was generally credited with various gender-equalizing measures in education, employment, and civil law. These rights helped the emancipation of women from the bondage of backwardness enabling women to play an active role in Iran's modernization and development programs. However, to initiate these measures, Reza Shah had to neutralize Iran's powerful Shiite clergy who considered gender-equalizing measures of the shah antithetical to women's status under the Shari 'ah Law. One of the most contested was the traditional Islamic garb, the *hijaab* (veil) that Reza Shah decreed its forced removal in state bureaucracies, ceremonies as well as the newly modern girl schools. The National Police played a controversial role in the forced unveiling of women in Iran winning for the police a reputation that did not endear the police to Iran's highly religiously conservative lower and middle class strata (Abrahamian 1982; Keddie 1981; Kusha 2000; Neshat 1982).

These reforms led to deeply seated religious and social resentment and even political reaction against the Pahlavi modernization schemes. Under the Directorate, General Mukhtari, the Municipal Police gained a notorious reputation for its oppressive and outright illegal internal intelligence gathering against the so-called subversive Iranian citizens and especially for police manhandling of the political dissidents. In 1941, the Allied forces invaded Iran and forced the shah to resign on behalf of his eldest son and heir apparent, Mohammad Reza Shah who subsequently assumed the title of the shah (Keddie 1999; Kusha 2000; Lenczowski 1992). The deposed shah was subsequently sent into exile in the Island of Morris, a protectorate of the British where he died in exile. Later his body was brought back to Iran and buried in Shah Rey Township with much fanfare as New Iran's Great Architect. After the 1979 revolution, a mob ransacked his place of burial and burnt it to the ground.

Under Muhammad Reza Shah (r. 1941–1979), the Iranian National Police was also responsible for internal security throughout the country. The police carried its internal security responsibilities in direct collaboration with a number of intelligence-gathering organizations that the Shah's regime had created in consultation with the American Federal Bureau of Investigation (FBI) and the American military advisors in Iran. In the rural areas, the National Gendarmerie was later created in 1944 and charged with law enforcement functions and responsibilities. In case of large operations against drug smugglers and interdiction operations, the National Police and Gendarmerie would collaborate with the army units. The most prominent among these was the Army Intelligence Unit and the National Information and Security Organization. Known by its acronym as the SAVAK, it was created through the Establishment of Security Organization Act (Kusha 2006), which was approved by the Iranian Parliament in 1957. This act was composed of five articles and gave a wide range of intelligence gathering and arrest and investigation powers to the SAVAK. To enhance the power of its directorate, it was given the administrative rank of the Assistant to the Prime Minister to be appointed directly by a decree of the Shah. Gradually, the SAVAK won a notorious reputation of a secret police organization involved in clandestine and illegal arrest, imprisonment, torture, and execution of hundreds of Iranian political dissidents from the mid-1960s until the overthrow of the monarchy in 1979. In fact, the hatred for SAVAK was one of the main impetuses to the revolutionary upheavals of the 1978–1979 period that led to the demise of the Pahlavi monarchy and the rise of the Islamic Republic.

Conclusion

Modern policing philosophy has not made much progress in Iran despite close to a century of attempts to structure a policing philosophy and typology akin to Western professionalism principles as articulated by the likes of Sir Robert Peel. This inability, as discussed in this chapter, has its deeply entrenched roots in Iran's historical longevity as well as in the social and cultural factors that have impeded the institutionalization of a more democratic set of relationships between the state and its organs (including the police) with tax-paying citizens. Islamization of police in postrevolutionary Iran has not resolved the problem of police despotism because Islamic Republic in Iran is republican in façade. In reality, it is a religious theocracy whose relationship with the average citizen is based on a set of religiously inspired rather than democratically inspired principles of governance. Modernization in both form and content is the historical outcome of the larger democratization of the social and legal relationships that regulate the structure of power and its utilization by the state and its main law enforcement organ, the police.

References

Abrahamian, E. (1982). *Iran between Two Revolutions*. Princeton, NJ: Princeton University Press.

Afary, J. (1994). Social democracy and the Iranian Constitutional Revolution of 1906–11. In J. Foran (Ed.). *A Century of Revolution: Social Movements in Iran*. Minneapolis, MN: University of Minnesota Press, pp. 21–43.

Alibabaie, G.R. (1385/1999). *Tarikh-e Artesh-e Iran: az Hakhamaneshi taa 'Asre-Pahlavi* (A History of Persian Army: From Achaemenids to the Pahlavids). Tehran, Iran: Entesharate Ashiyan.

Amaanat, A. (1997). *Pivot of the Universe: Nasir al-Din Shah and the Iranian Monarchy, 1831–1896*. Berkeley, CA: University of California Press.

Amnesty International. (2009). *Iran: Human Rights in the Spotlight on the 30th Anniversary of the Islamic Revolution*. Islamic Republic of Iran: Amnesty International.

Arjomand, S.A. (1984). *The Shadow of God and the Hidden Imam: Religion, Political Order and Societal Change in Shi'ite Iran from the Beginning to 1890*. Chicago, IL: University of Chicago Press.

Bagley, F.R.C. (1992). New light on the Iranian constitutional movement. In E. Bosworth and C. Hillenbrand (Eds.). *Qajar Iran: Political, Social, and Cultural Change, 1800–1925*. Costa Mesa, CA: Mazda Publishers, pp. 48–64.

Bakhash, S. (1978). *Iran: Monarchy, Bureaucracy, and Reform under the Qajars, 1858–1896*. London: Ithaca Press for the Middle East Centre, St. Antony's College.

Bakhash, S. (1981). Center-periphery relations in nineteenth-century Iran. *Iranian Studies*, 14 (Winter–Spring), 29–51.

Bakhash, S. (1992). The failure of reform: The Prime Ministership of Amîn al-Dawla, 1897–8. In E. Bosworth and C. Hillenbrand (Eds.). *Qajar Iran: Political, Social, and Cultural Change, 1800–1925*. Costa Mesa, CA: Mazda Publishers, pp. 14–33.

Ballantine, H. (1879). *Midnight Marches through Persia*. Boston, MA: Lee & Shepard.

Barak, G. (Ed.) (2000). *Crime and Crime Control: A Global View*. Westport, CT: Greenwood Press.

Bayat, P.M. (1992). The cultural implications of the Constitutional Revolution. In E. Bosworth and C. Hillenbrand (Eds.). *Qajar Iran: Political, Social, and Cultural Change, 1800–1925*. Costa Mesa, CA: Mazda Publishers, pp. 65–74.

Braga, A.A. et al. (2006). Problem-oriented policing in violent crime places: A randomized controlled experiment. *Criminology*, 37(3), 541–580.

Browne, E.G. (1893). *A Year Amongst the Persians*. London: A & C Black.

Crank, J.P. (2004). Police culture in a changing multicultural environment. In Q.C. Thurman and A. Giacomazzi (Eds.). *Imagining Justice*. Cincinnati, OH: LexisNexis, pp. 53–75.

Del Pozo, B. (2004). One dogma of police ethics: Gratuities and the "Democratic Ethos" of policing. *Criminal Justice Ethics*, 24(2), 25–47.

Dias, D.K. and Palmiotto, M.J. (Eds.) (2006). *World Police Encyclopaedia*. New York: Routlegde.

Dunham, R.G. and Alpert, G.P. (2010). The foundation of the police role in society. In R. Dunham and G. Alpert (Eds.). *Critical Issues in Policing*. Long Grove, IL: Waveland Press, Inc., pp. 1–16.

Ebbe, O.N.I. (2000). Nigeria: Post-traditional nation state. In G. Barak (Ed.). *Crime and Crime Control: A Global View*. Westport, CT: Greenwood Press, pp. 147–161.

Floor, W. (1973). The Police in Qajar Iran. *Zeitung der deutschen Morgenländischen Gesellschaft* 123, pp. 204–315.

Floor, W. (1992). Change and development in the judicial system of Qajar Iran, 1800–1925. In E. Bosworth and C. Hillenbrand (Eds.). *Qajar Iran: Political, Social, and Cultural Change, 1800–1925*. Costa Mesa, CA: Mazda Publishers, pp. 113–147.

Gilbar, G. (1986). The opening up of Qajar Iran: Some economic and social aspects. *Bulletin of the School of Oriental and African Studies*, 49(1), 76–89.

Goldstein, H. (1987). Towards community-oriented policing: Potential, basic requirements, and threshold questions. *Crime & Delinquency*, 33(6), 6–30.

Keddie, N.R. (1966). *Religion and Rebellion in Iran: The Tobacco Protest of 1891–1892*. London: Frank Cass.

Keddie, N.R. (1971). The Iranian power structure and social change, 1800–1969: An overview. *International Journal of Mathematical Engineering and Science*, 2(1), 320.

Keddie, N.R. (1981). *Roots of Revolution: An Interpretive History of Modern Iran*. New Haven, CT: Yale University Press.

Keddie, N.R. (1999). *Qajar Iran and the Rise of Reza Khan 1796–1925*. Costa Mesa, CA: Mazda Publishers.

Kusha, H.R. (2000). Iran: A developing nation state. In G. Barak (Ed.). *Crime and Crime Control: A Global View*. Westport, CT: Greenwood Press, pp. 81–101.

Kusha, H.R. (2006). Iran. In D.K. Das (Ed.). *World Police Encyclopedia*. New York: Routledge, pp. 390–396.

Kusha, H.R. (2011). A clash of modern professionalism and oriental despotism. Working Paper No. 33, New York: International Police Executive Symposium, May 2011.

Lane, R. (1992). Urban police and crime in nineteenth-century America. In M. Tonry and N. Morris (Eds.). *Modern Policing*, vol. 15. Chicago, IL: University of Chicago Press, pp. 1–50.

Lenczowski, G. (1992). Foreign powers' intervention in Iran during World War I. In E. Bosworth and C. Hillenbrand (Eds.). *Qajar Iran: Political, Social, and Cultural Change, 1800–1925*. Costa Mesa, CA: Mazda Publishers, pp. 76–92.

Maureen, P.K. (1992). Information technologies and the police. In M. Tonry and N. Morris (Eds.). *Modern Policing*, vol. 15. Chicago, IL: University of Chicago Press, pp. 349–398.

MHCIP. (2010). Iran Police News & Events. Retrieved on 7/1/2010 from http://news.police.ir/NCMS/Services

Nashat, G. (1982). *The Origins of Modern Reform in Iran, 1870–1880*. Urbana, IL: University of Illinois Press.

Nezam-Mafi, M.E. (1989). The council for the investigation of grievances: A case study of nineteenth century Iranian social history. *Iranian Studies*, 22(1), 51–61.

O'Hara. P. (2005). *Why Law Enforcement Organizations Fail: Mapping the Organizational Fault Lines in Policing*. Durham, NC: Carolina Academic Press.

Reichel, P.L. (2008). *Comparative Criminal Justice Systems: A Topical Approach*. Upper Saddle River, NJ: Pearson.

Reiss, A.J. (1982). Police organization in the twentieth century. In M. Tonry and N. Morris (Eds.). *Modern Policing*, vol. 15. Chicago, IL: University of Chicago Press, pp. 50–97.

Schafer, A.J. (2007). Thinking about the future of policing. In J.A. Schafer (Ed.). *Policing 2020: Exploring the Future of Crime, Communities, and Policing*. Washington, DC: The US Department of Justice.

Shuster, M. (1912). *The Strangulation of Persia*. New York: The Century Company.

Skolnick, J. (1994). *Justice without Trial: Law Enforcement in Democratic Society*. New York: Macmillan.

Stojkovic, S. et al. (2010). *The Administration and Management of Criminal Justice Organizations*. Belmont, CA: Cengage Learning.

Thomas, J.D. (2011). *Professionalism in Policing: An Introduction*. New York: Clifton Park.

Tolefson, H. (1999). *Policing Islam: The British Occupation of Egypt and the Anglo-Egyptian Struggle over Control of the Police, 1882–1914*. Westport, CT: Greenwood Press.

Uchida, C.D. (2010). The development of the American police: An historical overview. In R.G. Dunham and G.P. Alpert (Eds.). *Critical Issues in Policing: Contemporary Readings* (6th ed.). Long Grove, IL: Waveland Press, pp. 17–36.

Wallersteine, I. (1974). *The Modern World System I*. New York: Academic Press Inc.

Wickens, G.M. (1992). Shah Muzaffar al-Dîn's European tour, AD 1900. In E. Bosworth and C. Hillenbrand (Eds.). *Qajar Iran: Political, Social, and Cultural Change, 1800–1925*. Costa Mesa, CA: Mazda Publishers, pp. 34–47.

Witffogel, K.A. (1981). *Oriental Despotism: A Comparative Study of Total Power*. New York: Vintage Books.

Wright, D. (1977). *The English amongst the Persians during the Qajar Period*. London: Heinemann.

Yarshater, E. (1992). Observations on Nâsir al-Dîn Shah. In E. Bosworth and C. Hillenbrand (Eds.). *Qajar Iran: Political, Social, and Cultural Change, 1800–1925*. Costa Mesa, CA: Mazda Publishers, pp. 3–13.

Challenges of Police Reforms in Lesotho

2

CHELETE MONYANE

Contents

Introduction

In recent years, most studies on police reforms have incorporated new paradigms that cover issues such as community policing, development of police indicators, and police accountability (Frughling 2009). However, most police forces were reluctant to draw inputs from the work done by researchers and academics on police matters. In most cases, this research tends to be critical of police. This is because police reforms in most African countries are a deeply political endeavor—political interests are fundamental to the process of reform. For instance, in political systems where patronage is entrenched, police are tied to the apron strings of the political elite (Rauch and van der Spuy 2006). Police also have few trained professionals who can effectively apply their research findings in police practice (Fielding 1999; Perez and Shtull 2002). Added to this is the little research on police operations (Frughling 2009). Bayley (2010) argues that in a democratic society police ought to serve as neutral custodians of public order. They must be available, fair, and responsive at all times in the maintenance of law and order. Police are not only apolitical, but should also be immune from political interference. Professionalism is of utmost importance in the police. This entails training and the disciplinary codes of conduct.

The objective of this chapter is to provide an in-depth investigation into the challenges facing police reforms in Lesotho. There have been efforts to reform the Lesotho Mounted Police Service (LMPS). However, these efforts do not seem to have been fruitful. Problems of institutional transformation, shortage of human resources, and weak oversight remain unresolved. There were allegations that the reform process was meant to enhance control and dominance of ruling Lesotho Congress for Democracy (LCD) over the LMPS.[*]

Civic movements such as the Christian Council of Lesotho (CCL), the Development for Peace Education (DPE), the Lesotho Council of Non-Governmental Organizations (LCN), and the Transformation Resource Centre (TRC) have written authoritatively on the security sector reforms in Lesotho.[†] Much of their attention was, however, on the reforms of the Lesotho Defence Force (LDF) and the National Security Service (NSS) than a detailed analysis on reforms of the LMPS. They concluded that as a result of the absence of effective legislative instruments to capacitate the roles of oversight bodies and weak parliamentary portfolio committees, it is unlikely that the country will have accountable, transparent, and professional security forces. Over the years, there has been a significant improvement from the successive governments to recognize the role of civic movements in process of police reforms. Policy briefs have been circulated across the community councils and NGOs with the aim to capture the public views on police reforms (Masoabi 2004).

The chapter begins with the focus on the historical evolution and formation of the LMPS, discusses the reform initiatives introduced, and assesses the role of oversight and accountability bodies. It examines the role of civil

---

[*] A new coalition government was formed after the 2012 elections. It comprises of the All Basotho Convention (ABC), Lesotho Congress for Democracy (LCD) and the Basotho National Party (BNP).

[†] See Development for Peace Education 2010. *Police Reforms in Lesotho: A comprehensive Overview*. Christian Council of Lesotho. 2010 Understanding *the Nature of LMPS Reforms* and TRC 2010. *Police Reform in Lesotho, 1997–2010*.

society movements in the reform and presents the challenges facing the reforms. It concludes that there has been lack of political will to genuinely reform police as it has been evidenced by the minimal budget allocation for the reforms.

Understanding Police Reforms

According to Rauch and van der Spuy (2006), police reforms often involve changes in structure (from centralized to decentralized structural arrangements) and function (from an emphasis on defending regime security to the protection of citizen security). This forms the basis of legitimacy (from regime-based legitimacy to legitimacy based on popular consent and participatory modes of democracy). While this goal of fundamental change may be the one that the police leadership and practitioners must keep in mind, it is the one that seems unreasonably demanding in situations where governments themselves have limited capacity.

Across most democratic states, police are regarded as one of the cardinal pillars in support of democracy. Their actions are prescribed within the respect and promotion of human rights, support the rule of law, and maintain order (Hague 1993, 381), which means that police reforms are crucial for the consolidation of democracies. In situations where the authority is weak and institutions are unstable and dysfunctional, police reforming the police can be an arduous task (Rauch and van der Spuy 2006). Fruhling (2009, 466) argues that reforms of police fall under three broad categories. The first aspect entails the reorganization of police agencies through "decentralization, improved quality operations and oversight and disciplinary structures." Measures should be directed at improving efficiency, professionalism, and accountability. The second aspect entails the introduction of "new penal process codes that replace an inquisitorial and written procedure with an oral and accusatorial one." The third aspect entails the establishment of community policing structures (Fruhling 2009, 466).

Police reforms are important to instil respect for democratic values, human rights, and the primacy of civilian rule. Edmonds (1990, 110–112) argues that education and training for the police enables the foundation on which the "normative aspects of the professionalism are built." Police reforms are increasingly being recognized as an essential aspect of conflict management. A police force that enjoys the support of the community and that is capable of arresting insecurity can have a far-reaching impact in enabling lasting economic, social, and political development. Police reforms can further complement and "embolden other programming in the areas of security sector reform, rule of law and good governance" (Edmonds 1990, 110–112).

African governments such as Angola, Democratic Republic of Congo (DRC), Kenya, Mozambique, Namibia, Nigeria, Rwanda, and Sierra Leone undertook measures to modernize and demilitarize their police forces and strengthen their internal accountability mechanisms in the late 1990s and the early 2000s. In some African countries (Sierra Leone and Mozambique), policy briefs were copied from the Western models that were aimed at reforming the police. This was significant considering the colonial legacy, inefficiency, and corruption (Alemika and Chukwuma 2003). But police reforms in Africa need a concise understanding of the historiography and developments that occurred prior to their independence around the 1960s. This entails the fragile political institutions that were left behind by the departing colonial powers in the 1960s (Edmonds 1990). Hills (2000), at the conference on "Critical Issues for Police Studies in Africa," argues that African policing is confronted with problems of corruption and lack of accountability. Most institutions of African states are still headed by weak leadership. This has created more problems in the supervision of reforms in the security organs.

Police reforms in Southern Africa were integral in order to transform and improve their capacity to maintain law and order. Arguably, radical change was needed as a result of continuing violation of human rights, corruption within the police structures, and absence of accountability (Mothibe 1999). There was a need to ensure that the existing police organizations do not remain intact. It must be noted that as a result of the lengthy politicization of the security forces and the entrenched political activism within institutions of the state, it was unlikely that the excepted police reforms would be transformed overnight. Under these circumstances, reform exercises were motivated by the need to create legitimacy and credibility for the security sector. Police is the most direct and visible tool of the state to fight crime. The workload of the rest of the criminal justice system, that is, the courts and prosecutions, is determined by the activities of the police. This includes the number of crimes recorded and successfully investigated (Schonteich 2004, 220).

History of the LMPS

The global wave of democratization in the 1990s saw most African states undergoing profound political changes that entailed the embracement of political liberalization. Lesotho, too, was not immune from the effects of democratization on the global scale. What should be noted is that the emergence of these democratic systems in the 1990s did not yield any positive effects on Lesotho democratic institutions. Lesotho became independent as a parliamentary democracy in 1966 and uses a Westminster method of parliamentary governance inherited from Britain (Khaketla 1971). Governance does not have domestic roots in Lesotho because it is the replica of the British Westminster system (Matlosa 2003). This means that the state in Lesotho is a borrowed concept in both theory and practice entity that is framed along the Westphalian notion of the state. It is weak, dependent, and fragile (Makoa 1998; Mothibe 1998).

Lesotho is a democracy with low per capita income. It depends on the external sources of income such as migrant remittances, foreign aid, and the revenues from the Southern African Customs Union (SACU). Over the years, these external sources of income have declined. Most of the cash the people depend upon for survival comes beyond the country's borders. It has high levels of inequalities and high unemployment. Lesotho also has one of the highest HIV/AIDS rates in Southern Africa. The country performs poorly when measured against the aspects of the United Nations Human Development Index (HDI) such as life expectancy, mortality rates, and standard of living. It is the poorest country, with the lowest HDI of Southern Africa's "free nations," according to Freedom House (Breytenbach 2005).

In 1970, the Basotho National Party (BNP) under Prime Minister Chief Leabua Jonathan lost the election, as it won 23 seats against the 36 seats of the Basutoland Congress Party (BCP), or only 42% of the vote (Matlosa 1999, 172). However, his party remained in power as the constitution was suspended. During this period (1970s), the BNP government exercised strict control over recruitment into the military and police. It consolidated "its own power, not only against external threats but, most critically, against the internal opposition" (Mphanya 2004, 71).

Mothibe (1999, 47) argues that "the action set in motion an authoritarian agenda characterised by brute force, naked oppression and de facto one party rule." He further argues that the police force became highly politicized and acted as essential supporters of this civilian dictatorship in power. As a result of internal and external pressure to return the country to democracy, democratic rule was reintroduced in 1993. However, since the return to democratic rule, Lesotho has had numerous democratic breakdowns in 1994, 1997, 1998, and 2007.

The postdemocratic dispensation in the 1990s was greeted by a number of ugly political episodes. These included the assassination of the Deputy Prime Minister, the violent clashes between the military factions, the police mutiny, and the dissolution of the democratically elected government by King Letsie III (Mothibe 1999). In 1998, the country almost had civil war as opposition parties contested the election outcome. This political impasse was resolved through the military intervention led by South Africa under the auspices of South African Development Community (SADC) (Makoa 1999). However, the 2012 election results led to the emergence of coalition government of three parties as none of the main political parties was able to win an outright majority.

Lesotho's police force was formed in 1872. Since its formation, it was dominated by the sons of chiefs. The police officers provided protection to the magistrates and were interpreters and messengers. Since its inception, the police force was known as Basutoland Mounted Police (BMP). Similar to other former colonies, it was imposed by the British colonial masters. The BMP members were provided with military training and the Commissioner of Police was answerable to the Resident Commissioner (British colonial) but not to the Paramount Chief (Chief of Basotho). Its organizational values displayed the superiority of Britain over the colonized population (Mothibe 1999). The BMP became a colonial instrument used to suppress all forms of political challenges toward colonialism. This included challenges against the colonial institutions and policies. The senior leadership of the police were granted powers to arrest and hold suspects in detention for up to 48 hours without a warrant. They were further granted powers to administer oaths. The BMP relationship with the nation remained weak and enjoyed minimal cooperation. It became one of the influential forces during the colonial period as it performed both the military and law enforcement duties (Makoa 1997).

The BMP was renamed the LMPS after independence in 1966. Similar to the BMP, the LMPS performed dual roles, as the military and as the law enforcement organ of the state. When the LMPS was split to cater for the formation of the Police Mobile Unit (PMU), it started operating as a paramilitary force. Similarly, after the unconstitutional assumption of power in 1970, the LMPS suffered legitimacy crisis among the population as its predecessor. It backed the state of emergency declared by the Prime Minister Chief Leabua Jonathan. It was used to neutralize opposition, and torture and detain opponents to the regime for long periods without trials.

Police abuses and violations of human rights are eloquently documented in Khaketla (1971): *Lesotho 1970: An African Coup under the Microscope*. Similarly, a number of cases against the violations of human rights and police brutality are available in Maqutu (1990): *Contemporary Constitutional History of Lesotho*. According to the Lesotho Internal Security (Public Meetings and Processions) Act No. 15 of 1966 and the Internal Security (Arms and Ammunition) Act No. 17 of 1966, police had the powers to regulate public meetings, processions, and the acquisition of arms and ammunition. Police became a partisan institution identified with political party rather than as a neutral institution of the state (Mothibe 1999). This undermined their ethics of professionalism in the maintenance of law and order.

Without checks and balances over its operations, the LMPS became a law unto itself in the maintenance of the country's security policy. From the 1970s to the late 1980s, recruitment into the police became politicized. The recruits were requested to be card-carrying members of the ruling BNP. This was followed by the introduction of the *Sephephechana* (card-carrying members of the BNP were the only ones allegedly recruited to the police). A large number of BNP members were recruited. Over the years, the LMPS became politicized as officers were regularly seen in political rallies of the BNP. They were purportedly there not to maintain law and order but as participants (Machobane 2001).

In the post-1993 democratic dispensation, the biggest task was on how to create legitimacy for the police. Public opinion was divided because some people had been brutalized by the same police force for over 20 years. Nevertheless, the creation of legitimacy meant that there had to be open engagement with various political actors, civic movements, and other community groupings. There had been problems of accountability in the police over the years. Police were involved in cases of corruption and there were allegations of financial mismanagement within its senior echelons. This had developed during the lengthy period of civilian dictatorship under the BNP (1970–1986) and continued in military administration (1986–1993) (Machobane 2001).

The hive of return to democratic rule was short-lived. The members of the LMPS did not hesitate to wash their dirty linen in public against the government. There were accusations and counter-accusations by the rank and file members of the police. They complained about the poor working conditions and poor remuneration. This was worsened by unconfirmed allegations that the police officers were to be retrenched and replaced by the BCP members (Machobane 2001). There were inflammatory statements by the BCP members of parliament (MPs) and cabinet ministers. These included public utterances by the Prime Minister Ntsu Mokhehle that among the key enemies of democracy in Lesotho were the military and the police (Mothibe 1999). Consequently, the relations between the police and the government deteriorated rapidly.

Makoa (1997, 22) argues that in the post-1993, the BCP administration adopted a hostile attitude that contributed to the poor relations with the police and other security organs of the state. He argues that

> not only did the regime exclude its opponents from the administrative and governmental processes, but it also appeared determined to stoke political instability and violence. Examples of this double pronged policy [were] the purging of the civil service and the security forces, secret importation and stockpiling of weapons of war, and the training of BCP members in their use so that they could challenge the army and eradicate the opposition.

The BCP government soon became embroiled with the police in the early days of administration. The LMPS was struck by internal squabbles. There were differences of opinion between the junior and senior officers on how to end the strike leading to the infamous shooting at the Maseru Charge Office and subsequent mutiny by junior officers, that is, the junior officers were opposed to what they considered to be a high-handed approach adopted by their senior in trying to quell the strike and they refused to quell an illegal teachers' strike in 1995. This was irrespective of the government directives to stop the strike (Makoa 1997; Matlosa 1995). There were allegations that the striking teachers were mostly members of the main opposition party (the BNP). This was the party that the majority of the police members supported. Once again, the ethics of professionalism were compromised.

The problems between the police and the government reached a climax with internal police mutiny in 1997 (Southall 2003). However, the junior officers were those who were responsible (i.e., there was no unity of purpose in the police force regarding these actions). In response, the government directed the LDF to quell the mutiny and arrest the ringleaders. All those who participated in the mutiny were arrested. In an effort to guard against such a recurrence of mutinous behavior, the LMPS was stripped of its military image. The brown combat suits were abolished. This was followed by an official announcement that police officers would no longer carry guns while performing routine duties. The LMPS lost the veneer of being a combat force, as Makoa (1997, 1) correctly asserted "its most potent means of violence and coercion." Afterward, a certain degree of stability prevailed in the police.

During the 1998 political crisis, as the political protagonists contested against the election outcome that was in favor of the LCD, the military and the police took sides in support of the then-LCD government and the opposition parties. Factionalism and loss of discipline became prevalent in the police. Some junior members openly refused to perform their duties under command from their seniors. They accused Police Commissioner and Commander of the army of allegedly assisting the LCD to rig the elections. This led to divisions within the police. Some junior officers supported the opposition cause against the government. They complained about "the poor working conditions, lack of office stationery in police posts, shortage of police vehicles and the unclear chain of command from their superiors" (Commission of Inquiry in Political Developments in Lesotho 2001, 13).

The members of the police and the army joined the protesters in denouncing the then-LCD government. They were later involved in the violent clashes that resulted in the exchange of heavy gun fire in the capital town, Maseru. These clashes between the key organs of the state vested with the powers of maintaining law and order signaled the gravity of the problems within the security apparatus (Commission of Inquiry in Political Developments in Lesotho 2001).

Amid these developments within the police, there was no clear policy framework as to how the police reforms should be undertaken. Makoa (1996) argues that the major security reforms were directed toward military reforms as this was evidenced by the huge financial injection from the government. The financial allocation is the primary tool for any government and provides an insight into government concerns and priorities over time.

Reforms in the LMPS

Some of the problems that continued to bedevil the LMPS in the post-1993 democratic dispensation included the lack of accountability and the nonexistence of structures to ensure the adherence of the police force to civilian control. There were organizational problems due to the shortage of resources (Scher 2010).

Reforming the police involves the reconstruction of the material base of the police organization, human resource capacity development as well as more "cultural" aspects of reform. A reconstruction of the basic police infrastructure may involve rebuilding police stations; supplying paper, pens, and uniforms; putting communication systems in place; providing vehicles and petrol; or developing more specialist infrastructure involving forensic laboratories. A greater investment should be directed to the processes of recruitment, selection, and training of police personnel. The human resource development needs are great at all levels of the organization. This has to be from "foot patrollers to middle-level managers and executive officers" (Rauch and van der Spuy 2006, 19). However, often the needs tend to far outstrip the available resources. A greater prioritization of the resources as well as credible and feasible leadership is needed.

Prior to 1993, police matters were transferred from the Defence Commission and the Ministry of Defence (MOD) to the Ministry of Home Affairs. Its name changed from the Royal Lesotho Mounted Police (RLMP) and became the LMPS. This was an effort to create a more accountable and politically controlled police force (Mothibe 1999). Its service motto became *leponesa, mothusi, motsoalle* (police, helper, and friend) (own translation). This meant that the police were confronted with momentous task to display the high levels of professionalism. They were bound to act as change agents, resolve conflicts, maintain public order, and protect the people (Ministry of Home Affairs and Public Safety, Report 2008).

The major police reforms were introduced since the 1997 police mutiny. These were the White Paper on police reform, the 1998 Police Service Act, and the 5-year developmental plan known as *Beyond 2000: A Development Plan for the Lesotho Mounted Police Service 1998–2003* (Kingdom of Lesotho 1999; LMPS 1998). The 1998 Police Service Act provides for the administrative legal framework for the reform program. The development plan gives the provision for program of action for the easy implementation of reforms for 5 years.

The objectives of the White Paper were to create a more professional police force that is able to discharge law and order that is free from political manipulation. It emphasizes the need for the police to operate under the principle of the supremacy of civil authority. Hence, the LMPS mission reads as follows:

> To provide a high quality Police Service in Lesotho and in conjunction and consultation with the community, other organisations and agencies that seek to promote the safety and security of the individual, reduce crime, disorder and fear and enhance confidence in the rule of law. (Kingdom of Lesotho 1997, 2)

The White Paper outlines a new participatory approach that focuses on the following critical areas of the policing: police–community partnership, resource mobilization and utilization, the new police management, and the new directorate of police. It gives the Commissioner of Police more powers to decide, plan, and determine on how to utilize resources that are needed for policing through the approval of the Minister of Home Affairs (Kingdom of Lesotho 1997, 21).

In terms of the new management approach, the police are no longer directly seen as a department under the Ministry of Home Affairs, which is subjected to the bureaucratic red tape of the civil service. It is classified as the special unit within the ministry. This led to the formation of the Police Negotiating Council, which represents the interests of the police members and resolves their problems. To speed up the implementation of reforms as suggested in the White Paper, the Directorate of Police was formed in the Ministry of Home Affairs. The Directorate serves as an administrative arm to ensure that the reforms lead to an efficient and accountable service. It is under the leadership of the Principal Secretary and is independent from the LMPS (Kingdom of Lesotho 1997, 21).

Beyond 2000: A Development Plan for the Lesotho Mounted Police Service 1998–2003 sets out the plans and the framework on how to professionalize the police. It focuses on strategic guideline for crime management, police–community partnerships, the efficient management of resources, and the improvement of service delivery.

Oversight and Accountability Mechanisms

Opposition parties did not spare the government of criticism. They accused it of politicizing recruitment into the police. There were allegations that those who were closely aligned to the then ruling LCD were given preference for recruitment. There were also unconfirmed allegations of corruption within the senior echelons of the police (Kingdom of Lesotho 1997). Owing to this increasing political pressure and in an effort to assert its authority over the use of public resources, this saw the establishment of various oversight bodies to oversee the conduct of police.

The Constitution of Lesotho creates several provisions for the establishment of the Office of the Ombudsman. Its primary objectives are to investigate complaints against organs of the state [The Constitution of Lesotho 1993, Section 135(2) (a)]. The country also has the Directorate on Corruption and Economic Offences established under the Prevention of Corruption and Economic Crime Offences Act of 1999 (Berg 2005). Under the Prevention of Corruption and Economic Crime Offences Act of 1999, the Directorate is mandated to "investigate complaints, prosecute corruption subject to the Directorate of Public Prosecutions directive, prevent corruption and educate against evils of corruption" (Ministry of Justice: Human Rights and Rehabilitation, http://www.justice.gov.Is/news/anti_corruption.html, June 10, 2010). The Directorate is vested with the powers to investigate any form of complaint in the form of corruption.

Lesotho's constitution provides for the creation of offices of the Auditor General and the Attorney General. The Auditor General is vested with the powers to audit and report on the public accounts across the spheres of government annually. He is responsible over the financial oversight of the police. The Attorney General Office is mandated to "take necessary legal measures for the protection and upholding of constitution and other laws of Lesotho" [The Constitution of Lesotho 1993, Section 98(2)(c) and (b)]. The Attorney General oversees and heads the Director of Public Prosecutions, which has authority over the Directorate on Corruption and Economic Offences and serves an oversight body over the police.

The Lesotho Police Act of 1998 provides for an inspector of police to monitor police performance. It allows for the creation of the Police Complaints Authority (PCA). The PCA is vested with the powers to investigate public complaints on the police conduct. This serves as an internal accountability mechanism within the police. Bayley (2010) suggests that internal accountability within the police is crucial for the following reasons:

- It is difficult to properly investigate the police from outside, because the officers may be reluctant to fully assist with information and cooperate with the investigation process. Organizational culture tends to become resistant to those who are seen as outsiders.
- Internal investigations are more precise and accurate. They not only have the capacity to properly investigate the problems at the face value but can assess the factors that contributed to those problems.

Internal systems are effective and are likely to have a positive impact on the police officers. Problems are likely to be identified early and addressed quickly. This shows the significance of having effective internal accountability mechanisms in the police. But the salient question is: Does Lesotho oversight bodies have the capacity to effectively hold police accountable for their actions?

These constitutionally created oversight institutions are confronted with various problems. They are understaffed and underresourced, and lack the capacity to effectively execute their mandate. There is lack of trust, confidence in the capacity, and political neutrality. There is also poor coherence among these institutions with regard to working together. There is a weak link between the legislative organ (parliament) and these institutions as a result of poor accountability and shortage of resources. According to A and D,* "despite various meetings between these organs and parliament

---

* They were both part of the task team that was established to work closely with the MPs in order to ensure that there is proper coordination to avoid possible duplications in executing functions.

representatives, these bodies did not enjoy any support from the MPs as they were regularly criticized and had minimal support from the Speaker of the National Assembly." C further indicated that "most of the MPs did not really appreciate the importance that such bodies could play in consolidation of Lesotho's democracy." Lastly, D stated that "the MPs did not see the need for these bodies to be independent and financially viable to execute their mandate."

Lesotho's parliament does not have strong portfolio committees to monitor progress in these institutions (Poverty Reduction Strategy of Lesotho 2004/2005). According to A, "though these parliamentary bodies exist, they hardly meet to monitor the progress of these institutions." Similarly, D argues that "the most viable parliamentary portfolio committee is the Public Accounts Committee (PAC) while the rest only exists in name." These bodies do not have financial autonomy as a result of limited financial assistance from government (Ministry of Home Affairs and Public Safety, Report 2008, 14).

Role of Civil Society

Civil society movements play an important role in influencing the process of police reform. Haysom, Cachalia, and Molahleli (1993, 1) define civil society as

> critical component of democratic transformation in the third world is the development of a vibrant civil society, and not merely support for the formal institutions of multi-party democracy. Without the institutions of civil society, there will be no dispersal of power through society, nor will new state forms be accountable to the public. While it may be true that civil society itself requires a strong, resilient, democratic government; strong, robust and effective government also requires robust civil society institutions.

This means that any meaningful police reform requires an input from civil society (Rauch 1993). A strong capacity from civic movements is essential to push for monitoring and policy developments on police reforms. What makes civil society an essential ingredient for democracy is the fact that "it must be seen to improve the lives of people, to allow for self-exertion and release of people's creativity in the transformation of society for the better in all spheres of life" (Wamba-dia-Wamba 1994, 12).

Lesotho has a number of civil society organizations which emerged from as early as the colonial period (Matlosa 2003). The prominent ones are the CCL, DPE, LNGO, and the TRC. They are engaged in the variety of projects ranging from social welfare, emergency services, the environment, employment generation, and monitoring of human rights (Ministry of Home Affairs and Public Safety, Report 2008; Selinyane 1997). These civic movements have successfully advocated for the respect for human rights and accountability within the security organs. They have also advocated for fair labor practices across the civil service and the private sector. Their programs, as Matlosa (2003, 47) notes, have had a "positive impact on election-related aspects: the Lesotho electoral law, how to vote, the importance of voting and relationship between elections, democracy, human rights and participation responsibilities."

Furthermore, they continued to write regular monographs and organize seminars on the roles of police and military in democracy. They organized various rallies across the country to document public views on their trust in Lesotho's democratic institutions. They were actively involved in supporting the public awareness initiatives of the LMPS across the country on how to combat crime and provide assistance to victims of domestic violence. They played a significant role in leading the drive on how community policing should be introduced. They further continued to play significant oversight roles as watchdogs over the conduct of police. They assisted and encouraged the *Ha-Mamathe* communities in July 2007 to report against the incidences of brutality from the police counter crime prevention unit. It was allegedly reported that one person died and scores were left with serious injuries, following the unit operation in search of illegal firearms and stolen animals (Ministry of Home Affairs and Public Safety, Report 2008).

These civic movements also organized a series of sectoral and thematic position papers on how the government can undertake the police reforms over the years. These included raising concerns on how the government has to respond to the needs of the communities in combating crime. Through community consultations spearheaded by these civic movements, position papers provided objectives and strategies that had to be implemented but were forwarded to the Deputy Commissioner of Police: Administration and the Ministry of Home Affairs (Ministry of Home Affairs and Public Safety, Report 2008; Poverty Reduction Strategy of Lesotho 2004/2005). The salient question is: What happened to these commendable inputs spearheaded by the civic movements?

Nevertheless, although these civic movements are dedicated, their biggest shortcoming is the dependence on donor funding. Development partners such as the Development Cooperation of Ireland (DCI), the Department for International Development (DFID), the United Nations Development Programme (UNDP), the United Nations Children's Fund (UNICEF), and the European Union (EU) continue to play a significant role both technically and financially for the survival of these civic movements. South Africa's NGOs also made significant contributions both financially and to develop their staff capacity through conferences and training (Matlosa 2003).

The dependency on external sources has somehow narrowed their scope in terms of performing their oversight mechanisms over institutions of the state. This is because most of donor priorities in Lesotho are on poverty eradication and HIV/AIDS. So there is minimal attention directed to the issues of institutional reforms especially in the police. There is no official legislature in place to create working environment between the civic movements and the police. A particular reference can be made to the existing legislative instruments such as the White Paper and *Beyond 2000: A Development Plan for the Lesotho Mounted Police Service 1998–2003*. Although they recognize the roles that communities and civic movements should play in police reforms, there is nothing tangible that alludes to this. Civic movements are often mistreated and denied access to information by police. According to the Ministry of Home Affairs Report 2011, it was indicated that the majority of the civic movements do not have access to the trends and developments in the LMPS. According to A, "usually we do not like to work with some civic movements, they are weak and can be easily manipulated by the external agents to get information on the police."

Arguably, this means that civil society programs are influenced by donor priorities and conditions. The other problematic issue is that Lesotho's civil society is divided and fragmented. Most of them have similar objectives and strategies on how to combat poverty, elections, and democratic consolidation. Hence, Matlosa (2003, 46) argues that "... provides a much needed window of opportunity for donor funding." What has worsened these rivalries is the competition for donor funding. This has affected their progress on advocating for transparent police reforms. This has affected their roles of efficient watchdogs over the conduct of police.

Challenges of Police Reforms

The introduced police reforms as contained in the White Paper and *Beyond 2000: A Development Plan for the Lesotho Mounted Police Service 1998–2003* have had some positive results. Counter Crime, Stock Theft, and Child and Gender Protection units were established. Special training was further introduced to improve their professional conduct. Strategic locations that require police stations were identified and the existing facilities across police stations were improved (Poverty Reduction Strategy of Lesotho 2004/2005). A new crime management strategy that entails visible policing has been introduced. University graduates with special expertise are now being recruited to service as cadet officers. Domestic violence and child abuse crimes which were previously not given a special attention are now treated as a special priority. Mechanisms have been established in various police posts to address low staff morale. This has seen an improvement in the remuneration packages of police officers and performance monitoring mechanisms introduced (Ministry of Home Affairs and Public Safety, Report 2008, 13; *Work for Justice* 2006, 4).

To improve training, the Bramshill International Commanders Program was offered to few senior officers by the UK's National Police Improvement

Agency. There was an introduction of "lecture days." Regular sessions and lectures on policing methods and standards were conducted regularly on Wednesdays by the field training officers of the UK's National Police Improvement Agency for the LMPS police officers (Scher 2010). Despite these positive developments, some of the key challenges confronting police reforms entail the low public trust and confidence in police, the scourge of HIV/AIDS, poor infrastructure, weakness of oversight bodies, corruption, absence of monitoring and evaluation, lack of research, and absence of political will.

Public Trust and Confidence in the Police

The study conducted by the Afrobarometer in 2000 showed that 41% of the citizens had trust in the LMPS (Gay and Hall 2000). The main research method used in this study entailed bringing together a group of 10 senior personnel of the LMPS in a focus group discussion. The discussions were tape-recorded. Some of the quotes in the article were taken from these transcripts. The interviews were conducted on the range of issues on police reforms. The 2004 survey showed that 46% people had trust in the LMPS. In 2008, the Ministry of Home Affairs survey indicated that "48% of people trusted the LMPS" (Ministry of Home Affairs and Public Safety, Report 2008, 13). In 2011, the survey found that "43% of the people trusted the LMPS" (Ministry of Home Affairs and Public Safety, Report 2012, 26). This shows that there is a minimal faith and trust in the LMPS as an efficient crime combating organ of the state. The salient question is: Why is there such limited trust and confidence in the LMPS? According to A,

> the low levels of public trust and confidence in the LMPS is due to high levels of corruption within the senior echelons of the police, there have been widespread allegations that police are working with the criminal syndicates in stock theft and dagga smuggling.

This shows that much still has to be done to ensure that police reforms are able to instil faith and trust across the population. According to B,

> most of the LMPS leadership do not have significant expertise on policing policy matters. There is no constitutional or legal requirement that stipulates the criteria for the appointment of the National Commissioner of Police. There is no provision that explains explicitly whether that person should have expertise in crime and policing and any outstanding managerial expertise

Some of the previous police commissioners and management did very little to work with civic movements on policing matters. According to C, "there is absolute need to improve relationships between the police and most of the rural dwellers to instil public faith and trust in the LMPS." Some of the problems that have further eroded to the public trust in the LMPS are that police cannot effectively respond to crimes. According to D, "police take long time to investigate all the crimes and these results in delays in the handling of dockets over for prosecution." The LMPS' "Child and Gender Protection Unit is underfunded, understaffed, and lacks sufficiently trained personnel to deal with crimes" (http://www.lestimes.com/?p=4220 viewed on September 30, 2010). Victims of stock theft have accused police of allegedly providing guns to criminals. These allegations do not augur well for police reforms as envisaged in *White Paper and Beyond 2000: A Development Plan for the Lesotho Mounted Police Service 1998–2003*. Such community grievances, low public trust, and confidence will continue to pose a significant challenge for reforms coupled with the poor community–police relationships.

HIV/AIDS

Lesotho has high incidences of HIV/AIDS which are slightly over 23% (Ministry of Home Affairs and Public Safety, Report 2012). Moreover, combating HIV/AIDS in the LMPS still remains a difficult and sensitive issue. The LMPS continues to suffer the effects and impacts of the pandemic. According to B, "there are high rates of absenteeism and poor performance due to ill health and the demands of attending funerals continues to increase." There are no competent bodies and support structures to adequately address these issues within the police. The series of lectures introduced on HIV prevention has so far not yielded positive results. According to C, "the police by law cannot compel officers to declare their health status and these has had negative impacts on combating the disease." It is expensive to substitute the absent employees for the police force that has limited resources. According to A, "about 57% of the junior officers in my station resigned from active service as a result of HIV/AIDS related illnesses." What is problematic is that during transfers and deployments, some of the HIV/AIDS positive officers are transferred to faraway places from their families and do not get any support. Consequently, they end up resigning from the service.

Poor Infrastructure

Police stations are understaffed, underresourced, and inadequate. According to C, "in most police stations, some of the basic things such as stationery are not available. Due to lack of storage facilities, some of the exhibits are stored by the officers at their private houses." This was collaborated by D who indicated that "there are no storage facilities for exhibits and most of them end up disappearing." The LMPS does not have enough facilities for the safe storage of exhibits. D indicates that "some police stations are old, decrepit and some have not been renovated since 1993." Witnesses, victims, and perpetrators continue to denounce police as a result of missing and untraceable docket cases in police stations. This has resulted in the loss of confidence in the police and in frustration among the people who tend to take the law into their own hands.

There is no proper training as a result of the small size of the Police Training College (PTC). In order to make up for the shortfall, officers are often trained in South Africa and Botswana. According to B,

> the American Embassy has consistently assisted by sending officers to the U.S.'s International Law Enforcement Academy in Botswana. The officers were trained in courses that ranged from surveillance and detection to dealing with weapons of mass destruction and improvised explosive devices.

Furthermore, Interpol, the international police agency, contributed training modules in cybercrime and antiterrorism (Scher 2010). However, the fruits of these exercises are yet to be seen. According to B, "it has been difficult for the trained officers to impart their knowledge to their counterparts and in addition, most of the country's challenges are stock theft and the porous borders with South Africa, training in cybercrime and antiterrorism are not the key priorities for Lesotho." Added to poor infrastructure is the low staff morale in the LMPS. Police officers have consistently complained about poor salaries and benefits. According to B, this is caused by the "remunerations which are not at par with inflation and the inconsistent allowances."

Oversight Bodies

Parliamentary Oversight

According to F, "the parliamentary oversight bodies are weak and do not have the capacity to effectively execute their mandate." Similarly, G argues that "the compositions of the Lesotho's parliamentary committees are made of people who hardly understand the role of police in the democratic society." In addition, F indicates that "the majority of the parliamentary committees on national security do not have enough capacity to steer policing forward, to ensure that it becomes a credible and respected institution that is apolitical." There was a general agreement that various parliamentary committees responsible for oversight of the police parliament do not have sufficient capacity and execute their mandate. Over the years, they made marginal contributions to the normative aspects of professionalization of the LMPS and hardly in session to play their oversight role.

According to F, "there are no specialised internal oversight mechanisms to address the deficiencies arising from ill-discipline and other organizational matters as the existing ones are ineffective." Theoretically, these aspects are supposed to minimize the impunity in certain aspects where accountability is lacking. Practically, this has not been the case. Due to lack of communication with the LMPS, G indicates that "external bodies are not given enough powers to investigate, lack political support, and have shortage of human and financial resources." There has been limited assistance from the government with financial resources for them to effectively execute their constitutional mandate. The salient question is: Why? It is evident that the police are not regarded as one of the key cardinal organs in support of democracy in Lesotho. This is different from the military where there are rigorous mechanisms to retrain, professionalize, and improve financial rewards for top performers in different aspects of training.

External oversight bodies have not properly advocated and had influence over the speedy implementation of effective complaints system to maintain public trust and confidence in the police. They have not succeeded to serve as the fundamental agents over ill-treatment and misconduct of police. According to G, "this has been proved by the increasing number of civil cases pending in the courts of Lesotho against police brutality and corruption." However, the internal mechanisms can play a more proactive role in addressing the deficiencies and organizational matters. There is an urgent need to ensure that such mechanisms are supported financially by the state.

Police Complaints Directorate

While the body has been tasked to investigate the cases of misconduct by the police, it emerged that the body does not have enough capacity to effectively execute its mandate. According to D, "the PCD does not have skilled and experienced investigators within its ranks. This has undermined its role to adequately propose any meaningful reforms within the LMPS." There was a general agreement that the Police Complaints Directorate (PCD) is a toothless watchdog and has failed to bring any meaningful insights for the process of reforms. Although the PCA has its own researchers and investigators, it is unable to launch investigations independently. Its staff cannot take the citizens' complaints directly. According to D, "to make a complaint against a police officer, citizens are required to present the complaint personally to the minister of Home Affairs." While citizens could take complaints to the PCA, the agency is required by law to refer the complainant to the minister. Any complaint that comes to the commissioner is supposed to be forwarded to the minister. D indicates that "the minister has the discretion to either quash the complaint or refer it to the PCA for further investigation."

The problematic issues with these arrangements are that members of the public are faced with a tough job in trying to get an audience with the commissioner or minister. This process can be intimidating if the subject involves a complaint about the police. Second, given Lesotho's rugged and mostly rural terrain, just traveling to the capital city of Maseru is a significant undertaking. Currently, the system gives the minister, a political appointee, sole discretion to decide which cases would be investigated. Additionally, in other countries, some kinds of cases, such as deaths in police detention, warrant automatic referral to the PCA. However, Lesotho's Police Act has no such provisions.

According to D, "in 2009, about 20 complains were referred to the PCA by the minister. However, following their review, the PCA only pursued 14 cases. Furthermore, in 2010 only seven cases were completed and seven were still under investigation." Given such a minimal output for oversight over the police, this does not augur well for the reform process. It is evident that much still has to be done to improve the capacity of the PCA and to ensure that it executes its mandate effectively. The PCA does not have full investigative powers to examine complaints on police abuses. According to B, "the PCA does not have powers to receive relevant information, complaints without prior knowledge of the Commissioner of Police." In frustration, community members have accused it of failing to act against acts of torture, brutality, and criminal activities committed by the police.

PCA has often voiced its frustrations over the lack of cooperation from the police. This led to unnecessary delays in handling of cases of police brutality and corruption (Minister of Home Affairs and Public Safety, Lesao Lehohla, August 10, 2008). Perhaps much has to be done to ensure that the existing structures can discharge their functions independently. It would be essential that such bodies are given enough powers to carry out comprehensive investigations on police abuses free from police and executive interference. According to G, "such external bodies have to be well resourced, operate transparently and be given access to regular reports."

Judicial Oversight: The Role of Courts

Judicial oversight is an important form of scrutiny and constraint over the police. However, there has been an increase in the number of criminal activities conducted by the police. The courts have not adequately addressed these matters to set the precedent. This is because of the problems of poor coordination with other organs of the state. According to D, the "civil cases against the police have increased by over 50% but there are limited avenues for recourse." This is a useful missing link that could potentially provide an important source of information which could be credible for existing policy implications. The courts have not played an effective role over the police activities. According to H, "there is no judicial oversight over the activities of the police." According to *MoAfrika FM*, Radio Broadcast, November 26, 2006, there are a number of cases pending in the courts as a result of bribery and fraud against some police officers. The most significant example is the case of 28 senior police officers who were charged allegedly with fraud and forgery. The Assistant Commissioner of Police (Administration) has been suspended pending the finalization of his corruption trial. Whether these allegations are true or not for those within the senior echelons of the LMPS, they do not bound well for the successful police reforms and are likely to continue eroding the remaining public trust and faith in the police.

Corruption

Corruption and incompetence are rife. According to www.lestimes.com, viewed on May 10, 2010, "there is a culture of political patronage that perpetuates impunity and absence of accountability." The Directorate on Corruption and Economic Offences (DCEO) has not been effective with respect to the execution of its mandate. It is hindered by shortage of financial and human resources and poor infrastructure. Added to this are bureaucratic bottlenecks and poor professional skills. According to D, "most of the officers of the DCEO need more training on investigative methods on corruption." This was collaborated by G who argued that "while most of them do have legal backgrounds, corruption is more complex and there is a need for refresher courses for DCEO members." The other problem is that DCEO falls under the civil service structures and thus is subjected to the Public Service Regulations (Ministry of Home Affairs and Public Safety, Report 2011). According to D, "the other problem is the absence of legislative framework against corruption and economic offences. There is an urgent need to review the Prevention of Corruption and Economic Offences Act 1999."

Community Policing

Community policing forums have not been effectively introduced. Community policing is one important aspect for effective police reforms. In response to the escalating levels of stock theft, stock theft associations were established. Its intentions were to retrieve stock and mete out brutal capital punishment when the perpetrators were caught. Membership fees were introduced as insurance for the payment of bail and court fines if members were prosecuted (Scher 2010). According to F, "corruption became rife as some chiefs, police took advantage of the situation and demanded bribes while some chiefs allegedly received bribes for the sale of permits for stolen goods and animals." Corrupt police officers allegedly assisted in the prosecutions by giving false evidence that led to the acquittal of their collaborators who often use their licensed guns (Baker 2004; Buur 2003; Scher 2010). According to D, "these stock theft associations lack training, motivation and leadership." It means that they have failed to properly communicate and act as vehicles to enhance police effectiveness. The explicit aim of the stock theft units was to mete out "brutal capital punishment" to stock thieves, that is, these institutions involved the participation of chiefs (custodians of law and order). However, they later became instrumental in some criminal activities as some associations did transgress the law; that is, the associations were meant to operate within the law and their objectives should not be lumped with those which became wayward and became vigilante groups.

According to A, "there is no significant emphasis on the role that local communities are expected to play to ensure that local police are accountable." B indicates that "there are no community police forums in various police stations across the country." Lesotho does not have sufficient newspaper that gives an account of the developments in the police. There are no appropriate mechanisms for people to voice their grievances and problems from their communities in a coordinated manner especially on matters regarding the police. The existing newspapers are too small to devote sufficient time and do not have resources to crime reporting. According to F, "they do not have much influence across the society that could prompt to push for police reforms." *Leseli ka Seponesa*, the LMPS newspaper, merely reports on crime committed in urban areas with limited capacity. There are no policy frameworks within the senior administrative structures of the LMPS to improve its capacity on crime reporting [Transformation Resource Centre (TRC), Democracy Project Report 2006, 13, www.lestimes.com, viewed on May 10, 2001]. D indicates that "it is also not widely accessible for most people across the country."

Political Will

Political will is significant for successful reform process in any institution (Stone, Maxwell, and Keating 2001). There is absence of political will to genuinely reform the police. There is lack of consensus on the direction of the reform process even within the executive organ of the state. It is different from the proposed reform as outlined in the White Paper and *Beyond 2000: A Development Plan for the Lesotho Mounted Police Service 1998–2003*. Opposition parties have accused the government of politicizing police reforms. One opposition MP made public allegations that "those closely aligned to the then [ruling] LCD were secretly scouted and given preference in the recruitment process" (*MoAfrika* FM, Radio Broadcast, November 26, 2006). This was followed by the unconfirmed allegations that the ruling party MPs had initially submitted the names of the candidates who were to be recruited were allegedly submitted to the senior echelons of police. According to C, "most of the recruitments in 2008/10 did not have any ordinary Cambridge Overseas School Certificate (COSC) which is a pre-requisite for recruitment in the LMPS." Over the years, much financial injection was directed to the military than to the police.

In 1996/1997 budget, allocation of the military increased to M123.8 million (this was 9.1% of the total national budget and the third highest allocation received by any ministry) (Lesotho Budget Speech 1996/1997). In the 1997/1998 financial year, it was M147.1 million and was second to that allocated to the Ministry of Education. It further increased to M165.5 million in the 1998/1999 financial year. On the other hand, the police budget was slightly above M70 million in the 1997/1998 financial year (Lesotho Budget Speech 1998/1999). From 1999 to 2011, the military budget has increased by over M200 compared to the police (Ministry of Home Affairs and Public Safety, Report 2012). There has been a consistent financial injection in the military with the idea of creating professional and apolitical forces. Police reforms were not regarded as the top priority.

According to the former Prime Minister, the "Lesotho needed to have a strong viable military force so as to participate actively in the peacekeeping operations" (*MoAfrika* FM, Radio Broadcast, November 26, 2006). In most parliamentary debates, much attention on security sector reforms has been paid to improve the efficiency and more professionalization of the military. According to D, "the police are not seen as the key institutions that support of democracy in Lesotho, most of the attention is much more on the military." Similarly, C indicates that "the military is seen as a tool of influence and control among Lesotho's political elites." Such pronouncements by the politicians allude to the lack of political will to genuinely reform the police.

I am of the view that police reforms in Lesotho have to do with the resource endowment and how scarce resources are allocated. The state of economic growth and development is significant to drive the process of reforms. It is the economy that determines the amount of resources that the executive organ of the state can allocate to the LMPS. But the security budget seems to be in competition with other sectors for the scarce resources. Most of the resources are directed to the military. The salient question is: Most of Lesotho's problems are internal but why is there so much financial injection for the military? A strong viable police force that is well trained and well equipped could assist in curbing the stock theft and dagga smuggling to South Africa.

Research

Stone et al. (2001) argue that research has the prospects and potential to influence policies. But this has been another area that has not been improved in the LMPS. Although the research division exists, B indicates that "it lacks the capacity and financial resources to fully undertake its mandate." As a result of the new recruitment process, university graduates were recruited in police; one would have expected much more progress in terms of the research capacity. However, this has not been the case. Much has to be done to encourage them to engage in research activities that could be beneficial for police reforms. The police have hardly engaged the independent researchers on the best direction for the reforms. According to F, "little research exists on the progress and problems encountered the reforms and any possible solutions."

Furthermore, there is poor research capacity in the police on crime levels. This is worsened by poor coordination between various police stations. The methods of communication are outdated. According to A, "there is no accurate and reliable information on the accurate crime statistics and crime information." There is lack of expertise and crime exhibits are regularly sent to South Africa for analysis (Minister of Home Affairs and Public Safety, Lesao Lehohla, August 10, 2008; TRC, Democracy Project Report 2006). This often causes delays in the prosecution of cases and not much has been done to address this problem.

Monitoring and Evaluation

It emerged that there are no appropriate monitoring and evaluation mechanisms available in place. There is problem of shortage of resources to effectively ensure that such tasks are undertaken appropriately. This has been the major point of concern as it has been difficult to assess the extent of the progress that has been made with regard to police reforms. It has been difficult to attract any valuable inputs from the NGOs for expertise and to undertake appropriate citizen surveys in order to gauge the effectiveness of the work that has been undertaken. According to A, "the lack of monitoring and evaluation mechanisms within the LMPS has made it difficult to gauge what has been achieved in the terms of the reforms." Similarly, D indicates that "it has been difficult to know the kind of progress, how to avoid the duplication of some measures introduced and how they can be improved." In the absence of such mechanisms, it will be difficult to know the impacts, the amount of resources needed for the different programs, and the possible solutions in a cost-effective way.

Conclusion

Lesotho's police served as the guarantors of both civilian dictatorship and military rule that lasted for over 20 years. Through this period, the police became highly politicized, there was lack of accountability and the corruption was rife. After the 1993 elections, the incoming civilian governments did have a clear policy and strategic framework on how reform the police. Police were publicly rebuked as enemies of Lesotho's democracy. These tensions reached a climax with the junior police officers' mutiny in 1997 which paved the way for the reforms.

Police reforms are the democratic necessity in which the police should be held accountable for their actions. Police reforms help to improve accountability and transparency. The reforms must pave a way for improved quality operations, efficiency, and professionalism. Lesotho's police reforms as contained in the White Paper and *Beyond 2000: A Development Plan for the Lesotho Mounted Police Service 1998–2003* resulted in some significant improvements in the delivery of services. The police service was reorganized, the specialized units were established, and the visible policing was improved.

The greatest challenge for police reforms is the shortage of financial and human resources. Parliamentary portfolio committees have not advocated for the increased financial resources to support the reforms. Oversight agencies were created to monitor the actions and functions of the police. However, the record of the oversight agencies has been controversial. While the police directorate functioned efficiently within its closely delineated responsibilities, the PCA became a toothless watchdog. In the absence of any legislation to give the PCA some independence, especially authority to take complaints and launch investigations, it is likely to remain underutilized and as a potential tool of the incumbent minister. Added to this is their lack of independence as a result of shortage of funds. There are no appropriate monitoring and evaluation mechanisms available in place to assess the progress of police reforms. Finally, there is lack of genuine political will to effectively reform the police as more resources continue to be channeled to the military.

The conspicuously absent issue as to why police reforms in Lesotho are confronted by various challenges could, perhaps, best be explained with reference to placing the state at the center as the unit of analysis. While the Lesotho's state has the capacity and enjoys the monopoly of force to control its citizens, it has been unable to create the national consensus on issues of national importance. The state has failed to ensure that there is greater awareness on the importance of institution of police in the consolidation of democracy.

References

Alemika, E. and Chukwuma, I.C. (2003). *Civilian Oversight and Accountability of Police in Nigeria*. Lagos: Centre for Law Enforcement Education (CLEEN) Foundation.

Baker, B. (2004). Multi-choice policing in Africa: Is the continent following the South African pattern? *Society in Transition*, 35(2), 12–21.

Bayley, D. (2010). Understanding the evolving nature of policing: Trends and challenges. In *Conference on Politics, Theory and Methods of Policing Research: Innovations and Trends*. Monkey Valley, Cape Town, January 30–31.

Berg, J. Eds. (2005). Lesotho police. In *Overview of Plural Policing Oversight in Select Southern African Development Community (SADC) Countries*. Cape Town: Centre for Criminology, University of Cape Town, 9–11.

Beyond 2000: A Development Plan for the Lesotho Mounted Police Service 1998–2003. Maseru: Government Printers.

Breytenbach, W. (2005). Development and democracy in the Southern and Eastern African region. In Hansohm, D., Breytenbach, W., Hartenzberg, T., and McCarthy, C., Eds. *Monitoring Regional Integration in Southern Africa*, Vol. 5. Windhoek: Namibian Economic Policy Research Unit (NEPRU).

Buur, L. (2003). Vigilantism and the Policing of everyday life in South Africa. Paper Presented for ROAPE Conference: Africa: Partnerships as Imperialism, September 5–7, 2003, Birmingham University, Birmingham.

Commission of Inquiry in Political Developments in Lesotho, 2001. Maseru: Government of Lesotho Printers.

The Constitution of Lesotho (1993). Maseru: Government Printers.

Edmonds, M. (1990). Armed services and society. Inter-University Seminar, Special Editions on Armed Forces and Society. Boulder: Westview.

Fielding, R. (1999). *Understanding Police Reforms. The Case of Stop and Search*. Guildford: University of Surrey Press.

Frughling, H. (2009). *Recent Police Reform in Latin America*. Lanham: Lexington Books.

Fruhling, H. (2009). Research on Latin American police: Where do we go from here? *Police Practice and Research: An International Journal*, 10(5–6), 466.

Gay, J. and Hall, D. (2000). *Poverty and Livelihoods in Lesotho, 2000. More than Mapping Exercise*. Maseru: Sechaba Consultants.

Hague, R. (1993). *Comparative Politics and Government: An Introduction*. London: Macmillan.

Haysom, N., Cachalia, F., and Molahleli, E. (1993). *Civil Society and Fundamental Freedoms*. Report to the Commission of Inquiry into an Enabling Environment for Non-Governmental Organisations. Braamfontein: Centre for Study of Violence.

Hills, A. (2000). *Policing Africa: Internal Security and the Limits of Liberalization*. London: Lynne Rienner Publishers.

Khaketla, B.M. (1971). *Lesotho 1970: An African Coup under the Microscope*. London: C. Hurst & Co.

Kingdom of Lesotho (1997). *Kingdom of Lesotho Second Five Year Development Plan*, Vol. 1. Maseru: Government Printers.

Kingdom of Lesotho (1999). *Kingdom of Lesotho Third Five Year Development Plan*, Vol. 1. Maseru: Government Printers.

Lesotho Budget Speech, 1996/1997. Ministry of Finance. Maseru: Office of the Public Relations Officer (PRO).

Lesotho Budget Speech, 1998/1999. Ministry of Finance. Maseru: Office of the Public Relations Officer (PRO).

Lesotho Internal Security (Arms and Ammunition) Act No. 17 of 1966. Maseru: Government Printers.

Lesotho Internal Security (Public Meetings and Processions) Act No. 15 of 1966. Maseru: Government Printers.

Lesotho Mounted Police Service (LMPS) (1998). *Police Sector Reform*. Maseru: Government Printers.

Machobane, L.B.B.J. (2001). *The King's Knight: Military Governance in the Kingdom of Lesotho 1986-1993*. Roma: Institute of Southern African Studies (ISAS).

Makoa, F. (1997). Lesotho voter and elections: A note on the 1998 general election. *Lesotho Social Science Review*, 3(2), 22-29.

Makoa, F. (1998). Conflict and conflict resolution. *Lesotho Social Science Review*, 5(1), 9-17.

Makoa, F. (1999). The challenges of the South African military intervention in Lesotho after 1998 election. *Lesotho Social Science Review*, 5(1), 23-34.

Makoa, K. (1996). Political instability in post-military Lesotho. The crisis of the Basotho Nation-State? *African Security Review*, 5(3), 14.

Maqutu, W. (1990). *Contemporary Constitutional History of Lesotho*. Mazenod: Mazenod Institute.

Masoabi, P. (2004). Police complaints authority: Lesotho. Paper Presented at the Policing Oversight and Accountability Conference, Sandton, January 26-29.

Matlosa, K. (1995). Aid to Lesotho: Dilemmas of state survival and development, PhD thesis. University of the Western Cape, Cape Town.

Matlosa, K. (1999). Conflict and conflict management in Lesotho. *Lesotho Social Science Review*, 5(1), 1-14.

Matlosa, K. (2003). Political culture and democratic governance in Southern Africa. *African Journal of Political Science*, 8(1), 43-56.

Ministry of Home Affairs and Public Safety, Report, 2008. Maseru: Government Printers.

Ministry of Home Affairs and Public Safety, Report, 2011. Maseru. Government Printers.

Ministry of Home Affairs and Public Safety, Report, 2012. Maseru: Government Printers.

Ministry of Justice: Human Rights and Rehabilitation. Lesotho: Directorate on Corruption and Economic Offences. http://www.justice.gov.Is/news/anti_corruption.html, June 10, 2010.

MoAfrika FM, Radio Broadcast, November 26, 2006. Maseru: *MoAfrika* Morning Drive Show.

Mothibe, T. (1998). A modern history of Lesotho since 1968. Staff Occasional Paper. Roma: History Department, National University of Lesotho (NUL), 11.

Mothibe, T. (1999). The military and democracy in Lesotho. *Lesotho Social Science Review*, 5(1), 41-54.

Mphanya, N. (2004). *History of the Basutoland Congress Party (BCP)—Lekhotla la Mahatamoho*. Morija: Morija Museum and Archives.

Perez, W. and Shtull, R. (2002). Police research and practise: An American perspective. *Police Practice & Research*, 3(3), 169-187.

Poverty Reduction Strategy of Lesotho (2004/2005). Maseru: Ministry of Finance and Development Planning.

Rauch, J. (1993). State, civil society and police reform in South Africa. Paper Presented at the International Society of Criminology conference, Budapest, August.

Rauch, J. and van der Spuy, E. (2006). *Police Reform in Post Conflict Africa: A Review*. Pretoria: IDASA.

Scher, D. (2010). *Reining in a Rogue Agency: Police Reform in Lesotho, 1997–2010*, Innovations for Successful Societies. Princeton, NJ: Princeton University.

Schonteich, M. (2004). Revealing figures: A 10-year review of South African criminal justice performance. *South African Journal of Criminal Justice*, 17, 220–229.

Selinyane, N. (1997). Civil society and electoral politics and the retrieval of democracy in Lesotho. *Lesotho Social Science Review*, 3, 23–33.

Southall, R. (2003). Unlikely success: South Africa and Lesotho's election of 2002. *Journal of Modern African Studies*, 14(2), 45–57.

Stone, D., Maxwell, S., and Keating, M. (2001). Bridging research and policy. Paper Presented for an International Workshop Funded by UK Department of International Development. Radcliffe House, Warwick University, Coventry.

Transformation Resource Centre (TRC) Democracy Project Report, 2006. Maseru: TRC Library.

Wamba-dia-Wamba, E. (1994). Poverty and political participation. *SAPEM*, 7(10), 12.

Work for Justice, 2006. No. 74. Maseru, Lesotho: Transformation Resource Centre (TRC).

Websites

http://www.lestimes.com/?p=4220 viewed on September 30, 2010.

http://www.trc.org.ls/trc_programmes/info_comm/archives/2006/wfj74_screen.pdf viewed on August 23, 2010.

www.lestimes.com viewed on May 10, 2010.

www.lestimes.com/?p=2620 viewed on July 8, 2010.

The Soap Opera Rationale

A Complementary Information Management Construct in Police Work Practice

3

ERIK BORGLUND AND URBAN NULDÉN

Contents

Introduction

In the past 15 years, police work in Sweden has been changed from only reactive police work toward a more proactive approach. The proactive police work has been an important trend in modern police management. In the mid-1990s, the Swedish police introduced problem-oriented policing, and currently the Swedish police are working with the implementation of an intelligence-led policing. Both of these proactive approaches rest upon an idea that police work should be based upon decisions that are derived from various forms of structured analyses of information. This new way of carrying out police work creates a need to be better in dissemination of information in order to work proactively and implicitly to be better able to prevent criminal

61

activities (Brown and Brudney 2003). Brown and Brudney (2003) define the police as a learning organization or as a knowledge organization. In such capacity, information technology (IT) is often used as a means to manage huge amounts of information to acquire knowledge that is necessary for both operational and strategic decisions in proactive police work.

One of the fundamentals of the intelligence-led policing is to be able to produce high-quality bases for decisions. The bases for decisions are often reached by using IT to extract and analyze large data sets, and even information from various sources (Brahan, Lam, Chan, and Leung 1998; Oatley and Ewart 2003). Large data sets from different sources can also be used in knowledge management and information sharing (Chen, Zeng, Atabakhsh, Wyzga, and Schroeder 2003; Chen et al. 2002; Redmond and Baveja 2002).

In earlier research conducted by the authors of this article (Borglund 2004, 2005; Nuldén and Borglund 2006, 2012), police officers have been identified as being very active in the retrieval of information needed for their own work. Police officers make their operational and tactical decisions based on the information at hand—information retrieved from external information sources and the dispatch central. The police work can be described as knowledge intensive and is often time critical (Chen et al. 2002); in such work practice, accessibility of accurate and reliable information is important.

In the majority of the different IT solutions aimed to support proactive police work presented above (see, e.g., Brahan et al. 1998; Chen et al. 2002, 2003; Oatley and Ewart 2003; Redmond and Baveja 2002), one can see that all IT solutions have been based on a rationale where the proactive police work is very structured with a distinct start and finish. The IT systems which have been designed so far and developed especially for supporting the proactive police work, and which have been presented in research, support the structured way of carrying out police work, with characteristics similar to a project rationale. The proactive police work in Sweden is a rather new work practice (15 years); still many IT systems within the police are developed and designed to support a traditional reactive police work. It is important to increase the knowledge about proactive police work and the information management within that practice to be able to design IT systems aimed to support proactive police work. Based on an extensive data collection in the field of police work, we present a coexisting rationale. This coexisting rationale is less process-like and less structured. It is based on different rules and can be described to be more like a *soap opera*. The "soap operas emphasize the instability of closure and the inconsistency of the individual character. As unending narratives, soap operas depend on the narrative devices of deferral, contradiction, and repetition" (Archer 1992, 89). In this soap opera rationale, the police officers are acting more like bricoleurs, that is, they collect and search for information on a daily basis to acquire more knowledge and increase their ability to perform their work. They collect information to be better prepared and to reduce risks. The bricoleur is a person who solves situations with the tools available. The opposite of the bricoleur is the engineer who develops the optimal tool for every situation (Lévi-Strauss 1971). In the soap opera, the police bricoleurs collect bits and pieces of information that comes their way; the police bricoleurs never know when and where a certain piece of information can be useful. However, when they confront a situation, the sum of information collected and the experience gathered are the tools they have available to solve the situation.

When, for example, intelligence-led policing is introduced on a broad scale in the Swedish police, there is a need to increase the knowledge and competence on how to optimize information management within the police in all existing rationales. In this chapter, we do not claim that these two perspectives (the soap opera and structured project rationales) are mutually exclusive. Rather, we suggest that they coexist and the soap opera is a needed complement to understand the complexity of information management that exists in police practice. The purpose of this chapter is to present a set of properties that constitute the soap opera rationale and relate this rationale to a more structured project rationale.

This chapter is structured as follows: First, the applied research method is presented together with a description on how the research was carried out. The method section also includes a minor contextual description about the Swedish police and the proactive police work carried out in Sweden for a better understanding of the empirical data. The findings are presented, which are empirically based. How an information management rationale soap opera can look like is presented in the findings. The chapter then ends with a discussion about the two coexisting information management perspectives.

Research Method

The data collection and analysis has been a joint effort of two researchers: one that has a background in the police force and a visitor that investigated the police practice. The practitioner has 20 years of experience within the police domain, from three main areas of the police: patrol duty in Stockholm, operational work at the national Special Weapons and Tactics (SWAT) unit, and patrol duty in a smaller Swedish city. For the past 8 years, the practitioner has been doing full-time research and only minor police work; during that period, the police practice has been observed from both a practitioner's and a researcher's perspective. The second researcher has gained knowledge and experience from the police domain through participatory observation over a period of 4 years. The time spent in the field is equivalent to 25 weeks of full-time and first-hand observations following an ethnographical approach (Agar 1996; Ferrell and Hamm 1998;

Hammersly and Atkinsson 1995; Orr 1996). The observations have been made mainly as a "third" person in a two-officer patrol in the case of the visitor, and as one of the officers in the patrol in the case of the reflective practitioner. In Sweden, most officers work in pairs, which means that reference to a patrol means two officers in a police car. Notes have been taken during observations when possible. When it has been difficult to take notes due to a sensitive or chaotic situation or during night when it has been too dark, or when the officers glanced at the writing with suspicion, notes have been written down after the shift. Informal conversational interviews with officers during patrol have been conducted. Observations of operators, and listening to the conversations with both callers and patrols, have been performed at several different dispatcher centrals. The notes from the observations and interviews have been analyzed and categorized, and recategorized. The vast amount of data used in this research is to a large extent embedded in the experience of the researchers, and mainly in the experience of the practitioner. The analysis process is therefore not completely visible. The basis for the data collection during this research has been the police work practice.

In this chapter, we have used scenarios as a technique to "make work visible" (Suchman 1995) in order to present and exemplify how information management in the soap opera rationale can be seen. The scenarios are fictive but are based on real and common identified situations during the extensive data collection in the police work practice field. We do not intend to use scenarios as supplement to actual empirical data, rather to be better able to visualize the findings and the categorizations in the form of four properties of the soap opera rationale. Scenarios can be used in a variety of situations: "to present and situate solutions, to illustrate alternative solutions, to identify potential problems" (Bødker 2000, 63). Scenarios are often used to describe work practice (Carroll 2000).

The Proactive Police Work in Swedish Police

One of the possible reasons for the existence of the information management perspective, described in this chapter as soap opera, is the new proactive police work. To better understand the findings, some background knowledge of proactive police work is needed.

Around the world, several methodologies have been developed to enable a proactive police work, which is able to prevent crime before it happens. In Sweden, this has been named POP or problem-oriented policing. With POP, the police should be able to identify a problem area and then work in a structured way to reduce the problem. Intelligence-led policing is a method developed from the basic ideas of POP. In intelligence-led policing, intelligence serves as a basis for decisions and actions, rather than a source of problems.

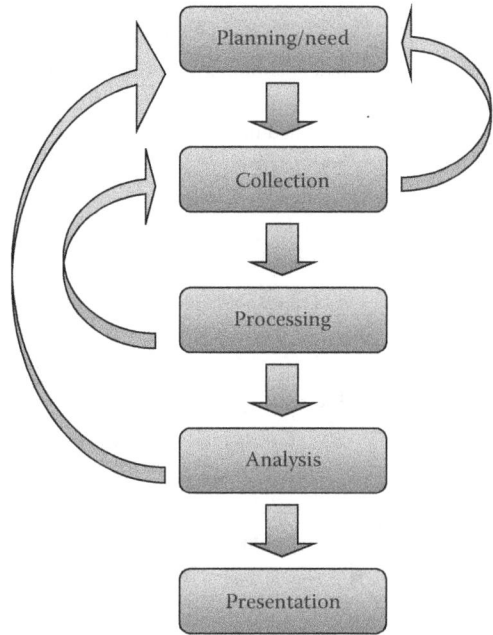

Figure 3.1 Intelligence process. (From Agrell, W., *Konsten att gissa rätt: under-rättelsevetenskapens grunder*. [The Art of Making Correct Guesses: Basics in Intelligence Science], Studentlitteratur, Lund, Sweden, 1998, p. 26. With permission.)

In Swedish police, intelligence is defined as "information processed and aimed for action."[*] It can be described as the art of making correct guesses (Agrell 1998). It includes the processes such as acquiring, capturing, analyzing, visualizing, and storing information, as well as the organizational and managerial structures that accommodate these processes. In Figure 3.1, the intelligence process is visualized.

The Swedish police have developed the PUM methodology (PUM—Swedish abbreviation for Police Intelligence Methodology; see Figure 3.2). PUM together with PNU (Swedish abbreviation for Police National Investigation routine) is the central component in the fight against "everyday crimes" and aims to increase the rate of solved crimes. PUM is developed from the fundamental ideas found in intelligence-led policing (e.g., Ratcliffe 2002, 2003). Figure 3.3 visualizes intelligence-led policing.

Police intelligence in Sweden is managed by the criminal intelligence services (KUT). In PUM, the goal is to carry out the initiatives taken by the police against criminal activities at the right time, using the right resources

[*] Interview with Head of Analysis section at National Criminal Investigation Department 2003-10-01.

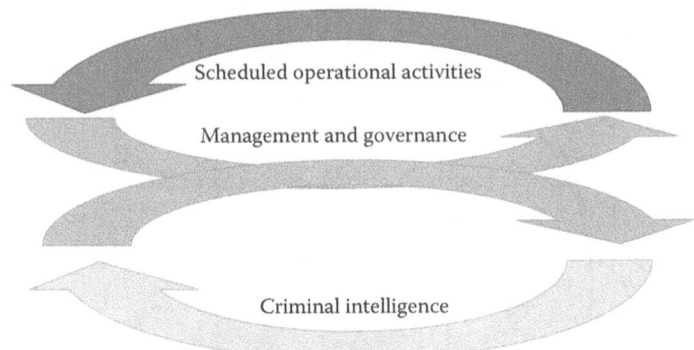

Figure 3.2 The PUM methodology.

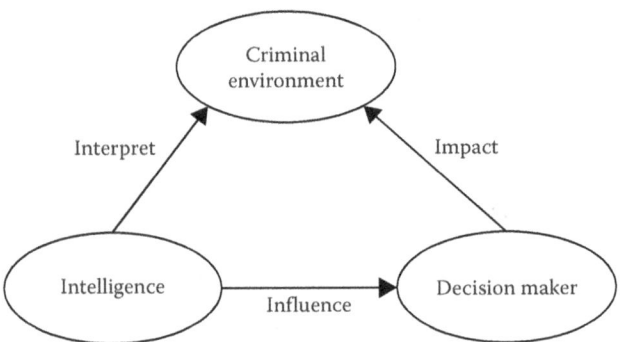

Figure 3.3 Intelligence-led policing. (From Ratcliffe, J. H., *Trends & Issues in Crime and Criminal Justice*, 1–6, 2003. With permission.)

and using the right method. PUM is based on three processes: management and governance, criminal intelligence, and scheduled operational activities. Altogether this means that all planned activities in the Swedish police should be based on criminal intelligence. As seen in Figure 3.2, PUM is a cyclic method, in which the intelligence process is an ongoing activity but still a governed and controlled activity.

In an intelligence process, it is important to receive information that could initiate an intelligence process. In the Swedish police, all police officers are responsible for writing intelligence entries, when they, during their work, receive any information that can be seen as an intelligence entry. It is the KUT units' responsibility to further analyze and assess the intelligence entry.

The KUT at national, regional, and local levels should be responsible for collecting and analyzing information, which is then presented to decision makers that are often commanding officers. It can be seen from Figure 3.3 that the intelligence units influence the strategic decision makers, who decide how to deal with the criminal environment based on the intelligence analysis.

In intelligence work, every bit and piece of information plays an important role. Bits and pieces of information are always present in modern police work. Sometimes the bits and pieces of information can be treated formally, for example, intelligence entries that are documented in a standardized way, but they can also be informal, for example, handwritten notes put on a whiteboard, or even small talk during a coffee break. For police intelligence, the intelligence entries are crucial for a high-quality qualitative work. The intelligence entry can either act as a trigger to start a further intelligence analysis or be used as one of many sources of information in the intelligence analysis process. Very often tip-offs are the basis of intelligence entries. A tip-off in police practice is almost always related to some sort of criminal activity or criminal person. When a tip is received and in some way recorded by the police, the tip is assessed. The assessment follows a system where the trustworthiness of the content and the source of the tip are assessed. The system results in a matrix of 4 × 4. This assessment method varies between police authorities. But a common assessment system is to rank the source of the tip with letters (A–D, where A is the most reliable) and numbers (1–4, where 1 is the most reliable).

Findings

In this section, we present the characteristics of the information management perspective described as soap opera. To structure the characteristics, the soap opera is divided into four different properties, which are all empirically grounded. Scenarios are used to visualize the four properties: repositories, routines, relations, and rituals.

Repositories

Bits and pieces of information are commonly used in the soap opera rationale. The bits and pieces of information are stored and kept in various repositories. In this chapter, a repository is meant to be understood as the place where bits and pieces of information are stored.

The common for the studied police authorities is that every police station has a physical place where they store the tip-offs and memos (*minnesanteckning* in Swedish). The memos are a kind of the bits and pieces of information, and they are often based on the documentation of tip-offs. The police officers take notes of situations worthy of documentation. In the studied police stations, we have found that these bits and piece of information are often found in binders with a register or index of some sort.

Another form of the bits and pieces of information is the intelligence entries. Today, it is common for police officers to write intelligence entries directly to the KUT unit through an intranet online form. Before the form is saved, and implicitly before it is delivered to the KUT unit, the police officers should print the intelligence entry on paper and put it into the binder. Of course, many of the bits and piece of information are not recorded in a system.

Bits and pieces of information can be judged by police officers, which is of common interest, or they can be given the status of high importance and be stored visually. Bulletin boards are such visual repository of bits and pieces of information. Such bits and pieces of information can be about criminals, police projects, changes in the legal system, and other police practice-related information. It can, of course, be the information in text, but pictures are also common. This information is commonly put up either on the bulletin boards or on the walls in the central areas of the police stations.

As stated earlier, the important bits and pieces of information in the proactive police work environment are the intelligence entries. Often you can find intelligence entries stored in separate rooms where information about, for example, a criminal gang or criminal individuals is stored in binders, as printouts attached on the wall, and so on. In this research, at one police station a special room has been arranged for intelligence entries, tip-offs, and similar bits and pieces of information about criminals. In the room, there was a notice board with photographs of criminals and notes on what vehicles the criminals were using and how they were linked to other criminals. The reason for storing this information in a special room was uncertain; the door was open and everyone at the police station had access to the room.

The Swedish police used software* to support analysis of intelligence, which makes it possible to print out large relationship sheets. Such sheets were found in the special room described earlier.

> Karen has just graduated from the police academy and is impressed by her older colleagues' knowledge about criminals. She thinks that almost every colleague knows where the most active criminals live and what vehicle they use. Karen has a "tip book" with a register (a–ö) where she writes down information about criminals, both those she meets during work, and those she gets information about by reading tips. In the "tip book" she also notes tips she receives when talking to criminals. Karen has realized that one of the factors for success in police work is to get information from criminals, who like to tip about other criminals.

In the scenario above, Karen uses a notebook to record bits and pieces of information. Karen's notebook is in her storage, but other police officers might store their bits and pieces of information in their local folder on the intranet.

---

* Analyst's notebook and iBase from the company i2 http://www.i2.co.uk/Default.asp.

Richard began his police carreer in Stockholm at one of the most known police stations, the Norrmalm precinct. At the Norrmalm precinct many of Richard's older colleagues had been investigated by internal affairs several times. This was one of the Norrmalm myths, that the precinct dealt with the most dangerous criminals and therefore the police officers were also reported for misconduct more often than police officers at other precincts. Richard was taught that police officers keep a copy of all their records in their lockers, because if one of them is under investigation it can be difficult to retrieve a copy of the record. Another aspect is to have access to the original record when it is time to produce evidence in court. When Richard first started to keep a copy of his records, he kept the records in paper in a binder in his locker. Today Richard keeps the records in the private folder he has on the police intranet. The records are not only police reports, they are also the forms that are filled as memos, basis for intelligence i.e. intelligence entries.

The repository can, as visualized by the scenarios above, be both digital and analog. Today there are police officers that use digital recorders and personal digital assistants (PDAs)/smartphones to record bits and pieces of information.

Routines

Police work and police practice are filled with routines. The routines can be either regulated or individually created. Each police station and local police authority is autonomous when it comes to, for example, how the intelligence entries and other form of bits and pieces of information should be recorded and how they should be stored. The routines on how to record intelligence entries include how to write, how to classify, and how to store the recorded intelligence entry. The routines can also be at national level. For example, there is a routine on how to distribute certain types of bits and pieces of information. If some intelligence entries are assessed and classified as trustworthy, there are routines describing how to distribute the intelligence entry to other police authorities. Another example describes the national routines on how to handle intelligence entries about serious organized criminality.

However, the routines do not need to be on a local or national basis; each police officer creates his or her own routines, which include his or her way of managing bits and pieces of information. Individual routines can show a huge diversity and every police officer creates his or her own routines.

Stephen often comes to work half an hour before his shift begins. He wants to have time to read through the binder filled with tips and look through the intranet. On the intranet the KUT has a password-protected folder where a collection of tips are presented, some partially analyzed. Stephen uses the extra half an hour to become updated on things that have happened since the last time he was on duty. Information is not a burden is his comment when he receives comments on working for free. The half an hour is often not enough to be fully updated, which is commented as: "The important information is very unstructured, and it's a pity that KUT doesn't make the tips searchable." Stephen is searching the national register of vehicles to print out the cars, which have been stolen since he worked last time.

In the scenario above, Stephen has created his own routines on how to get informed. One important source of this is intelligence entries. Other police officers created their own routines on how to record the tip-offs they receive, that is, when to write them down in the notebook or on the smartphone.

But there are routines not only on how to record and capture various bits and pieces of information, but also on when to delete stored and recorded bits and pieces of information. At national level, there are regulations on how long intelligence entries and similar information can be stored. There are also other types of time limits regarding the storage of bits and pieces of information, which can be both local and individual. Local routines can be that information placed on bulletin boards must be marked with the date when they were placed on the board, and after 14 days they will be removed. An individual/personal routine can be exemplified as police officers taking down their own added information on a bulletin board, or that they, after every third month, start to record bits and pieces of information in a new notebook.

Relations

Police officers often work in pairs in a patrol car. The time between assignments is utilized to talk about personal and police-related issues. This type of small talk also occurs at the police station during, for example, coffee breaks, meetings, and even in the gym. Small talk is an important channel of information distribution. When police officers meet and have small talk, bits and pieces of information are often distributed between them. Small talk in police community has been identified by Ekman (1999) as an important part of forming police work and police practice.

> Today Peter and John have been assigned to work together. John is working extra, and he and Peter normally work on different shift schedules. When they go driving, Peter notices a black BMW, and asks John to follow the car. John gets curious and asks why. Peter then tells him that there is a tip on that specific car that the owner often drives under the influence of alcohol. They continue to follow the black BMW to see if the driver does anything that is reason for the police patrol to pull him over.

Police officers share information and knowledge between them in an ongoing process. The above scenario is an example of how police officers acquire information in their work, from other police officers communicating intelligence entries in the shape of tips. In police practice, this research has identified that it is very common for police officers to share intelligence between each other. The importance of informing other officers is something both researchers have experienced. For example, when the reflective practitioner* arrives at the police station, his colleagues brief him on important things that have happened in the district. This verbal communication is not formal, rather small talk in hallways and around coffee tables.

> Andrew and Karen work together in a surveillance car. They drive in the center of the city. Karen notices one person standing in a corner and comments: "Is he waiting for a delivery?" Karen knows that she has read an intelligence entry about some people receiving narcotics in that neighborhood. Andrew answers: "No, I don't think so, I've heard it's 'Krille' that the tip was about. I was talking to 'Dirty John' yesterday and he said that the rumor among the criminals was that 'Krille' had received half a kilo of amphetamine." Karen asks Andrew if he trusts the information from "Dirty John" or if it was just some disinformation. Andrew is convinced that "Dirty John" was telling the truth because he had never fooled Andrew before. Karen and Andrew position themselves so they can observe people arriving at the corner, in order to observe and document any selling of narcotics.

In the scenario above, the intelligence entry is used as a source of information to carry out an operational analysis aimed to serve as a basis for decision of police action. The scenario also exemplifies that police officers in their relation to criminals obtain information, rumors, and tips about other criminals. Police officers obtain a lot of information from criminals, and some of this information can be disinformation. A police officer can, by having a good relation with criminals, obtain information that would never have reached the police otherwise. Despite this, many police officers display doubts in the intelligence entries that have their origin in tip-offs received from criminals. In this research, we also have found that the use of IT aids the communication process.

> Katrin and John is working night shift and so far there has been very little work to do, so they search for suspicious behavior amongst the people they meet. Far away they observe man dressed in dark clothing standing outside a small café. They cannot see his face from the distance, and Katrin and John do not want to drive up to the man, they temporarily pull over, and stand still for a while. They observe his actions, and after a while a black SAAB 9000 stop and the man enters the backseat of the car. Katrin notices the registration number that starts with HGT. John and Katrin follow the car and both of them get the feeling

---

* One of the authors of this chapter with a police background.

that something strange is going on. John who has many informants picks up his telephone and dials one of them. He asks the informant (a person that is classified as criminal) if he knows anything about a black SAAB 9000. John's informant tells him that the car belongs to Liv Nordberg, who is a Norwegian who sells methamphetamine. John thanks the informant, and Katrin and John follow the black SAAB a few kilometers before pulling over the car. The person in the dark clothes ran away from the SAAB, but is stopped by John. They find that this person carries 10g of Meta amphetamine.

Today, modern IT in the form of mobile phones is able to provide the police officers new ways to communicate with each other, and also to communicate with criminals. Traditionally, there have always been police officers that have had one or several informants that give information about criminal activities to the police officers. Before the use of mobile phones, the meetings were most often planned in detail, but today the communication between informants and police depend on the situation. In the scenarios above, we have presented situations where the police officers have obtained information from another police officer, but the information can also be obtained from informants who call the police officer to ask him/her about certain things.

Rituals

Uniformed police officers that work in larger police authorities start their day with a roll call. The roll call can be a lot like a ritual.

The A-shift starts their work at 15.00 this afternoon and they have gathered in the room for the roll-call. Every time there is a roll-call the majority of the officers sit at the same place. The more experienced and older colleagues have their places in the front and the "rookies" in the back. No one question this order. When the clock strikes 1500, everyone stops talking and turn their heads to the front of the room, where the duty officer sits. "Good afternoon everyone" says the duty officer and the rest of the officers reply: "Good afternoon." First, the duty officer presents the work teams of the day and you hear comments like: "oh yet another day where the strongest officers get to work together." When the practical details have been dealt with, the duty officer starts to read from a list of recently stolen vehicles, which is followed by an aloud reading from all new memos. Some police officers take notes in their own notebooks, but not all.

The above scenario is an example of how the ritual "roll call" can look like. In this research, we have found that very little differs between police authorities and police stations when it comes to roll calls. The roll call is almost always led by a superior officer. The roll call is an occurrence, but before every larger police operation the strategic commander gathers his or her officers for one last brief.

This was the final briefing before the Ministerial meeting in Åre, Sweden. Five hundred police officers have been placed in a hall designed for a maximum 350 officers. The County Police Commissioner started the presentation and welcomed all officers. After that the officer next in command holds his presentation, followed by the police operation commander who described how the police operation should be managed. After that, representatives from the intelligence unit were given time to present their information. They showed several pictures, read names, registration numbers on vehicles, and people that might be important to remember.

This scenario is an example of a traditional briefing during a larger police operation, which often involves a huge amount of bits and pieces of information that are pushed out to the audience. Often the highest ranked police officer starts the briefing and then a ceremony starts where each speaker has a lower rank than the previous one. Of course, other examples of how large police operations are managed can be found, but the police culture requires a certain structure and familiar rituals. During the above-presented roll calls, bits and pieces of information are distributed and communicated to a larger group of police officers.

Discussion

Based on the findings presented earlier, conclusions can be drawn as to what is the difference between the soap opera and the project rationale. In the soap opera rationale, the way to act in various situations is less regulated for the police officers, and sometimes not even recommended in law. The opposite is found in the project rationale where the acting is both legal and often heavily regulated. The project rationale is often about planned action, which results in regulated acting. The difference of time in temporal structure is big between the two rationales. In the project rationale, time is limited and follows an arranged temporal structure. In the soap opera rationale, the time can be seen as infinite. Police officers acting in the project rationale use known and official documents in their work, whereas those in the soap opera rationale use both official (known) documents and unofficial documents. As a real bricoleur, the police officers in the soap opera rationale use all available information resources to solve future situations. The information quality is seen as higher in official documents, which makes the overall interpreted quality of the information used lower in the soap opera rationale than the project rationale. The management of official documents and known information is carried out by information systems designed for that purpose. The unofficial documents are often not managed within a standardized and especially designed information system. They are more often managed in an ad hoc manner. The aim in the project rationale is action towards a certain goal. The soap opera is more about finding and acting in unexpected situations. The stringency is high in the project rationale and the opposite in the soap opera rationale. In a very structured rationale, like the project, the lexical space is controlled and well defined, whereas it is quite the opposite in the soap opera. In the latter, the lexical space is without regulations and undefined. In information systems used in the project rationale, the accepted vocabulary is only used. For example, the terms that are commonly used in police work information systems, and implicitly used in the project rationale, are crime scene, criminal, suspect, victim, and type of crime.

Conclusion

The purpose of this chapter is to present a set of properties that constitute the soap opera rationale and relate it to a more structured project rationale. In this chapter, four properties of the soap opera have been presented: repositories, routines, relations, and rituals, which can be seen as the fundamentals of this kind of information management.

In Table 3.1, where the characteristics of the two rationales were presented, it can be seen that the difference between the two rationales in light of accessibility, quality, and relevance, which we argue are fundamental to the information used in police work practice.

The accessibility of information can be seen to be higher within the soap opera rationale, because the information that is used within this rationale could be seen as existing everywhere. However, it is not a guarantee that the correct and needed information is accessible in this rationale. In the project rationale,

Table 3.1   A Summary of the Characteristics of the Two Rationales

Variable	Project	Soap Opera
Acting	Legal and regulated	Less legal and unregulated
Time	Delimited	Infinite
Information sources	Known Officially documented	Known/unknown
Information quality	High	Low
Type of information	Aggregated	Patterns
Characteristics of the goal	Guide Action	Find Unexpected
Level of stringency	High	Low
Type of supportive IT systems	Information systems	Manual routines Social software
Lexical space	Limited, well defined	Infinite, unlimited

Table 3.2 Accessibility, Quality, and Relevance in the Two Rationales

Information Properties	Project	Soap Opera
Accessibility	Context often dependent upon IT	High, but information not guaranteed to be relevant
Quality	High and controlled	Low and uncontrolled
Relevance	High, controlled, and centrally managed	High, individually managed, and based upon individuals' need

the accessibility depends on the context in which the information needs to be accessed. Currently, police officers depend upon various IT solutions to access information, and they cannot always access the information needed.

The quality of the information within the soap opera rationale is generally low compared to the project rationale. The information available and used in the soap opera rationale is not controlled and verified to the same extent as in the project rationale.

The relevance of information is different between the two rationales. One cannot say that the relevance of information is higher in one of the rationales; it is only different. In the soap opera rationale, the relevance of information is high and also related to the police officers and their need to act professionally. In the project rationale, the relevance of information is still high, but more controlled and official. One can say that in the soap opera rationale the information and its relevance are high and based on individual needs, and in the project rationale the relevance is controlled centrally by the police. This conclusion is summarized in Table 3.2.

The four properties of the soap opera rationale expose the challenges that one might face when trying to design IT supporting the soap opera rationale. The information management within the soap opera rationale is rather transient and situation dependent, even if it is possible to define the four properties of the soap opera rationale. A natural continuation of this research is to further investigate the requirements that soap opera places on information systems and to evaluate to what extent such information systems could increase the quality in proactive police work.

References

Agar, M. H. (1996). *The Professional Stranger and Informal Introduction to Ethnography*. San Diego, CA: Academic Press.

Agrell, W. (1998). *Konsten att gissa rätt: underrättelsevetenskapens grunder*. [The Art of Making Correct Guesses: Basics in Intelligence Science]. Lund: Studentlitteratur.

Archer, J. (1992). The fate of the subject in the narrative without end. In S. Frentz (Ed.), *Staying Tuned: Contemporary Soap Opera Criticism* (pp. 89–95). Bowling Green, OH: State University Popular Press.

Bødker, S. (2000). Scenarios in user-centred design—Setting the stage for reflection and action. *Interacting with Computers, 13*(1), 61–75.

Borglund, E. (2004). Information management in operative police practice: Using SSM as an analysis tool. Paper presented at the 27th Information Systems Research Seminar in Scandinavia, Falkenberg, August 14–17.

Borglund, E. (2005). Operational use of electronic records in police work. *Information Research, 10*(4), paper 236. Available at http://informationr.net/ir/10-4/paper 236.html.

Brahan, J. W., Lam, K. P., Chan, H., and Leung, W. (1998). AICAMS: Artificial intelligence crime analysis and management system. *Knowledge-Based Systems, 11*(5–6), 355–361.

Brown, M. M., and Brudney, J. L. (2003). Learning organizations in the public sector? A study of police agencies employing information and technology to advance knowledge. *Public Administration Review, 63*(1), 30–43.

Carroll, J. M. (2000). Five reasons for scenario-based design. *Interacting with Computers, 13*(1), 43–60.

Chen, H., Schroeder, J., Hauck, R. V., Ridgeway, L., Atabakhsh, H., Gupta, H.,... Clements, A. W. (2002). COPLINK connect: Information and knowledge management for law enforcement. *Decision Support Systems, 34*(3), 271–285.

Chen, H., Zeng, D., Atabakhsh, H., Wyzga, W., and Schroeder, J. (2003). COPLINK managing law enforcement data and knowledge. *Communications of the ACM, 46*(1), 28–34.

Ekman, G. (1999). *Från text till batong: om poliser, busar och svennar.* Stockholm: Ekonomiska forskningsinstitutet vid Handelshögskolan (EFI).

Ferrell, J., and Hamm, M. S. (Eds.). (1998). *Ethnography at the Edge: Crime, Deviance and Field Research.* Boston, MA: Northeastern University Press.

Hammersly, M., and Atkinsson, P. (1995). *Ethnography: Principles in Practice.* London: Routledge.

Lévi-Strauss, C. (1971). *Det vilda tänkandet.* Stockholm: Bonnier.

Nuldén, U., and Borglund, E. (2006). Police officers as users of information technology. Paper presented at the Proceedings of the Fourteenth European Conference on Information Systems, ECIS 2006, Gothenburg, Sweden, June 12–14.

Nuldén, U., and Borglund, E. A. M. (2012). Personas in uniform: Police officers as users of information technology. *Transactions on Human–Computer Interaction, 4*(2), 92–106.

Oatley, G. C., and Ewart, B. W. (2003). Crimes analysis software: "Pins in maps," clustering and Bayes net prediction. *Expert Systems with Applications, 25*(4), 569–588.

Orr, J. E. (1996). *Talking about Machines: An Ethnography of a Modern Job.* Ithaca, NY: Cornell University Press.

Ratcliffe, J. H. (2002). Intelligence-led policing and the problems of turning rhetoric into practice. *Policing and Society, 12*(1), 53–66.

Ratcliffe, J. H. (2003). Intelligence-led policing. *Trends & Issues in Crime and Criminal Justice,* (248), 1–6.

Redmond, M., and Baveja, A. (2002). A data-driven software tool for enabling cooperative information sharing among police departments. *European Journal of Operational Research, 141*(3), 660–678.

Suchman, L. (1995). Making work visible. *Communications of the ACM, 39*(9), 56–64.

Impact of Selection and Distrust in Construction of Professional Police Identity

4

LARS ERIK LAURITZ AND STAFFAN KARP

Contents

Introduction

The professional police identity is fundamental to understand how police officers conduct their work. In decision making and acting, police officers maintain an internal dialogue with the police identity. The decisions taken and how police officers act are dependent on the individual's interpretation of, and answer to, the question: *Who are we, what do others expect from us, and what is our mission?* It is, therefore, of great importance to reveal what constitutes the professional police identity and to deepen the understanding of how it is constructed. In this chapter, we show that improved knowledge about what comprises a professional police identity is crucial for a positive development in policing and better opportunities for police officers to act in secure and ethically defensible ways.

Professional Identities

Loftus (2010) summarizes the decades of ethnographic research on policing and concludes that the cultural mores learned in the socialization process have implications regarding how officers consider the public and how they act during their often life-long police career. Karp and Stenmark (2011) have showed that there is a very strong professional norm, defined by police officers in the field, regarding the knowledge and skills the profession requires and that this norm has an impact on police students from early on in their training. To examine the socialization process in police training, a more solid base for understanding the formation and content of a professional police identity could therefore be given. Professional identities are created when cultural values and norms (Stenmark 2005), as well as construed images, meet the professional regulations that guide the professional mission (Lauritz 2009). The perceived image, what others think of police officers, is a major contributor to self-perception. Dutton and Dukerich (1991) show how reflecting the organization's role, in view of others' perception of it, constructs new views about the social identity of police officers. Manning (2009) talks about policing as constantly revealing the emotions of others because the profession incorporates authoritative measures that are often aimed at restricting the freedom of others. These emotions are evoked in the minds of others, but they are understood by police officers, within a code that indicates the public position of police identity, that is, what police officers believe others think of them. Yim and Schafer (2009) show that such a perceived image is central to the police profession and it has an impact on both enjoyment and pride in their work to such an extent that it affects officers' general job satisfaction. Paes-Machado and De Albuquerque (2006) add a near-relative perspective on the issue when they describe police officers' families and other personal networks as crucial filters in the construction of the professional identity. Despite the perceived image not being regarded as an essential area for research, it has proved to be an important source for identity construction. Police officers, like other professionals, care about and take this into account in defining the definition of "who we are," the perceived image.

Identity construction also clarifies the "we and them" perspective. The culture binds the group together as an entity with a common language (Loseke 2007) and meaning, making the "we" important because it provides not only a secure feeling of belonging (Bruner 2002), but also uniqueness in relation to "them" or "the others." The often-expressed police categorization of others as either criminals or ordinary people contributes to the construction of their own group as something unique and special. It is suggested that the categorization of "we and them" is socialized in everyday training and practice (Van Maanen 1973). The negative notion of relations to others can already be socialized at training centers (Ford 2003). The possibilities for it are regular as it is common for police students to socialize with other police students, which has been emphasized as being one of the most enjoyable things in police training (Davey et al. 2001).

This categorization process, in which the police identity is defined as strictly separate from others via the definition of "we" in contrast to "them," can be seen as an obvious protection aid from the dangers of the profession (Fielding 1988) and the authoritarian aspect that is implied by the right to use force (Skolnick 2002) and enforce the law. In such a view, the categorization keeps the group together so that it can remain alert to the dangers and inappropriate external influences. But there is another side to the coin. The "we and them" attitude leads to the "blue code of silence," which Skolnick (2002) describes as originating from a great sense of, and need for, loyalty and friendship between police officers. The loyalty, especially, is asserted in small groups that can tightly connect individuals, which may, in turn, support corrupt behavior, since such friendships tie police officers to a small group of individuals and its specific values (Mink et al. 2000), with the risk that legal norms become relatively less important than group norms. By emphasizing and training critical thinking among police students, in order to convince new police officers to resist corrupt behavior, the education can contribute in making the police services a force that works for a democratic development of the society (Marenin 2004). The strong professional identity may also contribute to the often-described difficulties in managing the processes of change, for example, a culture promoting masculine, crime-fighting standards can be difficult to change into one promoting crime prevention—a frequently requested change (Davies and Thomas 2003).

That is why the question of where and when, the categorization that "we and them" stems from, is crucial in trying to gain an understanding of a police identity. Some of the studies (Van Maanen 1973; Fielding 1988; Mink et al. 2000; Skolnick 2002) find explanations in socialization and training processes, but also in the general, human need to belong. There are also explanations that stem from research on a certain personality trait found in police officers (Abrahamsen and Strype 2010). Lauritz (2009) grasped the core of the professional police identity among Swedish police students and police officers after only a few months in their new post. A series of three interviews with 10 students was carried out during the education period, and a fourth interview was carried out approximately 9 months after the completion of the education period. The study traced two evidently conflicting, but simultaneously complementary, ways of presenting the construed image. In one image, the police students and police officers see themselves as selected models. They present themselves as being selected via a highly competitive recruitment process, showing that they have qualities that others lack. The selected model has a conflicting presentation in an image of being in a profession distrusted by others, with a lack of confidence in the police in general. In this image, police officers are seen as prejudiced and hostile. In this chapter, we report on and discuss the results of a deeper analysis of the empirical material in Lauritz's study, focusing on the two perceived images—selection and distrust. In the earlier study, an initial structuring of the empirical material was accomplished using elements of coding and categorization from grounded theory (Glaser and Strauss 1971). In this chapter, we reanalyze the interviews to procure empirical evidence for the images and discover more about how the images of selection and distrust contribute to the construction of a professional police identity.

Selection and Distrust: The Pathway to a Strong Professional Identity

The two evidently conflicting, but simultaneously complementary, ways of presenting the construed image is as being, on the one hand, a selected model and, on the other, the distrusted, unwelcome intruder. In the following section, we present the results from the interviews.

Selection

In the first mentioned image, the informants present themselves as being selected via a highly competitive recruitment process, in which they have shown that they have qualities that others lack—qualifications engendering a clear sense of pride. The feeling of being qualified leads to the sense of being someone who others regard as worthy of imitating.

Pride in Their Success

There is very strong competition for admission to the Swedish Police Academy, with approximately 1 in 10 applicants being offered a place. The selection process is uniquely intense, comprising physical tests, knowledge tests, and interviews, in addition to basic requirements regarding education, grades, and earlier work experience. Every student has been successful in the competition. The interviews reveal that this is obviously a source of pride for the individuals, as Ida states:

> It is the feeling of being someone special, after acceptance to the police academy, as it is a long struggle to get here. Many apply, but only a few are accepted. That makes you feel special and selected.

Greta certainly shows how proud she is of being a police officer:

> Sometimes, when doing my sport, and new players come into the hall, they gaze at me as if they are thinking—she is going to be a police officer. Then I feel like, yes, I must behave properly, because she is staring at me and has eyes like saucers—it is as if she is saying: "She is going to be a police officer." Then you have to think about how you should behave. Nowadays, when I am in a pub, I am usually sober, whereas before I would get drunk.

Camilla is another informant who talks about pride when describing her feelings about being one of those selected:

> I will probably be very proud when I have completed my studies. At present I am very proud of having got into the academy.... We've been struggling so hard to get where we are.

Strengths of Police Officers

The feeling of being selected seems to contribute to a feeling of being in a group with superior personal qualities. In talking about other police students, as well as police officers, very positive judgments are common. In the first interview, Kasper already felt that his fellow students were a really competent group:

> Earlier, in most situations, I have judged my own capacity to be greater in most senses, compared to the group that I was in, but not in this group. Now I can lean back and see that the students surrounding me are also here for a special reason and they are the best at what they are doing. So, I really do not feel better in any way than anyone else.... Every police student has successfully passed the selection process. That makes us, kind of, like leaders, models for those who did not succeed, so to speak.... Here,... everyone is willing to dominate situations.

Ida talks about respect for the police in general, but she also extends the respect to her fellow students:

> But, I mean, respect, yes I have it. And I will always have it. I respect the students too, it's like, I look up to them.

In the same vein, Greta contributes a view that describes her future work experience as one that will give them even more knowledge, knowledge that is unattainable for people outside the police profession:

> It is like, when it comes to norms and values. I think you get a broader view of things. I may have seen A, then I know that B is that way, but, as a police officer, I can move further to C. But others stop at B, so I regard myself as being more knowledgeable.

The image of selection provides a sense of belonging to a highly qualified group—a group that has defeated many other applicants in the selection process. From an identity-perspective, the expressed feeling can be useful for understanding that the police identity is an identity well worth defending.

Distrust

As stated earlier, there is another view of police identity that clearly contradicts that of being selected and admired. The contradictory view is that of police officers as being unwelcome, lazy, and regarded as having, from the public's perspective, undesirable characteristics. The mass media are regarded as the main mediators of this image. The general opinion of the media as conveyors of news concerning police subjects is definitely negative. The epithets range from "not always in accordance with the truth" to "an abscess of society." Even more easily than the view of being selected, the sense of distrust provokes obvious defense mechanisms, even from students in their first semester.

Police Officers as Unwelcome

Camilla is one of the students who clearly explained the expected image of not being welcomed by ordinary people:

> I think that many people believe that the police are slack and not active enough. And people get annoyed when cyclists are fined just for riding without lights.

Generalizations, from the behavior of one or two police officers to the whole profession, are believed to be common. Some informants even worry about how to express themselves in social contexts to avoid others' generalizations. Jesper is one of the students who worry about provoking such a reaction:

> In some situations, you might say something that is not very clever, and the whole police force is held responsible for it.

Concerns about not making bad impressions are easily provoked when talking about relations between new police officers and other people. A common response to the sense of being presumably the center of attention for all citizens is that the police need to think about how they should behave and communicate. This feeling is one of several components that lead to the presentation of the police profession as a life mission, rather than a job.

Police Officers as Prejudiced, Lying Fascists

Another negative image is expressed by Kasper, who thinks that others believe that police officers are strongly prejudiced liars. In his opinion, people also regard police officers as corrupt, in the sense of always actively guarding against other officers being investigated for criminal activities, which is also Greta's opinion, expressed in the first interview with her:

> It is so bloody dense. The primary position is that police officers just stick together, covering each other's backs. In the public's mind, police officers always cover up other officer's mistakes and even crimes.

Annika makes a clear connection between what she believes is the public's view and how news is reported by the media:

> The public think that all police officers are fascists, running around, hitting poor demonstrators on their heads with batons, as that is what the media write about. It is always the police officers who are wrong. People who have no experience of their own of encounters with the police have a negative image of lazy police officers.

Annika, like many others, links negative reports from the mass media with the public's negative view of police work. She believes that the general public do not know how people work, but are presented with a picture by the media. This picture, according to the informants, is not correct. As new students at the police academy, the informants do not know much more about the police service than the general public, but they already use the argument that others do not know how good the Swedish police service is. It is one of the most common defense strategies in the interview material, which will be described and discussed below.

Another point of view parallels the one that regards the police as being unwanted and met with hostility by others. This way of looking at the police profession emphasizes an image in which violence is a common ingredient. There are only rare examples in which police students expressly state that police work involves frequent aggressive encounters or even fights, but when they describe situations that they expect to arise in an imagined work experience, elements of aggression and violence are often present.

Contact with the Public in Police Work

The two images—selection and distrust—continue to exist after a few months of work experience, but with regard to the latter, something clearly happens after quite a rudimentary experience. Some of the new police officers express surprise that most of their interactions with other people are very friendly. Jonathan gives one example of a common story in which he talks about people who have been fined, but who still show a significant amount of appreciation to the police:

> When you receive a "thank you" after imposing a fine on someone for urinating etc. … it certainly feels good to hear.

Apart from situations involving highly intoxicated people, there are only rare accounts of circumstances where the new police officers were met with disrespectful behavior from others. Jesper states:

> You might say that the most common response is appreciation. But, of course, it depends on when you work. On a Saturday evening people are too drunk, have mistreated people and quarrelled, and that makes the atmosphere worse. But otherwise, when a "Svensson" [average person] is pulled over for driving too fast or driving without seatbelts, and you have to act in an authoritative way, explaining the issue etc., then it is not unusual, even when issuing a fine, for them to say, "I appreciate your job officer."

Tommy explains the positive interactions by giving a description of good police behavior. He thinks that as long as police officers treat others in a good, respectful manner, they will also be met with respect:

> The funniest thing is realising, even if strange things happen in the profession and you meet annoying people, that most people are very positive towards us. So, when you meet people, and, for that matter, even criminals, you can have reasonably relaxed relations with them. In some ways it is surprisingly simple.

To sum up this section clearly, the informants expect police work to be a job that is characterized by some degree of violence and aggression. They also meet these elements in practice, but to a lesser extent than expected. Jonathan also emphasizes that the most common relations with others are built on mutual respect. However, in his case, it is complemented by a story from his experience, which shows how angry a situation can become when actually confronted with expressions of distrust:

> You usually have a good response to your actions. But, for instance, one Friday evening, when we had been patrolling the streets, it was bloody cold and windy. So, we decided to take the car and drive to McDonalds and rest in the car for a while. Then two men, around 45–50 years old, passed the car, and we heard them say—"It is certainly not surprising that the police are not very popular, they are just sitting in their cars, staring." That was, as I said, after we'd been walking around for one and a half hours before parking the car. I stayed calm, but my colleague was really pissed, so we approached them and it ended with them saying: "OK, but everyone is not like you then." But the first comment was not nice to hear.

Experiences of the Mass Media

Every informant has the opinion that the main objective of mass media in reports about police work is to discredit the police organization, individual police officers, and specific police actions. Here, Jonathan's statement, as a student, represents the main view of the mass media as chasing only negative headlines regarding police operations:

> The mass media only write about things when something has gone wrong. They never, or very, very rarely, write that the police have done something good, but they are quick to publish a story when there are big problems or someone is shot by a police officer. So, four out of five articles feel like they are negative. And that can affect people's opinions, I think.

In practice, the image of the mass media as striving to paint a negative image of police work is the predominant one. Camilla likens the mass media to an "abscess of society." And Kasper defends his negative image of the mass media, by shifting the responsibility for the shortcomings in the society's fight against crime to other authorities:

> In the mass media, we are always blamed for what the prosecutors do, namely, judging the criminals and doing something with all the evidence that we produce. But, instead, they write that police officers are lazy, and, yeah, if people believe that it is bad, because it is not true. They only do it to sell newspapers. So, it can feel unfair when we have arrested a criminal on 50 occasions and the prosecutor drinks his coffee and deletes things that he does not think should be investigated. This can then lead to a reduced investigation.... And a criminal in prison who is not treaded in the right way, and that also, undeservedly, affects the image of the police force.

The views expressed in the interviews range from Kasper's and Camilla's completely negative outlook to Tommy's point of view that the media are not only a negative part of the public debate but also constitute curious and important guardians of democratic values:

> There is quite a lot of media attention that is not very positive. Some is very negative and some is less so. But, above all, you do notice a lot of curiosity on the part of the media and the public. What are they doing? What is happening? Where are they? Everything from the media cannot be interpreted as discrediting, sometimes it is just curiosity.... But sometimes things get blown out of proportion without them being big issues.

Almost every informant at the time of the final interview had had at least some personal experience regarding their contact with the mass media. Regarding opinions about the media, the picture is now very different from the general view. The thoroughly negative portrait has been replaced with a positive one. None of the informants have anything essentially negative to say about their own contact with the media. On the contrary, their experiences have been characterized by mutual appreciation. Greta was pictured in a local magazine as one of the region's new female police officers:

> It is an article that a local newspaper wrote about police officers in sparsely populated areas. A friend and I were approached. It was a good, positive article.

Jesper gives an example where the Swedish police officers were criticized in a scientific journal but were offered a chance to defend themselves in the local news. Despite that opportunity, he also stresses that the best police news is usually negative:

> They gave us a chance to answer the accusations. They said: "This has been said, what is your response?" For me, that was good, but they usually write negative reports about the police profession.

When both relations to individual citizens and the mass media are discussed, there are obvious discrepancies between the expected image that is presented and the experienced counterpart. Regarding relations to citizens, the discrepancy can be described as the expectations containing more confrontation and violence than is later experienced. The relationship with the mass media starts almost with the expectation of war, where the media are depicted as the enemy who search for points with which to attack the police, in order to hurt the organization. This scene survives the entry into work experience, but then the war scene is combined with stories of friendship, mutual understanding, and benefits.

Even though it is incontestable that police work contains some elements of conflict, the results also suggest that the heart of police work is less imbued with conflict and aggression than is expected and imagined. Since the image of the enemy is seemingly exaggerated and even refuted after some experiences, it is easy to interpret the result as an indication that the image of the police profession as an isolated and criticized group is socially constructed.

Defenses

The defenses against criticism from the external world are easily triggered during all stages of the studied period. The most frequent defense is that others do not understand the difficulties faced by the police. This is seen when Greta, in the second interview, talks about a conversation with some friends who started to argue about poor police efforts:

> They started to get cocky about something they had heard, and I just felt like saying give up, you don't understand what you're talking about. They accused the police officers, but, I mean, they didn't understand half of it.

Another point of view is that economic and legal frames are seen as a hindrance to good, everyday police work. This dilemma has been described by Lipsky (1980), who believes that police officers, like social services' bureaucrats, are caught between the political demands for efficiency and the service receivers' demands for justice and compliance. Here, Kasper clearly expresses being put into a position between the decision makers and the public:

> I think most police officers make the best of every situation with the resources that are available to them. I think so, and, I mean, if people think that we do not take action against crimes such as a stolen bicycle or a burglary, then, well I have never met a police officer who did not want to investigate or take measures against a crime. And if this happens, the reason is a lack of opportunities.... It is not the police officer's fault, and not the police force's either, but the responsibility is in the hands of politicians, they are the ones who make the decisions and distribute the money.

Another common defense is that the problems are in the past they were once urgent, but today it is all history. In this context, Hans talks about police officers who lie in court—a phenomenon that was discussed in public at the time of the interview. He and his fellow students have discussed the issue:

> It happened more in the past. It may occur today, but not to the same extent. And we agreed, my fellow students and I, that we would not participate in such actions.

Thus, apart from references to others' lack of understanding of police work and to the political frames being insufficient, there is also a common defense stating that the problems belong to the past. There are some expressions in the interview material, stating that some things were bad in the 1980s and 1990s, but the police have dealt with most of these and this is now all in the past.

Discussion

So far, we have described a context where police students and new officers have a strong will to adhere to a sense of professional identity. In the interview material, this has been described as, at least partly, originating from two apparently contradictory sources—the sense of the group as having been selected after a hard competition, and therefore obviously being in some way ahead of other groups, and the sense of distrust that engenders a feeling that there is an outside enemy which upsets the positive feeling of selection.

The image of police officers as selected models fits quite well into the pattern of a profession which the applicants have dreamt of entering from early childhood (Lauritz 2009). As children they imagined the excitement in turnouts and admired the group of uniformed people given the mission of saving people in need and catching malicious thieves. Being a construct from early childhood, this view of the profession is not only obvious and strong, but also rather static and not easily adjusted (Berger and Luckmann 1967). The importance of the group seems to be a kind of starting point for the sense making that constructs the professional identity. For some of the informants, this is a major part of the reason they applied to join the police—for them, the profession appears to be a matter of teamwork, with a common goal and an expectation of good team sprit (Lauritz 2009).

In short, the image of being a selected model creates a sense of "WE," with capital letters, underlining the impression that police students and new police officers have a sense of belonging to a group, which gives them a great deal of pride and happiness. Because of the perceived value of the professional group, the students and new officers construct a sense of belonging that is well worth defending. In the empirical material, there are expressions that equate the work group with a beloved family. All informants appear to have found a sense of belonging to a group that is so valuable that they just want to remain in the group.

The parallel construction is "them," distanced from the police. This construct includes a perceived animosity from others toward the police. For the students, distrust can be seen as working with the selection to create an "outer enemy" from which the valued identity needs to be defended. But an interesting result is that, in their everyday life as police officers, the image is not manifested to the extent they expected during their education. Some informants are surprised to find a more friendly reaction from the individuals that they meet in practice. Experiences of the mass media are also positive, but the students' initial impressions, whenever the mass media are discussed, are that they only look for negative news, depicting the police organization as inefficient and corrupt, while police officers are criminals and lazy. Thus, the image of distrust seems to resist change to a great extent. At the beginning of their careers, none of the informants changed their critical point of view regarding the mass media, despite the entirely positive nature of their own experiences.

Some obvious defenses against considered aggressors are found in the interview material. The principal defense is that no one, outside the police force, understands the inner nature of the profession. Unless you are a police officer, you cannot understand the essence of the work they do. The mass media are largely responsible for the negative image of the police. The students' defenses are easily triggered, and only rarely do the students admit that any failings may be due to police inefficiency, the methods used, or officers' abilities. When shortcomings are admitted, they are introduced as exceptions; it is obvious that the perception is that only very few police officers are responsible for any mistakes.

The interplay between the sense of the "we," well worth defending, and the sometimes-aggressive sense of "them" seems to build a wall of suspicion against people outside the police profession. The wall of suspicion incorporates a means of defense against any aggressiveness toward the police force. The two concepts allow an interplay within the professional identity that contributes to its strong and clearly expressed nature, which includes strong ties between fellow students and colleagues. These strong ties, as previously mentioned, may be an essential tool in the sometimes dangerous and difficult police profession, but they also entail the risk of creating a kinship of corruption and a distance in relation to others that may contribute to increased aggression between the police and others.

In conclusion, our results provide strong empirical support for the perceived images of selection and distrust, traced in the study of Lauritz (2009), as significant constructors in the formation of a professional police identity. Further, we conclude that the constructors are reciprocal and reinforce each other in the process of constructing a professional identity well worth defending. One interesting question for future research is how the image of distrust develops throughout a career. If the day-to-day experience of encounters with the mass media and meetings with others continue to be mainly positive, does it affect the perceived image, or are the negative expectations so strong that they survive throughout a police officer's entire career? Finally, the practical implication of our conclusion is that the professional police identity must be a focal point during all stages of police training, as well as in everyday police work. The content of the professional police identity and the processes within its construction must be analyzed, reflected on, and discussed not only by researchers, but also by educators, students, and working police officers. How this can be achieved is beyond the scope of this chapter, but as we see it, it is a key question in developing policing for the future that will provide safety and security for all citizens in an ethically defensible way.

References

Abrahamsen, S. and J. Strype (2010). Are they all the same? Norwegian police officers' personality characteristics and tactics of conflict resolution. *Policing and Society: An International Journal of Research and Policy* 20(1): 99–123.

Berger, P. L. and T. Luckmann (1967). *The Social Construction of Reality: A Treatise in the Sociology of Knowledge.* New York, Anchor Books.

Bruner, J. S. (2002). *Making Stories: Law, Literature, Life* (1st ed.). New York: Farrar, Straus, and Giroux.

Davey, J., P. Obst, and M. Sheehan (2001). Demographic and workplace characteristics which add to the prediction of stress and job satisfaction within the police workplace. *Journal of Police and Criminal Psychology* 16(1): 29–39.

Davies, A. and R. Thomas (2003). Talking cop: Discourses of change and policing identities. *Public Administration* 81(4): 681–699.

Dutton, J. E. and J. M. Dukerich (1991). Keeping an eye on the mirror: Image and identity in organizational adaptation. *Academy of Management Journal* 34(3): 517–554.

Fielding, N. (1988). *Joining Forces: Police Training, Socialization, and Occupational Competence.* London, Routledge.

Ford, R. E. (2003). Saying one thing, meaning another: The role of parables in police training. *Police Quarterly* 6(1): 84–110.

Glaser, B. G. and A. L. Strauss (1971). *Status Passage.* Mill Valley, CA, Sociology Press.

Lauritz, L. E. (2009). Spirande polisidentiteter—en studie av polisstudenters och nya polisers professionella identitet. [Growing policeidentities—A study of policestudents and new police officers professional identity.] PhD diss., Umeå University, Umeå.

Lipsky, M. (1980). *Street-Level Bureaucracy: Dilemmas of the Individual in Public Services.* New York, Russell Sage Foundation.

Loftus, B. (2010). Police occupational culture, classic themes, altered times. *Policing and Society: An International Journal of Research and Policy* 20(1): 1–20.

Loseke, D. R. (2007). The study of identity as cultural, institutional, organizational and personal narratives: Theoretical and empirical integrations. *Sociological Quarterly* 48(4): 661–688.

Manning, P. (2009). Policing as self audited practice. *Police Practice and Research: An International Journal* 10(5–6): 451–464.

Marenin, O. (2004). Police training for democracy. *Police Practice and Research: An International Journal* 5(2): 107–123.

Mink, O., A. Dietz, and J. Mink (2000). Changing a police culture of corruption: Implications for the police psychologist. *Journal of Police and Criminal Psychology* 15(2): 21–29.

Paes-Machado, E. and C. L. De Albuquerque (2006). The family curriculum: Socialisation process, family network and the negotiation of police identities. *Australian & New Zealand Journal of Criminology* 39(2): 248–267.

Skolnick, J. (2002). Corruption and the blue code of silence. *Police Practice and Research: An International Journal* 3(1): 7–19.

Stenmark, H. (2005). *Polisens organisationskultur: en explorativ studie.* Umeå, Pedagogiska institutionen, Umeå universitet.

Karp, S. and Stenmark, H. (2011). Learning to be a police officer: Tradition and change in the training and professional lives of police officers. *Police Practice and Research: An International Journal* 12(1): 4–15.

Van Maanen, J. (1973). Observations on the making of policemen. *Human Organization: Journal of the Society for Applied Anthropology* 32: 407.

Yim, Y. and B. D. Schafer (2009). Police and their perceived image: How community influence officers' job satisfaction. *Police Practice and Research: An International Journal* 10(1): 17–29.

Human Rights and the South African Police Service

Are the Red Lights Coming On?

5

CORNELIS ROELOFSE

Contents

Introduction

South Africa is a young developing democracy, and the transition that led to the first democratic election in the country for all inhabitants was hailed as a miracle. The South African Constitution is also acclaimed, and considered as one of the most democratic and progressive constitutions in the world. The South African Police Code of Ethics stipulates that police officers must uphold the law and Constitution, and in fact should also protect the basic rights of citizens and migrants (South African Police 2011). This chapter looks at human rights and what, on the onset, appears to be recent increases in human rights violations by members of the South African Police. Examples of human rights violations by members of the police are frequent media features. Cases where the Right to Life, as enshrined in Chapter 2, Section 12 of the Constitution, has apparently been blatantly violated have been reported. One such report was the case of the death of a demonstrator in the Free State on April 23, 2011. South Africans were stunned by the violent and brutal attack on Andries Tatane, who died as a result of police action during service delivery protests in Ficksburg. A reporter from *Times Live* reported on the death of Mr. Tatane, who died at the hands of police officers in Meqheleng township, Ficksburg.

> The 33-year-old father of two died after being assaulted and shot by police—reportedly when he challenged them to spray him with a water cannon, instead of a group of elderly people. The community were protesting against an inadequate water supply, sewage spillages and the poor state of roads in Meqheleng township. (Mahlangu 2011, 1)

According to the report, the victim was shot at close range with rubber bullets and thereafter attacked and beaten by several officers. Another case of brutality has been reported in a daily paper, *The Star*. Hosken (2011a) reported that a *Pretoria News* photographer was assaulted by the police when he photographed police rescuing a suspected thief.

Another case that made the headlines is that of a photographer of a newspaper, incidentally also from the Free State. This time it was a photographer from the *Volksblad* (People's Paper) who was attacked and taken into custody by the police. He was later released after senior police officers intervened (Hosken 2011a).

Another bizarre case involved the ruthless killing of a woman, Jeanette Odendaal, who was shot in her car by a police sergeant in Kempton Park. The incident, according to an eyewitness, happened when Odendaal parked her car and accidently bumped into a police vehicle. She apparently was on her way to the police station to report a case. The car guard ran into the police station and reported the incident. The police officer came out and shot the woman while she was still in the car (Zwecker 2011).

Abuses such as using deadly force, assaults, torture, and rape are regular features in local media. This chapter attempts to answer a simple premise: whether there has been an increase in human rights abuses by the South African Police members, and whether the change in government leadership since the 2009 election has a possible bearing on this.

Definitions of Abuse

Citizens Against Police Abuse (CAPA), based in Louisville in the United States, defines abuse as follows:

> By police abuse, we mean the inappropriate and illegal use of police powers to coerce, harass, intimidate, arrest, assault and kill members of our community. Police abuse also occurs in the form of racial profiling, illegal roadblocks and illegal searches. (CAPA 2011, 1)

Police abuse is often perpetrated against victims of institutional discrimination, including racial minorities, informal economically active people such as street vendors, foreigners, homeless people, specific sexually oriented persons such as gays, and those who protest against poor service delivery or against political tyranny.

Statement of the Problem

The nature of police work is such that situations often arise where physical contact with protestors, perpetrators of crime, and detainees is unavoidable. Often the greatest provocation comes in the full sight of the media and the public. Police are also human and can therefore be subjected to stress and danger. The fact of the matter is that all too often stress and danger are not present when human rights violations such as assaults, torture, unlawful arrests, and the like are perpetrated. In an attempt to curb institutional and police abuse, conventions, protocols, laws, and codes are developed. Yet, notwithstanding these elaborate statutes, abuse is still going on. South Africa is a signatory to numerous human rights protocols and has a very elaborate Bill of Rights enshrined in the South African Constitution, Act No. 108 of 1996. Despite the constitutional protection of human rights, there have been many complaints about human rights violations in South Africa. Probably, the best summary of such complaints against the police comes from the US State Department's Country Reports on Human Rights Practices released in March 2009:

> The government generally respected the human rights of its citizens. However, the government, nongovernmental organisations (NGOs), and local media reported the following serious human rights problems: police use of excessive force against suspects and detainees, which resulted in deaths and injuries...." (US State Department 2009, 1)

Further reports of human rights violations come from a special rapporteur from the United Nations who made several observations and expressed concerns in a media statement about human rights after a visit to South Africa. The UN Special Rapporteur, after having visited the country for 10 days, said in a media release that allegations of police brutality in South Africa continue. In the media release, the Special Rapporteur lamented the fact that he could not get access to police holding areas for detained immigrants (Office for the High Commissioner of Human Rights 2007, 1).

These observations by the Special Rapporteur may raise issues under Article 9 of the International Covenant on Civil and Political Rights concerning the right to personal liberty. The findings and observations of the Special Rapporteur should sound alarm bells, and institutions such as the Human Rights Commission and Amnesty International (AI) should definitely monitor the situation. Xenophobia and the victimization of even South African citizens remain real threats to human rights in South Africa. The UN is supported by Harris who has the following to say about the South African Police Service (SAPS)'s handling of foreigners:

> Not only do the authorities neglect to pursue individual cases, [at times] they actively interrogate and victimize the victim further. This is done by means of a range of tactics, including verbal abuse, the destruction of valid documents, arresting the complainant, and sometimes, physical violence. Xenophobic attitudes and practices stand as a strong disincentive for foreigners to report crime and violence to the police.

AI added its voice to an increasing local and international awareness of what is happening in South Africa. AI reported incidents where the police abused the rights of street vendors, homeless people, and refugees. AI is of the opinion that this was done to clean up the areas around stadiums to the present South Africa as a clean and beautiful host of the Soccer World Cup. The South African law prohibits forced removals and such actions are clearly in violation of the Constitution (AI 2011, 1).

Even more indictments were brought against the South African Police by a researcher from the Southern African team, who raised the organization's concerns about the police and the leadership's attitude to torture as stated in the AI Report 2011—The State of the World's Human Rights.

> The methods employed by the police include "... severe beatings, electric shocks and suffocation torture while the person was shackled or hooded, and death threats." (Rayner 2011, 1)

The above citations are not only from media sources that may be labeled as biased or from opposition political parties, but also from reputable international organizations such as the United Nations and AI. The examples of human rights abuses and the opinions of international experts indicate that there are reasons for concern about the South African Police's actions. The critical debate here is whether these are isolated cases, or whether there is indeed a developing culture of disregard for human rights by police officers. One has to obviously be circumspect and should not attribute the actions of a small group of perpetrators to the entire police force. This chapter attempts to answer this critical point against the backdrop of political developments in South Africa. The first indicator to provide an answer to this question is to analyze the new approach to policing after 2007. The post-Polokwane leadership of the African National Congress (ANC), the ruling party in South Africa, indeed took a hard stance against crime. This development is scrutinized as part of the analysis of human rights abuses by police officers.

Methodology

The chapter is a desktop longitudinal analysis of official reports such as those of the United Nations, AI, the Human Rights Commission of South Africa, research reports, and media reports on police action. The author has been a public representative in the Limpopo Provincial Parliament, and was the National Strategist for a South African political party. This exposed him to the political arena in South Africa, giving some insights into South African political landscape. These insights were used to approach this delicate new era in South Africa's law enforcement policy changes since 2007. The chapter focuses on the period from 1994 to 2007 and from 2007 till date. As far as possible, comparisons have been drawn, not only of statistics but also of policy changes and their possible effects on police behavior.

New Approach to Policing

The new ANC leadership and ministers under the Zuma administration indeed ushered in a new approach to policing. In order to indicate the shift from police service to police force, it is imperative to discuss the political change that has occurred since 1994. It should be understood that former President Mbeki was of the opinion that South Africa did not have a crime problem. At the time, his deputy, Dr. Zuma, was implicated in the arms scandal that hinted on bribery and corruption. On June 14, 2006, President Mbeki relieved Dr. Zuma of his duties as deputy president. Mbeki told a joint sitting of Parliament that:

> In the interest of the honourable deputy president, the government, our young democratic system and our country, it would be best to release the honourable Jacob Zuma from his responsibilities as deputy president of the republic and member of the Cabinet. (BBC News 2005, 1)

Shortly thereafter, the National Prosecuting Authority announced its decision to charge Zuma with two counts of corruption. This started a protracted leadership struggle for the presidency of the ANC between Mbeki and Zuma and their respective followers. Zuma's followers, mainly from the South African Communist Party, Congress of South African Trade Unions, the ANC Youth League, and Young Communist League), asserted that there was a plot against Zuma to keep him from becoming the president of South Africa. This was spurred on by a number of events:

- Mbeki sacking Zuma as deputy president without the allegations being tested in a court of law
- Mbeki stating that the next president should be a female

Despite all the negative publicity and the protracted legal wrangles, Zuma defeated the incumbent president, Mbeki, at the ANC's Polokwane conference in December 2007. This feat was possible because of the organizational skills of the Zuma supporters. The "political plot" received support from the judiciary when Zuma attempted to have the charges of corruption against him dropped. Judge Nicholson mentioned in his judgment that there was political interference in the saga, although this was later overturned on appeal by the National Prosecuting Authority. Nonetheless, the observation by Nicholson led to Mbeki being recalled from office. He was replaced by "caretaker" President Motlantle. Zuma went on to become president of South Africa; having been elected in April 2009, he suspended Police Commissioner Jackie Selebi, who faced criminal charges on corruption and was found guilty but was granted leave to appeal, still in office. Selebi was succeeded by Bheki Cele, a former ANC Member of the Provincial Executive Committee in KwaZulu-Natal, and soon there was a policy change moving away from the service ideal to a hardened approach to crime. This new approach cannot be articulated more robustly than this quote of a statement made by the Deputy Safety and Security Minister, Susan Shabangu, who said of criminals:

> You must kill the bastards if they threaten you or the community. You must not worry about the regulations—that is my responsibility. Your responsibility is to serve and protect. I want no warning shots. You have one shot and it must be a kill shot.

This statement heralded in a new approach to policing. The consistent high levels of crime and public demand for action have solicited a forceful political response and concomitant policing approach. Wheatly's theory of the "Living Organism" (1995) clearly applies in the sense that the police "organism" developed stress as it struggled to match fighting crime within the constraints of the current statutory restraints. The deputy minister provided the right "medicine" to solve the impasse by stating thus: "You must not worry about the regulations—that is my responsibility." On March 10, 2009, when President Zuma announced his cabinet, he introduced the portfolio of Minister and Deputy Minister of Police, and no longer Safety and Security. The momentum was sustained by the Cabinet portfolio for Safety and Security that made way for the portfolio of Police. This introduced a shift from the service orientation to a police force, and policy changes were soon reflected in practice. One of the most obvious was the change affected to the ranks of the police. The service-orientated ranks of the "Police Service," such as inspectors, superintendents, and commissioners, made way for warrant officers, colonels, and generals. The Minister of Police was quoted by Politicsweb (2010, 1) as having stated:

> Police forces around the world are referred to as the Force and their ranks are accordingly linked to such designations. We have taken a stance as this government of fighting crime and fighting it tough. The rank changes are therefore in line with our transformation of the force, not only in terms of a name-change but change in attitude, thinking and operational duties.

The police are being gradually transformed. This transformation will inevitably inspire individuals with aggressive and hegemonic traits to act these tendencies out in policy and practice. The author is of the opinion that there is a slumbering potential for violent and discriminatory behavior within the police that will increasingly be portrayed as the new ideology takes hold. One should be aware that the change "… in attitude, thinking and operational duties …" will be interpreted in various ways. The premise is foundational in that some officers will interpret the political statements from an inherently aggressive predisposition and will not only "shoot the bastards" but also be robust toward suspects. The police by necessity must react to political direction, which in turn influences the organizational policy and culture. New recruits are especially vulnerable to organizational influences. The recruits are imports from society and already have personality traits that will either be drawn into subcultural deviance such as bribery, brutality, and ill-discipline, or be under the influence of good cops and be socialized to also become good cops. The irony is that the foundational socialization in the home and community will finally determine which way a young recruit will turn. It is appropriate at this stage to analyze police behavior in the pre- and post-2007 era.

Human Rights, 1994–2007

The transition from the old South African Police Force to the SAPS was a very delicate operation. After the 1994 election, the government was occupied with structural changes, such as the creation of nine provincial governments, dismantling the TBVC (Transkei, Bophuthatswana, Venda, and Ciskei—these were independent ethnic states under the apartheid government) state apparatus as well as those of the self-governing territories. This meant, *inter alia*, the amalgamation of 11 police forces, several defence forces, and former liberation movements into the new SAPS, and the South African National Defence Force. Officers from the previous regimes were taken up into the SAPS. One shocking incident former (pre-1994) regime officers of the Dog Unit letting their dogs loose on illegal immigrants shocked South Africa and the world. This incident had been broadcasted all over the world. Newham and Bruce were quoted in the *Sunday Independent* as saying that it is important to note that the Dog Unit incident was preceded by an attempt to extort money from the three men. One of the victims, Gilbert Ntimane, stated that prior to the incident, "The police … asked us for R300 but we didn't have it" (2002, 1). This statement reflects a regular occurrence in which foreign immigrants are systematically targeted for extortion. In some places, this is so common that immigrants refer it to as a "street tax." As the former police force was notorious for human rights violations, one can easily conclude that the former members have brought this culture into the SAPS. This may be the case, but since 1994 the police have applied affirmative action and also expanded its ranks, meaning that there has been almost 80,000 officers added to the force, and many of the former government's officers left the Force. The fact of the matter is that the transformed SAPS is also guilty of human rights violations. This extreme act of violence of the Dog Unit officers is not isolated. Cases of torture are frequently reported to the Independent Complaints Directorate (ICD),* a statutory body invoked by the Police Service Act, Act No. 68 of 1995, to investigate complaints against the police. A number of torture cases have been investigated by the ICD. Torture has been addressed by the international community.

Article 5 of the Universal Declaration of Human Rights and Article 7 of the International Covenant on Civil and Political Rights, both provide that no one may be subjected to torture or to cruel, inhuman, or degrading treatment or punishment. This led to the creation of Section 3 of the Convention against Torture and Other Cruel, Inhuman or Degrading Treatment or Punishment, which states:

> Each State Party shall take effective legislative, administrative, judicial or other measures to prevent acts of torture in any territory under its jurisdiction. (UN Office of the High Commissioner of Human Rights 1987, 1)

A researcher with Southern African team raised the organization's concerns about the police and the leadership's attitudes to torture in relation to the AI Report 2011—The State of the World's Human Rights. These concerns

---

* Now the Independent Police Investigations Directorate (IPID).

are, for instance, methods employed by the police which include "... severe beatings, electric shocks and suffocation torture while the person was shackled or hooded, and death threats." Researchers have also commented on the South African government's position regarding torture and it is obvious that such brutalities do not carry official approval. Pigou (2002, 1) for instance states the intention of the new government in South Africa when he notes:

> With the new political dispensation there has been a clear development of policy towards ensuring that policing in South Africa is conducted in a manner consistent with human rights and democratic values.

The question should thus be raised as to whether statute and policy run together or whether there is a developing schism? Clearly, there are a plethora of statutes and policies, but are they adhered to?

A report from the ICD issued in 2001 refers to 26 cases of torture that have been reported for investigation. The writer of the report (McKenzie 2004) states:

> I have had sight of the SAPS policy on torture and it appears to be a good policy as it is based on the principles of both the Constitution and the Torture Convention. ... In the majority of cases reported to the ICD, the Station Commissioners indicated that they were unaware that torture was being perpetrated in their own backyards ... if the Station Commissioners had been keeping an eye on interrogations of suspects, some of these malpractices could have been avoided.

This reflects a clear dereliction of duty as police standing orders have prescriptions for regular visits to holding areas. Station commissioners (now commanders under the new policy) must ensure that detainees are visited and that they can report abuse.

The ICD has conducted several torture investigations. The common forms of torture have been

- Assaults (where dangerous wounds were inflicted)
- Suffocation (commonly known as the tubing method where a victim is suffocated by a rubber tube or piece of plastic)
- The application of electrical shocks to the victim's body parts (McKenzie 2004, 1)

A case of torture and abuse that has been investigated by the ICD can be cited as an example of acts of abuse by the police being investigated:

> We investigated a case in which the police arrested the complainant on the basis that he could supply them with information about the identity of a suspect. He was allegedly suffocated with a plastic bag and electrical shocks

were also applied to his private parts. The complainant was also dangled from a helicopter in flight and threatened that he will be thrown out. He was subsequently thrown out of a moving vehicle. The complainant spent more than sixty days in hospital and for the rest of his life; he will not be able to manage his own affairs. He launched a civil claim against the Minister for Safety and Security and as a result of the ICD investigation, the matter was settled and he was awarded R2,7 million in damages. (McKenzie 2004, 1)

The ICD, by its own admission, does not have a comprehensive overview of reported allegations of police abuses. It is clear that the scope of torture is not known, but that incidents have occurred. According to Dibiah (2011, 1), Dikeledi Phiri, a national spokesperson for the ICD, said, "We have serious capacity problems and we are battling." We will get back to this point later in the chapter. Let it be mentioned though that the same reporter quotes from the National Treasury that concluded that the ICD only report on cases resolved within 6 months and that there is currently a backlog of 10,000 cases. It is clear that there is a massive problem in dealing with reported cases.

Human rights are entrenched in the Republic of South Africa (RSA) Constitution. Civilian oversight and other mechanisms such as the ICD are constitutional, and statutory provisions to monitor police actions exist as integral components of an elaborate policing monitoring system. The creation of a culture of Human Rights is an inherent desire of the laws of the RSA, but many violations occur, indicating that the core values are not thoroughly entrenched in the characters of some police officers.

Death in Custody or in Police Action (Right to Life—Section 11 of the South African Constitution)

Before venturing into the actual task and findings of the ICD, it is necessary to explain the constraints of the organization. Like with all crimes, there are a number of factors influencing the cases reported and investigated by the ICD:

- Public apathy and a lack of confidence so that many cases are not reported
- Staff shortages
- Inherent incompetence within the ICD itself

This means that what we see reported is not always the full picture of police violations. Shortages of investigators are directly linked to backlogs in dealing with complaints. The Open Society Foundation (OSF)'s Report of the Portfolio Committee on Safety and Security states that the ICD could not reach its target for investigating and finalizing cases due to a backlog from 1997. The national treasury assisted the ICD to develop a case-flow management system in 2006, but the backlogs were not eradicated (OSF 2009). In the same vein, Dibiah (2011) reports that Kwazulu-Natal Violence Monitor have raised concern that the ICD is not in a position to handle all cases due to shortage of staff. One can now look at the work of the ICD.

Gareth Newham and David Bruce (2000, 2) states that, "Police members' propensity towards violence is of particular concern." They also cite ICD statistics, indicating that more than 2500 people have died as a result of police action and in police custody since April 1997. In analyzing the data, they conclude that 70% of those killed are attributable to shootings by the police. They mention that "While a majority of these deaths are lawful within the realms of police work, an unacceptable number are still as the result of unjustifiable actions by police members." It means that from April 1997 until April 2000, an average of about 830 people were killed annually by the police. Obviously not all killings are unjustifiable, but for a constitutional state with a very good Bill of Rights, this is a very high figure. It creates the impression that the police are quick to draw their guns. Police action must also be juxtaposed to deaths in police custody.

Although the government has introduced significant reforms, inappropriate and excessive use of force by police remains a serious human rights issue. In order to evaluate the position, one must differentiate in deaths due to police action, for example, during arrest or crowd control, and deaths in police custody, for example, after arrest while in transport, in a police holding area or in a police cell. The average number of cases from 1997 to 2002 is 689 per annum. From April 2003 to March 2004, the ICD received reports of 383 deaths in police custody, with 20% of these deaths resulting from deaths in police cells. One should bear in mind that deaths in cells can also be as a result of natural causes as well as suicides. While it is encouraging that the reporting mechanism is in place, the high number of reported deaths, particularly in police custody, is worrying. In looking at the statistics on an annual basis, there is a 5% decrease from 2004/2005 to 2005/2006 in the reported number of deaths. From the 621 deaths reported in 2005/2006, 267 were identified as a result of natural causes and suicide, or from injuries sustained prior to detention. During the financial year 2006/2007, the ICD investigated 652 cases of death in police custody. This again reflects a slight increase over the previous year. In an analysis of the political situation in South Africa as far as politically inspired killings are concerned, the Country Reports on Human Rights Practices for 2006 released by the Bureau of Democracy, Human Rights and Labor indicated that there were no such killings by the government or its agents. The Report continues to say, however, that the police often use lethal force during apprehensions resulted in a significant number of deaths, and deaths in police custody were a problem, but that the government investigated and punished some abusers.

The Report furthermore states that the ICD reported "a worrying trend of on-going misuse and abuse of service issue firearms" by off-duty SAPS members "in disputes and circumstances totally unrelated to the business of the SAPS." The ICD's 2006 Report also noted a number of incidents resulting in deaths due to "excessive use of force by members of SAPS in which some of the suspects were unarmed and attempting to flee from arrest."

Human Rights Abuses after 2007 (Right to Life and Bodily Integrity—Sections 11 and 12 of the Constitution)

It has been stated above that the political change brought about by the new leadership that took control of the ANC in 2007 has ushered in a change in policing.

National, regional, and community newspapers in South Africa are reflecting numerous reports of alleged abuses by police officers. One of the most prominent cases is the already mentioned death of Andries Tatane. Shortly after this incident, a police officer shot a woman, who, according to bystanders, had accidently bumped into a police vehicle while parking her car.

At the official level, the ICD reports are also showing a sharp increase of complaints received for investigation. The total number of complaints in all categories for 2006/2007 was 5277 and increased to 6377 for 2009/2010. This represents a 20.85% increase over the previous year. For 2009/2010, a total of 860 deaths were reported, with 566 due to police action and 294 occurred while detainees were in police custody. Where there was a slight decrease (652–621) from 2004/2005 to 2005/2006, a dramatic increase of 38.48% occurred from 2005/2006 to 2009/2010. These statistics do not necessarily support a premise of increased human rights violations by the police, but it portrays a trend of an increasing number of cases being reported to the ICD. These tendencies must be closely monitored and analyzed as there is definitely a post-2007 surge. What can be clearly stated is that brutality reported in the media and complaints reported to the ICD are on the increase. The biggest indictment comes from a senior researcher of the Institute for Security Studies, Johan Burger, who is reported to have called for an inquiry into police action:

> Considering the ongoing and increasing scale of the problem facing the SAPS, it is arguable that a similar type of judicial commission of inquiry into the police is now urgently required. Police management have demonstrated that they are unable or unwilling to address these problems on their own. The time has now arrived for an independent judge to consider the root causes of the problem. (African.blog 2011, 1)

A matter to monitor closely is the increase in crowd action which, particularly the youth, continues to protest against poor service delivery. It can be taken for granted that complaints of deaths and injuries due to police action will increase. Unrest is spreading and the main bone of contention is the lack of service delivery by government as well as the redefining of provincial boundaries, which is also a political decision. The police have no control over these, yet they are confronted with increasing crowd control actions due to government's failure to deliver and the police will be under scrutiny for the manner in which they deal with the unrest.

Torture (Section 12 of Constitution)

It seems that torture is also being perpetrated regularly by members of the police despite the Bill of Rights stating in Section 12(d) that everyone has the right to freedom and security of the person, including not to be tortured in any way. The Parliamentary Portfolio Committee on Police in Parliament called on the nine provincial heads of the ICD to appear before them on February 18, 2011. In a question from the member of the official opposition these officials admitted, "... that every one of them was currently investigating reports of torture by members of the SAPS" (Kohler-Barnard 2011, 1). This is another aspect of human rights violations that must be scrutinized and vigorously monitored. The member of the opposition in a media release after the committee meeting states:

> According to today's testimony, torture appears to have been used in many instances to extract confessions or information out of suspects or, in some cases, the family members of assailants. We also received testimony that there are also systematic attempts to cover up these criminal actions, and that in many cases deaths in police custody are not being reported.

These are very serious violations, which cannot be ignored while arising out of the members of the ICD. The fact that violations are perpetrated, and then attempts are made to cover them up, is a very bad reflection on the police and on their disposition toward human rights.

Conclusion

Brutality reported in the media and complaints reported to the ICD are on the increase. There is a definite increase in the incidents reported in the media, as well as the number of complaints received by the ICD, as well as fatalities due to police action. Some acts such as the killing of Andries Tatane and Mrs. Odendaal seem blatant to the average observer. The cautious deduction is that there seems to be an increase in police brutality since 2007. The critical question will be whether brutality was spurred on by political statements and it would be interesting to follow court procedures of the two cases mentioned above and to hear what the police officers charged with murder will say in their defence.

As far as police brutality in general is concerned, the Human Rights Commission made the following statement:

> The Commission is concerned about what appears to be a trend around the country whereby the human rights of innocent residents are violated by the members of the police when they exercise their constitutionally-guaranteed rights. (Mushwana 2011, 1)

It should be stated that most police services around the globe are occasionally accused of human rights violations. Some are notorious for it such as the Zimbabwean police. It is important as a police performance indicator that the human rights violations in South Africa should be monitored and openly reported. The situations should be closely monitored and tendencies over the next 2 years will produce conclusive evidence. To answer the question in the title of this chapter: "Are the red lights flickering?" The author is of the opinion that we have definitely moved past amber. The concluding remarks substantiate this position.

References

African.blog. (2011) *The Case for a Judicial Commission of Inquiry into the South African Police Service*. Viewed at: http://www.the-african.org/blog/?p=473. Accessed on May 3, 2011.

BBC News. (2005) *South African Leader Sacks Deputy*. Viewed at: http://news.bbc.co.uk/2/hi/africa/4092064.stm. Accessed on May 10, 2011.

Bureau of Democracy, Human Rights and Labour. *Country Reports on Human Rights Practices for 2006*. Viewed at: http://www.state.gov/g/drl/rls/hrrpt/2006/. Accessed on June 24, 2011.

Citizens Against Police Abuse. (2011) *What Is Police Abuse*. Viewed at: http://www.louisvillepeace.org/capa/police_abuse.html. Accessed on May 10, 2011.

Dibiah, D. (2011) SOUTH AFRICA: *Man Killed by Police on Live Television*. Viewed at: http://www.iq4news.com/betty-dibiah/south-africa-man-killed-police-live-televisionion. *IQ4 News*. Accessed on June 24, 2011.

Hawker, D. (2011) Waiting for go-ahead to bury Janet. *Sunday Independent*. Viewed at: http://www.iol.co.za/sundayindependent/waiting-for-go-ahead-to-bury-janet-1.1063706. Accessed on May 3, 2011.

Hosken, G. (2011a) ICD to probe attack on photographer. *The Independent on Saturday*. Viewed at: http://www.tios.co.za/icd-to-probe-photographer-attacks-1.1022345. Accessed on May 3, 2011.

Hosken, G. (2011b) ICD to probe attack on photographer. *The Star*, February 7, 2011. Viewed at: http://www.thestar.co.za/icd-to-probe-photographer-attacks-1.1022345. Accessed on May 3, 2011.

Independent Complaints Directorate. *Annual Report 2004/05*. Pretoria: ICD.

Independent Complaints Directorate. *Annual Report 2005/06*. Pretoria: ICD.

Independent Complaints Directorate. *Annual Report 2006/07*. Pretoria: ICD.

Independent Complaints Directorate. *Annual Report 2009/10*. Pretoria: ICD.

Kohler-Barnard. D. (2011) Democratic Alliance (DA). *Media Release*. Viewed at: http://www.da.org.za/newsroom.htm?action = view-news-item&id = 6407. Accessed on June 7, 2011.

Mahlangu, I. (2011) Hundreds mourn Andries Tatane. *Times Live*. Viewed at: http://www.timeslive.co.za/local/article1036036.ece/Hundreds-mourn-Andries-Tatane. Accessed on May 3, 2011.

McKenzie, K. (2004) Paper delivered at a workshop for the drafting of a plan of action to prevent torture and ill treatment in Africa by the executive director of the Independent Complaints Directorate (ICD), Cape Town, February 12, 2002. Viewed at: http://www.info.gov.za/speeches/2002/020214946a1009.htm. Accessed on June 22, 2011.

Newham, G. and Bruce, D. (2002) *Racism, Brutality and Corruption Are the Key Human Rights Challenges*. Center for Study of Violence and reconciliation. *Sunday Independent*, December 10, 2000. Viewed at: http://www.csvr.org.za/index.php?option = com_content&view = article&id = 2122:racism-brutality-and-corruption-are-the-key-human-rights-challenges&catid = 139:media-articles&Itemid = 37. Accessed on June 23, 2011.

Open Society Foundation (OSF)'s Report. (2009) *Legacy Shadow Report 2004–2009*. Parliamentary Portfolio Committee on Police. Viewed at: http://www.osf.org.za/file_uploads/docs/police.pdf. Accessed on June 24, 2011.

Pigou, P. (2002) *Monitoring Police Violence and Torture in South Africa*. Viewed at: http://www.csvr.org.za/wits/papers/papigou1.htm. Accessed on May 5, 2011.

Powell, A. (2007) Police watchdog grossly understaffed. *IOL News*, January 3, 2007. Viewed at: http://www.iol.co.za/news/south-africa/police-watchdog-grossly-understaffed-1.363700. Accessed on June 23, 2011.

Rayner, M. (2011) *The State of the World's Human Rights*. Viewed at: http://m.timeslive.co.za/?i=3692/0/0&artId=4149956&showonly=. Accessed on June 7, 2011.

United Nations Office of the High Commissioner of Human Rights. (1987) *Convention against Torture and Other Cruel, Inhuman or Degrading Treatment or Punishment*. Viewed at: http://www2.ohchr.org/english/law/cat.htm. Accessed on May 10, 2011.

United Nations Office for the High Commissioner of Human Rights. (2007) *UN Special Rapporteur on Human Rights and Counter Terrorism Issues Preliminary Findings on Visit to South Africa*. Viewed at: http://www.hrweb.org/legal/cat.html. Accessed on May 5, 2011.

US State Department. (2009) *Country Report on Human Rights Practices released in March 2009*. Viewed at: http://www.state.gov/g/drl/rls/hrrpt/2009/af/135977.htm. Accessed on May 10, 2011.

Wheatly, M. (1995) The Heart of Organisation IONS' fourth annual conference, "Open Heart, Open Mind" in San Diego, CA, July 1995. Viewed at http://www.margaretwheatley.com/articles/unplannedorganisation.html 1995. 1–3. Accessed on July 31, 2012.

Zwecker, W. (2011) Cop shoots woman dead over bungled parking. *The Witness*, April 28, 2011. Viewed at: http://www.witness.co.za/index.php?showcontent&global%5B_id%5D=59766. Accessed on June 23, 2011.

Websites

Independent Complaints Directorate. Viewed at: http://www.icd.gov.za/media_statements/26052011.asp. Accessed on June 7, 2011.
South African Police. Viewed at: http://www.saps.gov.za/saps_profile/code_of_ethics/code_of_ethics.htm. Accessed on June 23, 2011.

Statutes

South African Constitution: Act No.108 of 1996.
South African Police Act: Act No. 68 of 1995.

The Evolving Nature of Community Policing

II

Community Policing
The Bahamas Model
Drawing a Thin Line
between Community
Policing and
Traditional Policing

6

PAUL A. ROLLE

Contents

Introduction

Community policing has essentially become the method for most Western democracies (Newburn 2003, 311). Additionally, Newburn (2003, 312) reports that much of the debates about community policing is rhetorical, yet much has to be done to understand these mostly experimental initiatives. The purpose of this chapter is to evaluate the impact of the Urban Renewal Project, a concept of community policing in Nassau, the capital of the Bahamas. After a general review of the policing models, and community policing generally, the author makes an analysis of the urban renewal concept in order to establish whether the approach is keeping within the definition of community policing as defined by Bayley (1988) and other criminologists, who conducted research on the subject of "community policing." In addition, he seeks to undertake an evaluation of the traditional policing models in order to establish if, in fact, there is a difference in outcomes compared to community policing initiatives.

There is a need to better understand how the projects impacted the city of Nassau because no evaluation study was conducted of them since they were implemented. The urban renewal policing model is essentially a new initiative that was introduced by the Royal Bahamas Police Force in 2002 to try and deal with these social issues that were thought to contribute to crime in Nassau (Bell 2005). The Royal Bahamas Police Force launched the Urban Renewal Community Policing Project in 2002. It was launched in conjunction with other partners such as the Ministry of Social Services, Ministry of Works and Housing, the Department of Environmental Health, and the National Insurance Board along with religious organizations, business partners, and members of the community. As the researcher looked at the preliminary results, it was concluded that there is value in furthering this research.

Policing Models

The movement toward community policing signals a major effort at transformational change to redefine how a police agency operates (Eck and Rosenbaum 1994, 14). Additionally, Eck and Rosenbaum (1994, 14) argue that transformational changes are very complex, long-term processes with many challenges and pitfalls. While much has been written about the overall philosophy and general principles of community policing, fewer efforts have been directed to provide leaders with specific information on what they need to focus on to make change happen in their police agency (Eck and Rosenbaum 1994, 15). According to Goldstein (1993), the police leaders who are contemplating the move to community policing need a realistic perspective to the principles of organizational change and a specific navigational tool that provides the elements required to transform a police agency into new ways of operating.

Policing contemporary communities consider policing not only in particular geographic areas, but also in specific groups within these areas (Jerrard 2005). Community policing, problem-oriented policing, and intelligence-led policing, all call on the police to be less reactive and more proactive (Goldstein 1987; Ratcliffe 2004, 25; Trojanowicz, Kappeler, Gaines, and Bucqueroux 1998). These policing strategies are all premised on the assumption that policing can and indeed needs to be improved (Newburn 2003, 311). Conversely, the concept of zero-tolerance policing, which calls on the police to be proactive in their approach to dealing with minor infractions of the law, has been criticized as not effectively reducing crime and solving problems (Burke 1998a, 669).

Definitions of Community Policing

Community policing is a vague concept that is easily claimed but difficult to define (Trojanowicz and Carter 1998, 51). Despite media reports of successes in changes in the police mode of operation, there is a need to answer the question: "What is the thing that is occurring?" Bayley (1988, 228–229) defines community policing as the new philosophy of professional law enforcement encompassing public relations campaigns, shop-front and mini police stations, rescaled patrol beats, liaison with ethnic groups, permission for the rank and file to speak to the press, neighborhood watch, foot patrols, patrol-detective teams, and door-to-door visits by police officers. Bayley (1988) in his definition goes back to fundamentals of community policing when he talks about mini police stations, neighborhood watch, and door-to-door visits, these represent policing in their most basic forms.

In modern democratic societies, the police bear the primary responsibility for ensuring public safety because law enforcement is viewed as the primary solution to crime (Bayley 1994, 143). However, Goldstein (1987, 1990, 21) argues that citizens and the police work together to identify the problems of the area and to collaborate in workable resolution of the problems. The police officers encourage the people in the community to solve their own problems with the help and cooperation of the police resources (Goldstein 1990, 21).

Goldstein's (1987) definition identifies the need for the police to solve problems with the help of the community and fits in well with the concept of problem-oriented policing. Thus, community policing is based on the joint efforts of citizens and police toward solving community problems. Goldstein (1987) does not give specifics as Bayley (1988) does, but sums up the purpose and objectives of community policing. However, Bayley (1994, 143) submits that experts on crime, including the police, understand very well that crime cannot be prevented exclusively through law enforcement.

Trojanowicz et al. (1998, 5) further explain the concept of community partnership as a new philosophy of policing based on the concept that police officers and private citizens working together in creative ways can help to solve contemporary community problems related to crime, fear of crime, social and physical disorder, and neighborhood decay. Trojanowicz et al.'s (1998) definition covers similar grounds as those identified by Bayley (1988) who also defines community policing as a new philosophy.

Finally, Friedman (1992, 4) proffered that community policing is a policy and a strategy aimed at achieving more effective and efficient crime control. These he identified as reduced fear of crime, improved quality of life, improved police services, and police legitimacy through a proactive reliance on community resources that seek to change crime-causing conditions (Friedman 1992, 4). However, Bayley (1988) in his definition opposes Friedman (1992) when he (Bayley 1988, 229) asserts that community policing is more a set of aspirations than programs. Nevertheless, all identified a need for greater public share in decision making (Friedman 1992; Goldstein 1997; Trojanowicz et al. 1998).

Zero-Tolerance Policing

In the 1980s, the expression "zero-tolerance policing" became pronounced as a method of law enforcement for many police forces mainly in the United States and received considerable attention from politicians and the media alike (Innes 1999). However, according to Crowther (1998), others condemned it as a move to oppress the poor and underprivileged in the community.

Zero-tolerance policing is said to have its philosophical origin in the "Broken windows" article published by James Q. Wilson and George L. Kelling (1982). In short, their thesis asserts that just as an unrepaired broken window is a sign that nobody cares and therefore leads to more damage; minor incivilities, such as begging, public drunkenness, vandalism, and graffiti, again if unchecked and uncontrolled, produce an atmosphere in a community in which more serious crime will flourish (Wilson and Kelling 1982). Over time, individuals may feel that they can get away with minor offences, which leads them to commit more serious offences (Wilson and Kelling 1982). According to Wilson and Kelling (1982), it is with the "broken window theory" that urban decay commences and disorder will eventually lead to fear of crime and the decline of neighborhoods in the following manner:

> A piece of property is abandoned, weeds grow up, and a window is smashed. Adults stop scolding rowdy children; the children, emboldened, become more rowdy. Families move out, unattached adults move in. Teenagers gather in front of the corner store. The merchant asks them to move but they refuse. Fights occur and litter accumulates. People start drinking in front of the grocery store and in time, an inebriate slumps to the sidewalk and is allowed to sleep it off. (Wilson and Kelling 1982, 32)

Wilson and Kelling's (1982) description of the broken windows theory is quite graphic and illuminating. It just shows how a neighborhood denigrates to a state where undesirables rule. The problems identified by Wilson and Kelling (1982) are exactly what community policing seeks to address. The philosophy of community policing requires that police departments develop a new relationship with the law-abiding people in the community, allowing them a greater voice in setting local priorities and involving them in efforts to improve the overall quality of life in their neighborhoods (Trojanowicz et al. 1998, 5).

Wilson and Kelling (1982, 32) do not suggest that incivilities and minor crimes in themselves lead directly to acts of violence and other forms of serious crime. They, however, suggest that many residents will invariably think that crime is on the rise and will modify their behavior accordingly (Wilson and Kelling 1982, 32). The principle of the broken windows theory, however, suggests that minor incivilities and low-level crime, if left unchallenged, will grow out of control and will in turn create an atmosphere in which levels of more serious crime will also increase, ultimately to a stage of being out of control (Wilson and Kelling 1982, 33).

William J. Bratton, the former Police Commissioner of the New York City, and Superintendent Ray Mallon of the Cleveland Constabulary in the United Kingdom both adopted the zero-tolerance police model (Dennis and Mallon 1997). Bratton and Mallon argued, for example, that "targeting the petty offenders on the streets can lead to substantial reductions in crime" (Burke 1998b, 667). Bratton (1997, 32) pointed out that homicide in New York declined by 50% during 1994–1996 and overall crime declined by 37%.

Bowling (1999, 531–554) argues that the striking reduction in homicide in New York City between 1991 and 1997 is based on circumstantial evidence of zero-tolerance policing. He points out that homicide rates were at an all-time high in 1990–1991 and had begun to decline before any radical changes in policing were instituted. Bowling (1999) further argues that the falling availability of crack cocaine, which spiked in New York in the mid-1980s, contributed to the decline in homicides. Bowling (1999) in his explanation seemingly sought to downplay the concept of zero-tolerance policing without giving much credit to it, but if there was an evidence to suggest other reasons besides zero tolerance, Bowling was correct to report and to give credit elsewhere.

Problem-Oriented Policing

"Problem-oriented policing" is an approach to policing in which discrete pieces of police business (each consisting of a cluster of similar incidents, whether crime or acts of disorder, that the police are expected to handle) are subject to microscopic examination (Goldstein 2001). Further, problem-oriented policing places a high value on new responses that are preventive in nature, are not dependent on the use of the criminal justice system, and engage other public agencies, the community, and the private sector when their involvement has the potential for significantly contributing to the reduction of the problem (Goldstein 2001). Additionally, Goldstein (2001) asserts that problem-oriented policing carries a commitment to implement the new strategy, rigorously evaluating its effectiveness and, subsequently, reporting the results in ways that will benefit other police agencies and that will ultimately contribute to build a body of knowledge that supports the further professionalization of the police.

The definition of problem-oriented policing as defined by Goldstein (2001) touches the core tenets of community policing (see, e.g., Friedman 1992; Goldstein 1987; Trojanowicz et al. 1998). All of these authors point to the fact that the police have to work in conjunction with the community in order to solve problems and prevent crime. Problem-oriented policing is not confrontational from the definition offered, but instead paves the way for the police to get involved in aspects of policing other than arrests (Goldstein 2001).

Tilley (1998) argues that problem-oriented policing is not limited to dealing with a particular problem, but has wide general applicability. He further argues that there is a consensus that crime and allied problems can only be addressed in partnership. The responsibilities of local authority and police authority for fostering community safety through partnerships create a potentially fertile ground for effective problem-oriented policing (Tilley 1998). As far as Tilley (1998) was concerned, effective crime prevention is synonymous with a stable society; it is a core activity, whose object is the preservation of lawful freedoms, through the creation of safer, less fearful communities.

Community Policing in the Bahamas

Community policing initiatives were decisively introduced in the Royal Bahamas Police Force following the 1984 Commission of Inquiry into drug trafficking in the Bahamas (Royal Bahamas Police 1985). This report, which was published by the Bahamas government, revealed widespread corruption throughout the police force and recommended that the police make significant changes to the way the force operated in order to restore the public's confidence and trust (Royal Commission of Inquiry 1984). Mr Bernard Bonamy was appointed as the new Commissioner of Police and he immediately adopted community-oriented policing as his new style of policing (Bahamas Police 1985).

The Urban Renewal Community Policing Project is a direct response to the past and current problems facing a number of inner-city communities in the Bahamas, such as crime, poor housing conditions, joblessness, illiteracy, homelessness, and human immunodeficiency virus/acquired immunodeficiency syndrome (HIV/AIDS) along with other social ills that contribute to crime and antisocial behavior (Farm Road Report 2002). Its objectives are to examine and improve the quality of life and the social and environmental conditions of high-crime communities; to involve the community in problem solving and empower the citizens to manage their community; to identify and tackle the main causes of social conditions that promote crime and deviant behavior; to prevent crime and reduce fear of crime in the community; and to identify the problems facing at-risk youths and to find alternatives for them (Farm Road Pilot Report 2002).

Methodology

Research Design

This research is qualitative in nature. The qualitative research design provides richer results, which are more explanatory in nature. The method allows the researcher to be closer to the data and helps the researcher to avoid errors in interpretation (Babbie 1990, 64). Additionally, Babbie (1990, 65) asserts that qualitative research helps the practitioners to clarify and explain results to provide richer relevant results, and to be more a part of the research process.

Data

For the analysis of effect of the Urban Renewal Project on crime in Nassau, the author used crime data for the Southern and Central divisions, where the Farm Road, Bain Town, and Grants Town Urban Renewal projects are located. In order to test the validity of the finding, the Northeast Division was used as a control since it did not have a project during this research. The Northeast Division is approximately the same size as the Southern Division (Bahamas Government 2000). The author evaluated the crime data for the years 2000 and 2001, which lie before the establishment of the Urban Renewal projects. The crime data for these 2 years were then compared to the crime reports for the years 2002–2004, in order to establish whether crime rates changed after the establishment of Urban Renewal projects in Nassau.

Some of the data were also gathered for this research through self-administered questionnaire surveys during the summer of 2005. The study population included 225 randomly selected households in each of the communities of Farm Road, Bain Town, and Grants Town. The goal of the survey was to evaluate the residents' perception of the urban renewal policing model and whether they felt safer with the method. Their responses are summarized in the following section.

Findings

The communities of Farm Road, Bain Town, and Grants Town are predominantly working-class and lower income communities in New Providence (Farm Road Pilot Study 2002). These are commonly referred to as "black belt," "grass root," and "over-the-hill" communities. The names of these communities are used as a political demarcation and differ from the names of the policing jurisdictions. These are represented on the police map in appendix (1) as the areas beats (2) 3, 6, 7, and 8. These are the areas locally referred to also as "old Nassau." Also, based on the 2000 census, quite a good percentage of the population of Nassau resides in these areas.

According to the Farm Road Community Project Report (FRCPR 2002), it was apparent that many residents live under substandard conditions. Most of the houses were constructed of wood and have fallen into a state of disrepair. The FRCPR also identified a problem with stray dogs, old burnt out structures, derelict vehicles, and a network of connected track roads that were used by criminals to attack victims (FRCPR 2002, 5). In addition to those already mentioned, the FRCPR report also identified some other critical social problems in the areas. These included, for example, high unemployment, overcrowded homes (in some cases as many as 20 individuals), little or no income for senior citizens, homes needing repair, and many individuals in need of medical care and assistance (FRCPR 2002, 7).

The Bahamas police then led the initiative of renewal in the Farm Road and Grants Town areas. In the first 6 months of the project, the police removed some 326 derelict vehicles from these areas according to the report (Farm Road Pilot Project Report 2002). Ferguson (2005) pointed out that these vehicles were in many instances used by individuals to sleep, hide weapons, and consume illicit drugs. Additionally, the FRCPR (2002) also reported that the police demolished over 200 derelict buildings in these areas.

During the summer of 2005, 225 residents were surveyed in each of the following communities: Farm Road, Bain Town, and Grants Town. The results from each of these communities were pretty much similar. On the question of whether the Urban Renewal was having a positive impact in their area, 125 residents of Farm Road, 100 residents of Bain Town, and 150 residents of Grants Town strongly agreed, whereas 75 residents of Farm Road, 125 residents of Bain Town, and 75 residents of Grants Town agreed. This is not surprising because out of all of these areas, Bain Town was the most depressed (Figure 6.1).

On the question of whether Urban Renewal is a good method to improve community–police relations, 150 residents of Farm Road, 125 residents of Bain Town, and 126 residents of Grant's Town strongly agreed, whereas 75 residents of Farm Road, 100 residents of Bain Town, and 99 residents of Grant's Town agreed. The overwhelming amount of residents in these three communities strongly agreed. This suggests that the model is a viable format and capable of making serious inroads to alleviate some of the problems in communities (Figure 6.2).

The final question asked was whether the residents felt safer with Urban Renewal. The results were pretty much the same as with those of the previous

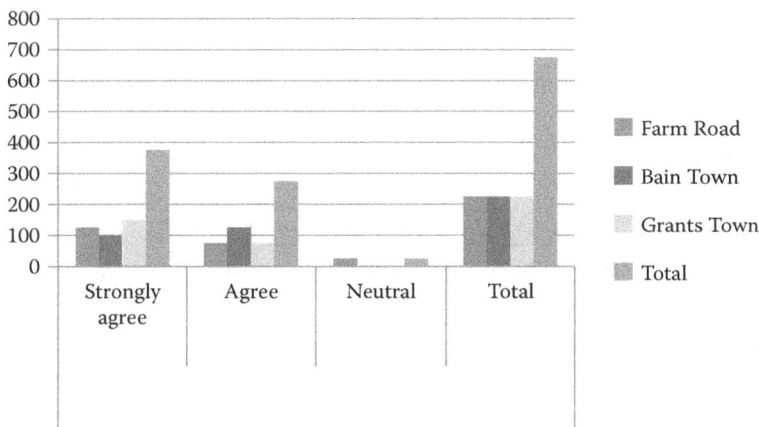

Figure 6.1 Projects having positive impact on crime in my area.

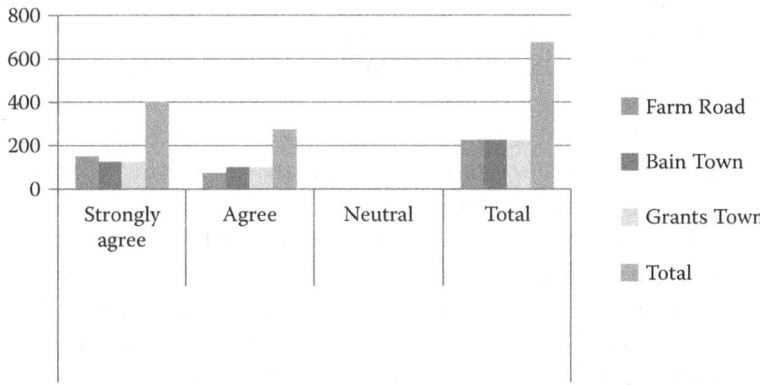

Figure 6.2 Projects are good methods to improve community–police relations.

questions. Four hundred and seventy-two residents strongly agreed that they felt safer. The remaining 203 residents surveyed agreed that they felt safer with Urban Renewal. It is interesting to note that none of the residents expressed discontent with the model. Many of the residents expressed overt gratification that the police attitude in their communities has changed from confrontation (Figure 6.3).

For the purpose of examining the level of crime in the areas, the Bahamas Police Annual Reports on Crime for the years 2000 through 2004 was analyzed with a particular focus on the Southern and Central divisions. Farm Road, Bain Town, and Grants Town fall into these policing divisions. These divisions also include other political divisions such as Englerston, Fort Charlotte, and Mount Moriah constituencies (Bahamas 2000 Census). The Urban Renewal projects do not apply to the latter, but they will form a part

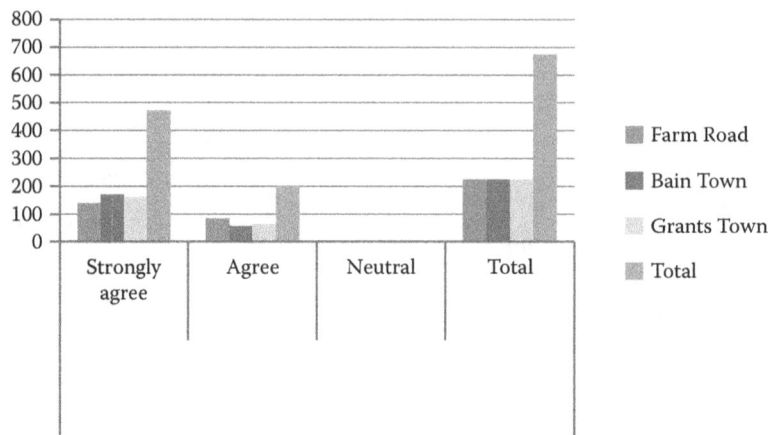

Figure 6.3 I feel safer now with urban renewal policing.

of the collective crime statistics since statistics are not collected based on political constituencies, but on policing divisions.

The crime data for the year 2000 indicate that 3692 serious crimes were recorded in these two policing divisions. Compared to other policing divisions in New Providence, this represents 44% of the total 8322 crimes in this island. In the category of crimes against the persons, 679 (55%) were recorded in the Southern and Central divisions. These divisions also recorded 28 (49%) homicides in New Providence. Also sexual crimes, which include rape and unlawful sexual intercourse, accounted for 64% of the total in New Providence and 49% of armed robberies were recorded in the Central and Southern divisions collectively (Bahamas Police 2000). In the category of crimes against the property for the Southern and Central divisions for the year 2000, a total of 3013 crimes were recorded (Bahamas Police 2000). Figure 6.4 represents 43% of the total crimes against the property for New Providence.

The crime figures for Nassau for the year 2001 reveals that there was a 21% decline in reported matters under 2000 (Bahamas Police 2001). The Southern and Central divisions accounted for 38% of the overall crimes reported; there were 36 homicides recorded in Nassau in 2001; 22 (66%) of them occurred in these divisions (Bahamas Police 2001). Additionally, 111 (43%) of the 258 sexual offences occurred in these divisions. As it relates to armed robberies, 200 (43%) of the 464 occurred in these divisions (Bahamas Police 2001). In the category of crimes against the property, 1389 were recorded in these divisions. This category accounts for 44% of the crimes in Nassau (Bahamas Police 2001).

For the year 2002, for Nassau the crime data for the Central and Southern divisions revealed that in the category of crimes against the persons, a total of 574 cases were recorded (Bahamas Police 2002). This represents 49% of

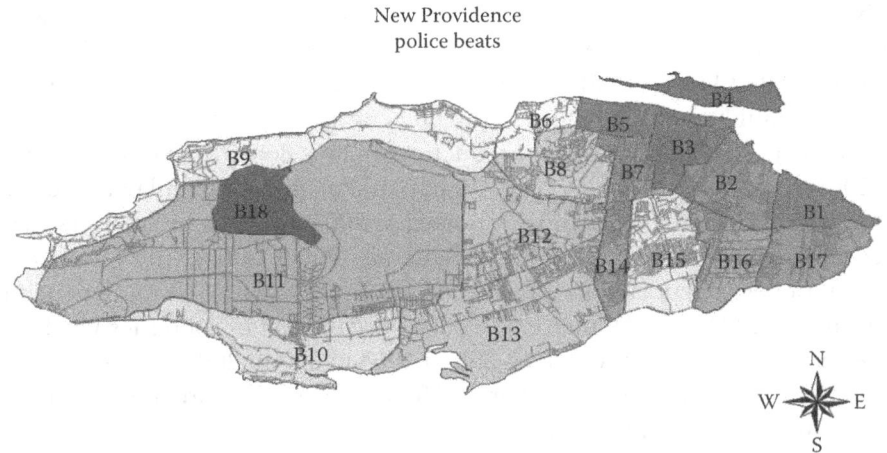

New Providence
police beats

Figure 6.4 Map of New Providence showing policing beats. (Courtesy of Research and Planning Section, Royal Bahamas Police Force, Nassau, the Bahamas.)

all crimes in this category for Nassau. These divisions recorded 10 homicides representing a 46% decline in that category for the previous year. This is a constant positive decline in the year 2000. In the case of sexual offences, these divisions recorded a total of 104, with Central recording 37 sexual offences and South recording 67 (Bahamas Police 2002). This accounts for 49% of all sexual offences for Nassau. The rape figures remained relatively unchanged with an increase of one over the previous year. When the figures for armed robberies were examined, the Southern and Central divisions recorded a total of 335 or 50% of the total for Nassau. The Central Division recorded 131 and the Southern Division recorded 204 (Bahamas Police 2002). An increase of 41% of armed robberies was recorded in these divisions over the previous year. Overall in Nassau for the year 2002, a 34% increase of armed robberies was recorded over the previous year. Robberies were tallied at 100 for these divisions or 57% of the total for Nassau (Bahamas Police 2002).

For the year 2003, the Southern and Central divisions recorded a total of 619 crimes against the person or 53% of the total for Nassau or a further (7%) increase over the previous year (Bahamas Police 2003). There were 17 homicides recorded in these divisions or 53% of the total for Nassau; these divisions recorded a total of 83 sexual offences or 44% of the total for Nassau (Bahamas Police 2003). There were 40 rapes in these divisions or 44% of the total recorded for Nassau (Bahamas Police 2003). This is a decline in the previous year. These divisions recorded a total of 361 armed robberies or 53% of the total for Nassau. Armed robberies increased minimally again in 2003. Robberies also increased to 126 (Bahamas Police 2003).

For 2004, figures are summarized as follows: The figures show an overall decrease of 9% in the reported crimes. An 8% decrease in property crimes in Nassau and a 13% decrease in crimes against the persons decreased were recorded (Bahamas Police 2004). Murder incidents declined 12% in 2003 and accounted for 4% of all crimes against persons (Bahamas Police 2004). Two manslaughters were recorded in 2004 compared to three in 2003, while rape reports yielded a significant reduction of 25%; 86 matters were reported in 2004 compared to 114 in 2003 (Bahamas Police 2004). Unlawful sexual intercourse rose (10%) over those reported in 2003, whereas 166 matters were recorded compared to 183 in 2004 (Bahamas Police 2004). The number of armed robberies reported in 2004 decreased by 14%, with 763 matters being reported in 2003 and 659 matters in 2004; a reduction in robberies yielded a 22% decrease in 2004, down from 258 in 2003 to 200 in 2004; and attempted robberies decreased by (10%), whereas 20 matters were recorded in 2003 and 18 in 2004 (Bahamas Police 2004).

It is necessary to reiterate the fact that the political divides differ from the policing divides. As Farm Road constituency falls in portions of both the Central and Southern divisions and Bain Town and Grants Town fall in other portions of the Southern and Central divisions. It is interesting to note that when the projects were introduced in these particular beat areas, crime was reduced. It would seem then that the concept of the urban renewal community policing model is an effective one in reducing crime. Nonetheless, in some instances, crime increased marginally in other beats where fewer police resources were allocated.

Interviews with Project Coordinators and Divisional Commanders

Ferguson (2005) argues that the project scheme should be force wide and every recruit should be introduced to the community policing concept. Trojanowicz and Carter (1988) also stressed the point that community policing strategies should be force wide. Ferguson (2005) sees a curriculum developed for community policing at the local police academy. He also stresses the need for a definitive policy on community policing in the police force and points out that community policing should not be specialized, but every officer ought to be able to switch at any time and perform those duties (Ferguson 2005). According to Dean (2005), the Farm Road project has enabled him and his officers to recognize that the purpose of policing is to help create safe communities with low levels of crime, fear, and disorder. Dean (2005) argues that the police response ought to be sensitive, caring, and professional. He says that the level of trust of the police has increased in his division. At first, it was a challenge of getting the other government agencies to cooperate with the police, but now it is a thing of the past (Dean 2005).

Dean (2005) highlights some of the successes of the Urban Renewal projects: the relationship among the police, community, civic organizations, and relevant government agencies has improved; crime has reduced; activities were created for young people such as marching bands and youth clubs, which help to decrease incidences of juvenile deviance; the community has developed more confidence in the police and is now reporting crime; and the police have received tremendous amounts of intelligence from residents in the community.

The next unit of interest for interview is the Grants Town Urban Renewal Project. Bowe (2005) stated that problem solving redefines the role of the police to focus on solving problems so the success or failure depends on how well the police are able to solve problems. Bowe (2005) does not believe that the police should solely rely on arrests made, summonses issued, and other quantitative issues. However, the police needs to be more accountable for their performance on behalf of the public, and as such both quantitative and qualitative measures are necessary (Bowe 2005).

However, Bowe (2005) suggests that the divisional commanders need to work closer with the Urban Renewal projects and since the divisional commanders are the advocate enablers and set the tone for the delivery of both law enforcement and social control, they have to appreciate this. Dean (2005) also expressed similar sentiments. Bowe (2005) asserts that projects are the support services in policing divisions and there ought not to be any division between projects and policing divisions. There is a need for more human resources so that officers may work flexible hours in order to increase their productivity (Bowe 2005). Additionally, Bowe (2005) advocates that each of the affected government agencies ought to appoint a liaison person for the Urban Renewal projects. In summary, Bowe (2005) contends that the projects are having a positive impact on the levels of crime. The relationship between the community and the police has also improved since implementation of the projects. She is optimistic about the progresses made so far in the project initiatives (Bowe 2005).

Seymour (2005) agrees that the projects are having a positive impact on crime in the Coconut Grove community. He believes that the projects are an excellent way to improve community relations with the police and that they are having that impact. Seymour (2005) disagrees that he is better able to manage the workload at his division since his officers were transferred to the projects, and is not satisfied with the work of the project team members.

Seymour (2005) further asserts that there was a significant improvement in forming partnerships with members of the community. He argues that members of the other agencies involved should be housed in the project offices so as to improve efficiency of the operation (Seymour 2005). The police force is involved in intelligence-led policing and intelligence from the project office needs to be improved (Seymour 2005). Additionally, Seymour (2005) complains that he gets information, but usually after officers in the projects have already taken action on matters that operational police officers should be dealing with.

Discussions

The objectives of Urban Renewal Community Policing Scheme are to examine and improve the quality of life and the social and environmental conditions of high-crime communities; to involve the community in problem solving and empower the citizens to manage their community; to identify and tackle the main causes of social conditions that promote crime and deviant behavior; to prevent crime and reduce fear of crime in the community; and to identify the problems facing at-risk youths and to find alternatives for them.

In 2002, crime rates in the Southern and Central divisions declined again in Nassau. During the same period, crime in the Northeast division rose to 1878. The year 2003 again saw a further decline in overall crime rates in the Southern and Central divisions where the Urban Renewal projects are located. Interestingly though, the Northeast division now recorded 1979 crimes, which is a further increase of 111 reported crimes. It is interesting to note that crime figures in the Southern and Central divisions also declined in the years 2003 and 2004. Further evaluation of the overall crime figures for Nassau revealed that the reported crimes increased in the Carmichael, West, and Southeast divisions (Bahamas Police 2002, 2003, 2004). None of these divisions had Urban Renewal projects during this review. It would seem then that the concept of the urban renewal community policing projects is an effective tool in reducing crime.

The concept of community policing is not a new one. However, what is necessary is for each community to tailor community policing to suit its own social, economic, and political structures. In the past, policing concepts have tended to isolate officers from the communities they serve, which can hamper crime control efforts. The Bahamas has the laws requisite for the government's agencies to remove derelict vehicles, clear bushy areas, and demolish abandoned dilapidated buildings. This legal authority, couple with the fact that the police have the overwhelming support from the political directorate, would have played a significant role in the police's success in achieving its objectives.

The Urban Renewal Community Policing approach provides a clear picture of what it means to work in partnership with citizens in tackling the root causes of crime and social disorder. The police have learned the importance of working in harmony with the relevant government agencies and the community. A project of such magnitude requires the total support of the government. This support is evident as the prime minister is intricately involved and has committed financial support to the project.

The results of the efforts by the Bahamian police clearly show a continual decline in crime and disorder in the city of Nassau. These results from the Urban Renewal Community Policing initiatives demonstrate the accuracy of the police in targeting those areas in Nassau that contributed to the significant proportion of the crime in that city. Once crime continues to decline, it is likely that residents in the various communities will begin to feel safe in their communities again.

Conclusion

Community policing is not a new concept, but it remains unclear exactly what community policing is and what it means. There is no universally accepted definition for the concept of community policing. Community policing has been described as a vague concept that is easily claimed, but difficult to define. However, a central role of the police is to deal with conflicts, disorders, and problems of coordination, which are necessarily generated by any complex materially advanced social order. The traditional method of policing, though functional in some sense, is more reactionary as opposed to solving problems and preventing crimes as does the community policing model.

Effective policing is preventing, reducing, and detecting crime, and providing safer communities and security for law-abiding citizens and their families. It is at the heart of any civil society. Be it zero tolerance, problem oriented, or community policing, neither can be effective without community involvement. While zero tolerance is closely linked to "the Broken Windows Theory" (Wilson and Kelling 1982), urban renewal community policing has also been grounded in this principle. The difference, however, is that unlike the forces that employed the zero-tolerance strategy such as New York Police Department that ends in labeling and community hatred of the police (Bratton 1997, 32), Urban Renewal has taken on a holistic approach of collaboration and community involvement in addressing the issues of crime and social disorder.

The findings from this research conclude that the strategies that were implemented by the Royal Bahamas Police Force since 2002 have been generating some positive results. The evidence for the first 3 years of the Urban Renewal Community Policing Scheme has seen significant benefits in terms of a total reduction in overall crime in each successive year. This is also coupled with the fact that social decay in these communities has been addressed and young persons have wholesome activities in which they can engage and receive training in the process.

It is necessary for the police in the Bahamas to identify their policing priorities and put the necessary policies and mechanisms in place to deal effectively with them. However, these must be properly disseminated throughout the police force so that every officer is aware of his or her expectations from both the organization and the community. This makes training an essential component in the process.

However, any subsequent success will be in the test as to whether crime continues to decline in Nassau. What is needed at the end of the day is a police service that is efficient and effective, and offers value for money. What is needed in the Bahamas is a police that enjoys wide public support and trust from the community. What is needed is a police service that rewards the skills and experience of its personnel and can recruit the best. Urban renewal community policing can only work if the local communities are empowered to engage in combating and beating crime and only if the citizens are placed at the heart of the renewal. The Royal Bahamas Police Force has done that and this leads to the significant successes achieved to date.

References

Babbie, E. (1990) *Survey Research Methods*. Belmont, CA: Wadsworth Publishing.

Bahamas Government (2000) Census of Population and Income, Department of Statistics, Bahamas Government.

Bahamas Police Act 1965.

Bayley, D. (1988) Community policing: A report from the devil's advocate, in J. R. Green and S. D. Mastrowski (eds.) *Community Policing: Rhetoric or Reality*. New York: Praeger, pp. 228–229.

Bayley, D. and Shearing, C. (1996) The future of policing. *Law & Society Review*, vol. 30, no. 3, pp. 585–606.

Bayley, D. H. (1994) *Police for the Future*. New York: Oxford University Press.

Bell, K. (Supt.) (2005) Personal Interview, April 4, 2005.

Bowe, C. (2005) Personal Interview, April 5, 2005.

Bowling, B. (1999) The rise and fall of New York murder, zero tolerance of crack decline? *British Journal of Criminology*, vol. 39, no. 4, pp. 531–554.

Bratton, W. J. (1997) Crime is down in New York, blame the police, in N. Dennis (ed.) *Zero Tolerance: Policing a Free Society*. London: Institute of Economic Affairs.

Brouder, J. P. (1995; Reprint 1997) *Comparisons in Policing: An International Perspective*. Aldershot: Avebury Ashgate Publishing Limited.

Bryman, A. (2001) *Social Research Methods*. New York: Oxford University Press.

Burke, R. H. (1998a) The socio political context of zero tolerance policing strategies in policing. *Policing: An International Journal of Police Strategies and Management*, vol. 21, no. 4, pp. 666–682.

Burke, R. H. (1998b) *Zero Tolerance Policing*. Leicester: Perpetuity Press.

Commonwealth of the Bahamas, *Report of the 2000 Census of Population and Housing*. Department of Statistics, Bahamas Government.

Community Policing Consortium (2005). http://www.communitypolicing.org/, May 18, 2005.

Crowther, C. (1998) Policing the excluded society, in R. H. Burke (ed.) *Zero Tolerance Policing*. Leicester: Perpetuity Press.

Dean, S. (2005) Personal Interview, March 30, 2005.

Dennis, N. and Mallon, R. (eds.) (1997) *Zero Tolerance: Policing a Free Society*. London: Institute of Economic Affairs.

Eck, J. E. and Rosenbaum, D. P. (1994) The police order: Effectiveness, equity, and efficiency in community policing, in D. P. Rosenbaum (ed.) *The Challenge of Community Policing: Testing the Promises*. Thousand Oakes, CA: Sage Publication.

Farm Road Community Project Report 2002.

Farm Road Pilot Study, 2002.

Ferguson, R. (Asst. Com) (2005) Personal Interview, April 4, 2005.

Friedmann, R. R. (1992) *Community Policing: Comparative Perspectives and Prospects*. New York: Harvester Wheatsheaf.

Goldstein, H. (1987) Towards community oriented policing. *Crime and Delinquency*, vol. 33, pp. 6–30.

Goldstein, H. (1990) *Problem Oriented Policing*. Philadelphia, PA: Temple University Press.

Goldstein, H. (1993) The new policing: Confronting complexity. Paper Presented at the Conference on Community Policing, August, National Institute of Justice, Washington, DC.

Goldstein, H. (2001) What Is Problem Oriented Policing? Centre for Problem Oriented Policing. http://www.popcenter.org/about-whatisPOP.htm

Innes, M. (1999) An iron fist in an iron glove? The zero tolerance debate. *The Howard Journal*, vol. 38, no. 4, pp. 397–410.

Jarred, R. (2005) Review: Hard cop, soft cop: Dilemmas and debates in contemporary policing. *Policing Journal*, vol. 78, no. 1, p. 87.

Leigh, A., Read, T., and Tilley, N. (1998) *Brit POP II Problem-Oriented Policing*. Crime Detection and Prevention Series Paper 93. London: UK Home Office.

Maxfield, M. G. and Babbie, E. (2001) *Research Methods for Criminal Justice and Criminology* (3rd ed.). Belmont, CA: Wadsworth Publishing.

Newburn, T. (2003) *Handbook of Policing*. Devon: Willan Publishing.

Ratcliffe, J. H. (2004) *Strategic Thinking in Criminal Intelligence*. Sydney, NSW: The Federation Press.

Reiner, R. (1985) *The Politics of the Police*. Sussex: Wheatsheaf Books.

Reiner, R. (ed.) (1996) Have the police got a future? in *Policing Public Order: Theoretical and Practical Issues*. Aldershot: Avery Publishing.

Report of the Commission of Inquiry Appointed to inquire into the Illegal Use of the Bahamas for the Transhipment of Dangerous Drugs destined for the United States of America, November 1983–December 1984. Nassau: Bahamas Government, 1984.

Royal Bahamas Police Force. (2002) Farm Road Community Project Report. Nassau: Bahamas Government, 2002.

Royal Bahamas Police Force Annual Report 1985. Nassau: Bahamas Government, 1985.

Royal Bahamas Police Force Annual Report 2000. Nassau: Bahamas Government, 2000.

Royal Bahamas Police Force Annual Report 2001. Nassau: Bahamas Government, 2001.

Royal Bahamas Police Force Annual Report 2002. Nassau: Bahamas Government, 2002.

Royal Bahamas Police Force Annual Report 2003. Nassau: Bahamas Government, 2003.

Royal Bahamas Police Force Annual Report 2004. Nassau: Bahamas Government, 2004.

Seymour, S. (2005) Personal Interview, April 6, 2005.

Trojanowicz, R. and Carter, D. (1998) *The Philosophy and Role of Community Policing*. East Lansing, MI: National Centre for Community Policing, Michigan State University.

Trojanowicz, R., Kappeler, V. E., Gaines, L. K., and Bucqueroux, B. (1998) *Community Policing: A Contemporary Perspective*. Cincinnati, OH: Alderson Publishing Company.

Webster's New World Dictionary (2003).

Wilson, J. Q. and Kelling, G. L. (1982) Broken windows: The police and neighbourhood safety. *The Atlantic Monthly*, vol. 249, no. 3, pp. 29–38.

The Community Involved and Planned Policing Model

7

An Alternative to Traditional Policing in Trinidad and Tobago

WENDELL C. WALLACE

Contents

Introduction

Crime prevention is dialectical in nature, that is, "being pulled in two different ways at once" (Rappaport 1981, 1) by the interests of the police and by those of community residents. However, as Rappaport (1981, 6) submits, "if we are dealing with problems that are dialectical by nature, then they will necessarily yield many divergent rather than one convergent solution...." Therefore, solutions to crime may not be found in the "bowels" of policing but may reside in the communities. This research was conducted as part of a larger national study to analyze the level of community involvement in the policing process in Trinidad and Tobago. Additionally, the study aimed to understand and reduce the nature/level of the dialectic in the policing process in the island. The results were then used to answer the call for increased levels of community involvement in the policing process. This call led to the creation of the Community Involved and Planned Policing (CIPP) model as an alternative construct to the traditional method of policing in the island. The research as well as the CIPP model is elucidated in this chapter.

The lack of community involvement in the policing process is a major factor that contributes to the escalating crime rates in Trinidad and Tobago. However, there are other contributory factors that contribute to the escalating crime rate in the island. Indeed, "there are other factors which cut across the diverse countries of the Caribbean (including Trinidad and Tobago) which heighten the vulnerability to crime and violence" (UNODC 2007, i). The result is that crime and violence as well as the present crime control methods present paramount challenges to the continued development of Trinidad and Tobago as a law-abiding society. As such, local policing strategies must be modernized and adapted to the evolving landscape of criminal activities. This modernization process must be conducted with the coproduction of crime reduction at the forefront of the reformation process and conducted via the involvement of local residents, police officers, and other stakeholders.

History of Community Involvement in Policing

Community involvement in maintaining law and order can be traced back to the communal system of policing in the Middle Ages as Anglo-Saxon codes of law placed certain obligations on the community. For example, the laws of Athelstan directed that a thief who fled "shall be pursued to his death by all men who are willing to carry out the king's wishes" (Riggs 1963, 46; cited in Rawlings 2003, 41). This became known as the "hue and cry." The Statute of Winchester (1285) "purported to reinforce this community based approach to the prevention of crime and the detection of offenders" (Rawlings,

2003, 42). The hue and cry was strengthened to require compensation of a robbery victim should the offender escape (Rawlings 2003). The Statute of Winchester also required all towns to establish a "watch" and householders were required to perform this duty. Watchmen were expected to guard the entrances to the town and patrol the streets maintaining order. However, the communal model of policing depended on the stable communities that existed under the feudal system. As feudalism declined during the fourteenth century and population mobility increased, the communal model of policing became less effective, resulting in a shift in the responsibility for policing from the community to officials (Rawlings 2003). Indeed, even after a system of justices of the peace, constables, and a professionalized watch became established, the responsibility for the detection of offenders, as recently as the nineteenth century, remained largely with the victim or the community.

Community Involvement in Social Problems

While in contemporary societies, community involvement is acknowledged as a significant tool to ameliorate social problems, prior to the 1960s little recognition was given to this (Filion 1999). The challenge to involve citizens in policy processes is a central theme in discussions about modernizing governance and reducing the "democratic deficit." These discussions about involving citizens and reducing the democratic deficit seem to be everywhere. Enthusiasm for the idea that citizens could and should be involved in policy processes is not new or confined to any one area of research. The public participation movement in urban planning that began in the late 1960s marked a watershed in making concerted efforts to open insular, expert-based, rational planning processes to citizens and civil society organizations (Filion 1999; Stroick 1998).

Despite the desire for greater levels of citizen involvement, the policy processes in which citizens are involved are not all the same and, consequently, the forms of involvement used may differ across policy stages. The reasons and mechanisms for involving citizens at the stage of identifying policy problems, for instance, may be quite different from those at the later stages of policy design or implementation. Recognizing that governing at the beginning of the twenty-first century would have presented new challenges for effective citizen involvement in policy processes worldwide, this research aimed to create, in a practical way, a different model of social control using citizen involvement interventions. To a large extent, the recognition of the need for public participation in the policy formulation processes has bypassed the Trinidad and Tobago Police Service (TTPS), and the organization remains largely insulated by public officials from citizen inputs.

This lack of involvement by community residents in policy formulation is neither a new phenomenon nor restricted to Trinidad and Tobago. Indeed, it can be traced back to 1987, when the Development Group for Alternative Policies submitted a report to the United States House of Representatives criticizing the Caribbean Basin Initiative, which was a pre-North American Free Trade Agreement (NAFTA). The criticism was based on six principles that had relevance not only for development but also for reform of the Criminal Justice System, particularly in policing. Of the six principles that were outlined, one principle spoke of a deficiency in the participation of the Caribbean people in defining and implementing the policies. Indeed, there is empirical evidence that high rates of organizational participation by local residents contribute to ownership and reductions in local crime rates (Simcha-Fagan and Schwartz 1986).

Community Involvement in Policing

A casual reading of the multiplicity of literature on community involvement in policing can create confusion and perplexity. This confusion arose as a result of the terminology used being highly diverse. Additionally, investigators who claim to be studying the problem frequently do not look at the same variables or employ the same methodologies, and even when they are investigating the same variables, different investigators may use completely different terms to describe and discuss the variables. As such, it is important to operationalize the term community involvement in policing so that the construct is neither esoteric nor mysterious. Involvement refers to the amount of physical and psychological energy that is devoted to an experience. In certain respects, the concept of involvement closely resembles the Freudian concept of cathexis. Freud believed "people (communities) invest psychological energy in objects and persons outside of themselves" (Astin 1984, 518). In other words, "people can cathect on their friends, families, schoolwork, neighborhood and jobs. Thus, the involvement concept closely resembles what the learning theorists have traditionally referred to as vigilance or time-on-task" (Astin 1984, 518).

In this chapter, community involvement in policing is operationalized as

> a process by which local people are empowered to become genuinely and continuously involved in defining and identifying crime and deviant activities which are of interest to them and in becoming part of the decision making process on those issues, so that they are involved in formulating, planning, developing, implementing and delivering policies and services aimed at taking action to alleviate and change them (Wallace 2012).

To put it simply, community involvement in policing refers to the amount of physical and psychological energies that communities collectively devote to the policing experience. Thus, a highly involved community is one which, for example, devotes considerable energy to ensure that the community is safe and reports criminal activities to the relevant authorities (crime stoppers, police, etc.). Such a community also spends much time working with other residents to reduce crime, seeks to forge relationships with the police, attempts to create a safe and secure environment using creative methods, participates actively in community organizations, and interacts frequently with the police and other residents with the aim of devising plans and policies to alleviate crime and deviance. Conversely, a typical uninvolved community neglects the community, spends little time in dealing with the community, abstains from communal activities, has infrequent contact with the police and other residents, and displays a general apathetic behavior to the community and crime-related issues. Therefore, as Astin (1984, 519) theorized, "involvement implies a behavioral component." Thus, what defines and identifies community involvement is what residents do somewhere along the continuum of policing, either individually or collectively, and not so much their thought processes. As such, community involvement in policing in Trinidad and Tobago should reflect five basic principles, which are as follows:

1. Involvement, as it refers to the investment of physical and psychological energies into various policing initiatives.
2. Involvement is what residents do somewhere along the continuum of policing (the object). That is, different communities will manifest different degrees of involvement in the given object, and the same community may manifest different degrees of involvement in different objects at different times.
3. Involvement can have either quantitative or qualitative features. The extent of a community's involvement in attending meetings aimed at social control, for example, can be measured quantitatively (how many hours residents spend at meeting) and qualitatively (whether the community contributes to the meetings or sits passively).
4. The extent of crime and deviance reduction associated with any policing program is directly proportional to the quality and quantity of community involvement in that program.
5. The effectiveness of any policy is directly related to the capacity of that policy to increase the levels of community involvement.

It is instructive to note that the last two principles are the key policing principles because they provide clues for designing more effective policing programs for residents. However, they are merely principles because they are subject to heuristic proof.

Historical Context of Policing in Trinidad and Tobago

To understand the genesis of policing in Trinidad and Tobago, we have to go further back into mid-seventeenth century to examine what the ideals of colonial policing were at that time and continue the examination of current policing systems in an effort to ascertain whether there have been any changes in the ideology as well as the methodology of policing. Speer (2004, 18) submits that early colonial policing was "prompted by semi-frequent slave revolts and that the first slave patrols and the slave codes that created them were established in 1649." Instructively, early agricultural mass production was different from mass commodity production and the agricultural process of production could not be concentrated in a factory. Therefore, the process required an abundance of cheap labor since modern farming tools were not available. Hence, mass enslavement became the favored tool. However, plantation owners constantly worried about revolts by the enslaved Africans, and it was this constant worry that helped create the slave codes (Speer 2004). By the 1750s, similar codes were enacted in almost every Caribbean colony. However, the spreading influence of democracy has encouraged nations to seek alternatives to traditional policing that leaves residents voiceless, and a broad consensus seems to have arisen concerning the way in which crime should be addressed. According to Lilly et al. (1995, 7), "crime is a complex phenomenon, and it is a demanding, intriguing, challenge to explain its many sides...."

From the inception of state policing in Trinidad and Tobago, the TTPS began using the British Colonial model of policing (or traditional policing) which had been developed in Great Britain and previously utilized in Ireland (Mastrofski and Lum 2008, 481; Mawby 2003, 15–40). Policing in Trinidad and Tobago is still generally conducted via the traditional method of policing. Instructively, an examination of the reformation process from the traditional to a more contemporary approach reveals that the process of change has been very slow in Trinidad and Tobago. Therefore, it appears that the TTPS "has ingested the tranquilizing drug of gradualism" according to Martin Luther King in his speech "I Have a Dream" delivered in Washington, DC, in 1963.

Traditional Policing

The traditional policing model tends to be only responsive to criminal and deviant events (Cordner and Sheehan 1999, 385–394) with little communal input (community involvement) toward proactive prevention of crime and problem solving. It is facilitated by "routine patrols, immediate response to calls, and follow-up investigations" (Cordner and Sheehan 1999, 385–394). The traditional policing method is therefore defined by police officers responding to specific requests from individuals or groups in the community with fast response to calls and follow-up investigations with little else in place to pro-actively deal with the root causes of crime.

Within this traditional policing model, police officers usually remain in police stations when not on patrol. They would respond when a call or an individual comes to report that a crime has occurred. Once the officer has responded to the crime, he would then take a report and deal with the matter or, depending on the nature of the incident, hand the investigation over to a detective. At this point, the officer would go back to his desk duty or patrol car and wait for another call to come in that a crime has occurred. As such, there is no real community involvement in crime reduction and intervention strategies. The traditional policing model usually consists of officers answer-ing calls for service and heavy reliance on deterrence through a visible pres-ence of the police on patrol. Indeed, with the traditional approach to policing, the officer has little interaction with the citizens within a community and can end up responding to crimes at various points in the community. The officer hardly knows anyone in the areas where he is responding nor do the citizens really know the officers.

With the traditional policing model, there is very little besides patrols in place so as to prevent crime from occurring. It is just a supply and demand sort of policing system. This type of policing tends to be only responsive to events, with little input toward the prevention of crime and the proac-tive problem solving. With the traditional policing model, "power emanates from the top with little concern of issues important to the local communities where such policing takes place and control is by the executive" (Miles and Sengupta 2006, 4). However, many social changes have occurred over the decades and traditional policing methods may not be as effective in address-ing the needs of the communities. Communities in the island have become more diverse and the problems have changed as drugs and violent crimes have become more common in urban communities. Additionally, the budget defi-cits of the late 1980s and the early 1990s prompted local legislators to seek out more creative solutions to provide policing services to the country. This led to the implementation of community policing in Trinidad and Tobago from 1996 (Deosaran 2000, 6; 2001, 6) to 2002. However, since 2002, policing in Trinidad and Tobago reverted to the traditional approach to policing. This meant that police officers had little interactions with residents in their com-munities and ended up responding to crimes at different times. Therefore, the officers hardly know anyone in the areas where they are responding nor do the citizens really know the officers. There is very little besides patrols in place to try to prevent crime from occurring and it is just a supply and demand sort of policing system.

Problems with Traditional Policing

As part of the author's doctoral dissertation, an assessment of policing and policing systems in Trinidad and Tobago was conducted between November 2010 and April 2011. Several problems and realities were identified as follows:

1. Local societies believe that the police can prevent crime and deviance by themselves. The reality is that the police cannot prevent crime by themselves. The police and the community are coproducers of crime reduction.
2. Local residents believe that they should not be included in crime prevention and intervention strategies. The reality is that police depend on community for legitimacy and support.
3. Societies by themselves can solve their problems. The reality is that a disorganized or dysfunctional community cannot protect itself; it is "unconscious" about its ability to solve its own problems.
4. There is a feeling of not belonging to a particular community, which is a transient behavioral pattern. The reality is that a safe communal environment is created by providing a sense of community and neighborhood ownership ... a "conscious community."
5. There is a feeling of hopelessness and marginalization among residents of certain communities who believe that they are constantly being used by politicians who are secure behind burglar-proof homes, security cameras, and armed security, and who believe that crime and deviance is not their problem as it does not affect personally. This is a myth. Crime is everyone's business.

Problems with Crime Fighting at Local/National Level

Many current approaches to policing, including those in Western democracies, are focused on crime fighting. The idea is seductively simple, that is, creating a set of criminal laws, then catching and punishing anyone found guilty of breaking these laws. Unfortunately, this approach to policing does not work well. For instance, while the number of crimes recorded by police forces across England and Wales declined by 8% in 2009/2010, the number of crimes that were solved also decreased by 10% (Flatley et al. 2010). It should be noted that in England and Wales only 1.2 million of the 4.3 million crimes recorded were solved (i.e., about 85% of crimes in England and Wales went unpunished) (Flatley et al. 2010).

One global, fundamental crime-fighting concept is that of fast response, and globalization has ensured that members of the TTPS are in concurrence with the concept. Again, the idea is seductively simple. If the police have fast vehicles and are alerted to a crime in progress, then they can race to the spot and apprehend the criminal in the act. Police investments in vehicles, radios, and other technology are high, and police officers like responding in fast cars, which are dashing and important. Unfortunately, statistics show that approximately only 3% of criminals are caught by fast police response in Trinidad and Tobago (Wallace 2012). Further, this figure may only rise to 5% even if police officers could respond at the speed of light. So the major financial investments in manpower and vehicles are made by police and political executives to achieve only minor, even miniscule effects, as their best efforts are ill-conceived and not concentrated on getting the police and the community involved as coproducers of crime reduction. Moreover, the public are now fully educated to the idea of fast response, even though it may be of little use. Most modern police agencies set the so-called response times, in which they guarantee response times and work hard to achieve them. However, the researchers submit that this is a classic example of missing the point, failing to measure outcomes, and concentrating instead on an internal system parameter that is easy to measure.

The traditional mode of policing in Trinidad and Tobago, then, is largely ineffective in catching criminals, despite valiant efforts by dedicated policemen over many years. The reason is simple that they are attempting the impossible. Trying to catch criminals during and after the event, when such crimes are occurring unpredictably over the social landscape, is a monumental task that requires universal knowledge. Police have neither the resources nor the universal knowledge. If, instead, police efforts were focused on peace operations, then much of the crime (not all) would be prevented from happening in the first place. If, instead of operating as crime fighters, police officers operated as peace officers, they could "turn down the flow at source," instead of trying to catch the waterfall (crime) in a teacup.

A Modern Approach to Policing

Modern policing differs from traditional policing in how the community is perceived and in its expanded policing goals of policing residents in a way that is not typical in traditional policing tactics. Police officers are often out in various communities before crimes are committed, for instance, getting to know adolescents and children or, for that matter, the adults in the community before they run into trouble. However, as policing became more centralized and Police station districts were demarcated to make policing more efficient, a shift from neighborhood policing to car patrolling peaked in the 1970s–1990s. It is submitted that an alternative to the traditional model of policing should be created and implemented in Trinidad and Tobago in an attempt to reverse the increasing trend of crime and that this model should be built on a community involvement criterion between the police and the communities they serve.

Theoretical Framework

In order to firmly ground the practical and, in some instances, abstract principles of the CIPP model to a theoretical base, several theories were analyzed. However, the two most succinct and applicable theories are discussed below.

Theory of Community Involvement

There is a strong theoretical case for the involvement of people who are affected by crime into the policing process. Community involvement is a process that provides private individuals with an opportunity to influence public decisions and has long been a component of the democratic decision-making process. Involving the various communities throughout Trinidad and Tobago in the policing process is a means to ensure that citizens have a direct voice in public decisions that affect them. Chen (2002, 1) submits that in some societies, "informal mechanisms of social control appear to play a more important role in controlling and preventing crime...." Therefore, greater levels of community involvement in policing are likely to have benefits for both police–community relations and actual levels of crime and disorder.

Burns and Taylor (2000) support the theory of community involvement in determining police intervention strategies when they posit that there are many arguments for community participation in decision making. In sum, the theory of community involvement can be applied to policing as its underlying focus is community involvement as a tool of solving social problems and crime is indeed a social problem (Burns and Taylor 2000). This fact has quite recently been realized in most countries and their policy makers have been quick to embrace and enforce this paradigm. For example, in 2003, the Home Office in the United Kingdom published a Green Paper on police reform ("Policing: Building Safer Communities Together") which contained a section on "increasing community engagement." Though the Green Paper did not define the term in a policing context, the paper spoke about providing better information to local areas and becoming involved in policing, either at a community level, through a business community, or by volunteering on an individual basis. The theory of community involvement can be used to understand the rationale for involving local residents in ameliorating their own crime problems as "co-producers of crime reduction" alongside police officers. The theory also lends theoretical support for involving local residents in the decision-making process in keeping with the evolution of policing from a professional model, to a reform model, to a community-based model, and, more recently, to a democratic model.

The Empowerment Theory

The roots of the empowerment theory emanated from the educational theory of Paulo Freire (1921–1997) who dedicated his life and teaching to the struggle of aiding oppressed and marginalized communities to achieve liberation (Demmitt and Oldenski 1999). Freire's theory has transformed the way in which policy makers viewed the poor and marginalized, and has been adopted and adapted in several different fields including law and criminal justice. The theory grew out of social reform movements which placed heavy emphasis on the value of clients, communities, and client self-determination. The empowerment theory posits that deterrence, law enforcement, and incarceration, by themselves, cannot resolve the underlying conditions that are the major causes of crime and social disorder. The theory submits that communities must accept and share responsibility with the police for social order, and both must work cooperatively to identify the problems and to develop proactive community-wide solutions. According to Rappaport (1981, 1984), the empowerment theory is a construct that links individual and communal strengths and competencies, natural helping systems, and proactive behaviors to social policy and social change.

This type of social control (crime) requires shared ownership, decision making, and accountability, as well as sustained commitment from both the police and the community. These new roles and relationships between the police and the community demand major shifts for both. The police must acknowledge that they cannot do the job alone, recognize that they have valuable resources available to them in the community, and understand the need to share power and decision making to solve community problems. Community problem solving takes on dimensions beyond the scope of any one individual agency or executive. In turn, communities, neighborhoods, families, individuals, schools, elected officials, local government agencies, organizations, churches, and businesses must become empowered to accept the challenge and responsibility to assume the ownership of their community's safety and well-being. Empowerment occurs when individuals or groups have a sustained commitment, appropriate information and skills, and an influence necessary to affect policies and share accountability for outcomes.

Instructively, empowerment can take place at three levels: the personal (Zimmerman 1995), the community or organizational (Peterson et al. 2002), and the sociopolitical (Moreau 1990). A disempowered person may not fully understand societal injustice and may unknowingly cause harm through his or her activities on behalf of a marginalized community (Sue and Sue 2003). Thus, the empowered person's activities within the community, in turn, will lead to a collective empowerment, where the community advocates for and is involved in social and political change (Carr 2003). While this may be useful as an initial step, the ultimate goal of empowerment is the sociopolitical liberation of marginalized communities having an increased stake in governing their communities (Carr 2003).

The empowerment theory is a particularly attractive and useful tool when analyzing community involvement in policing or when seeking to justify its usefulness because empowerment is an intentional, ongoing process centered in the local communities, involving mutual respect, critical reflection, caring, and group participation, through which voiceless people gain greater access to and control over issues that affect their well-being. Based on the postulations of academics such as Rappaport (1981, 1984) and Peterson et al. (2002), empowerment-oriented interventions are attractive to contemporary societies such as those existing in Trinidad and Tobago because they can be used to enhance community wellness, while aiming to ameliorate problems, provide opportunities for participants to develop knowledge and skills, and engage professionals as collaborators, instead of authoritative experts.

Method

The study explored the views of a sample of individuals recruited throughout Trinidad and Tobago, including the service providers (the police) and their clients (the residents of various communities). Overall, 6400 and 1663 questionnaires were distributed to household residents and police officers, respectively, using a stratified sampling approach. A concurrent survey of police officers and citizens was used in the study, as well as five focus group discussions. The concurrent survey of police officers and citizens within a single jurisdiction measured the view of police officers and residents at the same time using questionnaires that were largely similar. The dissimilarity was based on one question contained in the demographic section of the questionnaire. Police officers (who invariably reside in local communities as residents) were required to answer the questionnaires solely as police officers and not as residents of their communities with the exception of one question concerning their roles in the community as residents. Therefore, the study incorporated the major stakeholders in crime prevention and not only those operating within the criminal justice system or within the sociopolitical/communal system.

Because of the complexity and breadth of the objectives being evaluated and the wide range of the research questions, it was essential to the evaluation that multiple methodologies be used. As elucidated previously, the seldom-used concurrent survey approach was used to measure the views of both police officers and citizens within a single jurisdiction as Liederbach et al. (2008) found that this method is rarely ever utilized by researchers, but that it allows for the direct comparison of police and citizen views. Mail-out questionnaires were used in the study encompassing both open- and closed-ended questions, as well as scaled questions. The research also made use of focus group discussions. Both the quantitative and qualitative approaches were therefore utilized in the study. The processes outlined above did not limit the study, but served to enhance it because of the usage of different methodological approaches. The quantitative approach yielded content as it relates to data, while the qualitative approach yielded different themes or context.

The questionnaires were delivered to the community residents throughout the country by TTPost (the national mail service) and Remote Deliverers Inc. (a private mail distribution service to rural areas not serviced by TTPost). Both the mail distribution services distributed the questionnaires randomly to participants in 64 police station districts (precincts). The questionnaires to police officers were personally delivered to various police station districts, departments, branches, and units by the researcher. The questionnaires were then randomly distributed by a clerk at various police stations. Both the police officer and the resident questionnaires were returned to the researcher by self-addressed return envelopes via TTPost. There were 103 police officer respondents ($n = 103$) and 322 household respondents ($n = 322$).

Five focus group discussions were also conducted in five police station districts as part of the study to assist the researcher to gather qualitative data, which was difficult to otherwise gather and which could not have been elicited from the questionnaires. The focus group participants were recruited nationally by the researcher through the use of Internet and media advertising and by posting flyers advertising the focus group discussions on community notice boards. The five police station divisions used in the conduct of the focus group discussions were randomly chosen and the groups consisted of 8–13 persons of different ages, genders, ethnicities, education, and areas of residence.

Results

The quantitative data were collated and analyzed by the researcher using regression and correlation via the Statistical Package for Social Sciences (SPSS). The method used for the analysis of the qualitative data was the dot thematic mapping technique. The major findings are presented and briefly discussed below.

Focus Groups

The results from the five focus group discussions revealed that the level of community involvement in the policing process in Trinidad and Tobago was insufficient. The contextual themes revealed that there was a general consensus that the public does not feel sufficiently involved and that they have a peripheral role in the policing process throughout Trinidad and Tobago. There was a general consensus among the participants in the focus group discussions that a community involvement component in policing would greatly assist in reducing crime and deviance in the communities in Trinidad and Tobago. Only one individual posited the view that a community involvement component in policing will not reduce crime and deviance because some residents are afraid or unwilling to report crimes as they are benefitting from the proceeds of crime. There was a general consensus by at least 90% of the focus group participants that a locally thought-out, designed, and implemented "crime plan" would serve to reduce crime and deviant behaviors in Trinidad and Tobago. The remaining 10% were skeptical because local residents were still stuck in a colonial mindset and possessed a lack of faith and belief in any plan that is locally created. They were also skeptical about a local plan based on their perception of the extent of corruption, not only by police officers but within other segments of the society.

With regard to responsibility for reducing crime, the focus group responses varied enormously. The participants from the rural and semiurban areas were more likely to mention the role of the community and some were aware that they had worked in partnership with the police to reduce crime and disorder. There was a very strong feeling that parents were responsible for preventing their children from committing crimes and antisocial behavior. There was also a perception among most groups that schools had a role in preventing crime and that education in general should be improved as this might help to reduce crime. Participants from the 18–29 age groups generally believed that police officers had the major responsibility for crime control, while in the other categories there was a variance as to who had the major role in reducing crime. A few people mentioned the importance of community leaders in bringing the community together against crime; however, there were differences of opinion as to the meaning of the term "community leaders." There was a general consensus that the community as a whole was responsible for reducing crime.

Questionnaires

An evaluation of police officers' and residents' views of their level of responsibility for policing local communities revealed that no group (police officers or local residents) viewed themselves as having the sole responsibility or capacity to effectively manage crime. In terms of police officers' views that they (police officers) have their sole responsibility to police the local communities, 89% of the police respondents were not in agreement that it is their sole responsibility to police the communities. Almost 90% of the household respondents were not in agreement with the perception that the community residents acting alone have the responsibility to police their communities.

The evaluation of the possible impact of community involvement in policing on the policing process in Trinidad and Tobago showed that 70% of the police respondents strongly agreed that the introduction of a community involvement component into policing will have a positive impact on the policing process. Interestingly, only 7.2% of the household respondents believed that the introduction of a community involvement component into policing will positively impact policing. The variance in the figures among both groups seems to indicate that though community involvement in the policing process is a much touted concept in the literature, local residents do not agree that the introduction of a community involvement component into local policing will have a positive impact on the policing process and ultimately crime reduction. This may be related to issues of trust and confidence in the police as the study revealed that it (lack of trust and confidence in the local police) was the single largest hindrance (37%) to local residents assisting the police as "coproducers of crime reduction" in the island.

Relative to the level of community involvement in policing, 68% of the respondents (police officers) felt involved and active in the process of policing their communities when acting in their capacity as residents in their communities (police officers have a dual role in their communities as a resident and a police officer), while only 30.2% of the household respondents felt involved. Interestingly, almost 88% of the household respondents shared the view that community involvement in the policing process via a locally designed crime plan would reduce crime. However, only 60% of the police respondents agreed that community involvement in the policing process via a locally designed and implemented crime plan would reduce crime.

Discussion

The CIPP model is an alternative approach for creating and sustaining safer communities and reducing crime and deviance in Trinidad and Tobago. It should be noted that policing structures emerge according to a society's historical development and that while the character of police units all over the world might appear the same on cursory observations a closer examination, however, would reveal differences in organization, owing mainly to the historical and ideological antecedents of each society. The CIPP model is not the sole ownership of the researcher but much of it belongs to the hundreds of residents and police officers who were an integral part of the research. Many of the recommendations were garnered from the survey questionnaires and the incisive commentaries that were made during several focus group discussions throughout the island. These comments were painstakingly collected, collated, dissected, and massaged to create a model of policing, which is consistent with the thoughts of the public, with some inputs from the researcher. As such, the CIPP model reflects the voice of the people.

Importantly, the CIPP model should be viewed as an emerging and evolving local construct that seeks to understand and address the phenomenon of human conflict that manifests itself by the continuously increasing crime rates in Trinidad and Tobago. The principles of the CIPP model as an alternative method of policing are borrowed from the field of human resource management, called conflict management. Conflict management is the art, science, skill, and practice of preventing, controlling, and resolving conflict. Conflict management operates at any level from personal acrimony, through community and society, up to and including national and international conflicts. The principles of conflict management have been forged from hard experiences. In part, these experiences have been gained through the United Nations, the United States, the United Kingdom, and other interventions, some being less successful than others. Further principles and practices of conflict management have also emerged from policing at the local level. In both circumstances, and as is so often the way in human affairs, more has been learned the hard way from "doing it wrong." The CIPP model, like conflict management, builds on this hard-earned understanding.

The features of the CIPP model are as follows:

1. It attempts to create empowered, functional communities.
2. It utilizes security, policing, planning, technology, self-regulatory social controls, and criminology as tools of crime prevention.
3. It can be envisaged as a modern, state-of-the-art technique for reducing crime and involving communities in policing.
4. It uses contemporary crime prevention, analysis, and enforcement as collaborative problem-solving methods.
5. It starts with the creation of neighborhood profiles.
6. It is built on principles of community involvement in the policing process.
7. It is aimed at removing "voicelessness and hopelessness" from local communities.
8. It utilizes civilian infrastructure of the policing process along with traditional infrastructure mechanisms.

The CIPP model consists of the following six key tenets:

1. Community involved and community-based crime prevention and intervention strategies
2. Deployment of police for nonemergency interaction with members of the public
3. Active solicitation of requests for service not involving criminal matters

4. Creation of mechanisms for the grassroots feedback from the community
5. Civilian involvement/oversight of policing
6. Continuous partnerships between key stakeholders such as communities, NGOs, schools, and police officers

The CIPP model seeks to address the following issues:

1. *Developmental issues.* Crime and violence are developmental issues. The high rates of crime and violence in the island have both direct and indirect effects on human welfare in the short-run and longer run effects on economic growth and social development.
2. *Imbalance in resources.* The strongest explanations for the relatively high rates of crime and violence in Trinidad and Tobago and their continuous rise in recent years are drug trafficking and lack of involvement by residents in the policing process. The drug trade drives crime in a number of ways, for example, through violence tied to trafficking, by normalizing illegal behaviors, by diverting criminal justice resources from other activities, by provoking property crime related to addiction, by contributing to the widespread availability of firearms, and by undermining and corrupting societal institutions. However, it should be recognized that there is a trade-off between resources spent on combating drug trafficking and those spent on other forms of crime and violence prevention.
3. *An Overreliance on the criminal justice system.* Generally, there has been an overreliance on the criminal justice approach to crime reduction in Trinidad and Tobago to the detriment of other complementary approaches such as community involvement in policing which can be effective in reducing certain types of crime and violence. The public health approach, which focuses on modifying risk factors for violent conduct, is especially promising for addressing violence against women and youths in the island.
4. *Youth violence.* To address the issues of youth violence (usually a precursor to adult violence), local policy makers in the short run should borrow from the toolkit of evidence-based programs from other regions, such as early childhood development and mentoring programs, interventions to increase retention of high-risk youth in secondary schools, and opening schools after-hours and on weekends to offer attractive activities for youth to occupy their free time. While there are a multitude of programs in the island that address youth violence [Military-Led Academic Training (MILAT), Military-Led Youth Programme of Apprenticeship and Reorientation Training (MYPART), and Civilian Conservation Corp], few, if any, have been

subject to rigorous impact evaluation. In the medium and long run, impact evaluations should systematically document what works in youth violence prevention in the island.

The CIPP model will facilitate the creation of a Youth Involvement Unit (YIU) as part of the Community Involvement Unit (CIU) and will allow for the structured organization of youth activities such as police youth clubs, Police Athletic Leagues, drug awareness for youths, and youth-at-risk programs. The YIU will also have as a part of its structure a Juvenile Bureau to deal with youth delinquency. The aim of the YIU will be to foster positive, proactive relations with an often-ignored section of the community—the youths.

5. *Systematic reintegration of deportees.* Evidence from the local media shows that the average deportee is not involved in criminal activity, but a minority may be causing serious problems, both by direct involvement in crime and by providing a perverse role model for youth. More services should be offered to reintegrate deportees, along the lines of those provided by the Office for the Resettlement of Deportees in St. Kitts and Nevis. Options should be explored for deporting countries to shoulder a significant portion of the costs of these programs, in exchange for serious monitoring and evaluation of program impacts.

6. *Creative/alternative/novel approaches to crime prevention.* These different approaches mean that there are multiple possible entry points to engage in violence and crime prevention. In one instance, the most promising approach may be in the context of a squatter settlement/ghetto-upgrading project; in another instance, it may be in the context of a reform of the health service; in the other, it may be in the context of a reform of the criminal justice system. There is no one "ideal" approach. The common denominator is that successful interventions are evidence based, starting with a clear diagnostic about types of violence and risk factors, and ending with a careful evaluation of the intervention's impact that will inform future actions.

7. *Lack of communal involvement in the policing process.* Presently, policing in Trinidad and Tobago exudes a high level of noninvolvement and perceptions of voiceless among community residents in the policing process. The CIPP model aims to remove this "voicelessness" that pervades local policing and replace it with a system where local residents are no longer simply involved as the "eyes and ears" of the police, but are involved somewhere along the continuum of policing. This would be done via the creation of Community Enhancement Organizations (CEOs) in every police station district in Trinidad and Tobago to facilitate residents who feel safer in communicating their security concerns to nonpolice personnel; CEOs will be staffed by civilians.

Implementation of the CIPP Model

The CIPP model was created out of the desire of the researcher to facilitate an alternative approach to policing in Trinidad and Tobago which reflects a contemporary design based on the communal involvement of residents in the policing process. The model aims to remove the colonial legacy of voiceless citizens in policing. Three major issues were highlighted by the participants in the study and the operational and organizational requirement of the CIPP model answers the call for community involvement in policing. The major issues were identified as follows:

1. A lack of trust and confidence in the police, which leads to "the so-called dark figure of crime or those crimes not reported to the Police" (Fox 1996, 3)
2. A lack of community involvement by residents in policing their communities
3. A perception that the methods, equipment, and infrastructure used by the police are antiquated and outdated

A key component of the CIPP model would be the creation of CEO offices in every police station district throughout Trinidad and Tobago. These CEOs will be the civilian arm of the TTPS. The CEO offices will act as a network of service centers throughout each police station district and would coordinate and customize neighborhood services (police and social services) to satisfy the needs of the many diverse communities in the island. Each office will be staffed by nonpolice personnel within each community, namely:

- Community Crime Prevention Specialists (CPS)
- Community Resource Officer (CRO)
- CEO Administrators

The CEOs would act as a direct link between the communities and the police in a proactive manner. This is due to the nonreporting of crime to the police (dark figure of crime) as some community residents feel safer to communicate their safety and security concerns to nonpolice personnel. The CEO model is outlined in Figure 7.1. The aim of the CEOs would be to improve the quality of life for local residents and this will be facilitated via developing community partnerships that would bridge the gap between the communities and the police concerns. The CEOs would provide service related to the provision of safety and security of the communities by constantly liaising with the CIUs (staffed by police officers) in the respective police station divisions as well as with other NGOs. However, this would not be their only function as they would also provide information and services aimed at enhancing and revitalizing local communities in the following ways:

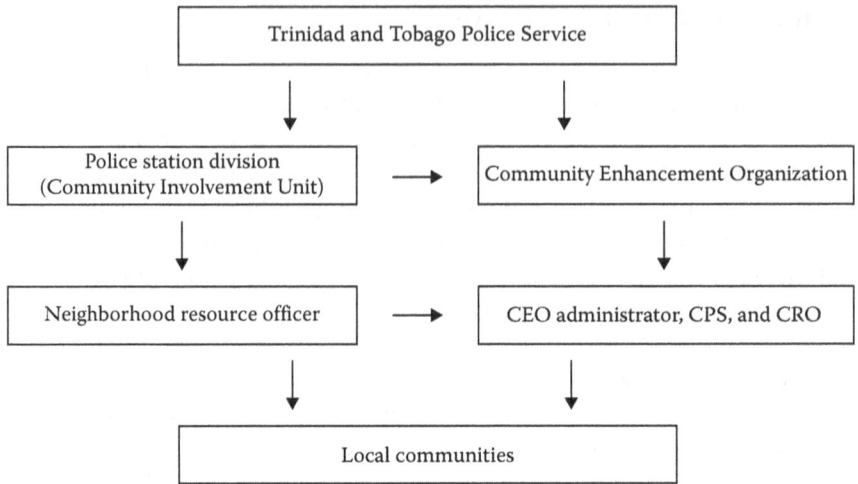

Figure 7.1 The community enhancement organization model.

1. Assisting in planning special events in the communities
2. Communicating between the regional corporations and neighborhoods and homeowners associations
3. Providing and listening to ideas aimed at improving community life
4. Providing information on local programs and services
5. Dealing with overgrown lots, derelict vehicles, unsafe buildings, and garbage collection issues
6. Providing guidance on social issues such as homeless persons, at-risk children, and domestic violence issues

The other component of the CIPP model would be the creation of CIUs in every police station division throughout Trinidad and Tobago. The CIUs will be based at each police divisional headquarter and will have as part of its organizational structure a YIU and Neighborhood Resource Officers (NROs) who would be patrol officers with special responsibilities for their area of jurisdiction (police station district). The CIUs will facilitate interaction with the CEOs.

With the implementation of the CEOs and the CIUs as part of the CIPP model, members of the TTPS and residents of the various communities will now share ownership, accountability, and decision making in the fight against crime and social disorder. The main aim will be to bring about effective, long-term solutions aimed at reducing crime and eliminating as "coproducers of crime reduction." It is the desire of the researcher that the CIPP model will remove the "colonial yolk of voicelessness" in policing which pervades Trinidad and Tobago's policing process. The researcher also hopes to facilitate an increase in the level of community involvement in the policing process via the CIPP model, and therefore decrease

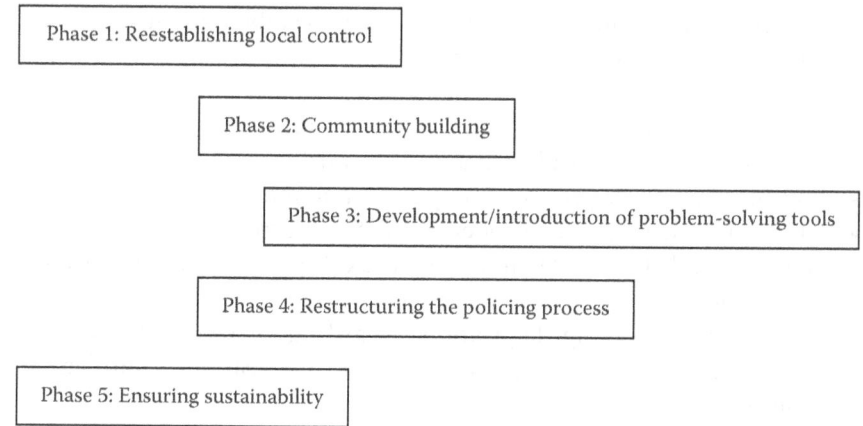

Figure 7.2 The CIPP model: The five-phase plan. (Adapted from Saville, G. J. et al., *Paper Presented in Winnipeg, Manitoba*, 2001. http://www.mppi.mb.ca/documents/Civitas1a.ppt.)

the "democratic deficit" in this liberal democracy. History will eventually determine whether the "collective efficacy" of community residents working alongside police officers in Trinidad and Tobago will provide the foundation for preventing and reducing violent crimes in local communities or whether the state formal social control mechanisms will continue to abound in the island.

The goal of the CIPP model is to create the capacity for building safe communities by involving local residents in the policing process. The process is divided into five phases. The CIPP model will begin with the creation of neighborhood profiles via community research and evaluation conferences, geographic mapping and identification of communities, and predictive crime mapping with geographic information systems. The creation of these neighborhood profiles will lead to the implementation of a five-phase plan of community involvement initiatives in the policing process aimed at creating safe, empowered communities by police/resident action. The five-phase plan of the CIPP model as an alternative policing approach is elucidated below (Figure 7.2).

The Five-Phase Plan

Phase 1: Short-term goal (6–12 months)—Reestablishing local control
Phase 2: Medium-term goal (6 months)—Community building
Phase 3: Medium-term goal (6–12 months)—Development/introduction of problem-solving tools
Phase 4: Long-term goal (after 30 months)—Restructuring the policing process
Phase 5: Ensuring sustainability

Phase 1—Reestablishing local control   The reestablishment of local control will be facilitated by the following:

- Meeting with all segments of local communities to listen to concerns, outline goals, and map a way forward
- Providing effective preventative patrols and emergency response
- Utilizing zero-tolerance/broken windows approaches
- Having visible foot, bike, mounted, and other nonvehicle patrols that are essential
- Introducing/enforcing legislation regarding abandoned lots and dilapidated buildings (police/community cleanup/beautification projects)
- Mobilizing a city safety program (starts here and moves outward)

Phase 2—Community building   Community building will be facilitated by police/community councils, planners, and representatives:

- "Coplanning" with police and policy makers to develop action-based strategies
- Introducing crime prevention through environmental design (CPTED)
- Introducing social and educational crime prevention programs (use of the media)
- Implementing restorative justice projects (peace-making approach focusing on social harm/love studies)
- Creating youth facilities (pathway guidance)
- Implementing school safety programs via at-risk programs
- Teaching parenting and conflict resolution skills
- Enforcing safe urban and rural design municipal regulations
- Facilitating community and neighborhood mobilization

Phase 3—Development/introduction of problem-solving tools   Problem-solving tools will include, but will not be limited to, the following:

- Creating CEO offices
- Introducing community CPS—residents
- Introducing CRO—residents
- Creating CIUs—police
- Introducing NRO—police officers
- Focusing on target hardening
- Situational prevention
- Mobilizing communities

Phase 4—Restructuring the policing process   The process of policing will be restructured to ensure the creation of a modern, responsive police service using the following mechanisms:

- Creating civilian oversight boards
- Expanding policing from being land based to sea based (marine patrols), which will ensure that all residents are involved in the policing process by providing access to residents who reside in yachts and on small islands off the mainland
- Expanding and modernizing of policing via vigorous recruiting and training and usage of contemporary technology, which includes the following:
  - Integrated databases
  - CCTV installation in all public spaces and on public transport (maxi taxis, buses, ferries)
  - CCTV headpieces and chest cameras for patrol officers
  - Integrated telephones for patrol officers (phone and radio)
  - Increased fines for providing false personal details to police officers
- Cooling crime hotspots by
  - Focusing attention on repeat offenders
  - Focusing attention on multiple complaint addresses
  - Introducing communal monitoring via CCTV (private electronic monitoring systems)
  - Ensuring celerity of punishment

Phase 5—Ensuring sustainability   To ensure sustainability, the following factors can be used:

- Creating an interconnected database of criminal elements and their profiles
- Introducing and enforcing modern laws from the simple to the complex (traffic/litter to parental responsibility)
- Fingerprinting at birth or contact with police officers (mandatory)
- Creating a DNA database
- Judicial expansion and strengthening (separate adult and juvenile legislation/infrastructure)
- Alternative sentencing
- Community rewards
- Institutional modification (number plates issued only at Transport Division)

Conclusion

In 1829, Sir Robert Peel submitted that "the Police and the people of the community are equal in terms of effective policing" (Braiden 1992, 108). It is therefore extremely necessary to have an effective relationship between both the groups in order for any crime control and prevention strategy to be successful. The CIPP model builds on this and contends that crime prevention is the responsibility of the total community. The CIPP model concretizes the view that the police and the community share ownership, responsibility, and accountability for the prevention of crime (Forrest, Myhill, and Tilley 2005, 1; Skolnick and Bayley 1986, 213). The aforementioned authors submitted that when the police work with the community and focus on their crime concerns, they form an effective relationship. It is therefore necessary for the police to respect all different types of cultures that make up the community in order to gain the respect from those individuals that make up the neighborhoods they are working in. Mutual trust between the police and the community is essential for effective and contemporary policing. The implementation of the CIPP model therefore requires a large investment in training with special attention to problem analysis and problem solving, facilitation, community organization, communication, mediation and conflict resolution, resource identification and use, networking and linkages, and cross-cultural competency. It is envisaged that the CIPP model will reduce the current dissonance that exists between the police officers and the communities they serve, positively impact policing, and act as an alternative to the traditional method of policing communities in Trinidad and Tobago.

References

Astin, A. W. (1984). Student involvement: A developmental theory for higher education. *Journal of College Student Development*, 40(5), 518–529.

Braiden, C. (1992). Enriching traditional police roles. In *Police Management: Issues and Perspectives*, edited by L. T. Hoover. Washington, DC: Police Executive Research Forum, p. 108.

Burns, D., and Taylor, M. (2000). *Auditing Community Participation: An Assessment Handbook*. Bristol: The Policy Press.

Carr, E. S. (2003). Rethinking empowerment theory using a feminist lens: The importance of process. *Affilia*, 18, 8–20.

Chen, X. (2002). Community and policing strategies: A Chinese approach to crime control. *Policing and Society: An International Journal of Research and Policy*, 12(1), 1–13.

Cordner, G. W., and Sheehan, R. (1999). *Police Administration*, 4th ed. Cincinnati, OH: Anderson.

Demmitt, A., and Oldenski, T. (1999). The diagnostic process from a Freirean perspective. *Journal of Humanistic Counseling, Education and Development*, 37(4), 232–240.

Deosaran, R. (2000). Community policing, public opinion and organizational climate. Paper Presented at Annual Meeting of the American Society of Criminology, November 15–18, San Francisco, CA.

Deosaran, R. (2001). Community policing, organizational transformation and benchmarking initiatives. Paper Presented at the 2nd Caribbean Conference on Crime and Criminal Justice, February 14–17, University of the West Indies, Mona Campus, Jamaica.

Filion, P. (1999). Rupture or continuity? Modern and postmodern planning in Toronto. *International Journal of Urban and Regional Research*, 23(3), 421–445.

Flatley, J., Kershaw, C., Smith, K., Chaplin, R., and Moon, D. (2010). *Crime in England and Wales 2009/10: Findings from the British Crime Survey and Police Recorded Crime*, 3rd ed. London: Home Office Statistical Bulletin.

Forrest, S., Myhill, A., and Tilley, N. (2005). Practical lessons for involving the community in crime and disorder problem-solving. Home Office Development and Practice Report #43. London: Research Development and Statistics Directorate.

Fox, J. A. (1996). *Trends in Juvenile Violence: A Report to the United States Attorney General on Current and Future Rates of Juvenile Offending*. Washington, DC: Bureau of Justice Statistics, United States Department of Justice.

King, M. L. (1964). Excerpt from the Speech "I Have a Dream." Delivered in Washington, DC.

Liederbach, J., Fritsch, E. J., Carter, D. L., and Bannister, A. (2008). Exploring the limits of collaboration in community policing: A direct comparison of police and citizen views. *Policing: An International Journal of Police Strategies & Management*, 31(2), 271–291.

Lilly, J., Cullen, F., and Ball, R. (1995). *Criminological Theory: Context and Consequences*. Thousand Oaks, CA: Sage Publications.

Mastrofski, S. D., and Lum, C. (2008). Meeting the challenges of police governance in Trinidad and Tobago. *Law, Policing*, 2(4), 481–496.

Mawby, R. I. (2003). Models of policing. In *Handbook of Policing*, edited by T. Newburn. Cullompton: Willan Publishing, pp. 15–40.

Miles, R., and Sengupta, P. (2006). *Working Paper: Building Gender-Responsive Community-Based Policing in Bangladesh*. Dhaka: Department for International Development, German Development Cooperation.

Moreau, M. J. (1990). Empowerment through advocacy and consciousness-raising: Implications of a structural approach to social work. *Journal of Sociology & Social Welfare*, 17, 53–67.

Peterson, N. A., Hamme, C. L., and Speer, P. W. (2002). Cognitive empowerment of African Americans. Race and Caucasians: Differences in understanding of power, political functioning, and shaping ideology. *Journal of Black Studies*, 32, 336–351.

Rappaport, J. (1981). In praise of paradox: A social policy of empowerment over prevention. *American Journal of Community Psychology*, 9(1), 1–25.

Rappaport, J. (1984). Studies in empowerment: Introduction to the issue. *Prevention in Human Services*, 3, 1–7.

Rawlings, P. (2003). Policing before the police. In *Handbook of Policing*, edited by T. Newburn. Devon: Willan Publishing.

Saville, G. J., Cleveland, G., and McLeod, R. (2001). The CIVITAS model: A comprehensive new approach for creating and sustaining safe civic places. Paper Presented in May, Winnipeg, MB. http://www.mppi.mb.ca/documents/Civitas1a.ppt (Retrieved on January 31, 2010).

Simcha-Fagan, O., and Schwartz, J. E. (1986). Neighborhood and delinquency: An assessment of contextual effects. *Criminology*, 24, 667–703.

Skolnick, J. H., and Bayley, D. H. (1986). *The New Blue Line: Police Innovation in Six American Cities*. New York: The Free Press.

Speer, T. (2004). Origins of modern policing. February 2004, *Issue*, 1(4), 1–20. http://www.utwatch.org/archives/issue/issue_1_4.pdf.

Stroick, S. M. (1998). Public involvement and community planning: The redesign of services for children and families in Southwestern Alberta. Doctoral Dissertation. University of Calgary, Calgary.

Sue, D. W., and Sue, D., editors. (2003). Socio-political considerations of trust and mistrust in multicultural counselling and therapy. In *Counselling the Culturally Different: Theory and Practice*, 3rd ed. New York: John Wiley, pp. 63–90.

UNODC. (2007). Crime, Violence, and Development: Trends, Costs, and Policy Options in the Caribbean, Report No. 37820, March 2007. A Joint Report by the United Nations Office on Drugs and Crime and the Latin America and the Caribbean Region of the World Bank. New York: UNODC.

Wallace, W. C. (2012). A concurrent analysis of the relationship between community involvement in policing and the policing process in various communities in Trinidad and Tobago: Towards a new social control model. Unpublished PhD dissertation. University of the West Indies, St. Augustine.

Zimmerman, M. A. (1995). Psychological empowerment: Issues and illustrations. *American Journal of Community Psychology*, 23, 581–599.

Community Policing
A Panacea or a Pandora's Box to Tackle the Rise in Crimes in Nigeria and South Africa

ADEWALE A. OLUTOLA

Contents

Introduction

To complement the efforts of the criminal justice structures in crime prevention, it is important to involve the communities in finding a solution to the menace of crime in the society. Visser (2003) defines community policing as both a philosophy and a strategy that is based on partnership between the community and the police to find creative solutions for contemporary community problems, crime, and other crime-related matters. In this definition, the thesis is the involvement of the communities in policing.

The fundamental basis of the involvement of the communities in crime prevention is admittedly the inability of the criminal justice systems to cope with the level of crime, to ensure justice, or to rehabilitate the offenders as well as the failure to deal with the root causes of crime in society. To this end, Schneider (2007) observes that crime prevention seems to be a philosophy, which, in many respects, is antithetical to that of the criminal justice system. This is because the criminal justice has been called upon to perform an impossible mandate of crime prevention (Burger 2007). It cannot be defended that the root causes of crime in the society (such as employment, dysfunctional family settings, inequality, poverty, and rural–urban drifts) are within the mandate of the criminal justice systems (Olutola 2012).

The increases in the global crime rates have been exacerbated by multidimensional factors, in which there is no quick fix solution. Increasing the budget of the criminal justice structures will not necessarily reduce the crime rate. Braithwaite (1989, 133) noted that:

> … criminal justice system cannot prescribe policies that will work to reduce crime; we cannot in all honesty say that the societies spending more on criminological research get better criminal justice policies than those that spend little or nothing on criminology.

This is still worse. All stakeholders need urgent brainstorming of some of the decisions of the courts of law that are in favor of human rights of an accused which is in contradistinction to the constitutional duty of the law enforcers and/or human rights of the victims of crime.

In Britain, for instance, former colonial master of Nigeria and South Africa, the House of Lords in the case of *Smith v Chief Constable Sussex Police* (2008) held that the case of the appellant could not be sustained against police officers who refused to prevent crime. Again, the case of *Anthony Martin v R* (2001) (also a British case) was nothing but an indirect support to criminalities. In this case, Mr Martin's home was broken into on six different times. On the seventh occasion he shot and killed one of the burglars and wounded the other. He was jailed for harming the burglars, his plea of self-defense was rejected by the court, and he was later denied parole because he posed dangers to the right to life of the burglars. Furthermore, Garside and McMahon (2006) note that the customary criminal justice policy is a totally irrelevant means of preventing crime and the government needs to explore a much broader policy antithetical to the present approach (criminal justice) in order to promote greater safety and security.

However, as appealing as community policing might be, it has failed in Nigeria and South Africa for different reasons. One of the reasons for the failure of community policing as a crime prevention scheme in Nigeria and South Africa can be traced to the historical development of the two countries. The idea of using the police force as a government institution was introduced by the British colonial power in Africa. The introduction of police as a government institution was for the protection and advancement of the economic and political interests of Her Majesty in England (Ibidapo-Obe 2005).

In order to achieve the Queen's imperial economic and political targets, the colonial power used maltreatment and suppression in the dealings with the local communities and whoever that resisted the expansion of the imperial power. Alemika (2007) notes that the colonial and apartheid police forces in Africa were reputed for brutality and impunity.

By using coercion and authoritarianism in the implementation of policies, the colonial power firmly severed the relationship between the local community and the police in Nigeria (Chukwuma 2000). Dixon (2004) emphasizes that, for a proper appraisal of community policing in South Africa, studies must reflect back to the era of the apartheid system of government. Dixon (2004) views the events organized by civil societies in the late 1980s as antipolicing activities and in opposition to the apartheid administration.

In this study, it was decided to focus on the following interviewees: police officers, magistrates in Criminal Courts Divisions, officers of National Prosecuting Authority, prison/correctional officers, and directors of nongovernmental organizations (NGOs) involved in crime prevention projects in each of the two countries (Nigeria and South Africa). These interviewees were interviewed because they were constitutionally recognized by the constitutions of Nigeria and South Africa as crime prevention clusters. Most importantly, the records of the two countries in terms of crimes (violent and nonviolent) are unacceptably high (Ekblom and Wyvekens 2004).

The aim of this chapter is to argue that community policing is not a solution to the increase in criminalities in Nigeria and South Africa. This is based on the experiences and the results of community policing in other countries such as the United States, Belgium, Australia, Singapore, Brazil, and Haiti. The reasons for the failure of community policing in each of the listed countries will be discussed, followed by an explanation of the Nigerian and South African situation based on the results of the empirical study.

Literature Review

Although a substantial amount of research has been done in the area of crime prevention, the idea of this chapter is to specifically deal with the assumption of whether partnership/community policing can be a solution to the increase in criminalities in Nigeria and South Africa.

Davis, Henderson, and Merrick (2003) have identified the following as some of the merits of community policing in crime prevention: (1) community policing promotes communication between police and citizens; (2) it ensures commitment to problem-oriented policing; (3) it permits the public to participate in setting police priorities and developing tactics; and (4) it empowers communities to help solve their own crime and disorder problems through sponsorship programs.

Dixon (2004) notes that although community policing has become a dominant philosophy in some countries such as the Netherlands and Sweden, other countries such as France and Austria seem not to be interested in the community policing models and have proved to be resistant to the principles of community policing. The same resistance was noted in the countries of Eastern Europe and the former Soviet Union that sees community policing as not only alien to their typical cultural, legal, and organizational traditions but also unattractive given these countries' political and economic situations. Second, it will be recalled that the former Soviet Union and countries of the Eastern Europe were the proponents of economic and political socialist theories, meaning that the State has the responsibility for the citizens' protection.

Another reason for the unattractiveness of community policing in the above-mentioned countries as noted by Davis et al. (2003) was that there is no single uniform model of community policing. It depends on how influential the local context is in shaping the development of community policing programs and the application of the program. Many perspectives on community policing exist, but each builds on assumptions and is only partially supported by empirical evidence. As a result, Ellison (2006) describes community policing as a plastic concept. Similarly Goris and Walters (1999) note that partnership or a community policing approach to locally based crime prevention, though becoming popular, is a fluid concept and often implemented without consistent theoretical foundation. Jagwanth (1994) emphasizes that for community policing to be effective, it must be seen as essentially a flexible strategy aimed toward the development of better policing practice.

Further, Shaw and Shearing (1998) noted that while community policing was supposed to be a measure, ensuring police reform in South Africa and guaranteeing a shift of focus in policing resources to poor areas, it has not done this. Rather, South African community policing has become a mechanism to achieve better bandit catching (meaning pursuit of criminals who escape or try to escape from the arms of the criminal justice structures) than the way of involving the police in wider strategies to enhance community involvement in crime prevention (Shaw and Shearing 1998).

In an article by De Vries (2008), it was observed that the high rate of crime in South Africa was complicated by the lack of police's effective management. This has resulted in citizens' frustration and a loss of faith in the abilities of the police to improve safety in their milieu. In Nigeria, as a result of police brutality, the relationship between the police and the citizens is short of cordiality. This has contributed to the difficulty in making community policing succeed in that country. Rather than community policing, Nigeria populace prefer informal policing. Scharf (1989) posits that informal policing is a policing style that originates from community-initiated policing. Such policing style originates from perceived failure of the state to provide the citizens with the protection they require (Alemika and Chukwuma 2003).

Three reasons have been identified for choosing informal policing over partnership policing: (1) informal policing is perceived to be the solution to the rise in the rate of crime; (2) it is taken to be the answer to the poor perception about the ability of the criminal justice systems to respond to the needs of the victims of crimes; and (3) the formal police service is inadequate (Sekhonyane 2002). Informal policing involves the activities of the people of a particular society engaging in their daily business and acting as watchdogs of the behavioral patterns of themselves and others, and intermittently taking corrective measures (Sekhonyane 2002). This is assumed to be more efficient and more effective for the society than the functions of policing given to a specialist body.

Community Policing in Other Countries

Davis et al. (2003) note that as countries of the world struggle to move in their level of political and economic development, from totalitarianism and tyrannical systems of governance to people oriented policing techniques, they search for an alternative additional form of policing to adopt. Quite a number of such countries, namely, the Unites States, Belgium, Australia, Singapore, Brazil, and Haiti, have found favor with community policing as a way to strengthen accountability of the police to citizens. The methods and results of community policing however differ from country to country.

Community Policing in the United States

In the United States, though, the idea of making the police and the citizens partners in the function of maintaining law and order in the society commenced before the popularity of the notion of community policing

(Davis et al. 2003). However, Ellison (2006) has identified some challenges to the full implementation of community policing in the United States. First, the traditional culture of policing continues to dictate police independence and crime fighting, while modern philosophy encourages using open systems approaches, building partnership, and solving problems. The principles of traditional policing and the new idea of community policing therefore could not be easily reconciled. Second, the police officers who are responsible for the implementation of community policing issues are said to be problematic and complex. Resistance to change and inherent reluctance to embrace change are the facts that police officers are traditionally conservative in nature, making them even more adverse to change.

Community Policing in Belgium

Several events led to the introduction of an alternative policing method in Belgium. In the late 1980s, Belgium witnessed a growing sense of insecurity caused by a number of high-profile violent events, street crimes, and social exclusion that could not be curtailed by the existing police and the criminal justice system. Goris and Walters (1999) noted that the Belgians reflected their unhappiness over government failure to address these safety issues by voting for more conservative political parties, which enables the right-wing parties to gain greater support and media attention. This consequently led Belgium to launch its "safety and crime prevention contracts" (Goris and Walters 1999). Central to the idea of "partnership" in crime prevention in Belgium was the networking of agencies, collaborating ideas, and involving the "community" in decision making and management.

As a result of the above situation, the Belgian government was not only seeking to strengthen the existing law enforcement but was also ready to try something different. The former Belgium government was also impressed by some successes recorded in other European countries about crime prevention especially in France, the Netherlands, and England (Goris and Walters 1999). These impressions established that communities could be important partners in the development of crime prevention programs.

Some scholars have attempted to answer the question whether the locally based crime prevention in Belgium actually prevents crime (Goris and Walters 1999), but there was no clear answer to this question. Goris and Walters (1999) point out some of the limitations to the success rate of Belgium idea of local approach to crime prevention such as (1) the fact that the crime prevention officials were elected by the residents for 6-year terms and were often susceptible to the changing demands of the electorates, which affects the contents and the quality of the prevention policy and (2) the fact that these crime prevention officials and the crime prevention workers who were often physically located within the offices of the local police made the public to view them as the partners or agents of the traditional police.

Community Policing in Australia

Homel (2005) opines that the history of crime prevention in Australia has been a continuous event. It is important to add here that Australia has never had a strong national crime prevention policy, except for the 1995 Safer Australia Initiative. Although the 1995 Safer Australian Initiative was short lived, it nevertheless attempted to define national crime prevention precedence under the leadership and support of a team of crime, business, and community "experts" (Homel 2005).

Crime prevention scheme in Australia is almost tantamount to a community project. Homel (2005) notes that in Australia, the national, state, and territorial governments have continuously adopted crime prevention strategy as a community development project. Community development project in Australia emphasizes the confidence that crime prevention in a particular community is not the duty of a sole entity but rather the result of the interplay of combination of structural determinants available in a particular community. Homel (2005) notes that if activities that promote crime could be removed from the society, then crime will be prevented.

One identifiable problem of Australian community or crime prevention initiative is the lack of continuity in the community crime prevention programs. An example is the 1996 Abandonment of the Safer Australia Initiative by the newly elected government in favor of another program—the National Campaign against Violence and Crime (NCAVC) (Homel 2005).

The experience of Australia at community crime prevention efforts had a number of implementation flaws. Most important of which were the lack of a clear and coherent central leadership at the various levels of government, frequent changes in the crime prevention methods, absence of commitment to research, and lack of an evaluation process designed to build up evidence-based crime prevention strategy (Homel 2005).

Community Policing in Singapore

Singapore is a multiethnic and multiracial society just as Nigeria and South Africa (Ganapathy 2000). Again, the modern police system in Singapore is fashioned after the British system of policing (Ganapathy 2000). Ganapathy (2000) notes that most of the functions performed by the Singapore police are similar to the British police functions, such as crime prevention, disorder and community security, protection of lives and property, maintenance of law and order, detection of crime, and apprehension of offenders (Section 8 of the Singapore Police Force Ordinances of 1958). These functions are also similar to the duties of the Nigerian and the South African police services [Section 4 of the Nigerian Police Act, Cap 359 Laws of the Federation of the Republic of Nigeria 1990, Section 205(3) of the 1996 Constitution of the Republic of South Africa].

One challenge for the Singapore Police Force (SPF) was how to ensure efficient performance of the above-listed functions in a multiracial and multireligious society of Singapore (a situation common to Nigerian and South African policing environments). It is important to point out that as appealing as the community involvement in policing might be, in Singapore the academics in that country have not produced any theory that can be tagged as Singapore criminological theory of crime prevention. Such theory will be important especially for the advancement of science of criminal justice and will broaden our understanding of other countries, which is an excellent way of knowing how others practice issues within the criminal justice system (Erika and Dammer 2001). Ganapathy (2000) points out that most of the crime prevention approaches in Singapore have relied essentially on social control through the theory of deviancy. The family has been called upon to preserve the traditional cultural values and bear the responsibility for socializing the children in the virtues of the ever-growing complex society (Ganapathy 2000).

Community Policing in Brazil

Brazil started community policing as a means of improving the traditional police duty of crime prevention, after the relative success that community policing recorded in the United States and Canada. In 1994, an NGO and social movement called VIVA Rio formed a strong partnership with the new commander of the military police. With the involvement of VIVA Rio, the military police who were previously in charge of street patrol and response to crime started the community policing attempt (Davis et al. 2003). Davis et al. (2003) noted that the planning process was a challenge because military police administrators were concerned that devoting a portion of staff to community policing activities would turn them away from the provisions of usual services.

Community policing in Brazil did not achieve the targeted ambition because police salaries were extremely low; the police were underequipped with regard to basic necessities such as vehicles, ammunition, and gasoline; police officers also received poor or insufficient training; they were feared by civilians and in turn feared the civilians; and the institutions that they worked in were often plagued by corruption (Davis et al. 2003).

Community Policing in Haiti

The January 2010 devastating earthquake that occurred in Haiti has annihilated whatever the structure of community policing left in that country. For a long period of time, Haiti was under the military rule (Davis et al. 2003). Therefore, it was not surprising that the Haitian police have always strived to protect the government and not the community (Davis et al. 2003).

Davis et al. (2003) observed that community policing failed in Haiti due to different reasons. One example is the frequent changes in the community policing commanders. Davis et al. (2003) note that the Canadian police commander in Haiti in 1998 described community policing in Haiti as a top priority. The Canadian police commander was later replaced by a French commander who saw community policing as just one of the policing techniques; this was a serious blow to the Haitian experience of community policing as it meant a tactical withdrawal of the support of international community to Haitian community policing. Davis et al. (2003) note that the hostile environment such as unstable government, extreme poverty, and non-functioning judicial system under which community policing was introduced in Haiti contributed to its down fall.

Methodology

Qualitative research approach was adopted for this study because of its relevance. First, there was a need to ask the research participants their perceptions of community policing and crime prevention in their respective areas (Prudence, Willem, Leseli, and David 2001). It was an exploratory study that aimed at comparing the results of the findings from the Nigerian and South African respondents' perspectives of their perception on community policing.

One advantage of adopting qualitative approach for this chapter is that such approach allows for a holistic study. This enables the researcher not to choose any particular crime but to research into community policing and crime prevention holistically. Taylor and Bogdan (1998, 8) noted that:

> in qualitative approach, the researcher looks at settings and people holistically; people, settings or groups are not reduced to variables, but are viewed as a whole.

In a qualitative approach, there are different techniques for gathering data. The researcher has adopted a qualitative technique of interview. One advantage of using the interview technique over questionnaire is that interview allows the researcher the opportunity to see and talk to the respondents and report his findings in writing and to have on the spot assessment of the happenings and challenges faced daily by these role players in an effort to ensuring a crime-free society (Hagan 2004; Oppenheim 2001).

In the process of data gathering, 20 crime prevention practitioners (respondents) were interviewed. This consisted of 10 respondents in each of the two countries (Nigeria and South Africa), namely, 4 senior officers of the South African and Nigerian police, 2 magistrates in the Criminal Court Divisions of the respective countries, 4 officers of the National Prosecuting Authority of the 2 countries, 4 prison/correctional officers of the 2 countries, 2 directors of social crime prevention, and 4 directors of NGOs actively involved in the crime prevention projects in the 2 countries. The officers interviewed for this chapter were purposefully selected. A letter of intro-duction was obtained from the Head of Department of Safety and Security Management of Tshwane University of Technology to all the selected Crime Prevention Departments of the two countries. Permission was later sought and granted by the respective respondents in the two countries. Thereafter, interviews were scheduled and conducted.

Choice of the Respondents

The respondents that were interviewed for the purpose of data collection in this chapter were representatives of the actual role players designated by the 1996 Constitution of the Republic of South Africa and the 1999 Constitution of the Federal Republic of Nigeria for crime prevention purposes in their respective countries. This gave the assurance that the data gathered are reli-able and valid in the sense that the participants had in-depth knowledge of the situation that was investigated. The researcher deliberately and purpose-fully decided on the list of the respondents because of the necessity to avoid haphazard informants or a kind of information the legal luminary will call hearsay evidence. Wengraf (2001) warns that a criminal justice researcher must avoid haphazard informants, and that it is always important to select research respondents with a purpose in mind.

The Questionnaire

In order to properly unknot the question whether community policing is a panacea or a Pandora's box to criminalities in Nigeria and South Africa, the researcher used in-depth interviews. This was done to gain practical infor-mation from respondents, in addition to the theoretical information found during the literature study.

An interview guide was used to ensure that respondents were asked the same questions with the same meaning (Oppenheim 2001). Unstructured, in-depth interviews were used as this allows for natural conversation (Champion 1993). The questions used were open ended to stimulate a discussion with a purpose in mind. Three questions were asked from the respondents, which are as follows:

1. Do you think crime prevention can be effective, if left with one component of criminal justice system? Please explain the reasons for your opinion.
2. How would you describe the communication and cooperation between the police, the judiciary, and the corrections in the field of crime prevention?
3. What sort of partnership role will you like to suggest between the criminal justice institutions, the organized business sector, and the community toward efficient crime prevention strategy?

Observation Method

In addition to the research technique of interviews, indirect observation was equally adopted for this study. Indirect observation was necessary in order to focus on the everyday and natural experiences of the respondents. A characteristic feature of the observation method of research is that it enables the researcher to gain an in-depth insight into the manifestations of reality. The target is not measuring in numbers, or gaining rules for behavior, but as De Vos, Strydom, Fouche, and Delport (2002) note, "... a qualitative researcher should strive at all times towards gaining feelings and impressions and experiencing the circumstances of the real world of the participants alongside them, and towards interpreting and sharing their activities."

An advantage of such technique, especially as it relates to this study, is that it gives the researcher a comprehensive perspective on the problem under investigation. It also gives the researcher the added advantage of studying the attitudes and behavioral patterns of the respondents in their natural situation.

Construction of the Interview Schedule

All the respondents interviewed for this research were senior officers with a very busy schedule in their respective departments. This made securing simultaneous appointments with all the respondents impossible. Having sought for and obtained the permission of the respondents, interviews for this research were conducted at times that each of the respondents was available. This strengthened the researcher's hand, in the sense that the research technique that had been earlier envisaged did not necessitate a group interview.

In addition, not using a group interview allowed the individual respondents to air their respective, independent opinions without any influence from other participants. The specific area covered in the research interview related to whether community policing is a panacea or a Pandora's box to criminality in Nigeria and South Africa.

Application of the Interview Schedule

The aforementioned research interviews and approvals were obtained telephonically or in some instances orally (face to face) after many follow-ups by the researcher to the offices of the respondents/interviewees. Appointment dates were scheduled directly with the respondents. The researcher conducted the research interviews with South African respondents first and later traveled to Nigeria to conduct similar interviews for the purpose of comparison of the data.

The research interviews were conducted at the offices of the respondents during office hours. Some of the interviews continued till after office hours as a result of interruptions and the busy schedule of the respondents. It took an average of 2–3 hours to interview each of the respondents. All the interviews were conducted and completed on the same day, with the exception of one interview that was continued on the following day.

Securing permission for the interview at the Department of Correctional Services in Pretoria (South Africa) was a little problematic, as the researcher was told that permission for research-related interviews could only be granted if the research theme was approved by the research section of the Correctional Services Department. However, this provision was later waived in the interest of the research. Obtaining permission for research interviews in Nigeria followed a similar pattern to that in South Africa. This made it easy for the researcher to complete the research interviews in Nigeria within a space of 6 weeks.

Gathering of Data

A tape recorder was used in the process of data collection. In order to ensure that the tape recorder was functioning properly, recordings were done for a few minutes and tested with the permission of the respondents before continuing. Equally, to ensure accuracy of the data collected and to avoid misinterpretation of the data, jottings were made of the responses.

In the process of data collection, the researcher observed that most of the respondents in the two countries had low morale and lacked public confidence in their ability to deliver optimally in terms of their constitutional duty of crime prevention. Most importantly though, the researcher believes that the answers provided by each of the respondents were true reflections of the situation and events in the two countries. The respondents were convinced that this research was for academic purposes and that it had nothing to do with politics. Some of the respondents had postgraduate qualifications (degrees) and knew that this research aimed to contribute to the advancement of the science of criminal justice.

Interpretation of Data

Having listened to the tape, the information was transcribed verbatim, without alterations to the language of the respondents. In the transcription process, similar and divergent opinions were listed in a table. This was done after coding of the data quantitatively into "agree," "strongly agree," "disagree," and "strongly disagree" categories. The methodology employed to interpret the data was to record the words of the respondents as a narrative and to list these responses to each of the questions.

Reliability and Validity

An important subject for a qualitative researcher is narrative advantage. In this study, the respondents are able to tell their story in the way and the manner in which they perceive the subject matter of the study. This gives recognition to the perceptions and experiences of the respondents. The experiences and perceptions of other people (i.e., those who did not participate in the research), and whether those responses are valid or reliable, are not important.

Generally, the literature revealed that scholars are divergent as to the precise meaning of the research tools "reliability" and "validity," and their application in both quantitative and qualitative studies. However, reliability and validity are the tools of an essentially positivist epistemology (Winter 2000). For a better understanding of these two research tools, especially as they were applicable to this research, some definitions and descriptions of reliability and validity by different scholars are presented.

On the one hand, Kirk and Miller (1986) suggest three techniques for measuring reliability in quantitative research: (1) the degree to which a measurement, given repeatedly, remains the same, (2) the stability of measurement over time, and (3) the similarity of measurement within a given time period. On the other hand, the term validity in quantitative research is argued by Winter (2000) as residing in a culmination of other empirical conceptions: universal laws, evidence, objectivity, truth, actuality, deduction, reason, fact, and mathematical data, to name just a few.

However, qualitative researchers consider the above definitions of reliability and validity by quantitative researchers as inadequate. Qualitative researchers view the concepts of reliability and validity differently. Golafshani (2003) defines reliability in qualitative research as the extent to which research results are consistent over time and an accurate representation of the total population under study. Adopting this definition as a parameter of evaluation of reliability, the researcher is confident that this study is reliable; this is because those that were selected for the purpose of data collection had not been selected haphazardly, but were representatives of the criminal justice structures of the two countries studied and were of high profile. Therefore, should this research be repeated using the same respondents, the same results would be obtained.

Furthermore, the important test for a qualitative research is its quality. Eisner (1991) notes that good qualitative research can help us "... understand a situation that would otherwise be enigmatic or confusing." Adopting this measure for this research, it is submitted that this research has helped in the understanding of the enigma or confusion regarding community policing situation in Nigeria and South Africa.

Research Findings (Nigeria)

The researcher confirmed the importance of community policing from the majority of the respondents interviewed in Nigeria. The respondents affirmed that crime prevention is the duty of every citizen and that it is the duty of the society to prevent crime, not exclusively the duty of the components of the criminal justice system. However, two of the respondents were not sure whether crime prevention is the responsibility of one component of the criminal justice system.

Eight out of the 10 of the respondents attested to the fact that crime prevention cannot be effective, if left as a duty for the criminal justice system only; community or partnership policing was suggested to be a solution to the rise in criminalities in the Nigerian society.

The following are some of the direct responses from the respondents on community policing in Nigeria (different respondents are indicated by R, followed by a number):

Do you think crime prevention can be effective, if left with one component of criminal justice system? Please explain the reasons for your opinion.

R1: It is unthinkable to assume that the police or the criminal justice system generally without the partnership with the community can ever succeed to prevent crime.

R2: The Nigerian society needs to cooperate (or work together) with the law enforcement agencies, if truly we expect the crime level to be reduced in this country (Nigeria).

R3: That is correct; remember that the Bible says that two is better than one because they have better rewards for their labor. Partnership policing will definitely reduce crime in Nigeria.

How would you describe the communication and cooperation between the police, the judiciary, and the corrections in the field of crime prevention?

R4: Truly, if Nigerians can consciously accept that crime prevention is not the sole responsibility of the criminal justice structures, then there will be a significant reduction in the crime rate in Nigeria.

R5: Honestly, I cannot say whether partnership or community policing can reduce the crime rate in Nigeria.

R6: No, it cannot. How do you think Nigerians can work with the Nigerian police? Ever since the prosecution and conviction of the former Inspector-General of the Nigerian Police for misappropriating public funds, the little trust that the Nigerians had in the Nigerian police had been erased.

What sort of partnership role will you like to suggest between the criminal justice institutions, the organized business sector, and the community toward efficient crime prevention strategy?

R7: I do not know, what others might say, but for me crime prevention is the duty of everybody still living and not that of the police alone; unfortunately, a good number of Nigerians have the erroneous idea that crime prevention is the duty of the police.

R8: Yes, joining hands with the criminal justice institutions is the solution to the ever-increasing rate of crime in Nigeria, but it is a known fact that the police are not trustworthy to work with.

R9: Crime rate is high in this country (Nigeria) due to the overdependence on the criminal justice institution to prevent crime.

R10: Yes, I think partnership policing will ensure the trust and confidence in the criminal justice system. This will invariably lead to reduction in the fear of being victimized in Nigeria.

Research Findings (South Africa)

On the other hand, the answers given by the respondents in South Africa are as follows: 7 out of the 10 respondents in the criminal justice structures of the South Africa assert that crime prevention is not the responsibility of one component of the criminal justice system, as the criminal justice system comprises many components and each of the components has a specific role to play to ensure a peaceful and anarchy-free society. However, three of the respondents in South Africa believe that the criminal justice institutions had the constitutional duty to prevent crime and must do their job.

The following are some of the direct responses of the respondents interviewed in South Africa on community policing vis-à-vis crime prevention:

Do you think crime prevention can be effective, if left with one component of criminal justice system? Please explain the reasons for your opinion.

R1: Truly, crime prevention can be better achieved in this country (South Africa), if the South African community stops to hide behind the criminal justice system and work in partnership with the police.

R2: Community policing will definitely reduce the crime rate in South Africa. Presently, there is a blaming game on the issue of the high crime rate. A man who assaults his wife will blame the police in South Africa; a court witness who refuses to attend court and give evidence will blame the court for miscarriage of justice. Parents who are supposed to instill morals into their children and did not, will blame the police, if their children commit crime in the society.

R3: Community policing can help a lot in crime prevention, but we do not have enough public awareness on community policing in this country.

How would you describe the communication and cooperation between the police, the judiciary, and the corrections in the field of crime prevention?

R4: Yes, we need to do whatever we need to do to reduce the crime level in South Africa. Criminals in this country can kill for a slice of bread; it seems that community policing is the way forward and we need to start immediately and commence the ideology.

R5: On a lighter note, is it possible even with community policing to have a crime-free society? The answer is capital "NO."

R6: No not at all. I will define crime prevention as preventing crime from occurring. If I am right in this definition, it means that community policing cannot prevent crime in South Africa. Remember that South Africa is a heterogeneous society, so how do we ensure that the black, white, colored, Indians, immigrants, male, female, old, and young will join hands with the criminal justice at the same level and 24/7 to prevent crime from occurring?

R7: No, it cannot. These terms are only the theories: community policing, sector policing, and neighborhood policing. None of these theories can reduce the crime level in South Africa.

What sort of partnership role will you like to suggest between the criminal justice institutions, the organized business sector, and the community toward efficient crime prevention strategy?

R8: As a member of a nongovernmental organization, I am aware of the importance of community policing in the efforts for crime prevention, but the same cannot be said of the majority of the ordinary citizens of this country.

R9: I will also suggest an active involvement of the local government. Cutting of grass, supplying electricity, and putting up CCTV camera wherever necessary will expose the criminals. The basic crime prevention services must be provided by each role player if we are to see a reduction in the rate of crime in this country.

R10: I agree. Community policing has a way of building trust and confidence with the law enforcers.

Discussion

In the interviews conducted with the respondents in the two countries for this study, the respondents almost unanimously agreed (15 out of 20) that to reduce crime levels in Nigeria and South Africa, there must be effective partnerships between the law enforcers and the communities.

The respondents did not controvert the above seemingly merits of community policing indicated earlier in this chapter and as listed by Davis et al. (2003). In actual fact, 15 out of the 20 respondents consider that community policing will additionally reduce the crime rate in Nigeria and South Africa due to its different theoretical qualities. It can therefore be deducted that on the one hand, the views expressed by the majority of the respondents in this study correspond to the information found in the literature (Braithwaite 1989; Davis et al. 2003; Dixon 2004; Goris and Walters 1999; Homel 2005; Garside and McMahon 2006; Schneider 2007; Shaw and Shearing 1998; Visser 2003). This then suggests that to reduce the crime levels in Nigeria and South Africa, the duo need to urgently gear up public/police awareness on the importance of partnership policing on crime prevention.

On the other hand, the practical experiences of the majority of the countries enunciated above (the United States, Belgium, Australia, Singapore, Brazil, and Haiti) where community policing have been tried and the high level of failure recorded in those countries, coupled with the fact that the average number of Nigerians and South Africans see crime prevention as the duty of the police and the criminal justice institutions, will suggest that perhaps the ignorance of the crime prevention practitioners in Nigeria and South Africa about community policing causes their belief that it is a solution to high crime rate in their respective countries. In view of experiences of different countries enunciated above, it is clear that community policing as a scheme of crime reduction in the contemporary time needs a further study and for now must be viewed and implemented with caution.

Conclusion

This chapter considers whether community policing model could be a solution to criminalities in the Nigerian and South African societies. The author has addressed the question from three view points. First, what community policing actually means in terms of the literature. The opinions of the scholars on community policing were also highlighted, coupled with the Nigeria and South Africa experiences of community policing. Second, the experiences of different countries that have tried community policing were also discussed. Third, the author interviewed the crime prevention practitioners in the two countries on the aptness of community policing to reduce the rates of criminalities. The author discovered that there was a perception among the crime prevention practitioners of the two countries that community policing will reduce the rate of criminalities in their respective countries.

In conclusion, the author wants to caution that community policing might not be a solution but rather a Pandora's box to the rise in the criminalities in Nigeria and South Africa. The crime prevention practitioners interviewed for this chapter seem to be ignorant of the experiences of different countries on community policing and the various hindrances to community policing as a crime-fighting device. More so, the researcher finds that the populaces of Nigeria and South Africa that ought to play a significant role in crime prevention see crime prevention as the constitutional duty of the criminal justice systems. Therefore, the author recommends a further research on community policing on how best the concept could be implemented in practice to achieve the optimal result, but for now the crime prevention practitioners of the Nigeria and South Africa must consider alternative crime prevention schemes aside from community policing if the rates of criminalities of their respective countries are to be reduced.

References

Alemika, E. and Chukwuma, I. (eds.). 2003. *The Analysis of the Poor and Informal Policing in Nigeria*. Lagos: CLEEN Publications.

Alemika, E. O. 2007. Police reform in Africa: Issues and challenges. IDASA, Police Reform in Post-Conflict African Countries Conference. Pretoria, March 12–15, 2007. Cape Town: Institute of Criminology.

Anthony Martin v R [2001] EWCA 2245.

Braithwaite, J. 1989. The state of criminology: Theoretical decay or renaissance. *Australian & New Zealand Journal of Criminology*, 22, 129–135.

Burger, J. 2007. *Strategic Perspectives on Crime and Policing in South Africa*. Pretoria: Van Schaik Publishers.

Champion, D. J. 1993. *Dictionary of American Criminal Justice Dictionary of Terms*. Chicago, IL: Fitzroy Dearborn Publishers, p. 25.

Chukwuma, I. 2000. Police transformation in Nigeria: Problems and prospects. *Human Rights Watch*, 17(11A), 9.

Davis, R. C., Henderson, N. J., and Merrick, C. 2003. Community policing: Variations on the western model in the developing world. *Police Practice and Research: An International Journal*, 4(3), 285–300.

De Vos, A. S., Strydom, H., Fouche, C. B., and Delport, C. S. L. 2002. *Research at Grassroots: For the Social Sciences and Human Services Professions*. Pretoria: Van Schaik Publishers.

De Vries, I. D. 2008. Strategic issues in the South African Police Service (SAPS) in the first decade of democracy. *Acta Criminologica*, 21(2), 125–138.

Dixon, B. 2004. Community policing: "Cherry pie" or melktert? *Society in Transition*, 35(2), 251–272.

Eisner, E. W. 1991. *The Enlightened Eye: Qualitative Inquiry and Enhancement of Educational Practice*. New York: Macmillan.

Ekblom, P. and Wyvekens, A. 2004. *A Partnership Approach to Crime Prevention*. Strasbourg: Council of Europe Publications.

Ellison, J. 2006. Community policing: Implementation issues. The FBI Law Enforcement Bulletin. *ProQuest Social Science Journal*, 75(4), 12–16.

Erika, F. and Dammer, H. R. 2001. *Comparative Criminal Justice Systems* (2nd ed.). Belmont, CA: Wadsworth/Thomson Learning.

Ganapathy, N. 2000. Conceptualising community policing, crime prevention and criminology: A Singapore perspective. *Australian & New Zealand Journal of Criminology*, 33(3), 266–286.

Garside, R. and McMahon, W. 2006. Does criminal justice work? The "Right for the wrong reasons' debate." [Online]. Available at: http://www.crimeandsociety.org.uk [Accessed on July 20, 2010].

Golafshani, N. 2003. Understanding reliability and validity in qualitative research. *Qualitative Report*, 8(4), 597–607. [Online]. Available at: http://www.nova.edu/ssss/QR/QR8-4/golafshani.pdf [Accessed on June 13, 2010].

Goris, P. and Walters, R. 1999. Locally oriented crime prevention and "partnership approach" politics, practices and prospects. *Policing: An International Journal of Police Strategies and Management*, 22(4), 633–645.

Hagan, F. E. 2004. *Essentials of Research Methods in Criminal Justice and Criminology*. Boston, MA: Addison-Wesley.

Homel, P. 2005. A short history of crime prevention in Australia. *Canadian Journal of Criminology and Criminal Justice* (April), 47(2), 355–368.

Ibidapo-Obe, A. 2005. *A Synthesis of African Law*. Lagos: Concept Publications.

Jagwanth, S. 1994. Defining community policing in South Africa. *South African Journal of Criminal Justice*, 7, 164–176.

Kirk, J. and Miller, M. L. 1986. *Reliability and Validity in Quantitative Research*. Beverly Hills, CA: Sage Publications.

Nigeria. 1990. *Cap 359 Laws of the Federation of Nigeria*. Lagos: Government Print.

Olutola, A. A. 2011. Crime prevention and the criminal justice systems of Nigeria and South Africa: A comparative perspective. PhD Thesis (Unpublished). Tshwane University of Technology, Pretoria.

Olutola, A. A. 2012. Long term crime prevention and the criminal justice systems of Nigeria and South Africa: A hopeless hope? *Acta Criminologican*, 2012(2), 17–30.

Oppenheim, A. N. 2001. *Questionnaire Design, Interview and Attitude Measurement.* New York: Continuum.

Prudence, M., Willem, S., Leseli, M., and David, B. (eds.). 2001. *Crime and Crime Prevention on Public Transport.* Pretoria: Unisa Press.

Scharf, W. 1989. Community policing in South Africa. In *Acta Juridica.* W. Scharf (ed.). Cape Town: Juta, pp. 206–233.

Schneider, S. 2007. *Refocusing Crime Prevention.* Toronto, ON: University of Toronto Press.

Sekhonyane, M. 2002. Violent justice, vigilantism and state's response. ISS Monograph Series No. 72, Pretoria, April 2002.

Shaw, M. and Shearing, C. D. 1998. Reshaping security: An examination of the governance of security in South Africa. *African Security Review*, 7(3), 3–12.

Smith v Chief Constable Sussex Police [2008] UKHL50.

South Africa. 1996. The 1996 Constitution of South Africa (Act 108 of 1996). Pretoria: Government Printer.

Taylor, S. J. and Bogdan, R. 1998. *Introduction to Qualitative Research Methods: A Guidebook and Resource.* New York: John Wiley & Sons.

Visser, A. J. 2003. Community policing as a crime prevention strategy for Cape Town City police. Master degree dissertation (Unpublished). University of Stellenbosch, Stellenbosch.

Wengraf, T. 2001. *Qualitative Research Interviewing: Biographic Narrative and Semi-Structured Methods.* London: Sage Publications.

Winter, G. 2000. A comparative discussion of the notion of validity in qualitative and quantitative research. *The Qualitative Report*, 4(3&4). [Online]. Available at: http://www.nova.edu/ssss/QR/QR4-3/winter.html. [Accessed on August 2, 2009].

Meeting with Citizens
New Local Dimensions of Dialogue between Citizens and Police Officers

9

MARTIN HRINKO AND PETRA BINKOVA

Contents

Introduction

Throughout the Czech Republic, one may find many enthusiasts who try to adopt and implement the tenets of the community policing (CP) philosophy. Nonetheless, there are still many of those who do not want to have anything to do with it and consider CP insignificant, which is a mere declaration for which there is no space in the real world. There are few reasons for such attitude. Some critiques are convinced that CP turns police service toward an inappropriate direction. Others claim that such concept cannot find any support among "the right" people or that there are not suitable conditions within the police organizational structure for it. Each of these arguments is partly correct, as one cannot expect that conditions for such a radical change would be created instantly.

Concerning the crime-fighting potential, the police in the Czech Republic underwent similar development as the police in most West European countries. As a result of it, the Czech police now represent a specialized body that is highly competent and qualified for professional crime fighting. The situation however seems opposite when it comes to dealing with those who are not involved in or connected to any criminal activity. It even seems that it is only a matter of time before regular citizens (to whom the police promised their help and protection*) become a passive audience of a performance to which they no longer understand. It is no surprise that the citizens' response to police work happen to be rather negative, particularly when it comes to the role of the police as a protective force. Because most police units in the Czech Republic as well as abroad are very much aware of such situation, they try to look for means to change it. It seems that CP has been a way to go. Yet, it is not an easy task to define CP in one paragraph, let alone one sentence. In short, it is a philosophy or a strategy that guides the police style and management at the local level and emphasizes the establishment of police–community partnerships and a problem-solving approach that is responsive to the particular needs of the particular community. Because the problems are most often local in nature, earning from local knowledge and experience is necessary. Officers' close interaction with local communities can only happen if the community and the police form a partnership of equality. They must also learn to trust each other while realizing the fact that whatever one does will also be in the best interest of the other.

Therefore, in the following section the authors aim to explain a very new approach for the Czech police which puts the police work in the country in line with those countries where various forms of CP practicing has already been an everyday practice for some years.

Police of the Czech Republic and Community Policing

The bond between the police (or their particular units) and local citizens had existed for many years. However, during the twentieth century, the police began to distance themselves from regular people and turned their focus on criminals and their increasingly more complex offences. The success of the police was then evaluated according to the number of captured offenders and solved crimes. The police have gradually become a service organization for illegal acting individuals and an actor in a not very publicly accessible police and thief game (i.e., investigating, clarifying, questioning, convicting, conspiring, and keeping up with the newest technologies). Offenders and the police, the two specialized and trained bodies connected to crime, were dealing with each other's agenda. Common people were left aside to passively observe their game.

Although the popular motto "the police as a service to the public" indicates that police officers must be aware of who is the contracting authority of their work, it does not reflect the gradual shift of the essence of their work.

---

* To help and protect is the motto of the Czech state police.

Receptive police, in turn, only points to the fact that there is not much of a chance to improve their reputation unless the police become more open and responsive to citizens. When it comes to community police, they cannot easily cope with their ambiguous classification and understanding of the term community in the Czech Republic; therefore, it most likely refers to social (communal) work. Fortunately, in 2003 the Czech Republic introduced the European Foundation for Quality Management (EFQM) model within the Czech police.* In accordance with the EFQM model standards, both the strong and weak points of the police were defined in order to determine their new priorities.

As a result, the Czech police announced the change of the concept of their work to become a real service for the public, that is, to provide CP rather than the previous service for the state. This almost 2-year conceptual work resulted in the successful implementation of the EFQM Excellence Model in the Czech police, as well as a strong relationship with the Dutch partners who acted as advisors during that period. The year 2005 thus marks the official (re)birth of CP philosophy within the Czech police system. But this was not merely the return to the old tradition. In fact, CP has been becoming increasingly popular particularly because the police forces worldwide are becoming aware of the contradiction between what they actually do and what they should do from the point of view of the public.

What still remains the key aspect of the CP strategy is the officer's local knowledge and his/her long-term close relationship with the community. Because the ability of the police to control crime through law enforcement based exclusively on their own resources is limited, CP allows the police to develop support for law enforcement actions by consulting with communities about their needs and fears. In other words, CP recognizes community problems that require community solutions and police strategies that are designed to encourage the community to become partners in controlling and preventing crime. All these observations, however, indicate that it is almost impossible to come up with one and final definition of CP since different individuals may perceive CP strategies very differently. This does not present any problem because it is somehow expected that CP programs that are needed to implement these strategies will vary from place to place, depending on various factors, such as social conditions and the capabilities of the police. Still, there is one important element that is always present. As in many other countries, the police in the Czech Republic are aware of the fact that they can only justify their own future meaningful involvement at the local level if they keep improving a close and collaborative relationship with the local citizens. One of the sources of inspiration to succeed in this has become

---

* Being preceded by the United Kingdom and the Netherlands, the Czech Republic became the third EU country to introduce the EFQM model.

the so-called problem-oriented policing (POP). According to this model, incidents that come to the attention of the police are only symptoms of deeper problems. To become more effective, police must seek to address the underlying conditions of crime, rather than reacting to incidents on an individual basis (Goldstein 1990). Although CP and POP are different models of policing, they are not mutually exclusive and can easily coexist side by side. POP emphasizes the importance of new responses and strategies* that are preventive in nature; it does not rely exclusively on law enforcement and engages other public agencies, the community, and the private sector when their involvement has the potential for contributing to the reduction of the problem (Braga 2008). This was, in fact, a starting point of a specific local project focusing on specific local conditions piloted by the Municipal Police Headquarters in Karviná in Moravia-Silesian Region which will be described in the following section.

Meeting with Citizens

The project started in Karviná in 2008 when the Municipal Police director and the Preventive Information Service employees decided to tackle the problem between majority of denizens and minority of socially inadaptable inhabitants in one quarter of Havířov.† This could only happen with the help of CP proactive strategies and relevant prevention experiences. The conflict between the two groups was connected to the fact that socially weak citizens living in the near-by regional capital city were offered a cheaper accommodation in that particular Havířov suburb in exchange for their flats for which they could no longer afford to pay the rent.‡ This offer was thankfully accepted by these citizens who then moved to the suburb that was up to that point inhabited exclusively by the local denizens. The inherently different way of life of the newcomers (late night life, frequent noise, leaving rubbish on public places, violating traffic regulations, petty crime such as theft and robbery) soon caused conflicts with the fairly conservative denizens. The Municipal Police director then visited the Mayor of Havířov to explain him the problem and to propose him an unprecedented revolutionary way to solve the problem. The solution was the Meeting with Citizens project that was based on the principle of the CP philosophy. The Mayor readily listened to such a new concept and decided to support the

---

* POP is widely known to utilize the SARA (Scanning, Analysis, Response, and Assessment) problem-solving method.
† The town of Havířov has approximately 20,000 inhabitants.
‡ This flat exchange was a project of the owners of the flats in the regional capital who wanted to use them for commercial purposes thus needed to "relocate" the socially weak somewhere else.

project and to allow the police to use gym inside the local elementary school building for the meeting. The police thus set up a suitable date, printed flyers, redistributed them to all citizens living in that quarter, informed the local media, and organized all necessary for the meeting to happen. The working title of the first session was "Meeting with citizens or how to solve problems at the local level."

The meeting was attended by the following invited members of the police:

- *Municipal Police director* who guaranteed a transparent engagement by the police top management. In addition, he/she has an equivalent position within the Municipal Police system as the mayor of the town. His/her presence thus represents a serious and sincere interest by the state police to solve citizens' problems.
- *Head of the local police unit* who is directly responsible for all police officers working in a given location. He was therefore able to answer questions addressing very specific issues and to directly react on the criticism of police work when it came to concrete matters. Moreover, as their superior officer, he/she could also guarantee implementation of suggested solutions by local police officers.
- *Local police officer* who is the one who works in a problematic location on an everyday basis; thus, his/her presence during the meeting was crucial. He had to introduce himself/herself to all citizens who were present during the meeting in order for them to know who they could contact or speak to right at the moment when any problem occurred.
- *Traffic police officer* who had an important role during the meeting when it came to questions of safety and continuity of the traffic flow and of adjusting the traffic signs and signals in a given location.
- *Police spokesperson* who acted as a moderator because of his/her experiences in structuring, timing, and overall dynamics of the negotiation process. He/she represented a neutral party and used various techniques to open or improve dialogue between disputing parties and aimed to help the parties reach an agreement (with concrete effects) on the disputed matters.

The local government was represented by the mayor of Karviná, the head of the Municipal Police, and the head of the Housing and Accommodation Department of the Town Hall. The invited *guest* was *the owner of the houses* in the conflict location who initialized the moving of socially weak citizens to the location inhabited solely by denizens. The meeting was attended approximately by 50 local citizens from different social classes. The meeting also attracted attention of different types of media; thus, the story of the innovative face-to-face approach described earlier reached the TV screens or pages of the local and regional newspapers. The media reactions as well as the reactions of those who participated in the first meeting proved that the project was a successful attempt to begin a permanent and open dialogue and a more effective collaboration between the police, local authorities, and citizens.

Since the very first meeting in 2008, the Meeting with Citizens project kept going on, and by now the local police solve most of the local problems as successfully as when the meeting happened for the first time. The Meeting with Citizens in Karviná that happened recently in July 2011 was attended by more than 170 locals (see picture no. 2). The structure of the meetings still remains the same and the length varies depending on the type of problems to be solved and the amount of citizens and their active engagement in the discussion.* Each new Meeting with Citizens project proves that the collaboration between the police and the citizens has been markedly improving. The police are being very active to react on citizens' incentives that bring satisfaction for all involved parties and help in creating a more friendly relationship between the police and the citizens and between the citizens themselves.

Meeting with Citizens or the Czech Version of Community Policing Expands Nationally and Abroad as an Example of Best Practice

Because the police officers in Karviná wished to share their innovative practice with their colleagues in other regions, they entered the project in the national competition of the best police projects organized by the Police Presidium called The Best Practice Award 2008. The project finished on the second place. One year later, Meeting with Citizens was awarded the third position in the national round of the competition called European Crime Prevention Award (ECPA).† In 2010, the project was selected by the Ministry of the Interior experts as one of the two Czech practices to be presented at the thematic seminar called Good Practices of Community in Conflict Management which was organized by the Hungarian Presidency and the EU Crime Prevention Network (EUCPN) in Budapest. Moreover, in 2010, the police activity inspired by Meeting with Citizens became one of the four basic evaluation criteria and an example of good practice for all police units managed within the Czech Regional Police Directorates.

---

* The average length of one meeting is around 3 hours.
† ECPA is a contest that aims to reward the best European crime prevention project. The national round is organized by the Czech Ministry of the Interior and the European round by EUCPN, the main objective of which is to promote crime prevention activity in member states across the EU and to provide a means through which valuable good practice in preventing crime could mainly be shared.

In 2009 and 2010, several Czech police officers and representatives of the Prague civic association called Open Society were selected to participate in a project focusing on the implementation of the CP philosophy into the practice of the Latvian Police. One might want to ask: Why Czechs? The answer to this question became obvious to all involved during the meeting between the Czech lecturers and the Latvian organizers. By the end of the meeting, they all agreed that the Czechs and the Latvians have a lot in common with regard to history, culture, and police practice. Consequently, the planning and the actual process of the implementation of the new Czech police philosophy (which is based on the Dutch model) appeared very comprehensible to Latvian colleagues. This had not been the case a year before when the Dutch delegation had tried to do the same. Many questions of the Latvians were similar to those of the Czechs when they had been learning the Dutch model. It became clear that the Czechs and the Latvians as representatives of the former East Bloc countries had to deal with and overcome many similar problems during their history of being (again) independent countries. This was the reason why the Czech delegation was so successful in Latvia and why the police practice based on the Czech project Meeting with Citizens is possible to be successfully implemented in Latvian conditions.

Conclusion

Since 2008, the Meeting with Citizens project has gone through a 4-year period of many positive experiences, and it still successfully continues its existence in Karviná region. There are plans to implement it soon in new regions in the Czech Republic. Based on those previous experiences, the project has been, compared to the first piloted meeting in Havířov, expanded and improved. The reaction of the police on the problems is now being monitored and evaluated. Based on these evaluations, it can be concluded that in all locations where the meeting took place, the situation considerably improved, the crime rate decreased, and the public respect for the police work noticeably increased.

In general, the above-described CP practice implemented in the Meeting with Citizens project can be seen as an example of a very new approach of the Czech police, which was introduced at the local level in a specifically selected region and which was later on launched all over the country. The author tried to describe the genesis and the background of the implementation process. Although one can find similar examples in other CP-experienced countries, there are always very distinctive features that must be taken into account in every particular country, region, or community. The project thus became valuable because its authors succeeded in implementing general rules while adding distinct characteristics not only into an everyday police practice but also into the lives of many citizens in the Czech Republic.

References

Braga, A. A. (2008). *Problem-Oriented Policing and Crime Prevention*. New York: Criminal Justice Press.

Goldstein, H. (1990). *Problem-Oriented Policing*. New York: McGraw-Hill.

Community Policing in Portugal
A Long and Winding Road

10

LUÍS FIÃES FERNANDES

Contents

Introduction

The policing and the police have been under a continuous effort to find new ways to achieve the best equilibrium between preventing crime, keeping public order, and providing better police service to community. This effort is challenged by ever-shrinking resources. Such effort of scientifically based improvement began in the 1960s, and by the 1990s such movement reached its peak and new terms such as "community policing," "problem-oriented policing," "hot spot policing," "broken windows policing," and "intelligence-led policing" turned into familiar vocabulary among police officers, community leaders, local and central authorities, and made their way into the political discourses about the police and the security (Bayley and Nixon 2010; Brodeur 2010; Jones and Newburn 2006; McLaughlin 2007; Newburn 2008; Reiner 2010; Williamson 2008).

By the mid-1990s, influenced by the French policing experience and by the public demand for better police services, the political discourse of the Portuguese politicians introduced the idea of a more attentive police to the citizens' needs. The police administrators accepted the idea and, by the late 1990s, the two main police forces in Portugal had implemented programs of *policiamento de proximidade* (Costa 1996), literally meaning proximity policing, a police that is closer to the ones that are policed (essentially it is community policing with Portuguese nuances).

This chapter aims to describe the process of adoption and adaptation of the community policing philosophy and practices in Portugal, focusing on the on-going process in the Public Security Police (PSP). The chapter is divided in two parts. In the first part, I will briefly put in context the actual police system in Portugal. In the second part, I will describe the current ongoing policing restructuring in the PSP.

The Portugal Policing Context: A Short Overview

From an historical perspective, the centralized police and the monopolization of the policing by the state are a recent phenomena in Europe. In Portugal, we can trace back the first proto-police to the fourteenth century.

In the twilight of the twelfth century, after a long period of war, Portugal became an independent kingdom. From 1211 on, with the consolidation of the king's power a reformation period started. According to the Portuguese medieval law, the king concentrated on all powers, but, sometimes, the king decentralized some of his power to the municipalities, namely, in matters concerning the security of the local community (Santos 1999).

In order to keep the security of the communities, King Dinis (1261–1325) appointed in every municipality an *Alcaide* [a word derived from the barbarian latin *Pretor* (Araújo 1853, 134), the captain of the castle, in a free translation]. The *Alcaide* was in charge of the castle and was responsible for the defense of the community (Ramos, Sousa, and Monteiro 2010, 47–77) as well as charged with ensuring the order maintenance and the administration of justice (Caetano 1981). Their responsibilities were to prevent crime and personal vendettas, keep the public peace, and uphold the law within the limits of the municipality.

Later, King Fernando (the first) created, in 1383, the first corps of *quadrilheiros** (literally someone that is part of a group of four) which comprised 20 citizens armed with a wooden pole with the mission to keep the peace in the city of Lisbon. The men were appointed by the municipality for 3 years, and can be considered the first Portuguese police officers. The *quadrilheiros* can now be considered the root of the Portuguese proto-police system.

Throughout the centuries, the jurisdiction over the police switched from local to central (in the twentieth century) and several police services were created. After 1974, the democratization of the State and its increased

---

* The *Quadrilheiros* patrolled the streets in groups of four and their mission was to guarantee the security of the area under their responsibility by keeping the public peace, preventing crimes, watch over vagrants and foreigners and inspecting the brothels and gambling houses (Cosme 2006, 29–31).

legitimacy* contributed partly for the enlargement of policing to new social sectors. The individuals' security and personal feelings of insecurity became the center of the police activity.

In order to fully understand the development of the proximity policing in Portugal, one has to understand how the main players in the police system interact and their jurisdictions, and have in mind that the Portuguese police system has a Napoleonic matrix. The Portuguese police system is substantially different from that of the British and can be described, in a nutshell, as fragmented (there are, at least, four main national police services), concurrent (some police services share the same legal jurisdictions), centralized command, and operational decentralization (each service has one national command/direction and several local branches, with varying levels of decentralization). The four main police agencies[†] are as follows:

1. The Gendarmerie (Guarda Nacional Republicana) is the largest police force under the Ministry of Internal Affairs with a strong territorial implantation in rural areas. This police force consists of military personnel under a double jurisdiction: of the Ministry of the Internal Affairs for policing matters (in peace time); and of the Ministry of the National Defense in case of war or crisis, and also for the purpose of standardization of the military doctrine, armament and equipment. Its main missions are public order, environmental protection, and civil protection.
2. The PSP (Polícia de Segurança Pública) is the second largest police body. It is a civilian police force under the Ministry of Internal Affairs with the territorial jurisdiction over the main urban centers. Its main missions are public order, criminal investigation, VIP protection, licensing and control of weapons and explosives, and private security regulation.
3. The Judiciary Police (Polícia Judiciária) is a criminal police service under the Ministry of Justice. Its main mission is to investigate serious and organized crimes.
4. The Immigration and Borders Service (Serviço de Estrangeiros e Fronteiras) is a security service under the Ministry of Internal Affairs. Its main missions include immigration and border control.

---

* This statement is made having in mind that Portugal went through a dictatorship for 40 years, ending in 1974 with the 25th of April revolution. Another important point to have in mind is that the dictatorship was protected by the political police that tried to neutralize every political dissidence.
† In Portugal, the current ratio police/100.000 inhabitants is around 466. The source used to determine the ratio was Eurostat (only 2009 data was available). According to the source, Portugal had 49.152 police officers (this number only comprises data from the GNR, PSP, PJ, and SEF).

The police system also comprises the Maritime Police* (Polícia Marítíma) and the Municipal Police, which is under the mayor (currently only about 33 municipalities have such a police service) and has jurisdiction within the boundaries of the municipality. Its main missions are to enforce general municipal laws, building and environmental laws, and traffic regulations.

The description allows to understand the difficult context of the proximity policing implementation. Such difficulty is generated inside the police system as its complexity, with several police bodies and the inevitable superimposition of jurisdictions, tends to be ungovernable (Teixeira, Lourenço, and Piçarra 2006, 109–120).

Portuguese-Style Community Policing

In the first years after the 1974 revolution, economy, inflation, unemployment, and the development of basic public services were the main priorities of the governments. The police system waited almost 10 years before major changes arrived. Increasing crime rates, mounting insecurity, shrinking public resources, and an ever-great demand from the public for more security led the government, during the 1990s, to make crime prevention and the policing reform a priority.

The main problem faced by the police was that old solutions no longer worked, and the new demands for service could not be met through traditional policing based on random police patrols and the idea of police omnipresence. Experience and common sense that long guided police administrators no longer prove effective.

The particular conditions of the Portuguese society might also explain why it took so long to adopt the community policing philosophy and principles:

- For 40 years, the police was used by the dictatorship as an instrument of population control. This led many people to distrust police and avoid any voluntary contact with its officers. The consequences were, and sometimes still are, a systematic lack of willingness of the citizens to get involved and support community initiatives conducted by the police.
- The I&D, as defined by Sherman (1998), were almost nonexistent in the Portuguese police system as most of the senior police officers thought that "police" (research about the organization and practices) was an exclusive domain of the police (officers), closed to the *academia*.
- The management style, essentially based in the idea of "budget administration," resisted to be replaced by a management style based on objective achieving and assessment of results.

---

* A police force under de Ministry of Defense. Its main missions are to enforce the laws and regulations in the area of maritime jurisdiction.

- Lastly, on the positive side, in the decades following the April revolution, the Portuguese society underwent fast and deep changes, coming closer to the European standards of living (Barreto 2002).

It was within this less than friendly environment that around 1995 the policing reform truly took off, with a set of stated objectives: to improve the relationship between the police and the public, and to reinforce the crime prevention and victims' protection. The police rhetoric (mainly by senior police officers) was one of the main obstacles to the transformation of the traditional policing. Proximity policing was thought as a kind of low-level policing that police officers would do when not responding to calls for service. At the same time, some police administrators also thought that proximity policing could be implemented with just a few minor organizational and training adjustments. Therefore, things that had to be changed in order for the reform to truly take place had their importance underestimated, or were systematically postponed.

The main problems were not about technical skills, training, or structural adjustments, but about culture and attitudes within the police. For most of the rest of the decade, proximity policing was more of a sound bite used by politician and police administrators than a real everyday practice.

In spite of such resistance, several policing programs directed toward schools, elderly, and victims were implemented. These programs were tailored to meet the special needs of different publics and were implemented through a series of different actions (such as school visits by police officers to speak about crime prevention, awareness programs against violence and drugs, and elderly assistance actions aiming to raise awareness about certain types of crime). These programs had a positive feedback from the public, but lacked a coherent structuring and were very dependent on the willingness and voluntarism of the individual commanding officers. Such personalization on the commanding officer had a major drawback: when a commander left (to another unit or position), most of the programs tended to be phase out. Furthermore, the programs also lacked evaluation by an independent body. These problems affected not only the PSP but also the Gendarmerie.

The Integrated Proximity Policing Program

The state of affairs described led the PSP, in the last quarter of 2006, to launch a pilot project called *Programa Integrado de Policiamento de Proximidade* [Integrated Proximity Policing Program (I3P)].* This program was a response to the necessity of managing strategically all the special policing programs that PSP had deployed throughout the past decade and reinforcing crime

---

* Find the official site at http://www.psp.pt/pages/programasespeciais/pipp.aspx?menu=1

prevention. The program departs from the evidence that the effects of policing on crime are complex (Sherman 1998), and only holistic solutions can solve crime problems and increase the feelings of security in the communities.

The I3P represented an effort to approximate (hence the use of the term "proximity policing") the police to the citizens. At the same time, the I3P aimed to provide adequate policing to the local security conditions, drawing on local resources through partnerships with other public and private bodies. The base assumption is that crime prevention only works with the contribution of a wide network of various institutions (Sherman et al. 1997).

The program was centered on the following four main objectives:

1. To increase the accessibility and proximity of the police to the citizens and to make policing available in the places where people naturally converge (transportation interfaces, shopping streets, entertainment places, etc.)
2. To strength police visibility and model patrolling tactics to local security conditions [using the right patrolling techniques (foot, bicycle, auto patrol, or a combination) and the right resources (rapid reaction teams, K9 teams, etc.] and to the needs of the people in a given location
3. To increase crime prevention potential through an efficient management of the available resources
4. To implement better working conditions for police officers, with better installations and policing equipment

Before expanding the proximity policing to all police stations, an assessment by an independent body was performed. The assessment used a population survey, which was done in two moments: during the initial I3P pilot deployment in 18 territorial police stations in 2006 and one year after deployment. The survey was performed by a research team from SociNova/CesNova (Human and Social Sciences Faculty of the Nova University of Lisbon) and aimed to (Lisboa and Dias 2008, 7)

- Understand how citizens interacted with the police and to what extent were they receptive to new strategies of policing
- Assess the program's impact on the fear of crime
- Assess how police officers assigned to pilot units relate to the population and the police organic structure

The survey concluded (Lisboa and Dias 2008, 7–11) that the respondents reported higher levels of feelings of security toward the city and the neighborhood where respondents lived or worked. The respondents that experienced fear of crime related that feeling with rumors mainly originated in the media.

Although crime rates in the pilot locations had not increased during the period and no significant increase in the victimization reported, an increase in awareness about the crime problems was noticed. The respondents also reveal very positive perceptions toward the police and the service provided. The policing was seen as important or very important for most respondents. Improvements in the knowledge of existing crime prevention programs were also noticed.

The police officers reported a good organizational climate and an increasing job satisfaction. The increasing membership by the police officers in local cultural or sporting associations revealed a greater community involvement. A decrease in the reporting of resource scarcity and lack of working conditions and training could also be observed. An enhanced knowledge of area residents and increased daily contacts were also noted. The police officers seem to value the proximity and the good relations they have with the population as well as with other community service.

The I3P full implementation comprised four phases:

1. The first phase was the strategic conception of the program, which involved brainstorming with practitioners and meetings with police managers and other stakeholders. After that, a strategic plan was prepared and approved by the police national director.
2. The second phase involved the training of the police officers who would be involved in the pilot projects.
3. The third phase was the assessment of the pilot projects. This assessment was done by an independent body (as we have seen).
4. The final phase was the full national deployment of the I3P.*

Portugal only relies on fully sworn police officers to deploy proximity policing within the community. The I3P is anchored at the local police stations that are the frontline police units responsible for providing the security services that the public relies on. These local units are commanded by *subcomissários* (lieutenants) who are the local program managers responsible for the coordination of the project within their area of responsibility. The local program managers are also responsible for the appointment of the local program supervisors and the proximity police officers.

The local program supervisors (up to the rank of sergeant) are responsible for the monitoring, guidance, and supervision of the different proximity teams and for the contacts between the police and the different stakeholders. The partnerships are a very important factor for the success of the I3P and may be established with various actors [central or local state agencies, nongovernmental

---

* At the time this chapter was written, these two last phases had not been implemented yet.

organization (NGO), etc.] in order to form a network of agencies capable of addressing to a problem from different angles and finding holistic solutions.

The core of the program are the teams of proximity police officers who were subjected to a special training before being deployed to the field. Their primary missions are foot patrol, the management and solving of low-level incidents, and the spotting of situations that have the potential of turning into criminal situations in the future. The proximity teams also liaise with local authorities and partner organizations in their territorial area of responsibility.

In spite of the weak effects such a policing strategy have on crime (Weisburd and Eck 2004, 52), it is important as a reassurance factor to risk groups (acting upon risk perception) as fear of crime is something that affects not only crime victims but also the individuals who think that they are at risk (Zedner 1997, 587). The proximity policing officers are teamed up according to certain roles/clients:

- *Proximity and victim support teams.* Their main mission is the policing of a certain sector within the jurisdiction of a police station. These teams direct their activities to the reassurance of older people in their residential areas, prevent domestic violence, support crime victims, and follow up *post facto* victimization* as well as identify problems that have the potential to degrade the feelings of security.
- *Safe school teams.* These teams are responsible for the safety and surveillance around schools, juvenile delinquency prevention, and identification of problems that have the potential to degrade the feelings of security within the school communities (students, teachers, parents).

Apart from these teams, the global policing strategy maintains and reinforces the coordination of these teams with the general policing activities such as criminal investigation, public order, and emergency dispatch through a constant intelligence flow.

Conclusions

Since the 1990s, there has been an increasing change in the ideas, culture, and practices within the PSP, materialized in the implementation of the I3P. The I3P can be seen, within the Portuguese context, as proximity policing of second generation: strategically planned, holistic approach to problems, flexible

---

* These objectives are in line with the conclusion expressed in the study carried out on the initiative of the European Crime Prevention Network (2004). *A review of scientifically evaluated good practices for reducing feelings of insecurity or fear of crime in the EU Member States*: European Communities.

and tailored to the local security needs of the community, and embracing part of the distinctive attributes of the community policing—proximity teams, empowerment, local tailor-made solutions, and wide network of partners.

Never before in the history of human kind did we, individually and as a society, achieve such high levels of security (in a wide sense). As policing is becoming increasingly pluralized in Portugal—as a large array of the central police and the municipal police along private security are engaged in the regulation and provision of security—it remains to be seen if the police system will be able to keep pace in the future with ever-increasing demands by the public for better service and ever-increasing budget cuts.

References

Araújo, A. H. de C. e. (1853). *História de Portugal* (Vol. Tomo IV). Lisboa: Viuva Bertrand e Filhos.

Barreto, A. (2002). *Tempo de Incerteza*. Lisboa: Relógio D'Água.

Bayley, D. H., and Nixon, C. (2010). The changing environment for policing, 1985–2008 (Executive session on policing and public safety). In *New Perspectives in Policing* (p. 16). Washington, DC: National Institute of Justice and Harvard Kennedy School.

Brodeur, J.-P. (2010). *The Policing Web*. New York: Oxford University Press.

Caetano, M. (1981). *História do Direito Português* (Vol. I). Lisboa: Editorial Verbo.

Cosme, J. (2006). *História da Polícia de Segurança Pública. Das Origens à Actualidade.* Lisboa: Edições Silabo.

Costa, A. (1996). *Para a modernização da actividade policial*. Lisboa: Ministério da Administração Interna.

Jones, T., and Newburn, T. (Eds.). (2006). Understanding plural policing. In *Plural Policing: A Comparative Perspective* (pp. 1–11). New York: Routledge.

Lisboa, M., and Dias, A. L. T. (2008). Organizações e Meio Envolvente: o Caso do "Policiamento de Proximidade." *Mundos Sociais: Saberes e Práticas*, Trabalho, Profissões e Organizações (p. 13). Presented at the VI Congresso Português de Sociologia, June 26, Lisboa, UNL/FCSH.

McLaughlin, E. (2007). *The New Policing*. London: Sage Publications.

Newburn, T. (Ed.). (2008). *Handbook of Policing* (Second ed.). Devon: Willan Publishing.

Ramos, R., Sousa, B. V. e, and Monteiro, N. G. (2010). *História de Portugal* (4.ª Edição.). Lisboa: A Esfera dos Livros.

Reiner, R. (2010). *The Politics of the Police* (Fourth ed.). Oxford: Oxford University Press.

Santos, A. P. R. dos. (1999). *O Estado e a Ordem Pública. As Instituições Militares Portuguesas*. Lisboa: Instituto Superior de Ciências Sociais e Políticas.

Sherman, L. W. (1998). *Evidence-Based Policing* (p. 15). Washington, DC: US Department of Justice, Police Foundation and Office of Community Oriented Policing Services.

Sherman, L. W., Gottfredson, D., MacKenzie, D., Eck, J., Reuter, P., and Bushway, S. (1997). *Preventing Crime: What Works, What Doesn't, What's Promising*. Washington, DC: National Institute of Justice.

Teixeira, N. S., Lourenço, N., and Piçarra, N. (2006). *Estudo para a Reforma do Modelo de Organização do Sistema de Segurança Interna. Relatório Preliminar.* Lisboa: Instituto Português de Relações Internacionais.

Weisburd, D., and Eck, J. E. (2004). What can police do to reduce crime, disorder, and fear? *The Annals of the American Academy of Political and Social Science, 593*(1), 42–65.

Williamson, T. (Ed.). (2008). *The Handbook of Knowledge-Based Policing. Current Conceptions and Future Directions.* Chichester: John Wiley & Sons Ltd.

Zedner, L. (1997). Victims. In M. Maguire, R. Morgan, and R. Reiner (Eds.), *The Oxford Handbook of Criminology* (Second ed., pp. 597–612). Oxford: Clarendon Press.

The Evolving Nature of Police Training and Personnel Management

III

Authoritative Language in Police Training

11

Style in Police Students' Memoranda

SOFIA A. ASK

Contents

Introduction

As part of an overarching Swedish project entitled "Texts with importance—Writing in education and professional practice," researchers at Linnaeus University are studying writing in the exercise of authority as it is performed in education and occupational life in three professions: police, teachers, and social workers. The term "exercise of authority" (in Swedish *myndighetsutövning*) means that decisions or measures are taken which express the power of the state to decide about some matter in relation to the citizens. Authority can be exercised both orally and in writing.

The exercise of authority by these professions is regulated in Sweden's basic law, administrative law, the Police Act, the Social Services Act, and the School Ordinance, and it is an important element in a well-functioning democracy. It can be crucial for the individual that authority is exercised in the correct way, since it affects the individual's life.

From a linguistic perspective, the exercise of authority in texts can concern, among other things, comprehensibility. One aspect of comprehensibility is the question of the stylistic level in formal texts; a register that is far too forced and bombastic does not further comprehensibility, and a tone that is too sloppy and informal can make the text seem less credible and thus less legally secure. This study considers how police students at Sweden's three police training colleges, in the texts they write as exercises, approach the writing practice of serving police officers and how they learn to balance the requirements of formal and comprehensible style in their written reporting.

Different Practices for Written Language

Nowadays, writing is a natural part of almost all professions and hence in most forms of professional training. Research has been done on the writing cultures of different professions (Anson and Forsberg 1990; Dias and Paré 2000; Freedman and Adam 2000), and there are empirical studies of how training is related and adapted to different professional writing cultures (Ask and Byrman 2009, 2010; Augsburger 1998; Ivanič 1998; Parks 2001; Schneider and Andre 2005).

Research on the significance of context for the individual's linguistic action can be found, for instance, in Freedman (1987), who has examined how law students enter the language worlds by which they are surrounded during their training. Similar studies in a Swedish context have been conducted by Blåsjö (2004) and Blückert (2010), who have studied how university students learn the typical text norms, specific genres, and technical language of their subject.

Being socialized into a professional language is a time-consuming process that depends on the context of the profession, as well as the content and practice of the training. Language and communication skills in speech and writing are important instruments in the work of the Swedish police, and students are therefore expected to develop a professionally sustainable writing competence during their training. How students in training programs that are heavily oriented to a professional career are socialized into a written discourse has not been studied much in Swedish research. My study as part of the project "Texts with importance" is, therefore, about police students' texts and how they are related to the professional discourse, and in this chapter I present some of the results that have been obtained.

Interim Texts in Swedish Police Training

Police training differs from other Swedish forms of professional training as regards the scientific focus, the length of training, and the orientation toward a future professional identity. It is not an academic program today, but it contains written elements and courses that require competence in academic writing and skills in the police discourse. Police training in Sweden is about to be reformed in a more academic direction, and the ability to write in a professionally oriented setting will therefore be valuable and in great demand.

The target language that the police students seek to learn can be found in texts written by their teachers and by serving police officers, and from these different texts, students who are less familiar with writing can acquire patterns and norms for their own writing. The student text as a genre can thus be regarded as an interim-language variant of professional police texts. Since the students derive patterns from authentic police texts, their texts will come close to the professional discourse on different levels, but they also contain traces of the teaching context and the specific conditions that affect writing in police training. If the ideal and the goal for the students' writing is the professional text—which need not always be the case in a training program that also includes other writing tasks than those strictly geared to professional practice—examining how close to or distant from that norm a student text is can be a possible measure of writing development in the textual worlds of professional training.

The texts produced during training are heterogeneous. Text norms or voices (Wertsch 1991) that are not associated with the profession stand out in the students' texts, which are both natural and expected. The texts that are produced can, of course, contain many types of heterogeneous elements. I use the term interim texts to describe the heterogeneity. This term is inspired by research on second-language learning, where it is customary to talk of interim language and target language (Kotsinas 1985). The target language is the language the learners are trying to acquire, while the interim languages are the varieties that the learners use on their way toward the target language. Interim language refers to all the levels and types of language mastery that exist in the span from knowing nothing at all to being fully fluent in the language.

Texts in a Police Investigation

The material assembled during a police investigation includes many different texts dealing with different aspects of the events that led to a crime being reported and a judicial process being started. In Swedish investigations, the three main types of text are the report (*anmälan*), the interview (*förhör*), and the memorandum (*avrapporterings-PM*).

The initial report that is filed can be described as the hub of the investigation. It is short and concise, giving information about the offence, the place, the time, and the people involved. The interview texts and memoranda elaborate on the narrative of what happened, although from different perspectives and in different ways. Other texts that occur are certificates from medical examiners, event reports, pictures, copies of diaries, notes, lists of seizures, memoranda to social authorities, decisions to take a person into custody in accordance with the laws on care, and so on.

Swedish police have to abide by *the objectivity principle*, which means that they must always be objective in reporting events and actions in their exercise of authority. In the memoranda written for an investigation, however, police officers can describe the experiences and emotions occasioned by taking part in an intervention. The writing police officers are free to write their memoranda as they themselves have perceived the events, that is, their own contribution, the behavior of the people involved, the setting, and the chronological development; they can include their narrative about this in the police discourse.

A patrol normally consists of two officers, and sometimes both of them write their own account of what they experienced at the scene of the intervention. This means that there are often two individually written texts describing what happened at the scene of the offence. Memoranda are particularly important judicial texts in the Swedish legal system because they are used as evidence when police officers are called as witnesses in trials.

Materials and Methods

In this study, I analyzed 50 Swedish police students' memoranda with the focus on how they conform to some of the guidelines for police writing. As regards style, the Swedish National Police Board has the following recommendations:

> Be alert to internal jargon. In formal texts it should be avoided or explained. If you must use technical terms for the sake of precision, you should explain them. [...] Avoid fashionable and slangy expressions. They attract unnecessary attention. (Swedish National Police Board 2007, 13)

Based on these guidelines, I analyze the memoranda texts here with regard to style. In my analysis, I proceed from the above recommendation concerning style in police texts, and the two categories that crystallize are *internal jargon and technical terms* and *fashionable and slangy expressions*. Through a close-up reading of the texts, I analyze how the training discourse relates to an envisaged professional discourse as regards stylistic register. My research question is: How does the style in the students' memoranda relate to the official guidelines for writing issued by the National Police Board?

It should be pointed out here that there are problems that I encounter as a layperson in a writing practice like this which I find unknown and inaccessible. In cases where I have been uncertain about my interpretations, I have consulted serving police officers and teachers in the police training program in order to better understand and correctly describe the professional discourse of which I have no firsthand knowledge.

Context: Police Students in Exercises and Text Production

The students whose texts constitute the material for this study are close to the end of their training (semester 4 of a total 5) and doing an exercise about domestic violence. They go through realistic practical exercises before they write the relevant texts. The process can be summed up as follows: A fictitious crime has been committed in an apartment used for exercises, and two of the police students receive a call telling them to go to the scene. There they meet actors who play the parts of the suspect and the plaintiff, and the police students perform an investigation at the scene and question the people. The way the police students perceive the events and the measures and decisions they take affect how much information they can obtain from the parties, and also the actual charge that may be brought. The charge in this case varies between assault and gross violation of a woman's integrity. After the exercise is over, the students write the texts that Swedish law requires in police matters concerning assault and violation of a woman's integrity. To assist them, the students have two computer systems used by the Swedish police: RAR (*Rationell Anmälningsrutin*, "Rational Report Routine") and DurTvå (*Datoriserad utredningsrutin tvångsmedel*, "Computerized Investigation Routine for Coercive Measures"). These are two digitally based tools that help the police in different ways to produce uniform, searchable, and checkable documents that are used by prosecutors, social authorities, and other stakeholders. They are thus authentic computer systems which the students will also use in their future professional life.

Be Alert to Internal Jargon and Technical Terms

The proximity to legal language and police practice means that the students' texts contain context-bound words that would really need to be explained to outside readers and laypeople. The students' texts are always created in an examination situation and that they want to show off their knowledge of sections of the law, police tactics, and investigation routines, and therefore forget their readers. Examples of context-bound words and expressions in the material are as follows:

1. *Husrannsakan i fara i dröjsmål* (search of premises due to risk of delay)
2. *Kollusionsfara* (risk of tampering with evidence)
3. *Målsägandebiträde* (assistant to the injured party)
4. *Skulle vi ha skrivit en SoL14:1§* (we should have written the Social Services Act 14:1§)
5. *En pl19 visitation genomfördes* (a pl19 search was carried out)
6. *Därefter informerade PaNN om fuk13 a–d och 14§§ för Charlotte* (PaNN then informed Charlotte about fuk13 a–d and 14§§)*

For the students, the exercise was not chiefly about writing a tenable text, but showing that they could act in the correct police manner and guarantee legal security in the given situation. The texts therefore show traces of the students' desire to display their knowledge to their teachers, who are the main recipients of the texts during the training period. These traces include references to sections of the law or technical terms that are self-explanatory in a legal context, not wholly transparent to the reader.

Avoid Fashionable and Slangy Expressions

In its directives, the National Police Board (*Rikspolisstyrelsen*) gives no examples of what could be regarded as fashionable and slangy expressions, saying only that such expressions "attract unnecessary attention" (National Police Board 2007, 13). The fundamental thing is that the police texts require a formal style that is appropriate for the exercise of authority. Police reports can become public documents at a later stage. In the analysis below, I show how students especially deviate from the public style when the cases concern violence and confrontation, and then they choose words and expressions that come close to fashionable and slangy expressions.

---

* *Search of premises due to risk of delay* means that the police can search a place without a warrant from a prosecutor in emergency situations where it is impossible to wait. *Risk of tampering with evidence* refers to the possibility that a suspect could sabotage an investigation by trying to get people to change their stories or by hiding or destroying evidence. *Assistant to the injured party* is the term for the counsel who assists the injured party. Writing a *SoL14:1§* means filing a report with the social services about a child who is in any kind of trouble. According to Section 19 of the Police Act an officer can search people who have been apprehended, which is what is meant by the phrase "a pl19 search was carried out." *Fuk13 a–d and 14§§* are the sections in the Investigation Ordinance which state that the police must inform crime victims of their rights.

It seems to be particularly difficult to achieve the right register for words to do with violence or the use of force in physical confrontations. When there is some kind of violent activity at the scene—whether by the police or by someone else—and the students have to describe it, they use words and phrases which show that they are uncertain about what is acceptable in the professional discourse. Clear descriptions of physical measures taken by the police are very important from the judicial point of view since the description of the events can determine whether a police officer who is accused of using excess force has acted within the law and used exactly the right degree of force required by the situation, and no more. It is hard for a police student to decide which words are stylistically and judicially expected in a public discourse. Can one write *vevar mot mig* ("takes a swing at me"), and is *stökig* ("rowdy") too weak a word when someone violently resists the police in their intervention? In the material, there are examples of words that can be said to stick out in a public discourse since they can be perceived as toning down what happened, as in the use of *stök* ("mess, rowdiness") or *bråk* ("noise, disorder, quarrelling") about violence, or the expressions may seem positively charged, such as *liv* or *livat* ("high life") in texts about gross violation of a woman's integrity.

Different forms of *bråk* and the associated verb *bråka* are by far the most frequent words in the students' descriptions of violence and confrontation:

1. *Bråk i lägenheten* (quarrelling in the flat)
2. *Bråkigt på platsen* (disorderly at the scene)
3. *Det har varit bråkigt i lägenheten* (it has been disorderly in the flat)
4. *Inget tydde på våld eller bråk* (there was nothing to suggest violence or quarrelling)
5. *Det har säkerligen varit bråk* (there has no doubt been quarrelling)
6. *Grannen har hört bråk* (the neighbor has heard quarrelling)
7. *Bråk och kvinnoskrik* (quarrelling and women's screams)
8. *Tecken på bråk* (signs of quarrelling)
9. *Lägenhetsbråk* (literally "apartment quarrelling")
10. *Skrik och bråk* (shouting and quarrelling)

The word *bråk* could be interpreted as what *Rikspolisstyrelsen* means by a word that does not "attract attention" and therefore works well in the context.

Forms of the verb *stöka* and the adjective *stökig* are the next most common ways to describe violent acts in the students' texts:

1. *Någon har ringt oss ang att det varit stökigt i lägenheten* (someone has phoned us to say that it has been rowdy in the flat)
2. *Vi fått ett samtal om att det har varit stökigt på platsen* (we received a call about how it had been rowdy at the scene)

3. *Vi fått ett samtal om att det varit stökigt i lägenheten* (we received a call saying that it had been rowdy in the flat)
4. *For att hjälpa [NN] med mannen som är stökig* (to help [name removed] with the man who is rowdy)
5. *Han började stöka lite* (he began to get a bit rowdy)
6. *Det varit stök på adressen* (there had been bother at the address)

Stökigt can be perceived as slightly milder than *bråkigt* and can therefore be said to risk trivializing what happened. *Liv* ("life" in the sense of "commotion") and the associated adjective *livat* that can mean "rowdy" but also "lively" and "merry" are also common expressions in the texts when the students seek to convey the idea that there has been violence or confrontation:

1. *Det var liv inne hos grannen* (there was high life in the neighbor's)
2. *Det blev liv ute i vardagsrummet* (it got rowdy out in the living room)
3. *Det varit livat i den aktuella lägenheten* (it had been rowdy in this particular flat)
4. *En person som ringt in och berättat att det har varit "livat" på platsen* (a person who called to say that there had been "high life" at the scene)

Stök and *livat* are colloquial and to some extent euphemistic descriptions of what in these cases is gross violation of a woman's integrity. The word *livat* is a particularly infelicitous choice since it suggests that something positive has happened. In one case, however (example 4), it is enclosed in quotation marks, which hints that the student felt that the word was perhaps not such a good choice and wished to indicate this in the text. Through "scare quotes," one can distance oneself from what is written and therefore signal irony or repudiation. It is also possible, of course, that *livat* is a direct quotation from some of the people involved, but quotations and statements are found mostly in interview texts and less frequently in memoranda. It is more likely that the quotation marks indicate the writer's stylistic uncertainty about the word.

When the police students have to describe their own physical actions, the words chosen tend to be down to earth and vague:

1. *Kollegan och mannen bråkar* (my colleague and the man quarrel)
2. *Jag och min kollega får gripa tag i Bengt-Göran för att lugna ner honom* (My colleague and I have to grab hold of Bengt-Göran to calm him down)
3. *Vi tog tag i honom för att få ut honom i köket* (We took hold of him to get him out of the kitchen)
4. *Efter visst tumult får vi på handfängsel på honom* (After a certain tumult, we got the handcuffs on him)

5. *Patrullen får dock använda milt våld och dra upp dörren* (However, the patrol had to use mild force and pull the door open)
6. *Vi får senare gemensamt med milt våld fösa ut Sven i korridoren* (We later had to use mild force together to push Sven out into the corridor)

When the police students describe their own physical action, they tone it down and make little of it. The meaning of "my colleague and the man quarrel" has nothing to do with quarrelling, if by that one means that two people are angry with each other and want to hit each other; it is a matter of a policeman trying to control a suspect in a violent confrontation. To "grab hold" or "take hold" of someone is a more neutral way of describing the same thing. Another vague wording is the phrase "mild force," which is also subject to interpretation. How mild is "mild force"? Who decides what "mild force" is? A similar vagueness can be found in the description "after a certain tumult we got the handcuffs on him," a phrase that could cause problems in a judicial process. "A certain tumult" can in practice be anything from vigorous, unexpected movements to physical assault.

When it comes to the violent behavior of the suspect, the words and expressions are less vague than when the police officers' own actions are described. At the same time, they can be perceived as slightly more colloquial. Quotation marks signal the writer's uncertainty about whether the word really is appropriate for the context, or could possibly be interpreted as a way to distance oneself.

1. *I samband med detta så brusade Bengt-Göran upp* (In connection with this, Bengt-Göran flared up)
2. *Han börjar veva mot mig* (He began to swing at me)
3. *Han "tänder" dock till* (He "blazed" up, however)
4. *Då "flyger" Bengt-Göran upp från stolen och går snabbt mot dörren* (Then Bengt-Göran "flew" up from the chair and went quickly toward the door)

The more concrete quality of the description of the suspect's violence may have to do with the fact that this violence justified the police intervention. It is thus important to be clear in the description of the aggressive acts of the suspect so that the coercive measures taken are justified and documented. It is the actions of the parties that provide the *constituent elements* that are present if an offence is to be considered to have been committed, and it is through documentation of these elements that a prosecutor can later initiate legal proceedings. Texts with many quotation marks around words that are not actual quotations are problematic, since they are imprecise and semantically vague.

Interim Language in Professional Training

The police students are, of course, students and thus have limited knowledge of writing in professional life, but they show in their memoranda how they try to achieve a formal, acceptable, and comprehensible register. As a whole their memoranda function in formal terms, but the style sometimes becomes colloquial. This kind of language is admittedly comprehensible, but it can affect the credibility and legal security of the texts. The students' interim language is heterogeneous, distant to varying degrees from the norms that exist for police writing. They sometimes lack the words and expressions that belong to official discourse, and then they take expressions from the internal jargon that they have become acquainted with during their training. The uncertainty in formulation occurs because the students need models of writing from which they can learn which words to use to document difficult confrontations involving the use of force by themselves and others. It is also judicially important: Police officers are sometimes reported for using excess force, and the descriptions of force can be an important source for the outcome of such cases.

The use of context-bound technical terms and fashionable or slangy expressions indicates uncertainty in relation to a target text that exists in the practice that the students aspire to gain access to. The fact that the writing situation is also part of an examination where things other than the actual writing are assessed no doubt influences how much effort the police students expend on choosing words and formulations. Writing exercises also means that the text will not be appraised by a prosecutor, which surely also affects the student's analysis of the receiver. At different places in the material, I can also see how the students make the fiction in the writing situation visible by stating explicitly in the texts that it is an exercise:

1. *Vårt fall avbröts då* (our case was then discontinued)
2. *Av tekniska skäl som hade med övningen att göra* (for technical reasons to do with the exercise)
3. *Vi skulle just gripa Roger när övningen avbröts* (we were about to apprehend Roger when the exercise was stopped)

Conclusion

The analysis shows that the police context was very important for the students, which means that the writing takes second place, even though these texts in professional practice can be crucial for whether a prosecutor will be able to initiate proceedings for an offence that has been committed.

All in all, the stylistic uncertainty the students sometimes display in relation to the guidelines issued by the Swedish National Police Board is due to the context in which they are writing. It is reasonable to assume that the students have had varying amounts of teaching in how to write their reports and how to find words for actions and events involving mental and physical violence. But police students need to acquire knowledge about what the descriptions of their own use of force can result in, and be aware that their memoranda may possibly be used in evidence. Texts in professional life must be stylistically acceptable, comprehensible to the receivers, and above all judicially tenable. Which register—everyday or more formal—is most comprehensible and simultaneously guarantees legal security is a question that remains. What is certain is that the police students' writing is an important field to continue researching. It might not be possible to find a solution for the exact written representation of everything the police see, hear, and do when violent events happen. But if those responsible for police training actively teach using good models from professional texts, the students may perhaps find modes of expression and stylistic levels that do not draw attention to themselves in the formal texts on which the exercise of their profession is based.

References

Anson, C., and Forsberg, L. (1990). Moving beyond the academic community: Transitional stages in professional writing. *Written Communication, 7,* 200–231.

Ask, S., and Byrman, G. (2009). Perspektiv och processverb i polisstudenters avrapportering. *Humanetten,* 24, 2–12.

Ask, S., and Byrman, G. (2010). Så slog han Anna med ett okänt antal knytnävslag i ansiktet: Reliefanalys av polisstudenters och polisers skrivande. In J. Smidt, I. Folvord, and A. Aasen (Eds.), *Rammer for skriving: Om skriveutvikling i skole og yrkesliv* (pp. 125–139). Trondheim: Tapir akademisk forlag.

Augsburger, D. (1998). Teacher as writer: Remembering the agony, sharing the ecstasy. *Journal of Adolescent & Adult Literacy,* 41, 548–562.

Blåsjö, M. (2004). *Studenters skrivande i två kunskapsbyggande miljöer.* Stockholm Studies in Scandinavian Philology, New Series, 37. Stockholm: Acta Universitatis Stockholmiensis.

Blückert, A. (2010). *Juridiska—ett nytt språk? En studie av juridikstudenters språkliga inskolning,* Dissertation. Uppsala: Uppsala University.

Dias, P., and Paré, A. (Eds.). (2000). *Transitions: Writing in Academic and Workplace Settings.* Cresskill, NJ: Hampton Press.

Freedman, A. (1987). Learning to write again: Discipline-specific writing at university. *Carleton Papers in Applied Language Studies,* 4, 95–116.

Freedman, A., and Adam, C. (2000). Write where you are: Situating learning to write in university and workplace settings. In P. Dias and A. Paré (Eds.), *Transitions: Writing in Academic and Workplace Settings.* Cresskill, NJ: Hampton Press, 31–60.

Ivanič, R. (1998). *Writing and Identity: The Discoursal Construction of Identity in Academic Writing.* Philadelphia, PA: Benjamins.

Kotsinas, U.-B. (1985). Invandrare talar svenska. *Ord och stil,* 15. Malmö: Liber förlag.

Parks, S. (2001). Moving from school to the workplace: Disciplinary innovation, border crossings, and the reshaping of a written genre. *Applied Linguistics,* 22, 405–438.

Schneider, B., and Andre, J.-A. (2005). University preparation for workplace writing: An explanatory study of the perceptions of students in three disciplines. *Journal of Business Communication,* 2, 195–218.

Swedish National Police Board. (2007). *Riktlinjer för skrivande inom polisen.* Stockholm: Rikspolisstyrelsen.

Wertsch, J.V. (1991). *Voices of the Mind: A Sociocultural Approach to Mediated Action.* London: Harvester Wheatsheaf.

Job Expectation, Adjustment, and Coping Mechanisms among Women in Two Police Forces in India

12

JISU KETAN PATTANAIK AND
VIDISHA BARUA WORLEY

Contents

Introduction

Historically, women have played an important role in India. Women warriors have fought courageously for the honor of their country. More recently, Kiran Bedi, the first woman to join the Indian Police Service in 1972, is continuing to make significant contributions toward the progress of Indian society even after her formal retirement from the service. Despite the critical contributions made by women, there has been little research aimed at understanding the acute difficulties faced by these women, who are very much a part of the society that still does not consider women to be at par with men, especially when it comes to their jobs as police officers, a traditionally male-dominated profession. Women entered the criminal justice system to control crime against women and children, and child abuse, and to provide better protection to women and juveniles (Horne 1980).

Sherman (1975) claims that women in policing have had an important political, social, economic, and psychological impact. The need for women police officers in British India was felt during the labor strike in Kanpur, India, in 1938 when women workers had to be controlled, and so women police officers were appointed in Kanpur in 1939 (Mahajan 1982). According to Ghosh (1981), the idea of introducing women into the police force in independent India was first mooted after the Partition of India and Pakistan in 1947 to deal with offenses that victimized women, as in kidnapping, abduction, and rape cases, and in relief camps that housed unattached women and children.

Highlighting the growing importance of women police officers, the National Police Commission (1980) pointed out that their role was crucial in rehabilitating delinquent girls, and in areas where the police came in direct contact with women. The visibility of women police officers would dispel any negative sentiments of distrust in the police and boost public confidence. Women police officers can also play an active role in community policing focusing on the public service aspect of policing.

Objectives of the Research Study

The objectives of the research study are as follows:

- What are the demographic and socioeconomic characteristics of the women police officers working in Orissa and Delhi?
- Which woman police force has a higher job expectation, Orissa or Delhi?
- To what extent are women police officers adjusted or maladjusted in the police organization?
- What changes in behavior have occurred after the women joined the police service?
- What coping strategies were adopted by the women police officers in both states to relieve their work-related stress?

Historically, Delhi is a cosmopolitan city that represents the mixed culture of the country itself. All women police personnel working in Delhi belong to different family backgrounds, religions, and ethnic groups. They are basically from Haryana, Punjab, Himachal Pradesh, and Uttar Pradesh. In Delhi, women police officers always live in a state of alertness and preparedness in view of the changing situation and high growth rate of crime, which pose a major challenge to criminal justice functionaries.

Orissa is an ex-feudatory state, dominated by traditional culture and folk-ways not much affected by modernity. Recently, some of the cities of Orissa are influenced relatively by modernization and urbanization. It is considered as economically backward state in comparison with other states of India. But it is culturally rich and full of natural resources. Women entered into police force in Orissa in order to control crime against women and children, but now they are performing all duties and functions which male police are doing in the state.

Therefore, it is very interesting to know as to what extent women police personnel are adopting modern law enforcement machinery in Delhi (cosmopolitan city) and Orissa (feudatory).

The purpose of this chapter is to provide a comparative empirical analysis of women police personnel working in two states in India, Delhi and Orissa, and examine their job expectations, their level of adjustment in the police departments, and their stress and coping strategies. It also proposes to explore the extent to which women police personnel are adapting and adjusting to the modern law enforcement setting in Delhi and Orissa.

Review of Literature

Research on women police officers was negligible till the 1960s when feminist writings began to highlight the unique role of women in the criminal justice system (Dick and Metcalfe 2007; Martin 1996). However, research on women police officers has been the subject matter of considerable interest among social scientists in the recent past. A 1971 national survey of major police agencies in the United States sponsored by the Police Foundation to determine how women were being utilized in police departments confirmed that there were very few women employees and that these few were deployed in limited tasks (Milton 1972). Connolly (1975) predicted that the use of women police officers in traditionally male roles would be a source of organizational conflict that would eventually bring about adaptive changes in policing. In a study of a pilot project involving 14 women police officers, Connolly (1975) found the evidence of conflict; she did not, however, find the evidence of organizational change. Bell's (1982) study concluded that women make competent and efficient police officers. Female officers have demonstrated that they can manage preventable violent situations and communicate with citizens, and their attitudes prove to be more effective than male muscle power. There is evidence that women police officers are more effective than their male counterparts in handling family fights. Homant and

Kennedy (1985) found that the women police officers show more concern, care, patience, and understanding in these situations. Ott (1989) inferred that the presence of women in the police force is particularly opposed by men as police work is stereotypically considered a male occupation. Hunt's (1990) study found that women police officers bring with them a culture of reformation that comes from feelings of care and sensitivity.

According to Young (1991), women police officers face a constant hostility "in the job" from fellow policemen who try to maintain control and dominance at the work place. He further comments that men perceive women police officers as weak individuals with no real ability for law enforcement. Brown and Campbell (1991) carried out a study on the Hampshire Constabulary in England. They found that most women officers were deployed either on foot or by car, were less likely to be part of special investigative units, prisoner management, marine sections, and traffic patrol, and did not have dog or air support.

Brewer (1991) notes that women may adopt various ways of coping, as in suffering in silence, going along with a joke that their male counterparts might have started, trying to become like the "boys," or bravely emphasizing their feminine characteristics. Brewer's (1991) formulation is significant because he emphasizes how women constructed their own gendered roles as either "Amazons" (strong, assertive warrior figures) or "Hippolytes" (more conventionally feminine). They were able to step out of the character when off duty and did not necessarily stick to a single script. Sutton (1995) conducted a study on women police officers and reported that 85% of women police officers from the New South Wales reported that in spite of significant organizational reforms, sexist mindsets and behaviors were very much prevalent within the service. Holdaway and Parker (1998) propose two types of conflict that women police officers experience: one is the stress between home and office work when family life interferes with workplace duties such as punctuality and overtime privileges; the other is the tension between work and home when family life suffers as a result of work as in being unable to take care of an ailing child at home.

In India, Mahajan's (1982) study on women police officers in the state of Punjab revealed that women's role in policing remains ambiguous and stressful. In another Indian state, Andhra Pradesh, the woman police force acts as an instrument of social change to raise the status of women in society (Shamim 1991). Shamim (1991) urged that women police need to be given independent charge of cases to bring them at par with their male counterparts. On a positive note, Natarajan (1996) observed that in Tamil Nadu, India, the full integration of women into policing is likely to occur soon. However, Bhardwaj (1999), on the other hand, lamented that women police officers in Delhi were dissatisfied with their status and role despite their valuable contributions in both traditional and modern areas of police work. Krishnamurthi (1996) demonstrated that women police officers in Nagpur, India, are prone to experience more stress, tensions, and conflicts in discharging their role in contrast to their male counterparts. Similarly, Banu (1995) found that a majority of women police officers in Chennai, India, experienced stress, and their life satisfaction and social support were at the minimum level. Pattanaik (1996) suggested that a majority of women police officers in Orissa have taken up their jobs with an altruistic motive. Even so, they experienced role conflict, were looked down upon by the male police officers, and faced more work-related problems compared to the male officers.

Methodology

This study is based on an exploratory-cum-descriptive research design. The research study adopts incidental sampling. Women police personnel from the rank of assistant subinspector to inspector working in Orissa and Delhi constitute the universe of the study. The first sample is composed of 40 women police officers, the second consists of 70 women police officers, and the final sample comprises 200 women police officers (75 from Orissa and 125 from Delhi) in the rank of assistant subinspector to inspector. In order to get information from the women police personnel, the principal researcher collected data in three phases in both Orissa and Delhi. All the subjects are residents of either Orissa or Delhi. The majority of the subjects are Hindus ($n = 175$; 87.5%), married ($n = 115$; 57.5%), and college graduates ($n = 105$; 52.5%), and live in joint families ($n = 105$; 52.5%) in both Orissa and Delhi. The age of women police personnel ranged from 23 to 43 years ($M = 31.81$; SD $= 7.59$) in Orissa and from 22 to 55 years ($M = 35.28$; SD $= 7.76$) in Delhi.

Procedure

First Stage

At the outset, 40 women police personnel from the states of Orissa and Delhi were asked to answer the following five questions:

1. What motivated you to join the police service?
2. According to you, what does a police officer expect from his job?
3. According to you, what does a woman police officer expect from her job?
4. Being a woman, what difficulties do you face as a police officer?
5. How do you overcome these problems?

After getting appropriate responses from all women police personnel, their answers were scrutinized and edited, and the initial job expectation checklist (JECL; 57 items with responses being "True" and "False") was developed. Similarly, the initial Police Behavior Scale (PBS; 49 items with responses being "Always," "Often," "Sometime," and "Never"), the initial Police Women Behavior Scale (PWBS; 43 items with responses being "Always," "Often," "Sometime," and "Never"), the initial Police Adjustment Scale (PAS; 46 items with responses being "Always," "Often," "Sometime," and "Never"), and the Women Police Coping Strategy Scale (WPCS; 56 items with responses being "True" and "False") were developed.

Second Stage

In the second stage, all the initial checklists/questionnaires containing the JECL, the PBS, the PWBS, the PAS, and the WPCS were administered to 70 women police officers (in both Orissa and Delhi).

In order to select and retain items for the final scale, item variance and item analysis (total item correlation) were conducted based on the responses received for the JECL and the WPCS. For the PBS, the PWBS, and the PAS, the quartile deviation, median, and magnitude of the total item correlation were done. Based on these values, the final items of the scales were selected.

Finally, all the questionnaires (containing all scales) were administered to 75 women police personnel in Orissa and 125 in Delhi. After receiving the questionnaires/checklists, completeness, and proper marking of the items were checked. The completed questionnaires were then individually scored (item-wise) and the total scores were awarded.

After that the final tabulation was done through the Statistical Package for the Social Sciences (SPSS) research in the Tata Institute of Social Science, Mumbai, India. Both parametric and nonparametric statistical methods pertaining to the study were computed for the analysis.

The Research Instrument

The research instrument used in the study was a questionnaire containing general background questions along with a JECL, a PBS, a PWBS, a PAS, and a WPCS. For the purpose of administering the tests, the women police officers were contacted through the Superintendent of Police (Orissa) and the Deputy Commissioner of Police (Delhi) and were asked to take part in the interview. The questionnaires were printed in a booklet form with self-contained instructions, which were administered in a group setting.

Analysis of Results

Socioeconomic Background

The distribution of ethnicity of women police officers in the study reveals that there is representation from all categories of the population in both Delhi and Orissa. Women from the "scheduled castes" (SC), "scheduled tribes" (ST), "other backward classes" (OBC), and "socially and educationally backward classes" (SEBC) are not attracted to the job of a police officer in both Delhi and Orissa. Women from these categories have showed less interest in the police service as the involvement of law and order problems creates the impression that these jobs are physically tough and demanding.

Thus, there was a maximum representation in the women police force of the general category compared to other categories in both Delhi and Orissa. The study revealed that in Orissa a majority of the women police personnel were from rural areas in contrast to Delhi where most women police personnel came from urban areas. The background of women police personnel plays a very important role in determining their performance, adaptability to the police environment, and their behavior toward the general public as well as the police staff. Looking into the marital status of women police officers, the study found that in Orissa most women police officers were unmarried ($n = 42$; 56%), while in Delhi most of them were married ($n = 83$; 66.4%).

Work-Related Problems

Police work involves a plethora of outdoor activities such as patrolling; providing security during important occasions, public functions, and rallies; crime fighting on the streets; and ensuring a safe and secure environment for the public in general. This crime-fighting and protective role, coupled with the fact that police officers have been predominantly male from the beginning, of the police profession is typically looked on as a masculine job. But slowly and steadily, with the advent of industrialization, urbanization, and rapid social changes, police forces all over the world have felt the need for women officers, and consequently women entered the occupation primarily to control crimes committed by and against women and children. Presently, women police officers around the globe are performing their duties and functions as efficiently as the male police personnel. However, the results of this study show that women are facing a lot of difficulties and problems both in the professional sphere and in the domestic front. This is due to gender discrimination, the rough and tough police subculture, the control by male colleagues, the attitude of male members, and the nature of the job itself that often requires long hours of work (Table 12.1).

Table 12.1 *t*-Test Showing the Difference of Test Scores of Women Police Officers in Orissa and Delhi on the JES

No.	State	N	Mean (SD)	*t*-Ratio
1	Orissa	75	19.33 (3.16)	$t = 2.38$ ($df = 198$; $p < .05$)
2	Delhi	125	18.24 (3.09)	

The study results show that while women police officers as a whole are facing problems in the states of Orissa and Delhi, women police officers in Orissa ($M = 19.33$; SD $= 3.16$) have higher job expectations than their counterparts in Delhi ($M = 18.24$; SD $= 3.09$), and the results are statistically significant at the $p < .05$ level. It may be because Orissa is a less developed state with a low population density and a lower rate of crime, whereas Delhi is a cosmopolitan state with a high population density as well as a higher crime rate that is increasing rapidly due to industrialization, migration from rural areas to urban belts, high social mobility, and slum culture. The "Crime in India" report, published by the National Crime Records Bureau, New Delhi (2007), suggested that Delhi reported significantly more number of crimes in the country. All these pose challenges for women police personnel posted in different police stations, police control rooms, railway stations, airports, and other allied offices. At the same time, the pressure of workload is much more in Delhi than in Orissa. Therefore, women police officers in Delhi are always living in a state of high alertness and preparedness to meet any eventuality and have less expectation out of their jobs than those in Orissa. Again, in Delhi, new types of crimes are emerging in the form of violent crime, organized crime, white-collar crime, cybercrime, and terrorism, which require sudden action by the police personnel to control crime. Thus, while the Delhi police job is more demanding, women police officers have less job expectation. On the other hand, while the Orissa police job is less demanding, the women police officers have higher job expectation.

Adjustment versus Maladjustment

Women police personnel also experience problems while maintaining a balance between family work and office work. Women police personnel, particularly those belonging to nuclear families, in the states of Orissa and Delhi are the worst affected. Their adjustment pattern in the police environment is poor. This is due to the fact that there is no extra help available in a nuclear family to do the family chores and look after the children.

It is evident from Table 12.2 that the family structure has a significant effect on the adjustment pattern of the women police officers. The higher score on the PAS shows that the women police officers had to make more adjustments at their workplace. Women police officers belonging to joint

Table 12.2   ANOVA Showing the Effect of Family Structure on Police Adjustment

No.	Family Structure	N	Mean (SD)	F-ratio
1	Nuclear	89	53.46 (19.46)	$F = 6.75$ ($df = 2/197$; $p < .01$)
2	Joint	105	44.60 (18.97)	
3	Extended	6	63.50 (24.03)	
4	Total	200	49.11 (19.88)	

Table 12.3   ANOVA Showing the Difference of Effect of Marital Status on Police Adjustment

No.	Marital Status	N	Mean (SD)	F-ratio
1	Unmarried	73	49.01 (19.89)	$F = 0.00$ ($df = 2/197$; $p > .05$)
2	Married	115	49.14 (20.09)	
3	Widow	12	49.41 (19.51)	
4	Total	200	49.11 (19.88)	

families ($M = 44.60$; SD $= 18.97$) are better adjusted to their workplace as opposed to those from nuclear families ($M = 53.46$; SD $= 19.46$). On the other hand, women police officers in extended families had to make the most adjustments ($M = 63.50$; SD $= 24.03$). These differences were found to be statistically highly significant at the $p < .01$ level (Table 12.3).

Married women police officers are prone to more stress and face problems in both Orissa and Delhi as their adjustment to the police environment is relatively low. This may be because married women police officers try to strike a balance between their domestic and professional roles which is very difficult, as the job of a police officer requires long work hours, at times extending to 24 hours a day. This study shows that married women police officers have a slightly higher adjustment problem ($M = 49.14$; SD $= 20.09$) as opposed to unmarried women police officers ($M = 49.01$; SD $= 19.89$). However, women police officers who are widows have scored the highest on the adjustment scale ($M = 49.41$; SD $= 19.51$), leading the researchers to infer that they might have the most trouble adjusting to the workplace.

Healthy and Unhealthy Coping Strategies

There are two purposes of coping: addressing the problem that causes pain and managing the emotion that results from the pain and suffering; thus, while one focuses on the problem, the other emphasizes the emotion (Folkman and Lazarus 1980; Lazarus and Folkman 1984). Coping strategies can be either healthy or unhealthy ways used by women police personnel in both Orissa and Delhi in order to seek relief from stress, strain, tension, anxiety, and depression that are related to their job. Some healthy coping strategies used by women police officers are intolerance of male colleagues' rough behavior, adjustment to the professional role, refusal to obey wrong orders of the superiors, mediation, physical exercise in the morning, avoidance of confrontation with colleagues, complaining to the boss whenever necessary, watching movies for relaxation, listening to music, considering difficult and adverse situations as an inevitable part of life, not getting involved in illegal activities, solving problems by properly communicating with their male partners, being aggressive if need be, accepting the limitations inherent in the work, discussing with friends about the problems in the job, debating with colleagues whenever right, cultivating belief and faith in the self, and critical assessment of problems.

Similarly, unhealthy coping strategies practiced by women police personnel include being submissive to male counterparts, revolting against male chauvinism, accepting male and female equality as an utopia, inequality, and dominance, maintaining silence in front of dominating male police officers, acceptance of harassment by superiors, working long hours, tolerating gender discrimination, neglecting personal interests, taking leave of absence when in trouble instead of dealing with the problem, considering the boss as being always right, and considering manipulation as the best policy (Table 12.4).

Women police officers from nuclear families ($M = 20.74$; SD $= 3.24$) used healthier coping strategies compared to their counterparts who belonged to joint families ($M = 20.62$; SD $= 2.71$). Higher scores on the WPCS indicated healthier coping strategies. On the other hand, women police officers that took the help of extended family members adopted the healthiest coping strategies ($M = 21.19$; SD $= 3.30$) (Table 12.5).

On examining the relationship between the personal characteristics of the women police personnel and their behavior, it was found that age had a significant negative relation to behavior (-0.17; $p < .01$). This means that older women exhibited worse behavior than the younger ones. Similarly, the older women police officers also adopted less healthy coping strategies (-0.13; $p < .05$) compared to the younger ones. Age at marriage and coping strategy also had a strong negative correlation (-0.12; $p < .05$). This shows that the younger a woman was at the time of marriage, the healthier was

Table 12.4   ANOVA Showing the Difference of Family Structure on Women Police Coping Strategy

No.	Family Structure	N	Mean (SD)	F-ratio
1	Nuclear	89	20.74 (3.24)	$F = 0.09$ ($df = 2/197$; $p > .05$)
2	Joint	105	20.61 (3.41)	
3	Extended	6	21.16 (2.71)	
4	Total	200	20.69 (3.30)	

Table 12.5   Relationship between Personal Characteristics and Personality Traits

Independent Variable	Dependent Variable				
	Job Expectation	Police Behavior	Police Women Behavior	Police Adjustment	Women Police Coping Strategy
Age	0.02	−0.17*	−0.09	0.09	−0.13**
Age at marriage	0.04	−0.04	−0.06	−0.00	−0.12**
Number of children	−0.01	−0.03	−0.05	0.00	−0.06
Years of service	0.10	−0.15*	−0.07	0.07	−0.15*

Notes: *Significant at .01 level.
**Significant at .05 level.

Table 12.6   *t*-Test Showing the Difference of Test Scores of Women Police Officers in Orissa and Delhi on the WPCS

No.	State	N	Mean (SD)	*t*-Ratio
1	Orissa	75	20.82 (3.23)	$t = 0.45$ ($df = 198$; $p > .05$)
2	Delhi	125	20.60 (3.36)	

her coping strategy. Years of service also showed significant relationships with police behavior (−0.15; $p < .01$) and coping strategy (−0.15; $p < .01$). This indicates that the less the number of years of service, the better was the behavior and more likely was the individual to adopt healthier coping strategies. This result is consistent with the findings of Butler and Cochrane's (1977) study which revealed that with increasing experience in the police profession, police officers exhibit an increased need to be independent of others in decision making, to argue their points of view, to do new and different things, and to ignore guilt and wrong doing. Again, it also reveals that with the increase of service in the police profession, the coping strategies become unhealthier.

From Table 12.6, it is quite evident that women police officers in both Orissa (20.82; SD = 3.23) and Delhi (20.60; SD = 3.36) adopt healthy coping strategies equally, and the difference is statistically insignificant ($p > .05$). Although healthy coping strategies adopted by these women police officers do not reach the optimum level of 31 (number of items in the WPCS = 31), the figures still indicate that they adopt healthier than unhealthier coping strategies.

Basically, a healthy coping strategy has a positive impact on human health and mind, while an unhealthy coping strategy has a negative effect. These healthy and unhealthy coping strategies are directly associated with police adjustment. Women police personnel who fail to adjust to the police workplace use more unhealthy coping strategies than those who adjust well.

Conclusion

This study was aimed at comparing job expectations, stress, adjustments, behavior, and coping strategies adopted by the women police forces in two Indian states, Orissa and Delhi, so that policy changes can be made accordingly. This study came to a number of conclusions. Women police officers in Orissa have higher job expectations than those in Delhi who are exposed to more dangerous situations, have longer work hours, and face greater rigor, thus reducing their expectations from the job. Women police officers from joint families also had higher job expectations as opposed to those from nuclear families, although the difference was not found to be statistically significant.

As far as adjustment is concerned, women police officers in Orissa are better adjusted than those in Delhi. This may again be due to the fact that Delhi, a metropolitan city, has greater pressure and complexities at work. Women police officers in joint families had the least difficulty adjusting to the work place as they got the support of other family members in taking care of the children and attending to household chores. Such support was not available to nuclear families. The situation was even worse in extended families where these women police officers had to rely on relatives to take care of their children, thus increasing stress and the resultant adjustment problems at the workplace. Also, married women police officers were found to have a slightly higher adjustment problem as opposed to unmarried women police officers. However, the most difficulties and adjustment problems were faced by widowed women police officers.

On examining police women's behavior, the researchers found that women police officers in Orissa showed better behavior and adopted healthier coping strategies than those in Delhi. It was also found that irrespective of the police force, younger female officers showed better behavior at the workplace and also used healthier coping strategies. Age at the time of marriage and years of service also showed significant statistical relationships with coping strategies. The younger a woman was at the time of her marriage and the less the years of service, the healthier was the coping strategy used. Women police officers from nuclear families also used healthier coping strategies compared to their counterparts who belonged to joint families. Women police officers that took the help of extended family members, in fact, adopted the healthiest coping strategies.

The presence of women police officers is of great significance in the present times; it is important to understand the various aspects of their work such as stress, adjustment, behavior, and coping strategies, as they are different from those faced by men. The involvement of more women in the police profession not only strengthens the police work but also helps in reducing crimes committed by and against women and children. They can strike a balance in the police profession. The authors recommend that personality testing at the time of recruitment should be made mandatory and women police personnel with better performance and better behavior should be identified and projected as role models for others. Necessary counseling by experts should be made as a routine arrangement in the police profession to reduce stress among police personnel. While little can be done to change the dangerousness of the work situation in Delhi, efforts can be made to give women police officers more support in both Orissa and Delhi. Child care services can be provided for the children of women police officers who come from nuclear families or depend on extended family members to take care of their children. A secure day care system can significantly reduce police stress at work, make officers better adjusted to their jobs, and lead to higher job expectations. In addition, members from less represented social categories can be encouraged to join the profession by aggressively pursuing recruitment from these communities and giving them good incentives, and explaining the altruistic purpose of the police profession. The profession should also be presented as having a good social status with power and authority so that women feel proud to be police officers and their families show support for their work.

References

Banu, A. (1995). Women police: A study of role stress, social support and life satisfaction. PhD dissertation, Madras University, Chennai, India.

Bell, D.J. (1982). Police women: Myths and reality. *Journal of Police Science and Administration, 10*(1), 112–120.

Bhardwaj, A. (1999). *Women in Uniform: Emergence of Women Police in Delhi.* New Delhi: Regency Publications.

Brewer, J. (1991). *Inside the RUC: Routine Policing in a Divided Community.* Oxford: Clarendon Press.

Brown, J. and Campbell, E.A. (1991). Less than equal. *Policing, 7,* 324–333.

Butler, A.J. and Cochrane, R. (1977). An examination of some elements of the personality of police officers and their implications. *Journal of Police Science and Administration, 5,* 441–450.

Connolly, H.A. (1975). Police women as patrol officers: A study in role adaptation. PhD dissertation, Department of Psychology, University of New York, New York.

Dick, G. and Metcalfe, B. (2007). The progress of female police officers? An empirical analysis of organizational commitment and tenure explanations in two UK police forces. *International Journal of Public Sector Management, 20*(2), 81–100.

Folkman, S. and Lazarus, R.S. (1980). An analysis of coping in a middle aged community sample. *Journal of Health and Social Behavior, 21,* 219–239.

Ghosh, S.K. (1981). *Women in Policing.* New Delhi: Light & Life Publishers.

Holdaway, S. and Parker, S. (1998). Policing women police: Uniform, patrol, promotion and representation in the CID. *British Journal of Criminology, 38*(1), 40–60.

Homant, R.J. and Kennedy, D.B. (1985). Police perception of spouse abuse: A comparison of male and female officers. *Journal of Criminal Justice, 13*(1), 29–47.

Horne, P. (1980). *Women in Law Enforcement.* Springfield, IL: Charles C. Thomas.

Hunt, J. (1990). The logic of sexism among police. *Women & Criminal Justice, 2,* 3–30.

Krishnamurthi, L. (1996). Role conflicts and tension of women police. *The Indian Journal of Social Work, 57*(4), 615–629.

Lazarus, R.S. and Folkman, S. (1984). *Stress, Appraisal and Coping.* New York: Springer.

Mahajan, A. (1982). *Indian Policewomen: A Sociological Study of a New Role.* New Delhi: Deep & Deep Publications.

Martin, C. (1996). The impact of equal opportunities policies on the experiences of women police constables. *British Journal of Criminology, 36*(4), 510–528.

Milton, C. (1972). *Women in Policing.* Washington, DC: Police Foundation.

Natarajan, M. (1996). Women police units in India: A new direction, *Police Studies, 19*(2), 63–76.

Ott, E. M. (1989). Effects of the male-female ratio at work. *Psychology of Women Quarterly, 13*(1), 41–57.

Pattanaik, J.K. (1996). Professional orientation and career aspiration of women police in Orissa: Some reflections on role conflict, a sociological analysis. MPhil dissertation, Sambalpur University, Orissa, India.

Shamim, A. (1991). *Women Police and Social Change.* New Delhi: Ashish Publishing House.

Sherman, L.J. (1975). Evaluation of policewomen on patrol in a suburban police department. *Journal of Police Science and Administration, 3*(4), 434–438.

Sutton, J. (1995). *Women in Policing: A Study of New South Wales Police.* Sydney, NSW: New South Wales Police Service.

Young, M. (1991). *An Inside Job: Policing and Police Culture in Britain.* Oxford: Clarendon Press.

Efficiency of Simulated Realistic Scenarios to Provide High Psychological Stress Training for Police Officers

13

JOHAN BERTILSSON, MITESH PATEL,
PETER J. FREDRIKSSON, LARS-FOLKE PILEDAHL,
MANS MAGNUSSON, AND PER-ANDERS FRANSSON

Contents

Introduction

In traumatic incidents such as the Columbine High School shooting (USA) in 1999; the Virginia Tech shooting (USA) in 2007; the Kauhajoki School shooting (Finland) in 2008; and the Utöya shooting (Norway) in 2011, police officers were faced with active attacker scenarios. Intervening in such ongoing events might be life threatening for the police officers involved, but may also be imperative for saving the lives of the victims. Incidents that evolve into large-scale killings are still rare (Greenberg 2007). However, what is less publicized is that regular police officers are frequently placed in threatening situations where immediate action needs to be taken under very uncertain conditions to save lives, like when someone screams out in terror from within an apartment. The danger involved in these and other police officer tasks is illustrated by the figures presented by Meyerhoff and colleagues: between 1989 and 1998, 682 police officers were killed in the line of duty in the United States (Meyerhoff et al. 2004). Hence, recent events highlight the importance of training regular police officers to handle rare but highly straining situations, where high psychological stress is commonly an associated component, since regular police officers are often the ones first to respond. Special Weapons and Tactics (SWAT) teams have the benefit of regular training, numbers, and better information, but SWAT teams generally arrive after regular police officer patrols to the scene and therefore often respond to contained situations, usually with a barricaded armed criminal with or without hostages.

However, the belief that actions under active threat conditions can be postponed without negative consequences until a well-trained SWAT team has arrived is often a misperception (Greenberg 2007). Active threat situations, like ongoing killing by an active shooter, can have a very fast killing rate. This means that regardless of the duration of an incident, immediate intervention is necessary to reduce the number of casualties that could otherwise be increasing by the minute (Greenberg 2007). Thus, the first police officers to respond may be faced with the very difficult decision whether to intervene immediately to save lives (Kelly et al. 2011). Relevant to these conditions, previous training under a few hours in strenuous conditions with elevated psychological stress has shown positive results on regular police officers and SWAT team members' performance when they are later forced to shoot under pressure (Oudejans 2008). An important question is, therefore, whether training in a realistic simulation of an active threat scenario is efficient enough to induce those high psychological stress levels, allowing regular police officers to practice to operate under such straining and stressful conditions (Meyerhoff et al. 2004; Nieuwenhuys, Caljouw, Leijsen, Schmeits, and Oudejans 2009; Oudejans 2008; Oudejans and Nieuwenhuys 2009). If this proves successful, then that would reveal an opportunity to systematically prepare professionals such as police officers, firefighters, and surgeons for rare but highly stressful events in advance, using realistic training scenarios adapted appropriately for each profession. Reality-based training, including decisions when to use firearms, is a relatively new educational approach. The objective is to allow police officers to acquire skills and competence by confrontation to situations relevant to their work while the high training realism simultaneously exposes them to the context-relevant stress associated with these situations in real life (Nieuwenhuys and Oudejans 2010; Oudejans 2008; Taverniers, Smeets, Ruysseveldt, Syroit, and von Grumbkow 2011).

The nature of active threat events presents police agencies with a unique set of problems. Police officers must attend to these events, knowing that they themselves may be deliberately targeted and that the perpetrators or terrorists are willing to die in their pursuit of inflicting the maximum level of loss and fear (Paton and Violanti 2008). In addition, the police officer arriving at the scene may be uninformed about the number, objective, weaponry, and actions of the armed perpetrators or terrorists. Such conditions of a large number of uncertainties are likely to induce psychological stress (Groer et al. 2010). The armed perpetrator or terrorist on the other hand may not act under the same uncertainties about the situation, but instead feel in control of the event and are often mentally prepared to die (Greenberg 2007). The mental state of an attacker can be erratic, ranging from thriving when in control over their victims to flee, shoot, or commit suicide in the first confrontation with police (Greenberg 2007).

Psychological stress is a natural human reflexive response evoked by perceived straining situations and the stress-evoked reactions can have both beneficial and negative consequences on performance. Lower stress levels potentially equate to better vigilance, performance, and greater chances of winning critical encounters (Vonk 2008). Elevated physical and psychological stress is associated with poorer decision making (Kassam, Koslov, and Mendes 2009), poor performance in shooting tasks (Oudejans 2008), and a major cause of friendly fire incidents during military operations (Meyerhoff et al. 2004). However, training at high psychological stress levels improves skill proficiency, leading to higher confidence and better performance (Murray 2004; Vonk 2008). Previous studies have demonstrated the importance and reliability of monitoring the heart rate for real-time investigations of the influence of increased stress (Carroll et al. 2000; Freyschuss, Hjemdahl, Juhlin-Dannfelt, and Linde 1988; Kassam et al. 2009; Murray 2004; Sawai, Ohshige, Yamasue, Hayashi, and Tochikubo 2007; Tidgren and Hjemdahl 1989; Vonk 2008).

The mental state under severe psychological stress is often described in emotions of feeling either challenge or threat (Kassam et al. 2009). The states of challenge or threat are identified from the individual's appraisal of how demanding a stressful situation will be, as well as their appraisal of their own personal resources to cope with the situation. Challenge occurs when an individual perceives that they have personal resources to cope with the demands of a task at hand, whereas threat occurs when demands outweigh perceived resources (Kassam et al. 2009). When perceiving a stressful challenge, the cardiac efficiency increases (i.e., increased cardiac output) and the peripheral resistance in blood vessels decreases (i.e., vasodilation), which increases circulation in the peripheral blood vessels and in the brain (Freyschuss et al. 1988). On the contrary, during a stressful threat, the efficiency in the cardiac cycle decreases and the peripheral resistance increases. This state may be seen as a physical reaction beneficial for the organism by minimizing or delaying possible blood loss due to risk of substantial physical damage. However, a drawback of this state is that at increasing stress levels, the lower blood flow reaching the periphery and the brain can cause a gradually increased loss of motor skills despite the higher heart rate (Grossman and Christensen 2004; Siddle 1995). Thus, the wrong state of mind could render police officers to physically perform less effective and make them handle their equipment poorly.

The study aim was to evaluate with scientific objective methods whether a realistically simulated active shooter scenario could effectively produce high levels of psychological stress in police officers, assessed with real-time monitoring of heart rate, thereby allowing better handling of such conditions in real life. Another aim was to investigate how simulated realistic scenarios over time generate psychological stress and how fast subjects physically recover from such stressful experiences. This study is, to our knowledge, the first in-depth analysis of the generation pattern and the magnitude of the psychological stress evoked under reality-based training of police officers while performing the exercises.

Methods

Ten healthy experienced police officers, who are both firearm and self-defense instructors (seven males; group average age 38 years, average height 1.81 cm, average weight 86.4 kg) volunteered to participate in the study. None had physical or cardiovascular problems or concerns. All participants gave signed consent and all tests were performed according to the Declaration of Helsinki.

Procedure

The objective was to expose the participating police officers to a highly realistic stressful scenario, where they themselves may feel pain when performing the exercise. The scene was set in an abandoned, three-level building unfamiliar to all participants. Each level had 20 rooms. The attacker(s) was positioned hidden in one or two of these rooms with three to four victims. The police entered the building in teams of two or four persons. The aim of the police officer team was to find the room(s) of the attacker(s) and work together to arrest or shoot the attacker if necessary.

On arrival, the participants were informed about the procedure. No participant had previously been trained to handle an active threat scenario. However, the participating police officers had on earlier occasions performed other training under stressful conditions, and to some extent were already acclimatized to perform under pressure due to their previous active career in the police force. Both police officers and attackers were armed with guns loaded with Simunition® paint cartridges (General Dynamics Ordinance and Tactical Systems Canada Inc.) and allowed to fire at each other. All participants in the exercise wore protective helmets. The police officers also wore their ordinary service equipment including lightweight ballistic vests.

Exercises Performed

Dry-Training

All started the training session by first performing the dry-training 2–5 times. The exercises were performed identically as in the police officer scenario—first in a two-person team and second in a four-person team. They were pushed to physically execute the procedure as they would if it were not practice. Officers moved at medium to fast pace through corridors, sometimes entering rooms with imagined perpetrators. The officers received instructional feedback if needed from instructors (in this case little instruction was needed).

Police Officer Team

The assessment was conducted as a highly realistic scenario. As part of a four-person team, the officers moved at medium to fast pace through corridors, looking for and entering the room with victims, and the attacker was equipped with a gun firing potentially painful paint bullets. Being hit with the Simunition paint bullets produced a short sensation of intense pain. All were assessed in the role of member in the police team at least twice. As part of the postevaluation, the performance was self-reviewed after trial completion, peer-reviewed by the other members of the team, and finally reviewed by the head instructors.

Cardiovascular Measurements

The participants were each equipped with a Polar Team System™ (Polar Electro, Sweden) heart rate recording device strapped on the torso below the Musculus Pectoralis Major. The equipment was put on in the morning before the transport to the chosen building for the exercise and removed in the afternoon when the training ended. The recording equipment needed no further attention until it was removed after all exercises were completed 4 hours later. Heart rate was recorded simultaneously in all 10 participants. Since all the participants performed the dry-training and police officer team exercises, they constituted their own controls regarding the different cardiovascular outcomes. All participants performed both exercises between 10.30 a.m. and 12.30 p.m. to minimized effects of circadian rhythm on the assessments made.

Analysis

The heart rate measurements were analyzed using the Polar Pro Trainer 5™ software (Polar Electro, Sweden). The heart rate was determined at three states when performing each task by response feature analysis (Matthews, Altman, Campbell, and Royston 1990):

- Start heart rate [steady-state heart rate in beats per minute (BPM) before the start of the exercise]
- Maximum heart rate [maximum heart rate recorded during the exercise (in BPM)]
- End heart rate [steady-state heart rate after the end of the exercise (in BPM)]

Values were also calculated illustrating the time (in seconds) taken to reach maximum steady-state heart rate level and recover from maximum steady-state heart rate. Finally, the heart rate change over time (in BPM/second) was calculated to illustrate the gradual increase and decrease in heart rate during the activation and recovery phases, respectively, during the exercise.

Statistical Analysis

Paired Wilcoxon matched-pairs signed-rank test (Exact sig. two-tailed) statistics were used to analyze the parameters recorded during (1) the dry-training exercise and (2) the police officer team exercise (Altman 1991). Nonparametric statistical tests were used as the Shapiro–Wilk test revealed that the obtained values were not normally distributed. In the statistical analyses were $p < .05$ considered significant.

Results

Heart Rate

Already before the start of the exercise, the mean heart rate was significantly higher ($p < .05$) by 7% in the participants when about to perform the police officer team exercise compared with the dry-training (Figure 13.1a). The mean heart rate at the start of the exercise was 83 BPM before the dry-training and 89 BPM before performing the police officer team exercise. The highest maximum

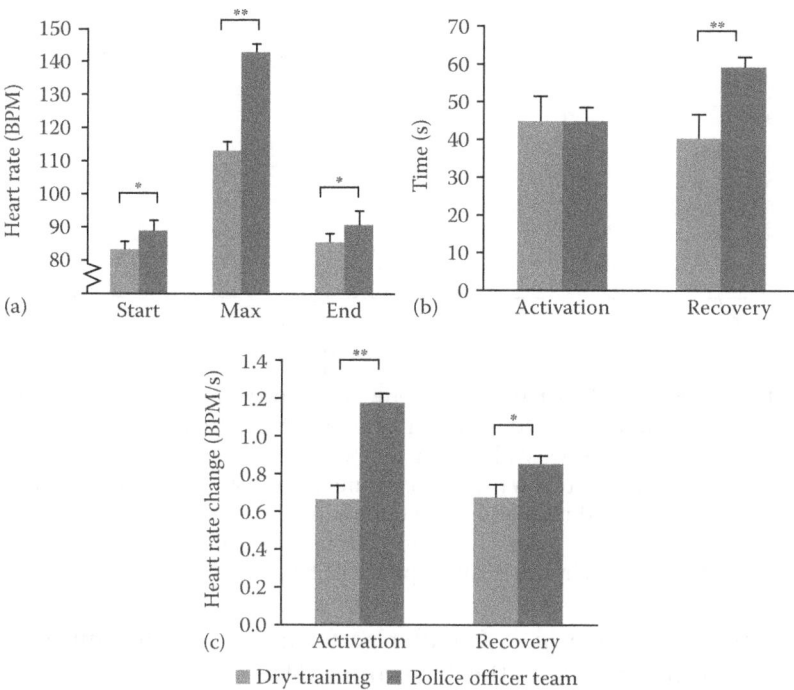

Figure 13.1 (a) Start—steady-state heart rate before the start of the exercise; Max—maximum heart rate recorded during the exercise; End—steady-state heart rate recovered to after the end of the exercise. (b) Activation: time taken to reach maximum steady-state heart rate. Recovery: time taken to recover from maximum steady-state heart rate. (c) Activation: gradual heart rate increase during the initial phase of the exercise; Recovery: gradual heart rate decrease during the recovery phase after the exercise. Mean + SEM (whiskers) values are displayed for all parameters. *p < .05; **p < .01.

heart rate was recorded when performing the police officer team exercise. The average peak value of 143 BPM was significantly higher (p < .01) by 27% than the value assessed during the dry-training (113 BPM). After completing the exercises, the mean steady-state heart rate recovered was significantly higher (p < .05) by 6% after performing the police officer team exercise compared with that after the dry-training. The mean heart rate was 85 BPM after the dry-training and 91 BPM after performing the police officer team exercise.

Time Taken for Maximum Change

The average amount of time to reach the maximum steady-state heart rate was almost identical (45 s) for the dry-training and the police officer team exercise, illustrating that the exercises including all physical activities were completed within the same time frame (Figures 13.1b and 13.2). However, the recovery to a steady-state level of heart rate after the exercises took

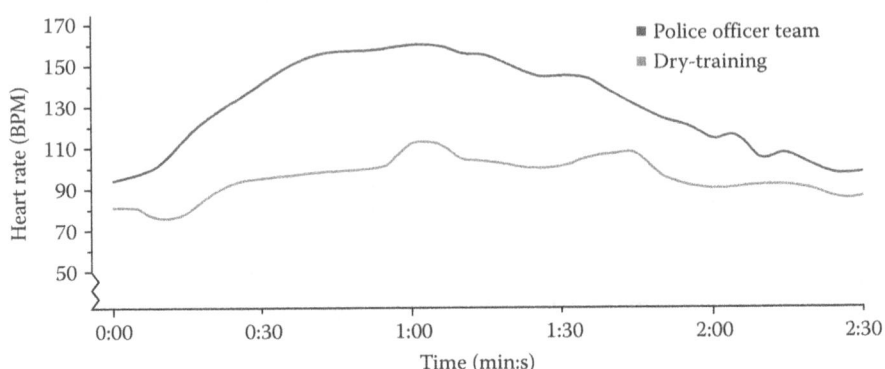

Figure 13.2 Recorded heart rate from one police officer while performing the dry-training and the police officer team exercise. Note that the physical stress performing the exercises was identical for both test conditions and that both exercises were implemented within the same time frame. In the figure, both exercises started at 00:00 min and were completed at about 01:10 min. Note the slightly higher pulse rate already before the start of the exercise and the fast increase in pulse rate during the initial phase of the police officer team exercise.

significantly longer time ($p < .01$) after performing the police officer team exercise (59 s) compared with the dry-training (41 s).

Rate of Change in Heart Rate

The rate of change in heart rate provides an estimation of heart rate activation or recovery intensity (Figure 13.1c). More intense changes in heart rate suggest increased excitability of the cardiovascular reactivity. Performing the police officer team exercise caused a significantly ($p < .01$) faster increase in heart rate (1.17 BPM per second) compared with the increase recorded during dry-training (0.67 BPM per second). Moreover, the rate of heart rate recovery was also significantly faster ($p < .05$) after performing the police officer team exercise (0.85 BPM per second) compared with the decrease recorded during dry-training (0.68 BPM per second).

Discussion

Most of us can recollect events where we suddenly became very clumsy when doing tasks under strict time constraints or in front of an audience. We might be mostly aware of this neurological reaction when we feel the negative side effects from it. However, it is also this neurological function that appropriately raises our attention and alertness at the right time and for the right reasons, and initiates the activation of sympathetic and autonomic reflexes, muscle reflexes, and CNS-controlled movement patterns aimed at saving our lives when the demands on "capacity" exceed the normal available resources. Thus, it is easy to understand that this neurological function has had a very important role in the survival of humankind, especially in the early stages of the development.

The study objective was to investigate whether this very essential neurological autonomic reaction in humans, commonly denoted as psychological stress or acute sympathetic stress response, can be produced not only in real life but to some degree also under artificial scenarios. If this is possible, it would mean that we could also design training programs utilizing the human CNS's ability to learn from repeated experiences, so the next time we encounter a similar situation we will have improved our ability to handle this condition. The neurological process we are studying has, depending on the level of arousal, gradually changing properties and effects on the autonomic system and the CNS. On low and moderate arousal levels, we mostly gain benefits in terms of increased attention and vigilance, faster reflexes, and better muscle forces. However, if the evoked arousal becomes too strong, it will be instead associated with negative side effects such as inability to perform fine and complex motor tasks. Moreover, one becomes more vulnerable to lose control of emotions and instead feel anxiety, fear, or panic, resulting in hypervigilance or fight, flight, and freeze states. Hence, it is in our interest to learn more about what type of motor activities someone who suffers severely from the effects of psychological stress is able to perform, given our natural biological strengths and limitations, whatever the cause for the psychological stress is. Based on such research, one would be able to write more correct action guidelines for handling of probable or known high psychological stress situations.

Occasionally, people may be exposed to life-threatening situations as part of their occupation. Police officers and military personnel might be the ones that first come to mind, but there are also substantial risks in a large number of other professions, such as high-rise construction workers. In many professions, correct decisions under strict time constraints must be made to save lives, such as in emergency health care. Often, however, the training for these professions emphasizes on the physical and technical aspects, while the psychological side is largely neglected (Oudejans 2008). Although the problems associated with psychological stress are well known among those working professionally with this issue, it is still a subject surrounded by a large amount of taboo in many professions and feelings of guilt and shame for not performing as well when it really mattered (Paton and Violanti 2008). Nonetheless, even highly trained athletes, SWAT team members, and experienced soldiers can suffer deteriorated performance due to psychological stress if the threat stimulus is sudden, horrifying, or unfamiliar to them (Meyerhoff et al. 2004; Murray 2004).

There are a number of opportunities to preemptively address the risk and consequences of psychological stress, which could be valuable in saving lives or preventing serious events from occurring. As illustrated by the scientific evidence presented in this study, it is possible to effectively induce a substantial amount of psychological stress in training scenarios if the training conditions are convincingly realistic. By using such custom-made realistic training, those who are trained will be allowed to repeatedly sense the feelings of psychological stress and become familiar to its physical and psychological effects. From these experiences, the individual may learn to handle their task more effectively since practicing with anxiety can prevent choking in perceptual-motor performance through acclimatization to the specific processes accompanying anxiety (Oudejans and Nieuwenhuys 2009). However, a certain degree of caution should also be respected not to inflict too much stress in the training scenarios too fast, so not to lead the trainee into the self-belief that he or she does not have the resources needed to handle the tasks (Atkins and Norris 2004). Moreover, it is also very important to train decision making and skills when the conditions may contain unknown elements or abrupt changes in the line of events (Schmidt and Lee 2011). Noteworthy, in this study all subjects included were already to some extent acclimatized to working under pressure, but still a strong psychological stress response was induced by the realistic scenario.

Physiological Characteristics of the Induced Psychological Stress

In this study, the peak heart rate increased substantially to an average of 143 BPM during the police officer team exercise from about 113 BPM during dry training. In the subject illustrated in Figure 13.2, the peak level was as high as 161 BPM. Adrenaline-induced heart rate increase by psychological stress to such levels has been associated with physiological consequences (Grossman and Christensen 2004; Siddle 1995). The physical effect of anxiety has been described in the shape of an inverted-U on performance (Schmidt and Lee 2011) depending on the task complexity concerning decision, perception, and motor act characteristics coupled with individual differences (Vonk 2008). The relationship between the level of psychological stress and the increased heart rate varies between individuals, depending on a number of factors such as previous stress experiences and physical state (Vonk 2008). However, typically, psychological stress that increases pulse rates above 115 BPM causes degraded fine motor control (Oudejans 2008; Siddle 1995). Furthermore, stronger stress activation to pulse rates above 145 BPM has been shown to cause degraded ability to perform complex motor control (Siddle 1995). At a very strong stress activation, the cognitive and physical performance degrades, resulting in hypervigilance, freezing, or ability to perform only very simple cognitive tasks and gross motor skills (Grossman and Christensen 2004; Siddle 1995; Vonk 2008). Hence, the performance deficits caused by psychological stress may render people unable to use equipment requiring certain fine motor skills or complex motor control

(Oudejans and Nieuwenhuys 2009). Thus, attention should be given to the design of equipment used by professions where psychological stress may occur, so it is suitable for handling under severe psychological stress and the physical repercussions associated with this state.

Furthermore, increased psychological stress could also have negative effects on memory recollection and decision making (Atkins and Norris 2004; Kassam et al. 2009). Interestingly, the assessing instructors in this study noted that the participants had clearly poorer or distorted memory recall of the events occurring while performing the stressful police officer team exercise than while performing the dry-training.

Training Scenario Requirements

The relevant attributes of the search-and-confront (limit or contain) rescue scenario used in this study are similar to those commonly displayed in media such as television news broadcasts. However, it would be wrong to imply that psychological stress effectively can be produced only in certain scenarios or only through a process of performing an elaborate series of action, executed in a specific order and time interval. Worth noting from this study is that the participants performed the same scenario several times, and it was first when the exercise was declared "real" that performing the scenario caused the participants to evoke strong emotions of raised attention and alertness. Thus, it is probably not any single detail in the physical design of the scenario or the sequence of actions made that raise psychological stress, for example, number of rooms to search, but more likely the sum of many subtle factors, such as the actions of the instructors, that make the participants strongly feel that "... this time is it really important that I perform well...."

In the design of the study, a number of precautions were taken so the effects recorded could be isolated to being exposed to the specific scenario used in the study. For example, the same subjects were exposed to the same physical conditions with and without the stressor factors present. Moreover, the study was designed so it was evident that the reactions recorded were linked to and only to the presence of these stressor factors. Note that our objective is not to compare the effects of being exposed to various psychological conditions. The design of the study strictly limited us to investigate the effect of being exposed to one specific scenario. However, this scenario is of special relevance for training of police officers.

One may speculate on the factors needed to produce a realistic scenario effectively inducing high levels of psychological stress under the training. In this study, many elements were deliberately kept unknown or unfamiliar to the participants, like the building itself, whether there were one or two attackers present, and in which of the large number of rooms (20 rooms), the attacker/s were positioned. The environment also contained sounds and movements from escaping victims. Another likely cause for feeling psychological stress could be the large risk for being hit by the painful Simunition paint bullets. The duration of the exercise, and thus the duration of which the realistic illusion had been maintained, could also be an important factor. As illustrated in Figure 13.2, a common pattern was the increased heart rate during the first 30–50 s of the exercise after which the reactivity reached a high steady-state level, with a slight peak when the attacker(s) was finally confronted. A further reason for feeling stress during the police officer team exercise was that their performance was evaluated by both the instructors and presented for their colleagues in retrospect. Thus, fear of failing or performing badly in front of other colleagues might have been a contributing social stress factor. Of note, this study revealed that real-time monitoring of cardiovascular activity during the exercise might be used as a mean to control the training scenario, by allowing the training instructors to add during the exercise, if necessary, more stressful elements to the scenario so the psychological stress aimed for is achieved.

One of the limitations in this study is that one cannot assume that all people will experience the same stress during high-pressure situations (Juniper, White, and Bellamy 2010) and feel the same stress when repeating the task. One has to assume that in a group of experienced professionals, some will be more experienced than others and will therefore enter these exercises better prepared than others. These experienced people may also gain smaller improvements by performing these exercises compared to persons for which these training scenarios are a novel experience. Still, we can conclude from the recordings of sympathetic and autonomic reactions that all subjects in the tested group systematically responded very strongly when participating in the exercise. Moreover, when comparing the findings from the two first repetitions of the police officer team exercise, many values were almost identical (performing test the first time: start—88 BPM, max—143 BPM, end—92 BPM; performing test the second time: start—87 BPM, max—145 BPM, end—88 BPM). One reason for why the state of mind was maintained in these repeated exercises might have been that the police officers changed their role when performing the team task. Hence, the experience of the event and the challenge to solve the new task might have produced a novel sensation when the task was repeated. The apparent need for the CNS to experience a new stressful scenario 5 times before it gives a much weaker activation of the stress response the sixth time can also be an explanation (Grossman 1995).

Another limitation with simulated scenarios are that they are not likely to evoke emotions as strong as those felt under real life threats and that this difference might still make participants taking part in simulated training not fully prepared to handle life-threatening events. Here, one approaches an ethical limit whether certain means should be allowed to address the issues with psychological stress, for example, use of alcohol or drugs to bring the effects of psychological stress under control in wartime conditions

(Grossman and Christensen 2004). In many countries, it would be regarded as deeply unethical to submit police officers or military personnel at least in peacetime to real life threats or even imply that they might be under such threats. Moreover, inflicting too much stress in the training scenarios too fast might forever break that person's self-belief in that he or she has the abilities and skills needed to handle the tasks, as mentioned earlier (Atkins and Norris 2004). Furthermore, as revealed in this study, also training scenarios inflicting much lower psychological stress levels produce strong enough sympathetic neurological responses so those who are trained will be allowed to repeatedly sense to some extent the feelings of psychological stress and become familiar to its physical and psychological effects.

Cardiovascular Activity as a Psychological Stress Marker

The psychological stress induced in the police officer team exercise was manifested by a continuously present substantially higher heart rate throughout the exercise, but this manifestation was also noticeable well before the start of the exercise and a long time after the exercise. Hence, as illustrated in Figure 13.2, the psychological stress alters the dynamical heart rate response pattern leaving residual effects also a long time after the exercise was declared complete. An elevated residual psychological stress effect after the completion of a reality-based exercise has previously been also reported by Tavernier and colleagues (2011), who found significantly higher cortisol levels both 5 and 20 min after completed exercises compared with baseline values.

The most noticeable effects of the psychological stress were the significantly faster increase in heart rate during the first 30–50 s of the exercise and the sustained significantly higher steady-state heart rate, about 30 BPM above the level recorded compared with dry-training. Of note, this elevated steady-state heart rate level was maintained and largely unchanged until the exercise was declared complete. Surprisingly, no abrupt increases of heart rate were recorded, suggesting that no strong startle reactions were induced, despite the police officers' abrupt confrontations with the attacker(s) during the latter phase of the exercise. One possible reason for this finding could be the knowledge that an attack would happen during the exercise, so the steady-state stress level adopted already included the psychological stress for this event. Importantly, the assessed heart rate reactions recorded highlight that operations under active threat conditions can also include heavy physical stress since the psychological load under threatening conditions are expressed as increased demand of cardiovascular reactivity.

The findings in this study illustrate the importance of using various information sources when investigating the effects of psychological stress. A common method to assess psychological stress is to take saliva samples before and after being exposed to stressful events and investigate its contents of cortisol. However, this study illustrates two problems with this approach. First, psychological stress is a dynamical process, which changes cardiovascular activity within seconds (Figure 13.2), or even shorter which demands high-resolution equipment to capture startle activations only visible in a few heartbeats (Vonk 2008). Hence, the information provided by discrete saliva samples may be limited in that it can confirm that an increase in the stress hormone production has occurred, but is unable to determine when it occurred and therefore not the triggering event for this reaction. Furthermore, discrete irregular sampling makes it difficult to determine characteristic properties describing a dynamic process, such as latency between event and recorded stress response, rate of increasing reaction, duration of reaction, and recovery rate. Second, it is likely that the mental state of mind and the duration of which a realistic illusion has been maintained are of importance for evoking a high-level stress response and for the properties of this evoked response. In that respect, it cannot be excluded that the procedure of repeatedly taking saliva samples for measuring the stress response may in itself influence the stress response recorded because the assessed subjects are repeatedly reminded of being participants in a scientific experiment.

However, to establish that the cause of the increased heart rate was psychological stress, one must exclude other reasons for the large increase in the heart rate recorded. The other likely reason for the increased heart rate is physical activity. However, the police officer team exercise was completed within an almost identical time as recorded for the dry-training (Figure 13.2). Moreover, the difference in the heart rate between dry-training and performing the police officer team exercise was very high (on average 30 BPM), which would have required very large increase in physical activity such as running instead of walking. In addition, elevated cardiovascular activity was captured already before the start of the police officer team exercise and also well after its completion. In addition, it is important not to rule out psychological cardiovascular elevations in dry-training. However, the purpose of the study was to induce high psychological stress levels through training in a realistic scenario compared with dry-training, and this objective was achieved. Hence, realistic scenario training combined with cardiovascular real-time monitoring of the police officers participating may provide a wealth of information that can be used to personalize training or facilitate recovery.

Conclusion

In certain professions can work-related events produce high psychological stress, which may cause degraded cognitive and physical performance, hypervigilance, freezing and render people unable to use equipment requiring fine motor skills or complex motor control. The consequences of this problem can to some extent be addressed by customizing the trained procedures and equipment so tasks are performed intuitively right also under high psychological stress. This study shows that recordings of heart rate may provide valuable information during this development of suitable training protocols and equipment, since the parameters has an ability to grade psychological stress levels and, thus, evaluate exercise efficiency and monitor improvements gained from participating in stress-based exercises.

When participants in this study performed an active shooter exercise without active stressor stimuli, the heart rate increased from an average of 83 beats per minute to 113 beats per minute, most likely mainly due to the physical activity. However, when the participants performed the identical exercise with active stressor stimuli, their heart rate increased significantly to an average of 143 beats per minute. Hence, it was possible to identify from the heart rate activation pattern whether the exercise only were physically straining or if the exercise also caused psychological stress activation (Figures 13.1 and 13.2), given that the physical tasks performed were identical. This means heart rate recordings may offer an alternative to the more complex cortisol method requiring taking saliva samples during the task monitored for later advanced laboratory analysis. Even if cortisol samples can provide useful information the method has a substantial drawback in that it cannot assess the fast changing dynamical process of psychological stress, for example, to find the triggering event for the stress reaction. Furthermore, discrete irregular sampling makes it difficult to determine characteristic properties describing a dynamic process, such as latency between event and recorded stress response, rate of increasing reaction, duration of reaction, and recovery rate.

The purpose of the study was to induce high psychological stress levels through training in a realistic scenario compared with dry-training, and this objective was achieved. Hence, realistic scenario training combined with cardiovascular real-time monitoring of the police officers participating may provide a wealth of information that can be used to personalize training or facilitate recovery. Of note, this study also revealed that real-time monitoring of cardiovascular activity during the exercise might be used as a mean to control the training scenario, by allowing the training instructors to add during the exercise, if necessary, more stressful elements to the scenario so the psychological stress aimed for is achieved.

References

Altman, D. (1991). *Practical Statistics for Medical Research*. New York: Chapman & Hall.

Atkins, V. J., and Norris, W. A. (2004). Survival scores research project: FLETC Research Paper (F. l. e. t. center, Trans.) (p. 54). Glynco, GA: US Department of Homeland Security.

Carroll, D., Harrison, L. K., Johnston, D. W., Ford, G., Hunt, K., Der, G., and West, P. (2000). Cardiovascular reactions to psychological stress: The influence of demographic variables. *Journal of Epidemiology & Community Health, 54*(11), 876–877.

Freyschuss, U., Hjemdahl, P., Juhlin-Dannfelt, A., and Linde, B. (1988). Cardiovascular and sympathoadrenal responses to mental stress: Influence of beta-blockade. *The American Journal of Physiology, 255*(6 Pt 2), H1443–H1451.

Greenberg, S. F. (2007). State of security at US colleges and universities: A national stakeholder assessment and recommendations. *Disaster Medicine and Public Health Preparedness, 1*(1 Suppl), S47–S50.

Groer, M., Murphy, R., Bunnell, W., Salomon, K., Van Eepoel, J., Rankin, B.,... Bykowski, C. (2010). Salivary measures of stress and immunity in police officers engaged in simulated critical incident scenarios. *Journal of Occupational and Environmental Medicine/American College of Occupational and Environmental Medicine, 52*(6), 595–602.

Grossman, D. (1995). *On Killing: The Psychological Cost of Learning to Kill in War and Society.* New York: Back Bay Books.

Grossman, D., and Christensen, L. W. (2004). *On Combat: The Psychology and Physiology of Deadly Conflict in War and Peace* (pp. 1–395). Millstadt, IL: PPCT Research Publications.

Juniper, B., White, N., and Bellamy, P. (2010). A new approach to evaluating the well-being of police. *Occupational Medicine (London), 60*(7), 560–565.

Kassam, K. S., Koslov, K., and Mendes, W. B. (2009). Decisions under distress: Stress profiles influence anchoring and adjustment. *Psychological Science, 20*(11), 1394–1399.

Kelly, R. W., Daddario, R., Waters, J. R., Alvarez, R., Andersen, J., Biddle, C.,... Riggio, M. (2011). *Active Shooter: Recommendations and Analysis for Risk Mitigation* (pp. 1–179). New York: New York City Police Department.

Matthews, J. N., Altman, D. G., Campbell, M. J., and Royston, P. (1990). Analysis of serial measurements in medical research. *British Medical Journal, 300*(6719), 230–235.

Meyerhoff, J. L., Norris, W., Saviolakis, G. A., Wollert, T., Burge, B., Atkins, V., and Spielberger, C. (2004). Evaluating performance of law enforcement personnel during a stressful training scenario. *Annals of the New York Academy of Sciences, 1032*, 250–253.

Murray, K. R. (2004). *Training at the Speed of Life, Vol. 1: The Definitive Textbook for Police and Military Reality Based Training* (Vol. 1). Gotha, FL: Armiger Publications.

Nieuwenhuys, A., Caljouw, S. R., Leijsen, M. R., Schmeits, B. A., and Oudejans, R. R. (2009). Quantifying police officers' arrest and self-defence skills: Does performance decrease under pressure? *Ergonomics, 52*(12), 1460–1468.

Nieuwenhuys, A., and Oudejans, R. R. (2010). Effects of anxiety on handgun shooting behavior of police officers: A pilot study. *Anxiety Stress Coping, 23*(2), 225–233.

Oudejans, R. R. (2008). Reality-based practice under pressure improves handgun shooting performance of police officers. *Ergonomics, 51*(3), 261–273.

Oudejans, R. R., and Nieuwenhuys, A. (2009). Perceiving and moving in sports and other high-pressure contexts. *Progress in Brain Research, 174*, 35–48.

Paton, D., and Violanti, J. M. (2008). Law enforcement response to terrorism: The role of the resilient police organization. *International Journal of Emergency Mental Health, 10*(2), 125–135.

Sawai, A., Ohshige, K., Yamasue, K., Hayashi, T., and Tochikubo, O. (2007). Influence of mental stress on cardiovascular function as evaluated by changes in energy expenditure. *Hypertension Research, 30*(11), 1019–1027.

Schmidt, R. A., and Lee, T. D. (2011). *Motor Control and Learning: A Behavioral Emphasis* (5th edition, Vol. 5). Champaign, IL: Human Kinetics.

Siddle, B. K. (1995). *Sharpening the Warriors Edge: The Psychology and Science of Training* (Vol. 1). Belleville, IL: PPCT Research Publications.

Taverniers, I., Smeets, T., Ruysseveldt, J. V., Syroit, J., and von Grumbkow, J. (2011). The risk of being shot at: Stress, cortisol secretion, and their impact on memory and perceived learning during reality-based practice for armed officers. *International Journal of Stress Management, 18*(2), 113–132.

Tidgren, B., and Hjemdahl, P. (1989). Renal responses to mental stress and epinephrine in humans. *The American Journal of Physiology, 257*(4 Pt 2), F682–F689.

Vonk, K. D. (2008). Police performance under stress. *Law and Order, 56*, Nbr. 10.

Development of Ghana Police Service Personnel and Performance

14

GERALD DAPAAH GYAMFI

Contents

Introduction

Professional policing was introduced by the British Colonial Authorities to the Gold Coast in 1821 (http://www.ghanapolice.info/history.htm). Historically, in 1874, the British who were then ruling the Gold Coast had a big war with the Ashantis named the "Sagrenti War." The British who were also ruling Nigeria and the West Indies at the time brought 700 Hausa men from Nigeria and some other troops from the West Indies to reinforce the existing number at that time to invade Kumasi when they found it difficult to defeat the Ashantis. Most of these men were killed by the Ashantis. After the war, the remainder of these men was mobilized by the British to form the then Gold Coast Constabulary. These men were trained by the British to use "brute force" in dealing with the public while serving the interest of the colonial administration. In 1894, 400 men out of the existing constabulary formed the Gold Coast Police by an ordinance that was promulgated in that year. This number increased to 22,129 as on February 2008. The service has a pyramidal organogram headed by the Inspector General of Police (IGP) who is appointed by the President of Ghana.

Since the era of the colonial authorities, the recruitment and selection requirements have almost been the same. Contemporarily, Ghana Police

Service is one of the public institutions in Ghana known for its bureaucracy as well as its well-structured staff recruitment and selection requirements.

Generally, enlistment into the Ghana Police Service is currently open to all able-bodied and sound-minded Ghanaians within the ages of 18 and 30 years. Based on the requirements, recruitment and selection into the police service could be categorized into under-cadets, general recruits, and escorts.

The selection requirements of the under-cadets include people who

- Are not more than 30 years old except certain professionals, for example, lawyers and medical doctors.
- Possess a degree or diploma from a recognized tertiary institution.
- Do not have any criminal records.

The selection requirements for the general recruits include people

- Who are between the ages of 18 and 25.
- Who possess a Senior Secondary School Certificate with a minimum of five passes including English and Mathematics.
- Whose minimum height limit is not below 5 feet 8 inches for males and 5 feet 4 inches for females.
- Who have physique and medically fit by all standards.
- Who have not been convicted for any criminal offence.

The escorts are to meet similar requirements as the general recruits without much emphasis on academic qualification and examination. When all the conditions stated above are satisfied, applicants would be required to undertake a written examination and would be expected to pass before being recruited into the service. The recruits are trained and they are expected to indicate some level of professionalism which could be translated into day-to-day mode of policing.

Problem Statement

The mass media ceased not to hammer on corruption on the part of the police personnel or how people were mistakenly killed or shot dead by police officers or umpteen attacks by armed robbers with even some police personnel found culpable. Serious crimes such as murder, robbery, narcotic drug peddling, and rape were perpetrated, and in some cases, some policemen who were supposed to enforce the law were found to be victims. Statistics from Ghana Police Service in 2008 showed that 68 police personnel were dismissed in 2006 and the same number in 2007 for misconduct. In discussing the alleged poor performance of the police, there were two schools of thought. The first school of thought argued that the selection requirements into the service were not based on very good person specification that affected the performance of the personnel of the service. The second school of thought also argued that the selection criteria had nothing to do with the performance of the personnel, but rather there were other motivational factors such as infrastructural development and remuneration which led to the underperformance and the subsequent accusations of the Ghana Police Service.

The questions frequently asked included were as follows: what were the bases or fundamental reasons for the loss of respect and how could the issues involved be addressed as the security and preservation of any sound society hangs on the security services of the nation, especially as it deals directly on a daily basis with the citizenry?

During the period of the study, the Ghana Police Service was under severe criticism by the general public as a result of their poor performance in the country in general, giving rise to questions about the relevance of the "integrity" attached to their motto "Service with Integrity." For a developing country like Ghana to attract investors, there must be peace and security in the country. Under the Police Service Act 1970 (Act 350), the Ghana Police Service has been mandated to perform its statutory functions of crime prevention, arrest and prosecution of offenders, maintenance of law and order, and ensuring the safety of persons and property.

Aims/Objectives

Ghana Police Service is the foremost state agency responsible for the maintenance of law and order in Ghana. The service has been widely described by some sections of the public as an entity that has lost grips of its functions, bringing into question a number of issues about its effectiveness or level of performance. It is for this reason that this study carefully examined the selection requirements for enlistment into the police service and the extent to which the selection requirements impact on the performance of the personnel. It is against this background that this study was undertaken in the year 2009 to ascertain whether the selection requirements of Ghana Police Service had any relationship with performance of the personnel of the service. This study therefore sought to

- Assess whether there was any significant relationship between the selection criteria and the performance of the police personnel.
- Find out whether the performance of the service was related to other factors than that of selection criteria.
- Suggest means of improving the performance of the service.

Justification

It was deemed that the research would inform the police service to reconsider its recruitment and selection procedures for improvement of its performance and suggest other means for appropriate capacity building program by the Human Resource Department of Ghana Police Service.

Literature Review

Selection is generally considered as a process that uses a methodical approach to identify the individuals who have the ability and the know-how to perform best out of all those who offer themselves for a job (Ash 2001; Price 2000); recruitment and selection process should not be considered in isolation but in the context of the overall human resource plan (Mukhwan 1978). The plan must cover areas such as potential for training, development and future promotion, flexibility and adaptability to possible new methods, procedures or working conditions, and how they fit into the organization's culture and social structure (Bratton and Gold 1999; Brumbach 1988). For organization performance, there is a need for a planned and systematic approach in order to select the appropriate staff and retain them for a reasonable length of time (Mattesen 1999).

Commenting on police selection requirements that could lead to effective performance, Cordner (1989) indicated that in order to be successful, police administrators should design selection requirements to meet the objectives of the police service, and if the administrators selected the wrong person, the output of the staffing process would be negatively affected. A study by Hsu et al. (2007) revealed that entrance examination taken by prospective employees has a significant positive effect on job performance.

Law enforcement workers are expected to work as professionals in order to keep pace with the pressures placed on them, and for them to give off their efforts to execute their tasks as professionals, they must be well motivated (Armstrong 2003). A study conducted in Russia showed that most of the police recruits thought corruption within the police service was justifiable and morally acceptable under certain circumstances when they were not well remunerated. This research was carried out when the policemen were perceived by the public and the media as being corrupt using their positions at work to extort money, goods, or services from victims (Adrian and Lee 2002). In Malaysia, when the police were underperforming and perceived to be corrupt, the President Datus Seri Najib made provision to motivate them to enhance their performance. He increased the remuneration of the personnel, resorted to the use of promotion on a time basis, provided logistics, and offered other incentives to enhance their efforts to fight crime (http://thestar.com.my/news/story.asp?file = 2010).

According to *Accra Daily Mail* news of June 2, 2005, it was reported that corruption in Ghana was so bad that one might think it had been institutionalized in the public sector, and most police and prison officers were ranked the highest bribe takers. *The Ghanaian Chronicle* reported on July 26, 2006, that some top police officers were allegedly involved in taking bribes. Anning (2006) indicated that the police was corrupt because the government lacked the political will to implement the various reports on police service such as Boyles Report (December 1971) which touched on pay, welfare, appointments, and promotions. Ghanaian policemen on peace missions abroad performed marvelously well that even in Kosovo some Ghana police personnel whose tour of duty had come to an end were requested to continue for another time period because of their performance, according to Stephen Canteen Cowboy, Leader of UN Mission in Kosovo, on June 14, 2006 (www.policeoracle.com/forum/forum-posts.asp?TID = 2053). The question that can be asked is as follows: Why such a performance on missions abroad? This could be attributed to the fact that when on mission the policemen are better motivated than when at post in Ghana.

Materials and Methods

In the year 2009, a team of five members including the author was constituted by their researcher to carry out the research after a consultation with some high ranking personnel of Ghana Police Service. The research took a multidesigned dimensional approach with a case study and a survey within the Ghana Police Service. The study was a descriptive one covering a wide range of cross section of the Ghana police personnel. The method and nature of collecting data involved both qualitative and quantitative techniques. The primary data were based on questionnaire and interview.

The fieldwork was undertaken within a period of 13 weeks. Four weeks were used for pretesting of the questionnaire. Nine weeks were devoted to the administration of questionnaire and interview of the subjects. In designing the instruments, experts from the Ghana Police Service were consulted. The questionnaire was pretested during a pilot study in the earlier part of 2009 to ensure that the questions asked were understood by the respondents. To ensure reliability, the respondents were interviewed by the team on some of the questions already asked in the questionnaire.

The population included all the police personnel in the Ghana Police Service (22,129). The sampling frame included the list of all police personnel within Accra from the following police units:

- Ghana National Police Headquarters
- Accra Regional Headquarters
- Accra South Divisional Headquarters—Ministries
- Accra Central Divisional Headquarters—Nima
- Kaneshie Divisional Headquarters—Kaneshie

Considering the sensitive nature of the study, the confidentiality of the respondents was highly assured. A multiphase sampling technique was used to select the police units and the personnel to participate in the study. The police population in Accra was stratified into five categories: Ghana National Headquarters,

Accra Regional Headquarters, Accra South Divisional Headquarters—Ministries, Accra Central Divisional Headquarters—Nima, and Kaneshie Divisional Headquarters—Kaneshie.

A purposive sampling technique was used to select the five categories based on the following: The National Headquarters was chosen because it was the hub upon which all policing activities in Ghana were done. The Regional Police Headquarters was selected in view of the fact that it was the Headquarters of all the Divisions in Accra. The three Divisional Headquarters were selected due to their strategic positions, nearness to big market places in Accra, and the possibility of handling crime-related cases.

One hundred copies of questionnaire were administered; out of which 72 were retrieved which included those from 10 senior officers and 62 junior officers. The data collection period was from April 30, 2009, to May 14, 2009. The main variables measured were the requirements of the recruitment and selection procedure of the Ghana Police Service and the performance of the police personnel. This included the height, academic qualification, aptitude test/entrance examination, rank, and age. Questions were also asked on the performance of the personnel and how it was related to the selection criteria.

Results

From the field survey, 2.8% of the respondents were indifferent on whether the height of personnel had something to do with performance. As indicated in Table 14.1, 29% agreed that the height of the personnel was related to performance, but 68% disagreed and indicated that it was a legacy from the colonial masters who because of the threat from the natives made it a requirement for their protection since they were to use "brute" force on the people, that is, the need for giants. While 62.5% agreed that academic requirement had influence on performance, 34.7% disagreed and 2.8% remained neutral. On the use of entrance examination as a requirement that had influence on performance, 40.3% agreed but 56.9% disagreed and 2.8% were undecided.

Table 14.1   Relationship between Entry Requirements and Performance

Factor	Strongly Agree (%)	Agree (%)	Disagree (%)	Strongly Disagree (%)
Height	9 (12.5)	12 (16.5)	12 (33.3)	25 (34.7)
Academic performance	25 (34.7)	20 (27.8)	8 (11.1)	17 (23.6)
Entrance examination	12 (16.7)	17 (23.6)	11 (15.2)	30 (41.7)
Other requirements	68 (94.4)	–	–	4 (5.6)

Table 14.2 Impact of Performance Factors

Factor	Frequency	Percentage
Motivation	15	20.8
Fair recruitment exercise	13	18.1
Recruitment requirement	12	16.7
Neutral	11	15.3
Training	9	12.5
Promotion	6	8.3
Individual attitude	5	6.9
All	1	1.4
Total	72	100

The result also indicated that 94.4% of the respondents joined the service after meeting all the entry requirements, but 5.6% disclosed that they joined the service even though they could not meet all the entry requirements. The majority of the personnel interviewed gave other factors including physique, health status, and command of the use of English language. When the respondents were asked to rate the following factors in order of importance with regard to how they impacted on their performance, the result was shown in Table 14.2.

The respondents were also asked to indicate in order of importance how the factors in Table 14.3 could bring about improvement in their performance and the result indicated as follows: motivation (29.2%), further education (23.6%), change of posting procedure (19.4%), training (16.7%), and change of job schedules (11.1%).

For the research team to know from the individuals their assessment of their own job performance, the result indicated as follows (Table 14.4): Excellent (26.4%), Very good (34.7%), Good (34.7%), and Average (4.2%).

The team also wanted to know the general performance of the police service in Ghana from the perspective of the personnel so the individual respondents were asked to assess the general performance of the service and the result indicated as follows (Table 14.5): Valid (2.8%), Excellent (9.7%), Very good (30.6%), and Good (30.6%).

Table 14.3 Performance Improvement Factors

Factor	Frequency	Percentage
Motivation	21	29.2
Further education	17	23.6
Change of posting	14	19.4
Training	12	16.7
Change of job schedule	8	11.1
Total	72	100

Table 14.4 Assessment of Overall Job Performance

Assessment	Frequency	Percentage
Excellent	19	26.4
Very good	25	34.7
Good	25	34.7
Average	3	4.2
Total	72	100

Table 14.5 Assessment of General Performance of Ghana Police Service

Assessment	Frequency	Percentage
Valid	2	2.8
Excellent	7	9.7
Very good	22	30.6
Good	29	40.3
Average	11	15.3
Below average	1	1.4
Total	72	100

Discussion

The men who were trained by the British were to use "brute force" in dealing with the public to serve the interest of the colonial administration and were to use some physical force on the people; therefore, physique, especially "height," was considered as the main factor in selecting the people for the then police force. The study revealed that the use of "height" as a factor should be discarded by the Ghana Police Service because the majority of the service men (68%) agreed that "height requirement does not have much significant impact on their performance." From the response received, the majority of the respondents preferred academic performance (45%) and entrance examination (29%) as the main criteria. This could emanate from the use of modern technology that involves Information and Communication Technology (ICT) for effective policing and the use of intelligence. Could physique be discarded outright? The constitution of Ghana mandates the police to use a minimal force and to defend themselves whenever attacked in the course of their duties, and this calls for personnel with good physical strength. Is there any correlation between "height" and "physical" strength? However, the use of "height" could leave out some people who do not meet the height requirement but have good physique and more intelligent and also have what it takes to do proper policing that could give credit to the police service in the eyes of the Ghanaian populace.

The view of majority of the respondents was that for good performance the police service should focus more on motivating the personnel (29.3%) and considered motivation as a factor that had tremendous impact on their performance. Fairness in selecting the people was also considered as a factor that influenced their performance probably because of tribal/political sentiments. Further education and training were considered as other factors that could enable them improve on their performance. Majority of the respondents considered their individual performance to be good (34%) or very good (34%). Generally, the research revealed that the performance of Ghana Police Service was good probably after considering their constraints that included logistics and poor condition of service.

Conclusion and Recommendation

The need for effective maintenance of law and order (peace and security) for the purpose of achieving socioeconomic development of the citizenry draws one's attention to the police service with particular reference to how the personnel discharge their duties. The result of the study revealed that there was appreciable level of relationship between the selection criteria and the performance of Ghana Police Service, particularly academic qualification and the use of entrance examination. It was also established that the selection exercise should be fair and equitable for better performance. However, the majority of the police personnel were of the view that the use of "height" as part of the selection criteria should be reconsidered by the police authorities. The study, therefore, recommended the following:

- The selection exercise should be fair to all Ghanaians.
- The use of "height" as a criterion for selection should be discarded.
- The police personnel should be encouraged to further educate and train themselves to meet the modern trend of policing.
- For improvement in their performance, the personnel should be better motivated.
- The logistics should be enhanced.

References

Adrian, B., and Lee, R. (2002). Attitude to corruption amongst police officers and trainees. *Crime, Law, and Social Change*, 38(4), 357–372.

Anning, E. K. (2006). An overview of the Ghana Police Service. *Journal of Security Management*, 4(2), 1–37.

Armstrong, M. (2003). *A Handbook of Human Resource Management Practice*, 9th Edition. Koga Page: London.

Ash, R. A. (2001). Selecting employee for fit: Personality and preferred managerial styles. *Journal of Managerial Issues* 13(4):500–517.

Bratton, J. and Gold, J. (1999). *Human Resource Management: Theory and Practice*. McMillan: London.

Brumbach, G. B. (1988). *Public Personnel Management*. Koga Page: London.

Cordner, W. R. (1989). *Introduction to Police Administration*, 2nd Edition. Anderson: London.

Hsu, Y., Chang, W. C., and Yang, V. (2007). *A Study on Recruitment and Job Performance in Product Design*. Education: Taiwan.

Mattesen, S. (1999). *Recruitment, Screening and Selection*. http://fcrc3.indstate.edu. Retrieved: March 3, 2009.

Mukhwan, W. (1978). Manpower planning for organization development. *Journal of Management Studies* 10(1):10.

Price, A. (2000). *Principles of Human Resource Management*. Blackwell: London.

Police Writing Techniques in Reported Interviews

15

GUNILLA K. BYRMAN

Contents

Introduction

> So you phone the police and they come and you talk to them and they write it down. And when you get these documents you try to piece it together: "Aha, so this is what happened?" But you're not functioning right at this stage. So you put it to one side and believe that everything is there. Then comes a prosecutor who reads through it and thinks, "That wasn't so serious." (Blixt, Hradilova Selin, and Westlund 2010, 45)

This quotation is from a study of citizens' contact with the judicial system. A Swedish woman who has been exposed to domestic violence reads the report on the investigation of her case and she gives her view of the text and the communication in the judicial system. "Aha, so this is what happened?" reveals that she does not think it is her experience of what happened that is documented in the investigation.

With this in mind, we acknowledge that police interviews are of vital importance in the Swedish criminal justice process. For the investigators themselves, the documented audiotaped and written interviews are an essential part of any investigation into a criminal offence, and an interview with a plaintiff or a suspect functions as evidence in itself. It is not only important for the police to get the statements of the interviewed persons right and in accordance with Swedish writing standards (*Svenska skrivregler* 2000), but it must also be tenable in the judicial process, since the prosecutor uses the interview reports as one source of evidence to decide whether or not to prosecute.

In this chapter, I discuss some problematic writing techniques, on both surface and deeper levels in the text, used by the Swedish police in writing investigative interviews. This should highlight the complexity in the linguistic process of transforming the interviewees' spoken words into a written readable text and the difficulties the police have in writing the interview.

My perspective is critical discourse analysis (cf. Coulthard 1996; Fairclough 2010), with a critical examination of the language used in the Swedish legal system. Studies on language in the legal context have been carried out by Heydon (2005, 2010) in Australia, Komter (2002, 2006) in the Netherlands, and Coulthard (1996, 2011) and Haworth (2010) in England. In Sweden, Jönsson (1988) and Gumbel (2000) have examined police investigators' writing from a linguistic perspective.

Jönsson compared audiotaped recordings and written interviews, showing that the police interview was a highly institutionalized and routine procedure, where the first priority for the police is to write a report. She also pointed out that in some police texts the content and perspective were corrupted so badly that this could have legal consequences, which means that in some cases Jönsson examined the police officer had added information and details in the text to get the narrative text into a better and more comprehensible shape. By comparing the audiotape and the written transcription, Jönsson concluded that the added details were not the words spoken by the interviewee.

Gumbel has suggested that the police reports are not only communicative tools in the judicial process, but also a reflection of the contemporary culture and the prevailing view of men's violence against women. She has studied the perspectives of the text, showing how the police officers' attitudes toward the men, distance, and the women, empathy, are expressed in the interviews (Gumbel 2000).

In a study (Ask and Byrman 2010) containing the same investigations of domestic violence as in this study, we have applied relief analysis, since this seems to be an efficient method for catching sight of the overall perspective of the officer and the text, to discuss how the constituent elements of the offense appear in the foreground and background of interview texts and how verbs are used to show the perspective in the texts. The results suggest that police officers need to use neutral reporting verbs and to write a fuller background for the interview texts to be credible and thus tenable in the continued judicial process (Ask and Byrman 2010). We have also noticed that a reported interview has always more or less obvious traces of the officer's attitudes, perspectives, and priorities in the text, which may corrupt the interview as evidence; in the Swedish legal system, this may restrain the prosecutor from continuing the judicial process (cf. Haworth 2010).

The aim of this study is to examine how the police, through different writing and retelling techniques, reproduce the interviewees' statements in the reported written interviews and the problems involved in this process. The focus is on the modes of presentation and the use of quotations and slashes in the texts. The questions are as follows:

- In what modes of presentation are the words of the interviewees reproduced in written interviews?
- What stylistic impact do the techniques have on the interviewees' statements and the texts as a whole?

I will introduce and discuss the modes of presentation in terms of narration (narrative), direct, indirect, and free indirect speech. In the texts the officers use quotation marks and slashes in a way that does not always agree with Swedish standards, and it can be disputed whether this is suitable in legal discourse. The interviews also construct a picture of the plaintiff's and the suspect's social status and mental state, which will be commented on briefly.

Techniques of Retelling and Writing

In the interview situation, investigators always have to choose how to frame and formulate the interviewee's statement. They can do this in different ways in the text by mixing *narration*, where the officer's perspective is prevalent, with *quoted* and *reported statements* from the interviewees, in different combinations and quantities. Quoted and reported statements can be reproduced in various ways (cf. Teleman, Hellberg, and Andersson 1999). In traditional stylistics, these techniques of quoting and reporting are named *direct, indirect*, and *free indirect speech*. In direct speech, the reader gets a sense of being near the speaker, and in indirect speech, a distance is established between the reader and the words of the speaker (Cassirer 2003).

In quotations, which normally correspond to *direct speech*, the officer reproduces the speaker's utterance as if it was a verbatim record; whether it actually corresponds exactly to the original utterance cannot always be established. For an example of a quoted statement, let us imagine a situation where a woman named Lena says:

(1) Yesterday Eric emailed: "Now I am staying here and waiting until you have made up your mind."

In the quoted sentence, references such as *I*, *now*, and *here* and the tense typically refer to the situation of the original utterance. In the example, *I* refers to Eric, not to Lena, who is reproducing it. A reported sentence, which corresponds to *indirect speech*, reflects in its structure the original speech act, but not always the exact wording. Generally, a reported sentence differs from a quoted sentence in that the personal pronouns and tense refer to the situation in which it is reported and can be reproduced in a subordinate clause or in some cases an infinitive phrase, for example, if Lena says:

(2) Yesterday Eric emailed that he would stay there and wait until I had made up my mind.

The narrator can also choose to integrate the other person's utterance into his or her text, given as a nominal below. The following example stands out as narration, often in the third person, and the narrator has the monopoly in the narration, as in:

(3) Yesterday Eric emailed an order for five new computers. Lena told me that today, but the company doesn't want to pay for them.

The reported sentences can change without any sharp border into descriptions of situations and courses of events. Especially unclear is the border between non-subordinated reported sentences and narrative, where the speaker in different ways shows the described person's view, what is called *free indirect speech*, for example:

(4) Why on earth had Eric emailed an order for five computers? He obviously knew that the company was in an economic crisis. But Lena defended his bold venture, because "she knew him."

Free indirect speech is typically in the third person and in the past tense. The effect is that the reader vaguely senses that it is the persons mentioned in the text, rather than the narrator, that e-mail, feel, and think. The vocabulary in general can be the interviewee's, not the narrator's; they are in symbiosis. If the officer uses this technique in the written reported interviews, this makes it difficult to keep the interviewer and the interviewee apart. The intensifier "on earth," the adverbial "obviously," the phrase "bold venture," and the quoted sentence "she knew him" create this impression.

A pure *narration* of this content could be something like this, mentioned here in the third person and in the present tense:

(5) Eric has emailed an order for five computers, though he knows the company has economic problems. Lena is encouraging him since she knows him well.

or in the past tense:

(6) Eric had emailed an order for five computers, though he knew the company had economic problems. Lena was encouraging him since she knew him well.

It is impossible to decide which technique would be the most functional in reported interviews, and the material shows that there is a mixture of all of them in authentic texts.

The Swedish Legal Context: Place, Time, and Power

According to Swedish law, any police intervention must be documented in writing. The Swedish police have different ways of recording statements from interviews. Sometimes, it is a verbatim record of the interview, which is always the case when a child is the injured party, but often it is a summary of what the interviewer considers the most important information.

The report is the start of the inquiry that follows. In the texts, the police have to show that the constituent elements of the offence exist. This means that the officer writing the texts retells and describes the criminal events and presents the interviewee's narrative, which is a complex process and not easy to do.

Time and space are problematic in the judicial process, since the principle of oral proceedings applies in Swedish courts. This means that witnesses and parties are questioned orally rather than having their statements read out. It is a consequence of the principle of immediateness, the requirement that the court should decide in the case on the basis of what has been seen and heard during the proceedings, because written language is considered more difficult for a listener to understand than speech (https://lagen.nu, February 6, 2011).

In assault cases, the prosecutor is in charge of the investigation. A prosecutor has to work with the investigation as a tool to decide whether or not to prosecute. If the prosecutor takes a case to the court, all investigative materials are considered known to the parties involved as a matter of principle. But everyone dealing with legal processes must realize that there is a difference between an interview room and a courtroom, as regards formality and audience. Furthermore, a long time could have passed since the crime was committed. Written investigations and hence the interviews are important for the prosecutors to decide whether to take the case to the court, but may not be crucial for the outcome of the court proceedings. The statements on the crime and the wording in the investigation can be questioned in the court and therefore the trustworthiness of the interviewees. The prosecutor has to instruct the police how to handle the investigation, and the police have to interview the parties in the case. Ask and Alison (2010) have examined the investigators' decision making, and they point out that information management is crucial for this, and in my opinion written language and verbal communication play a major role in decision making. That is why the language in the investigations has to be scrutinized.

The texts in an investigation are supposed to be understood by readers with very different skills and knowledge. The content and form of the retold course of events may be difficult for laypersons to understand, but the things stated there bear the stamp of truth because of their authority, content and form, and potential future consequences for those involved.

All written reported interviews are condensed and simplified, which is one of the reasons for writing them. It gives the prosecutor a brief summary of the course of events and shows the constituent elements of the crime. Written reported interviews are shorter and therefore not so time consuming for the prosecutors; hence, there is a good reason for producing written reports and making them clearly worded.

From a linguistic perspective, there are many problems that occur in a spoken discourse in the interview room and courtroom, where interviews take place in the legal context (cf. Haworth 2010). First, it is vital to record what was said during the original interaction, which requires the interviews to be presented in an adequate format. Second, comparisons between what was said during the interview and at the trial assume that an honest person will give a verbatim version of the course of events on two occasions, in different contexts, with different audiences, and above all after a long time. These factors will no doubt have an effect on the interviewee's statements. Third, the legal system assumes that the interviewer just asks the interviewee to say what happened, but in practice the interviewer has to show that the constituent element of the offence exists. To be able to do so, interviewers in most cases must put questions about what they think is relevant to the investigation. This defines the police in the role of questionnaire and the interviewee in the role of respondent. For this reason, there is no equal power relationship between the participants in the interview room, or for that matter in the courtroom (cf. Haworth 2010).

Data: Investigations of Domestic Violence

The data examined originate from 80 authentic investigations of domestic violence with different charges, containing the plaintiffs' reports, the reported interviews, and the police memoranda (360,000 words in 80 texts) from five police stations in Sweden (Ask and Byrman 2008). The examples are interviews chosen at random from two investigations in the corpus and can be described as representative of the corpus as a whole.

Domestic violence comes under public prosecution, and therefore, the prosecutor can take it to the court without the cooperation of the plaintiff, but if the injured party does not want to cooperate or perhaps wants to withdraw the complaint, it is not easy for the prosecutor to take it to the court. The fact is that only a small proportion of cases of domestic violence against women lead to a report being filed, and less than 50% go to prosecution (Lidholm 2002).

It is troublesome for the Swedish judicial system that so many cases are dropped. Apart from the fact that it is a difficult situation for the woman to report someone close to her, in my opinion there can be something in the way the reports are written, which makes it difficult to prosecute the case of domestic violence.

Data Analysis: Investigators' Writing Techniques

In this section, I will comment on the modes of presentation, which also include the use of quotation marks and slashes, in the reproduced interview with the plaintiff and suspect, and the impact they may have on the interviewees' statements and the texts as a whole, and hence in the continued judicial process. The features examined affect cohesion (i.e., how the sentences are connected to each other), inferences that the reader must be able to make in order to understand the situation and what happened, and also the use of perspective.

Besides, the data reported in the interview construct a picture of the interviewee, whether it gives an accurate view of the situation. Nevertheless this construction may influence the people in charge of the investigation, which will be commented on briefly.

The material comes from texts 44 and 10 in the corpus "Texts with importance" (Ask and Byrman 2008). In the first example concerning a couple in their 50s, both the plaintiff's and the suspect's interviews are discussed. The second example involves a young female plaintiff that has been hit by her ex-husband.

Middle-Aged Couple with Drug Problems

In the first interview, a female plaintiff has reported her cohabitant for having molested her. The police wrote the following account of the woman's statement. (In this and the following extracts the paragraphs are numbered in sequence for reference and to show when paragraphs are omitted.)

Text 44: Interview with the Plaintiff Maria
(January 25, 2007, 15:00–15:15, at the police station)

1. Informed that Tony [the suspect] has said that he threw a mobile telephone at Maria and that it hit her on the lip, Maria says that this is not correct. Tony hit her as she said in the first interview. He hit her in the face.
2. According to Maria, Tony has been drinking for a week. Maria thinks that he should get help. "This can't go on." When Tony is sober he is good. When he drinks he becomes "like crazy" if Maria "says the slightest thing wrong."
3. Twice before when Maria has reported him it has led to trial. Tony has been sentenced "to a month or so." At one of the trials Maria said to the judge that there was no point in sentencing Tony to prison. He needs care. Maria: "This is how I have had it for 14 years."

4. When asked about injuries Maria says that it hurts when she breathes (ribs), she has a red mark at her nose and on her lip and a big bruise on her wrist.

5. Maria does not remember how many times she has been forced to call for an ambulance when Tony has gone "ballistic." She has pleaded that Tony should be allowed to stay on for care, but he has come home in a taxi.

6. Tony is a periodical drinker. He can be without alcohol for a month or so, but then he drinks again.

7. Maria has applied for a restraining order. She is therefore asked how this is supposed to be arranged when she and Tony live at the same address. Maria: "I can't do that to Tony. He'll have to come home so that we can talk through our problems." (Maria does not want a restraining order).

8. Because of interruptions in telecommunications it has only been possible to hold a short interview with Maria. The police in X-town have promised to drive Maria to the hospital in X-town on the same day as this interview.

In the extract from a reported interview cited above, the presentation modes change constantly. The first paragraph is very complex with a lot of information about what has happened and the officer obviously read the suspect's statement aloud to her and asked her if it was correct. Maria's answer is reproduced by the officer as indirect speech in the first sentence. The second and third sentences in the paragraph appear to be narration written from the officer's perspective: "Tony hit her as she said in the first interview. He hit her in the face." These are constituent elements of the offence. The text imperceptibly glides from indirect speech in the first sentence to narration in the following, which gives it a vague impression of free indirect speech.

In paragraphs 2–5, the officer oscillates between the interviewer's and the interviewee's perspective, in a mixture of modes, for example, indirect speech ("According to Maria, Tony has been drinking for a week. Maria thinks that he should get help."), followed by a quotation ("This can't go on."), but the quoted statement is not explicitly referring to Maria. It seems isolated in the text. This is followed by the narration ("When Tony is sober he is good"); the next sentence is also narration, but it has two quotations mixed in: "When he drinks he becomes 'like crazy' if Maria 'says the slightest thing wrong.' " All this blended gives the impression of free indirect style, where the officer and the interviewee merge into one.

The reader must be good at making inferences to get a clear meaning out of paragraphs 2 and 3. For example, in "At one of the trials Maria said to the judge that there was no point in sentencing Tony to prison. He needs care. Maria: 'This is how I have had it for 14 years.' "; it is not easy to be sure whether she said these words to the judge or to the police officer that interviewed her. This illustrates that there is always a risk that the reader makes the wrong inferences, which can lead to a misinterpretation of the statement in the interview. Paragraph 3 is written in the same style.

Paragraph 4 reproduces an answer to a question from the interviewer and does so clearly. In paragraphs 5–6, the plaintiff's own language is revealed through a narrative, when she speaks about her cohabitant's alcohol problems and the consequences it has for his ability to control his aggression ("Tony has gone 'ballistic' "), with "ballistic" reproduced in quotation marks, a way for the officer to let us know that this is the plaintiff's usage. At the same time, the officer lets the narration slip into what seems to be direct speech, which gives the impression of free indirect style.

Paragraph 7 starts the narration with the officer's perspective followed by indirect speech and then with a quoted statement from the woman that is clearly worded as follows: "Maria: 'I can't do that to Tony. He'll have to come home so that we can talk through our problems.' " Then comes a comment in parentheses that she does not want a restraining order. Paragraph 8 explains why the interview lasted only 15 min. It was broken off due to a bad line, which is expressed in a bureaucratic way. It should also be pointed out that the plaintiff has not read through, or had the report read aloud, and approved of this interview as is required by law.

It seems as if there is no obvious thought behind when the interviewee should be quoted verbatim and when it is enough to use narration, direct speech, and indirect speech. The quotation marks rather become a tool for making the interviewee's presence feel genuine in the text, but there is not really a transparent system in the use of quotations. Two of the quotations are clearly attributed to Maria: "I can't do that to Tony. He'll have to come home so that we can talk through our problems." and "This is how I have had it for 14 years." Other occurrences show the interviewee's language, such as "ballistic," and her general thoughts about her situation and the relationship as a whole, such as "This can't go on."

Text 44: Interview with Suspect Tony
(January 25, 2007, 14:20–14:50, in the cell at the police station)

1. Tony denies being guilty of assault.
2. He states that he became jealous when Maria was talking on the telephone to Bo W-son who is a friend of both of them. Tony then threw Maria's mobile phone at her lip. She then scratched Tony on his left cheek and left ear. Tony shows the injuries to Prob. Const. M-daughter and D.I. K-man. The injuries consist of two small wounds on the left cheek and small marks behind the left ear.

[...]

5. Tony has a good recollection of the event. He does not normally have gaps in his memory when he drinks.

6. Tony thinks that their relationship is good, but when he and Maria drink, mistakes can arise. Maria has a "bloody awful temper" and they often provoke each other.

[...]

8. Nor has he threatened Maria. Tony believes that she only makes these accusations when she is on "the booze."

[...]

10. Tony states that when he gets his pension he normally drinks for about a week without stopping. He then drinks a few half-bottles a day. When he was arrested on Wednesday he had been drinking since Friday. According to Tony, Maria had gambled away a lot of money that Friday (19/01/07). Maria has also started drinking alcohol in the last few months and about a couple of long drinks a day. She then takes Sobril to strengthen the intoxication.

11. Tony was informed that Maria had applied for a restraining order. He thinks this is just "something she does when she's drunk." She has no need to be afraid of him. Tony thinks that they can be together when they are both sober.

[...]

13. Tony explained that he and Maria have a lot of things going on, for instance a flea market on Saturday and Sunday.

14. Read aloud and approved.

The first five paragraphs are pure narration. In paragraph 2, the female officer mentions herself and her colleague in the third person and in paragraph 5 she gives an account of the suspect's mental state: "Tony has a good recollection of the event. He does not normally have gaps in his memory when he drinks." Paragraphs 6 and 8 have a mixture of indirect speech ("Tony thinks that their relationship is good, but when he and Maria drink, mistakes can arise."), progressing into narrative with a quotation from Tony about her temperament ("Maria has a 'bloody awful temper' and they often provoke each other."). Paragraph 8 starts with narration ("Nor has he threatened Maria."), continues with indirect speech, and ends with yet another quotation that characterizes the suspect's language: "Tony believes that she only makes these accusations when she is on 'the booze.' " The blend of modes of presentation creates the impression of free indirect style, and paragraph 11 gives the same impression. In this interview, the quotations seem to be intended to reflect Tony's way of talking, for example, "bloody awful temper," "when she is on 'the booze,' " and "something she does when she's drunk."

Paragraph 10 gives an account of Tony's—but mostly Maria's—alcohol, drug, and gambling problems, which is reproduced in narration and indirect speech in a clear manner. This description of their problematic relationship is reinforced by paragraphs 5, 11, and 13, where Tony tries to lessen the seriousness of the assault by saying that she only wants a restraining order when she is drunk, but he says that she does not need to be afraid of him. He thinks their relationship is all right as long as they are both sober, and that they have shared activities such as the flea market.

The impression we get from these two interviews is of a couple with serious social problems. As Gumbel (2000) points out, the texts in investigations are not only the communicative tools in the judicial process, but also a reflection of the contemporary culture and the prevailing view of men's violence against women. She argues that the injured party is often constructed according to attributes concerning class and ethnicity, along with social problems, and the analyzed investigation is an example of this.

Ann and Her Jealous Ex-Husband

This report is about two young persons who have been married but are not living together any more. They have a child together, which is being taken care of by a stand-in family. Relatives (his brother and her mother) are in the young woman's flat in the evening when the assault happened. The ex-husband suspects that Ann has a relationship with his brother, who is jealous and assaults her. The extract from the interview describes when she came home after taking a walk with her ex-brother-in-law.

Text 10: Interview with the plaintiff
(January 30, 2007, 12:11–12.28, at the police station)

[…]
3. When Ann came home/in both John and her mother were angry because she had not come home. Ann tried to explain but John suggested that perhaps she had a relationship with Akko. There was some discussion and in the end she told John that "he had to get out of there" from her flat. John then grabbed her and hit her with his hand on the left side of her head. The blow which was hard hit her over the ear and caused real pain and that she felt as if she "was numbed." […] [She phoned the police after the assault.]
[…]
7. When the police were about to leave she called out that she wanted to talk to them, she had the feeling that they were not taking her seriously. The police came up and then she felt uncertain and could not cope with reporting what had happened. The police officers nevertheless wrote a report about the damage to the letter slit in the door.
8. Today she feels stronger mentally and wants to report him for assault and feels that she "can cope/manage to stick to what happened to her."
9. When asked about injuries: felt pain when she was hit, turned red and got numb/partly lost her hearing for a few days and that she feels humiliated. […]

12. Claim for compensation: wants to come back to this when she has talked to her counsel. As for the door/letter slit, the flat and door belong to Housing Company X. [...]
13. Ann states that she wants to bring up a previously reported event of abuse in 2005 which was closed because she could not cope with proceeding. A check in the register shows that Ann is referring to report KXXXXX-05, see separate interview. [This paragraph was crossed out in the original.]
14. Draft read aloud.

In this interview, the police have the same technique of blending different modes of presentation, which end up like free indirect speech, as in the extract from text 44 analyzed above. In addition, the officer has a dubious way of giving alternatives for the reader to interpret by using slashes: "When Ann came home/in both John and her mother were angry because she had not come home." and "got numb/partly lost her hearing for a few days." The phrase "can cope/manage to stick to what happened to her" is supposed to be direct quotation from the plaintiff, which it may be, but this way of reproducing it gives a vague impression that is hard to grasp and to interpret. The reader does not know whether it should be understood as meaning that she got numb or partly lost her hearing for a few days, or both. This technique of writing with slashes is not recommended by the Language Council of Sweden, which advocates using *or* or *and* instead of a slash, or simply rephrasing the sentence, which perhaps would be the most efficient way to do it in the text above (cf. *Svenska skrivregler* 2000).

A strange thing is that paragraph 13 is crossed out. From reading it, however, we can conclude that Ann had reported John once before in 2005. And on the night of this incident, Ann had not reported the assault, just the damage to the door and letter slit. We may well wonder why Ann felt that they did not take her seriously on that occasion.

This reported interview also constructs the plaintiff Ann as being hesitant, which may influence how she is treated and how successful her case will be in the end, all other things considered.

Discussion

The police technique of reproducing interviews in written reports by a mixture of modes of presentation—narrative, direct, indirect—gives a vague and unclear impression of the statements by the interviewees, and parts of the text sometimes slip into free indirect style. The officers use quotation marks and slashes in a way that does not quite conform to Swedish standards, which leaves the reader uncertain as to how the text should be interpreted. Slashes should be avoided at all times in legal texts like these, since they make the interpretation of the text difficult (cf. *Svenska skrivregler* 2000).

Sometimes quotation marks are used by the officers to mark a distance from the colloquial style of the interviewees, and at the same time this reflects the interviewees' language and way of talking. Sometimes the officers frame quotations with no reporting verb to identify the speaker and mix quotations with narration and indirect speech, all of which results in free indirect style in the texts.

This difficulty of transforming spoken words into written text is mentioned in the writing guidelines for the police (*Riktlinjer för skrivande inom polisen* 2007), but there is no guidance on how to deal with the problem in practice. The guidelines point out that writing in the police discourse is special, and the starting point is the interviewed person's spoken words. Police officers are instructed to reserve quotation marks for actual quotations. If they are reluctant to use some colloquial words or phrases, instead of putting them in quotation marks they should substitute words that they consider more correct for a formal text. Police are also advised not to use quotation marks when interviewees specifically state that they only have a rough recollection of what someone said, but the guidelines do not clarify exactly how such utterances should be reported.

If reported interviews are written in the mixed technique, it makes the meaning of the text vague, with the risk that the case will not be prosecuted because of this uncertainty. It may be disputed whether free indirect style is suitable at all in legal discourse, since it gives the impression of the officer of the interview and the interviewee apart, instead it feels as if they are in symbiosis. Free indirect speech therefore cannot be recommended in written interviews in the legal discourse, where criminal offences are investigated. Yet this is a stylistic feature commonly used in interview texts in all 80 investigations in the material.

The conclusion is that the techniques and the care with which the interview is reported can influence whether a perpetrator is prosecuted. One questionable stylistic feature is free indirect style, which the interviewer probably does not mean to use. Nevertheless, the effect of the carelessly quoted sentences with no clear indication of what exactly was said by the interviewee, and the mixing of quotation with narration and indirect speech leads to vagueness in the text and hence also in the statements of the interviewee. It should also be pointed out that most of the dialogue is not documented in the reported interviews. If that were the case, a verbatim record of the interaction would be much longer, normally at least 10 written pages for a 15-min dialogue. No doubt statements that the investigator considers unimportant are omitted in the writing up, which may have legal consequences.

Things happening during the interview are omitted, for example, all nonverbal features, the investigator's questions, discourse markers, and interruptions that can be significant for the interpretation of the statement (cf. Coulthard 1996). The interview should be read aloud to or read by the interviewee for approval, but sometimes this does not happen, whereas sometimes the text is only in draft form when approved by the interviewee, as appears quite often in the data examined in this study.

Admittedly, the writing situation for the police is not easy. They have to report the most trying events at all times, and they are often interrupted, since they may be ordered to new actions before they finished their ongoing writing job. Communication between the citizen and the police is constantly moving from spoken language to the language of the law, and this leaves traces in the texts. It may be one explanation for the mixture of modes of presentation and the use of quotation marks and slashes. Making the transformation from speech to written text is a difficult task that requires a lot of training to master and awareness of how the transition works.

Conclusion

Summing up the problem, it is a complex linguistic process to get spoken words into an appropriately written and tenable legal text. This ought to be carefully considered by the Police Academies and the police in Sweden, since police students get little training in this, and officers mainly learn to write plaintiffs' reports, interviews, and police memoranda by doing it in practice (cf. Ask and Byrman 2010). All these texts are important in an investigation, and ought to be taught carefully to all police students and the police, which does not happen today. It would save time and work, and it is in the police's best interest to get these texts right and judicially tenable. Ultimately, this study touches on matters of importance for the personal security and equality of all citizens in legal matters.

If the language in the investigations were generally handled with more care and awareness, it would perhaps be possible for the Swedish prosecutors to be more successful in court cases of domestic violence. The tendency that less than 50% go to prosecution (Lidholm 2002) is an embarrassing fact.

References

Ask, K. and Alison, L. (2010). Investigators' decision-making. In P.A. Granhag (Ed.), *Forensic Psychology in Context: Nordic and International Approaches*, 35–55. Cullompton: Willan Publishing.

Ask, S. and Byrman, G. (2008). *Texter med tyngd* [Texts with importance], (extracts from texts 10 and 44). Unpublished raw database with investigations of domestic violence (with protected identity of those involved), Linnaeus University, Växjö, Sweden.

Ask, S. and Byrman, G. (2010). "Så slog han Anna med ett okänt antal knytnävs-lag i ansiktet." Reliefanalys av polisstudenters och polisers texter ["Then he dealt Anna an unknown number of blows to the face." Relief analysis of police students' and police officers' writing]. In J. Smidt (Ed.), *Rammer for skriving: Om skriveutvikling i skole og yrkesliv*. [Frameworks for Writing: On the Development of Writing in School and Professional Life], 125–139. Trondheim: Tapir akademisk forlag.

Blixt, M., Selin, K.H., and Westlund, O. (2010). *Brottsoffers kontakter med rätts-väsendet: En fördjupande studie utifrån Nationella trygghetsundersökningen 2006–2008 och intervjuer med fokusgrupper*, 45 [Crime Victims' Contacts with the Judicial System: An In-Depth Study Based on the National Security Investigation 2006–2008 and Interviews with Focus Groups]. Stockholm: Brottsförebyggande rådet.

Cassirer, P. (2003). *Stil, stilistik och stilanalys* [Style, Stylistics and Style Analysis], 3rd ed. Stockholm: Natur och Kultur.

Coulthard, M. (1996). The official version: Audience manipulation in police records of interviews with suspects. In C.R. Caldas-Coulthard and M. Coulthard (Eds.), *Texts and Practices: Readings in Critical Discourse Analysis*, 170–171. London: Routledge.

Coulthard, M. (2011). Experts and opinions in my opinion. In M. Coulthard and A. Johnson (Eds.), *The Routledge Handbook of Forensic Linguistics*, 1st ed., 473–486. New York: Routledge.

Fairclough, N. (Ed.) (2010). General introduction. In *Critical Discourse Analysis: The Critical Study of Language*, 2nd ed., 1–21. Harlow: Longman.

Gumbel, I. (2000). *Hörd angående misshandel: Polisens protokoll vid förhör med misshandlade kvinnor och misstänkta män* [Questioned about Assault: Police Minutes in Interviews with Assaulted Women and Male Suspects]. Stockholm: Stockholms universitet, Institutionen för nordiska språk.

Haworth, K. (2010). Police interviews in the judicial process: Police interviews as evidence. In M. Coulthard and A. Johnson (Eds.), *The Routledge Handbook of Forensic Linguistics*, 1st ed., 169–181. New York: Routledge.

Heydon, G. (2005). *The Language of Police Interviewing: A Critical Analysis*. Basingstoke: Palgrave Macmillan.

Heydon, G. (2010). Forensic linguistics. In K. Allan, J. Bradshaw, K. Burridge, G. Finch, and G. Heydon (Eds.), *The Palgrave Companion to English Language and Linguistics*, 164–169. Houndmills: Palgrave Macmillan.

Jönsson, L. (1988). *Polisförhöret som kommunikationssituation* [Police Interrogations as a Communication Situation]. Linköping: Tema Kommunikation.

Komter, M.L. (2002). The suspect's own words: The treatment of written statements in Dutch court-rooms. *Forensic Linguistics*, 9(2), 168–192.

Komter, M.L. (2006). From talk to text: The interactional construction of a police record. *Research on Language and Social Interaction*, 39(3), 201–228.

lagen.nu (2011). https://lagen.nu/begrepp/Muntlighetsprincipen, February 6, 2011.

Lidholm, M. (2002). Att förebygga våld mot kvinnor i nära relationer: Lokalt brotts-förebyggande arbete [Preventing domestic violence against women: Local crime-prevention work]. Idéskrift 9 från Brottsförebyggande rådet. Rapport 2002:8. Stockholm: Brottsförebyggande rådet.

Riktlinjer för skrivande inom polisen [Guidelines for writing in the police] (2007). Revised ed. Stockholm: Rikspolisstyrelsen.

Svenska skrivregler [Rules for writing Swedish] (2000). *By the Language Council of Sweden*, 2nd ed. Stockholm: Liber.

Teleman, U., Hellberg, S., and Andersson, E. (1999). *Svenska Akademiens grammatik* [Grammar of the Swedish Academy]. 4, Satser och meningar, 850–874. Stockholm: Svenska Akademien.

The Evolving Nature of Police Operational Management

IV

Exploring System Transition in the Police Organization

The Case of the UK Police National Database

16

TESSA LAMBRI, LOUISE COOKE,
AND THOMAS W. JACKSON

Contents

Introduction

The National Policing Improvement Agency (NPIA) launched the Police National Database (PND) in June 2011. All 43 police forces in the United Kingdom, including the Child Exploitation Online Protection (CEOP), and the Serious Organized Crime Agency (SOCA) are now connected to the PND. The withdrawal of the Impact Nominal Index (INI) system set up in the interim in 2005 has meant that forces can only seek and acquire national police information on known offenders and individuals of interest from the PND. Media coverage of the PND launch was mostly favorable toward the initiative; however, civil liberties groups and senior MPs expressed concern at the scale of the database and the number of people who will be able to use it. For police forces and agencies, the PND is now at a critical stage—What will users think of the PND? Has it brought about any challenges to business practices and peoples' roles that were not anticipated? What impact has the transition from the INI to the PND had on the UK police forces? These research questions will be addressed in this chapter.

Background

The delivery of the PND has led to a series of significant change management issues, which include the transition from the INI system to the PND, the sharing of police information across force boundaries, and the challenges associated with implementing a new IT system. Access to police information in traditional communicative forms has been on a strict need to know basis. Neighboring police forces were in no more of an advantageous position than forces that were more geographically dispersed and physical force boundaries were no more or no less impeding in the sharing of police information (Newburn 2009). The well-known dictum "knowledge is power" is a contributory factor conceptually, in attempting to understand the various elements inherent in "police organizational culture"—a concept identified in both the Laming Report 2003 and the Bichard Inquiry 2004 as being a crucial factor in recent institutional knowledge failures (Dean and Gottschalk 2007). Ultimately, there is a greater risk in choosing not to share intelligence than there is to share intelligence in the most basic sense. The Bichard Inquiry which was the catalyst for developing the PND found that there were particular recommendations pertaining to the police service's information-handling practices, more specifically on record creation, retention, review, deletion, and the sharing of information under the Police Reform Act 2006. The remaining recommendations from the Bichard Inquiry were aimed at the social services and focused on improvements in employment-vetting procedures, new referral actions for child protection, and further training for staff involved in appointing people to work with children (Bichard Inquiry Report 2004).

INI to PND: Information System Transition

First of all, it is important to look at the recent transition from the INI system to the PND. From a business user acceptance perspective, managing the process of transition from one system to another is significant. Identifying any business benefits directly attributable to the system greatly depends on people engaging with it and accepting the system in line with its intended business use, and the long-awaited PND vitally enables the sharing and linking of police information for investigative purposes. It is, therefore, important that some initial research is carried out to provide insight and understanding of how the INI system was used by police forces before the PND and the expectations of future PND users following its recent implementation.

User acceptance testing is a technical term normally understood to occur before information system software is signed off as fit for purpose, and before a system can go live (Bocij, Chaffey, Greasley, and Hickie 2003). From a social and business perspective, this concept has been used for this research to specifically infer the understanding of how end-users of the PND will utilize the system contextually, but also how the PND will evoke changes in business processes and levels of resistance to such changes. Some resistance to change is inevitable, but this is particularly true with the introduction of new systems associated with business process reengineering (BPR), because of the new ways that work may be performed and the possible changes to people's job functions and roles (Beynon-Davies 2009). For definitional purposes, a business process can be described as "a set of logically related tasks performed to achieve a defined business outcome" (Boddy, Boonstra, and Kennedy 2005, 100). Boddy et al. (2005, 100) continue to define "'business process reengineering" or "business redesign" as "an organisational analysis approach to re-designing business processes." In essence, it is about identifying new or innovative ways of carrying out work or business as an organization—sometimes enabled or as a result of newly implemented IT technologies and capabilities. On a national level, police forces have recognized that BPR is a requirement for the PND, particularly in relation to the sharing and dissemination of police information under the data control measures put in place. It is, therefore, important that the primary objective of the PND, which is the sharing of police information, is not underplayed or negated by too strict security procedures when disseminating police data.

In order to manage the most critical determinant of technology effectiveness in organizations, it is necessary to understand how people use it to get work done. Technology is not valuable, meaningful, or consequential by itself; it only becomes so when people engage with it in practice (Marchand, Davenport, and Dickson 2000). Thus, it is important not to neglect technology use, as such neglect may encourage the onset of simplistic assumptions—that if people have technology, they will use it; that they will use it as designed; and that such use will produce the expected outcomes. With this in mind, the rationale underpinning this research on system transition from the INI to the PND was based on exploring the process of implementation and people's overall experiences and perceptions of the new system, and their adaption to new or altered working practices to support use of the system.

Research Methodology

This research uses a case study approach. Case studies allow in-depth exploration of one particular situation and facilitate the obtainment of "rich" data by multiple means (Robson 2011). The rationale for adopting a case study approach was based on acquiring data out of which concepts and theories could emerge, and future research directions can be subsequently identified. It would also enable decisions to be made about the research methods to use and a validation of their appropriateness (Robson 2011). Choosing to conduct small-scale research was based on gaining an in-depth and holistic understanding within a natural setting. Exploring key issues pertinent to current INI users and future PND users was important; therefore, the interview questions focused on the INI usage in various business units, its advantages and disadvantages, and users' expectations of the PND. The open-ended and flexible design of the questions allowed respondents to elaborate and also served the purpose of a checklist—guiding the topics to be covered during the semistructured interviews (Silverman 2005). The crucial point was that whatever the source of influence on what was already known about the topic of research, the concepts used to inform the design of the questions were treated as "provisional" and open to some alteration in how the questions were answered and in what order (Denscombe 2010).

The quest for achieving a representative sample was not required for the purpose of this small-scale case study. Based on the qualitative design of this research, the primary objective was to obtain empirical data using a cumulative sample approach, whereby nonprobability sampling is applied (namely, purposive and snowball sampling), to produce an exploratory sample, not a statistically representative one. The sample process for this study was essentially "discovery led" and the size and composition of the sample was not predictable from the start. This is a similar method used for theoretical sampling, which is closely aligned to the grounded theory research approach (Robson 2011). Idiographic research also positions itself in exploring particular events and providing the richest picture of what transpires using case study approaches (Cornford and Smithson 2006). The main idiographic principles relate to this research, one of which is to contextually understand phenomenon with emphasis on analyzing subjective accounts and experiences.

Participants

The police forces that took part in this research were identified through purposive sampling. All forces in England and Wales were contacted and invited to participate via their respective regional PND co-coordinators, who were asked to nominate the key INI and PND users. The forces that responded within the specified time frame were as a result asked to nominate participants. Snowball sampling began to occur whereby participants suggested other key users that could take part, and the sample began to increase in both size and scope. A mixture of police officers and police staff were interviewed, including office administrators, departmental managers, intelligence researchers, police detectives, and uniformed officers. A series of 15 interviews were carried out involving primary INI users and future PND users in forces. In total, participants from 12 police forces took part across England and Wales, which were the following:

- Bedfordshire
- Cambridgeshire
- Devon and Cornwall
- Dyfed Powys
- Essex
- Gwent
- Hertfordshire
- Leicestershire
- Northamptonshire
- Norfolk
- South Wales
- Wiltshire

Participants from the following force departments also took part:

- Force Intelligence Bureau
- Professional Standards/Vetting
- Police National Computer Bureau
- Public Protection Teams

Data Analysis

The methods used to analyze qualitative data largely differ from the deductive reasoning process often aligned to quantitative methods of data analysis. It is often the case that interviews of whatever nature will need to be recorded and transcribed for qualitative research purposes or for more prescriptive and statistical data analyses (Robson 2011). For this research, qualitative data analysis was appropriately used to enable the extraction of meaningful and occurring concepts that are distinct to the social or business setting being investigated. As such, the collection and analysis of data follows an inductive and logical approach, which is "discovery led," and is concerned with drawing wider inferences and arriving at more generalized statements about the topic (Silverman 2005). However, this can lead to some degree of crossover, often found in grounded theory approaches. The emergence of "theory" and "explanation building" generated from the research data provides some reinforcement of the findings being directly linked to "real-world facts" as much as possible (Denscombe 2010). While it is appreciated that case studies cannot achieve representativeness, they can, however, generate understanding of a "broader class of things," as well as unveil the various intricacies and subtleties of complex situations (Silverman 2005). The limitations or disadvantages of using a case study approach toward research and data analysis thereafter are in relation to the credibility of the generalizations made from its findings. For this research, efforts have been made to minimize this area of vulnerability by emphasizing the need to capture reality and experience with "unique" and pragmatic evidence that can help to develop and build theory; and to serve as a useful starting point for future research planning and design (Creswell 1994).

Results

The technique used to analyze the findings was consistent with the content analysis approach. The reason for choosing this technique was based on a systematic analysis of the data to capture the frequency of keywords to enable interpretation of the text in narrative form (Cornford and Smithson 2006). Furthermore, what was also of interest from an analytical point of view was the absence of keywords or concepts, which were regarded as just as important, as well as the capturing of these "one-off" views. Content analysis of all the data was initially carried out in two stages: the first stage involved the analysis of the data in relation to the questions on the INI system and the second stage analyzed the data relating to the PND. The purpose was to compare the usability of both systems, to understand how the introduction of the new PND system would impact organizational working practices, and to know whether the PND will be able to deliver the expected technical features and functions.

Stage 1: INI—Analytical Themes and Trends Identified (Based on Frequency)

1. Business processes
   a. Request generator—a time-consuming paper exercise, which is used to record the purpose of the INI request to the receiving force(s)
   b. Seeking authority to complete the request generator in the first instance
   c. Delays in receiving intelligence from the forces, particularly large urban forces, some of which have a backlog of INI requests to complete

2. System usability and capability
    a. Intelligence available to request from forces cannot be viewed
    b. Restrictive searching capability
    c. Data not instantly accessible
    d. Limited technical features and functions
    e. Easy to use/adapt
    f. Unintuitive system
    g. Reputational issues, that is, unreliable and inaccurate information
3. Operational and intelligence value
    a. Linking previously unknown intelligence from other forces
    b. Often used for force-vetting purposes
    c. Often used for risk assessment purposes
    d. Identifying information not available on PNC
    e. Good navigational tool to seek further information
    f. Mainly used for child protection and vetting purposes
4. Communication and collaboration
    a. Assists joint working with other forces/agencies working on similar (or same) enquiries
    b. Aids communication with other forces for preventative policing purposes

The themes emerging from the analysis of interview transcripts contain aspects that require highlighting in terms of the value and benefits of the INI system to end-users and to policing overall. Although there is usually a time lapse in receiving information from forces, the information derived from the INI is usually not available from other national police systems such as the PNC; the INI facilitates (albeit not instantly) the crucial linking of previously unknown intelligence held by other forces. The data also suggest that generally the INI system was easy to use and adapt to, but it appears that the common issues pertinent to INI users are that the system carries an inherent administrative burden. Technically, the INI system's searching capability is restrictive and unintuitive to current working practices, and there are reputational issues, which to an extent may have impacted on the limited use of the INI system across all business areas in the police organization.

In terms of making some recommendations based on this insight, negative perceptions of an IT system, whether as a result of speculation or "word of mouth" or from real tangible experiences, need to be rapidly identified and ameliorated through training and education in order to minimize the spread of such sentiment becoming a potential barrier to a system's use. Furthermore, organizations implementing new IT systems need to incorporate a significant presence of change management, communicating not only the envisaged strategic benefits of the system but also to staff how their roles and responsibilities could well be affected (Hughes 2010).

Stage 2: PND—Analytical Themes and Trends Identified (Based on Frequency)

1. Organizational factors
   a. Information Technology strategy for the PND
   b. Re-education on rationale for business process changes
   c. Training on new business processes required by the PND
   d. Confidential environment and strict access security measures
   e. An agreed national data-sharing protocol for the PND
2. System usability and capability
   a. Easy to use interface
   b. Overcomplicated system—unintuitive
   c. Better functionality compared to the INI system—wider search criteria include people, objects, locations, and events
   d. No "copy and paste" or printing functionality that impedes the electronic dissemination of data
   e. Automatic updates for forces are essential for business continuity and system credibility/reliability and data integrity reasons
3. Operational and intelligence value
   a. Better access to data from a national pool
   b. Benefits risk assessments
   c. Benefits intelligence assessments
   d. Identifies patterns of offending—nationally, regionally, cross-border
   e. Assists decision making and problem solving
   f. Has more emphasis on proactive policing
4. People impact
   a. Implications for working practices (and on roles and responsibilities of, particularly, administrative operators who are "passive" users)
   b. Analytical/intelligence handling skills required to assess/evaluate information from the PND
   c. Time gained in retrieving data will be spent deciphering relevant data
5. Information management capabilities
   a. Managing information in accordance with guidance and national policy on the "Management of Police Information"
   b. PND gives greater emphasis on assessing the relevance and value of data from the PND—but with information overload concerns
   c. The misuse of information and the potential ramifications—information use and disclosure practices

In contrast to the views expressed regarding the INI system, which were mainly in relation to delays in receiving data from the requested forces, the system's lack of technical functionality, and the "paper burden" of actually carrying out an INI search request, prospective users of the PND were collectively concerned about the quality and reliability of the data on the PND, in terms of whether forces on a national scale were regularly updating the system with current and up-to-date information. Furthermore, concerns were raised by police staff working in administrative support roles regarding their new responsibilities of assessing PND records following PND requests from operational police officers in their force. Such "passive" PND users, who were not previously required to perform the task of assessing a volume of information, are now required to decipher what is significant and relevant in response to the PND request, which could have serious risk implications for policing and safeguarding. Overall, participants recognized that to critically assess and evaluate information from police systems requires the application of specialist skills—skills in which not everyone in the police service is necessarily trained or required to have training. A force administrator in the Vetting Unit reinforces the following key point:

> The real work begins once you've performed a PND search. The onus is put on us to see what might be relevant in response to the request. I can see other administrators and myself seeking reassurance from managers and police officers as to what to choose to pass on—I didn't need to do this before with the INI system. We need training on how to do this for ourselves.

Another important issue, which needs addressing, is in relation to how data from the PND is practically disseminated once data records of interest have been located on the system. At the moment, the ability to print intelligence records from the PND is very limited, and records cannot be extracted in any electronic form. This could be a potential barrier of use for PND users in that such difficulties could not only dissuade the actual use of the system, but could also hinder a force's ability to easily share vital information from the PND—within their actual force. A Police Public Protection Unit supervisor expresses such concern:

> The PND is on a confidential network and this actually makes the sharing of police information quite cumbersome, especially when you have to prepare for Case Reviews with the Social Services or if you're liaising with another department in your force. You can't get the information out of the system once you've got it, and you can't print it either. There could be loads of records that I would need to go through and write down—it's not exactly a good use of my time and energy.

Davies (Boddy et al. 2005) developed the Technology Acceptance Model and identified the importance of evaluating the perceived use and the perceived ease of use. Davies (Boddy et al. 2005) suggests that acceptance of new technology in organizations is dependent on people recognizing its perceived usefulness and perceived ease of use. The two variables are understood to predict and influence users' attitudes—whether positively or negatively. The empirical study based on a survey questionnaire concluded that perceived usefulness has more effect than perceived ease of use, and that people are more likely to cope with a "difficult" system if it provides them with valuable information, but unlikely to use one whose only virtue is that it is *just* easy to use (Boddy et al. 2005).

PND "Most Wanted" Event: Bramshill Police College

Prior to the launch of the PND, the NPIA conducted a 2-day event at Bramshill Police College entitled "PND—Most Wanted." The purpose of the event was to "test" the PND in an operational environment by performing real searches on "wanted" people known or of interest to the police. It was anticipated that the PND would provide new information that would benefit current investigations and lead to new lines of enquiry. The aims of the event as outlined by the NPIA in the opening introduction were noted as follows:

1. Identifies good news stories for the launch of the PND
2. Provides evidence for effective operational use of the PND
3. Gives business assurance to different business areas
4. Encourages the increased use of the PND
5. Proves the value of the PND to the Association of Chief Police Officers (ACPO) leads in order to incorporate the PND into their national portfolios on police guidance and training
6. Learns lessons for PND Release 2
7. Provides evidence to the Home Office and Government Investment Board
8. Validates and proves the PND business case
9. Examines the data quality of information held on the PND

For a researcher, this was a unique opportunity to conduct participant observation, through actively contributing in the event, as well as observing the interactions of other participants from various police forces and law enforcement agencies. Observing the event was conducted informally through conversations with PND users. Primarily, this was a good opportunity to gain "real" insight into what users' thought of the PND, their experiences of using the system, and whether it provided them with tangible and useful information that was previously unknown. The research approach applied during this event largely relates to the study of people in naturally occurring settings in the "field," which capture their social meanings and ordinary activities, involving the researcher participating directly in the setting if not also in the activities (Silverman 2005). Overall, the data collected identified several key findings, which were considered significant from a user's perspective. Users were impressed with the availability and accessibility of police data from forces across England and Wales, but were not so impressed with the navigational layout of the system, particularly when the initial search returned a significant number of records. Also, records that were "access denied" did not state why the record could not be accessed—the reasons can be needing to accept specific intelligence handling conditions, the record(s) has not yet been uploaded by the owning force, or the technical issues that would need to be identified and resolved. On a more positive note, the majority of users commented on how the PND demonstrated enormous value to policing by its ability to link intelligence on a national level, and the speed in which searches were returned from millions of data records held on the system. Some of the interesting outcomes from the event are detailed below:

- A Serious and Organized Crime group currently under investigation was believed to be active in other parts of the United Kingdom. PND searches revealed that one member of the group was the subject of over 100 intelligence entries, which gave details of involvement in other offences.
- Domestic abuse—PND identified five forces that held information on a perpetrator with domestic abuse-related convictions
- Public protection and risk (violence)—An individual was acknowledged as being violent. Checks on the force crime system showed no trace. Checks on the PND confirmed that the name checked on PNC and local force system was actually an alias.
- Public disorder—An "AWOL" soldier was of interest to three police forces in relation to football violence.

Discussion

Organizations like the police service need to recognize that new technology is sometimes a convenient scapegoat for workplace dissatisfaction, and it is common to claim that resistance to change is a fundamental human trait (Hughes 2010). Another perspective would be to focus on the process of making the necessary changes in the police organization, by involving people in the selection of new technology and ensuring that the implementation of technology and surrounding factors are communicated across the organization. Training and the business and technical support available are also of importance, as well as how carefully the rollout is planned and executed (Beynon-Davies 2009). Furthermore, in terms of the technology itself, users will be questioning how well suited it is to their work, how easy it is to learn to use, how "forgiving" the system is of users' errors, and its reliability and efficiency (Boddy et al. 2005). Steps need to be taken by the police organization toward managing the effective use of new technology, and that resources and efforts are dedicated to developing appropriate user habits, as well as rewarding and recognizing the innovative use of technology, rather than simply focusing on what the technology is capable of (Bocij et al. 2003). In the case of the PND, "teething problems" are clearly apparent, but it is vital that early start-up problems are promptly resolved; otherwise issues of such nature could potentially lead to rejection of the new technology. In order to optimize the effective use of new technology, it requires users to have the necessary skills and training to be able to exploit the features and functions available to them. One of the most critical determinants of technology effectiveness is to evaluate how people use it to get work done (Boddy et al. 2005). User engagement with technology is just one aspect; other aspects relevant to technology usage and acceptance relate to police information behavior, their information management capabilities, and how both tacit (know-how) and explicit (know-what) knowledge are captured from police officers and police staff—as this contributes to the intellectual capital of the police organization.

The amount of information that police officers come into contact with astounding (Gottschalk 2006). The police service is a highly information-intensive organization (Newburn 2009); it must now work at creating and sustaining an organizational culture that promotes the sharing of information and knowledge. How people acquire and process information is determined by what their information needs are, their methods of information seeking, and how the information gathered is being purposefully applied (Merchand, Davenport, and Dickson 2000). Knowledge on the other hand in the context of policing refers to individuals' knowledge and it does not easily transform into organizational knowledge (Gottschalk 2006). Empirical studies have shown that the greater the anticipated reciprocal relationships are, the more favorable the attitude toward knowing sharing will be (Bock, Zmud, and Kim 2005).

A fundamental process of policing and law enforcement is conducting investigations. Investigations would grind to a halt if there were scant or limited information to develop or to act upon. The well-known data to knowledge continuum establishes the importance of making distinctions between data, information, and knowledge (Gottschalk 2005). For policing, "intelligence" is an inherent step in the "knowledge ladder," and refers to actionable information that has been organized, validated, and analyzed (Dean and Gottschalk 2007). Knowledge creation is, therefore, a continuous process of dynamic interactions between capturing the tacit and explicit knowledge of police officers and police staff, and is a nurturing and engaging process, which relies on access to relevant and appropriate information sources and systems (Dean and Gottschalk 2007). Knowledge management can be defined as a process or method to simplify and improve the process of sharing and understanding the knowledge within an organization, to effectively ensure that activities are in place, which facilitate the systematic and collective leveraging of knowledge throughout the organization (Middleton 2002). From an interdisciplinary perspective, knowledge management can be defined as "the effective learning process associated with exploration, exploitation and sharing of human knowledge (tacit and explicit) that use appropriate technology and cultural environments to enhance an organization's intellectual capital and performance" (Jashapara 2011, 14).

Conclusion

The research questions addressed in this chapter were based on exploring the perceptions and experiences of PND users since its implementation and identifying any issues, challenges, and concerns from both a user's and business perspective. In addition, this research aimed to examine the organizational impact of the transition from the INI to the PND.

From an organizational perspective, this research has found that the police must recognize the profound organizational changes evoked as a result of the PND. The changes that require particular attention are in relation to how information is shared; how it is stored, retrieved, and utilized; and the application of knowledge management initiatives such as sharing best practice, performance benchmarking, instilling responsibility and accountability for sharing knowledge, and formalizing such processes as part of the organization's core knowledge management values and principles (Turban and Ronson 2001). There are many challenges associated with designing and implementing knowledge management tools and initiatives in an organization. Failing to acknowledge the cultural and change management dimensions can lead to unsuccessful and futile implementation (Jashapara 2011). Another challenge would be the failure to adopt an appropriate organizational-wide strategy toward integrating knowledge management; police forces will have different views as to what knowledge management practically means in reality. Forces are aware of the central role of intelligence and knowledge to police work, by identifying what constitutes as knowledge management and where this knowledge exists, can assist in the design of a strategy to facilitate the application of knowledge that is acquired (Gottschalk 2006). Knowledge sharing and exchange is pivotal to successful knowledge management (Jashapara 2011). Research carried out by Seba and Rowley (2010) on knowledge management in police forces identified organizational culture as the main barrier to tacit knowledge sharing and exchange of expertise. On the basis of their findings, the authors suggest that the police organization develop further understanding of their organizational culture as part of the process of understanding how to create knowledge exchange cultures (Seba and Rowley 2010).

From a strategic and future planning perspective, the longevity of the PND should be considered particularly in relation to avoiding system futility. Areas that need to be considered are in relation to the sustainability of the PND in coping with the evolutionary demands of the twenty-first century policing. How can continuity and prolonged use of the system be ensured and to what extent, and what are the critical success factors to indicate how well the PND has become embedded along with the use of other core police systems such as the Police National Computer. Addressing these considerations require further exploratory research to be carried out in the form of a system performance evaluation—to assess the reliability and integrity of the PND within an operational context and by post-implementation reviews. Post-implementation reviews would be valuable in determining the success of the system in meeting its business requirements and whether it has delivered the anticipated benefits described in the project business case (Boddy et al. 2005). An additional reason for performing a post-implementation review is that lessons can be learnt from the project, best practice can be applied to similar projects in the future, and attempts can be made at avoiding the techniques that failed (Bocij et al. 2003). Future research can be built on this chapter by studying the evolutionary development of the PND in the context, its operational usefulness and acceptance as a valuable research tool; and whether the majority of PND users believe as stated by the Deputy Chief Constable of Durham Constabulary Mike Barton—that the system "does what it says on the tin" (NPIA 2011).

References

Beynon-Davies, P. 2009. *Business Information Systems*. Basingstoke: Palgrave Macmillan.

Bichard Inquiry Report, 2004. London: The Stationary Office (Viewed July 2011). Available from: http://www.bichardinquiry.org.uk/10663/report.pdf.

Bocij, P., Chaffey, D., Greasley, A., and Hickie, S. 2003. *Business Information Systems: Technology, Development and Management for the E-Business*. London: Prentice Hall.

Bock, G.W., Zmud, R.W., and Kim Y.G. 2005. Behavioural intention formation in knowledge sharing: Examining the roles of extrinsic motivators, social psychological forces and organizational climate. *MIS Quarterly*, 29 (1), 87–111.

Boddy, D., Boonstra, A., and Kennedy, G. 2005. *Managing Information Systems: An Organizational Perspective*. London: Prentice Hall.

Cornford, T. and Smithson, S. 2006. *Project Research in Information Systems*. Second Edition. Basingstoke: Palgrave Macmillan.

Creswell, J. 1994. *Research Design—Qualitative and Quantitative Approaches*. London: Sage Publications.

Dean, P. and Gottschalk, P. 2007. *Knowledge Management in Policing and Law Enforcement*. Oxford: Oxford University Press.

Denscombe, M. 2010. *The Good Research Guide*. Fourth Edition. London: Open University Press.

Gottschalk, P. 2005. *Strategic Knowledge Management Technology.* London: Idea Group Publishing.

Gottschalk, P. 2006. Stages of knowledge management in police investigations. *Knowledge-Based Systems,* 19, 381–387.

Hughes, M. 2010. *Managing Change—A Critical Perspective.* Second Edition. Basingstoke: CIPD.

Jashapara, A. 2011. *Knowledge Management—An Integrated Approach.* London: Prentice Hall.

Middleton, M. 2002. *Information Management—A Consolidation of Operations, Analysis and Strategy.* New South Wales: CIS.

National Policing Improvement Agency (NPIA). 2011. *Impact Forces Bulletin.* London: National Policing Improvement Agency.

Newburn, T. 2009. *Handbook of Policing.* Second Edition. Cullompton: Willan Publishing.

Robson, C. 2011. *Real World Research.* Third Edition. Chichester: Wiley Publishing Ltd.

Seba, I. and Rowley, J. 2010. Knowledge management in UK police forces. *Journal of Knowledge Management,* 14 (4), 611–626.

Silverman, D. 2005. *Doing Qualitative Research.* Second Edition. London: Sage.

Turban, E. and Ronson, J. 2001. *Decision Support Systems and Intelligence Systems.* London: Prentice Hall.

Exploring the Implementation of Head-Mounted Camera Technology in Volume Crime Scene Investigation

17

MARK BUTLER, TIM THOMPSON, AND ÉRIC BEL

Contents

Introduction

This chapter sets out the use of head-camera technology in operational Volume Crime Scene Investigation. It covers the design and background work needed to ensure that the requirements of this method complied with the participating UK Police Service's policy and procedures on photographic evidence capture. These procedures are regarded as being generic for all law enforcement departments. The head camera's effectiveness in capturing practice coupled with assisting the development of that practice is also discussed. Two research questions unfold from this concept: (1) How can technology of this type be implemented in the crime scene environment? and (2) What can be learned from this type of observation that will inform teaching and learning in higher education, professional training institutions, and police service training departments? Understanding crime scene practice is useful if the *practice* is to develop its expertise, a factor examined in other dynamic domains such as social work (Fook, Ryan, and Hawkins 1997). Literature in the field of crime scene examination and how examiners process the scene is limited; however, studies in recent years have explored the thought processes of examiners (Baber, Smith, Cross, Hunter, and McMaster 2006) and how practitioners come together as a team to tackle more complex crime scenes (Smith, Baber, Hunter, and Butler 2008). These studies have incidentally fed into learning and teaching.

Volume crime can be defined as crime that occurs with such frequency that the offences may be thought of as everyday police business. Defining volume crime precisely is problematic; however, a general description that encompasses vehicle-related crime, dwelling burglary, and criminal damage is thought of as being within this sphere (ACPO and NPIA 2009).

It is acknowledged that the term crime scene investigator is not uniformly accepted in all police services in the United Kingdom; indeed literature mentions that there are not only different titles in operation, such as forensic practitioner, forensic investigator, and scene of crime officer, but equally the role is different between police forces (Fraser 2007, 388–389). That said commonality is apparent. Holistically, the practice is one whereby the crime scene investigator is required to attend the crime scene location in order to observe, preserve, record, and recover forensic trace evidence and intelligence (Elmhirst 2010, 25–53). These include more general tasks such as photography and fingerprint examination at crime scenes or on recovered property. In the last decade, as a result of the DNA expansion project within the United Kingdom, police forces recruited staff to attend specifically volume crime (Fraser 2007, 338–339). These practitioners are known as volume crime scene investigators (VCSIs) whose sole responsibility is to attend offense locations classified as volume crime. The authors acknowledge that these practitioners in some instances play a supporting role in the forensic investigation of major crime.

Research shows that experts often leave out salient points when teaching, explaining, or communicating their decision making (Feldon 2007). In police and crime scene-related disciplines (Santtila, Korpela, and Häkkänen 2004), it has also been shown to be apparent. Understanding and observing the work of the VCSI is problematic for a number of reasons: gaining access into their working environment is heavily controlled for those outside the field of law enforcement, an aspect that has warranted study in its own right (Fox and Lundman 1974). The work even at volume crime level can often involve vulnerable members of the community, making data capture methods potentially restrictive, an area that parallels closely with social work (Wiles, Crow,

Heath, and Charles 2008). The willingness of the VCSI to be researched may be sensitive and requiring careful and open management. Therefore, research of this type requires collaboration and cooperation at different levels, with each stakeholder examining the value and risks from their own ontological position.

Literature Review

It is perhaps premature to suppose that VCSI research should need to consider all these stakeholders, when a great deal can be made of Crime Scene Report Forms through content analysis and follow-up interviews. Furthermore, research does not need to take part in a real-world setting, with simulated environments being useful where comparison of participants is being considered to identify specific areas to test for competency (Ericsson, Whyte, and Ward 2007). This aspect has already been proposed for crime scene examination staff (Butler 2009). However, observation of VCSI practice in the real-world environment arguably exposes truer interactions with those that have been a victim of crime or are actively involved in the investigation process, such as police officers or civilian investigating officers. The interaction with evidence or crime scene locations offers greater variation than simulated settings. An ethnographic approach using video and audio equipment explores these aspects and the sense constructed of how and when decisions and interactions are made (Clancey 2001). On this point, the Crime Scene Report Form is an important document and the subject of the previous study (Baber, Smith, Butler, Cross, and Hunter 2009). In this example, the goal was to understand how this document functions in recording the actions of the examiner and those that rely on the content and instruction contained within it.

Police knowledge in general has been argued as being largely tacit, despite extensive training being provided across all domains in the profession. Nevertheless, much knowledge that is needed to be effective (Holgersson, Gottschalk, and Dean 2008) is tacit (Holgersson and Gottschalk 2008). A feature related to good business suggests that the level of tacit knowledge is linked to innovative performance (Harlow 2008), with further studies suggesting that tacit knowledge is a worthy endeavor as it is separate from academic intelligence (Sternberg et al. 2001). A similar point is echoed in the field of forensic science (Doak and Assimakopoulos 2010). This is surprising due to the rigorous nature of the policies and procedures employed in this work. For example, Standard Operating Procedures serve as a method to standardize the work on grounds of safety and quality. This generally makes tacit knowledge explicit through good examples and a procedural approach (Baumard 1999).

The term *tacit* in essence means hidden or perhaps better explained by saying that certain kinds of knowledge come with practice or more specifically deliberate practice (Williams and Ericsson 2008). It is suggested that tacit knowledge is largely acquired by one of the two methods: (1) *directly*, perhaps through instruction of some kind even through narratives and talking about practice itself (Lundin and Nuldén 2007), and (2) *indirectly*, through personal self-reflection (Cianciolo, Matthew, Sternberg, and Wagner 2006). Capturing tacit knowledge or allowing it to be made overt is clearly problematic; even recognizing tacit knowledge comes with its own dilemma. Consequently, accepting and transferring theory across to volume crime scene examination research requires the thought as to when tacit knowledge may occur and indeed how, a question already posed in the domain of management (Armstrong and Mahmud 2008). For example, is it within the crime scene environment, conversations and swapping of narratives between practitioners, or even outside the world of work altogether? On this point, narratives in themselves should also be seen as data with different methods of addressing the data for research purposes. A holistic view offers a topographical perspective but may also be seen as a source that can be categorized (Bleakley 2005); in essence, narratives become a way to record tacit knowledge.

Head-mounted camera technology in this instance becomes a tool that stores practitioner knowledge, with the capacity to share it with others for example between peers, or from mentors and supervisors. The authors recognize that tacit knowledge is unlikely to be governed by the boundaries of the examination process, but nevertheless this is a pragmatic approach to explore whether head-camera technology can be used for this and other purposes.

Parallels to volume crime scene investigation can be observed in domains that mirror either the confidentiality of the work (Unsworth 2005) or indeed the practicalities of using such equipment in a hard dynamic environment (Childs 2005). It may even be used to observe the decision-making process (Omodei, Wearing, and McLennan 1997).

Video replay of this type of technology has found acceptance in the medical arena (Lyle 2003). Here, practitioners can offer commentary post action and in particular in the decision-making process. Furthermore, it has been suggested that it may even be useful as a methodology to hasten expertise in crime scene investigation (Fadde 2009).

Method

Participants

Four female VCSIs took part in this study over a 7-month period. One of the VCSIs had 12 months of prior experience in the role, whereas the other three had less than 4 months of experience. All VCSIs had undergone their education and training at a UK Higher Education Institution, obtaining a degree in crime scene science, before securing a post at a police force in the North East of England. Police service training afforded to the VCSIs was largely limited to operational procedures, and at no time had they used head-camera technology before.

Prior to the project going live, a project initiation document was written, detailing the outline of research, timescales, and a risk log. The risk log was detailed and incorporated documentation that would need to be signed by the members of the public giving consent for them to be recorded during the crime scene examination, for example, the complainant or key holder at a dwelling burglary or owner of a damaged motor vehicle. The video recordings generated were acknowledged as unused material and open for the defense council to view, if deemed necessary and pertinent. The project was signed off by a number of senior officers within the participating police force and also at an Association of Chief Police Officers (ACPO) level.

An operational handbook was written for the VCSI to view, should they wish to understand the project in more detail. It also had contact details of the first author and a list of requirements from the VCSIs during their crime scene examinations. In addition to the training provided, step-by-step guides as well as a troubleshooting guide were also incorporated in the handbook in the use of the equipment, should the equipment fail, or a complainant at the scene refuse to be recorded.

Training

The first author implemented a training workshop to ensure that the participants understood how the equipment worked and how the video files should be burned to CD or DVD. This process was collaborative, with the VCSIs offering solutions to ensure that the method used resembled the existing procedures. VCSIs were also instructed on speaking aloud during their operational examinations; the reasoning behind why this is important and how it would be analyzed formed the backdrop to the session. Reassurances were given to the VCSIs that provided language was generally appropriate and not offensive, minor indiscretions would be ignored. During these sessions, it was also explained that the material gathered would be used to learn about practice and also an opportunity for practice to be shared. The Chief Inspector and the Acting Inspector responsible for the project's implementation reiterated this sentiment and that the area Crime Scene Manager would be on hand to view and guide practice and not to use it as a tool for discipline.

Participants were also encouraged to write their reflections after every examination captured using the head-mounted camera or indeed any crimes that were pertinent. The training sessions covered the concept of a reflection, with VCSIs being encouraged to avoid retelling the events but instead put the events in context and focus on areas for development along with practices and procedures that went well. It was explained that reflection is difficult and certainly not instantaneous, and that we are more aware of the results of reflection than the process itself (Moon 1999). That said the process of reflection may generate creative solutions to existing problems. VCSIs were given a hardback notebook for their reflections; however, one VCSI chose to capture these on the Netbook provided.

Equipment

A PV800 Digital Video Recorder (DVR) and PV500 DVR and head-mounted bullet-style camera were used in this study, with all video data generated being stored onto a Secure Digital High Capacity (SDHC) memory card. On returning to the Scenes of Crime Department, a master copy and working copies were created before the memory card was formatted. Each video was subsequently catalogued and subjected to regular auditing. The Netbook with portable compact disk reading and burning facilities was available for the VCSIs or their supervisor to view the scenes, either together or independently. VCSIs could also view the scenes on the digital video recorder screen after the scene was attended and before the various disks were burned, archived, and formatted.

Calibration

Unlike mobile eye-trackers, head-mounted cameras do not require lengthy calibration; however, prior to each scene being examined, VCSIs centered the camera to ensure that head movement and eye-level perspective were represented in the display screen. While not capturing the detail of eye-tracking technology, an *own view perspective* allowed comprehensive coverage of the crime scene environment.

Data Collation and Processing

VCSIs provided verbal commentary during their scene examinations, and the audio in the video files was inputted into NVivo 9. NVivo 9 was used to collate all the video files, Crime Scene Report Forms, and transcriptions.

Each VCSI was interviewed twice for around an hour and a half for each interview during 7 months, as well as additional questioning during regular electronic mail communication. Other onsite visits also took place to check on the equipment, to replace batteries, or to observe the forensic laboratory at the police station used for the examination of property. These observations allowed access to other work the VCSIs were engaged in, which using a head-mounted camera would not be appropriate, for example, communication with other officers, colleagues, and telephone queries.

Table 17.1 Coding Framework for Missing Data Not Contained in the Crime Scene Report Form

Background intelligence	Coding reference examples are as follows: where articles were originally recovered from prior to the forensic examination, the aggrieved being a repeat victim, or information concerning previous crime scene examination visits. Plausible reasons why articles were targeted or which offending groups were most likely responsible were elicited through the information gathering phase of the examination but not always recorded. Additional detailed vocalized information captured in the verbal transcripts was also apparent, for example, serial numbers in property or specific detailed descriptions of property.
Evidence	Coding reference examples are as follows: direct evidence, for example, fingermarks, glove marks, and other trace evidence. Instances of "speculative" samples in the scene notes were confidently presented in the verbatim-transcribed accounts as "actual" evidence. Quality or evidential weight was also observed. Material recovered that may be considered for DNA analysis was not always recorded by circling the "Y" indicator on the scene notes.
Modus operandi	Coding reference examples are as follows: offender behavior or crime scene actions, for example, entry methods into location, property, and associated behavior such as search patterns and interference of locks, with either nearby objects or instrumentation brought to the location.

Interviews were initially largely unstructured to allow the VCSI to pass comment on what they felt was important; however, a semistructured interview framework was used after an initial 15–30 minutes.

Each Crime Scene Report Form was examined in detail and compared to the transcribed data. Missing material not contained in the report forms was pasted into a memo in NVivo 9 with links to the original data source. The memo was then coded, with three themes emerging: background intelligence, *modus operandi*, and evidence (Table 17.1). All missing data fitted into one of these three themes or nodes. A second researcher was used to ensure that the framework describing the three themes was robust, including the recoding of all coded references ($n = 47$) via a Kappa inter-rater reliability check. Discrepancies were few in number and resolved by reviewing each one in turn.

Results

Not all attempted scenes were successfully captured; specifically 20% of files were either not fully recorded or corrupt. These occurred largely early on in the study; however, by employing strict recharging practices of the DVR battery and ensuring that the DVR was warm before use or not left in the crime scene vehicle (the project was initiated in the winter months) vastly improved

Figure 17.1 Image showing VCSI applying a gel lifter to a vehicle jack handle.

the number of recordings. Image quality was not influenced by the use of fingerprint powders, jumping, or walking; furthermore, detail could still be observed in very low light levels (Figure 17.1).

Comments from VCSIs in Relation to Wearing the Head-Mounted Camera

VCSI 1: Fine, the only problem I find with it is that the things seem to move sometimes so like you have to check quite often how the, where the cameras pointing, but fine it doesn't bother me wearing it at all, I quite like it

Further questions were asked in relation to speaking aloud during the crime scene examination process.

VCSI 1: It don't bother me to be honest, I forget I've got it on
INT: Does the fact that you have to speak, does it help or hinder you …
VCSI 1: Erm no I think it helps to be honest 'cos it, I don't know it makes you think more I think
INT: In what sort, what sort of way?
VCSI 1: I don't know like when you, you tend to sort of go on auto pilot a bit don't you when you're going out to cars and things,… it just makes you think more …
VCSI 1: Makes you more conscious that you are videoing …
VCSI 2: I don't think it's been a problem at all no. Erm like I was saying the other day in, in, in a way it's, it's sort of helped me because it's helped me to slow down erm … and you know I learn a lot from

talking to people and talking out, you know talking out loud and what have you, whether if it's just in your head and you're silent at a scene, you know you might forget to do something or you might miss something whereas I find if I'm talking out loud, I know what I've done,…

VCSI 4: Yeah, no I don't have any problem with it except erm sometimes finding the time

VCSI 4: … you've got all the stuff to do when you come back with the head-cam, it's not too much that you would be, just ignore the narration and get on and do it, that would be fine

VCSI 4: I think speaking takes more time 'cos you're thinking about what you have to say for the narration, I mean it wouldn't bother me just wearing it, obviously you know you just get on with it don't you but erm, no it's the speaking thing 'cos you're consciously saying I'm going to do this, I'm just considering this, I'm going to move onto this next that kind of thing.

INT: … are you aware that somebody could look at it if they wanted to or?

VCSI 1: It wouldn't bother me at all

INT: Have you had a chance to have a look at anybody else's?

VCSI 1: I've had a sneaky look, (Participant 4) knows 'cos I told her yesterday

INT: (Participant 4) not bothered is she?

VCSI 4: Well I don't, at the end of the day it's like … As long as you're doing the job to the best of your ability

VCSI 1: No, no but it's only 'cos I wanted to see I was doing it right … But I, I just think it makes you think more …, it does effectively slow you down a little bit I think but because you're having to think about what you're saying and things, erm but I, I think that's a good thing because it does make you think, it does make you think more

INT: So what made you look? The fact that I'm coming today or?

VCSI 1: Erm, it was just purely out of, I suppose interest erm just to, just to see like what am I doing it right,…

The Interviewer confirmed that Participant 1 watched other VCSI videos not just to see how the head camera should be used or indeed the *speaking aloud* method, but also to view practice.

INT: So it wasn't how you conducted the examination, you were quite comfortable that you'd be doing it the same as everybody else, it was how you used the equipment?

VCSI 1: Yeah, but I must admit when I did watch them, I, I was watching what they did as well (9-second pause)

INT: So what were you looking for?

VCSI 1: Erm just to see what, what they were doing like a good example was, that I was watching erm one of (Participant 2) and she was out with (Participant 4) and 'cos (Participant 4) uses the flake powder like a hell of a lot she loves it,… and (Participant 2) was using this flake powder on a shed door. And she was like putting it on,…, but then she got her brush and was just painting like over it and I, 'cos I've actually spoke to (Mentor's name) about it later on, I didn't say that I'd seen (Participant 2) or anything, but I just said like I've seen somebody do that, is that like, I've never seen anybody do that before

INT: So you've put it on with a … magnetic wand

VCSI 1: Yeah the magnetic wand

INT: And then you use a brush

VCSI 1: Yeah and, and I've never seen anyone do that before to be honest

The interviewer asked what the response was from the mentor as follows:

INT: … that's not right, that's wrong?

VCSI 1: No, no, no 'cos it, you know, it's juts everyone does things different …)

VCSI 1: I never actually asked (Participant 2) about that

VCSI 1 retells the words spoken by the mentor and agrees that examiners will have their own methods and ways of examining.

VCSI 1: Yeah oh definitely yeah. So now it's just like oh that's, is that a new technique, I've never seen that before

INT: Are you going to speak to her (Participant 2) about it?

VCSI 1: Yeah, I, I, I probably would do yeah

INT: Are you going to try it?

VCSI 1: I'd be open to it yeah

INT: Right. So if you hadn't had seen the video, you would have maybe missed out on that, on that technique?

VCSI 1: Yeah definitely

INT: And has (supervisor's name) had a chance to have a look at your videos?

VCSI 1: He has yeah

INT: And what does he say about them?

VCSI 1: He was pleased with them, he give me a few pointers …

INT: What pointers did he give?

VCSI 1: He said that I should have taken erm like cuttings from the fence

INT: To match with instruments?

VCSI 1: Yeah, which I didn't know and I know I've spoken to erm (names of Participants 3 and 4) and they didn't know either (7-second pause)

VCSI 1: Yeah that was erm quite new to me that to be honest (15-second pause)

INT: Hmm, if (supervisor's name) hadn't have seen your video, (confirming) he didn't go out with you for the day or anything like that

VCSI 1: No, no I was on my own

INT: You would've missed that ...

VCSI 1: Definitely

Further examples also relate to DNA swabbing techniques where the supervisor makes specific comment on how the rim of a bottle should be swabbed. VCSI 1 recounts the conversation and has learned about different swabbing techniques on a variety of liquid receptacles. Interviewer wanted to explore whether the VCSI 1 was put off from the analysis of her practice.

VCSI 1: Erm no he just, apart from those comments, and I, I, I don't find them criticisms or anything at all

INT: No?

VCSI 1: I found them helpful to me ...

VCSI 1 also states that the supervisor has been complementary, and while he has not been able to view her practice in the field, he has been able to gain an appreciation from a variety of sources, one being the head camera. This aspect was also discussed by other participants.

Participant 4 commented in humor.

VCSI 4: Yeah, yeah exactly. (supervisor's name) always picks me up when he's watching my footage, he says you're using a zephyr on that thing

VCSI 4 explained to the Interviewer that the head camera has been a tool not only to explain which crime scene examinations have been done but also for the supervisor to acknowledge *work*, especially when little or no evidence has been recovered.

INT: ... if somebody showed you some written notes or something on socket (electronic database), they can't get a proper representation of what you've done, but with a headcam you can't really hide from it?

VCSI 4: No that's it!

INT: (Conversation in relation to good performance) So he's, he's made that judgement, maybe from talking to others, maybe from looking at your paperwork, and maybe from looking at your, your videos as well?

VCSI 1: Definitely

Participant 4 provides comment on the usefulness in reviewing the footage for self-development.

VCSI 4: Yes I have I look at the scene I think it's afterwards erm useful in that I can kind of look and think well maybe I could have used a different brush sometimes 'cos I just like, with ali (aluminium) powder, they teach you the zephyr brush in uni, you don't have to use the zephyr brush you can use the squirrel.

One aspect of the research was to explore whether the head-camera would capture more information than that contained in the Crime Scene Report Form. Differences between the content of the Crime Scene Report Form and the verbal commentary were analyzed and coded. It was found that more intelligence was recorded in the head-camera footage than that observed in the scenes of crime notes in all three of the following themes: (1) *modus operandi*, (2) background intelligence, and (3) evidence (Figure 17.2). The data were given to another researcher to test the terms of the constructed framework and the boundaries of the three themes.

The results of the inter-rater analysis are Kappa = 0.871 with $p < .001$. The measure of agreement is statistically significant and may be regarded as substantial (Landis and Koch 1977). There were no instances in our data where more information was contained in the Crime Scene Report Form that was not verbalized and captured in the transcription. We do, however, agree that this could become a possibility, but feel that it is unlikely to ever reverse the results.

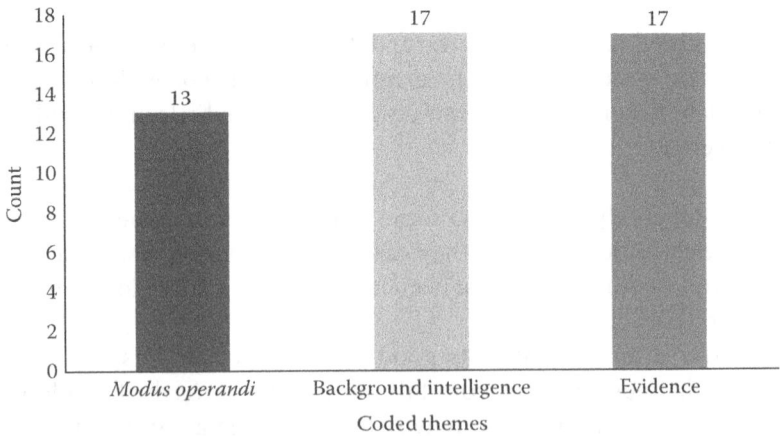

Figure 17.2 Chart showing the frequency of information assigned to a node not included in the Crime Scene Report Form ($n = 47$).

Discussion

It should be acknowledged that funding was not available to pay for overtime for each participant where the use and associated protocols of the head-mounted camera would result in a longer working day. Consequently, the true realism of a busy day may not have always been captured in the recorded material. It is proposed that the implementation of reflections is optional to that of the head-mounted camera and no doubt the reduction of administration could be significant if reflections were deleted from the policy. That said the content of the interviews was drawn heavily from the reflections and a factor to be discussed in future work. The purpose of the recordings was not to eliminate the need for other recording methods, such as Crime Scene Report Forms and photography. This issue has already been explored in depth (Baber et al. 2009). This research also did not seek to challenge examination behavior, rather than to ascertain where this behavior originated. It was not the authors' position to suggest that practices and procedures were incorrect. Furthermore, it was never in the remit of the study to compare the quality of the examinations between the four participants. This helped to build trust and fostered openness between the VCSI participants, other police employees, and the researchers.

None of the VCSIs passed strong negative remarks in relation to wearing the equipment; indeed there were a number of strong positive benefits such as thoroughness and being forced to slow down. Issues in relation to the time that it took to carry out the administration of the video footage were mentioned and this should not be ignored. Where there was a busy day, this did impact on whether the head camera was utilized, with Participant 4 commenting that *speaking aloud* slowed her down. This was also remarked on by Participant 1. This is however juxtaposed with the benefits of slowing down and taking in more of the environment. VCSIs offered a solution for future work, suggesting speaking aloud to be removed or limited to reduce the impact on their administration tasks.

While rich data were derived from the reflections, the process of thinking and writing certainly added to the administration tasks of the day. The quality of the recordings was such that, provided the calibration of the bullet camera was carried out effectively, practice could be observed in detail.

Field notes were also taken from meetings and interviews from the supervisor of the area the VCSIs were based. Interestingly, while his/her early feelings were not made overt, he/she later expressed that he/she did not realize that the recordings would be quite so useful. One particular example was in relation to viewing the examination of property by Participant 3. The property contained folded lead in a sports holdall; while there was no forensic material recovered from the property, the supervisor was able to inspect visually the type and in particular the surface construction of the bag and recommended the VCSI to return and remove the handle for subsequent DNA analysis. The VCSI questioned this as it was not a usual protocol; however, the supervisor was able to place the examination of the property into a wider context of other related offenses.

This aspect provides support for a community of practice, where knowledge is shared and passed on with the aim of improving *situation awareness* in the future. It should be recognized that knowing what is happening and the influences that may impact at this moment in time is different and distinct from the physical or oral actions in implementing what should be done (Wickens 2008).

The material captured with the head-camera technology was also more than that expressed in the Crime Scene Report Forms. In many instances, there are some relevant cultural practice reasons why this is the case. The coded theme Evidence had a number of instances where the VCSI saw what they believed to be fingermarks on the surface of items being examined. These did not always translate across to the report form, with often a generic "speculative search" phrase being utilized instead.

Practitioners in this particular police service had access to other technology that was able to scan unenhanced fingermarks, lifted from surfaces with a gelatin lifter. A useful additional feature was that the VCSIs also used this technology to capture potential DNA material, should the fingermarks be insufficient for further examination. On this point, there were instances where confirmation of whether DNA was recovered by circling the appropriate section on the form was not implemented. There appeared to be a culture of recording fact-based remarks other than that expressed in the section where the *modus operandi* or briefing information was required. Exploring this reasoning was not part of the research. However, its presence supports the notion that to make judgments on VCSI development from solely the Crime Scene Report Forms can limit the opportunity to observe innovation or challenges. Consequently, the head-mounted camera with audio recording is able to capture justification of actions during the scene examination.

Conclusion

It was also recognized that when participants communicated with each other their competence developed. Using head-mounted cameras to capture VCSI performance has been shown to be a useful tool to aid development. Furthermore, the video data may be used as a mechanism for sharing awareness and facilitating the spread of knowledge in relation to practice. Being careful to not overburden the examiner with additional administration duties in relation to the use of this technology is the key to its effectiveness and survivability. Speaking aloud during the examination was found to add time to the scene examination and should not be underestimated. While no specific quantifiable measure was possible, it was a strong factor that emerged from the interviews. The positive from this was a sense of thoroughness, with justifications for actions being made overt.

The authors suggest that the technology could be considered in the following circumstances: Those new in service or within a probationary period as defined in this study, with a recommendation that any implementation should seek strategic support, committed to positioning this as an opportunity for sharing knowledge. The authors also acknowledge that openness to using head-camera technology may not be welcomed by all practitioners and that this research used new technology with new members of staff.

One specific area believed to have future use is for practitioners to gather video material as evidence for annual appraisals or personal development reviews. A framework linking to the National Occupational Standards or requirements specific to the place of employment could be accrued by the practitioner. This has a number of advantages over existing systems that rely predominantly on reviewing exhibits, documentation, and photographs from the attended scenes. The authors wish to make it clear that this technology should not replace these methods but instead sit alongside them. In some instances, it is foreseen that this will reduce the burden of supervisors gathering evidence. Head-camera technology should not be a direct substitute for onsite observation by mentors or supervisory staff, and it is accepted that scenes in which no evidence is found may still show complex decision making or indeed creative thinking. Nevertheless, a mentor or supervisor may happen to choose a day to observe practice which is unchallenging. We feel that a library of recorded scenes allows the examiner more freedom and opportunity to collate evidence of their competence in a dynamic environment. It can sit alongside other methods and serve as a repository to share practice and even innovation. It does, however, require careful construction and maintenance.

References

ACPO, and NPIA. (2009). *Practical Advice on the Management of Priority and Volume Crime* (2nd ed.). London: National Policing Improvement Agency.

Armstrong, S. J., and Mahmud, A. (2008). Experiential learning and the acquisition of managerial tacit knowledge. *Academy of Management Learning & Education, 7*(2), 189–208.

Baber, C., Smith, P., Butler, M., Cross, J., and Hunter, J. (2009). Mobile technology for crime scene examination. *International Journal of Human-Computer Studies, 67*(5), 464–474.

Baber, C., Smith, P., Cross, J., Hunter, J., and McMaster, R. (2006). Crime scene investigation as distributed cognition. *Pragmatics & Cognition, 14*(2), 357–385.

Baumard, P. (1999). *Tacit Knowledge in Organizations*. London: Sage Publications.

Bleakley, A. (2005). Stories as data, data as stories: Making sense of narrative inquiry in clinical education. *Medical Education, 39*(5), 534–540.

Butler, M. (2009). Identifying Expert Performance. *Police Professional,* (144), 18–19.

Childs, M. (2005). Beyond training: New firefighters. *Disaster Prevention and Management, 14*(4), 558–566.

Cianciolo, A. T., Matthew, C., Sternberg, R. J., and Wagner, R. K. (2006). Tacit knowledge, practical intelligence, and expertise. In K. A. Ericsson, N. Charness, P. J. Feltovich, and R. R. Hoffman (Eds.), *The Cambridge Handbook of Expertise and Expert Performance* (pp. 621–626). New York: Cambridge University Press.

Clancey, W. J. (2001). Field science ethnography: Methods for systematic observation on an arctic expedition. *Field Methods, 13*(3), 223–243.

Doak, S., and Assimakopoulos, D. (2010). Tacit knowledge: A needed addition to SOPs in a forensic science. *Forensic Science Policy & Management: An International Journal, 1*(4), 171–177.

Elmhirst, O. (2010). The crime scene. In P. C. White (Ed.), *Crime Scene to Court: The Essentials of Forensic Science* (3rd ed., pp. 25–53). Cambridge: Royal Society of Chemistry.

Ericsson, K. A., Whyte, J., and Ward, P. (2007). Expert performance in nursing: Reviewing research on expertise in nursing within the framework of the expert-performance approach. *Advances in Nursing, 30*(1), E58–E71.

Fadde, P. J. (2009). Instructional design for advanced learners: Training recognition skills to hasten expertise. *Educational Technology Research Development, 57*(3), 359–376.

Feldon, D. F. (2007). The implications of research on expertise for curriculum and pedagogy. *Educational Psychology Review, 19*(7), 91–110.

Fook, J., Ryan, M., and Hawkins, L. (1997). Towards a theory of social work expertise. *British Journal of Social Work, 27*, 399–417.

Fox, J. C., and Lundman, R. J. (1974). Problems and strategies in gaining research access in police organizations. *Criminology, 12*(1), 52–69.

Fraser, J. (2007). The application of forensic science to criminal investigation. In T. Newburn, T. Williamson, and A. Wright (Eds.), *Handbook of Criminal Investigation* (pp. 388–389). Devon: Willan Publishing.

Harlow, H. (2008). The effect of tacit knowledge on firm performance. *Journal of Knowledge Management, 12*(1), 148–163.

Holgersson, S., and Gottschalk, P. (2008). Police officers' professional knowledge. *Police Practice and Research: An International Journal, 9*(5), 365–377.

Holgersson, S., Gottschalk, P., and Dean, G. (2008). Operational knowledge of patrolling police officers. *International Journal of Management and Enterprise Development, 5*(1), 49–62.

Landis, J. R., and Koch, G. G. (1977). The measurement of observer agreement for categorical data. *Biometrics, 33*(1), 159–174.

Lundin, J., and Nuldén, U. (2007). Talking about tools—Investigating learning at work in police practice. *Journal of Workplace Learning, 19*(4), 222–239.

Lyle, J. (2003). Stimulated recall: A report on its use in naturalistic research. *British Educational Research Journal, 29*(6), 861–878.

Moon, J. A. (1999). *Reflection in Learning & Professional Development: Theory & Practice.* Oxon: Routledge.

Omodei, M. M., Wearing, A. J., and McLennan, J. (1997). Head mounted video recording: A methodology for studying naturalistic decision making. In R. Flin, E. Salas, M. Strub, and L. Martin (Eds.), *Decision Making under Stress: Emerging Themes and Applications* (pp. 161–169). Aldershot: Ashgate.

Santtila, P., Korpela, S., and Häkkänen, H. (2004). Expertise and decision-making in the linking of car crime series. *Psychology, Crime & Law, 10*(2), 97–112.

Smith, P. A., Baber, C., Hunter, J., and Butler, M. (2008). Measuring team skills in crime scene investigation: Exploring ad hoc teams. *Ergonomics, 51*(10), 1463–1488.

Sternberg, R. J., Nokes, C., Geissler, P. W., Prince, R., Okatcha, F., Bundy, D. A., and Grigorenko, E. L. (2001). The relationship betwen academic and practical intelligence: A case study in Kenya. *Intelligence, 29*(5), 401–418.

Unsworth, C. A. (2005). Using a head-mounted video camera to explore current conceptualizations of clinical reasoning in occupational therapy. *The American Journal of Occupational Therapy, 59*(1), 31–40.

Wickens, C. D. (2008). Situation awareness: Review of Mica Endsley's 1995 articles on situation awareness theory and measurement. *Human Factors, 50*(3), 397–403.

Wiles, R., Crow, G., Heath, S., and Charles, V. (2008). The management of confidentiality and anonymity in social research. *International Journal of Social Research Methodology, 11*(5), 417–428.

Williams, M., and Ericsson, K. A. (2008). From the guest editors: How do experts learn? *Journal of Sport and Exercise Psychology, 30*, 653–662.

To What Extent Are All Policing Problems Wicked?

18

NEIL COOK

Contents

Introduction

The *Oxford Dictionaries Online* defines a problem as "a matter or situation regarded as unwelcome or harmful and needing to be dealt with and overcome," and in a policing context, the most common situation considered as unwelcome that requires a police response is the commission of a crime. Various specific crime types will be explored to provide illustrations to support the assertion that all plural policing problems are actually Wicked, but that they are Tame or Critical problems when they are considered singularly.

The roots of problem solving using a logical sequence of steps, sometimes known as the scientific method, can be traced back through notable thinkers such as Galileo in the sixteenth century to Aristotle in the fourth century BCE. Many guides and books have been published to advise on problem solving, and one such popular tome is Kepner and Tregoe's *The Rational Manager* (1965). *The Rational Manager* approach advises problem solvers to use the "action sequence for problem analysis and decision making" using a linear sequence of stages. Conklin (2001), among others, has summarized the traditional approach of problem solving by using the "waterfall model" as

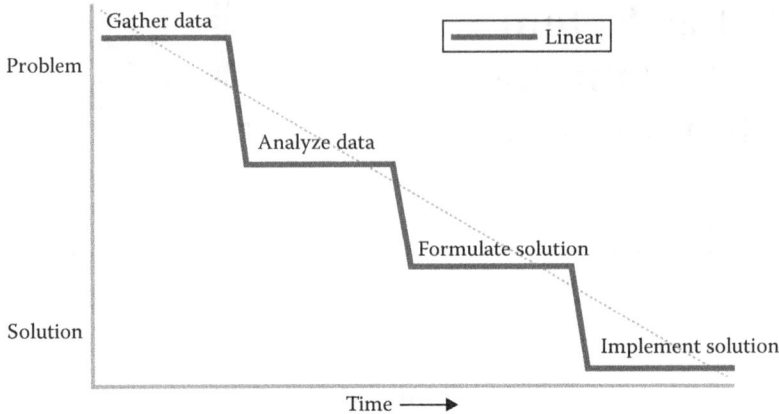

Figure 18.1 Waterfall model of problem solving. (Reproduced from Conklin, J., http://cognexus.org/wpf/wickedproblems.pdf. With permission.)

an illustration, which has the following four stages: gather data, analyze data, formulate solution, and implement solution (Figure 18.1). The idea of this approach appears to move in sequence through these four stages to arrive at destination "problem solved."

It is important to note the assertion that these four stages can be deployed in a linear sequence to arrive at a solution and that formulating a solution does not come before the data have been collected and analyzed. Whether this procedure is an observed reality regardless of problem type will be explored in this chapter. Preliminarily, the ability to classify problems as Wicked, Tame, or Critical is a central component to this task, and so efforts must be taken to establish the meaning of each term before moving forward.

Problem Typology

Churchman (1967) first introduced the concept of "Wicked" problems to the literature by referring to a seminar by Professor Horst Rittel. Wicked and Tame problems were then further discussed in the context of planning in the field of social policy (Rittel and Webber 1973). This is not to say that Wicked problems did not exist prior to this point, but more that our awareness became more attuned to them. They now had a label. Tame and Wicked problems are essentially at different ends of the spectrum of solvability. Tame problems are characterized as simple puzzles, with a possible example being a Rubik's cube. While there are allegedly 43 quintillion (10^{18}) possible starting positions, there is only one solution (Vaughen 2011). The task of solving a Rubik's cube may not be easy depending on your personal prowess, but by applying a set procedure, the cube can be solved in as little as the current record of 6.65 seconds.

A clear distinguishing feature of Tame problems is that we know what success will look like before we start. In the case of the Rubik's cube, all the sides must have uniform color. Once this condition is satisfied, we know we have solved the problem. Therefore, there is a predetermined stopping point, and importantly the Tame problem remains solved even after this stopping point. Essentially, Tame problems can be solved by the application of a scientific method involving the logical progression through the steps shown in the "waterfall model." Rubik's cubes have been solved before, a method to solve it has already been formulated, and it is possible to learn to apply a technique to solve it again and again.

For Rittel and Webber, Wicked problems are characterized by 10 criteria that are succinctly summarized by Grint as

> complex, rather than just complicated, it is often intractable, there is no uni-linear solution, moreover, there is no "stopping point" it is novel, any apparent "solution" often generates other "problems", and there is no "right" or "wrong" answer, but there are better or worse alternatives. In other words, there is a huge degree of uncertainty involved. (2005, 1473)

The exact original criteria will be examined in more detail later.

Conklin notes that

> these criteria are more descriptive than definitional. The point is not so much to be able to determine if a given problem is wicked or not as to have a sense of what contributes to the "wickedness" of a problem. (2001, 9)

For the purpose of this examination of policing problems, a more simplistic view may be taken at times, for if a problem fits most of the Wicked criteria, then it can be considered to be Wicked for ease of discussion. However, Conklin recognizes that life is not so clear-cut when going on to say, "It may be convenient to describe a problem as wicked or tame, but it's not binary—most problems have degrees of wickedness" (2001, 11). In Rittel and Webber's own words, "The search for scientific bases for confronting problems of social policy is bound to fail because of the nature of these problems" (1973, 155). In line with previous bodies of work in fields such as product design and software engineering, it will be argued that any traditional sequential method of problem solving will not be successful against a Wicked policing problem (De Grace and Stahl 1990; Guindon 1990). Wicked problems cannot be solved. A third class of problems was added by Grint (2005) entitled Critical. These are extremely urgent in nature requiring immediate attention, but have great clarity as to what action is needed. They could be considered to be Tame problems with an immediate deadline making them akin to a crisis. Grint (2008) combines the three problem types with Etzioni's (1964) types of power—coercive, calculative,

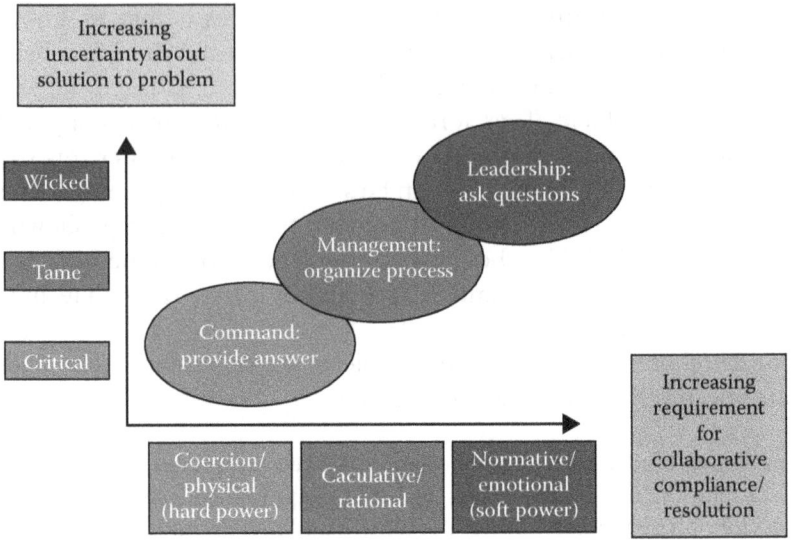

Figure 18.2 Framework for problems and authority. (Reproduced from Grint, K., *Clinical Leader*, 1, 2, 2008. With permission.)

and normative compliance—and provides a total framework of problems, power, and authority as shown in Figure 18.2.

A much abbreviated summary of the above would be that it shows what approach is most associated with the problem type. Critical problems are most often associated with coercion, whereby the commander takes control of the crisis and is relied upon to provide the answer and avert imminent disaster. Managers are expected to apply the standard operating procedure to resolve a Tame problem, whereas the leader is associated with asking the right questions in a collaborative effort to tackle a Wicked problem. Just to complicate the task of characterizing policing problems as particular types further, Grint argues that problems are subjective, or possibly to paraphrase a known saying that "Wickedness is in the eye of the witness":

> fixing a broken leg is the equivalent of a Tame Problem—there is a scientific solution to that and we know how to fix them. Or rather, suitably qualified medical professionals know how to fix them. So to such people your broken leg is a Tame Problem, but if you run (sorry, crawl) into a restaurant for your broken leg to be fixed it will become a Wicked Problem because it's unlikely that anyone there will have the knowledge or the resources to fix it. Thus the category of problems is subjective not objective—what kind of a problem you have depends on where you are sitting and what you already know. (Grint 2008, 12)

The argument will be made that problems are actually objective and changing personal perspective on a problem does not alter the problem itself, but it might guide you to a more appropriate solution. Just because you do not know how to do something, it does not mean that it cannot be done. Not knowing how to complete a Rubik's cube does not suddenly transform the problem from Tame to Wicked. Objectively, the cube can still be solved, just not by an individual, and whether someone else solves it or not is irrelevant. No criteria for "wickedness" come into being just by handing the cube from an expert to a novice; there is no penalty for experimentation, and no more Wicked problems appear through attempts at solving it. So the argument would be made that a broken leg is Tame regardless of the location you happen to be; the knowledge to solve the problem is in existence: call for a doctor. Whether anyone present can actually solve it does not alter the problem type as the problem is solvable.

In policing terms, a distinction can be made between proactive and reactive policing, typically with the former looking at prevention and the latter at detection. Both areas will in turn be examined to see what problem type a typical crime may be characterized as using the Tame, Wicked, or Critical framework. This will then allow an assessment to be made as to what extent policing problems are of each type.

Reactive Investigations—Single

The investigation and detection of crime is a very important reactive function of the police. It is argued that the immediate aftermath of a crime, such as murder, is a Critical problem as there is a shortage of time to secure and preserve any available vital evidence according to the "Golden Hour" principle. This principle effectively states that if CCTV, forensics such as DNA, or witnesses are not identified and preserved as soon as possible, then they may be lost forever to the investigation. While it is clear what must be done to preserve such evidence, and we can envision what success will look like before we proceed, due to the time pressure involved, the problem could best be described as a Critical one, which lies within the realm of the commander. The image of the police officer directing action at the crime scene is compelling and congruent with the criticality of the problem.

Where there are primary crime scene considerations for recovering evidence that would otherwise be lost in a race against the clock, as guided by this "Golden Hour" principle, the crime problem can be classed as Critical regardless of the severity of the actual crime. So just as a murder was used as an example above to illustrate a Critical problem, an offence of shoplifting could also be classed as Critical if the same time pressure existed. The use of the word "crisis" in the context of shoplifting would be unsavory to most police officers.

Once the time pressure has finally evaporated, the police will transition to conducting their inquiries in a timely manner based on a standard operating procedure. Again, taking murder as an example, there is a how-to guide entitled the ACPO Murder Investigation Manual (2008) that includes step-by-step instructions of what to do in each stage of an inquiry. Returning to our three-problem typology, a Tame problem is essentially being described. We know what success will look like before we start when the perpetrator has been identified and put before the courts, we can apply the set procedure laid out in the Murder Manual to achieve that success, and we can conclude once the investigation is complete that the stopping point is self-evident. Once the investigation is finalized and the murder is solved, it remains so, notwithstanding appeals that can be raised through the courts. While murder investigations can be resource intensive and prolonged, they are still methodical and routine based which may account for their high detection rate of 86% (Mitchell and Babb 2007) when compared to the overall crime detection rate of 27%. Therefore, it could be argued that crimes being investigated, after an initial period against the clock, become Tame as they are ultimately about gathering the available evidence using documented best practice.

The argument that problem types can be objective is again revisited. Student officers investigating their first offence would still be investigating a Critical and then a Tame problem. This situation would remain even if they did not have the knowledge, capacity, or capability to deal with the investigation, as knowledge is available and the problem has been solved many times before to a satisfactory standard. While it is agreed that the expert and the novice can look at a problem and see different things, it is argued that the true problem is unchanged by the outside perspective taken. The perspective may alter the approach taken but does not alter the problem itself.

Proactive Investigations—Single

A popular model used in guiding the police during proactive investigations is the problem analysis triangle (Figure 18.3), which is based on Cohen and Felson's (1979) "routine activity theory." Essentially, where an Offender, Victim, and Place intersect, there will be a crime. In order to prevent that crime, one of the factors must be removed. It could be a Manager altering a location to design out crime possibilities using "target hardening," a Guardian being present to look after victims via high visibility policing, or alternatively a Handler focusing on an offender to deny them the opportunities. There is a substantial similarity between the problem analysis triangle and the fire or combustion triangle shown in Figure 18.4. The combustion triangle demonstrates the three necessary components that intersect to create a fire. Any two are not sufficient independent of the third.

Both triangles suggest that if the goal is to prevent a crime or fire from occurring, or even continuing, then one of the constituent parts must be removed to

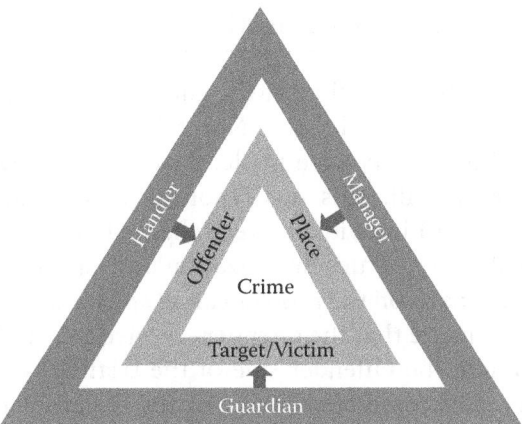

Figure 18.3 Problem analysis triangle. (Reproduced from Eck, J. E., www. popcenter. org. With permission.)

Figure 18.4 Combustion triangle.

break the chain. The parallel similarities between the two triangles should be self-evident. The suggestion is that depriving Oxygen and sufficient Heat of an appropriate Fuel can stop a fire. Therefore, by removing any potential Victims from a relevant Place with potential Offenders present prevents the crime.

A typical proactive police operation may involve targeting a drug dealer, which is an offender-centric approach. This operation may involve surveillance work to gather sufficient evidence to lead to an arrest and support a prosecution. The goal is known from the start, case law is set to guide the police, and guides are available on best practices. A similar problem will be seen before and the same process can be rolled out again. All of the above leads to the conclusion that proactive policing can be seen to address individual Tame problems. An examination will now be made to see if the same problem analysis triangle that appears to be useful to Manage individual Tame problems which can also now assist the police with combating larger scale drug dealing.

Proactive Investigations—Plural

Operation Tennyson was launched at the end of October 2002 and resulted in 16 addresses being searched across North Manchester under the Misuse of Drugs Act, and 30 arrests were made. Part of the operation focused on an area of Cheetham Hill. This was reported in the *Middleton Guardian* on December 2, after 10 individuals were charged. This operation involved the surveillance of a large drugs organization and can be seen as a scale-up Offender-based approach on the problem analysis triangle. By gathering sufficient evidence to ensure that the offenders receive a custodial sentence, the police seek to handle the Offender side of the triangle and stop the crime from reoccurring. This could be seen as treating the problem as a Tame one, by managing a process.

Nevertheless, the operation was heralded as a success with a large number of convictions, removed a gang from the streets of the community, and enhanced community relationships by sending out positive reassurance messages. However, the problem was not solved. In 2006, Operation Centreback culminated in the execution of 34 simultaneous search warrants in the same Cheetham Hill area of North Manchester, with 19 arrests for drug-related offences. This was reported by the *Manchester Evening News* on March 3, 2006. It could be suggested that this operation made little impact on a larger scale too. The very next day, as the news was broken, gangs from Birmingham and Newcastle were found to be in the area trying to take control of the vacated drugs turf.

In addition, the very same operation had to be repeated in the same area to combat the same problem yet again. Operation Eye involved 500 police officers and ended with 25 arrests from 30 executed search warrants conducted on October 5, 2010, which was reported in the *Manchester Evening News*. The police evaluation of Operation Eye conducted in August 2011 concluded:

> In the months that followed crime returned to its previous level, indicating the impact of the police operation was short term and that further operations or sustained activity will be required to keep crime at a low level.

It is proposed that the main reason why the tactic failed to make a dent in the larger problem is because the policing problem of preventing drug dealing is not a Tame problem, but is in fact Wicked, and that scaling up the problem does not allow for the same scaled-up simple solution offered by Management via our trusty problem analysis triangle. Even though the police subjectively saw the problem as a Tame one, it did not make it Tame. The argument is that the problem was objectively Wicked all along, and any attempt to view or deal with it as a Tame problem was in vain. The difference between the Police's problem analysis triangle in Figure 18.3 and the Fire

Service's combustion triangle in Figure 18.4 now appears. The combustion triangle can be scaled up and it still accurately reflects the environment. As a Tame problem, even with a large fire, the model holds true; removing one of the three components permanently stops the fire. The suggestion being made is that drug dealing, as a Wicked problem, is not stopped by removing one set of Offenders. The Offender side of the triangle is deep and self-replenishing, and can remain intact despite police intervention so that crime will continue.

The complex issue of drug dealing is a policing problem that has existed for years and has persisted even with zero tolerance approaches and police force initiatives. Single-mode solutions have been tried and have effectively failed. For example, drug dealing has many factors that affect the problem shaped by society, which largely fall outside the ability of the police to influence alone. Police crackdowns and tougher enforcement do not appear to be making much impact in the longer term. If the problem was Tame, then surely it could be solved and wiped out completely, but this drug-free land does not appear to be on the horizon. The police problem of preventing drug dealing will now be compared against the criteria for a Wicked problem as originally defined by Rittel and Webber (1973).

Rittel and Webber's Original Wicked Problem Criteria

The prevention of drug dealing scores well across the board compared to the original criteria of a Wicked problem, and some of the more important criteria will be examined in detail below.

There is no definitive formulation of the problem in that we do not know why it occurs or completely understand all the interrelated components. If all the factors that affect a problem are truly understood, then the problem is understood and appropriate action can be taken. Part of the essence of a Wicked problem is that the search for a solution often takes place before the problem is fully understood. It could be argued that we do not know all the reasons why drug dealing occurs, and so focusing solely on an enforcement approach will not address the other factors in play. Another consequence of this is that the "waterfall model" will never assist in solving a Wicked problem. We would never move past the "Gathering data" stage as more factors would come into play ending up with a state of "paralysis by analysis."

The solutions are not true or false but are good or bad. For instance, to stop heroin dealing, it would be possible to burn all the existing poppies, but the consequence would be devastating to the medical profession requiring morphine from the same crop; therefore, this solution might be rejected as bad.

Every attempt counts significantly. Every police attempt to combat the problem of drug dealing will alter the landscape in which they work; if the police use and expose a particular tactic, then they will be unable to use that tactic again in that area, and probably also elsewhere, as the criminal fraternity will have received an education courtesy of the police and will alter their actions to negate the police tactic's effectiveness. This means that unlike using a Rubik's cube, we cannot rescramble our policing environment and "have another go." Any attempted action leaves a footprint and becomes part of the problem.

Every wicked problem can be seen as a symptom of another problem, and can be described or framed differently. If you view drug dealing as a consequence of a lenient justice system that lacks a suitable deterrent, then this problem is a function of this further problem. However, drug dealing could equally be seen as a failure on the part of the education system to instill aspiration and enable legitimate opportunities. These views are not mutually exclusive, and framing the problem in a different way may change the approach adopted.

Wicked problems have no stopping rule. This is the only criterion that does not appear to fit at first glance with the original list. While there is a conceivable stopping point, with the complete eradication of drug-dealing, it is simply not achievable with the available resources or time available. So while there may be a vision of what our drug-free Utopia looks like, there is no road map to get us there. So we are left attempting to achieve a reduction in drug dealing down to a level that we can view as tolerable; tolerance of drug dealing is not usually something for which chief constables are renowned. Reviewing the prevention of any particular crime in general against the above set criteria for the definition of a Wicked problem shows a massive overlap. It is argued that as proactive policing problems are scaled up, they transform from being Tame problems where a single-mode approach focusing on an Offender, a Victim, or a Place may have success to being Wicked problems where the issue is a lot more complex and there is no available blueprint for success.

Drug Dealing as a Wicked Problem: Further Examples

An open-source online search of local media in the Greater Manchester Police area reports at least 36 dedicated drugs operations in the past 5 years that utilized long periods of surveillance work and culminated in simultaneous drugs warrants being executed and multiple arrests being made. All details recorded are taken directly as originally reported in the respective newspaper. Greater Manchester Police is divided into 12 geographical divisions, and all of them have conducted such an operation in the past 5 years, with most being represented multiple times. It should come as no surprise that a plain-clothes drugs operation is a recognized tactic used by the police to tackle networks of drug dealing throughout the force area, with the aim of disrupting and bringing the offenders to justice. However, the argument is made that it is a single-mode approach best used against Tame problems.

On the Rochdale Division of Greater Manchester Police, the same cycle of proactive drugs operations can be seen. In May 2008, the police entered the strike phase of Operation Alligator leading to 15 arrests for supplying drugs, as reported in the *Rochdale Observer*. In May 2009, Operation Perryville led to 30 addresses being searched and 20 people being charged for dealing drugs. Storey (2009), writing in the *Rochdale Observer* on May 15, 2009, noted that the Operation "makes a total of 1,146 drugs-related arrests in Rochdale in the last 12 months." Surely with this amount of activity and number of arrests, it is confirmed that the problem is Wicked and thrives despite police action. An extract from the evaluation of Operation Perryville notes that

> the indirect impact of this extensive disruption has also been substantial in parts of Rochdale, where it has contributed to a fall in crime on the targeted Rochdale North and South [Neighbourhoods] ... However, while there is a demand for drugs and a willing cohort of dealers to supply, the threat to the Division remains prominent.

While it is noted that police arrest activity is not a true measure of an area's drug problem; an average of more than three arrests a day for drug offences sustained over the course of a year is at least an indicator that drugs are still readily available after Operation Alligator's clampdown on the supply chain. If the drug problem was a Tame one, then it could have been solved through Alligator or Perryville, and there would have been no need to conduct Operation Frond in December 2010 which used over 100 officers to affect 13 drug arrests, and most recently an unnamed operation in August 2011 which accounted for a further 10 drug-related arrests. The drug problems remain despite the police's continued efforts.

The Salford Division also exhibits the same pattern, but may perhaps assist in further illustrating a particular point in the Tame or Wicked typology. The *Salford Advertiser* documents the police operations in August 2006 with 20 arrests, Operation Marengo in October 2007 with 21 arrests, and a further 18 arrests in April 2008, before a more significant operation in June 2008. This combined operation involving the Serious Organised Crime Agency, Greater Manchester Police, and Cheshire Police into drug smuggling started in June 2008 and ran for 2 years, which resulted in 17 people being jailed for a combined total of 170 years. This was fully reported in the *Salford Advertiser* (Keeling 2011). The point to be made is that by virtue of the custodial sentences that convicted drug dealers receive, we can know that they are not in the vicinity any more. For example, of the 27 offenders charged in relation to North Manchester's Operation Eye, 17 were still in custody a year later. So if the problem was truly Tame, and we have removed the Offender side from our problem analysis triangle, then it should mean that we have solved the problem.

Further operations in Salford include Operation Merton with 12 arrests in June 2009 and an unnamed operation with 10 arrests in March 2011, and would indicate that drug dealing has continued unabated. Our drug problem does not seem to have gone away, even after removing our fifth group of offenders. Therefore, it is proposed that the Offender side of the triangle replenishes itself quicker than the police can arrest and remove them. This idea will be explored later.

Two further examples will be cited from the Bolton and Oldham divisions, respectively, before moving on to examine the end results of all these operations. Operation Chives occurred in Bolton in 2008 and ran in the *Manchester Evening News* under the headline of "Cops smash Bolton drug ring" on April 7, 2009, when the remaining 14 offenders were convicted. The story contains the interesting statement that "Operation Chives follows two previous successful crackdowns on drugs in Bolton." How successful were these crackdowns if it has to be repeated a third time? Operation Chives cannot be said to have been more successful than its predecessors as evidenced by the need for Operation BRAD (Bolton Residents Against Drugs) which was initiated on June 30, 2011, and reported by the *Manchester Evening News*. A progress check on September 1, 2011, recorded that Operation BRAD had achieved 59 arrests in 48 raids over 56 days. A speculative suggestion would be that this too will not be the last drugs operation aimed at the area.

The examples found in the Rochdale, Salford, and Bolton divisions all support the assertion shown in the Cheetham Hill example that repeated drugs operations have been conducted in the same areas without altering the drug problem substantially. They effectively just change who is doing the drug dealing. The Tame problem approach, through Management, of simply removing the Offenders to prison does not affect or address the Wicked problem lurking beneath. The two cited operational evaluations admit as much.

One final series from Oldham will be used before moving on, as it has two illustrations that characterize the problem effectively. The Oldham Division of Greater Manchester Police had already seen 10 people charged with drug dealing after 14 arrests as reported by the *Oldham Chronicle* on December 21, 2009. This was followed by Operation Rescind on March 30, 2011, with 16 arrests for drugs from 16 separate addresses. June 2011 saw Operation Barmah, which resulted in a further seven people arrested for supplying drugs. Next is the ironically named Operation Rescind 2 on July 21, 2011, which resulted in another 15 drugs arrests, as reported by the *Oldham Advertiser*. The operation name suggests an attitude that "Operation Rescind was so successful that it should be repeated." The assertion has been made repeatedly that this approach of attempting to treat large-scale drug dealing as the Tame problem is wrong and that large-scale problems become Wicked. In addition, if the problem were Tame, then a successful operation would not have to be repeated; the problem would remain to be solved.

With the above in mind, it is perhaps interesting to read that the Superintendent in charge of Operation Rescind 2 is quoted in the *Oldham Advertiser* (Greer 2011) as

Today shows that the desire to rid our communities of the blight of drugs is continuous and we will go back and keep tackling the issue in the same area as many times as necessary until the problem is dealt with.

The questions to be answered here are as follows: Can the problem ever really reach the status of "dealt with" or are the police just putting on a brave face when they actually realize they are faced by an unsolvable Wicked problem? If problems are subjective, then why have not the police's attempts to reframe drug dealing as Tame been successful? While the main measure of success referred to above has been whether the drugs operation had to be repeated, it would be naive to suggest that a drugs operation is only successful if it stops drug dealing permanently. Police action can have other ultimate aims. However, this measure of success was used as it illustrates the difference between a Tame and a Wicked problem, and can help us decide which problem type drug dealing actually is. A doctor would not be expected to declare an operation to amputate a limb as a success if it had to be repeated the following year. This is because surgery can be viewed as a Tame problem. Procedures are documented and taught and can be repeated with an expectation of success. Human patients are not in the habit of regenerating limbs after an amputation; the problem limb once solved remains solved.

The police have never so far stated that the drug problem in a given area is unsolvable. Instead the common themes seen in every police spokesperson statement reported in the media aftermath of the operation are as follows: it sends a clear message to the community that drugs will not be tolerated, it demonstrates police commitment to taking action, it provides reassurance to the community that criminals will be arrested and convicted, and more information and intelligence are required from the community to continue the fight against crime.

While this report has focused entirely on drugs operations as an illustration of the principle being proposed, evidence exists to demonstrate that the police use the same Tame operational approaches repeatedly to attempt to address Wicked problems across all crime types and in all areas. It is a belief that evidence of a continual cycle of police operations targeting offences like serious acquisitive crimes such as robbery and burglary could have been suggested as a substitute or supplement, and that this evidence would not be peculiar to Greater Manchester Police and would be replicated across the country. The idea of taking an isolated proactive Tame police problem and scaling it up and making it into a collective Wicked problem lead us to a reexamination of reactive policing

Reactive Investigations—Plural

It was previously asserted that the investigation of any individual crime, even arguably the most serious crime of all murders, is a Tame problem. Investigation skills can be taught in the classroom, officers can apply what they learn from their previous jobs to the next one, and following the same procedure each time can lead to success; single-crime investigations can be successfully managed.

According to the Ministry of Justice's Crime Statistics Bulletin for the financial year of 2009/2010, the police recorded 4.34 million crimes (Ministry of Justice 2010). There is no possible way with the police's current resources that all of these crimes could be effectively investigated. The police therefore need to decide what to investigate. There appears to be no right answer here, which is hopefully the hallmark of a Wicked problem lurking beneath. Should the police investigate every crime regardless of the chance of a positive result? Should the investigation be in proportion to the severity of the crime? How do you equate and rank the severity of each crime? When would you know you had the optimum solution? There is no best or even optimum solution available, although it is possible to have better or worse solutions to the resources problem. For most people, investigating crimes in the order that they are reported and then wiping the slate clean at the end of the day are less preferable than prioritizing murders and serious assaults even if it means that some minor crimes were not investigated at all.

One possible explanation for this apparent shift of a reactive investigation from being a Tame problem when concerned about an individual crime to a Wicked problem when the investigation is scaled up is because the focus changes from "How do I investigate this crime?" into "How do I choose which crime to investigate?" The former allows for a recipe-style investigation by numbers, while the latter has a very real opportunity cost of making a decision; whichever victim does not get an investigation loses again. Reviewing the available literature on this topic does not yield any variance in opinion. Most texts mention in passing the view that policing matters overall are of a Wicked nature: "they cannot solve crime—a wicked problem" (Grint 2010, 23). Hopefully the contribution on offer here is the duality of the problems; the problem type depends on scale.

Summary

Essentially, the argument has been made that in isolation a proactive policing investigation can be treated successfully as a Tame problem by following the approach espoused by the problem analysis triangle, in which directly targeting one contributory factor may resolve the problem. Similarly, a single reactive policing investigation can also be treated as a Tame problem as previous experience can be used to guide the next investigation and it can be prescripted to follow all available lines of inquiry. Therefore, as Tame problems, they have been reduced to mere puzzles for the police to solve. However, the argument of scale has been applied which transforms these policing problems from Tame puzzles to Wicked monstrosities when they are combined together. The assertion is that policing problems are in fact Wicked when considered in their entirety. The consequences of this assertion are that police problems are solvable when taken in isolation, either by detection or by prevention, but when the problem is scaled up sufficiently, it transcends the police's ability to solve it, and the problem may not ever be solved even with outside help (Figure 18.5).

If there were any form of choice involved, it would appear to make sense to choose to tackle policing problems as a collection of Tame ones. The argument has been made that the problem type is fixed, regardless of what the subject would prefer it to be. It might appear that the suggestion is being made that if every individual Tame problem were solved, then this would solve the overall Wicked problem too. However, decades of global policing history would suggest otherwise that this is an illusion, and that their individual solution does not contribute significantly to solving the overall collective problem. The assertion is also that on some level all crime types have both Tame and Wicked components, in that a single crime is an individual unit and is Tame that can be solved, but it forms a part of the larger Wicked problem that cannot be solved (Figure 18.6).

Picking the whole problem apart, one Tame crime at a time has little impact on the underlying issues that lie at the heart of why the crime actually occurs, which is the root cause. Just like fighting with the multiheaded mythical beast, removing a Tame head one at a time has little effect overall as the Wicked beast regenerates and the problem persists. So despite "successful" police drugs operations arresting the offenders, the courts convicting them, and the Tame aspect of the problem being addressed, the Wicked drug-dealing problem overall continues. The conclusion to draw

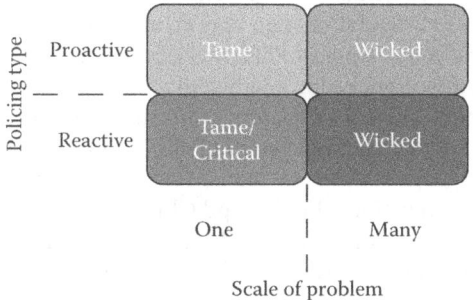

Figure 18.5 Problem scaled-up matrix.

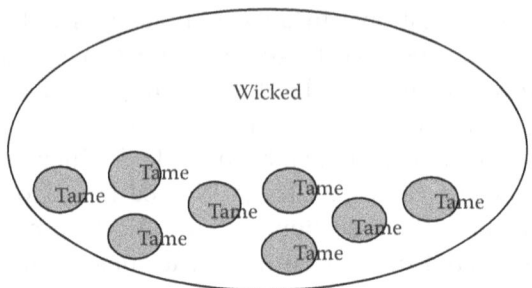

Figure 18.6 Duality of policing problems.

from the above is not that the police are fighting a losing battle against Wicked problems that cannot be solved, but that the police need to work more with partner agencies to engineer novel clumsy approaches for a resolution to many of societies' ills. This is in fact showing an understanding of the very nature of leadership. For if the police leaders already knew what course of action to take, then the problem would be characterized as Tame as opposed to Wicked (Grint 2010).

Police leaderships should understand the true nature of the problems that they face and work collaboratively with partners to pioneer new approaches. The current approaches only lead to the same successful results for Tame problems; Wicked problems require something different. A critical follow-up question is as follows: At what point do Tame problems become Wicked when scaled up? If this problem-type tipping point could ever be identified, it could be key in determining the most appropriate approach to a given policing problem by identifying the largest "chunk" that could be successfully resolved as a Tame problem.

References

Association of Chief Police Officers (2008). *Manual of Murder Investigation.* Bedfordshire: National Centre for Policing Excellence.

Churchman, C. (1967). Wicked problems. *Management Science,* 14(4), B141–B142.

Cohen, L. and Felson, M. (1979). Social change and crime rate trends: A routine activity approach. *American Sociological Review,* 44, 588–605.

Conklin, J. http://cognexus.org/wpf/wickedproblems.pdf.

De Grace, P. and Stahl, L. (1990). *Wicked Problems, Righteous Solutions: A Catalogue of Software Engineering Paradigms.* Englewood Cliffs, NJ: Prentice Hall.

Eck, J. E. www.popcenter.org.

Etzioni, A. (1964). Modern Organizations. Englewood Cliffs, NJ: Prentice Hall.

Greer, S. (2011). Fifteen arrested as police mount drugs raids in Oldham [*Oldham Advertiser*]. Retrieved on September 10, 2011, from http://menmedia.co.uk/old-hamadvertiser/news/crime/s/1441429_fifteen-arrested-as-police-mount-drug-raids-in-oldham.

Grint, K. (2005). Problems, problems, problems: The social construction of leadership. *Human Relations*, 58, 1467–1494.

Grint, K. (2008). Wicked problems and clumsy solutions: The role of leadership. *Clinical Leader*, 1, 2.

Grint, K. (2010). *Leadership: A Very Short Introduction* (1st Ed.). Oxford: Oxford University Press.

Guindon, R. (1990). Designing the design process: Exploiting opportunistic thoughts. *Human-Computer Interaction*, 5, 305–344.

Keeling, N. (2011). Man jailed as police smash cocaine gang [*Salford Advertiser*]. Retrieved on September 10, 2011, from http://menmedia.co.uk/salfordadvertiser/news/s/1423915_man-jailed-as-police-smash-cocaine-gang.

Kepner, C. and Tregoe, B. (1965). *The Rational Manager: A Systematic Approach to Problem Solving and Decision Making*. New York: McGraw-Hill.

Ministry of Justice (2010). *Criminal Statistics: England and Wales 2009 Statistics Bulletin*. Retrieved on March 30, 2011, from https://www.gov.uk/government/uploads/system/uploads/attachment_data/file/217947/criminal-statistics-annual.pdf.

Mitchell, H. and Babb, P. (2007). *Crimes Detected in England and Wales 2006/07*. Home Office Statistical Bulletin 15/07. London: Home Office.

Rittell, H. and Webber, M. (1973). Dilemmas in a general theory of planning. *Policy Sciences*, 4, 155–169.

Storey, K. (2009). Police raids seize drugs and £30,000 [*Rochdale Observer*]. Retrieved on September 10, 2011, from http://menmedia.co.uk/rochdaleobserver/news/s/1115268_police_raids_seize_drugs_and_30000.

Vaughen, S. (2011). *Counting the Permutations of the Rubik's Cube*. Retrieved on March 30, 2011, from http://faculty.mc3.edu/cvaughen/rubikscube/cube_counting.ppt.

Examining Police Integrity
Categorizing Corruption Vignettes

19

DAVID JENKS, LEE MICHAEL JOHNSON,
AND TODD L. MATTHEWS

Contents

Introduction

Law enforcement is a crucial aspect of the criminal justice system, and the integrity of those who work within it is essential. All democratic societies recognize the important role of the police in maintaining the rule of law (Bayley 2002). Bundled within this role is that police officers live within the constraints of the law. Police are mandated to uphold the law through statutes, court decisions, and departmental rules of conduct. The boundaries created by the constitution, state, and department dictate acceptable police behavior. When officers violate the established boundaries, they partake in police deviant behavior (Ivković 2005b). When officers do not violate these boundaries, they exhibit integrity. Klockars and associates defined police integrity as "the normative inclination among police to resist temptations to abuse rights and privileges of their occupation" (Ivković and Shelley 2008, 60).

Police deviance has serious social consequences including a decline in public support for police, loss of trust in the rule of law, and a general mistrust of police. Taken in context with the necessity of community involvement for effective policing, a loss of public support could be catastrophic to the community. Inconsistent practices of law enforcement often reduce the community's confidence in police and willingness to aid in investigations because the relationship between law enforcement and the public is strongly affected by the perceived legitimacy of the police organization (Bayley 2002; Ivković 2005b). Further, how the police are viewed often coincides with a general perception of the entire criminal justice system. Highly publicized cases of police corruption or misconduct are especially harmful to public views of the police. Bayley (2002, 134) noted that this type of high-profile incident was the exception, not the rule: "Although the public is most concerned about dramatic infringements of the rule-of-law, such as brutality, planting false evidence, and lying in courts most of the liberties taken by police are more mundane, routinized, and difficult to detect."

With so much at stake then, it is vital that police officers possess a great deal of integrity. Police agencies are constantly striving to improve recruitment, application, and training procedures, and to identify the individuals best suited to fulfill the roles of the police officer. It is therefore imperative to understand the nuances of officers' perceptions of corruption to disseminate the most complete information as possible. Although researchers have argued that the environment of integrity may be *more important* than selection and training (Klockars, Ivković, Harver, and Haberfeld 2000), it certainly has an impact worth examining. It follows that it is also important to focus on how officers perceive different types of corruption so as to direct future research and also practitioners to allocate limited resources in the areas that are most problematic. It is within this context that the current analysis was launched. This chapter explores whether past research on police officers' perceptions of integrity, specifically the vignettes outlined in Klockars et al. (2000), may be reconsidered using a different method of categorization.

Police Deviance

The vignettes in Klockars et al.'s (2000) instrument describe the instances of police deviant behavior ranging in seriousness, if they were placed on a single conceptual scale, from working a second job to the unnecessary use of force. It is plausible that these vignettes are differentiated by hierarchical degrees of seriousness along the conceptual scale and also that the vignettes cluster categorically—a possibility explored in the current analysis. Literature on police deviance often conceptualizes and defines police misconduct, corruption, and brutality as types of police deviance. Thus, it is important to first review these distinctions.

Police misconduct is defined as police officers' violations of formally written rules, standard operating procedures, regulations, and criminal and civil law (Lynch and Diamond 1983). Not all forms of police misconduct are highly scrutinized because of the general lack of well-defined and upheld rules. Operating norms within agencies sometimes differ from the law or written departmental rules (Barker and Roebuck 1973), thus making it problematic to have one controllable standard. This point has been debated more recently by Ivković and Shelley (2008) who argued that officer integrity was linked directly to agency integrity.

Although corruption falls under the class of police misconduct, it is also large enough to be a single category. Definitions of corruption are influenced by the values and orientation of the researcher, officer, police department, policy, and criminal statute (Barker and Carter 1994). According to Barker and Roebuck (1973), corrupt acts that are criminal are therefore deviant by definition. However, as defined in the literature, corruption is not *always* criminal, and as a result, controversies surround the actions of what constitutes acceptable behaviors. For example, a free cup of coffee is commonly viewed as a courtesy and is therefore not a form of corruption, while other stakeholders may define the very same behavior as such. Questions arise when the free cup of coffee becomes a free snack, a free meal, and so on. Even as the behaviors become deemed more problematic, corruption is difficult to detect because many officers and administrators fail to identify or report potentially corrupt activities. Additionally, both offenders and victims who partake in corrupt activities generally benefit so there are typically few complainants, when an officer takes cash in lieu of making an arrest. Failure to draw attention to these unwanted activities creates obstacles within the justice system and for conducting research.

While definitions vary, personal gain appears to be a crucial element in views of police corruption. Police themselves tend to view serious violations of integrity as only the activities that are engaged in for personal gain (Barker and Roebuck 1973; Ivković 2005a, 2005b; Klockars et. al. 2000). Herman Goldstein, an early theorist on police corruption, also argued that corruption involved the misuse of police authority in a manner designed to produce personal gain (Goldstein 1975). According to Barker and Carter (1994, 47):

> Corrupt acts contain three elements: (1) They are forbidden by some law, rule, regulation, or ethical standard: (2) they involve the misuse of the officer's position; and (3) they involve some actual or expected material reward or gain. The material reward or gain can be in the form of money, goods, services, and/ or discounts.

Ivković (2005b, 549) defined police corruption as

> an action or omission, a promise of action or omission, or an attempt of action or omission, committed by a police officer or a group of police officers, characterized by the police officer's misuse of the official position motivated in significant part with the achievement of personal gain.

Excessive force and brutality, however, are often distinguished from corruption and are included instead under what Barker and Carter (1994) identified as abuse of authority. Abuse of authority was defined as having three types: physical abuse (i.e., excessive force and brutality), psychological abuse (i.e., harassment), and legal abuse (i.e., violating citizens' rights). Corruption may also be conceptually divided according to whether it serves selfish or altruistic interests. In research by Martin (1994), municipal officers in Illinois perceived accepting bribes, planting weapons on suspects, stealing property, and using drugs as the top of the most serious forms of police misconduct but perceived stopping suspects to harass, performing illegal searches, and conducting unauthorized records checks to be much less serious forms of police misconduct (the same or even less serious than accepting free coffee). Compared to most public opinion polls, officers were more likely to believe that illegal searches were not only acceptable behavior but justified in many cases to illustrate their authority (Martin 1994). Some police misconduct is done not for personal gain presumably, but in the name of public good. Illegal searches and other "bending of the rules" may be seen as necessary to fight crime. Martinelli (2006) noted that this type of behavior was termed "noble cause" corruption and was frequently used by officers performing their daily duties.

In law enforcement, "occupational deviance" has become the leading framework for understanding police misconduct and corruption. Police occupational deviance is defined as both the criminal and noncriminal deviant acts committed during normal work activities or under the guise of an officer's authority (Barker 1990). Occupational deviance is generally exhibited in the forms of police misconduct and police corruption which are applied to the role of police officers as an employee rather than the duties of policing (Barker and Carter 1994). The role of an officer is strongly influenced by the perception of occupational environment. Each occupation has its own distinctive norms, standards, and rules of conduct. Individuals who share common work environments also share similar occupational deviant behavior. For example, sleeping on the job is a common deviant behavior found among individuals who work night shifts such as nurses, police officers, and the military, and employee theft and deception is deviant behavior common in the retail and service industries (Barker and Carter 1994). There are many forms of deviance that can only be committed by those in a given occupation such as law enforcement. For example, only police officers can threaten to make an arrest and can accept money instead of issuing traffic citations. The one element that ties all of these acts together is that they are engaging in behavior that is provided by their occupation (Barker and Carter 1994).

Measuring Police Integrity

Research on police integrity has occupied a significant place in the criminal justice literature for many years. Understanding the previous work builds a strong framework for studying all forms of police behavior including the use of force, misconduct, and corruption. Prior research includes examinations of officer's attitudes toward various violations of police integrity. Thus far, studies using data from Klockars et al. (2000) and Ivković (2003) examined specific violations of integrity. Micucci and Gomme (2005) analyzed officer's perceptions against one variable—the use of force. Marché (2009) constructed an economic model that evaluated agency size and resources and their effects on perceptions of corruption. Jenks (2009) examined officers' perceptions of moonlighting. Ivković (2005a, 2005b) expanded the use of these data in comparative studies, and Schafer and Martinelli (2008) focused on supervisory position.

Previous research examined police officers' perceptions toward separate hypothetical vignettes, which contribute to the understanding of how police view single cases of integrity. However, little research has more generally examined officers' perceptions of corrupt behavior. The current analysis furthers the exploration into police officers' perceptions of police integrity by examining if perceptions of different vignettes make up a larger construct of behaviors generally viewed as corruption. It is important to know if groupings of scenarios make up clear measures of integrity instead of assuming that all of the vignettes are equally valid outcome measures of police integrity.

Klockars et al. (2000) ranked case scenarios based on officers' perceptions of offense seriousness, appropriate and expected discipline, and willingness to report. In accordance with that ranking, the authors argued that four case scenarios (off-duty security business, accepting free meals and discounts on beat, accepting holiday gifts, and cover-up of police driving under the influence of alcohol DUI accident) were considered least serious offenses, while other case scenarios (bribes from a speeding motorist, crime scene theft of watch, theft from found wallet, and use of excessive force) were considered most serious offenses. This categorization leaves the three case scenarios (supervisor misusing release time, 5% kickback from auto repair shop, and free drinks to ignore late bar closing) as midrange serious offenses. This classification was based on officers' perceptions of the vignettes and will be compared to the results of the current analysis.

Methodology

Sample and Data

The data for this analysis were collected as part of a cross-national survey study of police integrity by Klockars (1999) under a grant from the US National Institute of Justice. This dataset is the largest and most comprehensive of its kind, and as such, it is still being utilized by researchers who are studying officers' perceptions of corrupt behavior (see, e.g., Ivković 2005a; Jenks 2009; Marché 2009). The current analysis is based on the data provided by 3230 sworn police officers in 30 agencies across the United States [see Klockars et al. (2000) for a complete overview of the sample].

Participants were selected through convenience sampling, which was utilized for three primary reasons (Haberfeld, Klockars, Ivković, and Pagnon 2000; Micucci and Gomme 2005). First, a random sample could not reasonably be drawn from a population that included nearly 18,000 agencies (Walker and Katz 2008, 63) of varying sizes,* mandates, functions, organizational structures, and systems of governance and political accountability (Micucci and Gomme 2005, 492). Second, police cooperation is suspect and difficult to obtain when studying any type of police behavior that could be considered corrupt (Haberfeld et al. 2000; Micucci and Gomme 2005). Third, expanding the knowledge of police behavior that was underreported and underrecorded was not "readily amenable to achievement through random sampling techniques" (Haberfeld et al. 2000; Micucci and Gomme 2005, 492).† The sample does not include state police agencies and includes only one sheriff's office and one county police agency. Thus, the sample overrepresents municipal police agencies. The sample also overrepresents police agencies from the Northeast region of the United States, although it does contain some agencies from the South, Southeast, and Southwest. Further, although it was stressed that participation would be kept confidential, many agencies did not accept the invitation to participate in the study. These agencies may have feared revealing potentially unbecoming information. Thus, the sample also disproportionately represents police agencies that are more receptive to research.

---

* For a complete review of the effect of agency size on officer's perceptions using Klockars et al.'s (2000) data, see Marché (2009).
† For a more detailed description of these reasons, please see Haberfeld et al. (2000) and Micucci and Gomme (2005).

The purpose of the original research was to collect quantitative data that can be used to search for answers to the following five questions (Klockars et al. 2000):

1. What is the level of knowledge of organizational rules governing corruption?
2. How strongly does the occupational culture support these rules?
3. To what extent does the Code protect officers who violate agency rules prohibiting corrupt behavior?
4. What punishment is accepted for violation of these rules?
5. To what extent are the views of the individual officer different from the norm of the occupational culture?

These data were collected via a self-administered anonymous questionnaire that presented 11 different hypothetical case scenarios, as displayed in Figure 19.1. A traditional approach to studying perception of crime severity has been through the development of vignettes. Case scenarios provide the opportunity to analyze respondents' perception in a range of topics while focusing on their opinions and behavioral intentions. Each scenario was followed by seven questions asking participants to rate the seriousness of the behavior, the type of disciplinary action required, and the likelihood of reporting the behavior, as displayed in Figure 19.2. The scenarios are based on Barker and Roebuck's (1973) typology of police corruption and were familiar to citizens and representative of a modern-day industrialized society, and special attention was paid to the issues of cultural neutrality when creating the hypothetical situations. Participants were asked to assume the role of the officer in each scenario—one who has been a police officer for 5 years with a satisfactory work record and no history of disciplinary problems. To ensure respondents' confidentiality and participation, participants were only asked to answer the questions about their perceptions, not their personal experiences.

The questionnaire also consisted of a limited number of questions about participants' agency size, rank, length of service as an officer and at the current agency, type of assignment, and supervisor status. Demographics such as age, race, and sex were excluded, and a limited number of questions were asked to decrease the chances of participant identification and increase the response rates. It was thought that officers would be less likely to answer the questions about corruption if any identifying characteristics were included (Klockars et al. 2000, 6). The final questions that were directly asked include the following: "Do you think that most police officers would give their honest opinions in filling out this questionnaire?" followed by "Did you?" Eighty-four percent of respondents reported that they thought most officers answered the questions honestly. Ninety-seven percent reported

Corruption Case Scenarios

Case 1. A police officer runs his own private business in which he sells and installs security devices such as alarms, special locks, and so on. He does this work during his off-duty hours.

Case 2. A police officer routinely accepts free meals, cigarettes, and other items of small value from merchants on his beat. He does not solicit these gifts and is careful not to abuse the generosity of those who give gifts to him.

Case 3. A police officer stops a motorist for speeding. The officer agrees to accept a personal gift of half of the amount of the fine in exchange for not issuing a citation.

Case 4. A police officer is widely liked in the community, and on holidays local merchants and restaurant and bar owners show their appreciation for his attention by giving him gifts of food and liquor.

Case 5. A police officer discovers a burglary of a jewelry shop. The display cases are smashed and it is obvious that many items have been taken. While searching the shop, he takes a watch, worth about 2 days' pay for that officer. He reports that the watch had been stolen during the burglary.

Case 6. A police officer has a private arrangement with a local auto body shop to refer the owners of the cars damaged in the accidents to the shop. In exchange for each referral, he receives a payment of 5% of the repair bill from the owner.

Case 7. A police officer, who happens to be a very good auto mechanic, is scheduled to work during coming holidays. A supervisor offers to give him these days off, if he agrees to tune-up his supervisor's personal car. Evaluate the supervisor's behavior.

Case 8. At 2:00 a.m., a police officer, who is on duty, is driving his patrol car on a deserted road. He sees a vehicle that has been driven off the road and is stuck in a ditch. He approaches the vehicle and observes that the driver is not hurt but is obviously intoxicated. He also finds that the driver is a police officer. Instead of reporting this accident and offense, he transports the driver to his home.

Case 9. A police officer finds a bar on his beat which is still serving drinks a half hour past its legal closing time. Instead of reporting this violation, the police officer agrees to accept a couple of free drinks from the owner.

Case 10. Two police officers on foot patrol surprise a man who is attempting to break into an automobile. The man flees. They chase him about two blocks before apprehending, tackling, and wrestling him to the ground. After he is under control, both officers punch him a couple of times in the stomach as punishment for fleeing and resisting.

Case 11. A police officer finds a wallet in a parking lot. It contains the amount of money equivalent to a full-day's pay for that officer. He reports the wallet as lost property, but keeps the money for himself.

Figure 19.1 Klockars' (1999) instrument—Scenarios.

they answered the questions honestly. The police officers who did not report honestly were excluded from the analysis.

Descriptive statistics were computed to provide more details on the sample (see Table 19.1). A majority (59.8%) of respondents worked in very large agencies of over 500 employees, while many of the remaining officers worked in medium-sized agencies of 76–200 employees. Sixty-nine percent of respondents held the rank of patrol at the time of survey completion, while the rest were relatively evenly divided between the ranks of sergeant,

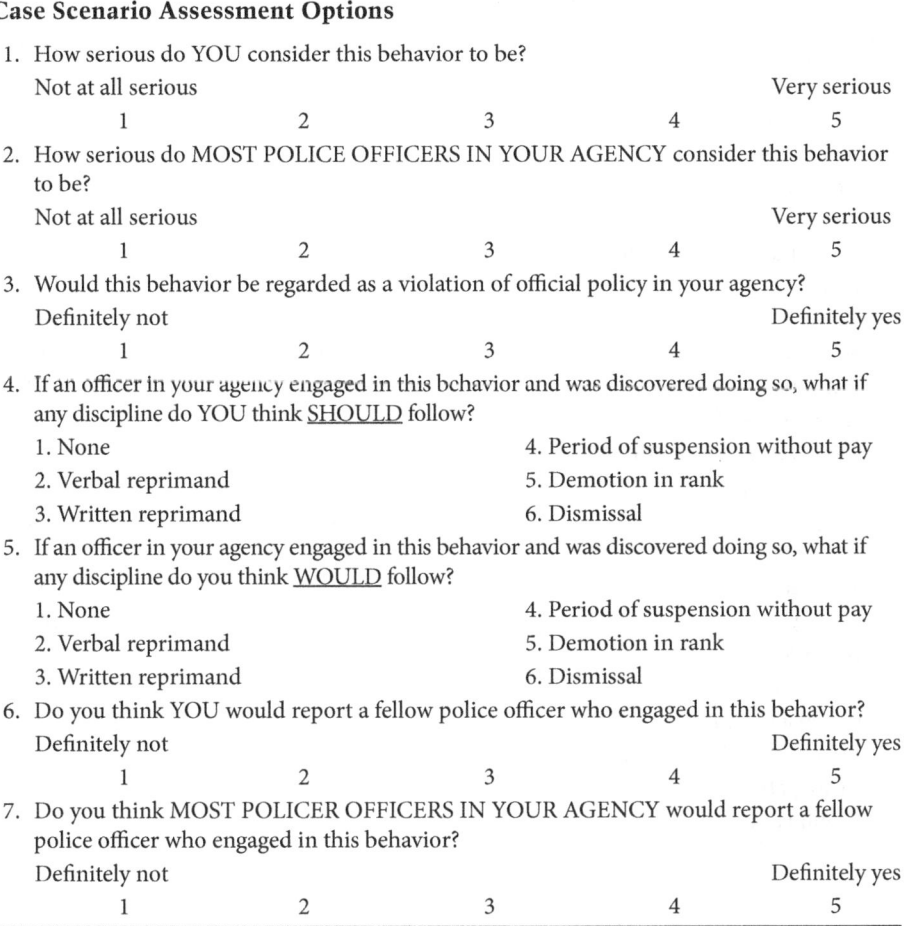

Case Scenario Assessment Options

1. How serious do YOU consider this behavior to be?

   Not at all serious   Very serious

   1   2   3   4   5

2. How serious do MOST POLICE OFFICERS IN YOUR AGENCY consider this behavior to be?

   Not at all serious   Very serious

   1   2   3   4   5

3. Would this behavior be regarded as a violation of official policy in your agency?

   Definitely not   Definitely yes

   1   2   3   4   5

4. If an officer in your agency engaged in this behavior and was discovered doing so, what if any discipline do YOU think <u>SHOULD</u> follow?

1. None	4. Period of suspension without pay
2. Verbal reprimand	5. Demotion in rank
3. Written reprimand	6. Dismissal

5. If an officer in your agency engaged in this behavior and was discovered doing so, what if any discipline do you think <u>WOULD</u> follow?

1. None	4. Period of suspension without pay
2. Verbal reprimand	5. Demotion in rank
3. Written reprimand	6. Dismissal

6. Do you think YOU would report a fellow police officer who engaged in this behavior?

   Definitely not   Definitely yes

   1   2   3   4   5

7. Do you think MOST POLICER OFFICERS IN YOUR AGENCY would report a fellow police officer who engaged in this behavior?

   Definitely not   Definitely yes

   1   2   3   4   5

Figure 19.2 Klockars, 1999 instrument—Assessment questions.

detective, or command staff. Regarding the length of service, the highest percentage of officers were on the job between 6 and 10 years, with rather even percentages falling between 3 and 5 years, and in each of the categories over 10 years. Finally, 78.4% of respondents reported that their assignment was to be on either patrol, call, control, or traffic, with 10.5% assigned to investigative or detective responsibilities and 11.1% serving administrative or other assignments.

Current Study Design

Factor analysis was employed to determine whether the 11 vignettes used historically in the literature are accurate representations of behaviors that officers typically view as corruption. The intention here is to discover if

Table 19.1 Sample Descriptive Statistics

Variable	Frequency	Percentage
Agency size ($N = 3232$)		
Very small (less than 25)	93	2.9
Small (26–75)	215	6.7
Medium (76–200)	739	22.9
Large (201–500)	251	7.8
Very large (more than 500)	1934	59.8
Rank ($N = 3174$)		
Patrol	2190	69.0
Sergeant	369	11.6
Detective	380	12.0
Command staff	235	7.4
Length of service ($N = 3185$)		
Less than 1 year	132	4.1
1–2 years	248	7.8
3–5 years	495	15.5
6–10 years	777	24.4
11–15 years	522	16.4
16–20 years	448	14.1
Over 20 years	563	17.7
Type of assignment ($N = 3176$)		
Patrol/on call/control/traffic	2489	78.4
Investigative/detective	335	10.5
Administrative/other	352	11.1

officer integrity, as indicated by the ratings of the seriousness of integrity infractions, can be globalized to these 11 vignettes. The use of data collected from a convenience sample with very limited measures of predictor variables is less problematic as the primary purpose of the current study is to explore the measures of integrity, not to propose the causal models that can be generalized. Klockars et al. (2000) identify the scenarios as 10 cases of corruption (including working off-duty) and 1 of excessive force. These case scenarios are presented in Figure 19.1. Excessive force can be viewed either as a category of police deviance in itself or as a severe form of corruption. Regardless, excessive force is a violation of integrity, and therefore, the scenario is included in this analysis to measure integrity. Another scenario describes working off-duty at a security business. This behavior is not necessarily corrupt for many agencies and could even be encouraged in some situations as an additional source of revenue in a profession that has long been plagued by relatively low pay and benefits (Jenks 2009).

Table 19.2 Descriptive Statistics for Integrity Indices

	Mean	SD	Alpha Score
Off-duty business ($N = 3131$)	10.32	5.47	0.193
Receiving meals ($N = 3156$)	16.30	6.09	0.883
Receiving holiday gifts ($N = 3144$)	18.28	7.04	0.916
Ignoring officer DUI ($N = 3133$)	19.27	6.77	0.895
Using excessive force ($N = 3147$)	24.84	6.63	0.894
Supervisor misusing release time ($N = 3152$)	24.59	6.22	0.887
Auto shop kickback ($N = 3158$)	28.10	6.07	0.896
Accepting free drinks after hours ($N = 3159$)	26.95	5.80	0.876
Stealing from found wallet ($N = 3164$)	30.66	5.14	0.857
Ignoring speeding ($N = 3163$)	30.51	4.38	0.785
Stealing from business ($N = 3143$)	32.78	3.80	0.821

Police Integrity Measures

Police integrity is defined as police officers' perceptions regarding the seriousness of corruption cases. Eleven indices were constructed based on officers' responses to the corruption case scenarios (minus working off-duty). Officers used the same set of seven questions to assess each corruption case scenario (Figure 19.2), which provides standardized multi-item measures of officers' reactions to all scenarios. Coded responses to the seven questions in a case scenario were summed to create one measure. In items 4 and 5 of each case scenario, the verbal and written reprimand options were combined into one category in order to maintain categorical coding consistency with the other items (i.e., 5 categories per question or 35 per case scenario). Table 19.2 reports the means, standard deviations, and Cronbach's alpha scores for the 11 indices. The alpha scores were very high, ranging from 0.785 to 0.916, suggesting that each index is measuring one dimension of corruption.

In addition, a general integrity index was constructed *a priori* by summing all 10 case scenario index measures. The overall index scores ranged from 70 to 350, with a mean of 252.4 and standard deviation of 40.32, and the Cronbach's alpha score for the overall index was also high: 0.877 (also in Table 19.2). While this alpha score implies a global integrity measure, factor analysis is a much more adequate method for exploring general integrity.

Results

Responses to each of the 7 questions were combined into an additive index for all 11 vignettes. A factor analysis of all 11 additive indices was conducted using principal component analysis with varimax rotation. The analysis yielded two factors explaining a total of 60.1% of the variance for the entire set of variables.

Table 19.3   Factor Analysis of Vignettes Indices

Vignette	Unrotated		Rotated	
	F1	F2	F1	F2
Off-duty business	0.394	0.535	0.082	*0.659*
Free/discounted meals	0.573	0.599	0.207	*0.803*
Holiday gifts from merchants	0.638	0.458	0.333	*0.712*
Cover-up of police DUI	0.670	0.141	*0.516*	0.450
Supervisor holiday for tune-up	0.695	−0.012	*0.612*	0.329
Excessive force on car thief	0.739	−0.145	*0.716*	0.235
Auto repair 5% kickback	0.786	−0.111	*0.740*	0.288
Bribe from speeding motorist	0.783	−0.138	*0.750*	0.262
Crime scene theft of watch	0.771	−0.268	*0.803*	0.143
Drinks to ignore late bar close	0.805	−0.208	*0.804*	0.212
Theft from found wallet	0.791	−0.324	*0.848*	0.104

Note: Initial eigenvalues: total component $1 = 5.468$, % of variance 49.705; total component
       $2 = 1.147$, % of variance 10.431.
Betas larger than 0.5 are indicated in bold.
F1, Factor 1; F2, Factor 2.

The first factor was labeled corruption due to the high number of incidents which are as follows: crime scene theft of watch, bribe from a speeding motorist, theft from found wallet, free drinks to ignore late bar closing, 5% kickback from auto repair shop, supervisor holiday for tune-up, excessive force on a car thief, cover-up of a police DUI accident, and holiday gifts from merchants. This first factor explained 49.7% of the variance. The second factor derived was labeled not corrupt. This factor was labeled as such due to the high loadings by the following factors: off-duty security system business and free meals and discounts on beat. The variance explained by this factor was 10.4%. The Kaiser–Meyer–Olkin (KMO) and Bartlett's test of sphericity both indicate that the set of vignettes are at least adequately related for factor analysis. Substantively, this means that we have identified two clear patterns of response among officers—one pattern of responding to vignettes commonly viewed as corruption and the other pattern of responding to vignettes not commonly viewed as corruption (Table 19.3).

Conclusion

Over the years, it has been difficult to research and understand police integrity. While there have been obvious legal boundaries dictating acceptable police behavior, it is now clear that researching officers' perceptions toward varying levels of police misconduct can be beneficial. It is essential to understand police officers' perception of violations of integrity, especially behavior consisting of misconduct and corruption, in order to create the structural foundation for stronger policies regulating police integrity. The analysis indicates that officers' perceptions encompass a wide variety of corrupt behaviors, but also includes two vignettes, referring to having an off-duty business and accepting free meals and other gratuities as a courtesy, which are not typically regarded as corrupt.

Due to study limitations, results must be interpreted with caution. The integrity measures used in this analysis are limited in that they do not assess all aspects of police integrity. As Klockars et al. (2000) pointed out, the corruption case scenarios almost entirely consist of misconduct committed for personal gain (one case involves excessive use of force). Other violations of integrity such as abuse of discretion, rudeness to citizens, and other forms of misconduct usually not motivated by personal gain were not observed (Klockars et al. 2000). In addition, while the dataset used in this analysis contains the largest, most comprehensive, and most recent data available on police officers' perceptions of integrity, it was drawn from a nonrandomly selected sample and is somewhat dated (10 years old). The convenience sample was taken mostly from municipal agencies in the Northeast region of the United States. Further, because some agencies and individual officers chose not to participate in the study, the sample was biased toward police agencies and officers that are more receptive to research and less fearful of analyses of their perceptions. The responses of the officers who volunteered may not represent the perceptions of those who were excluded or chose not to participate in the survey. Clearly, future research is needed to collect and analyze the current data from different types of police agencies across varying regions of the United States.

This study has important research and practice implications. To begin with, since the study establishes that not all 11 vignettes typify behavior that is viewed as corrupt, some integrity measures are viable options in researching police integrity, while others are not. It becomes apparent that the most appropriate integrity measure to be used in research depends on the particular needs and goals of the research. For example, some researchers or agencies will be interested in examining a specific corruption problem, while others are interested in activities more readily considered corruption. Thus, some scenarios are useful but limited. Focusing on a specific corrupt act may not be adequate to indicate officers' risk of engaging in corruption; a perception of the seriousness of the case could be an exception to the way an officer usually perceives corruption. For example, it is possible that officers tend to tolerate free meals and working off-duty because they believe that these activities are not a violation of the rules (even though they often are). If this is true, situational variables may sometimes predict officers' perceptions more than individual propensities. It is therefore foreseeable that researchers and agencies will eventually exclude vignettes that have historically been included. The current trend in research using this type of data is to include vignettes that this analysis illustrates are not viewed as corruption by police officers. The development and use of more appropriate vignettes is, then, another useful option in researching the integrity of police officers and developing policies and practices aimed at boosting integrity/reducing corruption.

Police administrators have tackled the issue of corruption by creating stricter hiring policies, thoroughly screening applicants, and aggressively removing officers who appear to be morally deficient (Haberfeld et al. 2000). A revised instrument using only the vignettes that are viewed as serious corruption would better measure and assess the level of integrity of police officers and evaluate the effectiveness of initiatives intended to increase the integrity of police officers. Agencies may wish to address integrity from a more practical framework, rather than incorporate issues that officers do not relate to the issues of integrity in their experiences or observations. A more practical view of integrity is also more adaptable as opposed to relying on theoretical definitions where clear lines cannot be drawn. Integrity itself is vague and opaque, and should be treated as such, rather than case- and context-bound over time. This is not to say that if police officers do not think that an act is corruption, then *it is not* corruption. The current analysis identifies patterns in the data; it does not establish what is substantively true. The proposition that accepting gratuities is not at least mildly corrupt, or unethical, is dubious. Gratuities could stand as symbolic bribes, putting the officer in a conflict of interest. Thus, an argument could be made that the excluded vignettes really *do* reflect corruption, at least in some form or to some extent. Regardless, it should be clear that the nature of police corruption and officers' integrity cannot be assumed, but rather must be thoroughly conceptualized and researched.

The current analysis seems to clearly note, however, that there are two integrity constructs in the data. Crudely, these may be conceptualized as light versus serious types of integrity violations. Off-duty work and free coffee and meals represent "conflict of interest" behaviors that could make officers more beholding to some citizens over others, not severe infractions (with a side business only potentially being a conflict of interest, if it interferes with work). These behaviors are definitely in the gray area of police deviance. At face value, the remaining items that load together look more like "serious misconduct" as they involve more extreme cases of corruption for personal gain, unprofessional behavior, and abuse of authority. These behaviors are much less in the gray area, if at all. Researchers could still use all of the 11 measures in studies of corruption, but if they choose to use composite measures, they could examine "conflict of interest" and "serious misconduct" separately. Police involvement in conflict of interest behaviors could still be a problem, and they could also correlate with the more serious violations, so it would be informative to examine them as well. Further, low integrity on one composite measure but not on the other would help agencies see more specifically where they are having problems. The general point to be made is that it is important that researchers and practitioners recognize distinctions and commonalities across corrupt behaviors when explaining, assessing, and attempting to increase police officer's integrity.

References

Barker, T. (1990). Peer group support for police occupational deviance. In T. Barker and D. Carter (Eds.), *Police Deviance*, 2nd edition (pp. 45–57). Cincinnati, OH: Anderson.

Barker, T. and Carter, D. (1994). *Police Deviance*, 3rd edition. Cincinnati, OH: Anderson.

Barker, T. and Roebuck, J. (1973). *An Empirical Typology of Police Corruption*. Springfield, IL: Charles C. Thomas Publisher.

Bayley, D. (2002). Law enforcement and the rule of law: Is there a tradeoff? *Criminology & Public Policy* 2, 133–154.

Goldstein, H. (1975). *Police Corruption: A Perspective on Its Nature and Control*. Washington, DC: Police Foundation.

Haberfeld, M., Klockars, C., Ivković, S., and Pagnon, M. (2000). Police officer perceptions of the disciplinary consequences of police corruption in Croatia, Poland, Slovenia, and the United States. *Police Practice and Research: An International Journal* 1, 42–72.

Ivković, S. (2003). To serve and collect: Measuring police corruption. *The Journal of Criminal Law & Criminology* 93, 593–649.

Ivković, S. (2005a). *Fallen Blue Knights: Controlling Police Corruption*. New York: Oxford University Press.

Ivković, S. (2005b). Police (mis)behavior: A cross-cultural study of corruption seriousness. *Policing: An International Journal of Police Strategies & Management* 28(3), 546–566.

Ivković, S. and Shelley, T. (2008). The contours of police integrity across Eastern Europe: The case of Bosnia and Herzegovina and the Czech Republic. *International Criminal Justice Review* 18(1), 59–82.

Jenks, D. (2009). Police corruption or police productivity? Moonlighting in US agencies. *Critical Issues in Justice and Politics* 2(2), 87–104.

Klockars, C. (1999). *Police Corruption in Thirty Agencies in the United States*, 1997 (ICPSR Version). Washington, DC: National Institute of Justice.

Klockars, C., Ivković, S., Harver, W., and Haberfeld, M. (2000). *Measurement of Police Integrity*. Washington, DC: National Institute of Justice.

Lynch, G. and Diamond, E. (1983). Police misconduct. In S.H. Kadish (Ed.), *Encyclopedia of Crime and Justice*, Vol. 3 (pp. 915–919). New York: The Free Press.

Marché, G. E. (2009). Integrity, culture, and scale: An empirical test of the big bad police agency. *Crime, Law and Social Change* 51, 463–486.

Martin, C. (1994). *Illinois Municipal Officers' Perception of Police Ethics*. Chicago, IL: Illinois Criminal Justice Information Authority.

Martinelli, T. J. (2006). Unconstitutional policing: The ethical challenges in dealing with noble cause corruption. *Police Chief* 73(10), 1–6.

Micucci, A. and Gomme, I. (2005). American police and subcultural support for the use of excessive force. *Journal of Criminal Justice* 33, 487–500.

Schafer, J. A. and Martinelli, T. J. (2008). First-line supervisors' perceptions of police integrity: The measurement of police integrity revisited. *Policing: An International Journal of Police Strategies & Management* 31(2), 306–323.

Walker, S. and Katz, C. M. (2008). *The Police in America: An Introduction*, 6th edition. New York: McGraw-Hill.

Representations of the Police in the British Media

"Hard" Cops and "Soft" Cops

20

IAN MARSH

Contents

Introduction

The focus of this brief overview is on the way that the media represent the criminal justice system, and in particular how the police are presented in our mass media. It considers real-life or factual representations and also how the police are portrayed in fictional accounts and presentations. It is not always easy to separate out what is fact from fiction—and fictional programs such as dramas and soap operas will usually try and make their "fiction" as realistic as possible. As Mason puts it: "Audiences 'commuting' between the realms of factual news and entertainment programming has implications for public perceptions of law enforcement agencies, the courts and prisons as well as offenders and victims" (2003, 5).

In addition to the massive interest the general public have with crime and criminals, there is also a deep fascination with how these crimes and criminals are discovered and dealt with by the criminal justice system—with how the police go about catching and charging offenders (and with how the courts and judiciary sentence them and with what happens to those offenders who enter the penal system).

A country's criminal justice system is a massive operation. Home Office data on police powers and procedures in England and Wales showed that in 2008/2009 the police made almost 4000 arrests for recordable crime each day (1,456,347 a year) and stopped and searched over 4100 people each day (Home Office 2010). And the Ministry of Justice data for 2009 showed that 1,693,200 defendants (4638 each day) were proceeded against in courts in England and Wales, with 1,405,900 being sentenced by those courts (Ministry of Justice 2009). However, in spite of these quite dramatic figures, most people still only have a fairly limited experience of the police and the criminal justice system. As with our knowledge and understanding of criminal behavior, so our understanding of the criminal justice system is derived largely from the mass media we consume. Crime stories are a staple of many forms of our media, and these stories often focus on crimes that have reached the stage of getting to court. There is a tremendous interest in "who gets what" from within our criminal justice system. And because the media will almost inevitably focus on the more spectacular crimes and those that lead to the most severe punishments, the picture portrayed by the media about law enforcement and punishment is liable to be distorted in a similar way.

While it is understandable that the media focuses on solved crimes (through covering the trials and courtroom drama), Leishman and Mason (2003) point out that this coverage can give the wider public the impression that most crime is solved and that the police are pretty effective in detecting crime—impressions that the information on the actual clear-up rates of all crimes committed demonstrates to be way off the mark. The crimes covered by the media are more solvable because, as mentioned above, they are the more serious sorts of crime, such as murder and sexual offences. And these are the crimes that are usually solved by the police—because they will spend considerable resources on high-profile and serious crimes and because such crimes are often relatively easy to solve as the offender (in the case of murder) will more often than not have had some previous association (and often a close association through marriage or family ties) with the victim. This sort of media coverage might reassure the public that the police are effective at catching criminals, but can also lead to criticism when they fail to solve crimes. However, Leishman and Mason make the point that "the lack of emphasis in the media on unspectacular unrecorded, unsolved property crimes can be seen to let the police 'off the hook' for underperformance in such areas" (2003).

British Crime Surveys (Kershaw et al. 2000, Nicholas et al. 2007) found that television or radio news was cited by most people (nearly three-quarters of the population) as their major source of information about the criminal justice system, with newspapers also having a significant impact. So it would seem fair to conclude that how the media portray the police, the courts, and judiciary, and our penal system will have a major influence on public knowledge and public opinion.

The Police–Media Relationship

In introducing the chapter on "policing and the media" in the fourth edition of *The Oxford Handbook of Criminology* (2007), Robert Reiner, one of the foremost academic writers on the media and policing, highlights the collaborative nature of the relationship between the police and the journalists and the broadcasters. He cites the comment of Sir Robert Mark, Commissioner of the Metropolitan Police in the early 1970s, that the police and the media relationship could be compared to "an enduring, if not ecstatically happy, marriage." Reiner describes the relationship between the police and the media as one of "mutual dependence and reciprocal reinforcement." On the one hand, and as we have highlighted above, the way that the criminal justice system, including and in particularly the police, has dealt with offenders has always been a significant part of the mass media content, in both factual and entertainment contexts. On the other hand, though, the police are concerned with how they are portrayed by the media; and, more specifically, with creating and encouraging a positive police media image, as they are aware that public support and cooperation will help them in enforcing the law.

It is self-evident that in order to solve crimes the police need to collect relevant information, and the public are one of the most important sources of information for the police when investigating crime. This is notably the case with regard to some of the more serious crimes, such as murder investigations, when the police make use of the media as part of their investigation strategy— for instance, through using the media to appeal for information that might help them solve the crime. Innes (2001) makes the point that the police can use the media as a means of mass communication for informing the general public that a crime has occurred and witnesses need to be identified. One of the earliest and longest running "reality television" programs, *Crimewatch*, is based on this idea, but appeals to the public from bereaved victims and/or senior police officers can also be made via newspapers. And these communications, whether through television or the press, are presented by the police in a way that they will persuade people to come forward with information— either as witnesses or perhaps through suspecting someone of an offence or being an acquaintance of an offender. This form of public appeal is relatively cheap and easy for the police to use as well as having, as Innes puts it, an "important symbolic function ... (that is) important in producing a sense of public legitimacy for the institution of policing." However, police use of the media in this way can cause difficulties—such appeals can generate an enormous amount of information, much of which will be irrelevant to the particular enquiry, and they can also lead to an expectation that the particular case should be solved by the police. More seriously, there have been problems with media appeals where relatives of a victim have made a public appeal and later been found to have been involved in the offence itself. A notable example of this was the case of Tracey Andrews who was found guilty, in 1997, of murdering her fiancé after claiming that he had been killed in a "road rage" attack and who had used the media to appeal for witnesses to this supposed road rage attack.

In the United States, a similarly notorious example was the case of Susan Smith who, in 1994, reported to the police that her car had been stolen by a black man who had driven her car away with her two young sons (aged 3 years and 14 months, respectively). Smith made a tearful television appeal for the rescue and return of her sons, but a few days later confessed to letting her car roll into a lake and drown them. She was convicted of murder in 1995 and sentenced to life imprisonment. In Smith's case, the police had been suspicious of her before the appeal and let it go ahead as a means of expediting their investigation.

There are also overlaps and similarities between the job of a police officer (and in particular a detective) and a journalist. Leishman and Mason (2003) provide a number of examples that make this point. Both jobs can involve working odd and long hours, pressure to get "results," and a need to meet deadlines; in both cases, rules and regulations have to be followed which might get in the way of a "result"—journalists have to work within laws of libel and contempt and police officers within regulations governing the stopping, searching, arresting, and so on of suspects. And while there might be a lot of bureaucratic and routine work for those employed in both areas, they are also faced with quite dramatic events in the course of their work. In addition, informants can and do play an important and useful role for journalists and police officers. Leishman and Mason also look at the crossover that exists between the nature of police work and news gathering—in spite of some antagonism between the two professions, what the police do overlaps with what makes news, which "drives a sense of dependency between police and members of the media, uneasy though this may be at times." The nature of the police–media relationship has inevitably been affected by recent changes in the media industry, particularly by the technological developments that have enabled a massive increase in media outlets. The 24-hour continuous news programs on satellite television have increased the demand for news stories and the time available to delve into such stories; as the police are an important source of news stories, this has increased the media demands on them. Technological advances have also impacted on the accountability of the police. Mawby (2001) considers how the use of lightweight cameras, including on mobile phones, has increased the scrutiny which the police are subject to. For instance, amateur filming of the policing of demonstrations or police dealing with incidents can be used on news programs and through the Internet.

In his examination of media images of policing, Mawby (2003) considers why these images matter. He cites Reiner's categorization of media representations of policing (and law and order more generally) under the headings of either "hegemonic" or "subversive." The first sees the police as being in a dominant position with regard to the media in that they can choose and filter the information they provide, and the media treatment of the police can play an important role in fostering a positive and favorable image of the police. By contrast, the "subversive" position suggests that the media can be a threat to authority and can undermine respect for the police; in the past, it has done this by exposing police malpractice and corruption, for instance, in the late 1960s when exposure of corruption in the Metropolitan police led to some of the most senior police officers in the country being imprisoned, through to the reporting of "institutional racism" in the police highlighted by the Macpherson Report into the murder of Stephen Lawrence (1999). Mawby suggests that these quite distinct headings and positions indicate the importance of examining media images.

As we have seen, for many people, the media, and particularly television, is how they find out about the police. Policing is popular on television, with police programs having attracted high viewing figures for many years [Mawby (2003) cites *Frost* and *Heartbeat* as being in the top five watched programs in 1999]. Police programs can also inform the wider public about the nature and future of policing; they can, as Mawby quotes, "fulfil a symbolic role, providing a commentary on policing and on society, and offering interpretations of the police in society" (2003).

Television Dramatizations of Policing

In this section, I will provide a potted history of the way the police have been represented in the media, and particularly in television drama. Leishman and Mason (2003) argue that since the formation of the "modern police" in the nineteenth century, the police have always been concerned with presenting a positive image to the general public. In the early days of organized policing, universal public support was by no means there for even a centralized, government-run police force. Histories of the origin and development of formal, modern policing in England and Wales illustrate the concerns about and opposition to the police. While there had been institutions of law enforcement going back to medieval times, with watchmen and constables performing community policing-type functions from the thirteenth century, it was not until the late 1700s that more organized forms of local policing, such as foot patrols and horse patrols, developed in London. Emsley (2005), among others, suggests that it was concern about crime and disorder, highlighted by the growth of industrial capitalism and the consequent growth of urban industrial cities, that led to a fear among "respectable" society of a new and potentially dangerous urban working class and a demand for better, more coordinated policing of the capital and elsewhere. These concerns and social changes led, then, to Robert Peel introducing legislation in 1822 for the creation of the Metropolitan police force in London. The model of the Metropolitan police was soon copied elsewhere in the country and, following further legislation in 1857, the formation of local police forces was made obligatory for local government throughout the country.

However, while there was support and even affection for the new English "bobby" (named so after Robert Peel), there was also a good deal of opposition, and often hostile opposition, to the new police. Emsley refers to police officers being regularly assaulted by the public and having to patrol with cutlasses in some of the "rougher" working class areas, with certain areas virtually left to themselves and unpoliced. In view of these reactions and worries, it is not surprising that the police were concerned from the start with promoting and maintaining a positive image of themselves and their role in society. And to some extent, the police did win the public over and became an accepted and acceptable part of British society; indeed Emsley cites a comment from *The Times* in 1904 talking of the police as "a great human mechanism, perhaps the greatest of its kind." The development of a sort of admiration for, and certainly acceptance of, the new police was in part at least due to the portrayal of them in both fiction and newspaper reporting of the time.

From these early days, the new police were represented in two main ways—as an approachable patrol officer helping to prevent crime through his (early police officers were invariably male) presence on the streets or as a skilled detective, working, almost Sherlock Holmes-like, to solve major crime. This combination, or division, of images has been continued through to the present day in media presentations of police and policing—a combination of a soft police service and hard law enforcement (Leishman and Mason 2003). The plots in the comedy series, *Thin Blue Line* (a British sitcom set in a police station, which ran between 1995 and 1997, and starred Rowan Atkinson), for instance, center around the different approaches to law enforcement of the morally principled, but often bumbling, everyday policing epitomized by Inspector Fowler and the more devious "results at any cost" style of Detective Sergeant Grimshaw.

Indeed this dual approach in policing—of service against force and of soft against hard policing—has led to a tension that is still apparent in the police service today—the uniformed bobby on the beat against the more hidden work of the plain-clothed detective. In her discussion of the way the role of the police has been portrayed by the media, Jewkes (2004) considers two "mediated ideals" of the police, representative of these two styles of policing. Here, we will consider these two ideals in a little more detail—on the one hand, illustrated by Police Constable (later Sergeant) George Dixon in the *Dixon of Dock Green* series that ran from 1955 to 1976 on BBC One who exemplified community policing at its best and, on the other, by Detective Inspector Regan and Detective Sergeant Carter, the no-nonsense crime fighters, in *The Sweeney* (which ran for four series from 1975 to 1978 on BBC One), whose style of and approach to investigating and arresting major criminals often skirted on the margins of legality.

Of course, there have been many more television and film representations of police and policing which we will not be able to consider in this brief overview. Police detective films, for instance, have been a popular staple of cinema films for years—and many of these films portray police officers kicking out against authority and the constraints placed on them in doing their job (a theme central to *The Sweeney* television drama). Films such as *A Touch of Evil* and *The Big Heat* in the 1950s, through to the glut of police detective films in the 1960s and 1970s, including *Bullitt*, *Klute*, and *Chinatown*, portrayed the leading police officers as heroic crime fighters. Probably, the seminal film of this ilk was *Dirty Harry* (1971), starring Clint Eastwood, which focused on the conflict between crime solving and following the rules, and was followed by other vigilante cop films such as *Lethal Weapon* and *Die Hard* in the 1980s and 1990s (Leishman and Mason 2003). Here, though, our focus will be on British television representations, and in that context *Dixon of Dock Green* and *The Sweeney* provide sort of extreme almost stereotypical examples of the role of the police officer and of different styles of policing.

Jewkes (2004) and other commentators have highlighted and examined the key role that the *Dixon of Dock Green* series played in setting a benchmark for television portrayals of the police. The series and, particularly the character of Dixon, created a symbolic representation of the "British bobby." In his discussion of media images of the police, Mawby (2003) argues that in the early days of the series, Dixon was viewed as a realistic portrayal of policing, but that toward the end of its run, it was widely viewed as irrelevant and outdated—with tougher police series such as *Z Cars* (1962–1978); *Softly, Softly* (1966–1976); and, as mentioned, *The Sweeney* seen as providing a more modern and accurate picture of policing.

During the period when these early police television series were shown, there was a change in the construction of policing, reflecting changes in the police's relationship with the wider public. The last three series mentioned above, and especially *The Sweeney*, were made at a time when there was more questioning of (and dissatisfaction with) the police. Mawby (2003) sees the central characters as "symbolic of their respective times"—the late 1950s and less settled mid-1970s—with the optimism of Dixon and his pride in his job replaced by the cynicism of Regan.

George Dixon originally appeared in a film, *The Blue Lamp* (1950), and although only playing his part for the first 20 minutes of the film (until he was shot), the popularity of his character led to the drama series *Dixon of Dock Green*. As mentioned above, the series was seen as a realistic portrayal of day-to-day policing, a realism that was accentuated by it focusing on the everyday aspects of the job, rather than the spectacular or comic aspects that tended to be highlighted in films. Leishman and Mason (2003) describe the Dixon character as the "embodiment of all that was good and dependable" and this was reinforced by his final monolog at the end of each episode where he "would use the night's story as a reminder to his audience to stay on the straight and narrow." This caring approach sits in stark contrast to the harsher image presented by later series such as *The Sweeney*. In comparing the two styles of police program, Reiner (1994) sees *Dixon* and *The Sweeney* as thesis and antithesis, respectively:

> The thesis, represented by *Dixon*, presents the police primarily as carers, lightning rods for the postwar consensual climate. Its antithesis, *The Sweeney*, portrays the police primarily as controllers, heralding the upsurge of a tough law and order politics in the late 1970s.

Before considering *The Sweeney* as illustrative of a harder style of policing, there were other police drama programs that presented a different view of policing to the *Dixon* model and we will refer to the *Z Cars* series that overlapped with *Dixon* for a number of years. Leishman and Mason (2003) suggest that Reiner ignores the importance of *Z Cars* by interpreting it as essentially a transition between the two styles of policing represented in his comparison of *Dixon* and *The Sweeney*. Leishman and Mason argue that *Z Cars* was "a world away from the stately pace of *Dixon*"—it attacked the conventions of the older series and portrayed a different world of policing set in a fictional estate, Newtown, based on the large new town of Kirkby on the outskirts of Liverpool—which was the first area of the country where Unit Beat Policing (with police in panda cars rather than on foot patrols) was practiced. Indeed, the success of *Z Cars* was largely due to its perceived realism. The first episode, in 1962, introduced the four police constables who were the patrol officers featured in the series—they were not of the same high moral standards that George Dixon continued to exemplify. To use Leishman and Mason's description of them:

> Lynch is depicted as a "lady's man and uses the police telephone to check on the odds for his horses, while Steel argues with his wife, Jayne, who has a black eye received in retaliation for throwing a hotpot supper at him..." Fancy Smith, an imposing Lancastrian, who explains to two young girls attempting to get into a nightclub, "Anyone who spoils my patch with trouble gets the back of my hand" ... dour Scotsman Jock Weir, introduced to the audience on a stretcher semi-conscious after a rugby match. Assuring his superiors of Weir's suitability for the job, (Sergeant) Watt tells them "He can handle himself in a bundle." (2003, 57)

Both *Z Cars* and *Dixon of Dock Green* attracted high-viewing figures; however, *Z Cars* attacked and undermined the "too good to be true" world of George

Dixon and its "warts and all" portrayal of the police laid the ground for a range of other series, including *Softly, Softly*; *Barlow at Large*; and *Barlow*.

Leishman and Mason (2003) describe *The Sweeney* as "perhaps the ultimate celebration of the police breaking the rules in order to obtain a conviction." It was the first police drama to acknowledge police corruption, or at least rule bending, as part and parcel of everyday policing. As mentioned earlier, it was clearly a product of its times, and the late 1960s and the early 1970s were a time when public confidence in the police was being undermined in a number of ways and in particular through concerns over police corruption. Robert Mark, Commissioner of the Metropolitan Police from 1972, established a department to investigate complaints against police officers, and during his 5-year term, 500 officers were dismissed or required to resign. Although scandals and corruption were not unique to this period, what was new as the revelation that they were systematic and widespread and went to the very top of the police force. Some of Scotland Yard's most senior officers were found guilty and given lengthy jail sentences in the 1970s, including the Commander of the Flying Squad Ken Drury and the Head of the Serious Crime Squad Wallace Virgo, the two most senior officers to come before British courts.

The publicity surrounding these and other high-profile cases affected the relationship of the police with the wider public. In a similar vein, the publicity surrounding the way the police handled demonstrations and industrial disputes excited concern and widespread criticism. In their handling of political demonstrations, over the Vietnam War and apartheid, for instance, the police were criticized for being too heavy handed; increased media coverage served to sharpen such criticism. Perhaps most dramatic were the television and news pictures of the policing of the miner's strike of 1984/1985. The policing of this strike was very confrontational (indeed one "event" is popularly referred to as the "battle of Orgreave") and polarized the police from "ordinary" working people. And the inner-city riots and disorders of the early 1980s in Brixton (London), Toxteth (Liverpool), Moss Side (Manchester), and elsewhere reflected an increased alienation between the police and the sections of the population.

All of these events were filmed and appeared in our living rooms almost as they occurred and they could be seen as signifying and encouraging a move away from traditional notions of policing and the image of the local bobby toward a more militaristic and reactive form of policing. *The Sweeney* was influenced by, and to some extent, a product of these sociopolitical influences and their presentation in the media. After the success of a one-off television film, thirteen 1-hour programs were made under the title of *The Sweeney* (taken from cockney slang—Sweeney Todd/"The Flying Squad").

Although not as heavily violent as films of the time such as *Dirty Harry* or of more recent portrayals, *The Sweeney* presented crime fighting as a battle—taking place in the "urban jungle of London" (Leishman and Mason 2003).

The rule bending by Regan, Carter, and other members of the "squad" was confined to what was needed to catch villains, with the official procedures seen as red tape getting in the way of the police's attempts to save and shield the public from crime and criminals. As with other commentaries on the importance of *The Sweeney*, Leishman and Mason cite Regan's rant from an episode called *Abduction*:

> Try and protect the public and all they do is call you "fascist." You nail a villain and some ponced up, pinstriped Hampstead barrister screws it up like an old fag packet on a point of procedure and then pops off for a game of squash and a glass of Madeira. He's taking home thirty grand a year, and we can just about afford ten days in Eastbourne and a second-hand car. No. it's all bloody wrong my son. (2003, 75)

The Sweeney certainly broke the mold in terms of television portrayal of the British police, and in finishing this section, we will mention some more recent examples of police dramas. Any review of police drama on British television would be incomplete without mentioning *The Bill*, which in terms of longevity has been Britain's most successful police program. First broadcast in 1984, *The Bill* finally outstripped *Dixon of Dock Green* in August 2005, and it went on until August 2010 when the last episode was shown. Over its many years, it adapted to meet the challenges of the highly competitive world of television drama and was being shown for two 1-hour episodes per week by the end of its run, with each episode attracting over 4 million viewers, and it was broadcast in over 50 countries worldwide. *The Bill* recounted the goings-on in and around a fictional Metropolitan police station, Sun Hill, located in the East End of London (based on the "real" London Borough of Tower Hamlets). It was unusual in police dramas in that it adopts a series, soap opera format and did not focus on one aspect of police work only but rather on the lives and work of officers on one shift of the uniform division and on the work of detectives based there.

In terms of the division between "soft" and "hard" policing and the portrayal of these different police styles exemplified by *Dixon of Dock Green* and *The Sweeney*, respectively, *The Bill* established a kind of midway position and balance between the two poles as well as accommodating both the uniformed and detective sides of policing (Leisham and Mason 2003). Indeed, Reiner (2007) argues that *The Bill* can be interpreted as the "synthesis of the dialectic" that was represented by the police portrayals in *Dixon* and *The Sweeney*. It shows a range of contrasting images of police work, from community constables to rule-bending detectives. Reiner also comments that *The Bill* represented the "spectrum of contemporary policing in terms of gender, race, organizational specialism and rank." This approach was developed and can be found in a number of other, more recent police programs which we are not able to consider here (programs such as *Heartbeat*, *Midsomer Murders*, *Morse*, *Juliet Bravo*, *The Gentle Touch*, and *Prime Suspect*).

Taking on Reiner's argument, Leishman and Mason (2003) suggest that as *The Bill* developed in the 1990s and into the 2000s, it became a "new synthesis" of police representations in the media. It began to highlight more disturbingly corrupt police characters, while the "ordinary" police officers began to be portrayed with serious moral failings and personal flaws. As Leishman and Mason put it:

> Ever the synthesis, *The Bill* has come to define the virtually real territory of a contemporary TV copland, where the moral certainties of *Dixon* are long gone and television cop heroes have become people whose virtue is relative rather than absolute. (2003, 103)

Reality Television and the Police

So far, I have focused on fictional representations of the police, and in conclusion I will refer briefly to the police reality programs of recent years—what might be termed "factional representation." Again, given the confines of space in an introductory overview, I will focus on one major example of this genre—*Crimewatch UK*. *Crimewatch UK* began on BBC in 1984 and is broadcast on a monthly basis; it uses dramatic reconstructions and surveillance film of crimes to try and gain information from the public that will help the police to solve particular crimes. It was developed from a popular German program *Aktenzeichen XY* which had been running since 1967. The format has been adopted in other countries, in the United States; for instance, *America's Most Wanted* became the longest running program in the history of the Fox Television Network (running from 1988 until June 2011). As with *Crimewatch*, it aims to assist law enforcement in catching offenders who are wanted for various crimes, usually focusing on the most serious crimes and on the most wanted fugitives (often relating to the FBI Ten Most Wanted Fugitives list). The discussion will be based on the more in-depth analysis of the program offered by Jewkes (2004), in which she examines some of the myths about crime that she argues it helps to perpetuate.

From its beginning until 2007, *Crimewatch UK* was presented by Nick Ross, however, and tragically, it became the subject of police and media attention in 1999 when Ross's copresenter, Jill Dando, was the subject of a violent murder. As well as continuity of presenters, the format of the program has remained virtually the same since 1984. There are reconstructions of a few (usually three or four an episode) serious crimes, plus appeals to the public for information about offenders and suspects from a range of crimes across the country, and there are updates on crimes and offenders that are covered in previous program—particularly where some progress has been made in catching offenders. Jewkes comments that this continuity and reference back to previous episodes and crimes serves the purpose of "congratulating the audience for helping to secure convictions, making them feel absolutely integral to the show, and further giving the (inaccurate) impression that *Crimewatch* is largely responsible for solving serious crime in the UK." (2004, 153)

It is difficult to measure the success of the program; in 2000 the *Crimewatch* team claimed that since 1984 there had been 582 arrests resulting directly from the program. However, it is difficult to substantiate such claims as many of those arrests may well have occurred without the program anyway.

Jewkes (2004) goes on to emphasize the inherent tension between information and entertainment that lies at the heart of *Crimewatch* and, indeed, "reality" television programming in general. While specific items might not be included just for entertainment value, program editors are aware that there has to be some visual and journalistic impact so as to make "good television." This tension between entertainment and "its public service remit," as Jewkes puts it, is illustrated by the sort of crimes that are represented on the show—basically the most uncommon (statistically) crimes such as murder and rape are those which are most often featured, while the more common but less spectacular property crimes and corporate crimes are rarely shown.

However, it is clear that *Crimewatch* has been important in helping the police improve their public relations through demonstrating the police and the public working together to investigate and solve real crimes, as Jewkes comments:

> The benefits to (the police) in terms of the warm feelings induced by watching the police and public working together to solve crimes arguably outweighs all other benefits of the programme. (2004, 163)

Each program includes up to 30 officers from across the United Kingdom making statements and appeals and taking part in interviewers with the presenters. This helps to lend a "personal touch" to the investigations and presents the human face of the police service, hopefully acting as an encouragement to informants and witnesses to contact the police with information.

While very popular and clearly having some positive impact on the relationship of the police with the wider public and on solving particular crimes, *Crimewatch* has been criticized for contributing to the fear of crime through its emphasis on and dramatic reconstructions of violent and sexual crime. Leishman and Mason (2003) acknowledge that it is difficult to establish whether the program does engender an increased fear of crime, but refers to British Crime Survey information that suggests that *Crimewatch* has helped to create a climate of fear of crime. *Crimewatch* has also been criticized for its reliance on police information and for the fact that the police largely determine the content of the program; indeed, without police cooperation it would not exist.

References

Emsley, C. (2005). *Crime and Society in England 1750–1900*, 3rd ed. Harlow: Longman.
Home Office (2010). *Police Powers and Procedures, England and Wales 2008/9*. London: HMSO.
Innes, M. (2001). Crimewatching: Homicide investigations in the age of innocence. *Criminal Justice Matters*, 43, 42–44.
Jewkes, Y. (2004). *Media & Crime*. London: Sage Publications.
Kershaw, C., Budd, T., Kinshott, G., Mattinson, J., Mayhew, P., and Myhill, A. (2000). *The British Crime Survey*. London: Home Office.
Leishman, F., and Mason, P. (2003). *Policing and the Media: Facts, Fictions and Factions*. Cullompton: Willan Publishing.
Macpherson, W. (1999). *The Stephen Lawrence Enquiry: Report of an Enquiry by Sir William Macpherson of Cluny*. London: Home Office.
Mason, P. (2003). Introduction: Visions of crime and justice. In Mason, P. (ed.) *Criminal Visions: Media Representations of Crime and Justice*. Cullompton: Willan Publishing, 1–12.
Mawby, R. (2001). Promoting the police? The rise of police image work. *Criminal Justice Matters*, 43, 44–46.
Mawby, R. (2003). Completing the half-formed picture? Media images of policing. In Mason, P. (ed.) *Criminal Visions: Media Representations of Crime and Justice*. Cullompton: Willan Publishing, 214–237.
Ministry of Justice (2009). *Sentencing Statistics: England and Wales 2009 Statistical Bulletin*. London: Ministry of Justice.
Nicholas, S., Kershaw, C., and Walker, A. (2007). *The British Crime Survey 2006–2007*. London: HMSO.
Reiner, R. (1994). The dialectics of Dixon. In Stephens, M., and Becker, S. (eds.) *Police Force, Police Service*. London: Macmillan, 11–32.
Reiner, R. (2007). Media-made criminality: The representation of crime in the mass media. In Maguire, M., Morgan, R., and Reiner, R. (eds.) *The Oxford Handbook of Criminology*, 4th ed. Oxford: Oxford University Press, 302–337.

Emerging Issues

Urgent Police Interviews with Suspects of Terrorism under PACE
Risks and Mitigation

21

KARL ROBERTS

Contents

Introduction

Since the events of 9/11 and 7/7, there has been much research and debate concerning the policing of terrorism. There has been recent interest in the way in which police carry out interviews with terrorist suspects, the tactics used, the risks and opportunities for the investigation, and the methods of best practice (Roberts 2011). One topic that has not so far been explored is the police use of urgent interviews (as defined by English Law) with terrorist suspects. This area is of some interest because of the context in which these interviews take place and because the relevant legislation allows some relaxation of the usual controls placed upon police interviews. This chapter therefore explores urgent interviews with terrorist suspects as defined within English Law; it argues that the context in which these interviews are done raises a number of possible risks to the integrity of a police investigation and considers how some of these risks may be mitigated. The chapter begins with a discussion of the relevant legislation.

The Law

Police investigations in England and Wales are governed by a range of legislation, in particular the Police and Criminal Evidence Act (PACE; UK Home Office 1984), the Regulation of Investigative Powers Act (RIPA; UK Home Office 2000a), and the European Convention on Human Rights (ECHR; Council of Europe 1953). Particularly relevant to police interviews with criminal suspects is PACE that covers all aspects of the detention, treatment, and questioning of criminal suspects. Section 41 of the Terrorism Act (UK Home Office 2000b) and code H of PACE govern police interviews with those detained under the Terrorism Act.

In general, the legislation provides all detained individuals with the right to have their arrest notified to another individual, the right to legal advice, and the right to be interviewed at a location designated for detention, such as a police station, without unnecessary delay. Legislation exists however to suspend some of these rights under certain circumstances. The relevant legislation is Annex B Code H of PACE—delays to interview under Terrorism Act (TACT) Schedule 8. This legislation allows that police may delay notification of arrest and/or access to legal advice and carry out an interview in a nondesignated place if the person detained has not yet been charged with an offence and if an officer of Superintendent rank or above has reasonable grounds for believing the exercise of the above rights that may result in one or more of the following:

Interference or harm to persons and/or evidence
Serious loss or damage to property
Alerting of others in particular co-offenders
Hindrance to the recovery of property
Interference with the gathering of information
A risk of a legal advisor passing on information to others

In these circumstances, the police may carry out a so-called *urgent interview*. The legislation is however clear that urgent interviews must cease once the relevant risk has been averted or all of the questions necessary to avert the risk have been put to the detainee.

PACE code H requires that a record be made of the interview, where possible in the form of a tape recording or contemporaneous notes; however, where this is not possible, the notes made during the interview may be written up by the interviewer as soon as practically possible following the interview.

The practical upshot of this legislation is that where there is a perceived threat to public safety and/or to the integrity of an investigation, some interviews, those deemed urgent, with terrorist suspects may take place without notification and without legal representation in nondesignated detention centers, and may be recorded only with notes written up (in some cases) after the interview.

In those circumstances when an urgent interview is allowable, without the benefit of legal representation for the suspect, much of the onus to protect the suspect's rights rests with the police interviewer. The next section will consider the urgent interview context by exploring the impact of terrorism and the threat of terrorism on individuals and how this might affect the interview process.

The Urgent Interview Context

Terrorism is designed to achieve political change using fear as a weapon (Burleigh 2008). Terrorist atrocities produce many strong emotions in observers including fear, grief, anger, frustration, sadness, a sense of powerlessness, a desire for revenge, and a desire to *do something* (Sprang 2003). As human beings, police officers involved in counterterrorism work are not immune from these emotions; indeed as a result of their investigative duties, it is possible that these emotions might be exacerbated. For example, police officers are typically exposed to details about a terrorist act way beyond the experience of most members of the public (e.g., precise details about victim injuries); they may find themselves the focus of great political and media pressure to obtain "results" in the aftermath of a terrorist act, and there is frequently fear that the terrorists are plotting another atrocity or fear of what might have happened had the police not thwarted a planned attack. There can also be, in some quarters, little sympathy for a "terrorist" suspect and a belief among some members of society that terrorists by dint of their actions forfeit their human rights (Burleigh 2008). It is in this context that urgent interviews with terrorist suspects are carried out.

Urgent interview by definition is done when there is a need for information to be obtained from an individual very quickly. This need for urgency, when considered in the psychological context described previously, may lead to a number of potential risks to the interview process. Anger, fear, feelings of powerlessness, and a desire for revenge are powerful emotions that in the context of urgency may make the use of tactics not normally associated with police interviewing such as threats, overt aggression, and even, *in extremis*, torture which seem more acceptable and even desirable to some. Indeed some commentators have argued for the limited use of torture and other extreme approaches to terrorist interviewing (Dershowitz 2002). Dershowitz argument is particularly applicable to urgent interviews; he cites a so-called ticking bomb scenario—a situation where there is a need for urgency to protect lives in the face of a possible atrocity—where the information needs of law enforcement outweigh any of the human rights that would normally be accorded to an individual. In such circumstances, Dershowitz argues that investigators could use any means at their disposal to elicit information, including torture.

There is a risk then that in the highly emotive and pressured context when urgent interviews take place for some police officers, in a desperate need for information, to utilize robust and aggressive means to obtain it. This risk may be compounded by the lack of normal safeguards for the suspect and legal representation during the interview and the tacit support from some sections of the society for the use of robust measures. In the next section, we will consider the impact of such "robust," interview practices.

Utility of Robust Interview Practices

Threats, overt aggression, and torture all work on the basis that raising an individual's discomfort is likely to make them more compliant as regards providing information; essentially the suspect is encouraged to trade information in return for an end to their suffering (Rejali 2007). However, such tactics frequently fail to obtain reliable information (Gudjonsson 2003) and often do much damage to community and even international relations (Rejali 2007; Roberts 2011). This is not withstanding the fact that some individuals who may have been considered suspects and who may be subjected to such treatment may be innocent of any involvement in terrorism (Sands 2008; Stafford-Smith 2007).

From a psychological perspective, the so-called robust interview practices run the risk of increasing the vulnerability of the suspect so that much of the information collected during the interview may be unreliable and potentially misleading (Gudjonsson 2003). This happens because the experience of threats and aggression increases an individual's anxiety that serves to increase an individual's fear and also their uncertainty and doubt about events they have experienced. In this state, the individual is often very sensitive to the reactions of an interviewer—looking for signals from the interviewer that their responses are acceptable and that their discomfort is coming to an end—and is prone to tailor answers to questions in order to obtain favorable reactions from the interviewer (Gudjonsson 2003). In the case of urgent interviews, these psychological responses of the interviewee may be further compounded because as we have seen, urgent interviews are likely to take place in highly emotive contexts where the individual may already be in a state of high anxiety brought about by fear of being arrested and the trauma of the arrest itself—arrests of terrorist suspects may involve large numbers of, often armed, police officers due to the need to protect police officers from potential threats.

The creation of high levels of anxiety may also serve to increase an individual's suggestibility, making it more likely that they will begin to accept information provided by the interviewer and to confabulate accounts of events based upon that information (Gudjonsson 2003). As stated, the ultimate upshot of robust interview practices is a risk the interview will produce unreliable information and in some cases this may culminate in a false confession—a confession of guilt by an innocent person. Clearly unreliable information and false confessions are highly undesirable as they result in significant damage to the creditability of the police and the criminal justice system (Gudjonsson 2003).

As well as the potentially negative impact of robust methods on the anxiety levels experienced by a suspect, there is an impact upon the likelihood of their cooperation with police and their perceptions of the legitimacy of the police (Roberts 2010, 2011). Of relevance here are notions of procedural justice (Tyler 1989).

Tyler (1989) has noted that all individuals hold a series of expectations concerning how they wish to be treated during interactions with authorities. He identified four classes of procedural justice expectations:

1. Voice in the interaction—individuals expect to be able to express a viewpoint and feel that their information is valued.
2. Neutrality in the interaction—individuals expect an absence of bias in their treatment by the authority.
3. Respectful treatment in the interaction—individuals expect to be treated in a manner that protects their rights.
4. Trustworthiness of the authority—individuals expect to be treated in a sincere way with concern for their needs and where their needs are addressed.

Research has demonstrated that the extent to which procedural justice expectations are met has a powerful influence upon the perceived legitimacy, trust, and confidence in an authority and the likelihood an individual will cooperate with the requirements of the authority (Tyler 1989; Tyler and Blader 2003). Skogan (2006) has also demonstrated that there is an asymmetric effect of negative and positive encounters with the police upon the confidence individuals have in the police. Negative encounters have a much greater impact upon an individual's confidence than do positive encounters, where negative encounters appear to significantly reduce confidence, whereas positive encounters appear to have a more limited impact.

Following this, it can be said that what police officers do during an interview is crucial in determining a suspect's perception of the police and potential for cooperation. A robust or aggressive interview style is highly likely to compromise procedural justice expectations, challenging expectations of trust, fairness, and voice. This will likely reduce an individual's perceptions of police legitimacy and reduce the prospect of their future cooperation, including cooperation during the urgent and any subsequent interviews. It may be argued that this is a small price to pay, should further terror attacks be prevented especially if the person is ultimately convicted of terrorist charges. However, risking losing an individual's cooperation so early in the interview process may severely limit the potential for information collection that may lead to other offenders.

Also not all persons who are interviewed for terrorist offences, including those who experience an urgent interview, are ultimately charged, and these individuals are likely go back into the communities from where they came. Local interest in an individual's experiences is likely to be high; indeed a terrorism arrest is often reported very quickly by the media who may devote significant coverage to the event (Nacos 2007). Following their release, it would therefore be expected that at least some individuals subject to an urgent interview will discuss their treatment by police with other members of their community. Other community members will have procedural justice expectations akin to those of the suspect given the ubiquity of such expectations (Tyler 1989). Reports of negative experiences will therefore challenge these expectations with the risk that parts of the community, if not the whole community itself, may begin to lose their belief in police legitimacy, and this may predicate a reduction in cooperation with the police (Roberts 2010). It is also possible that an individual's negative experiences may also be seized upon by those who would make political capital to damage the reputation of the police and/or may become a means of recruiting others to a terrorist cause (Sands 2008).

Risking the loss of community cooperation is not trivial. Central to the United Kingdom's counter terrorism strategy Contest (UK Home Office 2011) is engagement with local communities to prevent terror attacks. Engagement, it is hoped, will encourage members of local communities to discourage individuals from involvement in terror groups and to provide intelligence about those suspected of involvement in terrorism. Robust and aggressive urgent interview tactics could negatively impact upon these attempts to engage with communities. Loss of perceived police legitimacy and cooperation from the community is a significant challenging for the Contest strategy.

Finally, it is worth making the point that a key performance indicator of policing today is public confidence in the police (UK Home Office 2009). It is known that public confidence is strongly related to the extent that procedural justice expectations are met and to notions of police legitimacy (Tyler 1989). The negative effects of robust urgent interview measures may have an additional negative impact on judgments of overall police performance.

To summarize, the emotive nature of the urgent interview situation, for both the interviewer and the suspect, may increase the risk of interviewers utilizing robust interview approaches in their legitimate desire to obtain information quickly. The use of such interview tactics is not without risks to the reliability of the information that can be obtained, to the welfare of the suspect, and ultimately to the perception of the police by the community. The ultimate risk of robust tactics is to reduce the reliability of information obtained and to reduce the perceived legitimacy of the police resulting in reduced cooperation from individuals and communities.

The chapter will now move on to consider potential solutions to the risks identified above and suggest some ways of carrying out urgent interviews that balance the legitimate needs of police to obtain information quickly while minimizing the risk of obtaining unreliable information and damaging procedural justice expectations.

Conducting the Urgent Interview

Urgent interviews in counterterrorism are arguably one of the most difficult situations a police interviewer may encounter and represent a powerful test of professionalism and integrity. Due to the lack of usual legislative controls, there are many risks to the integrity of police investigations and the public perception of the police, should an urgent interview be carried out inappropriately. In the following section, suggestions are made which may mitigate some of the risks. These are based upon extant psychological research and police best practice. To preempt, urgent interview approaches advocated here are based upon clearly articulated aims and objectives that conform to a suspect's procedural justice expectations through the development of rapport and sensitivity to their sociocultural characteristics.

Interview Planning

Clearly articulated aims and objectives allow judgments to be made about the relative success of any interview, where success is the extent that these are achieved (Roberts and Herrington 2011). An interview plan should therefore contain details about why the interview is being conducted, what it seeks to achieve, and the topic areas and questions that will be asked (Ord, Shaw, and Green 2008). For urgent interviews, planning of this sort is particularly important because PACE code H clearly states that urgent interviews should cease when all the relevant questions to avert the risk have been asked and/or the risk has been averted whether the suspect answers these questions. Interviewers are not permitted to stray into other topic areas not relevant to averting the risk at hand, for example, issues related to an individual's guilt of an offence, their background, attitudes, or interests unless these topics are clearly relevant to the risk.

As urgent interviews typically follow sudden dramatic events, limited planning often results in leading to ill-defined aims and objectives and poorly identified interview topics and questions (Shaw, pers. comm.). The impact of this is to make it very difficult for interviewers to identify when to stop the interview (where all the relevant questions have been asked) and assess its success (Ord et al. 2008). Where interviewers are unable to identify the end point of an urgent interview, there is a risk that they continue and ask questions not relevant to averting the risk. To continue an urgent interview in this way is a breach of the terms of PACE code H and could ultimately lead a court to question the legality of any evidence obtained following such questioning. Indeed some individuals convicted of terrorism offices have cited their experiences during urgent interviews in their appeals post conviction. For example, those convicted of the 24/7 attempted bombings on the London Underground, though their appeals were not upheld, and cited potential illegalities in the urgent interview questioning (*Daily Mail Online* 2008).

Ultimately, the suggestion here is that interviewers need, even in the high pressure situations of urgent interviews, to be cognizant of the purpose of the interview and to clearly articulate a plan; otherwise they risk breaching the legislation.

Interview Personnel

Selection of personnel to carry out an urgent interview is important. As detailed above, this is a high pressure situation, where there is a risk of interviewers adopting nefarious tactics as a result. This is compounded where interviewers are inexperienced and/or have had insufficient training (Shaw, pers. comm.). To mitigate this risk, it is suggested that, where possible, the interviewers should be trained to advanced suspect interviewer level; this is referred to in the UK National Investigative Interviewing Strategy as PIP level 2 specialist interviewers (NPIA 2009). This level of training provides interviewers with advanced knowledge of interview methods, rapport building, and psycho-logical processes such as responses of suspects to anxiety, suggestibility, and the impact of interviewer behavior on suspects. Interviewers with this level of training are more able to identify the impact of their actions on the suspect, to understand the suspect's response, and to have knowledge of approaches to interviewing which take account of these issues (see below). It is also suggested that interviewers are likely to carry out urgent interviews would benefit from training in recognizing and dealing with their own responses to trauma and anxiety as these emotions are likely to be the motivators for the more "robust" interview approaches described above. An ability to recognize and deal with one's own distress is likely to allow individuals' greater ability to control these emotions and enable interviewers to take a more controlled approach to the interview (Roberts 2009, 2010).

Where possible it is suggested that investigators give consideration as to who is best suited to carry out the interview, that is, what interviewer characteristics do they consider which will be most productive with a particular suspect. Some individuals might relate much better to a man or a woman or indeed to a younger or older interviewer. The racial characteristics of the interviewer may be relevant as maybe their regional accent, religion, or physical appearance. Where investigators feel that such issues are relevant, selecting an interviewer with the preferred characteristics might be beneficial in terms of building rapport and trust with the suspect (Roberts and Herrington 2011).

In the United Kingdom, the so-called TACT arrests are often very traumatic for the suspect featuring as they often do (for very good security reasons), armed police in riot gear aggressively entering the suspect's home often during the early hours of the morning resulting in significant anxiety on the suspect's part. Those responsible for the arrest may often be perceived negatively by the suspect as a result of the implied threats and what may be perceived as intrusion. As such the police officers actively involved in the arrest may struggle to generate rapport with the suspect. It is therefore argued that the individuals responsible for the urgent interview should, as far as possible, not be involved in the arrest or in searches of the suspect or their property (Roberts 2009, 2010). It is also suggested that the urgent interview take place away from the property, in a vehicle or other location that is not in the middle of police activity. This is likely to reduce some of the emotion experienced by a suspect compared with them being within the property and observing police activity there, and increase the likelihood that the interviewer may develop some rapport with the suspect.

Suspect Characteristics

It is suggested that interviewers should spend some time familiarizing themselves with everything that is known about the suspect prior to the interview; this includes issues such as their background, interests, and any particular vulnerabilities such as mental health status, fears, and anxieties (Roberts 2010). This will allow interviewers to begin to predict likely behavioral responses from the suspect during the interview and to consider possible approaches toward them. Essentially, interviewers should tailor their approach to the specific characteristics of the suspect to maximize the possibility that they can build rapport with them as this will maximize the chance of obtaining information from them (Roberts and Herrington 2011). It is acknowledged that this is only usually possible when an arrest is planned or when an interviewer is privy to intelligence and other information prior to an arrest. Clearly, the amount of information about different individuals will vary and there are likely to be some individuals for whom limited information is available prior to an arrest.

As some urgent interviews may require a police officer to interview an individual from a different cultural background from their own, it is important for interviewers to give some consideration to the suspect's cultural background (Gelles, McFadden, Borum, and Vossekuil 2006). Throughout their life span, an individual's culture presents them with various examples of what is and is not acceptable behavior across a range of situations. These behavioral exemplars coalesce into an individual's cultural scripts. Cultural scripts can be considered to be cognitive schema or mental models, containing beliefs and expectations about how the individual and others should behave. Cultural scripts are important in governing behavior across situations and important among them are religious, moral, and ethical scripts (Hofstede 2001). Knowledge of a suspect's cultural background is therefore useful as it will allow interviewers to have an understanding of the suspect's modes of communication, to make predictions about the likely behavior and reactions of the suspect during the interview, and to identify the sorts of interviewer behavior that the suspect will find acceptable and unacceptable. Ultimately cultural knowledge will help police design interview approaches that maximize the likelihood that the suspect will engage with them and provide the required information during the urgent interview (Gelles et al. 2006).

A lack of knowledge or appreciation of different cultural scripts is not a trivial point as it can lead to significant problems during an urgent interview (Gelles et al. 2006). For example, lack of cultural knowledge often leaves interviewers perplexed by some of the behaviors, or beliefs expressed by a suspect with many interviewers regarding such behavior or beliefs as challenges to their authority (Gelles et al. 2006). This can and often does provoke attempts by the interviewer to challenge the behavior and even question or attempt to change the beliefs (Gelles et al. 2006). Use of such tactics during an urgent interview, while being a clear breach of PACE code H (interviewers must only ask questions that are relevant to the identified risk), is also likely to result in a complete breakdown of communication. Communication breakdowns in such circumstances as challenges of this sort are often perceived by individuals as threats to their identity (Breakwell 1983; Roberts 2010). This is because cultural scripts, in particular religious beliefs, are an important aspect of any individual's identity (Breakwell 1983) and challenges to identity in an encounter with an authority (the interviewers) compromise procedural justice expectations leading to noncompliance with the authority's wishes (Tyler and Blader 2003).

During an urgent interview, it is also important for interviewers to monitor the behavior of the suspect. This is likely to inform interviewers about the suspect's attitude toward the police, the reaction to the questions, and the areas that they find threatening. This can help interviewers to further tailor their interview behavior toward the suspect and may help planning for any subsequent interviews (Roberts and Herrington 2011).

Interviewer Behavior

A large body of literature points to the utility of rapport-based interview approaches over those involving threats in obtaining reliable accounts from suspects during police interviews (Bull and Milne 2004; Ord et al. 2008). As such interviewers are advised to utilize this form of interviewing for urgent interviews. Threats or aggressive approaches toward the suspect, as described above, are generally counterproductive and do not enhance the likelihood of obtaining reliable information even in the context of urgency and so these should be avoided. It is accepted that some suspects are likely to be hostile to the police, but adopting an aggressive approach to such individuals will only serve to increase their hostility.

Rapport is important in any interview because it engenders trust between a suspect and an interviewer, minimizes the risk of a suspect experiencing excessive anxiety, and maximizes the likelihood that a suspect will answer questions and disclose relevant information, thereby reducing the risk of collecting unreliable information (Fisher and Geiselman 1992; Kebbell, Milne, and Wagstaff 1999; Milne and Bull 1999; Shepherd and Milne 1999). However, one obvious question is, how can rapport be developed with an individual in the context of an urgent interview?

Typically, rapport is developed by personalizing the interview, showing empathy for the suspect and their situation, and actively listening and paying attention to their needs and behavior (Fisher and Geiselman 1992; Milne and Bull 1999). In addition, it is important for the interviewers to explain the situation to the suspect and to, as far as possible, try to allay any concerns (Shepherd 1991).

In developing rapport during urgent interviews, interviewers should attempt to consider the legitimate needs of the suspect. The suspect may be fearful and uncertain, some individuals may have little knowledge or experience of law enforcement, and others may come from other cultures in which policing is not rooted in liberal democratic values, and so may genuinely fear for their lives or expect that they will be subject to torture. Attempts to reassure them during the urgent interview are likely to help engender trust as these may allay some of these fears. In the case of Islamist extremists, for example, taking some steps to be respectful of their religious needs such as reassuring them that in police custody they will be accorded the right to pray may be useful. Asking suspects how they feel and if they need anything is also useful as again this shows some attention to them as individuals.

Importantly, rapport building should not be the sole activity, and it is important that interviewers ask legitimate questions during the urgent interview. Essentially, these questions need to be focused upon the immediate situation and the need to alleviate risks as defined by PACE. It is advised that suspects be informed of the purpose of the interview and that direct questions concerning what they may know should be asked. Direct questions will illustrate the urgency of the situation; however, suspects should be given time to answer the questions as quickly firing questions at the suspect and/or repeating the same question will allow limited time for reflection and may increase anxiety reducing the prospects of the questions being answered. Similarly, although the situation is likely to be one of high pressure and a suspect will need to be kept focused upon the issue at hand, interrupting the suspect excessively will serve to damage rapport and may also reduce the likelihood of a response (Gelles et al. 2006; Roberts 2011; Savage and Milne 2007).

Interviewers should maintain a calm demeanor when addressing the suspect as displays of anger and frustration are unlikely to result in a flow of information. If the interviewer can build rapport with the suspect, it may be possible to present the suspect with a calm rationale as to why they should provide information; potentially if rapport building is successful, the suspect may wish to work with the interviewer to protect others (Roberts and Herrington 2011).

It is noteworthy that many would-be terrorists do not subject their fantasies of terrorist violence, martyrdom, and the impact of the activities to reality testing and frequently suspend critical thinking in the context of the planning of a terrorist atrocity (Horgan 2005; Rogers et al. 2007). Essentially, noncritical thinking patterns that serve to minimize the suffering of others and justify the atrocity are common (Horgan 2005). These thinking patterns may remain unchallenged until these individuals are apprehended by police where the would-be terrorist is asked to account for themselves. When apprehended, these individuals are faced with the uncomfortable reality where the possible consequences of their actions may become available to them, perhaps through questions or comments by police officers, or the individuals considering their situation. Fear or guilt and remorse may be experienced by some of these individuals and a rapport-based supportive interview environment may provide the conditions in which these individuals are most likely to share information. It is of course acknowledged that there are individuals who are focused upon their terrorist activities and who, regardless of the approach, will not provide any information to the police, however, *a priori*, interviewers will not necessarily know who these individuals are and, through the use of a rapport-based approach, the urgent interview may allow investigators the opportunity to identify such an individual.

Ultimately, a rapport-based approach is advised for urgent interviews as this is most likely to allow the police to obtain relevant and reliable information. An additional benefit of such approaches is that treating individuals with respect is consistent with procedural justice expectations and so will minimize the risks of reduced legitimacy and cooperation that follow compromising these expectations. Also, rapport developed at the urgent interview stage is also likely to enhance suspect cooperation during any later full suspect interview.

Summary and Conclusions

In England and Wales, the legislation, PACE code H, allows for urgent interviews of terrorist suspects under certain conditions and is specific as to the purpose of the urgent interview. In particular, urgent interviews should stop when all questions relevant to ending a specific risk have been put to a suspect, whether the suspect chooses to respond and/or when the risk has been eliminated. Urgent interviews do not give the suspect the same rights as those normally available during police interviews under PACE, and so the onus is on the police interviewer to protect the rights and well-being of the suspect. Urgent interviews, however, are not without risks, related to the context of the interview—one of fear, uncertainty, and even anger following a terrorist atrocity, in which interviewers may find themselves under a great deal of pressure from others to obtain results. Threatening and otherwise oppressive interview tactics are a risk in these contexts, especially given the unsupervised (due to the lack of legal representation) nature of the urgent interview. Such robust interview tactics may lead to unreliable information, damage to the well-being of the suspect, and damage to the reputation of the police, particularly as they violate procedural justice expectations.

In this context, adequate planning of the urgent interview is vital and clear aims and objectives for the interview need to be identified. A consideration of the characteristics of the suspect, selection of persons to carry out the interview, the approach they should take toward the suspect—one that is focused upon rapport, supporting the legitimate needs of the suspect and their procedural justice expectations—and the topics and questions that need to be covered form an important part of this planning process. Ultimately, even in the high-pressure context of urgent interviews, the principles of good investigative interviewing apply, and it is with reference to these that investigators can hope to obtain the maximum amount of information from the interview, minimize the risks to the integrity of the police investigation, and maximize cooperation from suspects and the communities from which they come.

References

Bull, R., and Milne, R. (2004). Attempts to improve police interviewing of suspects. In G. D. Lassiter (Ed.), *Interrogation, Confessions, and Entrapment*. New York: Kluwer, pp. 181–196.

Burleigh, M. (2008). *Blood & Rage: A Cultural History of Terrorism*. New York: HarperCollins.

Council of Europe (1953). *European Convention for the Protection of Human Rights and Fundamental Freedoms, as amended by Protocols Nos. 11 and 14*, November 4, 1950, ETS 5. http://www.refworld.org/docid/3ae6b3b04.html (accessed August 26, 2013).

Daily Mail Online (2008). *London 21/7 Bombers Lose Appeal Bid*. http://www.daily-mail.co.uk/news/article-1016533/London-21-7-bombers-lose-appeal-bid.html (accessed December 23, 2009).

Dershowitz, A. M. (2002). Want to torture? Get a warrant. *San Francisco Chronicle*, January 22.

Fisher, R. P., and Geiselman, R. E. (1992). *Memory-Enhancing Techniques for Investigative Interview: The Cognitive Interview*. Springfield, IL: Charles C Thomas Publishing.

Gelles, M., McFadden, R., Borum, R., and Vossekuil, B. (2006). Interviewing Al-Qaeda-related subjects: A law enforcement perspective. In T. Williamson (Ed.), *Investigative Interviewing: Developments in Research, Rights and Regulation*. Devon: Willan.

Gudjonsson, G. H. (2003). *The Psychology of Interrogations and Confessions: A Handbook*. 2nd Edition. Chichester: Wiley.

Hofstede, G. (2001). *Culture's Consequences, Comparing Values, Behaviors, Institutions, and Organizations across Nations*. Thousand Oaks, CA: Sage Publications.

Horgan, J. (2005). *The Psychology of Terrorism*. London: Frank Cass.

Kebbell, M. R., Milne, R., and Wagstaff, G. F. (1999). The cognitive interview: A survey of its forensic effectiveness. *Psychology, Crime & Law*, 5, pp. 101–115.

Milne, R., and Bull, R. (1999). *Investigative Interviewing: Psychology and Practice*. Chichester: John Wiley & Sons, Ltd.

Nacos, B. L. (2007). *Mass-Mediated Terrorism: The Central Role of the Media in Terrorism and Counterterrorism*. Lanham, MD: Rowman and Littlefield.

National Police Improvement Agency (NPIA) (2009). National Investigative Interviewing Strategy, NPIA Briefing Paper. London: HMSO.

Ord, B., Shaw, G., and Green, T. (2008). *Investigative Interviewing Explained*. 2nd Edition. Chatswood, NSW: LexisNexis.

Rejali, D. (2007). *Torture and Democracy*. Princeton, NJ: Princeton University Press.

Roberts, K. A. (2009). *Investigative Interviewing and Islamic Extremism*. Paper Presented at the 2nd Annual Conference of the International Investigative Interviewing Research Group, April 14–16, Middlesbrough.

Roberts, K. A. (2010). Ethical police interviews with Islamist terror suspects: The significance of suspect behavioural, cultural and identity characteristics. In D. Antonius, A. Brown, T. Waters, M. Ramirez, and S. J. Sinclair (Eds.), *Interdisciplinary Analyses of Terrorism and Aggression*. Cambridge: Cambridge Scholars Publishing, pp. 182–203.

Roberts, K. A. (2011). Police interviews with terrorist suspects: Risks, ethical interviewing and procedural justice. *British Journal of Forensic Practice*, 13(2), 124–134.

Roberts, K. A., and Herrington, V. (2011). The psychology of suspect interviews—An international perspective. In J. Kitaeff (Ed.), *The Handbook of Police Psychology*. New York: Taylor & Francis, pp. 383–401.

Rogers, M. B., Loewenthal, K. M., Lewis, C. A., Amlot, R., Cinnirella, M. C., and Ansari, H. (2007). The role of religious fundamentalism in terrorist violence: A social-psychological analysis. *The International Review of Psychiatry*, 19(3), 253–262.

Sands, P. (2008). *Torture Team*. New York: Palgrave Macmillan.

Savage, S., and Milne, R. (2007). Miscarriages of justice—The role of the investigative process. In T. Newburn, T. Williamson, and A. Wright (Eds.), *Handbook of Criminal Investigation*. Devon: Willan Publishing, pp. 610–628.

Shepherd, E. (1991). Ethical interviewing. *Policing*, 7, 42–60.

Shepherd, E., and Milne, R. (1999). Full and faithful: Ensuring quality practice and integrity of outcomes in witness interviews. In A. Heaton-Armstrong, E. Shepherd, and D. Wolchover (Eds.), *Analysing Witness Testimony: A Guide for Legal Practitioners and Other Professionals*. London: Black stone Press, pp. 124–146.

Skogan, W. (2006). Asymmetry in the impact of encounters with police. *Policing & Society: An International Journal of Research and Policy*, 16, 99–126.

Sprang, G. (2003). The psychological impact of isolated acts of terrorism. In A. Silke (Ed.), *Terrorists, Victims and Society: Psychological Perspectives on Terrorism and Its Consequences* (Wiley Series in Psychology of Crime, Policing and Law). Chichester: Wiley, pp. 133–161.

Stafford-Smith, C. (2007). *Bad Men: Guantánamo Bay and the Secret Prisons*. London: Weidenfeld & Nicolson.

Tyler, T. R. (1989). The psychology of procedural justice: A test of the group value model. *Journal of Personality and Social Psychology*, 57, 830–838.

Tyler, T. R., and Blader, S. L. (2003). The group engagement model: Procedural justice, social identity and cooperative behaviour. *Personality and Social Psychology Review*, 7, 349–361.

UK Home Office (1984). *Police and Criminal Evidence Act London*. London: HMSO.

UK Home Office (2000a). *Regulation of Investigatory Powers Act (RIPA)*. London: HMSO.

UK Home Office (2000b). *Counter Terrorism Act*. London: HMSO.

UK Home Office (2009). *The New Performance Landscape for Crime and Policing*. London: HMSO.

UK Home Office (2011). *The UK Counter-Terrorism Strategy CONTEST*. http://www.homeoffice.gov.uk/counter-terrorism/uk-counter-terrorism-strat/ (accessed March 18, 2011).

Counterterrorism Legislation in the United Kingdom

22

A Review of the Impact of Control Orders

IMRAN AWAN

Contents

Introduction

The overall symmetry of counterterrorism policies, legislation, and practices has been radically transformed following the review into the UK counterterrorism agenda (HM Government 2011). The reforms include reducing the length of precharge detention, the abolishment of control orders for Terrorism Prevention and Investigation Measures (T-PIMs), and finally having "reasonable suspicion" before stopping and searching someone under the Terrorism Act (Lewis 2010). Fenwick and Choudhury's (2011, V) study into the impact of counterterrorism legislation and policies involved a number of in-depth interviews and focus groups which sought to explore the perception of both Muslims and non-Muslims across Britain about counterterrorism laws and policies in general. They state that

> Counterterrorism measures are contributing to a wider sense among Muslims that they are being treated as a "suspect community" and targeted by authorities simply because of their religion. Many participants, while not referring to specific laws or policies, felt that counterterrorism law and policy generally was

contributing towards hostility to Muslims by treating Muslims as a "suspect group," and creating a climate of fear and suspicion towards them.

Many of the UK reforms concerning counterterrorism legislation discussed above have come at a time where the present government has come under fierce opposition from civil liberty groups to uphold its pledge that they would reexamine all counterterrorism policies which have been deemed to be hard-line approaches that risk stigmatizing communities (Spalek 2010). The chapter examines one such policy (control orders) and reviews the impact they have had on communities and their overall effectiveness in light of the rights of individuals to freedom of movement, freedom of association, freedom of communication; the right to liberty; and the right to a private family life.

The UK government has been in the process of enacting a number of antiterrorism laws following the 9/11 and 7/7 attacks. This includes the Anti-Terrorism, Crime and Security Act (ATCSA) 2001, the Prevention of Terrorism Act 2005, and the Terrorism Act 2006. The problem with such legislation is that they have had the potential to stigmatize communities and risk alienating them as the police are given further powers which they could abuse (Gearty 2005).

Control orders were a controversial regime which, the British government assured the public, was needed to prevent future terrorist activity. However, it is clear that while control orders attempted to "control" terrorist suspects and prevent further atrocities, they also had the potential of breaching the rights and liberties of individuals. Indeed, while the Prevention of Terrorism Act 2005 replaced Part 4 powers under the ATCSA 2001 and created control orders that could be used against suspected terrorists regardless of their identity, they were limited and could be imposed for a period of up to 12 months at a time when their legality could also be challenged. Furthermore, control orders created measures to supervise suspects through electronic tagging or by requiring them to remain in their homes (Fitzpatrick 2003). The restrictions included house arrest, who a person can speak to or meet, or when a person can leave his/her house. If a control order was breached without reasonable excuse, it would result in a prison sentence of up to 5 years, a fine, or both.

Control orders also created rules in relation to appeals against nonderogating and derogating orders. Part of the Act created provisions for an independent annual review and three-monthly reporting to Parliament on the powers of the Home Secretary when exercising the use of a control order (Flynn 2005). In the aftermath of the London bombings on July 7, 2005, the government announced that more new antiterror legislation would follow. The resulting Terrorism Act 2006 has also been the subject of a legal, moral, and political debate. The chapter examines the legislation in relation to control orders in more detail.

The Prevention of Terrorism Act 2005

As noted above, the Prevention of Terrorism Act 2005 was introduced as a result of the terrorist bombings in London in July 2005. The main purpose of the 2005 Act was to provide for control orders, which imposed restrictions on individuals suspected of being involved in terrorism. The control order regime imposed severe restrictions on a suspected individual's freedom of movement, and the government argued that control orders were nevertheless important tools in the fight against terrorism, but promised that they would only be used after careful political and legal decision making.

The system of control orders repealed Part 4 powers of the ATCSA 2001 and gave broader powers to impose certain conditions on individuals and prohibits certain movements, for example, access to the Internet, house arrest, and curfews (Turner 2010). Other restrictions included a person surrendering his/her passport, the need to report to a specific place and at a specific time, restrictions on the place a person lives at or stays, who they were allowed to meet, on all modes of communication (including telephone calls), and restrictions on their movement which often led to serious questions as regards the rights of individuals to freedom of movement (Middleton 2011).

The Control Order Regime

Control orders were brought in by the Prevention of Terrorism Act 2005 as a preventative measure to prevent further terrorist activity. They gave the Home Secretary wide powers to detain suspected terrorists. So long as the Home Secretary has "reasonable suspicion" that a person is involved in terrorist activity, they will be entitled to impose certain restrictions in order to prevent a terrorist attack. The Prevention of Terrorism Act 2005 also allowed for two control orders to be used. The first are control orders that derogate from the European Court of Human Rights and the second are control orders that do not derogate.

During the debate on the Prevention of Terrorism Bill, the Home Secretary at the time Charles Clarke informed the House of Commons that

> at the top end, the obligations that could be imposed include a requirement for the individual to remain in a particular place at all times, or similar measures that amounted to a deprivation of liberty. The place in question could be the individuals own home or his or parents home. It could even in certain circumstances be in accommodation owned and managed by the government. (Clarke 2005, 152)

This amounted to quite a severe restriction on a person's life when he/she has not yet been convicted of any offence. What control orders really did was to put suspects under house arrest. Some of the restrictions imposed included monitoring suspects' activities throughout the day, who they can speak to, and who they can meet. They also had to relinquish their passport (Starmer 2007). There were restrictions on their telephone calls, travel, and use of the Internet. The police could also visit their home from time to time, and the suspects would also be electronically tagged (Fenwick 2008).

Under Section 2(1)(a), the Home Secretary only needed "reasonable suspicion" that someone may be involved in a terrorist activity to apply for a control order. Critics argued that the section was too wide and gave scope for mistakes and inaccuracies. In most cases, as we shall see, it was almost impossible to argue against the imposition of the order on the basis that the police had inaccurate evidence. Innocent people could be detained on evidence that may not necessarily show that they were involved in a terrorist activity, but on which the Home Secretary bases a "reasonable suspicion." The legal procedure therefore required the only justification that the Home Secretary required was to show that the control order was necessary because national security is at risk if this particular terrorist suspect is not detained (Middleton 2007).

This meant that, even if an innocent person was detained under the Prevention of Terrorism Act 2005 on the basis of weak evidence, the Home Secretary did not need to fear any accountability. Once the Home Secretary had "reasonable suspicion" that this person may be involved in a terrorist attack, as long as they can prove that there was "some risk," whether the risk is slight would not matter. As a result, there have been a number of controversial cases where control orders have been implemented (Mendelle and Naseem 2008). For example, in *MB v Secretary of State* (2006), the Home Secretary had argued that, once she had "reasonable suspicion," the courts did not need to look at how and why she had reached that decision, or look at the evidence obtained. However, Mr Justice Sullivan proceeded to rule that this was wholly unfair and did not meet the criteria set out in the Human Rights Act 1998. The case clearly showed that the courts would insist on examining the evidence and would not simply accept the Home Secretary's word. Moreover, the courts were not prepared to act as a rubber stamp on the executive.

In *Secretary of State for the Home Department v JJ* (2006), the wide powers of the Home Secretary were again under question. The argument consisted of whether Article 5 (the right to liberty) had been breached. The terrorist suspects in question had been isolated in such a way that they were not allowed to have any contact with relatives, friends, or family. As Kier Starmer states,

> they had to remain from 16.00 until 10.00 (18 hours) under curfew without stepping out as far as their yards, gardens or even communal corridors. They also had to wear an electronic tag 24 hours a day and to allow the police and/or monitoring company access to the premises any time. There was also a rule that no visitors should be allowed to the premises without Home Office approval, only to be given on production of the name, address and photo identity of the would-be

visitor, and a rule that the individual subjected to the control order should not agree to meet anyone in the six hours that they were allowed off their premises, again unless they had Home Office approval to do so. (Starmer 2007, 124)

However, the courts held that, in respect of the seriousness of the threat posed in this case, there had been no breach of Article 5 of the Human Rights Act 1998. This was because the nature of the evidence suggested that the individuals involved were likely to pose a threat. Article 5 allows for "(c) the lawful arrest or detention of a person effected for the purpose of bringing him before the competent legal authority on *reasonable suspicion of having committed an offence or when it is reasonably considered necessary to prevent his committing an offence or fleeing after having done so*" (emphasis added).

Moreover, the government had also been previously criticized in the case of *Chahal v UK* in 1996. Here, the government wanted to deport suspected terrorists to countries where there was a possibility that they may suffer torture and ill-treatment. The government had argued that Mr Chahal should be deported to India because he was suspected of being involved in terrorist activities. But because he risked torture and ill-treatment, the European Court of Justice held that he was not to be deported.

Clearly, the person in charge of the control order process (the Home Secretary) regarded the judiciary as an obstacle to their main purpose, which was seen as the maintenance of security, not the preservation of civil liberties. As a result, Starmer argues,

Until July 2005, the Government accepted that it could not deport non-nationals suspected of terrorism to countries such as Algeria, Jordan and Libya because there was a real risk that they would face death, torture or ill-treatment on their return. (Starmer 2007, 125)

However, as he goes on to say:

A few weeks later, that all changed. In August, nearly all non-nationals were taken off control orders and detained. In his press conference on August 5, 2005, the Prime Minister announced that "the rules of the game are changing" and that new grounds were to be published for deporting such individuals. Countries with well-documented histories of human rights abuse would be invited to promise not to torture anyone sent back to them by the United Kingdom. (Starmer 2007, 125)

At the time, John Reid, the Home Secretary, argued:

When I see and hear all of these things then I sometimes feel that so many people who should be foremost in recognizing the serious nature of the threat just don't get it. We cannot afford any misunderstanding, in any quarter about the nature and scope of the threat which we are facing. (Reid 2006, 7)

In another case, the *Secretary of State for the Home Department v AL* (2007), Ouseley J held that, based on the evidence the Home Secretary had at his disposal, the control order was both proportionate and necessary. In this case, the person involved (AL) had an intention to travel abroad to engage in terrorist activity. The restrictions the Home Secretary imposed included reporting to a police station daily, surrendering his passport, and providing the Home Secretary details of any employment he had. The court agreed that the control order was proportionate because it would prevent (AL) going abroad and participating in these terrorist activities. Again, the point is worth making that the individual was not charged but only suspected of being involved in terrorist activities.

More recently, the Abu Qatada case has again raised important questions as regards the conflict between the judiciary and the British government. The cleric posted a number of sermons and videos in 2002 and was allegedly a keen sympathizer of the Al-Qaeda narrative. As a result, he was detained in 2002, and since then the UK government has attempted to deport him to Jordan and finally succeeded when assurances were given by authorities in Jordan that Qatada would receive a fair trial. Prior to this decision the European Court of Human Rights had ruled that Abu Qatada should be released under strict bail conditions which included him adhering to a 22-hour curfew, and as such he is not allowed to leave his address for longer than a 2-hour period, and any visitors he may have must have gone through a preapproval system. Similarly, he had no access to any electronic sources such as the Internet.

The UK Attorney General Dominic Grieve has argued that although Abu Qatada poses a serious threat to national security but that he should not be detained without a fair trial. The Attorney General stated:

> We obviously don't have indefinite internment without trial in this country. Individuals enjoy the right to liberty and government is bound by the rule of law and has to observe it. (Travis and Meikle 2012)

Indeed, the former Home Secretary David Blunkett with respect to the Abu Qatada case has argued:

> It is an unholy mess. We are left in the absurd position of not being able to remove a man even though everyone accepts he won't be tortured, not being able to keep him in prison because his human rights trump the protection of the British people, and a government that has watered down control orders so that they are more lax than was previously the case. (Travis and Meikle 2012)

As illustrated above, a wide-ranging conflict was beginning to emerge between the judiciary and the government, with the judiciary questioning the evidence needed for a control order and regarding the legislative requirement of "reasonable suspicion" as too wide (Middleton 2007). On the other side, the previous Home Secretary at the time had argued that control orders were necessary because of the terrorist threat faced by the United Kingdom. Lord Carlile (the independent reviewer of antiterror legislation) at the time reported that, in 2005, there were 18 control orders, of which 9 were still subsisting. Furthermore, he acknowledged that a balance between civil liberty and national security was needed and believed that it was being achieved (Carlile 2010).

At the same time, however, Lord Carlile argued that in all cases where control orders are used, (1) they should be scrutinized closely; (2) the Home Office should create a procedure whereby officials and representatives of the control authorities meet regularly to monitor cases in order to achieve consistency and to protect national security; and (3) the police should give clear and unequivocal evidence that the person is involved in terrorist activity. The Home Secretary subsequently informed the House of Commons that he believed that Lord Carlile's report endorsed the control order system and the government has said that it accepted Lord Carlile's findings and would implement his recommendations.

However, control orders came under increased scrutiny from human rights campaigners, who argued that the right to private and family life, the right to freedom of thought, the right to conscience and religion, the right to freedom of expression, the right to freedom of movement, the right to freedom of association, and the right to a fair trial are all breached by control orders (Gearty 2007; Kostakopoulou 2008). Indeed, the right to private and family life has had an impact on individuals' families, especially restrictions on communications with children and spouses.

Furthermore, critics argued that the right to freedom of association was breached by the intense surveillance, isolation, and lack of social interaction that control orders could impose (Arden 2005).

There has also been an argument that control orders caused psychological and mental distress. For example, Mahmoud Abu Rideh, a terrorist suspect, held under a control order stated, "My kids worry that when they get back from school I will be gone and they might not find me gain. My wife can't sleep. She is asking me not to go out again" (Gillan and Yafai 2005).

Control orders should only be used in exceptional circumstances and be proportionate. If the orders were used in such a manner, they may have achieved what they were aiming for, which is prevention and disruption of future attacks. The requirement of "reasonable suspicion" however was too wide a test. Though there is a need to tackle the threat of terrorism, this should not consist of the erosion of civil liberties (Gearty 2008). The Human Rights Act 1998 is enshrined in the UK law as a way of making sure that legislation is compatible with people's rights. The government's first response to a terrorist attack has been to enact legislation that potentially curbs civil liberties. This subverts the traditional criminal justice process, mainly by undercutting habeas corpus and the right to liberty. Following the UK government review into counterterrorism legislation, control orders were abolished for T-PIMs.

Terrorism Prevention and Investigation Measures

As noted above, control orders led to the detention without trial of both foreign nationals and British citizens. The fact that the Home Secretary had "reasonable suspicion" was enough evidence for issuing a control order. However, the government was criticized for this new power as it breached the Human Rights Act (Fenwick and Choudhury 2011). The new system of T-PIMs, as the government argues, will strike the right balance between liberty and national security. The previous system of control orders could be imposed without any time limit and individuals would be effectively under house arrest and not know the charge against them.

Some of the key proposals of T-PIMs include the following: (1) a limitation of holding a suspect without charge (i.e., based on a premise of conducting a more thorough investigation followed by possible charge and conviction); (2) a suspect will be allowed to use a mobile phone and the Internet, subject to conditions allowing for a greater freedom of association; and (3) T-PIMs will expire after 2 years unless new evidence emerges of involvement in terrorism. Moreover, the focus is now on evidence that is more robust where previously there was a requirement for the Home Secretary to show "reasonable suspicion"; this has changed to include the phrase "reasonable belief."

Thus, T-PIMs will not forcibly remove suspects (objectionable to many minority communities who have felt that counterterrorism legislation has marginalized and stigmatized them), meaning that suspects will now be required to stay at home overnight for up to 10 hours where previously it had been 16 hours. However, the impact of such reforms, as critics argue, remain kafkaesque because they in fact mean that suspects will continue to be electronically tagged, report regularly to the police, and could face exclusion from particular places as well as the prevention of travel overseas. Furthermore, the current system cannot escape the stigma attached to control orders and will continue to have the potential of fostering alienation of the Muslim communities in Britain and potentially act as a recruitment tool for extremist groups (Githens-Mazer and Lambert 2010; Murdie 2007).

Conclusion

Control orders had a huge impact on communities and in particular on civil liberties. Following the terrorist attacks of July 7/7, the British government enacted antiterror legislation in the view that it hoped it could combat the threat of terrorism. However, there is no substantial evidence that suggests that control orders have made people in the United Kingdom more safe, and indeed it has arguably made people less safe. The threat from terrorism should not mean that people's individual freedoms are curtailed (Spalek and Lambert 2008).

Since 9/11, it is correct to say that we are in a new political age and that the civil liberties we once enjoyed must—according to the government—be reassessed. Terrorism has changed, and terrorists are now using complex international networks and making suicide bombers. However, the legacy and impact of control orders appears to have alienated many Muslim communities as shown by recent studies (Fenwick and Choudhury 2011) and the government must ensure now that T-PIMs do not have the same effect.

References

Arden, M. (2005). Human rights in the age of terrorism, *Law Quarterly Review* 121 (October): 604–627.

Carlile, L. (2010). Sixth report of the independent reviewer of the Prevention of Terrorism Act 2005. Presented to Parliament pursuant to section 14(3) of the Prevention of Terrorism Act 2005. Available from http://www.homeoffice.gov.uk/publications/counter-terrorism/independent-reviews/lord-carlile-sixth-report?view=Binary [accessed June 10, 2011].

Chahal v UK [1996] ECHR 54.

Clarke, C. (2005). Prevention of Terrorism Act, House of Commons Debate, vol. 431 col. 152 (February 22) Available from http://www.publications.parliament.uk/pa/cm200405/cmhansrd/vo050222/debtext/50222-05.htm [accessed May 10, 2012].

Fenwick, H. (2008). Proactive counter-terrorist strategies in conflict with human rights, *International Review of Law, Computers & Technology* 22 (3): 259–270.

Fenwick, H. and Choudhury, T. (2011). The impact of counter-terrorism measures on Muslim communities, Equality and Human Rights Commission Research Report no. 72. Available from http://www.equalityhumanrights.com/uploaded_files/research/counter-terrorism_research_report_72.pdf [accessed June 20, 2011].

Fitzpatrick, J. (2003). Speaking law to power: The war against terrorism and human rights, *European Journal of International Law* 14 (2): 241–264.

Flynn, E. (2005). Counter terrorism and human rights: The view from the United Nations, *European Human Rights Law Review* 10 (1): 29–49.

Gearty, C. (2005). 11 September 2001, counter-terrorism, and the Human Rights Act, *Journal of Law and Society* 32 (1): 18–33.

Gearty, C. (2007). Rethinking civil liberties in a counter-terrorism world, *European Human Rights Law Review* 2: 111–119.

Gearty, C. (2008). The superpatriotic fervour of the moment, *Oxford Journal of Legal Studies* 28 (1): 183.

Gillan, A. and Yafai, F. (2005). Control order flaws exposed, *The Guardian* (March). Available from http://www.guardian.co.uk/politics/2005/mar/24/uk.terrorism [accessed April 10, 2010].

Githens-Mazer, J. and Lambert, R. (2010). *Islamophobia and Anti Muslim Hate Crimes: A London Case Study*. European Muslim Research Centre. Available from http://centres.exeter.ac.uk/emrc/publications/IAMHC_revised_11Feb11.pdf [accessed June 19, 2011].

HM Government. (2011). Review of counter-terrorism and security powers. Home Office. Available from http://www.homeoffice.gov.uk/publications/counter-terrorism/review-of-ct-security-powers/sum-responses-to-cons?view = Binary [accessed on June 14, 2011].

Kostakopoulou, D. (2008). How to do things with security post 9/11, *Oxford Journal of Legal Studies* 28 (2): 317.

Lewis, P. (2010). Peace campaigner, 85, classified by police as domestic extremist (June). Available from http://www.guardian.co.uk/uk/2010/jun/25/peace-campaigner-classified-domestic-extremist [accessed June 10, 2011].

MB v Secretary of State (2006) EWHC 1623.

Mendelle, P. and Naseem, A. (2008). Human rights and terrorism, *Justice of the Peace*, 172: 486.

Middleton, B. (2007). Control orders: Out of control?, *Criminal Lawyer* 173: 3–5.

Middleton, B. (2011). Rebalancing, reviewing or rebranding the treatment of terrorist suspects: The counter-terrorism review, *Journal of Criminal Law* 75 (3): 225–248.

Murdie, A. (2007). Terrorism, human rights and the inquisition, *Justice of the Peace*, 171: 231–234.

Reid, J. (2006). Security, freedom and the protection of our values. Speech by Rt Hon John Reid MP, Home Secretary, August 9, 2006. Available from http://www.demos.co.uk/files/johnreidsecurityandfreedom.pdf [accessed February 5, 2011].

Secretary of State for the Home Department v AL (2007) EWHC 1970.

Secretary of State for the Home Department v JJ (2006) EWHC 1623.

Spalek, B. (2010). Community policing, trust, and Muslim communities in relation to new terrorism, *Politics & Policy* 38 (4): 789–815.

Spalek, B. and Lambert, R. (2008). Muslim communities, counter-terrorism and de-radicalisation: A reflective approach to engagement, *International Journal of Law, Crime and Justice* 36 (4): 257–270.

Starmer, K. (2007). Setting the record straight: Human rights in an era of international terrorism, *European Human Rights Law Review* 2 (February): 123–132.

Travis, A. and Meikle, J. (2012). Abu Qatada: Attorney general says government must follow rule of law, *The Guardian* (Tuesday February 7, 2012). Available from http://www.guardian.co.uk/world/2012/feb/07/abu-qatada-attorney-general-law [accessed January 21, 2013].

Turner, A. (2010). Stop and search, *Criminal Law & Justice Weekly* 174: 434.

A Tale of Three US Cities

23

Police Accountability and Urban Indians in Albuquerque, Portland, and Duluth

EILEEN M. LUNA-FIREBAUGH

Contents

Introduction

The American Indian nations are sovereign. They have been deemed by the US courts to be "domestic dependent nations" with the right to make and enforce their own laws[*] and to hold their police accountable to their own rules. The American Indian nations also have the authority in certain circumstances (e.g., in contracting with local law enforcement) to define and/or restrict the

---

[*] *Johnson v. McIntosh*, 21 US (8 Wheat.) 543 (1823); *Cherokee Nation v. Georgia*, 30 US (5 Pet.) 1 (1831); *Worchester v. Georgia*, 31 US (6 Pet.) 515 (1832).

activities of local law enforcement in Indian Country.* This is generally not the case in urban communities, where Indian tribes and nations are in competition with states and cities as to how policing is to be conducted.

The experiences of urban Indians† with the police are remarkably similar from city to city. Regardless of the location, urban Indians, individually and collectively, often experience a level of disconnect with police departments and the city power structure. This disconnect is evidenced in statistics, stories, and reflections. It is necessary to address this disconnect if urban Indians are ever to take their proper place in urban society.

This chapter focuses on data compiled from studies of Albuquerque, NM; Portland, OR; and Duluth, MN. These studies were conducted by this author to examine the community satisfaction of the public with their police complaints systems. The studies did not specifically relate to the urban American Indian communities in those cities. However, the information obtained provides a greater understanding of the relationship between American Indians and their police departments.

The cities chosen for this chapter have large urban Indian populations and are surrounded by Indian Country. The communities are widely distributed geographically, with one in the Pacific Northwest, one in the Southwest, and one in the Great Lakes region. They are of different sizes and differ demographically. Their urban Indian populations are historically well established and diverse. The surrounding reservations and pueblos are near enough to send workers, who live on Indian land, into the cities for work. Throughout the twentieth century, these cities were also employment centers for Indians, from geographically widespread areas, who voluntarily moved to urban areas for educational or employment opportunities, or were relocated through governmental action.‡

In each city, the author surveyed members of the urban Indian community and community organization representatives regarding their perceptions of and experiences with city administrations. The experiences of urban Indian communities with the police of their cities were strikingly similar. The alienation of urban Indians, regardless of tribe, was evident, their

---

* 18 USC Section 1151 The term "Indian country," as used in this chapter, means (1) all land within the limits of any Indian reservation under the jurisdiction of the US government, notwithstanding the issuance of any patent, and, including rights-of-way running through the reservation, (2) all dependent Indian communities within the borders of the United States whether within the original or subsequently acquired territory thereof, and whether within or without the limits of a state, and (3) all Indian allotments, the Indian titles to which have not been extinguished, including rights-of-way running through the same.

† The term Indian is generally used throughout the United States by the indigenous population to refer to themselves and is the term used in law. The term Native American is also used by some. I use the term Indian as it is the legal term and also the term used by my family and tribe.

‡ Canby (2009, 28).

relationships with the police were strained, and the communities were highly disaffected.

The Albuquerque study of the police complaints system began in 1996 and was funded by the city. The city of Albuquerque published the report as a public record in 1997. The urban Indian community, even though central to the life and image of Albuquerque, was not a pivotal part of the call for a study.

The Portland study was conducted in 2007. The report was funded by the city of Portland. It was published in 2008 as a public record by the Mayor's Office. As with Albuquerque, the urban Indian community was not central to the call for a study.

The Duluth police accountability study was conducted in 2010. The final report has not yet been published. Here, unlike Albuquerque and Portland, the urban Indian community was central to the call for a study. The study was contracted by the Duluth Task Force for Improved Community Police Accountability (DTFICPA), which included a number of urban Indian and reservation-based activists, as well as non-Indian organizations and members of the Duluth Police Department. This study was funded by grants and other funds obtained by the Task Force, not through city funding. In Duluth, there were some American Indian community and organizational activists connected with the city administration and the police department. However, the observations and experiences of most urban Indians and organizations were similar to the other two studies and were not positive.

Police Accountability and the Concept of Continuous Improvement

The concept of accountability of government and, in particular, of police is one that is fully entrenched in democratic societies. In the United States, the right of the public to know the public's business and to participate in the decisions as to how that business is carried out has been the basis of the development of the concepts of police accountability and civilian oversight of law enforcement.[*] The police are accountable for many things including the manner in which they treat people and the integration of the community into the policing process. The rise of civilian oversight of police agencies grew out of this sense that the community has a proper role to play in policing and in how this role is performed.

The concept of continuous improvement, or total quality management, is a management philosophy focused on an effort to expose and eliminate root causes of problems. Usually, this involves many incremental or small-step

---

[*] See, for example, the works of Samuel Walker and of Eileen Luna-Firebaugh, on civilian oversight of police.

improvements rather than one overwhelming innovation. In Japan, the word for this concept is *Kaizen*, which is Japanese for "improvement" or "change for the better."

These studies conducted by the author revealed that the cities over time have been committed to the concept of continuous improvement. This concept proceeds from the premise that an effective governmental system (in this instance police accountability system) needs to include processes that encourage and achieve continuous improvement, that is, systematic, ongoing efforts to improve an organization's performance against the attributes of quality which are most important to involved citizens, employees, city officials, and the community.

Continuous improvement proceeds from a position of acceptance. It views improvement as incremental rather than as revolutionary or tumultuous. It enhances the stability of a system and encourages the development of community confidence in the process of change.

Continuous improvement goes under many different names—total quality management, sustainable business excellence, continual process improvement, and best practice. Whatever terminology is used, though, the essential features remain the same:

WHO—all stakeholders in the organization should have the opportunity to be involved; to ensure a systematic approach, clearly defined responsibilities and resources are needed.

WHEN—continuous improvement is undertaken as an ongoing cycle, which is repeated over and over. As requirements and the service delivery change, organizations need to respond with new ideas and new ways of working.

WHAT—the focus is on the key processes an organization uses to meet the needs of stakeholders.

WHY—continuous improvement makes good policy sense. It is about working smarter in striving to achieve our stated goals, particularly when it is so easy to become overwhelmed by the day-to-day demands of keeping the organization going.

Findings of the Three Accountability Studies

There are 564 federally recognized tribes in the United States, with a national representation of American Indians at just over 2,447,989, or 1.5% of the total according to the 2000 US census.* Approximately 60% of American Indians in the United States are urban based. These urban populations are the result of both the voluntary and imposed relocation of American Indians. Many of these people identify as American Indians, even if they no longer

---

* 2000 Census retrieved form http://www.census.gov/main/www/cen2000.html.

participate in life on reservations or in tribal activities. For many, urban activities centered on American Indian centers and services have become the foundation of their identities as American Indians. The American Indian populations who self-identified as American Indians in the selected cities of Albuquerque, Portland, and Duluth ranged from 2.8% to 5.1%.

The City of Albuquerque, New Mexico (Study of 1996–1997)

The native population in and around Albuquerque, NM, is very much a part of the fabric of the city. The total population of American Indians in New Mexico was 211,178 in 1998, or 10.6% overall. There are 5 Indian reservations and 19 pueblos in New Mexico, with 8 pueblos in close proximity to the city of Albuquerque. In 1998, at the time of this study, the American Indian population in Albuquerque was 2.6%. This percentage increased over time, and in 2008 the number of American Indians residing or working in Albuquerque was 5.1% of the city's population. The urban Indian population of Albuquerque is long standing, with some 160 tribes represented. The city is the hub of American Indian life in central New Mexico with many large federal agencies that serve the native population. The governmental center for the state's 19 pueblos is located on tribal land within the city's boundaries.

Regardless of the geographical integration of the Native American population and the city, the integration of tribes and tribal citizens with the city's power structure was noticeably lacking. This was evident in the community satisfaction study done in 1996. Outreach to the American Indian community was largely lacking in Albuquerque. This was the case even though American Indians were reported as being overrepresented among those who had issues with the police.[*] There was also a lack of involvement in the operations of the city, which was manifested in the low American Indian response rate to the study. Only 2% of the respondents to the survey identified as Native Americans, a lower percentage than the then overall Indian population of 2.6% in Albuquerque.

The Albuquerque study showed that racial and ethnic minorities held less favorable attitudes about police than Whites. American Indians as individuals and American Indian organizations in general expressed their concerns that "incidents involving conflict (e.g., use of force)" (Luna and Walker 1997) mostly occurred against low-income, minority males who however seldom registered complaints against police personnel.

This evidence of disconnect was also evident in the lack of Native American police officers. In 1998, only five (1.4%) of the Albuquerque police officers identified themselves as Native Americans. There were no significant

---

[*] Albuquerque Indian Center interviews conducted by the author in 1998.

differences in officer survey responses based on race or ethnicity, and their responses did not suggest that racial and ethnic conflict were issues within the APD. Though the Albuquerque Police Department (APD) appeared to have problems with what one officer described an "old boy network." This description correlates closely to what Jerome H. Skolnick has described as "Code Blue."[*]

The City of Portland, Oregon (Study of 2007–2008)

The native population of Oregon is relatively small (45,211 or 1.6%) and approximately 89% of this population is urban. There are nine tribes in the state, but none are geographically close to the city of Portland. Portland has the largest urban Indian population in Oregon, with 2.8% of the population identifying as Native American, representing more than 200 tribes.[†] Approximately 6785 American Indian residents reside in Multnomah County, where Portland is located, and more than 85% of these residents live within the Portland city boundaries.

The city is a hub of Native American services and activities along the Columbia River border with Washington. A number of Oregon tribes and organizations have offices and service programs in Portland. The Columbia River Inter-Tribal Fish Commission, which represents the interests of tribes in Washington, Oregon, and Idaho, is located in Portland, as are the central offices of the Affiliated Tribes of Northwest Indians and the Northwest Regional Office of the Bureau of Indian Affairs.

Unfortunately, as with Albuquerque, the integration of tribes and tribal citizens within the city's power structure was noticeably lacking. The 2007 study showed that there was little outreach to the American Indian community, nor was the community involved with police administration or operations.

During the study, interviews of Native American Agency administrators and community spokespersons were conducted at community centers and in private settings. There was unanimity among those interviewed that there was no outreach by police administration to the native community. There were no representatives of the American Indian community on any board or commission that focused on the police. This was the case even though American Indians were overrepresented among those having complaints against police and those who have issues with police.

[*] Skolnick (2002).
[†] 2006–2008 American Community Survey, retrieved from http://factfinder.census.gov/ servlet/ADPTable?_bm=y&-geo_id=16000US4159000&-qr_name=ACS_2008_3YR_ G00_DP3YR5&-ds_name=ACS_2008_3YR_G00_&-_lang=en&-_sse=on.

The interviews conducted in the American Indian community indicated that Indians in Portland did not feel comfortable talking with the police, nor in seeking police assistance. Representatives further stated, "There is no readily available brochure about the police complaint process" (Luna-Firebaugh 2008). Others stated, "There was no personal contact by the police complaint office. Everything has to be online or in writing" (Luna-Firebaugh 2008).

The city asked the Indian Center to help with recruiting Native American commission members, but the experience was not uniformly positive. Spokespersons for the American Indian community stated that staff or community members of the Indian Center had not been invited to participate in any kind of "Indian awareness" for police training, nor in squad room meetings. Neither the police nor the police complaint office had asked to come to a community meeting to talk about police issues. Brochures had never been provided for distribution in their centers.

The Indian Center stated they knew approximately 100 native persons who were dissatisfied with police contacts. However, Portland relies on the city's online website to disseminate information regarding the filing of complaints. This computerized approach generally did not assist Native Americans. The Native American Center administrators estimated that 90% of native community members did not have access to computers in their homes and transportation issues restricted their ability to get to a computer. The native activists believed that, due to administrative hurdles, only two American Indians actually managed to file a complaint during the target period of the study (2005–2007). The two who did manage to file were told that there was not enough information to support their case, despite providing the officer's name, business card, license plate, and time/date of incident.

During the target years of the study (2005, 2006, and 2007), American Indians filed approximately 1.2% of the complaints received, a significantly lower percentage than their representation in the Portland population. There were eight Native American complainants who responded to this survey. Not all of these answered all questions. The numbers that follow reflect the discrepancy of response. However, even taking that into consideration, the responses of Native American complainants to the Satisfaction Survey were not positive:

- None of these American Indian complainants who responded to the survey reported that they were satisfied with the police complaint process.
- Less than a half (three of eight) reported that they were treated with respect by the investigator.
- Less than a half (three of eight) reported that the investigator asked fair questions.
- Only two of the seven respondents stated that witnesses to their incident were interviewed.

- Only one of the six respondents stated that enough information was gathered by the police complaint investigator to make a fair decision.
- Only two of the six respondents indicated that information obtained from them was carefully considered prior to a decision on their complaint.

Only three (0.033%) of the Portland police survey respondents indicated that they were Native Americans. This percentage was significantly lower than the American Indian population of Portland.

There were no significant differences in officer survey responses based on race or ethnicity. In general, more than three-quarters (76.4%) of the police respondents who had received complaints believed that the outcome of the investigation was what they deserved, and more than 90% believed that the investigation was fair. Neither race nor ethnicity seemed to affect the subject officers' opinions of the investigation.

The City of Duluth, Minnesota (Study of 2010)

Duluth, MN, is the major urban center for Northern Minnesota. The Native American population in Minnesota is 1.2%. In 2000, the Native American population of Duluth is 2984, or 3.4% (http://www.helloduluth.com/Census.Cfm). There are 14 Indian reservations in the state, with 6 being in close proximity to Duluth.

The Fond du Lac tribe is on the border of the city. A tribal casino, tribal offices, and service programs are on trust land in the downtown area. The Bureau of Indian Affairs is also located within city boundaries. Duluth is the home of the Center for the American Indian and the American Indian Community Housing Organization. Mending the Sacred Hoop (MTSH) and the Program for Aid to Victims of Sexual Assault (PAVSA) are national organizations committed to service to Indian victims of sexual assault. The "Duluth Model" is used throughout the nation and the world to structure Domestic Abuse Intervention Programs (www.theduluthmodel.org).

The city of Duluth recognizes this urban American Indian presence to some extent. However, full involvement of the American Indian community in policing and police administration is not evident. The Duluth Police Department and the city administration have made efforts to connect with the American Indian community. There is an active American Indian Commission. A number of American Indian activists were founders and members of the DTFICPA that was instrumental in initiating the 2010 study.

MTSH conducted a Safety and Accountability Audit in 2008. The study focused on the problems facing American Indian women victims in contending with the Duluth police and justice system. This study reflected a substantive move by the professional American Indian community to bring community awareness to problems and to affect change within the Duluth Police Department.

Leslie Beiers, Head of the Criminal Division for the St. Louis County Attorney's Office (in which the city of Duluth is located), wrote an introductory letter for the 2008 MTSH study, in which she states,

> The horrific, wrenching stories of so many Native American women and their experiences with the "system" in which I've spent most of my adult life working, were shocking and saddening to me ... I became more committed and more hopeful that significant changes can be made. (St. George and Harris 2008, 6)

This awakening was echoed in the words of John W. Beyer, Duluth Deputy Chief of Police, who wrote in the introduction to the MTSH study, "Participating in the safety audit itself was challenging both personally and professionally because it was difficult to hear from victims that they believed the police department had failed them" (St. George and Harris 2008, 5).

Although efforts were made to connect the American Indian community with the city's power structure, they have not been completely successful. The City of Duluth relies on the computerized filing of complaints against police personnel. Few in the Native American community have unrestricted access to computers. This was emphasized by the disproportionate numbers of American Indians who answered the study survey online (18) and who completed hard copies (115).

While problems continue to exist, some changes have occurred. The Center for Indian Resources (CIR) is an urban service program of the Fond du Lac tribe. CIR officials reported that Duluth police in the past had failed to recognize tribal court orders. The organization met with the Duluth Police Chief, after which the department began recognizing these orders.

However, the 2010 police accountability study indicates that the American Indian community and the police remain disconnected, while perhaps more hopeful that change can occur. Unlike the cities of Albuquerque and Portland, the American Indian community responded to the Complaints Satisfaction Survey in significant numbers, with 14.3% identifying as American Indian. This number of respondents contrasts positively with the 2.8% who are identified as Native Americans by the city of Duluth.

The responses to the Complaints Satisfaction Survey indicated that American Indians were generally not satisfied in their contacts with the Duluth police:

- Less than one-third (28.8%) of the American Indian respondents believed that Duluth police officers were fair in their dealing with the public, and only 29.8% reported that the officers were professional, courteous, and helpful.
- Just over one-third (39.2%) of the respondents reported that they had confidence in the Duluth Police Department.
- Just over one-third (35.7%) of American Indians who filed complaints reported that they were interviewed as part of the investigation.
- Only one-fifth (21.2%) of the American Indian complainants who responded to the survey reported that they were satisfied with the outcome of the police complaint process.

Only 2 of the approximately 150 Duluth police officers are American Indians (1.3%), a percentage well below the native population of the city of Duluth. Both of these officers responded to the survey. Neither officer expressed any particular concerns with the Duluth Police Department, nor with the complaint system.

The Duluth study found that American Indians held less favorable attitudes about police than Whites and were willing to take a stand against what they saw as misconduct. Native Americans reported that they filed complaints against the police at a fairly high rate. More than 11.1% of the Native American survey respondents reported that they had filed at least one complaint during the years from 2005 to 2010.

Individual Points of Contrast

The studies addressed in this chapter occurred over a period of 12 years. Much can change in that time. However, there has been no research published over this time period that brings these issues of American Indians and the police to light. These data indicate that there are some commonalities over time in these three cities:

- There was little outreach into the communities conducted by the police departments or the city administrations. Where relationships existed, they were generally with organizations and activist individuals, seldom with grassroots community members.
- The idea that the complaint system needs to be accessible to all who might need to access it is fundamental. Computer access is not universal, and in communities of color, it is severely lacking and/or not compatible.
- The survey results were consistent with national trends regarding the attitudes of communities of color toward the police. While the American Indian community in Duluth was not as disaffected as

were those in Portland and Albuquerque, all three communities were, at the time of the studies, largely unhappy with, and distrustful of, their police departments.

- In all three cities, there were relatively few Native American police officers, even though the cities reported that they had made efforts to recruit.

Effects of the Police Accountability Studies

Change in public policy is hard to measure, particularly over relatively few years. Sometimes the best that one can do is to look at objective quantitative information. When numbers are examined, they show that the integration of American Indians into the police infrastructure improved where a study was done, which emphasized the activities with the Native American communities, and where the urban Indian community was focused on integration into the city administration and police ranks.

In Duluth, the study is less than a year old. It is notable however that the urban Indian community and the reservation-based community of Fond du Lac remain closely involved with the study implementation process. Duluth has benefited from the previous studies in that it organized its study process to include representation from both Fond du Lac and urban Indian organizations. The police department has consciously attempted to involve American Indians in police policy and has looked to urban Indian organizations, such as MTSH, to help to guide its community interaction.

In Portland, the percentage of the city's Native American population is 2.8%. Very soon after the completion of the community satisfaction study, the number of Portland police personnel who are American Indians grew, from 3 in 2007 to 5 in 2010. Unfortunately, this number remains less than a percent (0.52%) of Portland police personnel. However, the distribution of American Indians throughout the police ranks is interesting to note. Of the total of five Portland police personnel who are American Indians, two have been promoted to detective and one to sergeant. There are an additional two who are patrol officers.

Quantifiable change for American Indians in Albuquerque has not been positive since 1997. The city's American Indian population has increased, from 2.6% in 1997 to 5.1% in 2008. However, while the number of American Indian police officers in 1997 was 5, this dropped to 4 in 2010. The percentage of American Indian police officers remains significantly below 1% (0.033%). As was the case in 1996–1997, there has been little or no attention to the recruitment or hiring of American Indians into the police ranks. This echoes the expressed attitudes of city personnel at the time of the study.

It further echoes the urban Indians' lack of focus on integration into city administration or police ranks which was evident during the time period of the study.

Conclusion

It is possible to draw a number of conclusions from these studies. Most importantly even now, in the first years of the twenty-first century, most urban Indians remain invisible to, and on the outside of, elements of the urban power structure, even those sworn to "protect and serve." Yet it is also possible to conclude that continuous improvement can occur and be encouraged.

The continuous improvement model as discussed previously is conditioned upon the concept of and commitment to change. It is a continuum, based on previous accomplishment, and oriented toward progress. The continuous improvement model is defined by the idea that the job is not done. It presupposes the willingness of organizations and individuals involved in an enterprise to look for ways to expand their influence and to improve situations. The best practices analysis in this study shows that police accountability is a journey, not a destination. In some cities, police accountability to American Indian communities is farther along than others. But the journey remains under way in many cities.

During the 13 years from 1997 to 2010, three cities developed or reaffirmed their commitment to police accountability and service to all communities. Unfortunately, while urban Indian populations have increased, the numbers of Native American police personnel and their percentage of representation in the ranks have not increased. There has been little advancement in the idea of focused recruitment or targeted activities that aim to empower the urban Indian communities. The study conducted in 2010 does show positive change over the 1997 and 2007 studies. Perhaps the improvement indicated by the 2010 study shows a municipal willingness to change and a commitment to constructive improvement that may be a cause for hope.

References

Canby, W. C. (2009). *American Indian Law in a Nutshell*. St. Paul, MN: Thomson/ West.

Luna, E. (1997). Special issues for evaluating projects on Indian tribal lands. In M. R. Burt (Ed.), *Evaluation Guidebook* (pp. 233–245). Washington, DC: Urban Institute.

Luna, E. (1999). Police accountability in the American Indian community. *Georgetown Public Policy Review*, 4:2.

Luna, E. and Walker, S. (1997). *A Report on the Oversight Mechanisms of the Albuquerque Police Dept. Prepared for the Albuquerque City Council* (Public Document number OC-5). Albuquerque, NM: City of Albuquerque City Council.

Luna, E. and Walker S. (2000). Institutional structure v. Political will: Albuquerque as a case study in the effectiveness of civilian oversight of police. In A. Goldsmith (Ed.), *Civilian Oversight of Policing: Governance, Democracy and Human Rights* (pp. 83–104). Portland, OR: Hart Pub.

Luna-Firebaugh, E. (2008). *Performance Review of the Independent Police Review Division*. Portland, OR: City of Portland Oregon Mayor's Office. Retrieved from www.portlandonline.com/auditor/index.cfm?a = 245276&c = 44653.

Luna-Firebaugh, E. (2010). *A Study of Police Accountability*. Duluth, MN: Duluth Task Force for Improved Community Police Accountability.

Luna-Firebaugh, E. and Walker, S. (2005). Law Enforcement and the American Indian community: Challenges/obstacles to effective law enforcement. In L. Gould and J. I. Ross (Eds.), *Native Americans and the Criminal Justice System* (pp. 117–134). Boulder, CO: Paradigm Publishers.

Martyn, H. and Schindler, M. (2001). *Giving Power Back to the People: A Six Step Continuous Improvement Model*. Brisbane, QLD: Australian Library and Information Association Conference. Retrieved from http://conferences.alia.org.au/tafe2001/papers/martyn.schindler.html.

Skolnick, J. H., Code blue, *The American Prospect*, November 30, 2002, Retrieved from www.prospect.org/cs/articles?article = code_blue.

St. George, R. and Harris, S. (2008). *Safety and Accountability Audit of the Response to Native Women Who Report Sexual Assault*. Duluth, MN: Mending the Sacred Hoop.

Stone, C. and Bobb, M. (2002). *Civilian Oversight of the Police in Democratic Societies. Global Meeting on Civilian Oversight of Police*. Los Angeles. Retrieved from http://www.vera.org/content/civilian-oversight-police-democratic-societies.

Walker, S. (2005). *The New World of Police Accountability*. Thousand Oaks, CA: Sage Publications.

Medical Examination of Mentally Disordered/ Mentally Vulnerable Detainees in Police Custody in England and Wales

24

DAVID LOWE

Contents

Introduction

The research in this chapter focuses on the medical examinations carried out by Force Medical Examiners (FMEs) on mentally disordered or mentally vulnerable detainees in police custody in England and Wales. The research was carried out on behalf of the UK's Faculty of Forensic and Legal Medicine (FFLM) between November 2010 and May 2011. The reason why only FMEs in England and Wales were subjects of the research rather than the whole of the United Kingdom is that they are governed by the Police and Criminal Evidence Act 1984 (PACE), which does not apply in Scotland or Northern Ireland. Due to previous miscarriages of justice regarding the treatment of mentally disordered and vulnerable detainees in England and Wales, it was decided to assess the impact PACE had had on the treatment of mentally disordered and vulnerable detainees. In addition to this, the FFLM wanted to measure the FMEs' qualifications to examine mentally disordered or vulnerable detainees, and in so doing, the FFLM felt that it was important to know not only the frequency and time spent examining such detainees when in police custody but also the condition of and the medical facilities available in the rooms the FMEs used to carry out the examinations.

PACE was introduced in January 1986 to govern police actions regarding the searching of individuals, the searching of premises, police conduct during investigations (including powers and conduct during arrest, the rights of persons to legal advice, and the questioning of suspects in police custody), and the treatment of detainees in police custody. The part of PACE and the accompanying Codes of Practice relevant to this research is to cover the treatment of detainees in police custody, in particular the treatment of mentally disordered or mentally vulnerable detainees. The Codes of Practice define a mentally disordered or vulnerable detainee as a person of any age who is incapable of understanding the significance of questions or their replies [PACE Codes of Practice Code C Annex E (1)]. This definition is designed to cover a variety of mental conditions suffered by detainees in police custody, thereby ensuring that the detainee receives the appropriate care while in police custody.

It was the point that regarding the appropriate care mentally disordered or vulnerable detainees received in police custody, the FFLM was interested in gathering data. This chapter examines how as a result of the research findings the FFLM brought about changes in FME practice at police station custody suites. The changes introduced by the FFLM were in relation to FME's training to examine mentally disordered or vulnerable persons, improving the condition and facilities of the FME consultation rooms at custody suites and FME recording practices when carrying out examinations on all categories of detainees to determine if they are fit for interview or fit for detention.

Background to the Research

Pre-PACE: The *Lattimore* and *Kisko* Cases

Until PACE was introduced in England and Wales, there were no statutory safeguards in place guiding police action regarding the treatment of persons suffering mental disorder or vulnerability while detained in police custody. Two classic English miscarriage of justice cases, *Lattimore* and *Kisko*, highlight the problems that existed for this category of detainee in police custody prior to PACE. Interviewed by police officers without the presence of an appropriate adult or a legal representative, both Lattimore and Kisko made admissions during their respective suspect interviews. As a result of their admissions, both men were convicted of murder: Lattimore in 1972 and Stefan Kisko in 1975. In both cases, the UK Court of Appeal (CA) held that the admissions of the respective defendants were brought about due to oppressive interviewing. Due to the severe oppressive tactics deployed by the interviewing officers, the Lattimore case was influential in members of the 1981 Phillips Commission recommending the introduction of PACE and the formation of an independent prosecuting body (that became the Crown Prosecution Service in 1986) (Zander 2003, xiii–xiv).

In *R v Lattimore* (1975) 62 Cr. App. R. 53, Colin Lattimore, an 18-year-old with a mental age of an 8-year-old, was arrested in 1972 for the murder of Maxwell Confait. During his police detention, no appropriate adult was present nor was he examined by an FME regarding his fitness for interview. During his interview, Lattimore confessed to killing Confait. At first instance, he was convicted of manslaughter, as the court accepted his defense of diminished responsibility. In upholding Lattimore's appeal, the CA stated that if the police had not relied solely on the admission but also examined other evidence present, that evidence would have shown that Lattimore could not have committed the murder (Webster 2002). Stephan Kisko, an adult with a mental age of a 13-year-old, was arrested for the rape and murder of a young girl, Lesley Moleseed. Like Lattimore, Kisko did not have an appropriate adult nor was he examined by an FME to see if he was fit for interview. Being open to suggestibility, during the sixth interview Kisko admitted to the investigating officers raping and murdering Moleseed. In 1992 his conviction was quashed by the CA. Being critical of the police relying solely on the evidence of Kisko's admission, the CA stated that crucial to the conviction being quashed was the fact that Kisko was unable to produce semen, yet semen was found in Lesley Moleseed's vagina and underwear. Even though DNA evidence was relatively unheard of in 1975, Moleseed's underwear with semen stains on it found at the crime scene was retained by the police. In 1992 the DNA found on the underwear was matched with a sample taken and retained on the UK's DNA database. As a result, the actual offender was traced, arrested, and convicted of Moleseed's murder (Jenkins 2007). These high-profile cases raise the concern of how many other persons suffering from mental disorder or vulnerability during this period were convicted based solely on the evidence of their admission.

Key Rights Introduced by PACE Regarding Mentally Disordered/Vulnerable Detainees

PACE transformed how the police in England and Wales looked after persons detained in police custody. Not only do the police now have statutory powers and obligations, but their actions have to conform to the Codes of Practice that accompany PACE. The Codes of Practice have been introduced to assist police officers applying PACE when carrying out their duties. Although a police officer's failure to comply with the Codes of Practice does not render their action unlawful, it can lead to the acquittal of a defendant [Section 67(10) PACE]. PACE and the Codes of Practice brought in two important developments relating to how all categories of detainees are dealt with while in police detention. This includes the treatment of the mentally disordered or vulnerable detainee.

Approximately 25% of the UK's population experience some form of mental disorder in a given year (Herrington and Roberts 2012, 2), and one consequence of this is the number of detainees suffering from mental disorder or vulnerability being widespread among individuals in police custody in England and Wales, with as many as 45% of detainees having learning difficulties (Herrington and Roberts 2012, 3). Therefore, having such statutory safeguards in place to protect the mentally disordered or vulnerable in police custody is important. However, the first few years after PACE commenced did not provide the intended aegis for all suspects suffering from mental disorder or vulnerability. In *R v Paris, Abdullah and Miller* (1993) 97 Cr. App. R. 99, a case also known as the Cardiff Three, the three defendants were arrested, interviewed, and later convicted of murdering a sex worker in 1986. The UK CA upheld the three defendants' appeals finding the Miller's admissions inadmissible. Not only Miller had a low IQ, but at the time he also suffered from levels of anxiety (O'Mahoney et al. 2012, 4). Without an appropriate adult presence (although a legal representative was present during the interviews), the CA was critical of the police style of questioning. The Court held that during the interview the officers were not questioning Miller but were shouting at him for what they wanted him to say [*R v Paris, Abdullahi and Miller* (1993) 97 Cr. App. R. 99 at p. 103]. This case was instrumental in bringing about a change of attitude in the application of PACE by police officers, especially custody suite staff (O'Mahoney et al. 2012, 5–6).

Such a change of police attitude toward applying PACE provisions is important as a significant development in PACE regarding mentally disordered or vulnerable detainees is the right to have an appropriate adult present (Paragraph 2 Annex E PACE Codes of Practice Code C). The Codes of Practice clearly state that where a person is mentally ill or mentally vulnerable [under section 1(2) Mental Health Act 1983] and may not understand the significance of what is said by the police, an appropriate adult will be called (Note 1G Code C PACE Codes of Practice). Although in all cases he examined in which the detainee was juvenile an appropriate adult was called for, disconcerting is that in England and Wales Reiner found that on many occasions the services of an appropriate adult were not called on by the police for detainees suffering from mental disorder or were mentally vulnerable (2010, 217). This is disconcerting because the role of the appropriate adult is not to act as a passive observer, but PACE states that they are to be active, with their main purpose being to advise and facilitate communication between the police and the mentally disordered or vulnerable detainee who is being interviewed (Code C PACE Codes of Practice, paragraph 11.17).

The person who can act as an appropriate adult for the mentally disordered or vulnerable detainees is

1. A relative, guardian, or other person responsible for his/her care or custody.
2. Someone experienced in dealing with mentally disordered or mentally vulnerable people but who is not a police officer or employed by the police.
3. Failing these, some other responsible adult aged 18 or over who is not a police officer or employed by the police [Code C PACE Codes of Practice Code C paragraph 1.7(b)].

For many mentally disordered detainees, the appropriate adult can be a qualified social worker, but invariably he/she is a trained volunteer from an adult service organization. Pierpoint's study on appropriate adults reveals that the training of the volunteer appropriate adults is very basic (2006, 225). While the volunteers may be well intentioned, Pirepoint found that one consequence of their training being so basic is that many of them do not provide the protection needed when assisting the mentally ill detainee (2006, 226–228). Her recommendation is that appropriate adults should be joined by a mandatory legal adviser in the interview room (2006, 232). Her recommendation should be seriously considered as Sanders et al. (2010, 24) found that even the "professional" appropriate adults can misunderstand what is happening, fail to spot incriminating answers given by the detainee in interview, and feel just as intimidated as the suspect when in the presence of police officers. This is an important issue as fully trained appropriate adults have access to the custody record of mentally ill detainees so as to ensure that they are receiving the appropriate treatment while in custody, including ensuring the detainee has been examined by an appropriately qualified FME and question the custody officers as to which medical treatment the detainee has had.

This leads to the second right PACE introduced regarding mentally disordered or vulnerable detainees—the right to be examined by a registered medical practitioner to assess if detainees suffering from mental illness are either fit for custody or fit to be interviewed (PACE Codes of Practice Code C Paragraph 5 Annex E). In England and Wales, the medical practitioner was invariably the FME. As many of the FMEs employed by police forces in England and Wales were found to be doctors with little or no training in mental illness, amendments were made to PACE in the Police and Magistrates Court Act 1994 allowing state registered nurses trained in treating mental illness as well as FMEs examine detainees to assess if the detainee was either fit for custody or fit for interview. It is important that mentally disordered or vulnerable detainees are correctly examined by suitably qualified FMEs or medical practitioners when determining their fitness for interview as such detainees are susceptible to suggestion by interviewing officers, resulting in them giving responses they think the officers want to hear (Padfield 2000, 129).

It is also important that mentally disordered or vulnerable detainees are examined regarding their fitness for detention or interview by an FME in person at the custody suite and that the FME does not give advice to the police over the telephone as post-PACE there is still an overreliance by the police on the FME's findings. FME practices, such as advising custody officers over the telephone only, under PACE should no longer occur (Jacobson 2008, 14). A good example of the consequences of an FME failing to attend the police station to examine a mentally disordered or vulnerable detainee is seen in *R v Aspinall* (1999) TLR 86, Crim. LR 741. On arrival at the custody suite, Aspinall informed the custody officer that he suffered from schizophrenia and, correctly, the custody officer called an FME to examine Aspinall. Following a telephone conversation with the custody officer and Aspinall, the FME noted that Aspinall was a schizophrenic on medication, and while anxious, he was lucid in thought and orientated in time and space. Over the telephone the FME considered that Aspinall was fit to be interviewed. As a result, he was interviewed without the presence of an appropriate adult or a legal practitioner as he told the custody that he did not want them to be present. At first instance, the trial judge allowed Aspinall's interview evidence to be admitted as he had been rendered fit for interview by the FME. As a result, he was convicted and given a custodial sentence. However, the UK's CA rejected the decision of the court of first instance and held that the interview was inadmissible. The key to their decision was that while a mentally disordered person may appear normal, regardless of this fact, PACE was clear that the safeguards should be put in place and at least an appropriate adult should have been present. While PACE has improved the situation for the mentally disordered or vulnerable detainee in police detention, mistakes are still being made. Citing a Home Office study, Sanders et al. (2010, 203) found that large numbers of detainees died at their own hands, many of whom displayed warning signs but had been declared fit for either detention or interview by the FMEs. They also found that as custody officers want to process all detainees as quickly as possible they "… sometimes try to deliberately keep appropriate adults away from suspects suffering from *mild* disorders or disabilities" (Sanders et al. 2010, 203; my emphasis).

Research Methods

Research Aims

The aim of the research was to ascertain

1. FME's qualifications to conduct examinations of mentally disordered or vulnerable detainees.
2. The frequency FMEs conducted examinations on mentally disordered and vulnerable detainees.
3. FME's opinions of the facilities they had to conduct examinations of mentally disordered and/or vulnerable detainees at police stations.

Questionnaire

As the research was being carried out on their behalf, Chair of the FFLM granted access to the FMEs in England and Wales. However, there was only a short timescale in which the primary research was conducted, and being located all over England and Wales, it was compounded by the geographical location of the FMEs. As a result, quantitative methods were the only viable option open to the researcher. The option taken was to a design and send out questionnaires as they are an economical and effective way of collecting large amounts of data over a short period of time (King and Wincup 2008, 31).

   When drafting the questionnaire, the aim was to combine one that contained a descriptive and exploratory purpose. By description, the data were obtained giving certain characteristic traits of the FME sample. Combining with exploratory questions, the data were obtained revealing FME's knowledge and attitudes toward their role and the conditions they worked in when examining mentally disordered or vulnerable detainees (Bayens and Roberson 2011, 106–107). With the assistance of the Chair of the FFLM, a questionnaire consisting of 13 questions was drawn up and piloted. Question selection and the number of questions were important so as to not deter respondents from completing it. Therefore, the questionnaire not only had to contain medical accuracy but also had to be the right length to encourage completion by the respondents. From their numerous usage of survey questionnaires, Ditton et al. (2000, 147) point out that the quality of the data received from a questionnaire is a function of the types of questions asked. The aim of this research was to have a small number of questions of sufficient quality from which meaningful data were gathered. To help achieve this, the questions were based on the three main categories: behavior, opinion, and knowledge. Bayens and Roberson describe the aims of these categories as follows:

1. Behavior questions—aimed at descriptions of actual experiences, activities, and actions by participants that would have been observable had the researcher been present.
2. Opinion questions—aimed at finding out what people think about something, usually from the aspects of life they have participated in. These questions tell the researcher about people's goals, intentions, desires, and values.
3. Knowledge questions—determine what factual knowledge the respondent has. They are not opinions or feelings, but they represent what is known (Bayens and Roberson 2011, 125).

When piloting the questionnaire, the FFLM Chair ensured that the question construction was accurate in relation to medical terms and practices. The questionnaire consisted of a combination of closed-ended questions with Liggett five-scale answers and open-ended questions allowing for qualitative responses. When piloting the questionnaire with a few of the FMEs, it was checked with the respondents if the questions were relevant, as well as the time it took for respondents to complete it.

Respondent Sample Size

With the FFLM Chair granting access to all the members of the Faculty, the research covered all the FMEs who were governed by PACE in England and Wales. To further encourage the responses, the FFLM Chair e-mailed all of the members of the Faculty with his/her personal endorsement that this research was being carried out on behalf of the FFLM. This clearly assisted, as 108 completed questionnaires returned from the FMEs including practicing physicians, sexual offence examiners, and forensic pathologists that comprised a sample size of 89 FMEs employed by the 42 Home Office police forces in England and Wales. This comprised 21% of the total number of the FMEs employed in England and Wales.

Results of the Data from the Questionnaire

FME Qualifications to Examine Mentally Disordered or Vulnerable Persons in Police Custody

The first two questions were asked to respondents for details of their qualifications and training in mental illness; this included those who had a diploma in treating the mentally ill. Of the 89 FMEs in England and Wales, only 36 (40.4%) received the training and possessed the diploma in treating the mentally ill, with 25 (28%) stating that they had received some form of training in dealing with mentally disordered or vulnerable detainees. However, 28 (31.5%) had received no training at all in examining mentally disordered or vulnerable detainees. This was a major cause for concern as it could result in mentally disordered or vulnerable detainees in police custody being examined by the FMEs without any training or qualifications in dealing with mental health. This situation may change in the near future as 36 (40%) of the respondents who did not possess the diploma in treating the mentally ill indicated that they have taken steps to undergo the training required for the diploma.

The latest piece of research covering an FME's qualification to deal with mentally disordered or vulnerable detainees in the United Kingdom to draw a comparison found that only 18% of FMEs employed by the Metropolitan Police (London and Greater London area) possessed a Diploma in Medical Jurisprudence (Savage et al. 1991, 151). It is possible that the FMEs who do not possess the relevant certification are still capable of performing a satisfactory mental health assessment. The National Criteria for England (The National Reference Group 2009, 1) looks at specific categories of practitioners seeking approval from those with specific psychiatric training to those with general practice experience, forensic physicians, and those falling outside the scope of the Act. In respect of general medical practitioner experience (GP), criterion A states that such practitioners should be members of the Royal College of General Practitioners or Psychiatrists and have had at least 3 years' experience in a principal or salaried post, and undertaken a substantial amount of time in the diagnosis of mental disorder.

Regarding the FMEs in this research, of those who do not have any qualifications relating to examining mentally ill persons, some may be eligible for such certification if they have membership of the FFLM. Under FFLM membership if the respondents have been an FME full time for a period of 6 months or part-time over a 12-month period during which time they carried out four supervised assessments under section 12(2) Mental Health Act 1983, consultants may also be eligible for approval to examine mentally disordered detainees under the Act. Alternatively, if the FMEs have 4 years post registration experience in the relevant areas of mental illness or disorder that includes 4 months in a supervised psychiatric training post, then under their FFLM membership, the FMEs are deemed as suitably qualified to examine mentally disordered or vulnerable detainees in police custody.

There are a number of bands into which such nonapproved FMEs fall to make them satisfactory and competent practitioners for such assessing mentally disordered or vulnerable detainees. For these FMEs to be deemed as satisfactory and competent, they must provide written evidence of any relevant training they have undergone or show that they have undertaken at least 15 assessments of fitness for mentally disordered or vulnerable detainees for custody or interview within the previous 12 months. Approval is not automatic. Every FME applicant is appraised by the FFLM on merit in relation to experience, training, qualifications, and references, as the body itself sees it as important that regarding their fitness for custody or interview, mentally disordered or vulnerable detainees are examined and assessed correctly.

What did come out of this research is the complex system of ascertaining whether an FME is qualified to carry out examinations on mentally disordered or vulnerable detainees. As a result of this research, the FFLM has decided to standardize qualifications for the FMEs working in the custody suites in England and Wales. This will not only make it easier for the FFLM to differentiate FMEs who are qualified to examine mentally disordered or vulnerable detainees, but it will also assist the police custody staff in selecting a suitably qualified FME and subsequently court officials and lawyers, should a case go to court. Also as a result of this research, the FFLM has decided that FMEs who let their approval lapse should not carry out examinations on mentally disordered or vulnerable detainees until their approval to do so is renewed. As a result, the FFLM is compiling a list of suitably qualified FMEs available to assist the police in selecting an FME with the relevant training in mental health to attend the examination.

Frequency FMEs Are Called Out to Examine Mentally Disordered or Vulnerable Detainees

While in 1991 only 5% of FME callouts were related to psychiatric disorder, this research found that this figure had risen. The data revealed that in 16.67% of the cases in which custody officers requested for the services of FME respondents, mentally disordered or vulnerable detainees were to be examined. One problem that did come out of the data was regarding the term "fit for interview." There was no breakdown in the categories of detainees used by FMEs when making their records of examinations to ascertain a detainee's fitness for interview that they carried out at custody suites. Fitness for interview examinations were requested by the police not only for detainees who were mentally disordered or vulnerable, but also for detainees who sustained physical injuries, who were drunk, or who were under the influence of drugs.

As a result of this research, the FFLM has begun to change the recording practices of the FMEs when they examine fitness for detention or fitness for interview, ensuring that FMEs are now specific about the condition of the detainee they examined, that is, whether the detainee was drunk or was suffering from mental disorder or vulnerability.

Conditions of the FME Examination Rooms in Custody Suites in England and Wales

Designed to draw comparisons with previous research carried out in relation to the treatment of mentally disordered or vulnerable persons, respondents were asked to comment on the conditions and facilities in custody suits in England and Wales. This was an important issue for the FFLM. In the questionnaire, the FMEs were given three categories regarding the conditions of FME examination rooms in custody suites: basic, good, and excellent. Basic condition was described as working in a small examination room containing minimal medical supplies to meet FME requirements and having average hygiene. Good condition was described as a decent size FME examination room, containing more than basic medical supplies to meet FME requirements with good level of hygiene. Excellent condition was described as a well-proportioned FME examination room containing a wide variety of medical supplies to meet virtually all FME requirements with a very high standard of hygiene. The responses revealed that 53% of the FMEs rated the custody suites, the rooms, and the facilities where they examined detainees as basic.

One of the FMEs added in the qualitative responses that of the five different custody suites he/she attended, three were basic, one was good, and one was excellent. From the responses given, the variance in conditions of FME examination rooms appears to be dependent on the actual police station building. Some of the custody suites were located in older buildings and were not really suited for an FME's modern-day requirements. In contrast, some of the FMEs work in newly built bespoke custody suites that are either a separate building or attached to traditional police stations. The data showed that the FMEs working in the newly built custody suites have excellent facilities regarding the detention and treatment of detainees. Similar data were found in a report by Owen and Flanagan (2008) and Payton-James et al. (2008). Finding a total lack of hygiene in three London police stations that were built over 50 years ago, Owen and Flanagan stated that these custody suites were inappropriate for the collection of forensic samples (2008, 5). In addition to this, Owen and Flanagan found that there were no controlled drugs cabinet at Peckham station (2008, 10), and most of the medication held on site in all three custody suites were out of date (2008, 10). As a result of the research, the FLLM has recommended to the respective police authorities to allocate a larger percentage of their budget to the conditions and facilities of FME examination rooms.

Length of Time Spent Examining Mentally Disordered or Vulnerable Detainees

This research found that 79% of the 89 FMEs in England and Wales spent between 10 and 20 minutes examining detained persons. This was in line with the study of Savage et al. (1991, 57), which found that 70% of the FMEs researched took on average 15 minutes to examine a detained person in police custody. In this research, one FME spent on average 15 minutes with a detainee, but when it came to mentally disordered or vulnerable detainee, he/she would spent 30 minutes for a mental health assessment. Another FME could spend up to 2 hours if it was a mental health assessment or if the detainee or complainant had been sexually assaulted. Another FME stated that his/her examination took on average 20 minutes per detainee, but added that this figure increased regarding an examination of a detainee with a mental health condition. One of the FMEs stated that an average time spent examining detainees was between 10 and 15 minutes, but added that psychiatric cases take much longer.

The longer an examination taken by an FME on the fitness to detain or the fitness to interview of a mentally disordered or vulnerable detainee, the more pressure the custody officers feel regarding the time such detainees spend in custody. Section 41(2) PACE states that a person can only be kept in police detention without charge for up to 24 hours. This can be extended to 36 hours with a superintendent's authority (section 42 PACE) up to a maximum of 96 hours for indictable offences with a warrant granted by a magistrates' court (section 43 PACE). Having a mentally disordered or vulnerable detainee eats into that time, the time that could be spent processing the detainee and releasing them before the first 6-hour review is due. Sanders et al. (2010, 203) found in their research that after detention has been authorized, the custody clock is running down adding pressure on custody officers to process cases as quickly as possible. As seen from the data in this research, up to an extra hour is added to the time in custody where a mentally disordered or vulnerable detainee is examined by an FME (this is not including the time lapsing from the custody officer calling the FME to the time taken for the FME to arrive at the custody suite and preparing the FME examination room). Regardless of the pressure custody officers may be under, the time taken by the FMEs examining mentally disordered or vulnerable detainees demonstrates how they take their role seriously and are desirous of maintaining professionalism.

The Variance in England and Wales Police Forces as to Who Examines Mentally Ill Detainees

This research found that 56.3% of the 42 police forces in England and Wales run contractually based forensic medical services. Baksi (2009) found that one problem with police forces contracting out medical services is the potential for a standoff between the FMEs and the Metropolitan Police over the terms of a new contract the FMEs were expected to sign. The stand-off was caused by the FMEs who were feeling that the new terms inter-fered with their impartiality when examining detainees in police custody (Baksi 2009, 2). A number of police forces in this research were contracting medical services out to other health-care professionals such as nurses and paramedics. From a number of the FME's responses, there appears to be a degree of resentment by the FMEs toward medical personnel they perceive as less qualified than themselves. The FMEs that raised this resentment saw the move to contracting medical services out to less qualified medical staff as no more than a cost reduction exercise by the police authorities of the respective police forces taking this route. A Somerset FME stated that foren-sic medical services were going through a difficult phase. Expanding on this, he said that outsourcing of services resulted in private companies making money out of the care of vulnerable people who needed better, rather than worse services.

Changes Brought about as a Result of This Research

While only being a short questionnaire, consisting of 13 questions, it pro-vides a snapshot of the current situation in the United Kingdom regarding the FMEs' examination of mentally disordered and vulnerable detainees in police custody in England and Wales. From the data the question-naire produced, the FFLM has already begun to put in place the following changes:

1. Standardizing the qualification of the FMEs to examine mentally disordered and vulnerable detainees in police custody. This will not only allow the FFLM to carry out a skills audit of their members, but assist the police when requiring an FME to examine a mentally dis-ordered or vulnerable detainee and, should a case subsequently go to court, it will assist the court officials and lawyers.
2. Recording practices when the FMEs examine detainees in police cus-tody for their fitness to be interviewed or their fitness to be detained. This has been broken down so the FMEs now record the category of detainee they examine. This includes mentally disordered or vulner-able detainees.
3. Bringing about pressure on relevant police authorities to provide the finance to enable the respective police force's FME examination rooms in custody suites to be upgraded beyond basic facilities. This includes improving the hygiene of the room and ensuring the medi-cation and medical supplies that are within date.

What this research also shows is that for changes to be introduced in policing practice, there does not have to be a grand design research project. A short, simple questionnaire sponsored and designed with the assistance of the body requesting the research can have just as much impact in bringing about change. For this research, the three changes that have been introduced will not only assist custody officers and police staff in ensuring that they have an FME qualified to examine a mentally disordered or vulnerable detainee, thereby reducing the potential for any evidence obtained from that detainee being rendered inadmissible at future trials, but also help in ensuring that the protection of PACE and its Codes of Practice is in place for mentally disordered and vulnerable detainees in England and Wales.

References

Baksi, C. (2009) Doctors put police station detainees at risk, *Law Society Gazette* 32 (7), 5–9.

Bayens, J.G. and Roberson, C. (2011) *Criminal Justice Research Methods*. Boca Raton, FL: CRC Press.

Ditton, J. et al. (2000) Crime surveys and the measurement of problem: Fear of crime, in Jacobson, J. (editor) *No One Knows: Police Responses to Suspects with Learning Disabilities and Learning Difficulties* (pp. 67–82) London: Prison Reform Trust.

Herrington, V. and Roberts, K. (2012) Addressing psychological vulnerability in the police suspect interview, *Policing 6* (1), 1–10.

Jenkins, R. (2007, November 13) Conviction too late for victim of "worst miscarriage of justice" of all time, *The Times*, p. 2.

King, R.D. and Wincup, E. (2008) The process of criminological research, in King, R.D. and Wincup, E. (editors) *Doing Research on Crime and Justice* (2nd edition; pp. 1–15) Oxford: Oxford University Press.

The National Reference Group (2009) *The National Criteria for England* (Revised October 2009) available at www.guideweb.rg.uk (accessed June 10, 2011).

O'Mahoney, B.M. et al. (2012) To challenge, or not to challenge? Best practice when interviewing vulnerable suspects, *Policing 6* (2), 1–13.

Owen, J. and Flanagan, C. (2008) *Report on an Inspection Visit to Police Custody Suites in Southwark Basic Command Unit 21st–22nd April 2008 by Her Majesties Inspectorate of Prisons and Constabularies*. London: HMSO.

Padfield, N. (2000) *Text and Materials on the Criminal Justice System* (2nd edition). London: Butterworths.

Payton-James, N. et al. (2008) Provision of forensic medical services to police custody suites in England and Wales, *Journal of Forensic and Legal Medicine 3* (1), 27–37 doi:10.1016/j.jflm.2008.09.002.

Pierpoint, H. (2006) Reconstructing the role of the appropriate adult in England and Wales, *Criminology & Criminal Justice 6* (2), 219–237.

Reiner, R. (2010) *The Politics of the Police* (4th edition). Oxford: Oxford university Press.

Sanders, A., Young, R., and Burton, M. (2010) *Criminal Justice* (4th edition). Oxford: Oxford University Press.
Savage, S. et al. (1991) *Forensic Medicine Services in the Metropolitan Police Area.* Portsmouth: Institute of Police and Criminological Studies/Health Information Research Service, University of Portsmouth; cited in Kelly et al. The role of the police surgeon, *Policing 9* (2), 148–159.
Webster, R. (2002 January 20) The new injustices, *New Statesman 97* (3).
Zander, M. (2003) *The Police and Criminal Evidence Act 1984* (4th edition). London: Sweet & Maxwell.

Cases Cited

R v Aspinall (1999) TLR 86, Crim. LR 741.
R v Lattimore (1975) 62 Cr. App. R. 53.
R v Paris, Abdullahi and Miller (1993) 97 Cr. App. R. 99.

A Comparative Study of a Centralized and a Decentralized Police System

25

The Plan for Adopting a Decentralized Police System in South Korea

JINWOO PARK AND PETER JOHNSTONE

Contents

Introduction

It is widely accepted among historians that the concepts and practices of modern American police system were originated from the English heritage. Whereas this may not be the complete picture of all policing influences as this overview frequently bypasses the significant influence of France on the English system directly and the US system indirectly, the overall major influence remains located within the early night watch system and the subsequent Metropolitan Police Act of 1829. In England, beginning around AD 900, ordinary citizens played the role of law enforcement with intent to protect their family members and neighbors from criminals and outlaws (Jones and Johnstone 2011). Ten males over the age of 12 formed a group called tithing, and each tithing was responsible for detecting and apprehending its members in case of a criminal event. In turn, 10 tithings were clustered into a hundred, and a constable appointed by a local nobleman was in charge of directing the hundred (Alpert and Dunham 2010). It is believed that the constable was the first law enforcement official who had greater responsibility than simply aiding one's fellow citizen. There also existed night watchmen who patrolled the cities and villages at night to detect criminals and fires, and in such cases, they reported to the constable (Abadinsky and Winfree 1992).

Just as tithings were grouped into hundreds, the hundreds were clustered into shires, which correspond to the concept of counties today, and each shire was supervised by a shire reeve (or sheriff), who was selected by the king. The shire reeve, a chief law enforcement official for the county, performed a wide variety of functions, such as crime investigation, arrest of criminals, and tax collection. In England, the system of sheriffs, constables, and night watchmen continued into the 1700s without significant changes. One noteworthy fact regarding the establishment of early policing system in England was that it was initiated spontaneously by the community members with intent to protect their neighborhoods from both internal and external threats.

In Colonial America, the English police system of sheriff, constable, and night watchmen was easily adapted to the colonies by early settlers. The county sheriff, selected by the local governor, played a primary role in enforcing laws and regulations, especially when the colonies were relatively small and rural. The American sheriffs performed similar task to those of England; their duties included arresting criminals, serving subpoenas, and collecting taxes. Meanwhile, constables and night watchmen performed a wide range of tasks in the larger urban cities and towns, such as Boston, Philadelphia, and New York (Alpert and Dunham 2010). The night watchmen were responsible for reporting fires, raising hue and cry, arresting suspicious persons, and patrolling the streets. Likewise, the constables performed a wide variety of tasks, including taking suspects to the court and terminating health hazards. Even though the sheriffs, constables, and night watchmen carried out the role of law enforcement officials, the manner in which they were organized and operated were far from the concept of modern police system as it is perceived today. In summary, during the early stages of developing a police system for the United States, there were two main influences: an informal system that reflected internal controls suitable for burgeoning agricultural communities, which was most prominent and effective in New England and Southern colonies, and a formal system. The formal system supplemented the informal system in Colonial America and comprised the courts, the government, the sheriffs, and the local constables. Despite ridicule and community disapproval, this formal system continued until the American Revolution and its vestiges remain today (Jones and Johnstone 2011).

Development of Modern Police System: From England to the United States

The English policing system of sheriffs, constables, and night watchmen, which continued largely unchanged for more than 500 years since its establishment, faced significant challenges in the mid-eighteenth century (Alpert and Dunham 2010). During that period, the Industrial Revolution led to the rapid development of large cities in England and the rest of Europe. For example, the population of London nearly doubled from 1750 to 1820 as many people left rural areas and congregated to the city seeking economic opportunities. Rapid industrial growth and unprecedented influx of large population into the cities were inevitably accompanied by a breakdown in social control. A wide variety of problems, such as crime, urban riots, public health, and unemployment, disrupted the city, and the early constable–watchmen system of law enforcement was no longer capable of dealing successfully with those aggravating problems. Consequently, the middle and upper classes, who were concerned about these social problems, recognized the need for more preventive and protective measures and began to seek alternative solutions.

Among various alternatives, the most convincing proposal was replacing the ineffective constable–watchmen system with more powerful and centralized police force. At first, the idea of creating organized and uniformed police force was opposed by numerous politicians and citizens due to the potential threats of excessive governmental control over citizens. However, the advocates of a police force eventually prevailed over the opposing party largely based on the pervasive social disorder and the fear of crime experienced by London citizens. After the perceived successes of the Bow Street Runners and the formalized policing of the River Thames in 1798 (Jones and Johnstone 2011), there followed years of debate that culminated in the first London-wide police force created by the then Home Secretary, Sir Robert Peel. The London Metropolitan Police shared a wide range of similarities with modern police agencies as we see today around the world. They are both uniformed and paid officers, whose primary role is prevention of crime.

During the same time period, the cities and towns in the United States also faced similar problems to those in England: disorder and crime. In addition to these problems, American cities also experienced a unique racial tension, which was largely caused by foreign immigrants, such as Irishmen, Germans, and a growing population of black slaves in the southern states (Alpert and Dunham 2010). These racial and ethnic conflicts led to numerous riots, and when the riots were accompanied by the ever-increasing crimes, such as homicides, robberies, and thefts, citizens felt a loss of social control. By that time, it was apparent that the outdated constable–watchmen police system could not handle the complex problems in the large cities. When the American political forces encountered the demand for an alternative police system, it was natural and easy for them to examine and adopt the police system in England, which was suffering from similar problems.

However, the American police departments did not adopt the London Metropolitan Police system exactly. Instead, they borrowed certain aspects of the system selectively, with most notably the adoption of the preventive patrol concept and uniformed officers. Unlike the highly centralized London police, however, American police system pursued a decentralized style of local and municipal governments. While the London police were perceived as an extension of national government, American police departments were largely under the control of different local and municipal political factions. In the United States, political leaders selected and recruited police officers, whereas London Metropolitan Police hired officers who met certain objective criteria (Jones and Johnstone 2011).

Because American people put great emphasis on human rights and freedom, they were opposed to the notion of centralized police force, which has great possibility of governmental control over them. In fact, the police forces were viewed as delegates of citizens, who were given the right to use force on behalf of the ordinary citizens for more effective and better protection of the citizens' rights. For this reason, local and city residents preferred to have police departments under their immediate control with primary focus on serving the citizens' interest (Marion 2002). Consequently, American police departments differed considerably depending on the political factions and local governments in power.

Contemporary Law Enforcement Agencies in the United States

The law enforcement system in the United States basically consists of three different levels of agencies depending on the jurisdictions and boundaries of authority in which they operate: local, state, and federal agencies.

Throughout American history, police activities have been viewed as primarily the responsibility of local and municipal governments. Indeed, state constitutions permit local governments to organize, recruit, train, operate, and pay police forces to protect their citizens (Abadinsky and Winfree 1992). Local police departments are generally in charge of ordinary protective duties such as enforcing laws and regulations, apprehending criminals, preventing crimes, and restoring public order. As of September 2008, there were 12,501 local police departments in the United States with 593,000 full-time employees, and they accounted for approximately 52% of all local and state law enforcement employees combined. Among these agencies, more than 50% of all departments employed less than 10 full-time officers, whereas only 5% (638 agencies) employed more than 100 full-time officers. Surprisingly, those 638 agencies out of the total 12,501 departments employed 61% of all local police officers. To reiterate just one department, New York Police Department, employed 36,023 full-time sworn officers (Bureau of Justice Statistics 2011).

Because of the huge variation in size among departments and environments in which they operate, it is almost impossible for the agencies to establish one single standard of operation. In fact, the operation of police departments varies in a wide variety of aspects, including officer selection, training procedures, organization, budgeting, and department policies. For example, while larger police departments tend to apply higher standards in their officer selection process, smaller departments implement less screening methods in the process. To be specific, police departments serving more than 1 million people used psychological evaluation (100%), written aptitude test (100%), personality inventory (85%), and polygraph examination (77%) more frequently than departments serving less than 2500 people. These smaller departments required psychological evaluation (48%), written aptitude test (20%), personality inventory (38%), and polygraph examination (10%) less frequently. Likewise, the number of training hours required for new officers differs significantly among agencies from 691 hours for the smallest departments to 1783 hours for the second largest departments (Bureau of Justice Statistics 2010). Organization and administration of the larger departments are also substantially different from those of smaller departments. In large urban police departments, such as New York Police Department (NYPD), they are divided into subunits depending on a geological and functional basis with strong chain of command, and each officer usually performs one single specialized duty (Abadinsky and Winfree 1992). On the other hand, in smaller departments, the structure is much simpler, and it is not uncommon for one officer to perform multiple duties at the same time.

Similar to the local police departments, county sheriffs also play a significant role in providing law enforcement services to the citizens. As of 2008, there exist a total of 3063 sheriffs' offices across the nation, and they employed around 31% of all local and state officers (Marion 2002). County sheriffs perform conventional law enforcement tasks, such as responding for calls for service, enforcing traffic laws, and providing patrol. In addition to these traditional functions, county sheriffs are also engaged in court-related duties such as providing court security. Moreover, around 75% of all sheriffs' offices are responsible for operating at least one county jail (Marion 2002). In general, the sheriffs in the Western states provide a full range of services and possess some degree of political power, whereas the sheriffs in the Eastern states provide only limited services. With a few exceptions, most county sheriffs are elected officials.* For this reason, they are usually supported by organized political parties, and obtaining the position of a sheriff depends more on political royalty than one's competence to perform the task (Abadinsky and Winfree 1992).

State Law Enforcement Agencies

With the exception of Hawaii, all other 49 states in the United States have a certain form of state law enforcement agency established and operated by the state government (Anderson, Mangels, and Dyson 2003). In 2008, state law enforcement agencies employed 93,148 full-time officers, and accounted for 8% of all local and state full-time employees (Bureau of Justice Statistics 2008). Although the title and structure of each agency vary substantially from state to state, in general, state police agencies can be divided into the following two groups: full-service agencies and partial-service agencies.

Full-service agencies are authorized to perform a full range of tasks ranging from regulating the state's highways to enforcing all state criminal laws. Probably, the best-known example of the full-service state police agency is the Texas Rangers. In the states with full-service authority, state police officers are responsible for maintaining law and order throughout the state, especially in the rural areas with lower population density where local or county police forces are not available. However, in a majority of the cases, local police departments and county sheriff's offices are still the primary enforcer of the laws and provide most everyday services to the citizens. In contrast, state police mainly assists local law enforcement agencies that lack adequate resources to perform certain tasks. They may engage in state-wide criminal investigations or may be asked to perform certain duties on request.

---

* In Hawaii; Rhode Island; and the five boroughs that comprise New York City, Nassau County, and Westchester County (New York), Dade County (Florida), and Denver County, the sheriff is appointed.

Unlike the full-service agencies, the power of the partial-service state agencies is limited by either jurisdiction or types of crimes they are authorized to control. These agencies usually enforce the traffic-related laws on the state's highways, and they are also in charge of the issuance and management of driver's license and motor vehicle inspections. Some of these agencies have an independent criminal investigation bureau to investigate major crimes and state-wide crimes. They also provide certain services to support the local police agencies. For example, forensic laboratories are operated by the state police in most states and provide services regarding the evaluation of evidence to local police departments that lack these facilities (Bureau of Justice Statistics 2010).

Along with the primary state police agencies, highway patrols, and investigative units, there are more than 350 state-level special jurisdiction law enforcement agencies that exercise a certain degree of investigative and policing powers under specific circumstances. These agencies either serve a special geographic jurisdiction or have special investigative or enforcement responsibilities. For example, state park rangers maintain the law and order and prevent crimes against visitors in a state's public park system. Likewise, some states allocate state police officers to the state-run university and college campuses, and they perform law enforcement duties within the campuses. On other occasions, some agencies are responsible for the enforcement of just one specific type of laws such as alcohol/tobacco laws, agricultural laws, or narcotics laws (Marion 2002).

Federal Law Enforcement Agencies

As American society became more complex and dependent upon technology and transportation, many offenses have become interstate, and the jurisdiction of one state was no longer sufficient to deal with such interstate offending (Falk 2010). Because the United States has not had a national police force such as those now being developed in many European countries, there was traditionally no countrywide agency that could deal with burgeoning cross-border criminality. This resulted in the growing belief among Americans that the federal government needed to take responsibility for investigating nationwide crimes. Consequently, the US congress authorized various federal agencies to enforce specific laws across the entire nation.

As of 2004, there exist 65 federal law enforcement agencies in the United States, and they employed approximately 105,000 full-time officers authorized to carry firearms and make arrests in the territory of the United States (Bureau of Justice Statistics 2006). The Department of Homeland Security (DHS), which was created after the terrorist attacks in November 9, 2001, employed the largest number of officers, and they accounted for about 40%

of all federal law enforcement officers. Under the DHS, the US Customs and Border Protection (CBP) is, *inter alia*, responsible for protecting the nation by preventing terrorist attacks, illegal weapons, illegal drugs, and materials dangerous to agriculture from entering the United States. Next, the Department of Justice was the second largest employer, and it accounted for approximately 35% of all full-time federal officers. The department includes agencies such as the Federal Bureau of Investigation (FBI); the Federal Bureau of Prisons (BOP); the Drug Enforcement Administration (DEA); the Bureau of Alcohol, Tobacco, Firearms, and Explosives (ATF); and the US Marshalls Service (Bureau of Justice Statistics 2006). In addition to these large agencies, numerous less-known agencies under various branches of the federal government perform specific federal law enforcement tasks.[*]

History and Development of Korean Police System

Before the fourteenth century, there was no official police organization in Korea, and military personnel were in charge of maintaining peace and social order (Hinton and Newburn 2009). In 1471, a well-organized semi-military police agency, named "Po Do Cheong," was formally created to deal with an increasing problem of pervasive thievery. The officials, called "Po Do Ri," were responsible for apprehending thieves and patrolling streets at night. Each Po Do Cheong was headed by an army general, and he exercised almost unlimited authority within its jurisdiction. Inconsistent with its original emphasis on controlling crime, however, Po Do Cheong had changed to take on more actions as a military army (Shin 2010).

In 1894, Po Do Cheong was abolished and replaced by a modernized national police force, called "Kyeong Mu Cheong" (Bureau of Police Affairs), as part of the reform movement to colonize the Korean peninsula by Japanese government. The paramilitary and centralized Bureau of Police Affairs duplicated the Japanese police system, which itself followed a continental European policing style. Provincial police bureaus, police stations, and mini-police stations were established across the nation, and a new rank system was employed. During that period, Japanese personnel had significant impact on policing in Korea, and Japanese military police personnel were deployed in major cities to investigate anti-Japanese movements.[†] In 1910, Japan officially annexed Korea, and the Korean police was placed

---

[*] For example, the US Postal Inspection Service, the Internal Revenue Service (IRS), the National Park Service, the US Capitol Police, the Bureau of Diplomatic Security, and the US Fish and Wildlife Service.

[†] A law was enacted to permit Japanese personnel to be hired as police officers working for Korean government, and by 1908, approximately 40% of police officers in Korea were Japanese (1863 out of total 4991 police officers) (Hinton and Newburn 2009, 78).

under the direct control of the Japanese Governor General. Since then, the centralized national police in Korea was used by the Japanese government to suppress and rule Korean citizens, and the police personnel were often brutal and violent on implementing their duties (Hinton and Newburn 2009). They performed civilian police work along with other tasks, including collecting information and promoting the use of Japanese language. Numerous Korean people were tortured and killed by the Japanese-led police force until the end of World War II.

The Japanese government's 35-year colonial occupation of the Korean Peninsula finally came to an end with the Japan's surrender to the Allies in 1945. After independence, the United States controlled the South, and the Soviet Union occupied the North. The US Army Government in South Korea established the Korean Police on October 21, 1945, and a series of structural and functional policing reforms were followed. Police duties were restricted to controlling crime, maintaining social order, and gathering information on communists (Hinton and Newburn 2009). Numerous Korean people were hired as new police officers to fill the space once occupied by the Japanese personnel. However, without adequate background checks and no specific employment suitability criteria, lots of unqualified people and criminals were recruited (Shin 2010). Furthermore, facing the shortage of human resources, the US Army Government decided to fill high-ranking positions with those former Korean police officers who had worked for the Japanese government. In fact, 82% of newly hired high-ranking police officers were these former police officers (Shin 2010).

Three years after the US Army Government's reign ended, the Republic of Korea was established in 1948, and the national police were reorganized under the direct control of the Ministry of Home Affairs. Two years later, political and ideological tensions between the South and North eventually resulted in the outbreak of the Korean War. During wartime, along with ordinary police duties, the Korean police actively participated in military operations including fighting against enemy forces. As a result, during the 3 years of the Korean War, over 10,000 police officers were killed, and a large number of officers were injured (Shin 2010). The active involvement of the Korean police in the Korean War made it almost impossible to develop a politically neutral and democratized police force. Moreover, the unstable society after the war made the Korean government utilize the police as an effective political tool to maintain power and authority.

Following the successful military coup by Park Chung-hee in 1961, who became the president, consecutive military regimes were established up until 1993. During this period, Korean government was essentially authoritative and dictatorial, and government depended deeply on the police to control citizens and to suppress demonstrations and political opponents. Military personnel were appointed to high-ranking police positions, and many police officers were deployed to gather information concerning antigovernmental movements. As public demonstrations against authoritarian military governments increased significantly, numerous police personnel were engaged in breaking up and arresting the demonstrators. The abuse of human rights and excessive and brutal use of force by the police were common,* and this led to further public outcry against the government.

As Korean society was swiftly democratized, however, the necessity to stop the political manipulation of the police by a ruling government and to assure the autonomy of the police was increased. As a result, in 1991, the Police Act was enacted, substantially modifying the structure of the Korean police. The current Korea National Police Agency (KNPA) was established as an independent agency, outside of the direct control from the Ministry of Interior. In addition, the National Police Board, which consists of seven civilians, was created to assure political neutrality of the police. The Board provides advice and recommendations on budget, equipment, and administration policy. In 1999, the Korean police implemented a major reform movement, called "Operation Grand Reform 100 Days," to establish police legitimacy and to improve relationships with the public.† Police administrators adopted a new operational theme focusing on the service roles of the police and the importance of police–citizen partnerships. Consequently, various programs were initiated, including a citizen's police academy and volunteer community patrol program. Similarly, a police reform committee was created under the KNPA to provide a plan for police reform in 2003, and the Korean police continue to strive to regain police legitimacy and to improve the image of the police (Hinton and Newburn 2009).

The Contemporary Police System in South Korea

As of 2009, a total of 99,554 sworn police personnel and 3,842 civilian officers were working for police agencies in South Korea. Unlike the law enforcement officers in the United States, who are employed and paid by individual agencies, the entire police officers in South Korea are employed by a single national government. The national government is responsible for the selection, training, and management of the entire police force within the country (Korea National Police Agency 2010).

---

* For example, during a 1987 police interrogation of an antigovernment student organization, Pak Chong Chol, a 21-year-old Seoul National University student, died after being held under the water and forced to swallow it.
† This reform was heavily influenced both by President Kim Dae-jung's massive national reform movement emphasizing the importance of democracy and human rights and by the popularity of community policing in the United States.

The Korea National Police Agency

Unlike the decentralized police system in the United States, South Korea has sustained a highly centralized national police system since its establishment of modern police force in 1894. The National Police Agency is located in Seoul, the capital city of South Korea, and is led by the Commissioner General. The Commissioner General is the highest ranking position in the force. The Commissioner General is appointed by the President of South Korea from a pool of four deputy commissioners. The National Police Agency generally performs tasks concerning administration and management of the entire national police force, so it is uncommon for the agency itself to engage directly in regular law enforcement activities (with the exception of national security threats or nationwide issues). In practice, the National Police Agency is responsible for the formulation of general policy, distribution of resources, and supervision of metropolitan and provincial police agencies.

The National Police Agency largely consists of seven bureaus—Administration, Safety, Investigation, Security, Intelligence, National Security, and Foreign Affairs—and four divisions—Planning, Information and Communication, Traffic Management, and Inspection. In addition, a total of four national police training institutions are being operated under the direction of the National Police Agency. The National Central Police Academy is responsible for training new recruits, whereas the Police Training Institute provides in-service training courses for continuing officers. The National Police University is in charge of selecting 120 high-school graduates each year and training them to be police leaders. It also provides training courses for police executives and supervisors. Finally, the Police Investigation Academy is a specialized training facility that provides professional and contemporary investigation skills and theory classes for crime investigators.

Metropolitan and Provincial Police Agency

The entire territory of South Korea is geographically divided into seven metropolitan cities and nine provinces. Each metropolitan city or province operates its own police agency, so a total of 16 metropolitan and provincial police agencies are under the direct supervision and control of the National Police Agency.* With minor variations, these agencies have a similar organizational structure to that of the National Police Agency and are responsible for administering police stations and subpolice stations within their

---

* Gwangju and Daejeon Provincial Police Agencies were established in 2007.

geographic jurisdiction. The head of metropolitan or provincial agency is either Deputy Commissioner or Assistant Commissioner depending on the size and population of the jurisdiction in which they serve. For example, Seoul Metropolitan Police Agency and Gyeonggi Provincial Police Agency, which are the first and second largest agencies in South Korea, respectively, are directed by the Deputy Commissioner. In contrast, the other 14 metropolitan and provincial police agencies are headed by the Assistant Commissioner.

Although the major task of the metropolitan and provincial police agencies is administration and supervision of local police stations within their jurisdiction, unlike the National Police Agency, it is very common for them to be directly engaged in law enforcement activities concerning province-wide crimes. For instance, each metropolitan and provincial police agency operates criminal investigation unit to deal with crimes, such as drug and organized gang crimes. Given that local police departments are not capable of dealing with these types of crimes due to resource restraints, metropolitan and provincial level investigation units play an important role in the law enforcement against these crimes. Likewise, metropolitan and provincial police agencies also operate highway patrols, and they are responsible for enforcing traffic laws and securing road safety on the highways within their jurisdictions. In addition, some larger metropolitan police agencies operate Special Weapon and Tactics (SWAT) to detect and prevent terrorist threats and attacks. They are also responsible for dealing with complicated cases including crimes involving hostages.

Local Police Stations and Subpolice Stations

As of 2010, there were a total of 247 local police stations across the nation, and they were under the direct control and supervision of metropolitan or provincial police agencies to which they were attached.* Each police station is categorized as a first-, second-, or third-level station, depending on the size of population within the jurisdiction. A police station is classified as the first level when its serving population is more than 250,000. A second-level police station is in charge of a midsized city where the population is between 150,000 and 250,000. Finally, a third-level police station is located in a rural area with

---

* Three new police stations—Anyang Manan, Bucheon Ojeong, and Yongin Suseo station—opened as recently as in July 2010. Also, note that the number of local police stations within a metropolitan or provincial police agency varies significantly depending on the size of each agency. For example, while Gyeonggi Provincial Police Agency operates 41 police stations, Jeju Provincial Police Agency operates only 3 police stations.

a population fewer than 150,000. Most police stations are categorized as the first level due to the fact that over two-thirds of Koreans live in metropolitan areas. There are multiple police stations in some larger cities, but generally there is one police station per city. Each local police station is directed by a senior superintendent, and he/she is responsible for administering and supervising the department and its officers.

A local police station generally consists of five sections—Administration, Safety, Investigation, Security and Traffic, and Intelligence and National Security—and an inspection division.* The function of local police stations is very similar to that of the local police departments in the United States. They provide ordinary law enforcement services to their citizens. A unique characteristic of Korean police system is the operation of subpolice stations since its establishment (Hinton and Newburn 2009). Each police station operates varying number of subpolice stations depending on the population in the jurisdiction. Currently, there are 423 regional patrol stations and 1517 mini-police stations across the country. Regional patrol stations are generally located in urban areas with high population density, whereas mini-police stations tend to be operating in areas with a smaller population.† These subpolice stations operate 24 hours a day and 7 days a week on a three-shift or four-shift system. In general, a senior inspector is responsible for the management of a regional patrol station, and mini-police station is headed by an inspector.

More than 40% of the total police officers in South Korea are assigned to subpolice stations, and they perform a wide variety of tasks. The major duty of subpolice stations is prevention of crime by providing intensive patrol services within their beats. They are also in charge of responding to calls for service. Upon detecting a criminal event, they immediately engage in apprehending criminals and perform a brief investigation of the suspects. In addition, they perform the task of enforcing traffic laws and regulations and act as community policing officers having direct contact with the residents and providing various services. It is believed that the subpolice station system plays a significant role in deterring crime and maintaining a low rate of crime in South Korea and improves citizen satisfaction about the police.

---

* The actual organizational structure of each police station varies depending on the characteristics of a specific jurisdiction. For instance, some police stations distinguish Security section from Traffic section and operate two independent sections rather than one section.

† There were 825 regional patrol stations and 529 mini-police stations in 2006. Since then, the number of regional patrol stations declined significantly, whereas the number of mini-police stations increased substantially. This trend shows that the newly adopted regional patrol station system replacing mini-police station since 2003 was not viewed successful.

Issues about Adopting a Decentralized Police System in South Korea

Since the establishment of the first modern police force in 1894, South Korea has experienced a series of periods characterized by extremely unstable societal and political circumstances. Korea peninsula was ruled by the Imperial Japanese government for nearly 35 years in the early twentieth century, and shortly after the independence, ideological conflicts and political intervention of the United States and the Soviet Union led to the Korean War between the South and the North. The dynamics of extreme political instability and social disorder continued throughout consecutive military regimes up until the early 1990s. The unique conditions of South Korea characterized by national security threats from the North and the demonstrations against the authoritative military governments have resulted in the political manipulation of police force as an effective tool to protect the governments and to suppress the citizen's opposition (Chungbuk Research Institute 2010). As a result, Korean police were generally considered as a limb of the ruling governments, which lacked political neutrality and democratic principles. However, as Korean society began to be rapidly democratized since the early 1990s, the necessity for preventing the abuse of authority and for securing political neutrality of the Korean police increased significantly at the same time. Consequently, numerous scholars and political figures began to assert the necessity of separating police force from the direct control of the national government and adopting a decentralized police system to accomplish the democratization of Korean police (Hinton and Newburn 2009).

In addition to the political neutralization of the police, the controversy of adopting decentralized police system was fueled by the discrepancy between the administration of a local government and a centralized national police force. South Korea adopted a system of self-governing local body in 1991 when the municipal assemblymen were directly elected by citizens for the first time. Later, in 1995, mayors and governors of counties and provinces were elected directly by residents, which eventually led to the era of local governments. The system of local governments has continued in South Korea, and the fifth election of governors and mayors took place in June 2010. Prior to 1995, mayors and governors in South Korea were appointed by the governmental officials. However, the administration of police has been still under the direct control of national government, and this is a huge contradiction given that almost two decades have passed since the initiation of the local government system. Currently, with the exception of Jeju province, provincial and local governments have no authority or responsibilities for operating police departments in their regions (Shin 2010). The centralized police system in South Korea makes it almost, if not entirely, impossible for police departments to provide law enforcement services adequate to the unique demands and conditions of each local government (Shin 2010). For this reason, the adoption of decentralized police system has been considered as a prerequisite to provide effective and customized law enforcement services.

On the other hand, opponents of a decentralized police system have posed substantial questions about the necessity and effectiveness of adopting a decentralized system given the unique characteristics of South Korea. In support of this, countries established on the basis of federalism, such as the United States, have traditionally embraced the concept that each state has the authority to administer its own autonomous state and local government. Consequently, in those countries, law enforcement activities have also been perceived to be the responsibilities of the state and local governments. This is not the model that South Korea has followed where a centralized model, characterized by a strong chain of command, has dominated throughout the country's history. Furthermore, the unique political situation of the Korean peninsula (and sustained potential threats by the North) requires a policing model that can effectively respond to policing issues associated with threats to national security. Furthermore, although recent events would suggest that it is unlikely in the short term, should the North and South unify in the future; a national police force would be significantly more effective in dealing with any large-scale social disorder than the fragmentary response that local forces might provide.

So far, various historical and political factors surrounding the issues about adopting a decentralized police system in South Korea have been explored. Before ultimately reaching to a detailed discussion of adopting a decentralized police system in South Korean social contexts, it is essential to examine the advantages and disadvantages of the centralized and decentralized police system in general. Recognizing the benefits and drawbacks of each system will provide some backgrounds conducive to a more in-depth discussion about South Korean police system in specific.

Advantages and Disadvantages of a Centralized and a Decentralized Police System

A centralized national police system has a wide range of advantages. First, because organization and administration of police force is universal throughout the entire nation, it is possible to respond more swiftly to emergencies and national security threats under the direct control of the central government. Second, cooperation with other police departments and other agencies is much easier than in a decentralized police system, so the performance of police duties can be readily supported by such external forces. Third, due to the fact that the authority of national police applies to the entire country, officers can deal with a broad range of crimes across different juris-dictions. Fourth, a single national organization facilitates the establishment and management of facilities that require a huge amount of budget, such as training institutes or crime laboratories (Chungbuk 2010). Fifth, it is pos-sible to appoint a skilled and trained officer to a specific position on demand. Finally, police officers can perform their duties free of any administrative intervention by local political parties, thus assuring internal organizational stability (Shin 2010).

Conversely, a centralized police system has multiple disadvantages at the same time. To begin with, instead of focusing on traditional police responsibilities to protect citizens and properties, police might be politically manipulated by the central government to perform duties in favor of the government's interests (Shin 2010). Accordingly, police might be viewed as a representative of the central government rather than a representative of the community they serve. Historical events that took place in countries adopting a centralized police system have clearly demonstrated the political manipulation of police in reality (Chungbuk 2010). In addition, hierarchical organization produces an authoritative and suppressing impression to cit-izens. Second, a centralized police system makes it difficult to implement policing strategies appropriate to specific regional circumstances due to mul-tiple reasons including budget. Third, because police officers do not have inti-mate connections with the community members they serve, it is difficult to understand and provide law enforcement services that community members actually need. Finally, the transfer of high-ranking officers is frequent, so they are usually not highly concerned with the local interests (Shin 2010). In addition, officers who are asked to work in rural areas are susceptible to low morale if they are required to separate from their family.

Not surprisingly, the major disadvantages of a centralized police sys-tem can be translated into the advantages of a decentralized police system. Given the contradicting theoretical basis on which the two police systems were established, it is reasonable that the decentralized police system has the advantages, the lack of which the centralized police system was criticized for. It is possible to accomplish political neutrality of the police force by prevent-ing direct intervention from the central government. However, in countries with a centralized police system, it is almost impossible for the police force to be free from external political influences. For instance, high-ranking offi-cers in South Korea are appointed by the president following recommenda-tions by the Commissioner General and the Secretary of the Ministry of the Public Administration and Security. Consequently, support from powerful political parties is viewed as a critical element to be promoted into high-ranking positions, so political figures exercise substantial influences on the police administration. Under the decentralized police system, however, each police department is attached to and managed by a local government and is independent from the central government. Therefore, it is unlikely that local police departments are open to the same level of potential political influence by the central government; each local police department can operate a flexible organization adequate to the unique characteristics and specific needs of the area it polices. As a result, it is possible to provide customized law enforcement services in response to the circumstances of each community. Unlike the centralized police system, decentralized police officers are hired by local governments, and they are paid by the community members they serve. Moreover, once they become a police officer in a certain jurisdiction, it is common that they work for a long period or continue their entire career in one jurisdiction. Consequently, police officers tend to feel a higher degree of attachment to the community they serve, and in turn, they have greater responsibility to secure safety and order of the community; community members are also more favorable to police officers and are willing to cooperate to police duties (Shin 2010). Also, a decentralized police system increases the opportunity of community members to participate in police activities both directly and indirectly. Community members can provide their opinions about specific policing policies and participate in decision making. In addition, supervision and direct control by community members contribute to prevent police corruption and abuse of authority. Finally, combining police administration and general public administration reinforces the efficiency of the local government and enables local governments to provide complete administrative services to citizens.

Decentralized police systems also produce a series of disadvantages. First, it is difficult to respond to a number of intranational and transnational crimes. As information and communication technology and transportation have developed rapidly, police activities, such as crime investigation and traffic law enforcement, have also become a nationwide matter. In this context, local police forces that have restricted authority within a certain jurisdiction are not capable of dealing with more complex and transient criminality. In addition, given the absence of a national police headquarters, cooperation with other police departments or other governmental agencies is more difficult. Second, because police departments are attached to local governments, police officers are highly exposed to the influences of local political parties (Chungbuk 2010). Considering that mayors and governors are political figures that belong to a specific party, there is a substantial risk that they might operate police departments arbitrarily. In addition, the appointment of a police chief largely depends on who becomes a mayor or governor, so appointments are highly influenced by local elections and can result in political corruption of police (Chungbuk 2010). Third, financial problems of some local governments might result in low-quality policing services. Conversely, local governments with plentiful resources are able to provide high-quality services and the discrepancy of quality of policing services among local governments could lead to the overall societal dissatisfaction and instability across the country (Shin 2010). Finally, the absence of a national organization and the relatively small budgets of local police departments make it difficult to establish and operate training facilities or criminal laboratories (Chungbuk 2010).

A Plan for Adopting a Decentralized Police System in South Korea

The current police system in South Korea is significantly different from that of the United States in almost every aspect. Unique historical and political circumstances in South Korea have resulted in the formation and operation of a centralized police system since its establishment as a nation state. As Korean society began the process of democratization rapidly in the early 1990s, the demand for adopting a decentralized police system has increased.

Since the establishment of the Republic of Korea in 1948, the effort to adopt a decentralized police system has been continued with each government. However, it had always been curtailed at the initial stages of planning and discussion and had never been actualized until the establishment of the Kim Dae-jung administration in 1998. Prior to the early 1990s, national security threats from the North and consecutive military regimes significantly restricted the efforts and debates to adopt a decentralized police system. The implementation of a decentralized police system was one of his key presidential election pledges. After he took office, the ruling political party began to actively participate in creating a plan for adopting a decentralized police system.

The Kim Dae-jung administration established several key principles for adopting a decentralized police model in South Korea. First, police duties should be divided into national police duties and local police duties; national police duties to be performed by national police officers or to be delegated to local autonomous police forces. In contrast, local police duties are to be conducted independently by local autonomous police forces. Instead of adopting a complete decentralized police system like the American system, a compromised police system of national police force and local autonomous police force was proposed. Second, considering the geographical aspects of the country, the tendency of cross-region crime, special security threats from the North, and the poor financial status of local governments, autonomous police forces should be established in metropolitan cities and at the province level. Third, police committees are to be established to ensure democracy and fairness of police administration. A national police committee is to be established under the direction of the prime minister, and it is responsible for administering national police agency. Similarly, metropolitan mayors and provincial governors are to establish local police committees to administer local autonomous police agency. Both police committees are in charge of making policies and standards of policing in their jurisdiction, and national and local police committees have a supervisory authority upon national and local police agencies, respectively. Fourth, national and local police agencies have an obligation to collaborate with each other, and local police agencies are not subordinate to the national police agencies in general. However, in cases of national emergencies and large-scale riots, national police chief can direct and command local police chief.

Based on these principles, the Kim Dae-jung administration prepared a bill for adopting a decentralized police system in 1999; however, the bill was never submitted to the National Assembly. The failure to move this forward can be attributed to various reasons. Primarily, conflicts among agencies prevented the adoption of a decentralized police system, that is, conflicts between the central government and local governments, conflicts between the ruling political party and the opposition party, and conflicts between police and prosecutor's office. For example, local governments strongly opposed to the bill due to the potential financial burdens adoption would impose (Shin 2010). In addition, the Democratic Party led by President Kim Dae-jung failed to hold a majority in the following election, so the political power to pass the bill was significantly reduced. Meanwhile, there also existed internal opposition among police officers on the ground that their status and job security would be weakened. Many police officers considered potential assignment to a rural office to be a demotion compared with duties in large cities. All the circumstances described above made the issue highly controversial, and the bill was eventually abandoned by the end of the Kim Dae-jung administration (Shin 2010). Despite the failure during the Kim Dae-jung administration, the succeeding Roh Moo-hyun administration continued to strive to adopt a decentralized police system upon taking office in 2002. Specifically, a Police Innovation Committee was established in the National Police Agency, and a Decentralized Police Task Force Team was established in the Presidential Committee on Government Innovation and Decentralization. These groups studied police systems in France, Spain, and Italy, and eventually submitted a government plan for adopting a decentralized police system in 2004 (Shin 2010). Subsequently, the Decentralized Police System Promotion Bureau, which consists of both central and local governmental officials, was created to implement the plan, and as a result, Decentralized Police System Act was written. After minimal revision through the Legislative Office, the Act was finally submitted to the National Assembly in November 2005 (Shin 2010).

The most significant difference between the Decentralized Police System Act and the bill proposed during the Kim Dae-jung administration was that local autonomous police department were to be established at the local government level instead of at the metropolitan city and province level. However, the

Roh Moo-hyun administration also acknowledged the necessity of a national police force given the history of South Korea in that it had maintained a centralized national police system throughout its history. Consequently, a compromised and dualistic police system was proposed to minimize the negative opinion and to minimize objections against implementation. Specifically, South Korean policing would comprise two forces; a national police and a local autonomous police coexisting in a certain jurisdiction while performing different duties. A national police force with responsibility for tasks that require uniformity throughout the entire country, such as intelligence, national security, foreign affairs, and major crime investigation, and a number of local autonomous police forces engaged in patrol, crime prevention, traffic law enforcement, governmental facility security, and special judicial police activities. Both forces are designed to be equal and parallel in relationship, and not one agency is subordinate to the other agency. Local autonomous police officers are to be hired directly by mayors and governors of counties, and they hold the status of local governmental officials. Basically, each local government is accountable for the budgets necessary to establish and operate a local autonomous police force, but at the initial stage, the central government could provide subsidies for successful establishment of the new system (Shin 2010). In addition, given the financial restraints of local governments, the national police will provide training courses for the new local autonomous police officers. Finally, the Decentralized Police System Act mandated interchanges of personnel between the national police and the local autonomous police to reinforce connections.

In addition to the Act, the Roh Moo-hyun administration planned to conduct pilot operations of a decentralized police system in selected local autonomous governments. Evaluating a total of 39 candidates, the government selected 17 local governments across the country (Shin 2010). One local government from each metropolitan city and province was chosen with the exception of Seoul metropolitan city and Gyeonggi province where due to size two local government forces were established. Pilot operation of the decentralized police system was planned to examine the suitability of the model in real settings so that if any problem is detected it could be revised prior to the application to the entire country. Under the assumption that the Decentralized Police Act would be passed as planned, the pilot operation was supposed to initiate in the second half of 2006. However, the Act did not pass in the National Assembly, and the plan for pilot operation was automatically abandoned (Chungbuk 2010).

The primary reason for the failure of the Act was the conflicting viewpoints of the central government and the metropolitan city and provincial governments. As mentioned earlier, the Roh Moo-hyun administration planned to establish local autonomous police departments at the local government level. However, the Cooperation Meeting of Metropolitan City

Mayors and Provincial Governors was strongly opposed to the central government's plan, and instead, it is proposed that local autonomous police department be established at the metropolitan city level and at the province level (Shin 2010). Their assertion particularly focused on publicizing the potential problems of the police system proposed by the central government. Specifically, it is criticized that the central government's plan would not be able to respond to a wide range of crimes or a large-scale demonstration in a timely and effective manner. Furthermore, they criticized that the central government's plan would lead to a significant discrepancy in the quality of policing services among local governments given the various financial statuses of local governments.[*]

Consequently, 12 members of the National Assembly including You Gi-jun made and submitted their own decentralized police system bill actively adopting the opinions of the Cooperation Meeting of Metropolitan City Mayors and Provincial Governors. The conflict between the central government's bill and the opposition party's bill aroused significant political debates and prevented either one of the bills from passing the National Assembly. As a result, both bills were automatically abandoned at the end of the 17th National Assembly session in 2007.

Meanwhile, independent of the Decentralized Police System Act, local autonomous police department was first established in Jeju Special Self-Governing Province by a special law in 2006 (Chungbuk 2010). Unlike the Roh Moo-hyun administration's plan, however, Jeju autonomous police department was attached to Jeju Province instead of at the local government level. Thirty percent of the new autonomous police officers were hired by the national police officers, and the remaining were planned to be hired directly by the Jeju Special Self-Governing Provincial Governor (Shin 2010). From the outset, it was proposed that Jeju autonomous police officers would focus on performing duties closely related to the community, such as crime prevention, traffic management, and local security. Additionally, they would hold special judicial police authority to enforce laws relevant to environment, health, and education. However, they do not have the authority to investigate crimes, so they have an obligation to transfer criminal investigations to the national police. The establishment of Jeju autonomous police produced several positive results. For instance, they contributed to maintain public order particularly in tourist spots by preventing illegal activities (Chungbuk 2010). In addition, they played a significant role in improving traffic safety facilities and preventing traffic accidents. But establishment of the local force also presented some problems especially in relation to funding; they have found recruitment of local people challenging. It was intended that the initial force would comprise

---

[*] The percentage of financial independence for local governments varies from 92.7% (Jung-gu, Seoul) to 7.1% (Shinan, Shandong).

120 sworn officers; however, by November 2009, only 82 officers had been appointed. Moreover, even though these officers have special judicial police authority, the lack of professional knowledge and equipment has made it difficult for them to perform some duties effectively (Chungbuk 2010). To make matters worse, cooperation with national police has not been achieved to the degree anticipated or needed. Despite the problems, the establishment of Jeju autonomous police holds a significant meaning in South Korean police history as a first step toward a decentralized police system.

In 2008, President-elect Lee Myung-bak took over the administration from Roh Moo-hyun. The Lee Myung-bak administration announced that the former government's plan for adopting a decentralized police system would be embraced for the most part. One noticeable difference, however, would be the appointment of a Public Order Cooperation Officer to facilitate collaboration between national police and local autonomous police forces. The appointment is not universally supported though as some view the role as potentially ineffective and duplicitous (Shin 2010). Other than the issue of the Cooperation Officer Lee Myung-bak's administration accepted the majority of the proposal within the Decentralized Police System Act. However, since 2010 the situation has changed considerably with the enactment of the Special Law for Restructuring Local Administration System in April 2010. According to this legislation, the existing 230 local governments are to be combined and reorganized into a total of approximately 70 larger local governments, and as a consequence of this law, the decentralized police system plan designed had to be reconsidered. As the discussion about reconstructing local administration system continued, enactment of the Decentralized Police System Act was also postponed.

Conclusion

A survey of 12,000 governmental officers and police officers conducted in 1995 revealed that approximately 70% of the subjects were in favor of adopting a decentralized police system in South Korea (Shin 2010). Likewise, another survey conducted as recently as October 2010 also indicated that more than 55% of the subjects supported a decentralized police system (Chungbuk 2010). Generally, it is believed that adopting a decentralized police system will contribute to the political neutralization of the police and enable police departments to provide customized policing services to the community, improve public perception of the police, and establish better relationships with community members (Shin 2010). Given the result of surveys and efforts of successive governments since the 1990s, it is apparent that both police officers and politicians have recognized the need for adopting a decentralized police system in South Korea. Therefore, the fundamental issue is not whether to adopt the system, but how to adopt the system in South Korean contexts.

Among the several controversial issues, the biggest issue has been at which level a decentralized police system should be adopted. Both the Roh Moo-hyun administration and the Lee Myung-bak administration agreed that a decentralized police system needed to be introduced at the local government level instead of at the metropolitan city or province level. Both accepted that in order to provide a high-quality citizen-oriented policing service and one that would actively react to the needs of the community, the establishment of a local autonomous police department in each local government region was essential. However, considering the specific conditions of South Korea, such as small territory, national security threats from the North, increasing wide range of national and international crimes, and low level of financial independence of local governments, it appears to be appropriate to introduce a decentralized police system at the metropolitan city level and at the province level initially, and then more gradually implement local autonomous police forces across the entire country.

Whether placing a local autonomous police force under the direct control of a local government or operating it as an independent agency from the government is an issue of significant importance for South Korea. Given that mayors and governors belong to political parties, it is perhaps inevitable that local autonomous police forces might be significantly influenced by political interests and the political neutrality of a police force might be substantially impeded if it is attached directly to local governments (Shin 2010). In fact, a survey reported that 78% of the subjects supported a system independent from local governments indicating high concerns about political influences (Chungbuk 2010). However, even a police system independent from local governments is not completely free of political influences. Therefore, it is crucial to make a systemic strategy to assure political neutrality of local police forces. One potential remedy is the operation of an independent citizens committee with supervisory authority over local police administration.

Additionally, how to secure budgets necessary for operating a local autonomous police force is also a critical issue. In principle, local governments are held accountable for preparing budgets, but it is almost impossible to meet the financial burden given the poor financial status of most local governments (Shin 2010). To make matters more complicated, there are substantial disparities in financial status among local governments. Therefore, for the present, it is necessary that the central government provide local governments financial subsidies so that the quality of policing services among local governments can be balanced.

Criminal justice systems are social institutions that respond to the cultural requirements of each distinct human society. However, at the same time, humankind does not exist within hermetically sealed social and cultural enclaves. There are constant cross-cultural exchanges of ideas, moral preferences, and techniques of social and political control. Even in the midst of great diversity, humankind is one, and individual societies do not hesitate to borrow from other institutions that offer the solutions to pressing human problems. (Jones and Johnstone 2011, 385)

South Korea has maintained a centralized national police force since its establishment in 1894. Unique historical and political conditions in South Korea required central governments to operate a powerful police force that could exercise authority throughout the entire country. Given the social and historical context of South Korea, introduction of a decentralized police model, such as that operated in the United States, is impractical. A combined policing model that utilizes both centralized and decentralized forces appears to be the most viable option for South Korea. In order to succeed in the implementation of a combined model, cooperation between national and local government and national and local autonomous police forces is essential. It is hoped that this can be achieved for the benefit of all users of police services in the country.

References

Books

Abadinsky, H. and Winfree, L.T. (1992) *Crime & Justice: An Introduction*, Chicago, IL, Nelson Hall.

Alpert, G.P. and Dunham, R.G. (2010) *Critical Issues in Policing*, Long Grove, IL, Waveland Press.

Anderson, J.F., Mangels, N.J., and Dyson, L. (2003) *Criminal Justice and Criminology: A Career Guide to Local, State, Federal and Academic Positions*, Lanham, MD, University Press of America.

Falk, G. (2010) *The American Criminal Justice System*, Santa Barbara, CA, Praeger.

Jones, M. and Johnstone, P. (2011) *History of Criminal Justice* (5th Edition), Waltham, MA, Anderson.

Hinton, S.M. and Newburn, T. (2009) *Policing Developing Democracies*, Abington, Routledge, p. 104.

Marion, N.E. (2002) *Criminal Justice in America: The Politics behind the System*, Durham, NC, Carolina Academy Press.

Shin, H.K. (2010) *Municipal Police*, Incheon, Republic of Korea.

Reports

Bureau of Justice Statistics. (2006) *Federal Law Enforcement Officers, 2004*. Washington, DC, US Department of Justice.

Bureau of Justice Statistics. (2008) *Census of State and Local Law Enforcement Agencies*. Washington, DC, Bureau of Justice Statistics.

Bureau of Justice Statistics. (2010) *Local Police Departments, 2007*. Washington, DC, US Department of Justice.

Bureau of Justice Statistics. (2011) *Census of State and Local Law Enforcement Agencies, 2008*. Washington, DC, US Department of Justice.

Chungbuk Research Institute. (2010) *A Study of the Introduction and Establishment of an Autonomous Police System*, Cheongju, Chungbuk University Press.

Korea National Police Agency. (2010) *Korean Police Annual Report 2010*, Seoul, Korean National Police Agency.

Consolidated Abstracts

Chapter 1   A Clash of Modern Professionalism and Oriental Despotism: The Case of Iran, 1878–1979

Police modernization history in Iran dates back to the late-nineteenth- and early-twentieth-century administrative reforms of the Qajar dynasty reaching their most comprehensive form under the Pahlavids. With the historical overthrow of the monarchy in Iran in 1979, police are being Islamized. This chapter argues that although modernized in form, police in Iran have remained despotic in content due to a historical clash between the forces of Western professionalism and Oriental despotism in the traditional Iranian conception of state and policing. It concludes that the incompatibility between form and content in modern policing will only be resolved through democratization of the conception of state and, by extension, of the police in Iran.

Chapter 2   Challenges of Police Reforms in Lesotho

Policing studies have evolved globally. Today, it has become a vibrant area of inquiry in which scholars from various disciplinary backgrounds converge to engage in issues relevant to social order. Police reforms are essential because of their implications for consolidation of democratic institutions. Reforms entail reorganization of the police force to ensure efficiency and professionalism. Police reforms in Lesotho were introduced in 1997 after an internal mutiny by junior officers. The chapter looks at the challenges facing police reforms in Lesotho. Attention is drawn to the critical analysis of internal institutional constraints within the police force in Lesotho. Support agencies and oversight bodies were introduced to monitor the activities of the police in order to ensure adherence to common standards. However, the record of the oversight agencies remains controversial. While the police directorate functioned efficiently within its closely delineated responsibilities, the Police Complaints Authority (PCA) remained toothless and was unable to provide any meaningful oversight or accountability. The PCA does not have the authority to register complaints and launch investigations. Oversight bodies and civic movements do not have sufficient human and financial capacity. There is no appropriate legislative framework that recognizes their contributions. Added to this is the absence of the political will to genuinely reform police as evidenced by a minimal budget allocation for the reforms.

Chapter 3   The Soap Opera Rationale: A Complementary Information Management Construct in Police Work Practice

In the past 15 years, police work in Sweden has changed from only reactive police work to a more proactive approach. Proactive approaches have been supported by many different IT solutions based on a structured rationale. We present a coexisting rationale more to be like a soap opera based on lengthy data collection in the field of police work. This chapter shows how information management can be seen in the soap opera and the project rationale, and a set of four properties that constitutes the rationale soap opera: repositories, routines, relations, and rituals.

Chapter 4   Impact of Selection and Distrust in Construction of Professional Police Identity

Police culture is often described as strongly unifying, leading to a feeling of a strong professional identity. The main reasons for these descriptions, as suggested in police research, are due to the profession's shared risks and the role of authoritarianism. In this chapter, two complementary reasons are presented, both manifested in the image that police students and officers believe others have of them. The students' images are formed from the feelings of being selected and the notion that others distrust them. In conclusion, our results provide strong empirical support for the images as significant constructors in the formation of a professional police identity.

Chapter 5   Human Rights and the South African Police Service: Are the Red Lights Coming On?

South Africa is considered as a young and developing democracy. It moved from oppressive policing to a community approach directed by internationally recognized human rights. This chapter critically analyzes the transition of police practices within two distinct eras, namely, from 1994 (after the first democratic elections) until 2007 and then from 2007 till date. The reason for the distinction between the two periods is the leadership change that took place after the African National Congress' conference in Polokwane, Limpopo Province, in December 2007. At the conference, Dr. Jacob Zuma, the current South African President, defeated Mr Thabo Mbeki and became the president of the ANC. He then became the president of South Africa in 2009. He was the *de facto* president of the country since the 2007 confer- ence and influenced policy based on the Polokwane resolutions. Soon a hard stance against crime and criminals was adopted, leading to drastic policy changes such as changing the cabinet portfolio for Safety and Security to Police, introducing military ranks for the police, and starting a "war" against criminals. The chapter looks at police brutality pre- and post-2007 in order to deduce whether there has been an increase in human rights violations in light of these changes.

Chapter 6   Community Policing: The Bahamas Model Drawing a Thin Line between Community Policing and Traditional Policing

Over the years, much research has been conducted on examining the impacts of traditional policing and community policing models being employed in developed countries. Very little or no studies have been done on this in developing countries. As a result, a barrier exists on this account between the developed and the developing countries, which hinders the spread of knowledge about the advancements being made. This study examined the urban renewal community policing model in The Bahamas using representa- tive field survey data collected during 2007 in New Providence. The evidence from this research does support continued investment in police innova- tions that call for greater focus and streamlining of police efforts, combined with an expansion of strategies for policing beyond simple traditional law enforcement.

Chapter 7   The Community Involved and Planned Policing Model: An Alternative to Traditional Policing in Trinidad and Tobago

The policing system in Trinidad and Tobago largely reflects the tradi- tional colonial model as a remnant of its past English heritage. This study examined the extent to which police officers and community residents are involved in policing their communities. The study utilized the seldom-used concurrent survey model within a single jurisdiction via focus group discussions and mail-out surveys to gather data on the efficacy of a system of policing that involves police officers and community residents as coproducers of crime. The findings of the study indicated that a higher level of community involvement in the policing process was desirable. As such, the Community Involved and Planned Policing (CIPP) model was developed as an alternative to the traditional policing model in Trinidad and Tobago.

Chapter 8   Community Policing: A Panacea or a Pandora's Box to Tackle the Rise in Crimes in Nigeria and South Africa

This exploratory study examines whether community policing is perceived to be a solution to the rise in criminalities in Nigeria and South Africa. The author takes a qualitative approach to this. Ten crime prevention practitioners from each of the two countries were interviewed. The study revealed the perception that community policing could lead to a decline in criminalities in the two countries. However, in view of the experiences of other countries in community policing, the author concludes that community policing is not a solution to the rise in criminalities in Nigeria and South Africa. The root causes of crimes must be rigorously addressed.

Chapter 9   Meeting with Citizens: New Local Dimensions of Dialogue between Citizens and Police Officers

In this text the authors present, explain, and assess one of the most successful preventive projects of the police from the Czech Republic that is called "Meeting with Citizens," which was implemented in 2008 in the town of Karviná in Moravia-Silesian region. In order to solve specific local problems, local police officers applied an entirely new approach that was inspired by the philosophy of community policing. Their tactic was shown to be a very effective one and, therefore, has been practiced from that time in many other conflict communities or locations. Such a proactive attitude of the police officers shows the police as an institution in a greatly positive light, especially in the eyes of the citizens. Moreover, the project had already been awarded with several prestigious national and international prizes. At present, the project's main objectives and goals are being further advanced in its original location and implemented in the other areas.

Chapter 10   Community Policing in Portugal: A Long and Winding Road

The origins of the Portuguese police can be traced back to the fourteenth century. Since that time, the Portuguese police system went through several changes. At the end of the 1990s after more than 20 years of democracy, the two main Portuguese police forces (the Public Security Police and the Gendarmerie) adhered to the values of community policing. Within this framework, the Public Security Police is currently developing a new program called Integrated Proximity Policing Program. Launched in 2006, this program can be seen, within the Portuguese context, as proximity policing of second generation.

Chapter 11   Authoritative Language in Police Training: Style in Police Students' Memoranda

This chapter considers how 50 Swedish police students approach the writing practice of serving police officers and how they learn to balance the requirements of formal and comprehensible style in their written reporting. The police students' memoranda were analyzed with the focus on how they conform to the guidelines for police writing issued by the Swedish National Police Board. The analysis shows that the students' memoranda function in formal terms, but the style sometimes becomes colloquial. This kind of language is admittedly comprehensible, but it can affect the credibility and legal security of the texts. The results indicate that police teachers and trainers need to focus more on language use and writing skills of the students in order to ease the transition from educational training to writing in occupational settings.

Chapter 12   Job Expectation, Adjustment, and Coping Mechanisms among Women in Two Police Forces in India

Women have historically played an important role in India. Women warriors fought courageously for the honor of their motherland. More recently, Kiran Bedi, the first woman to join the Indian Police Service in 1972, is continuing to make significant contributions toward the progress of Indian society even after her formal retirement from the Services. Despite the critical contributions made by women, there has been little research aimed at understanding the acute difficulties faced by these women, who are very much a part of the society that still does not consider women to be at par with men, especially when it comes to their jobs as police officers, a traditionally male-dominated profession. The purpose of this chapter is to conduct a comparative empirical study of women police personnel working in two states in India, Delhi and Orissa, and examine their job expectations, their level of adjustment in the police departments, their behavior, and their coping strategies. The study indicates that women police officers in Orissa adopt more positive coping strategies than their counterparts in Delhi. The authors attribute this to various factors such as the stress of urban living and the nuclear family structure that is more prevalent in Delhi as opposed to Orissa. All the subjects in this study are residents of either Orissa or Delhi.

Chapter 13   Efficiency of Simulated Realistic Scenarios to Provide High Psychological Stress Training for Police Officers

Violent encounters may put police officers under strong psychological stress, which influence the ability to perform mental and physical tasks. The objective of this research was to investigate the efficiency (peak stress) and structure (generation, recovery patterns) of stress evoked from realistic training scenarios, by monitoring heart rate changes. The heart rate recordings revealed significantly higher psychological stress while performing realistic exercises to levels where fine motor skills are known to be degraded and complex motor skills are affected. Hence, well-designed realistic training scenarios may provide suitable training conditions for police officers to train in how to handle physical and psychological consequences of high psychological stress.

Chapter 14   Development of Ghana Police Service Personnel and Performance

This deductive study that was based on the administration of questionnaires and interviews of Ghana Police personnel in Accra to evaluate the extent to which the performance of the personnel was related to the selection requirement of the service revealed that there was a positive relationship between the selection requirements and the job performance of the personnel to some extent. However, it was also revealed that using "height" as a selection requirement, which was relevant when the police was a force during the colonial era, has outlived its usefulness and should be discarded. The study also revealed that the performance of the police personnel could be enhanced if they were developed through learning and better selection methods.

Chapter 15 Police Writing Techniques in Reported Interviews

This study considers how 50 Swedish police officers write the interviews in investigations of domestic violence. Investigators in the police have four different linguistic possibilities for reproducing interviewees' words from written reported interviews in the investigations. The police use the following narrative techniques: narration, direct, indirect, and free indirect speech. The results suggest that the rendering of the interviewees' voices is more or less trustworthy, depending on which technique is used, and the writers should be aware of free indirect speech, because this technique makes for hazy distinctions between the writer and what was heard, which can jeopardize and alter the interpretation of the statements of the interviewees and thus the tenability of the continued judicial process. Yet, free indirect speech is a rather common strategy in the studied material.

Chapter 16 Exploring System Transition in the Police Organization: The Case of the UK Police National Database

This chapter addresses the recent implementation of the Police National Database (PND) and explores the impact of system transition from the Impact Nominal Index (INI) system that was set up in the interim in 2005. The aim of the research was to gain understanding of the users' perceptions and early experiences of using the PND, as well as the identification of organizational challenges and changes to business processes following its implementation. This chapter reports on the findings obtained during the interview of police officers and civilian staff in several police forces in England and Wales. A total of 12 forces took part and 16 police representatives participated in the research. This research found that there are important change management issues that require consideration, such as effectively communicating to the staff how their roles and responsibilities could be affected as a result of the PND. Information sharing is at the heart of the PND; this research has identified mitigating factors that cause difficulty in the dissemination of police information. Maximizing the PND's potential in the police organization requires acknowledgment of the various organizational and cultural changes evoked as a consequence of sharing and accessing information on a national scale; this will play a role in ensuring that the PND is sustainable, has longevity like other core police systems, and has the ability to cope with the evolutionary demands of twenty-first century policing.

Chapter 17 Exploring the Implementation of Head-Mounted Camera Technology in Volume Crime Scene Investigation

This chapter presents the potential of head camera technology for capturing Volume Crime Scene Investigation practice. Four female Volume Crime Scene Investigators (VCSIs) collectively recorded 55 crime scenes over a 7-month period. Video recordings and interview data were analyzed using NVivo9 software. Head-mounted camera technology did survive its deployment in the field of Volume Crime Scene Investigation, although there are limitations to its use. Qualitative examples show that it can enhance training by being a mechanism to capture tacit knowledge. Future work is now proposed for using head-mounted camera technology to better understand crime scene practices.

Chapter 18 To What Extent Are All Policing Problems Wicked?

Both proactive and reactive criminal investigations conducted by the police are examined using the Tame or Wicked problem typology proposed by Rittel and Webber. It is proposed that all plural policing problems are actually objectively Wicked, but that they are Tame or Critical problems when they are considered individually. Proactive drug operations conducted by Greater Manchester Police over the past 5 years across five divisional areas are reviewed to show that they have little long-term impact and illustrate that single-mode "elegant" solutions may not be the most effective approach once the problem passes a certain scale threshold.

Chapter 19 Examining Police Integrity: Categorizing Corruption Vignettes

A growing body of literature on integrity of police officers focuses on their perceptions of corruption vignettes. The current analysis examines these vignettes using the factor analysis by Klockars et al. survey data of police officers in the United States. The results indicate that the historically used vignettes can be divided into two factors: one that reflects more serious and the other that reflects less serious, corrupt behavior. The vignettes regarding an off-duty business and accepting free meals and other gratuities may not be perceived as corruption. Their implications on research and practice are discussed.

Chapter 20 Representations of the Police in the British Media: "Hard" Cops and "Soft" Cops

Although criminal justice systems and institutions are massive operations involving many millions of people in various capacities, most people's understanding of how they "work" is largely derived from the mass media. This chapter looks at the way the media represent the police and policing in Britain—in both real-life and fictional contexts. It starts by considering the collaborative nature of the relationship among the police, the journalists, and the broadcasters before considering different TV dramatizations of policing and, in particular, the contrast between the image of a "soft" police service and a "hard" law enforcement agency. The chapter ends with a consideration of the nature and role of police reality television, using the *Crimewatch UK* program as illustration.

Chapter 21 Urgent Police Interviews with Suspects of Terrorism under PACE: Risks and Mitigation

In the United Kingdom as in other legislatures, the police can, under certain circumstances, carry out urgent interviews with suspects of crime. Urgent interviews are designed to protect the public from harm by averting other serious offences and/or the escape of other offenders. This chapter explores the use of urgent interviews in counterterrorism. It introduces the legislation governing their use [the Police and Criminal Evidence Act (PACE) code H] and identifies the risks associated with urgent interviewing in counterterrorism. Considering relevant research and best interviewing practice, the chapter provides recommendations as to how the various risks may be mitigated.

Chapter 22 Counterterrorism Legislation in the United Kingdom: A Review of the Impact of Control Orders

The European Court of Human Rights ruled in 2012 that Abu Qatada should not be deported from Britain back to Jordan, because of the fear that he may be tortured, which raised important issues in respect of the impact of counterterrorism laws in the United Kingdom. Abu Qatada was described as a radical "Islamist" preacher who had been held in prison and placed under curfew for more than 6 years. As a result, the European court ruled that Abu Qatada be granted bail by the UK Special Immigration Appeals Commission in the United Kingdom in February 2012. In light of this ruling, it is important to examine the conflict between the judiciary and the UK government (albeit that Abu Qatada would eventually lose his appeal against deportation). The objectives of this chapter are to examine the impact of the UK government's control orders that have allowed individuals to be held under house arrest and strict curfews. In the aftermath of the London bombings on July 7, 2005, the British government announced the introduction of control orders. Control orders created measures to supervise suspects through electronic tagging or by requiring them to remain in their homes. However, following the government review of counterterrorism legislation in 2010, control orders have been abolished, and in their place the government has enacted the Terrorism Prevention and Investigation Measures (T-PIMs). The chapter adopts a case-analysis approach, examines the legacy and impact of control orders, and argues that they have been both controversial and ill-defined, and risk alienating the Muslim communities.

Chapter 23   A Tale of Three US Cities: Police Accountability and Urban Indians in Albuquerque, Portland, and Duluth

Experiences of urban Indians with police are remarkably similar across the United States. Urban Indians, individually and collectively, often experience a level of disconnect with police departments and the city power structure. Three studies conducted from 1997 to 2010 indicate that most urban Indians remain invisible to, and on the outside of, the urban power structure. However, continuous improvement can occur and be encouraged. During the above-mentioned period, Albuquerque, Portland, and Duluth developed or reaffirmed their commitment to police accountability and service to all communities. Improvement has occurred, which may indicate a municipal willingness to change and hopefully a commitment to constructive improvement.

Chapter 24   Medical Examination of Mentally Disordered/Mentally Vulnerable Detainees in Police Custody in England and Wales

This chapter examines the treatment of mentally disordered or vulnerable detainees in police custody in England and Wales by Force Medical Examiners (FMEs) regarding their fitness for detention or fitness for interview. The research was requested by the UK's Faculty for Forensic and Legal Medicine as they wished to gather data on the qualification of their members to examine mentally disordered or vulnerable detainees in police custody. As a result of this research, the Faculty introduced changes to the FMEs' qualifications, how the FMEs' record examinations were carried out at custody suites, and upgrading of facilities in the consultation rooms used by the FMEs at police stations in England and Wales.

Chapter 25 A Comparative Study of a Centralized and a Decentralized Police System: The Plan for Adopting a Decentralized Police System in South Korea

This chapter explores the origins and historical development of two distinctive police systems—centralized and decentralized police systems. In the United States, local government establishes its own police departments to provide law enforcement services. State and federal agencies are responsible tackling for statewide or nationwide crimes, and they assist local agencies when required. Policing in South Korea is governed by one single national police agency. As the Korean government is planning to implement the decentralized police system in the near future, this chapter explores how to adopt the decentralized system while minimizing potential negative effects within the South Korean social context.

International Police Executive Symposium, IPES, www.ipes.info

The International Police Executive Symposium (IPES) was founded in 1994. The aims and objectives of the IPES are to provide a forum to foster closer relationships among police researchers and practitioners globally; to facilitate cross-cultural, international, and interdisciplinary exchanges for the enrichment of the law enforcement profession; and to encourage discussion and published research on challenging and contemporary topics related to the profession.

One of the most important activities of the IPES is the organization of an annual meeting under the auspices of a police agency or an educational institution. Every year since 1994 annual meetings have been hosted by such agencies and institutions all over the world. Past hosts have included the Canton Police of Geneva, Switzerland; the International Institute for the Sociology of Law, Onati, Spain; Kanagawa University, Yokohama, Japan; the Federal Police, Vienna, Austria; the Dutch Police and Europol, The Hague, The Netherlands; the Andhra Pradesh Police, Hyderabad, India; the Center for Public Safety, Northwestern University, Evanston, IL; the Polish Police Academy, Szczytno, Poland; the Police of Turkey (twice); the Kingdom of Bahrain Police; a group of institutions in Canada (consisting of the University of the Fraser Valley, Abbotsford Police Department, Royal Canadian Mounted Police, the Vancouver Police Department, the Justice Institute of British Columbia, the Canadian Police College, and the International Centre for Criminal Law Reform and Criminal Justice Policy); the Czech Police Academy, Prague; the Dubai Police; the Ohio Association of Chiefs of Police and the Cincinnati Police Department, Cincinnati, OH; the Republic of Macedonia; and the Police of Malta. The 2011 annual meeting on the theme of "Policing Violence, Crime, Disorder and Discontent: International Perspectives" was hosted in Buenos Aires, Argentina, on June 26–30. The 2012 annual meeting was hosted at the United Nations in New York on the theme of "Economic Development, Armed Violence and Public Safety" on August 5–10. The 2013 annual meeting on the theme of "Global Issues in Contemporary Policing" was hosted by the Ministry of Interior of Hungary and the Hungarian National Police on August 4–9.

There have also been occasional special meetings of the IPES. A special meeting was cohosted by the Bavarian Police Academy of Continuing Education in Ainring, Germany; the University of Passau, Germany; and the State University of New York, Plattsburgh, NY, in 2000. The second special meeting was hosted by the police in Kerala, India. The third special meeting on the theme of "Contemporary Issues in Public Safety and Security" was hosted by the Commissioner of Police of the Blekinge Region, Sweden, and the president of the University of Technology on August 10–14, 2011.

The majority of participants in the annual meetings are usually directly involved in the police profession. In addition, scholars and researchers in the field also participate. The meetings comprise both structured and informal sessions to maximize the dialogue and exchange of views and information. The executive summary of each meeting is distributed to participants as well as to a wide range of other interested police professionals and scholars. In addition, a book of selected papers from each annual meeting is published through the CRC Press/Taylor & Francis Group, Prentice Hall, Lexington Books, and other reputed publishers. A special issue of *Police Practice and Research: An International Journal* is also published with the most thematically relevant papers after the usual blind review process.

IPES Institutional Supporters

Shri Balasubramaniyum, Director General of Police, Kerala Police, Police Headquarters, Trivandrum, Kerala, India. E-mail: manojabraham05@gmail.com

Dr. David E. Barlow, Professor and Dean, College of Basic and Applied Sciences, Fayetteville State University, 130 Chick Building, 1200 Murchison Road, Fayetteville, NC 28301, USA. Tel: +1 910 672 1659; Fax: +1 910 672 1083. E-mail: dbarlow@uncfsu.edu

Dr. Diana Bruns, Chair, Criminal Justice & Sociology, Southeast Missouri State University, One University Plaza, Cape Girardeau, MO 63701, USA. Tel: +1 573 651 2178. E-mail: dbruns@semo.edu

Craig J. Callens. Royal Canadian Mounted Police, 657 West 37th Avenue, Vancouver, British Columbia V5Z 1K6, Canada. Tel: +1 604 264 2003; Fax: +1 604 264 3547. E-mail: bcrcmp@rcmp-grc.gc.ca

Dr. Irwin Cohen, Department of Criminology & Criminal Justice, University of the Fraser Valley, 33844 King Road, Abbotsford, British Columbia V2 S7 M9, Canada. Tel: +1 604 853 7441; Fax: +1 604 853 9990. E-mail: irwin.cohen@ufv.ca

Connie Coniglio, Australian Institute of Police Management, Collins Beach Road, Manly, New South Wales 2095, Australia. Tel: +61 2 9934 4800; Fax: +61 2 9934 4780. E-mail: cconiglio@aipm.gov.au

Mark E. Correia, PhD, Dean, College of Health and Human Services, Indiana University of Pennsylvania, 216 Zink Hall, Room 105, 1190 Maple Street Indiana, PA 15705-1059, USA. Tel: +1 724 357 2555. E-mail: mcorreia@iup.edu

Setlhomamaru Dintwe, Department of Police Practice, UNISA, Florida Campus, Corner Christiaan De Wet and Pioneer Avenues, Private Bag X6, Florida 1710, South Africa. Tel: +27 011 471 2116; Cell: +083 581 6102; Fax: +27 011 471 2255. E-mail: dintwsi@unisa.ac.za

Dr. John A. Eterno, NYPD Captain (Retired), Department of Criminal Justice, Molloy College, 1000 Hempstead Avenue, PO Box 5002, Rockville Center, NY 11571-5002, USA. Tel: +1 516 678 5000, Ext: 6135; Fax: +1 516 256 2289. E-mail: mailto:jeterno@molloy.edu

Dr. Mario Gaboury, School of Criminal Justice and Forensic Science, University of New Haven, 300 Boston Post Road, West Haven, CT 06516, USA. Tel: +1 203 932 7260. E-mail: rward@newhaven.edu

Blaine Goodrich, Baker College of Jackson, 2800 Springport Road, Jackson, MI 49202, USA. Tel: +1 517 841 4522. E-mail: blaine.goodrich@baker.edu

Mal Hyde, Commissioner, South Australia Police, Office of the Commissioner, 30 Flinders Street, Adelaide, South Australia 5000, Australia. E-mail: mal.hyde@police.sa.gov.au

David A. Jenks, PhD, University of West Georgia, Pafford Building 2309, 1601 Maple Street, Carrollton, GA 30118, USA. Tel: +1 678 839 6327. E-mail: djenks@westga.edu

Valibor Lalic, Defendology Center for Security, Sociology and Criminology Research, Srpska Street 63, 78000 Banja Luka, Bosnia and Herzegovina. Tel/Fax: +387 51 308 914. E-mail: lalicv@teol.net

James Lewis, Cyber Defense & Research Initiatives, LLC, PO Box 86, Leslie, MI 49251, USA. Tel: +1 517 242 6730. E-mail: lewisja@cyberdefenseresearch.com

David Lowe, LLB Programme Leader, Law School, John Moores University, Law School, Redmonds Building, Brownlow Hill, Liverpool, L3 5UG, UK. Tel: +44 (0) 151 231 3918. E-mail: d.lowe@ljmu.ac.uk

Dr. Harvey L. McMurray, Chair, Department of Criminal Justice, North Carolina Central University, 301 Whiting Criminal Justice Building, Durham, NC 27707, USA. Tel: +1 919 530 5204, +1 919 530 7909; Fax: +1 919 530 5195. E-mail: hmcmurray@nccu.edu

Dr. Gorazd Mesko, The Faculty of Criminal Justice and Security, University of Maribor, Kotnikova 8, 1000 Ljubljana, Slovenia. Tel: +386 1 300 83 39; Fax: +386 1 2302 687. E-mail: gorazd.mesko@fvv.uni-mb.si

Richard Myers, Professor, College of Natural and Social Sciences, University of Maine at Augusta, 46 University Drive, Augusta, ME 04330-9410, USA. E-mail: rmyers@maine.edu

Edmundo Oliveira, PhD, Professor, 1 Irving Place University Tower Apt. U 7 A 10003.9723 Manhattan, New York, NY, USA. Tel: +1 407 342 2473. E-mail: edmundooliveira@cfl.rr.com

Naoya Oyaizu, Deputy Director, National Police Academy, Police Policy Research Center, Zip 183-8558: 3-12-1 Asahi-cho Fuchu-city, Tokyo, Japan. Tel: +81 42 354 3550; Fax: +81 42 330 3550. E-mail: PPRC@npa.go.jp

Stephen Perrott, Department of Psychology, Mount Saint Vincent University, 166 Bedford Highway, Halifax, Nova Scotia, Canada. E-mail: Stephen.perrott@mvsu.ca

Kris Pillay, Professor and Director, School of Criminal Justice, College of Law, University of South Africa, Preller Street, Muckleneuk, Pretoria, South Africa. E-mail: cpillay@unisa.ac.za

Mr Kamalendra Prasad, Inspector General of Police, National Institute of Criminology and Forensic Science, MHA, Outer Ring Road, Sector 3, Rohini, Delhi 110085, India. Tel: +91 11 275 2 5095; Fax: +91 11 275 1 0586. E-mail: direc-tor.nicfs@nic.in

Cliff Roberson, Professor Emeritus, Washburn University, 16307 Sedona Woods, Houston, TX 77082-1665, USA. Tel: +1 713 703 6639; Fax: +1 281 596 8483. E-mail: roberson37@msn.com

André Souza, Senior Researcher, International Council on Security and Development (ICOS), Visconde de Piraja 577/605, Ipanema, Rio de Janeiro 22410-003, Brazil. Tel: +55 21 3186 5444. E-mail: asouza@icosgroup.net

Drs. Perry Stanislas and Hirsh Sethi, The Faculty of Health and Life Sciences, School of Applied Social Sciences, De Montfort University, Hawthorn Building, The Gateway, Leicester, LE1 9BH, UK. Tel: +44 (0) 116 257 7146. E-mail: pstanislas@dmu.ac.uk, hsethi@dmu.ac.uk

Sean Tait, The African Policing Civilian Oversight Forum (APCOF), 2nd floor, The Armoury, Buchanan Square, 160 Sir Lowry Road, Woodstock Cape Town 8000, South Africa. Tel: +27 21 461 7211; Fax: +27 21 461 7213. E-mail: sean@apcof.org.za

S. Caroline Taylor, Professor, Foundation Chair in Social Justice, School of Psychology and Social Science, Social Justice Research Centre, Edith Cowan University, 270 Joondalup Drive, Joondalup, Western Australia 6027, Australia. E-mail: c.tay-lor@ecu.edu.au

Important Publications for POLICING and LAW ENFORCEMENT

Published

Contemporary Issues in Law Enforcement and Policing
Edited by
Andrew Millie and Dilip K. Das
Catalog no. 72153, 2008, 248 pp.
ISBN: 978-1-4200-7215-0
$85.95 / £54.99

Global Trafficking in Women and Children
Edited by
Obi N.I. Ebbe and Dilip K. Das
Catalog no. 59432, 2008, 272 pp.
ISBN: 978-1-4200-5943-4
$119.95 / £76.99

Criminal Abuse of Women and Children
An International Perspective
Edited by
Obi N.I. Ebbe and Dilip K. Das
Catalog no. 88033, January 2010, 396 pp.
ISBN: 978-1-4200-8803-8
$124.95 / £79.99

Urbanization, Policing, and Security
Global Perspectives
Edited by
Gary Cordner, AnnMarie Cordner, and Dilip K. Das
Catalog no. 85573, 2010, 475 pp.
ISBN: 978-1-4200-8557-0
$133.95 / £85.00

Police Without Borders
The Fading Distinction Between Local and Global
Edited by
Cliff Roberson, Dilip K. Das, and Jennie K. Singer
Catalog no. K10281, January 2011, 328 pp.
ISBN: 978-1-4398-0501-5
$129.95 / £82.00

Forthcoming

The Evolution of Policing
Worldwide Innovations and Insights
Edited by
Melchor de Guzman, Aiedeo Mintie Das, and Dilip K. Das
Catalog no. K16314, November 2013
600 pp., ISBN: 978-1-4665-6715-3
$119.95 / £76.99

Examining Political Violence
Studies of Terrorism, Counterterrorism, and Internal War
Edited by
David Lowe, Austin Turk, and Dilip K. Das
Catalog no. K20372, December 2013
c. 450 pp., ISBN: 978-1-4665-8820-2
$99.95 / £63.99

Police Reform
The Effects of International Economic Development, Armed Violence, and Public Safety
Edited by
Garth den Heyer and Dilip K. Das
Catalog no. K21383, January 2014
c. 400 pp., ISBN: 978-1-4822-0456-8
$129.95 / £82.00

Policing Major Events
Perspectives from Around the World
Edited by
Martha Christine Dow, Darryl Plecas, and Dilip K. Das
Catalog no. K20365, August 2014
c. 450 pp., ISBN: 978-1-4665-8805-9
$89.95 / £57.99

To order these or other titles, please visit our website at
www.crcpress.com

CRC Press
Taylor & Francis Group

A Call for Authors

Advances in Police Theory and Practice

AIMS AND SCOPE:

This cutting-edge series is designed to promote publication of books on contemporary advances in police theory and practice. We are especially interested in volumes that focus on the nexus between research and practice, with the end goal of disseminating innovations in policing. We will consider collections of expert contributions as well as individually authored works. Books in this series will be marketed internationally to both academic and professional audiences. This series also seeks to —

Police Reform in China

- Bridge the gap in knowledge about advances in theory and practice regarding who the police are, what they do, and how they maintain order, administer laws, and serve their communities
- Improve cooperation between those who are active in the field and those who are involved in academic research so as to facilitate the application of innovative advances in theory and practice

Mission-Based Policing

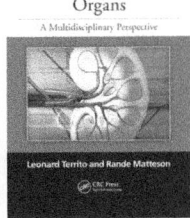
The International Trafficking of Human Organs
A Multidisciplinary Perspective

The series especially encourages the contribution of works coauthored by police practitioners and researchers. We are also interested in works comparing policing approaches and methods globally, examining such areas as the policing of transitional states, democratic policing, policing and minorities, preventive policing, investigation, patrolling and response, terrorism, organized crime and drug enforcement. In fact, every aspect of policing, public safety, and security, as well as public order is relevant for the series. Manuscripts should be between 300 and 600 printed pages. If you have a proposal for an original work or for a contributed volume, please be in touch.

Series Editor
Dilip Das, Ph.D., Ph: 802-598-3680
E-mail: dilipkd@aol.com

Dr. Das is a professor of criminal justice and Human Rights Consultant to the United Nations. He is a former chief of police, and founding president of the International Police Executive Symposium, IPES, www.ipes.info. He is also founding editor-in-chief of *Police Practice and Research: An International Journal* (PPR), (Routledge/Taylor & Francis), www.tandf.co.uk/journals. In addition to editing the *World Police Encyclopedia* (Taylor & Francis, 2006), Dr. Das has published numerous books and articles during his many years of involvement in police practice, research, writing, and education.

Proposals for the series may be submitted to the series editor or directly to –
Carolyn Spence
Senior Editor • CRC Press / Taylor & Francis Group
561-317-9574 • 561-997-7249 (fax)
carolyn.spence@taylorandfrancis.com • www.crcpress.com
6000 Broken Sound Parkway NW, Suite 300, Boca Raton, FL 33487

Index

Note: f and t denote figures and tables in the text